KU-008-255

Kingfisher
Geography
Encyclopedia

Kingfisher
Geography
Encyclopedia

TED SMART

General Editor Sue Grabham
Senior Co-ordinating Designer Tracy Killick

Editors Claire Berridge, Jane Butcher,
Charlotte Evans, Nina Hathway, Ann Kay,
Linda Sonntag, Jill Thomas
Assistant Editor Julia March
Editorial Assistant Virginie Verhague

Cartographer Alan Whitaker
Cartographic Editors
Tara Benson, Annabel Else
Assistant Cartographic Editors
Nicola Garrett, Victoria Hall
Cartographic Services
Cosmographics, Lovell Johns Ltd
Base Map Artwork Malcolm Porter

Senior Designer Janice English
Designers Paul Calver, Dawn Davies,
Earl Neish, Andy Stanford
Additional Design Branka Surla, Smiljka Surla

Additional Art Preparation Shaun Deal,
Roy Flooks, Mark Franklin, Matthew Gore,
Mel Pickering, Janet Woronkowicz

Writers Sean Connolly, Antony Mason,
James Muirden, Linda Sonntag,
Phil Steele, Jill Thomas

Picture Research Su Alexander, Elaine Willis
Artwork Archivist Wendy Allison
Assistant Artwork Archivist Steve Robinson

Publishing Director Jim Miles
Art Director Paul Wilkinson

Production Manager Linda Edmonds
Production Assistant Stephen Lang

Indexer Hilary Bird
Glossary and Phonetics Daphne Ingram
Proofreader Penny Williams

Geographical Consultants
Keith Lye, Dr David Munro, Julia Stanton
Natural History Consultant
Michael Chinery
Social Geography and History Consultant
Professor Jack Zevin

KINGFISHER
Kingfisher Publications Plc
New Penderel House, 283-288 High Holborn,
London WC1V 7HZ

First published by Kingfisher 1995 as *Kingfisher Encyclopedia of Lands and Peoples*
Copyright © Kingfisher Publications Plc 1995
This edition published 1999

This edition produced by The Book People Ltd,
Hall Wood Avenue, Haydock, St Helens, WA11 9UL

All rights reserved. No part of this publication may be reproduced, stored in a
retrieval system or transmitted by any means, electronic, mechanical, photocopying
or otherwise, without the prior permission of the publisher.

A CIP catalogue record for this book is available from the British Library

ISBN 1-85613-582-9

Colour separation by Newsele s.r.l. Milan, Italy
Printed in China

FOREWORD

With almost 200 independent countries in the world, how do you get to see them all in a lifetime? Luckily, you have the ultimate travel machine right in front of you. Within seconds, at the turn of a page, the *Kingfisher Geography Encyclopedia* can take you wherever you want to go. That means anywhere in the world, from tiny atolls in the Pacific Ocean to alpine meadows in Europe, from the steamy rainforests of South America to the frozen tundra of Siberia.

Over the following 640 pages, you will travel through mountains, deserts, forests and plains, spotting the many animals and plants that live in these very different environments. You will meet the people of these lands, learn how they dress, enjoy themselves and earn their living, even discover the food they eat and the language they speak. You will see how nations have developed over the centuries, find out about their wars against other nations and their battles for independence and economic success. And throughout you will be guided by locator globes and beautiful relief maps showing towns, rivers, roads, mountains and many other features.

Within the *Kingfisher Geography Encyclopedia* there are literally thousands and thousands of facts about every country in the world. This staggering collection of images and information required an enormous effort from an enthusiastic team of writers, editors, designers, picture researchers, production supervisors, and many, many others. You are about to see the results of their effort and dedication for yourself as you 'travel' the world. Sit back, turn the pages an enjoy the trip!

CONTENTS

EUROPE 5-128

AFRICA 129-256

NORTH AMERICA 257-320

CONTENTS

AUSTRALIA AND THE PACIFIC ISLANDS
EARTH IN SPACE 513-576

REFERENCE/INDEX 577-640

THE GEOGRAPHY ENCYCLOPEDIA

When you venture into the pages of this encyclopedia you will begin a journey around the globe. It will take you across rugged mountains, scorching deserts, frozen wastelands, lush rainforests and rolling grasslands to reach faraway destinations. On the way you will meet many different peoples with their varied traditions, languages, politics, religions and ways of life. Locator globes and detailed relief maps will guide you around more than 180 independent countries, while the reference section provides you with a mass of useful facts and figures about the world. A detailed timeline sums up the major historical events across each continent. These two pages suggest how to get the most out of your *Geography Encyclopedia* and describe some of its many special features.

ENDANGERED WORLD
Find out which of the world's animals are in danger and why.

THE TEXT
Let the text transport you to each corner of the globe. It will introduce you to new landscapes, peoples, cultures and traditions.

LANGUAGE SCROLLS
Learn how to say hello and goodbye in a variety of languages. Pronunciation guides are given in brackets.

FACTS AND FIGURES
Look up all the essential information on each country – its size, religions, exports, population, currency and much more.

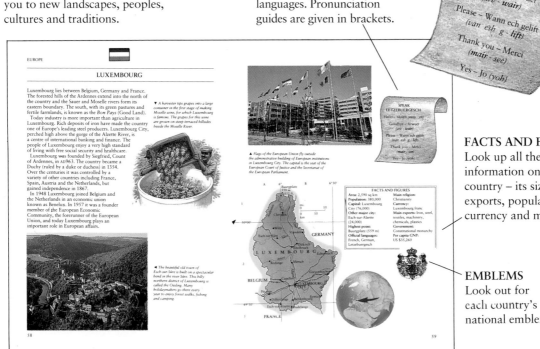

EMBLEMS
Look out for each country's national emblem.

MAPS
Find the capital, highest point, major towns and important transport routes on each country's detailed relief map.

FEATURE BOXES
Explore famous sites and the history behind them. Read about exciting events, traditions and religious festivals. Find out about important leaders and the roles they have played in world history.

THE RUINS AT KILWA KISIWANI
The ruins of a mosque lie on the tiny island of Kilwa Kisiwani, near Kilwa Kivinje. Between the 1100s and the late 1400s this island was the most important Islamic centre on the Swahili coast. It was at the height of its power in the 1200s when Arab traders exported gold, ivory and hides to Arabia and India. The traders brought their Muslim faith and built beautiful mosques in the style typical of Arab architecture. The domes and arches were specially shaped so that the air inside the mosques remained cool and refreshing.

LOCATOR GLOBES
A red arrow positions each country within its continent.

FACTS AND FIGURES
Area: 112,090 sq km
Population: 5,595,000
Capital: Tegucigalpa (679,000)
Other major city: San Pedro Sula (461,000)
Highest point: Cerro Las Minas (2,849 m)
Official language: Spanish
Main religion: Christianity
Currency: Lempira
Main exports: Coffee, bananas, timber, meat, sugar, shrimps, lobsters
Government: Republic
Per capita GNP: US $580

FLAGS
The latest flag for each independent country is shown.

FOOD BOXES
Find out about some of the tastiest traditional dishes in the world.

TANZANIA People and History

N'DIZI YA NA NYAMA
N'dizi ya na Nyama is a tasty stew made of beef, coconut milk, tomatoes and unripe bananas or plantains. A plantain is similar to a banana, but must be cooked before it is eaten. Bananas are widely grown in Tanzania and are often used in cooking.

Tanzania is made up of two countries that joined together in 1964 – Tanganyika on the African mainland and the island country of Zanzibar. Its peoples are as varied as its scenery and wildlife. There are well over 100 ethnic groups. Although the different peoples have their own languages, most Tanzanians also speak Swahili.

During the early Middle Ages Arab traders settled along the coast of what is now Tanzania. They intermarried with the Africans who lived there, spreading the Muslim faith that is still practised by one third of Tanzania's people. The Swahili culture, a mixture of African and Arab traditions, was also developed. In the 1600s the sultans of Oman, a country on the Arabian peninsula, took control of Zanzibar. They planted cloves and traded in ivory and slaves brought from the east African interior.

Late in the 1800s Germany ruled Tanganyika, while Zanzibar came under British rule. After World War I the British governed both countries until the mainland gained independence in 1961. Zanzibar gained independence in 1963 and Tanzania was formed in 1964 by its first president, Julius Nyerere.

Unlike many other African countries, Tanzania has not suffered from ethnic violence. Although it is very poor, has undergone war with Uganda and endured serious economic problems, Tanzania has tried to solve the difficulties in its own way. Recently great efforts have been made to improve farming, healthcare and education. Today Tanzania has one of the highest literacy rates in Africa.

◄ Children celebrate at a Muslim wedding. Tanzanians follow Islam, Christianity and traditional African beliefs in about equal numbers.

► Porters carry fossilised brachiosaurus bones. They are among the 250 tonnes of dinosaur bones found at Tendaguru, just north of Lindi, between 1909 and 1913. The fossils were all shipped to the Berlin Museum in Germany.

▲ A Makonde carver works on a wooden sculpture. The Makonde people, who live on the coast and along the Mozambique border, are famed for their skill at wood carving.

THE RUINS AT KILWA KISIWANI
The ruins of a mosque lie on the tiny island of Kilwa Kisiwani, near Kilwa Kivinje. Between the 1100s and the late 1400s this island was the most important Islamic centre on the Swahili coast. It was at the height of its power in the 1200s when Arab traders exported gold, ivory and hides to Arabia and India. The traders brought their Muslim faith and built beautiful mosques in the style typical of Arab architecture. The domes and arches were specially shaped so that the air inside the mosques remained cool and refreshing.

206

207

N'DIZI YA NA NYAMA
N'dizi ya na Nyama is a tasty stew made of beef, coconut milk, tomatoes and unripe bananas or plantains. A plantain is similar to a banana but must be cooked before it is eaten. Bananas are widely grown in Tanzania and are often used in cooking.

COLOUR PHOTOGRAPHS AND ILLUSTRATIONS
Over 3,000 colour photographs and illustrations give a detailed picture of life in all the countries of the world.

USING THE MAPS

The box below contains a map key. It explains what the different symbols on the maps in this encyclopedia mean. For example, a square marks a capital city and a black line marks a road. On the right is a sample map. The lines of latitude and longitude are marked in degrees. The letters and numbers between the lines are the grid references. They help you to find places on the map by identifying the square in which they are found.

The scale bar on a map helps you to measure distances. On this map 2.2 centimetres equals 200 miles and 1.4 centimetres equals 200 kilometres.

The town of Antserañana is marked by a circle. The circle is in grid reference B1. To find it, all you have to do is look down the map from B and across the map from 1.

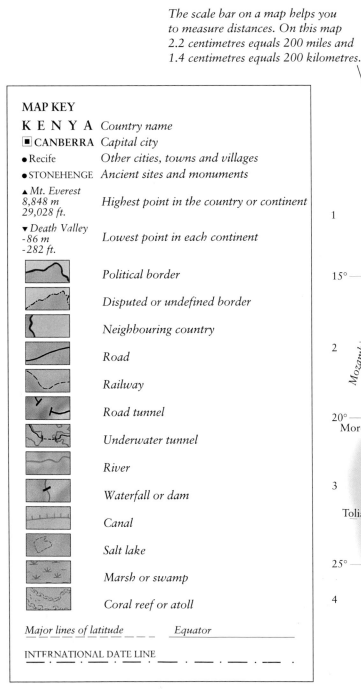

MAP KEY

K E N Y A	Country name
■ CANBERRA	Capital city
● Recife	Other cities, towns and villages
● STONEHENGE	Ancient sites and monuments
▲ Mt. Everest 8,848 m 29,028 ft.	Highest point in the country or continent
▼ Death Valley -86 m -282 ft.	Lowest point in each continent
	Political border
	Disputed or undefined border
	Neighbouring country
	Road
	Railway
	Road tunnel
	Underwater tunnel
	River
	Waterfall or dam
	Canal
	Salt lake
	Marsh or swamp
	Coral reef or atoll

Major lines of latitude ——— Equator

INTERNATIONAL DATE LINE

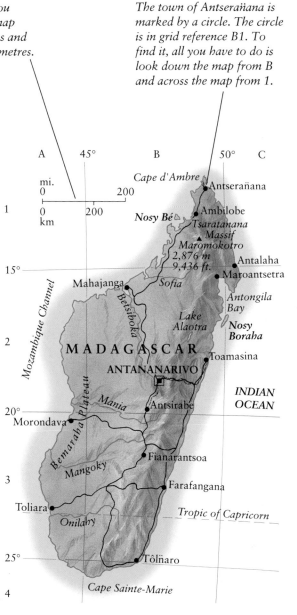

EUROPE

Arctic Circle

Tropic of Cancer

Equator

EUROPE *Geography*

Europe is the smallest continent in the world apart from Australia. It stretches westwards from the Ural Mountains to the Atlantic Ocean. The Urals form the border with the continent of Asia, which is part of the same landmass. Europe's coastline is deeply indented, with many peninsulas, bays and islands. The largest island is Great Britain, just off its northwest coast.

The most northerly areas lie in the cold, snowy wilderness above the Arctic Circle. From there, the great arm of Scandinavia curves south around the Baltic Sea. Much of central Europe is an enormous plain, once covered in trees, but now largely cleared for farmland. Summers are hot and winters bitterly cold. This plain stretches from Russia across to France and southeastern England, taking in the countries of Poland, Germany, the Netherlands and Belgium. In the west the climate is milder, affected by rain-bearing winds from the Atlantic Ocean and a warm ocean current called the North Atlantic Drift.

Southern Europe is divided from the north of the continent by the towering mountain ranges of the Pyrenees, Alps and Carpathians. The lands around the Mediterranean Sea enjoy mild winters and warm summers. Olives, oranges, lemons, grapes and cotton grow well in these areas. In the far southeast rise the arid, rugged mountains of Greece, with its many rocky islands.

In the southwest the Iberian Peninsula juts out into the Atlantic Ocean. Much of it is a hot, dry plateau. It is separated from North Africa by the narrow Strait of Gibraltar.

▲ *The Iron Gates are spectacular walls of rock in the Samaria Gorge, on the Greek island of Crete. This is Europe's longest ravine. Crete is one of the largest islands in the Mediterranean Sea.*

▶ *The ice of Norway's Jostedal Glacier melts into the sparkling blue waters of a lake. It is the largest glacier on the European continent. Other famous European glaciers are the Mer de Glace and the Aletsch, both in the Alps.*

NORTH ATLANTIC OCEAN

Ir

B.
Bis.

D.
Iberia
Peninsu.
Tagus
Mese

Strait of Gibra

6

◄ *Molten lava pours from a vent on Mount Etna. This volcano, which towers over 3,300 metres above the island of Sicily, is the highest in Europe. It is thought to have been active for more than two and a half million years. Some of the most active volcanoes in Europe are found around the Apennine Peninsula.*

7

EUROPE *Political*

Throughout its history Europe has had a great influence on world politics. It was the ancient Greeks who first created a democracy, in about 450BC. This system, where the government is chosen by the people, is widespread today. During the Middle Ages the Roman Catholic Church held great political influence across Europe. By the 1700s power had shifted away from the Church into the hands of a few nations such as Spain and Great Britain. They grew rich from exploiting Asia, Africa and the Americas. Many of these colonies did not gain their independence until this century.

▲ *The flags of the European Union fly outside the headquarters of the Council of Europe in Strasbourg, France.*

Both World War I (1914-1918) and World War II (1939-1945) began in Europe. After World War II the continent split into communist countries in the east, led by the Soviet Union, and non-communist nations in the west, supported by the United States of America. Europe became the centre of a power struggle between communist and non-communist countries. This was known as the Cold War. In the 1980s reforms in the Soviet Union and eastern Europe led to the collapse of communism there. New states emerged when the Soviet Union, Yugoslavia and Czechoslovakia broke up. The Cold War ended, but conflict between ethnic groups and economic problems caused new tensions in eastern Europe.

Fifteen western European nations had joined the European Union by 1995. This organization was first set up in the 1950s. Today it is working to unify the different countries of Europe politically and economically.

◀ *Germany's Berlin Wall is knocked down in 1989, marking the end of the division of Germany into East and West. The wall had been built in 1961 by the communist German Democratic Republic (East Germany).*

◄ *Queen Elizabeth II of England* (far left) *greets King Olav V of Norway* (second left) *during a state occasion. Sweden, Spain, Denmark, Netherlands, Luxembourg, Belgium, Monaco and Liechtenstein also have monarchs. Today European kings and queens have limited powers. Real control lies with each country's government.*

KEY TO MAP

1 ANDORRA
2 BELGIUM
3 NETHERLANDS
4 LUXEMBOURG
5 SWITZERLAND
6 LIECHTENSTEIN
7 MONACO
8 VATICAN CITY
9 SAN MARINO
10 CZECH REPUBLIC
11 SLOVAKIA
12 AUSTRIA
13 HUNGARY
14 SLOVENIA
15 CROATIA
16 BOSNIA-HERZEGOVINA
17 YUGOSLAVIA
18 ALBANIA
19 MACEDONIA
20 MOLDOVA
21 LITHUANIA
22 LATVIA
23 ESTONIA

EUROPE *Plants and Animals*

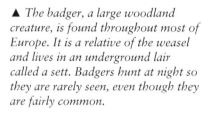

On this crowded continent wild plants and animals have to compete for space with human farms, settlements and industries. Even so, with its many climates and habitats, Europe supports a rich variety of wildlife.

The cold lands around the Arctic Circle are home to reindeer, geese and snowy owls. A little farther south the mosses and lichens of the tundra, which is frozen for most of the year, give way to forests of spruce and birch. These spread through northern Europe and are roamed by bears and wolves.

In the milder climates of northwestern Europe, mixed woodlands of oak, ash and beech are home to squirrels, deer, wild boar and many kinds of birds. Seabirds such as gulls, auks and gannets breed around the rocky Atlantic coastline. Many types of fish can be found in the Atlantic Ocean, including cod, herring, salmon, sardines and sturgeon.

The grasslands of central Europe are largely used for farming, but also support many small mammals and birds. Great hawks and eagles prey on the partridges, quails, mice, moles, rats and other small creatures in this region.

Farther south, the mountain range known as the Alps has its own wildlife, such as burrowing mammals called marmots and the goat-like chamois. Alpine flowers include the deep-blue gentian and the tufted, white edelweiss. On Europe's southernmost fringes, around the Mediterranean Sea, olive trees, cypresses and umbrella pines flourish. Snakes, lizards and tortoises are among the animals that bask in the warm sun of this region.

▲ *The badger, a large woodland creature, is found throughout most of Europe. It is a relative of the weasel and lives in an underground lair called a sett. Badgers hunt at night so they are rarely seen, even though they are fairly common.*

▼ *Powerful Atlantic salmon leap up a waterfall as they travel upstream to breed. Atlantic salmon spawn (lay their eggs) in the rivers of northwestern Europe. The young salmon spend a year or two at sea before returning to the same stream where they themselves hatched.*

▲ *The colourful peacock butterfly is common all over Europe, except in the Arctic. It can live in woodlands, gardens and even mountain areas. The beautiful eye markings on the wings are designed to scare off hungry birds.*

◀ *The puffin is a seabird that lives around the Atlantic coasts of Europe. Its beak becomes striped in blue, red and yellow during the breeding season. The puffin feeds on small fish, including sand eels. It nests in burrows.*

▲ *The green lizard is the second largest lizard in Europe after the ocellated lizard. It can be up to 45 centimetres long. Green lizards are found across southern and central Europe. They live in rocky places or on scrubland, feeding on insects, slow worms and other lizards.*

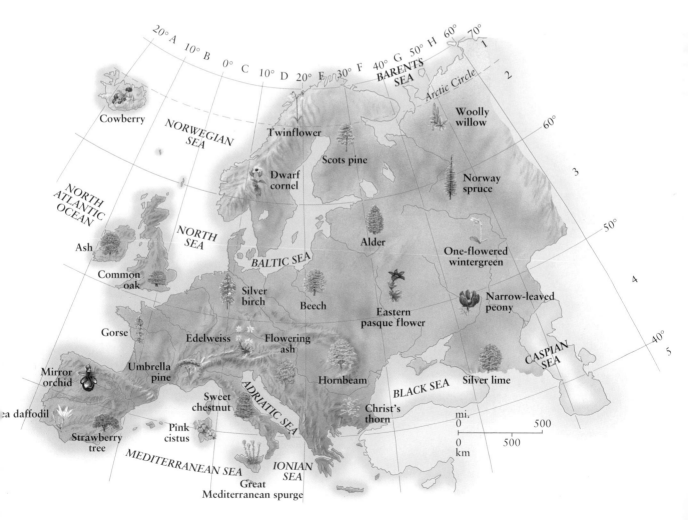

11

ICELAND

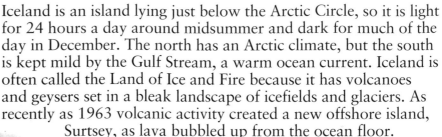

▼ *Black rocks rise from the shallow waters of Lake Myvatn in northern Iceland. They were formed from the cooled lava of ancient volcanoes. Iceland has over 200 volcanoes, many of them active.*

Iceland is an island lying just below the Arctic Circle, so it is light for 24 hours a day around midsummer and dark for much of the day in December. The north has an Arctic climate, but the south is kept mild by the Gulf Stream, a warm ocean current. Iceland is often called the Land of Ice and Fire because it has volcanoes and geysers set in a bleak landscape of icefields and glaciers. As recently as 1963 volcanic activity created a new offshore island, Surtsey, as lava bubbled up from the ocean floor.

Iceland was settled by Vikings from Norway around AD870. In AD930 Icelanders founded a parliament, the Althing. This still survives today and is the oldest parliament in the world. In 1262 the island came under the rule of Norway and from 1380 it was ruled by Denmark. Iceland became independent in 1944.

The country depends on fishing for its economy. Trawlers sail the North Atlantic and Greenland Sea in search of cod, herring, capelin and haddock. Farming is difficult in the harsh landscape, but sheep, dairy cattle and sturdy Icelandic ponies are raised in the lowlands. There is little industry so many goods have to be imported. The cost of living is therefore high, but most Icelanders have low heating bills. Almost boiling water from underground springs is pumped directly to 85 percent of people's homes. Spring water also heats greenhouses so that tomatoes and flowers can be grown throughout the year. The hot springs offer Iceland cheap energy without pollution.

▼ *Icelanders bathe in a pool heated naturally from a hot spring. In the background a power station pumps the hot spring water directly to people's taps and radiators.*

FACTS AND FIGURES

Area: 103,000 sq km
Population: 263,000
Capital: Reykjavik (101,000)
Other major city: Kopavogur (17,000)
Highest point: Hvannadalshnukur (2,119 m)
Official language: Icelandic
Main religion: Christianity
Currency: Krona
Main exports: Fish and fish products, shellfish, crustaceans, animal feed, aluminium, iron, steel, diatomite
Government: Constitutional republic
Per capita GNP: US $23,670

▲ Almost half the population lives in or near the seaport of Reykjavik, Iceland's largest city and main commercial and cultural centre. Reykjavik is the most northerly capital city in the world.

▼ Skidoos (motor skis) are used to cross Iceland's northern snowfields. They are an effective and enjoyable means of transport in a country that experiences heavy snowfalls during the winter months.

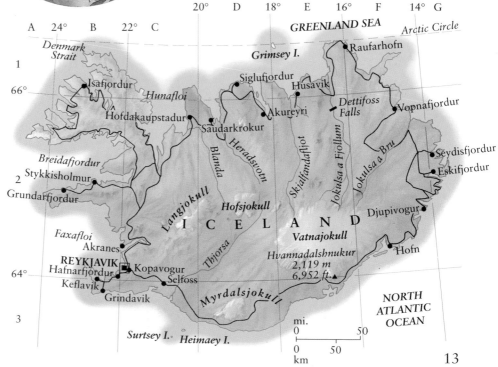

NORWAY

The Kingdom of Norway stretches above the Arctic Circle to Europe's most northerly point, North Cape. There, it is dark all day in mid-winter while during the brief summer the sun still shines at midnight. This part of the country is known as the Land of the Midnight Sun.

Norway has a rugged coastline with deep sea inlets called fiords. They form natural harbours, protected from the rough seas by chains of islands. The coastal areas are kept ice-free by warm ocean currents, while inland the forested mountains and steep valleys receive heavy winter snow.

Norwegians share a common history with their Scandinavian neighbours, Sweden and Denmark. In the early Middle Ages they were Vikings, the seafarers and warriors who sailed to Iceland, Greenland and North America. Norway has been ruled by both Denmark and Sweden, but gained independence in 1905.

For centuries most Norwegians have lived along the coast and made their living from the sea. Dried fish was already an important export in the Middle Ages and shipbuilding began to develop as a major industry in the 1600s. Both these industries are still important today and Norway's shipping fleet is one of the most modern in the world. Since oil was discovered in the North Sea in the 1960s the Norwegians have also become experts at oil rig construction. Norway's swiftly flowing rivers produce hydroelectric power and its forests provide timber for wood and paper. Some trees are grown especially for commercial purposes.

FACTS AND FIGURES
Area: 386,960 sq km
Population: 4,312,000
Capital: Oslo (460,000)
Other major city:
Bergen (213,000)
Highest point:
Galdhopiggen (2,469 m)
Official language:
Norwegian
Main religion:
Christianity
Currency:
Norwegian krone
Main exports: Oil and oil products, natural gas, ships, fish, paper, wood pulp, machinery
Government:
Constitutional monarchy
Per capita GNP:
US $25,800

▼ Children gather around a spinning wheel in a primary school classroom in Oslo, Norway's capital. They are being shown how to spin wool in the traditional way. However, today most wool is spun by machines.

▲ This stave church in central Norway is almost 1,000 years old. It was built shortly after the Vikings were converted to Christianity. Between 1000 and 1300 wooden stave churches were built all over Norway. They are so-called because of the four staves, or wooden corner posts, around which they are built.

B 12° C 16° D 20° E 24° F 28° G 32°

1

North Cape

Hammerfest

Vadso
Kirkenes

70° NORWEGIAN
SEA

Tromso

RUSSIA

A 8°

Vesteralen

FINLAND

2

68°

Lofoten Is.

Harstad
Narvik

3

Bodo

66°

Arctic Circle

4°

Mo

NORTH
ATLANTIC
OCEAN

64°

4

Steinkjer

5

Kristiansund

Trondheim
Fjord

62°

Alesund

Andalsnes

Trondheim

SWEDEN

N O R W A Y

Jostedal
Glacier
Sogne
Fiord

Galdhopiggen
2,469 m
8,100 ft.

Lillehammer

6

Bergen

Hamar

60°

Hardanger
Fiord

Honefoss
Drammen

OSLO
Moss

7

Haugesund

Stavanger

Skien

Fredrikstad

58°

Kristiansand

NORTH
SEA

mi.
0   200

0   200
km

Skagerrak

▼ *The blue waters of the
Geirangerfiord in central
Norway are so deep that
large ships can travel far
inland. The Norwegian
fiords were carved out of
the rock by glaciers during
the Ice Age.*

◄ *Fish are sorted at a
processing plant in Tromso.
The Norwegians have exported
dried fish since the early
1200s. Today's catch of
herring, whiting, cod and
haddock is frozen and
canned as well as dried in
the traditional way.*

SWEDEN *Introduction*

Sweden forms the eastern part of the Scandinavian Peninsula. From the icy wastes of the Arctic the country stretches south towards Denmark. There are mountains along the border with Norway, descending to lowlands along the coast. The long Baltic coastline is broken into many islands. In the centre and the south of the country there is a maze of lakes that were gouged out of the landscape more than 10,000 years ago during the last Ice Age.

Sweden is one of the larger countries in Europe, but also one of the most thinly populated. More than half the land is covered in forests of spruce and pine. These woodlands are home to wolves, bears, lynx and red deer. They also provide timber for Sweden's highly profitable furniture and paper industries. The fertile farmland in the south produces most of the country's food. Rich iron ore deposits in Lapland are another of the country's valuable resources – some of the ore is used for steel production in Sweden, but most is exported abroad. Rivers are harnessed to produce hydroelectric power for these and other industries. Sweden's wealth of natural resources has made it a prosperous country.

Swedes have one of the best standards of living in the world. They pay high taxes, but have many welfare benefits including free healthcare and pensions. In the early 1990s Sweden's high wages made it difficult for the country's industries to compete with goods produced in other countries. So in 1991 a new prime minister, Carl Bildt, introduced stricter controls on public spending to deal with this economic problem. However, Sweden remains one of the wealthiest countries in Europe.

ENDANGERED WORLD — The badger-like wolverine is now protected in Sweden. It has been hunted as a pest and for its fur.

◄ *Stockholm, the capital of Sweden, lies on the Baltic Sea coast. It is built on 14 small islands that are connected by about 50 bridges. Stockholm's cathedral and Gamla Stan (Old Town) date back to the Middle Ages.*

FACTS AND FIGURES

Area: 449,960 sq km
Population: 8,716,000
Capital: Stockholm
(685,000)
Other major cities:
Goteborg (434,000),
Malmo (237,000)
Highest point:
Kebnekaise (2,111 m)
Official language:
Swedish

Main religion:
Christianity
Currency: Krona
Main exports: Vehicles,
machinery, iron, steel,
paper products
Government:
Constitutional
monarchy
Per capita GNP:
US $26,780

▼ *Summer sunshine warms the fields near Uddevalla in southern Sweden. The land is very fertile here and farmers grow wheat, oats, sugarbeet and potatoes.*

◄ *In the far north a Sami (Lapp) herder cares for his reindeer. Today only a small number of Sami people live a traditional nomadic way of life, keeping reindeer for their meat, milk and hides. Most Sami earn a living from farming, fishing or mining.*

SWEDEN *People and History*

The Sami (Lapps), who live north of the Arctic Circle, are descended from the first inhabitants of Sweden. Germanic peoples moved into the area about 2,000 years ago and most Swedes are descended from them. Like their Scandinavian neighbours in Norway and Denmark, the Swedes became Viking seafarers. From about AD800 they raided the coasts of Europe and founded settlements as far away as eastern Russia.

In 1397 Sweden was united with Norway and Denmark under Danish rule. It regained independence in 1523 under the leadership of Gustavus Vasa, who was crowned King Gustav I. Sweden became the most powerful nation in northern Europe, winning numerous victories in battle under King Gustavus Adolphus during the early 1600s and King Charles XII in the early 1700s. In 1818, after a brief period in which parliament ruled, Jean-Baptiste Bernadotte was elected to the Swedish throne. He had fewer powers than previous monarchs. The present Swedish royal family is descended from Bernadotte, but today the power of government lies with a democratically elected parliament called the Riksdag. Since 1993 the Sami have also had their own council, which is called the *Sameting*. In 1995 Sweden became a member of the European Union.

Today most Swedish people live in towns and cities, working in service or manufacturing industries. Many farm labourers also have part-time jobs in nearby towns. The Swedish government is well known for its fair treatment of workers and for excellent social services. Wages are generally high and the Swedes spend more of their earnings on holidays than any other nation in the world.

▲ *This is a model of the* Vasa *warship, which sank in Stockholm's harbour at five o'clock on August 10, 1628. It was raised from the seabed in 1961. Most of its contents, such as 4,000 coins, meat, butter and neatly folded sailors' clothes, had been preserved by the salt water. The original ship is in Stockholm Museum.*

SPEAK SWEDISH

Hello – Hej *(hay)*

Goodbye (formal) – Adjö
(a - yair)

Goodbye (informal) – Hej då
(hay - daw)

Thank you – Tack *(tak)*

Yes – Ja *(yah)*

No – Nej *(nay)*

▲ *This head of a Viking warrior is a silver charm from the AD900s. It was found at Aska, a small town near Kristianstad. The Swedish Vikings set up trading posts in Russia and the Ukraine. They also explored some of the rivers of eastern Europe.*

**JANSSON'S FRESTELSE
(Jansson's temptation)**

An onion and anchovy mixture is layered in between thin slices of potato to make this popular Swedish dish. Fresh cream is poured on the top and the pie is baked until it is golden brown.

▲ *People dance around a maypole to celebrate Midsummer's Eve. This festival marks the return of summer, when the daylight hours are long and nights very short. In Lapland, above the Arctic Circle, it stays light for 24 hours a day for part of the summer season.*

▶ *King Carl XVI Gustav, Queen Silvia and the royal family attend a state occasion. The heir to the throne is Crown Princess Victoria (second from left).*

FINLAND

There are thousands of islands and lakes in this scenic country. Almost two thirds of the land is forested and in some areas home to bears, wolves and arctic foxes. In the northernmost part of Finland, beyond the Arctic Circle, the country takes in part of Lapland. The Sami (Lapps) in this area are descendants of the earliest known peoples to settle in Finland. A small number still live in the traditional way. However, most of the population live in the south and are ethnic Finns who migrated from the Ural Mountains in Russia around 2,000 years ago. There are also some people of Swedish descent.

The history of Finland has been shaped by its two powerful neighbours, Sweden and Russia. Sweden started to gain control from the 1100s. Russia invaded in 1809 and the country became part of the Russian empire. However, when the Russian Revolution broke out in 1917 Finland declared its independence.

The prosperity of modern Finland is built on the development of its natural resources. The dense forests provide large supplies of timber for furniture and paper-making. Many of these products are sold abroad, accounting for about a third of Finland's exports. To ensure future supplies and to protect the environment, trees are continually replanted under a strict conservation policy. The country also makes use of its enormous water supplies – about a quarter of Finland's power is generated by hydroelectric schemes. The lakes and rivers provide plentiful trout and pike. Sea fishing is also a major industry.

FACTS AND FIGURES

Area: 338,150 sq km
Population: 5,067,000
Capital: Helsinki (502,000)
Other major cities: Tampere (175,000), Turku (160,000)
Highest point: Mt Haltia (1,328 m)
Official languages: Finnish, Swedish
Main religion: Christianity
Currencies: Euro, Markka
Main exports: Timber, vehicles, paper products, machinery, ships, clothes, furniture
Government: Constitutional republic
Per capita GNP: US $22,980

◄ *Finland has about 60,000 lakes, most of them in the central part of the country, which is known as the Lake District. The lakes were gouged out of the landscape by glaciers during the Ice Age more than 10,000 years ago.*

A 20° B 24° C 28° D 32°

1

70°

Mt. Haltia
1,328 m
4,357 ft

NORWAY

Lake Inari

mi.
0   100
0   100
km

2

Ivalo

68°

LAPLAND

SWEDEN

Kolari

3

Arctic Circle

Rovaniemi

66°

Tornio   Kuusamo

RUSSIA

Gulf
of
Bothnia

Oulu

4

Lake Oulujarvi

Raahe

Kajaani

64°

Kokkola   F I N L A N D

Jakobstad   Iisalmi   Lake Pielinen

Vaasa

5

Kuopio

Seinajoki   Joensuu

Jyvaskyla   Varkaus

62°   Savonlinna

Mikkeli

Pori   Tampere

Rauma   Hameenlinna   Lahti   Imatra

6   Lappeenranta

Riihimaki   Kouvola

Aland Is.   Turku   Salo   Kotka

60°   HELSINKI

Mariehamn   Gulf of Finland

BALTIC
SEA

7   ESTONIA

▲ The capital, Helsinki, is dark in the middle of a winter day. Like other Arctic countries, Finland is dark for most of each day in winter and light throughout midsummer nights. This is because of its northerly location.

▲ Cross-country skiing is a popular winter sport in Finland. With snow on the ground for up to seven months a year, many Finnish children learn to ski as soon as they can walk. For centuries skis and sleds offered the only practical way of crossing snowy forests and wildernesses.

◄ One of Finland's major shipbuilding yards is at Turku, where the Gulf of Bothnia meets the Gulf of Finland. Finnish shipyards specialize in icebreakers and ferries that cross the rough northern waters.

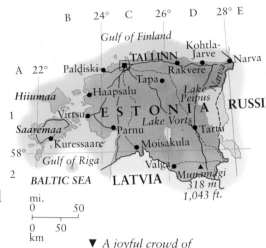

THE BALTIC STATES

ESTONIA is a flat country and almost half of it is farmland. There are many forests, cultivated for the country's timber, paper and furniture industries. Peat bog covers some areas. Estonia also includes over 800 islands in the Baltic Sea.

The ancestors of today's Estonians were people who settled here and formed independent states thousands of years ago. In the 1200s the Teutonic Knights, religious crusaders from Germany, conquered the land and converted its inhabitants to Christianity. Over the centuries that followed Estonia was ruled by Danes, Swedes, Poles and Russians, but the people kept the Estonian culture and spirit alive. They broke free of Russian rule in 1918, but Russia, as the communist Soviet Union, took over again in 1940. Estonia remained under Soviet rule for the next 50 years. This was a time of heavy industrialization and suppression of the Estonian language and customs. Estonia declared itself independent when the Soviet Union broke up in 1991. Today Estonians are free to enjoy their national culture and traditions again.

▼ A joyful crowd of Estonians wave national flags. They are celebrating their independence from the Soviet Union in 1991.

LATVIA is a country of low, forested hills, lakes and streams. This was another of the Baltic States to break away from the Soviet Union in 1991. The Latvians (or Letts) had known centuries of rule by Germans, Poles, Swedes and Russians. Latvia was independent from 1918 until 1940, when it became part of the Soviet Union. During the years of communism many Latvians (like other Baltic nationals) were sent to labour camps in Siberia. At the same time thousands of Russians settled here. The Soviet Union took farms into state ownership and set up factories. Heavy industry has caused serious pollution and Latvia has a strong environmental movement that is working to combat this.

The Latvian people also have a distinct culture. Their language is one of the oldest in Europe and singing in choirs is a highly popular tradition.

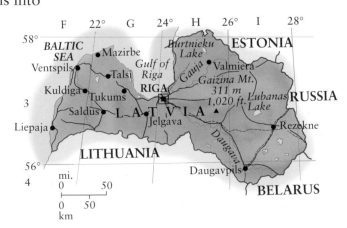

LITHUANIA's coast has white sand dunes and popular holiday resorts. Inland, a plain with lakes and forests rises to hills in the west and southeast. Large areas of swamp have been drained to increase farmland. Farm products include cereal crops, flax, sugar beet and potatoes. Cattle and pigs are also raised. Most Lithuanians, however, live in cities and work in industries such as construction, chemical production, food processing and shipbuilding. Traditional singing and dancing are important to the people and huge festivals take place each year.

People have lived here since prehistoric times. Historical records show that trade was flourishing around 50BC, when amber was sold to the Romans. In the 1200s the Lithuanians fought off German crusaders and kept their freedom. The country was united with Poland in 1569, but in 1795 came under Russian rule. Like the other Baltic States, Lithuania was independent from 1918 until 1940, when it became part of the Soviet Union. The Soviets industrialized the country and many Lithuanians flocked from rural areas to get jobs in the new factories. Lithuania declared independence when Soviet communism collapsed and the Union broke up in 1991. The first democratic elections were held the following year.

FACTS AND FIGURES

ESTONIA/LATVIA/ LITHUANIA
Governments: Republics
Main religion: Christianity
Main exports: Food, chemicals, manufactured goods

ESTONIA
Area: 45,100 sq km
Population: 1,517,000
Capital: Tallinn (503,000)
Official language: Estonian
Per capita GNP: US $2,750

LATVIA
Area: 63,700 sq km
Population: 2,586,000
Capital: Riga (911,000)
Official language: Latvian
Per capita GNP: US $1,930

LITHUANIA
Area: 65,200 sq km
Population: 3,730,000
Capital: Vilnius (593,000)
Official language: Lithuanian
Per capita GNP: US $1,310

▲ *St Anne's Church and the Church of the Bernardines is in Vilnius, the capital of Lithuania. About 90 percent of Lithuanians are Roman Catholics.*

DENMARK *Introduction*

Denmark consists of a mainland and nearly five hundred islands. The mainland is called Jutland. It is a long peninsula that extends northwards from Germany and divides the stormy waters of the North Sea from the Baltic. The biggest island is Sjaelland. Danish territory also includes two distant, self-governing provinces – the vast Arctic wilderness of Greenland and the rugged Faeroe Islands, which lie between Scotland and Iceland.

Almost completely surrounded by sea, Denmark has a mild climate with strong winds. It is a flat, low-lying, green land. There is little wild vegetation in Denmark because farmland, which is the best in Scandinavia, takes up most of the countryside. Denmark is farmed intensively – chemical pesticides, fertilizers and modern machinery are used to get the highest yield from the land. Danish produce, especially butter, cheese and bacon, is exported throughout the European Union. Fishing fleets bring in mackerel, herring and cod.

Oil and gas are drilled in the North Sea, but Denmark has few mineral resources on land. However, the Danes have developed wind turbines to harness wind power and generate electricity. These turbines are now exported, along with more traditional Danish crafts such as glass, silverware and furniture. Danish goods are noted for both their quality and high standards of design.

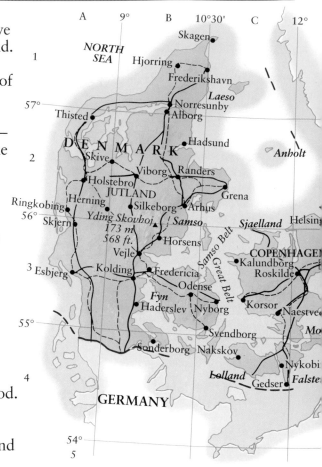

◀ *A tractor goes to work on Fyn island. Its fertile clay soil supports grain crops, oil-seed rape and sugar beet. There is also rich pasture for cattle. On the horizon a wind turbine generates electricity.*

► *Queen Margrethe II and her husband greet crowds in Copenhagen. The Queen succeeded her father in 1972. When she ascended the throne, her husband, a French count called Henri de Laborde de Monpezat, became Prince Henrik of Denmark.*

30' E 15° F

50

50

EDEN

BALTIC SEA

Bornholm

Ronne ●

FACTS AND FIGURES

Area: 43,080 sq km
Population: 5,189,000
Capital: Copenhagen (1,343,000)
  Other major cities: Arhus (272,000), Odense (181,000)
  Highest point: Yding Skovhoj (173 m)
Official language: Danish

Main religion: Christianity
Currency: Danish krone
Main exports: Meat, fish, dairy products, electrical equipment, machinery, transport equipment
Government: Constitutional monarchy
Per capita GNP: US $25,930

DANISH PASTRIES
These sweet rolls are rich, flaky and often iced. The Danes eat them at any time of day, but particularly at mid-morning with cups of strong coffee. Delicious Danish pastries have become popular in many parts of the world.

► *The picturesque New Harbour in Copenhagen was built during the 1670s. Boats bob in front of the beautiful waterfront buildings, which are kept perfectly restored.*

DENMARK *People and History*

There were people living in this land 100,000 years ago, then during the last Ice Age most life perished. The ice slowly melted around 8000BC, small plants grew and wandering herds of reindeer came to eat them. The animals were soon followed north by nomadic hunters. In about AD800 Danish and other Scandinavian seafarers called Vikings began raiding the coasts of Europe. The Vikings ruled England in 1016, then expanded their empire into Germany. In 1397 Denmark united with its neighbours Norway and Sweden, but over the centuries that followed there were several wars between the three Scandinavian countries and Denmark lost much of its territory. Its present boundaries were decided in 1920.

Today Denmark is a country of peace and prosperity. Its social welfare schemes ensure free healthcare, education, pensions and other benefits. About 85 percent of the population lives in towns and cities and the majority works in service industries. Almost all enjoy a high standard of living. Traffic pollution is a problem in the cities, but many Danes, including the royal family, are helping to reduce this by using bicycles. In rural areas most people are farmers. Farms in Denmark are privately owned, although some farmers have set up co-operative dairies and slaughterhouses where ownership, work and profits are shared among a group. Danish farming practices are renowned throughout the world for their efficiency.

▲ *Danes in traditional costumes gather before a folk dance. There are about 150,000 members of folk dancing clubs in Denmark. They meet regularly in farm buildings and dance to the sound of the violin.*

◄ *As evening falls the illuminations are switched on to create a magical world at the Tivoli Gardens. Copenhagen's famous pleasure gardens offer entertainments such as ballet, restaurants and fairground attractions. They are named after the famous Tivoli Gardens in Italy and were opened in 1843.*

▶ *An infant class gathers around the teacher at a school in Alborg, northern Jutland, to listen to a story. Some of the world's favourite children's stories come from Denmark.* The Ugly Duckling *and* The Snow Queen *were written here by Hans Christian Andersen about 150 years ago.*

SPEAK DANISH

Hello – Goddag
(go - day)

Goodbye – Farvel
(fah - vel)

Thank you – Tack
(tahk)

Yes – Ja *(yah)*

No – Nej *(nie)*

THE GUNDESTRUP CAULDRON

This silver bowl was found in a lake at Gundestrup in Jutland. Historians believe that it dates from between 100 and 300BC. However, its origins remain a mystery as it combines many European styles. The cauldron is likely to have been made by Celtic peoples because it is decorated with Celtic gods. Large areas of present-day Germany and Hungary were Celtic from 100 to 300BC and peoples in Denmark were influenced by the Celtic culture at this time.

▲ *Egeskov Castle, on the island of Fyn, rises directly out of the water. Constructed on wooden stakes sunk into the bed of the lake, it was built as a fortress in 1554. Today the castle houses a vehicle museum containing horse-drawn and old cars.*

UNITED KINGDOM *Introduction*

The United Kingdom (UK) is a union of four lands. England, Scotland and Wales take up the island of Great Britain, while the province of Northern Ireland consists of six counties in Ireland. The UK also has close economic and political links with self-governing territories such as the Isle of Man, in the Irish Sea, and the Channel Islands, off the coast of northwest France.

The UK is an industrial nation with a large population for its size. However, outside its crowded towns and cities there is dramatic and beautiful countryside, including the heather-covered glens of Scotland, the deep valleys and mountains of Wales and the rolling, grassy fields of England and Northern Ireland. A mild and wet climate makes much of the land green and fertile.

The sea has played an important role in the history of this island nation. During the 1700s and 1800s the British Navy was the most powerful fleet in the world. British control of the seas enabled it to build a vast overseas empire and become a great trading nation.

Today the UK is still a major industrial power, but its political influence on world affairs has declined. Although the UK is a monarchy, real political power lies with parliament. During recent years many people in Scotland and Wales have campaigned for separate parliaments. In Northern Ireland some of the inhabitants want to be part of the Republic of Ireland. Since 1969 this has caused a bitter civil conflict, but a cease-fire in 1994 brought hopes for peace.

SPEAK WELSH

Good Morning – Bore da
*(bo - ra **dah**)*

Goodbye – Hwyl *(**hoo** - ill)*

Please – Os gwelwch yn dda
*(oss **gwell** - ooh un thah)*

Thank you   Diolch
(dee - olh)

Yes – Ie *(yeh)*

No – Nage *(**nah**-geh)*

▼ *The remains of Hadrian's Wall run across bleak hill countryside in northern England. The wall was built by the Roman Emperor Hadrian between AD122 and 126. It defended Roman Britain from bands of fierce northern warriors.*

FACTS AND FIGURES

ENGLAND/WALES/
SCOTLAND/N IRELAND
Population: 57,826,000
Main religion:
Christianity
Currency: Pound sterling
Government:
Constitutional
monarchy
Per capita GNP:
US $17,760

ENGLAND
Area: 130,420 sq km
Capital: London
(6,680,000)
Official language:
English

WALES
Area: 20,770 sq km
Capital: Cardiff
(279,000)
Official languages:
Welsh, English

SCOTLAND
Area: 77,170 sq km
Capital: Edinburgh
(438,000)
Official language:
English

N IRELAND
Area: 14,120 sq km
Capital: Belfast
(284,000)
Official language:
English

► *The Houses of Parliament, seat of the UK's government, rise from the banks of the river Thames in London. They were built between 1840 and 1870. Dominating the buildings is the clock tower, which houses a famous bell called Big Ben. The UK's form of parliamentary democracy has been used as a model by many other nations throughout the world.*

UNITED KINGDOM *Geography*

The United Kingdom (UK) takes up much of the British Isles, a group of islands lying off the northwestern coast of Europe. There are many small islands, but the two main ones are Great Britain and Ireland. The changeable but mild climate of the British Isles is affected by the Atlantic Ocean. The western coasts receive a high rainfall from the ocean winds, but the eastern coasts are drier.

The Highlands of Scotland have wild and spectacular scenery. They contain the UK's highest mountains and long lakes called lochs. The twin island chains of the Hebrides lie in the Atlantic Ocean off Scotland's west coast. Farther south the land descends to the great river Clyde. This area, known as the Central Lowlands, has low, rolling hills and good farmland. Higher hills and moorland mark the borders with England. Across the sea from Scotland the province of Northern Ireland includes farmland, deep sea inlets and Lough Neagh, the largest lake in the British Isles.

Northern England is divided by the limestone and granite heights of the Pennine range. In the northwest there are mountains and sparkling lakes. Wales is a beautiful land of green valleys, meandering rivers, grassy plains, hill farms and bleak mountains. The Cambrian Mountains cover much of the country. They are dotted with small lakes and waterfalls.

Most of central England is a rolling plain, while in the east flat lowlands border the North Sea. In the densely populated southeast, ranges of chalk hills called downs rise above fertile farmland. The southwest of the country has large stretches of heather-clad moorland. Atlantic waves beat on the rocks of the rugged southwestern peninsula.

▼ *The Giant's Causeway is an extraordinary headland on the northwest coast of Northern Ireland. Its hexagonal (six-sided) columns are formed from a volcanic rock called basalt.*

▼ *Much of the English countryside is a patchwork of small fields. They are green with pasture and golden with wheat or rape. Hedgerows and woodland divide the landscape.*

◄ *The magnificent snow-capped mountains of the Scottish Highlands rise above Loch Eil. This wild and beautiful region of Scotland contains the highest mountains of the UK. The highest of all is Ben Nevis at 1,343 metres. The mountains attract many climbers and hill walkers.*

► *A whitewashed house and thatched barn face the open sea on the island of North Uist in the Outer Hebrides. The Outer Hebrides are a chain of islands off the west coast of Scotland. Much of the land there is low and treeless, battered by gales from the Atlantic Ocean.*

◄ *The dark Mynydd Du (Black Mountain) towers above the county of Powys in South Wales. Most of Wales is mountainous. The Cambrian Mountains cover almost two thirds of the country. The only flat lands are along the English border and around the coast.*

31

UNITED KINGDOM *Economy*

The United Kingdom (UK) was the first nation in the world to change from an agricultural economy to an industrial one. This process started in the late 1760s and was called the Industrial Revolution. During the 1800s industries such as textiles, iron and steel-making, shipbuilding and heavy engineering were developed. They were fuelled by coal, which was the UK's biggest natural resource at that time. Until the 1980s these industries were the backbone of the economy. The UK is still a major industrial nation, but the products that it manufactures have changed. Newer industries such as electronics, food processing and chemicals have grown in importance. Most people now work in service industries such as administration, finance, education, healthcare and tourism. Today the UK's most important natural resource is the large fields of oil and natural gas that lie beneath the North Sea.

Only about two percent of the population is employed in farming. However, much of the country is intensively farmed to provide food for its inhabitants as well as for export. Large areas of fertile soil in southern and eastern England produce grain, fruit and vegetables. Dairy cattle graze on the green pastures of western England and sheep feed on the uplands of Scotland and Wales. Much of the UK's ancient forest and woodland has been destroyed over the years, but large conifer plantations now produce timber for building and paper-making. Fishing boats sail from ports all around the coast and the UK's fishing fleet is the fifth largest in the European Union.

▲ *Whisky is checked for quality as it matures in a wooden cask. This drink is made from malted barley. It is mashed with spring water and then fermented. Whisky is an important export for Scotland and Northern Ireland (where it is spelt whiskey).*

▶ *A steel mill glows with white heat in Sheffield, an industrial city in northern England. The UK is a major producer of steel and related products. Stainless steel knives and forks once made the name of Sheffield famous around the world.*

ECONOMIC SURVEY

Farming: The UK's chief crops are barley, potatoes and other vegetables, wheat and sugar beet. Sheep, beef and dairy cattle, pigs and poultry are raised.
Fishing: The UK fishing fleet contains about 11,000 vessels. Catches include cod, haddock, herring and plaice.

Mining: Petroleum and natural gas are leading resources. Coal and iron ore mining has declined in importance.
Industry: The UK is the world's fifth most important trading nation. The importance of manufacturing has recently declined relative to service industries.

▼ *A miner checks the shearing machine at Tower Colliery in Wales. Since the 1800s coal has been one of the most successful industries in England and Wales. However, increased competition from abroad and the use of other fuels has led to its decline. In recent years most UK coalmines have been closed down by the government. Tower Colliery was reopened when the miners joined together to buy it in 1994.*

▲ *An offshore oil rig drills in the North Sea. The oil is then transported by pipeline to the mainland. As other industries decline, oil remains one of the UK's most important sources of income.*

▶ *The Bank of England is one of the most important financial institutions in the world. Founded in 1694, it was once an ordinary bank. Today it manages the government's bank account and issues nearly all the UK's banknotes.*

UNITED KINGDOM *People*

▼ *Primary school pupils gather for morning assembly. The children's wide range of backgrounds reflects the many different peoples that live in the UK today. Britain provides free schooling, which is funded by taxes.*

The United Kingdom (UK) is not a large nation, but its history has made it home to a wide mixture of peoples, cultures and religions. The English form much the largest group. Others include the Welsh, Scots, Irish and Jews. Many people have ancestors who came from parts of the former British empire – India, Pakistan, Bengal, Hong Kong, Africa and the Caribbean.

More than four fifths of the UK's inhabitants live in England. Most of them live and work in towns or cities. At weekends and holiday times the main roads are crowded with people visiting the countryside or taking a trip to the coast. Gardening and watching or playing sport are other favourite outdoor leisure-time activities.

Although the UK is a modern land of airports, motorways and sprawling suburbs, many ancient customs are still carried on here. English Morris dancers wear traditional costume to perform at occasions such as May Day. At a Welsh festival called the Eisteddfod poets and musicians compete for honours every year. Wild celebrations and Scottish dancing mark the occasion of Hogmanay (New Year's Eve) in Scotland.

The UK has a rich literary and artistic heritage. Over the centuries its countries have produced many great poets, playwrights, novelists, painters, architects and musicians. The English language has spread around the world from North America to Australia. It is spoken throughout the British Isles, but with many different regional accents. Other languages spoken include Welsh, Scots Gaelic and Irish Gaelic.

◄ *Heavyweight Welsh rugby players scramble for the ball while the crowd roars and sings. Team sports are popular throughout the UK, with fans following football, rugby and cricket. Other popular sports include golf, angling and horse-racing.*

◄ Thousands of people spill across a park in Edinburgh, Scotland, during the annual arts festival. The main festival includes some of the world's greatest orchestras, theatre companies and artists. An unofficial fringe festival offers a chance for small theatre groups, experimental artists and comedians to perform.

► Yachts sail near Cowes, on the Isle of Wight, during the town's annual sailing regatta (race-meeting). Cowes is England's best-known yachting centre and Cowes Week is an important sporting event. All through the week, yachts of all nations race for prizes.

◄ Crowds of people cheer and wave flags at the Last Night of the Proms in London's Albert Hall. This popular season of classical concerts always ends with the same ritual – the singing of Land of Hope and Glory and Rule Britannia.

UNITED KINGDOM *History*

The United Kingdom (UK) was formed in 1801. It was made up of the countries of England, Scotland, Wales and the whole of Ireland. After 1921 southern Ireland was no longer part of the Union. England, Scotland and Wales are collectively known as Great Britain.

The recorded history of Great Britain begins with a Roman invasion in 55BC. By the AD100s the Romans had conquered much of Great Britain, apart from the far north. Roman traders and soldiers helped introduce Christianity and also established many towns. The Roman empire declined in about AD400 and Germanic peoples called Angles and Saxons invaded the land that became England. Vikings from Scandinavia overran parts of northern and eastern England, while Celtic peoples ruled Wales and Scotland. In 1066 the Normans (Vikings who lived in northern France) conquered England.

During the Middle Ages England was often at war with its neighbouring countries. However, England and Wales were united in the mid-1500s and Scotland joined them in 1707, forming the union of Great Britain. From the 1500s Britain won a vast overseas empire. Its scientists and engineers fuelled the change from an agricultural to an industrial society in the 1700s. Britain's political power declined in the 1900s, although it played a leading role in two world wars. By the 1960s most of Britain's colonies had become independent. In 1973 it joined the European Economic Community (now the European Union).

▲ *Stonehenge, in southern England, was probably raised between about 2700 and 1400BC. Archaeologists think that the site was used for religious ceremonies. It may have acted as a gigantic calendar because the stones are lined up according to the movements of the Sun.*

◄ *Cottages with old timbers and thatched roofs may be seen in some English villages. Many of them were built in the 1500s and 1600s. This was a time of growing prosperity for the country, in spite of a civil war during the mid-1600s.*

► *London's Limehouse Dock bustles with activity in 1828. Britain was the first country in the world to develop industry in the Industrial Revolution of the 1700s. Canals, steamships, railways, coal mines, iron works, potteries and textile mills continued to be built throughout the 1800s.*

◄ *Women check shells at a munitions factory during World War I (1914-18). Before this, few British women went to work. During the war women had to carry out many of the jobs usually done by men, who were away fighting. This change in their role helped women to win the right to vote for the first time in 1918.*

► *Protestants known as Orangemen parade in Northern Ireland. They belong to the Orange Order, which gets its name from William of Orange. In 1688 this Protestant prince defeated James II, a Roman Catholic, in a struggle for the English throne. Over the centuries differences between the Roman Catholic and Protestant religions have caused conflict in Northern Ireland, but a cease-fire was declared in 1994.*

REPUBLIC OF IRELAND *Introduction*

The Republic of Ireland takes up most of the island of Ireland. This independent country is also known by its Irish name Eire. It is sometimes called the Emerald Isle because of its lush countryside, which is kept green by rain from the Atlantic Ocean. The Republic's neighbour, Northern Ireland, is part of the United Kingdom.

The Republic's west coast is rugged, with cliffs, craggy inlets and small offshore islands. Low mountains around the coasts give way to central lowlands, with pasture and black peat bogs. There are many lakes (called loughs) and rivers teeming with trout and salmon.

The last 800 years of Ireland's history involves its struggle against English control. This has often involved violence and bloodshed. The southern part of the island finally gained its independence in 1921 and the Irish Free State was formed. This eventually became the Republic of Ireland in 1948.

The Republic's exports include butter, cheese and other dairy products, natural fibres, whiskey and beer. It also has an important fishing fleet that trawls the waters of the Atlantic Ocean for cod, haddock and plaice. Although farming is vital to the economy, three out of five people live in towns or cities. Some of them work in the manufacture of textiles or glass, while many others are employed in the growing service sector.

IRISH STEW
The country's best-known dish is a stew made from lamb or mutton. It is simmered in hot water with potatoes, onions, carrots, leeks and pearl barley. Potatoes have been a staple food in Ireland since the 1800s. Irish stew is traditionally served with dumplings made from suet.

FACTS AND FIGURES

Area: 70,280 sq km
Population: 3,563,000
Capital: Dublin (916,000)
Other major city: Cork (175,000)
Highest point: Carrauntoohill (1,041 m)
Official languages: Irish, English

Main religion: Christianity
Currencies: Euro, Punt
Main exports: Livestock, dairy products, whiskey, machinery, chemicals, manufactured goods
Government: Constitutional republic
Per capita GNP: US $12,100

◄ *The wild countryside around Galway is typical of much of the Republic of Ireland's farmland. The farmhouses are low and whitewashed, with thatched roofs. Stone walls divide fields grazed by sheep and cattle. The region's unspoilt beauty attracts many tourists.*

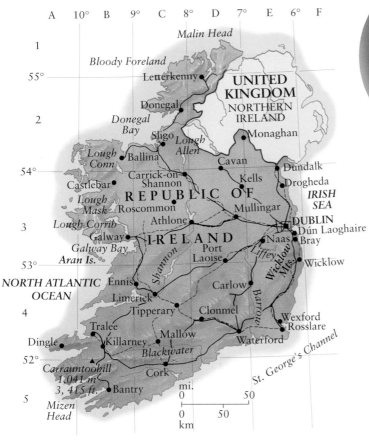

A 10° B 9° C 8° D 7° E 6° F

1

Malin Head

Bloody Foreland

55° Letterkenny

UNITED KINGDOM

NORTHERN IRELAND

Donegal

2 Donegal Bay

Sligo

Monaghan

Lough Allen

Lough Conn Ballina

Cavan

Dundalk

54° Castlebar Carrick-on-Shannon

Kells

Drogheda

REPUBLIC OF

Lough Mask Roscommon

Mullingar

IRISH SEA

Lough Corrib Athlone

DUBLIN

3 Galway IRELAND

Naas Dún Laoghaire

Galway Bay Port Laoise

Bray

Aran Is.

53° NORTH ATLANTIC OCEAN Ennis

Liffey

Wicklow

Shannon

Wicklow Mts.

Limerick Carlow

4 Tipperary

Barrow

Clonmel

Wexford

Mallow Waterford

Rosslare

Dingle Tralee Killarney

Blackwater

52° Carrauntoohill 1,041 m 3,415 ft. Cork

Bantry

St. George's Channel

5 Mizen Head

mi.
0   50

0   50
km

▼ Two fishermen pull a lobster pot back into shape before going to sea once again. Shellfish accounts for nearly a third of the Republic of Ireland's earnings from fishing.

◄ Students gather for a graduation ceremony outside Trinity College, Dublin. This is the oldest university in the Republic of Ireland, founded in 1591. There are three other universities in the Republic.

REPUBLIC OF IRELAND *People and History*

It is thought that people first arrived on this island from Scotland around 6000BC. Today the Irish people are known for their warm hospitality and storytelling. Popular pastimes include horse-racing, folk music and dancing. However, the Republic is a strict society. Law-making is influenced by the Roman Catholic Church and divorce is illegal. Many people in the Republic are calling for some of these laws to be changed.

From 400BC Celtic peoples came to Ireland from mainland Europe. They were followed by the Vikings from Scandinavia in the AD700s. In 1171 Henry II of England invaded Ireland and won lands around Dublin. During the 1600s the English seized land in the north and gave it to Protestants from England and Scotland. Eventually Protestants outnumbered Catholics in the north. In 1921 the Catholics of the south split from the Protestant north. Their lands were named the Irish Free State and were self-governing, but loosely linked to the United Kingdom (UK).

In 1922 fighting broke out. This was between the Irish Republican Army (IRA), Catholics who wanted Ireland to be an independent republic, and those who wanted to maintain ties with the UK. In 1949 the Irish Free State gained independence as the Republic of Ireland. However, from the late 1960s a terrorist war raged in Northern Ireland between the IRA and Protestant Loyalists (loyal to the British government). Many died during the years that followed, but in 1994 both sides declared a cease-fire and peace talks began.

▼ *The* Book of Kells *is an illuminated (illustrated) manuscript of the Bible's Gospels. It was produced by Christian monks around AD700. The pictures are brightly coloured and decorated with real gold.*

◄ *These workers are digging peat in the traditional way, with long spades. Peat forms in wetlands called bogs. It is made up of partly decayed plants that have formed thick, matted layers over thousands of years. Blocks of peat are dried and used in the home as fuel for cooking and heating. Peat is also burned in power stations.*

◄ Hurling is a fast and dangerous game. It is played with sticks called hurleys and a ball made of cork and covered in leather. Two teams of 15 players try to score goals at opposite ends of the field. Some players wear helmets to protect themselves against injury. The hurling cup final is held in Dublin each September.

► An Irish folk group entertains drinkers in Dublin. The musicians play an accordion, a fiddle and a bodhrán or hand-drum. The men are wearing traditional kilts. The Irish enjoy laments (sad songs) as well as wild dance tunes called jigs and reels.

SPEAK IRISH

Hello – Dia dhuit
(dee - ah **gwit**)

Goodbye – Slán leat
(slarn **lat**)

Please – Le do thoil
(leh doh hol)

Yes – Sea (shah)

No – Ní shea (nee hah)

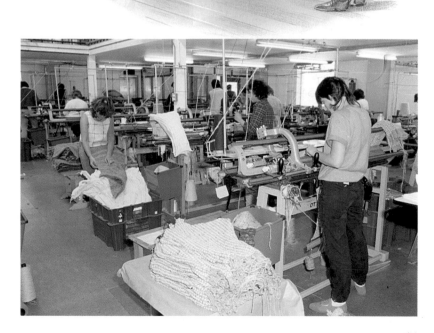

► Textiles are finished off at a factory near Donegal. The manufacture of textiles, especially linen and wool, is an important industry in the Republic. Linen comes from the flax plant and is woven into material for tea towels, clothing and furnishings.

GERMANY *Introduction*

Germany lies at the heart of Europe. Surrounded by nine other countries, its natural boundaries are two stretches of coastline in the north, the river Rhine in the southwest and the Bavarian Alps in the southeast. It is a fertile land, with wide, flowing rivers and thick forests. Germany has rich natural resources, which have helped to make it one of the world's leading industrial nations. The German people have greatly influenced the culture of Western Europe, especially its music, literature and architecture. German scientists have made many important discoveries in chemistry, medicine and physics.

People have lived here since ancient times. For most of its history this has been a divided land made up of many small states. After World War II (1939-1945) Germany was separated into two parts – the Federal Republic of Germany in the west and the German Democratic Republic in the east. In 1990 the two parts were reunited amid great celebration from peoples of the East and West.

Germany is a federal republic made up of 16 states that are called *Länder*. Every state has its own regional government and sends delegates to the Bundesrat or Federal Council. Each state may make its own laws on education and local government, but national laws are passed by the Bundestag or Federal Assembly (parliament). The leader of the government is called the Chancellor and the head of state is called the President.

FACTS AND FIGURES
Area: 356,730 sq km
Population: 81,187,000
Capital: Berlin (3,438,000)
Other major cities: Hamburg (1,661,000), Munich (1,237,000)
Highest point: Zugspitze (2,963 m)
Official language: German
Main religion: Christianity
Currencies: Euro, Deutsche Mark
Main exports: Machinery, transport equipment, textiles, chemicals, iron, steel, minerals, wine, lignite
Government: Constitutional republic
Per capita GNP: US $23,030

ENDANGERED WORLD

The rosalia longhorn beetle used to be hunted because of its beauty. It is now rare.

◀ *Munich is the third largest city in Germany. It is famous for its many museums, attractive public buildings and large number of breweries.*

A 6° B 7°30' C 9° D 10°30' E 12° F 13°30' G 15°

DENMARK

Flensburg
North Frisian Is.
BALTIC SEA
Fehmarn
Sassnitz
Rügen

1

54°

NORTH SEA

Kiel
Rostock
Greifswald
Lübeck

2

East Frisian Is.
Wilhelmshaven
Bremerhaven
Hamburg
Schwerin
Neustrelitz

53°

Oldenburg
Bremen
Müritz Lake

NETHERLANDS

Weser
Elbe
Lüneburg Heath

POLAND

3

Osnabrück
Hanover
Brandenburg
BERLIN

52°

Münster
Bielefeld
Hildesheim
Braunschweig
Potsdam
Oder

Rhine
Hamm
Paderborn
Magdeburg

4

Duisburg
Essen
Dortmund
Kassel
Göttingen
Dessau
Halle
Leipzig
Cottbus

Düsseldorf
Ruhr
G E R M A N Y
Erfurt
Weimar
Dresden

51°

Wuppertal
Cologne
Marburg
Gotha
Jena
Gera
Chemnitz

Aachen
Bonn
Fulda
Zwickau
Ore Mts.

5

BELGIUM

Mosel
Wiesbaden
Frankfurt
Coburg

CZECH REPUBLIC

50°

Mainz
Darmstadt
Würzburg

LUXEM-BOURG

Trier
Mannheim
Heidelberg
Erlangen
Bohemian Forest

6

FRANCE

Saarbrücken
Nuremberg

49°

Heilbronn
Regensburg

Karlsruhe
Rhine
Stuttgart
Danube
Ingolstadt

7

Offenburg
Ulm
Augsburg

48°

Freiburg
Black Forest
Ravensburg
Munich

AUSTRIA

8

Lake Constance
Bavarian Alps
Zugspitze 2,963 m 9,721 ft.

SWITZERLAND

mi.
0 — 100
0 — 100
km

▼ *Germans celebrate becoming one nation again on October 3, 1990. From 1945 to 1990 Germany was divided into two nations – East and West. Germany is now trying to overcome the differences between the two.*

► *The river Rhine slowly winds through a gorge in western Germany. The Rhine is Germany's longest river and is one of the world's busiest waterways. Large barges use it to transport fuel, timber and grain. Tourists visit the central part of the river to see its many castles and beautiful scenery.*

GERMANY *Geography*

▲ *Berchtesgaden is a ski resort set high up in the Bavarian Alps. Many mountaineers go there to climb Mount Watzmann (in the background). Other visitors bathe in the salty, local springwater as a health cure.*

Germany's low, sandy coast, dotted with its many offshore islands, looks out onto the grey, stormy waters of the North Sea and the Baltic Sea. The two seas are linked together by the Kiel Canal, a busy shipping channel. Inland the landscape gently rises, reaching a wide, flat plain that stretches right across northern Germany. This region is drained by several broad rivers, such as the Oder, Elbe and Weser. Along the wide river valleys and seacoasts the soft and fertile soil supports crops of rye, oats and potatoes. Parts of the plain are wild heathland, unsuitable for farming. Other areas have been planted with trees for timber. In the west lies the valley of the river Ruhr, where rich deposits of coal and metal ores are mined.

Central Germany is often called the Central Highlands. This is a rugged landscape of plateaus, forested mountains, steep gorges and rushing rivers. In the far west of the country there is a series of hills, lying in ridges. Sheep graze the high, rocky pastures and vineyards cover the hillsides. The valleys between the ridges have Germany's most fertile soils. Fields of crops such as wheat and barley stretch along the rivers.

In the southwest lies the Black Forest, named after its dark fir and spruce trees. This region is rich in bubbling mineral springs and many famous health resorts have developed there. In the extreme south of the country are the soaring Bavarian Alps. The highest point in Germany, the Zugspitze, is in this region. There are also many beautiful lakes and tourists visit all year round to enjoy the scenery and the snowy mountain slopes.

◀ *The Mosel River loops backwards and forwards through fertile land near Germany's border with Luxembourg. Vineyards along its steep banks produce the famous Mosel wines, which are exported to countries all over the world.*

► *The small town of Lichtenberg lies near Dresden, in eastern Germany. It nestles in the foothills of the Ore Mountains which border the Czech Republic. This is an area of rolling farmland, forest and rocky heath.*

◄ *Fields of wheat and oil-seed rape stretch among woodland on the north German plain. This broad, almost flat region of land was once covered in dense forest. It is now one of Germany's most productive farming areas.*

► *A river cuts through the Black Forest in the southwest. Many walkers and holidaymakers visit these dramatic wooded hills in the summer months. However, large parts of the forest have been damaged by acid rain. Environmental groups are trying to protect this and other areas.*

GERMANY *Economy*

Germany is Europe's leading industrial nation. Its major cities are international centres of trade and banking. It is Europe's largest car manufacturer and a world leader in the production of chemicals for medicines, plastics and paints. A wide range of other industries produce electrical goods, tools, computers, textiles and precision instruments. Germany's most important industrial region is the Ruhr Valley.

Among Germany's best known exports are beers, wines and sausages. In western Germany most farms are small and many are only operated part-time. In eastern Germany large farms that were run by the state are now being broken up and sold to individuals.

After World War II Germany's cities and factories were devastated and the country was divided. West Germany was helped by the United States of America, Britain and France to rebuild its economy. In 1957 it became a founder member of the European Economic Community (today's European Union). Under communist rule, East Germany had state-run industries. It spent a lot of money on creating jobs and on social welfare, but had very few consumer goods. After reunification in 1990 the east joined the same economic system as the west, which caused unemployment and high prices in the east. However, many economists believe that these problems can be solved by Germany's strong economy.

▲ *An open-cast mine just south of Cologne produces lignite, also called brown coal. It is used as fuel for power stations. Cologne is an important industrial centre. Large quantities of black coal are also mined in this region.*

◄ *Germany's government meets in Bonn in 1994. After World War II the country divided and Bonn became the capital of West Germany. When East and West Germany reunited in 1990 Berlin became the country's state capital.*

▼ *A worker harvests sugar beet on the north German plain. Germany grows large quantities of root crops for animal fodder and cereals to make bread and beer. It is one of the world's main producers of sugar beet, barley and rye. However, Germany is not self-sufficient in food and a third of its food has to be imported.*

ECONOMIC SURVEY

Farming: Leading crops include barley, oats, rye, potatoes and sugar beet. Grapes (for wine), hops and tobacco are grown in the central uplands and the southwest. The southeast has the best pasture for livestock. Farmers raise cattle, horses, pigs, poultry and sheep.

Fishing: Catches include cod, pollack, salmon and mussels.

Mining: Germany has reserves of hard coal, lignite, iron ore, potash and other minerals.

Industry: Includes iron and steel, cement, chemicals, transport equipment and vehicles, consumer goods, precision instruments, optical goods, textiles and electronics.

◄ *A robotic arm fits batteries into a Mercedes car on the assembly line. This factory near Stuttgart is one of the most highly automated in the world. The cars it produces are renowned for their quality, performance and reliability. They are exported all over the world.*

► *One of the world's largest inland ports is at Duisburg. It is built where the river Ruhr flows into the river Rhine. Enormous warehouses and loading bays handle chemicals, steel and textiles produced in the factories of the Ruhr Valley, Germany's chief industrial region.*

GERMANY *People*

Most Germans are of northern or central European descent, united by a common language. Since the 1950s many people from Turkey, Italy and Yugoslavia have also come to the country to work. Germany's population of about 80 million makes it the second most populated country in Europe after Russia.

Education has always been very important to the Germans. Germany was one of the first countries to set up a state education system for everyone. Their schools and universities, as well as business corporations and factories, are much respected throughout the world. Germans are also famous for their support of the arts. Germany has produced many great composers, including Beethoven and Wagner. A group of German designers, known as the Bauhaus, had a huge influence on modern architecture.

Very few Germans work on the land. Most people live in or near the towns and cities where the country's many thriving industries are based. However, although this is a modern nation of urban-dwellers, old customs have not been forgotten. Some Germans still wear national dress for special occasions, especially in southern areas. Medieval traditions are preserved by townspeople who regularly perform plays that were written centuries ago.

Political protest has been common in western Germany since the 1960s. Today thousands of young Germans often gather to protest about modern issues. These include pollution, nuclear power and the rise in racism that has recently occurred in Germany and in other parts of Europe.

WURST
Wurst means sausage and Germany is said to have over 1,500 different kinds! Every region has its speciality, often sold as a snack on the street with a roll and a large dollop of mustard. Bratwurst is long and served grilled. Weisswurst is boiled. Frankfurters are named after the city they came from – Frankfurt. All sorts of spicy sausages, salamis and cold hams are served at a typical evening meal.

◄ *Guests fill one of the many huge tents and halls set up for Munich's most famous annual festival, the* Oktoberfest. *At the two-week-long festival people come to enjoy the beer, brass bands and good food in large quantities.*

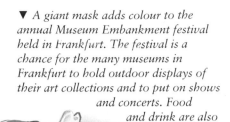

▼ A giant mask adds colour to the annual Museum Embankment festival held in Frankfurt. The festival is a chance for the many museums in Frankfurt to hold outdoor displays of their art collections and to put on shows and concerts. Food and drink are also provided.

▲ An athletics event opens at the international stadium in Stuttgart, southern Germany. Sport is a popular leisure activity across Germany and many people belong to sports clubs. Supported by the government, German sports associations have produced many world-class athletes, footballers, skiers and tennis stars. Football is Germany's most popular sport.

◄ A family stops for a rest while hiking in the Bavarian Alps. Walking and youth-hostelling are very popular pastimes in Germany. At weekends city parks are busy with joggers, cyclists and other fitness enthusiasts. Germany's many lakes and rivers are ideal for canoeing, rowing, sailing and swimming.

49

GERMANY *History*

By 1000BC Germanic and Celtic peoples, who probably came from Russia, were living across the region that is now called Germany. In the AD400s a Germanic group called the Franks defeated the Romans, who were fighting to control this area. In AD800 the great Frankish ruler Charlemagne revived the Roman empire here. He controlled vast lands that included most of France and northern Italy. When his empire broke up Germany was divided into independent states, which elected an emperor. The region came to be called the Holy Roman Empire and the Austrian Habsburg family ruled it almost continuously from 1438 until 1806.

In 1517 Martin Luther, a German monk, became the leader of a movement called the Reformation. He criticized the Roman Catholic Church and demanded reforms. His followers were known as Protestants, meaning 'those who protest'. Religious and political disagreements led to war (1618-1648), dividing Germany into Protestant and Roman Catholic states. In 1871 Germany was united under Otto von Bismarck, prime minister of an area called Prussia.

Germany's defeat in World War I (1914-1918) left the country in crisis, crippled by inflation. The Nazis (National Socialists) came to power, promising to make Germany great again. Led by Adolf Hitler, the Nazis aimed to create a master race and killed millions of Jews, Poles, Russians and political opponents. Germany was defeated again in World War II (1939-1945) and divided into East and West. The Berlin wall was built to separate East and West Berlin. In 1990 East and West Germany were reunited.

▲ *Ulm Cathedral was founded in 1377, but not completed until 1890. Its steeple is the tallest in world, rising almost 161 metres above the city. In the Middle Ages Ulm grew wealthy through trade as it was an important crossing point over the river Danube.*

▶ *Johannes Gutenberg examines a sheet of a Bible that he printed around 1450. Gutenberg invented the first successful printing press. Before this books in Europe were usually copied out by hand, so they were very expensive. With the new presses books could be printed rapidly, helping the spread of information and ideas.*

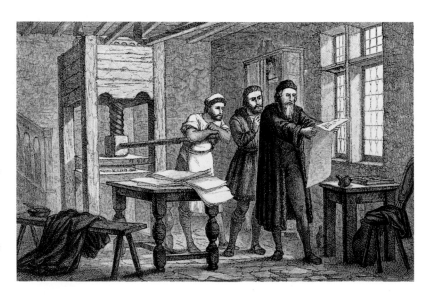

► *Linderhof castle was built by Ludwig II, king of the southeastern region of Bavaria. The castle was built at great expense and decorated with painted ceilings and gilded angels. It was completed in 1878. Ludwig's extravagant, eccentric ways led his government to declare him insane in 1886. He drowned a few days later.*

WAR-TORN COLOGNE

After Germany's defeat in World War II (1939-1945) many of its cities lay in ruins. Cologne *(above)* was almost completely destroyed by United States and British bombers. Miraculously, Cologne's magnificent cathedral *(background)* survived the bombardment.

After the war the damaged areas of cities such as Cologne were quickly rebuilt. A lot of the old buildings were replaced with modern, postwar designs. Some historic buildings were restored to their former glory, particularly in the eastern parts of Germany. In many cities bombed churches, once they had been made safe, were left standing as a reminder of the terrible consequences of war.

▲ *East German bricklayers build the Berlin Wall in 1961. The wall was put up by the communist East German government to separate East Berlin from West Berlin and stop people leaving East Germany. In 1989 there were many protests and the people of Berlin started to pull the wall down. The following year East and West Germany were reunited.*

BELGIUM

ENDANGERED WORLD

The copper butterfly lives in Belgium's coastal lowlands. It is at risk because of the draining of marshes.

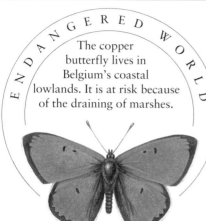

Flat farmland reclaimed from the sea forms much of Belgium's coastal lowlands. These rise to fertile plateaus in the centre of the country and to the wooded hills of the Ardennes in the southeast. The Meuse and Schelde rivers have been important trade routes for centuries.

Belgium has few natural frontiers and has often been a battleground for neighbouring nations such as France, Germany and Britain. For much of its history Belgium, with the Netherlands and Luxembourg, has been part of region known as the Low Countries. During the Middle Ages the Low Countries became rich through trade, but long years of war and foreign rule followed. Belgium finally became an independent nation in 1830. It soon became wealthy through industry and from new colonies on the African continent. Although Belgium suffered great destruction during World Wars I and II, recovery was rapid. Today the country is one of the most heavily industrialized places in Europe and steel manufacturing is its most important industry. Belgium has close economic links with other European countries and its capital, Brussels, provides a base for the Council and Commission of the European Union.

Most Belgians share the Roman Catholic faith, but are divided into two distinct ethnic groups. The Dutch-speaking Flemings live in northern Belgium and the French-speaking Walloons live in the south. To reduce tensions between the two, Belgium has created separate regions that have considerable control over local matters.

FACTS AND FIGURES
Area: 30,530 sq km
Population: 10,010,000
Capital: Brussels (951,000)
Other major city: Antwerp (466,000)
Highest point: Botrange (694 m)
Official languages: Dutch, French
Main religion: Christianity
Currencies: Euro, Belgian franc
Main exports: Iron, steel, machinery, transport equipment, chemicals, processed food, cut diamonds, textiles, plastics
Government: Federal constitutional monarchy
Per capita GNP: US $20,880

▶ *Petrochemicals are produced at this factory in the industrial centre of Antwerp. The city is a centre of the Belgian chemical industry, where products include plastics, paints, fertilizers and coal tar, which is used in making soap.*

► *A brilliantly patterned carpet of begonias decorates the Grand-Place, a square in the centre of Brussels. This magnificent display of flowers is created there every other August. Large numbers of plants and flowers are grown in the Belgian countryside.*

NORTH SEA

NETHERLANDS

Zeebrugge
Ostend
Nieuwpoort
Bruges
Evergem
Torhout
Roeselare
Tielt
Ypres
Kortrijk
Menen
Mouscron
Tournai
Ath
Halle
Waterloo
Mons
La Louvière
Charleroi
Philippeville
Dinant

Antwerp
Turnhout
Mol
Sint-Niklaas
Mechelen
Maaseik
Ghent
Aalst
Hasselt
Louvain
BRUSSELS
Tienen
Wavre
Liège
Eupen
Verviers
Botrange
684 m
2,277 ft.
Namur
Malmédy
Marche-en-Famenne
Bastogne
Neufchâteau
Arlon

Leie
Schelde
Sambre
Meuse
Ardennes

B E L G I U M

FRANCE

GERMANY

LUXEMBOURG

mi.
0   50
0   50
km

◄ *The finishing touches are given to a batch of handmade chocolates. Belgium is famous for luxury foods such as chocolates and pâté, as well as for its strong beers and fried potatoes.*

NETHERLANDS *Introduction*

This country is often called Holland, although in fact that name only applies to two of its twelve provinces. The word Netherlands means lowlands. This is an appropriate name because the country is almost entirely flat and much of the land lies below sea level. There are large areas of polder, which is land that has been reclaimed from the sea, rivers and saltmarshes. Reclamation has occurred over hundreds of years. The delta region of the southwest, formed by the mouths of several rivers, is protected against flooding by a series of vast dams and floodgates.

The flat landscape of the Netherlands is cut by a network of rivers, canals and dikes. Cattle graze the green fields, while barges make their way up and down the waterways. The land is also crossed by many motorways and road bridges. This is one of the world's most crowded countries and the majority of its population lives in urban areas. Spreading suburbs and high-rise flats are found in most cities, but city centres often look as if they have changed little for centuries. There are fine old brick houses beside canals and bridges that date back to the 1600s. Cyclists are a common sight in both the towns and the countryside as the narrow streets and lack of hilly ground make bicycles the ideal form of transport.

The Netherlands is famous all over the world for its dairy produce, greenhouse vegetables, cut flowers, bulbs and seeds. Dutch factories produce a wide range of goods from electrical appliances to textiles and chemical products. Amsterdam, the capital, is also a major centre for diamond cutting and polishing.

FACTS AND FIGURES

Area: 41,530 sq km
Population: 15,287,000
Capital: Amsterdam (1,092,000)
Other major cities: Rotterdam (1,070,000), The Hague (495,000)
Highest point: Vaalser Berg (321 m)
Official language: Dutch
Main religion: Christianity
Currencies: Euro, Guilder
Main exports: Dairy products, flower bulbs, vegetables, petrochemicals,
Government: Constitutional monarchy
Per capita GNP: US $20,590

ENDANGERED WORLD

The pond bat roosts in old buildings. The chemicals used to protect timber have threatened its survival.

◄ *The Dutch parliament buildings are in The Hague. Parliament, called the States-General, is made up of two chambers. The Netherlands is a monarchy, but real political power lies with its democratically elected government.*

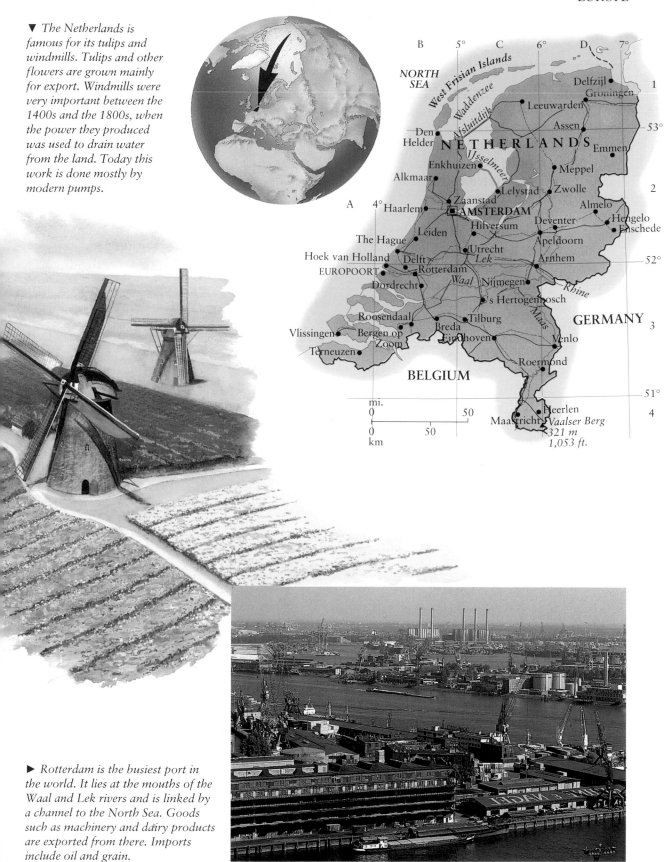

▼ The Netherlands is famous for its tulips and windmills. Tulips and other flowers are grown mainly for export. Windmills were very important between the 1400s and the 1800s, when the power they produced was used to drain water from the land. Today this work is done mostly by modern pumps.

B 5° C 6° D 7°

NORTH SEA

West Frisian Islands

Waddenzee

Afsluitdijk

Den Helder

Delfzijl

Groningen

Leeuwarden

Assen

53°

NETHERLANDS

Emmen

IJsselmeer

Enkhuizen

Meppel

Alkmaar

Zwolle

Almelo

Lelystad

Zaanstad

Hengelo

A 4° Haarlem

AMSTERDAM

Enschede

Leiden

Hilversum

Deventer

2

The Hague

Utrecht

Apeldoorn

Hoek van Holland

Delft

Lek

Arnhem

52°

EUROPOORT

Rotterdam

Waal

Rhine

Dordrecht

Nijmegen

's Hertogenbosch

Maas

Roosendaal

Tilburg

GERMANY 3

Vlissingen

Bergen op Zoom

Breda

Eindhoven

Venlo

Terneuzen

Roermond

BELGIUM

51°

mi.
0   50

Heerlen

4

0   50
km

Maastricht Vaalser Berg
321 m
1,053 ft.

► Rotterdam is the busiest port in the world. It lies at the mouths of the Waal and Lek rivers and is linked by a channel to the North Sea. Goods such as machinery and dairy products are exported from there. Imports include oil and grain.

NETHERLANDS *People and History*

The people who live in the Netherlands today are known as the Dutch. They are mainly descended from Germanic peoples called the Franks, Frisians and Saxons, who all settled here about 2,000 years ago.

The Netherlands, Belgium and Luxembourg form a region called the Low Countries. By the 1300s the French dukes of Burgundy were in control of this area. In the early 1500s the Low Countries joined the immense empire of the Habsburg family, whose lands included Spain and Austria. By this time many Dutch people had joined the Protestant religion and resented being ruled by Spain, a Roman Catholic country. In 1568 they rebelled against the Habsburgs. After many battles independence was finally won in 1648.

During the 1600s the Netherlands became one of the world's leading sea powers and acquired a large overseas empire. Trade with the Dutch East Indies (Indonesia) brought great wealth. Land was reclaimed from the North Sea and fine cities were built in this country. Great painters such as Rembrandt and Vermeer helped to create a golden age for the arts.

At the end of the 1600s Dutch power began to decline. Belgium broke away from the Netherlands to become a separate nation in 1830. In this century the Dutch have built up close economic links with their neighbours and prospered. They became one of the first members of the European Economic Community in 1957.

Today most Dutch people live in cities and work in service industries or manufacturing. They have a high standard of living, but space for housing is limited in this crowded country. People make use of the Netherlands' many waterways for watersports such as sailing and swimming. When the canals freeze over in the winter they are used for ice-skating.

SPEAK FRISIAN

Hello – Hoi *(hoy)*

Goodbye – Oant sjen
(ont syen)

Please – Asjebleaft
(*ash - yeh - bleeft*)

Thank you – Tankje wol
(*tank - ya vol*)

Yes – Ja *(yah)*

No – Nee *(nay)*

◄ *Ships crowd into the harbour of Rotterdam in 1615. During the 1600s Dutch merchants and explorers sailed the world, bringing back riches and finding new shipping routes.*

▼ A pole-vaulting championship is held every year in Friesland, in the north. Some champions have vaulted across distances of 14 metres. In times gone by, farmers used poles to get over the dikes (banks) that crossed their land. This developed into the sport that the people of Friesland enjoy today.

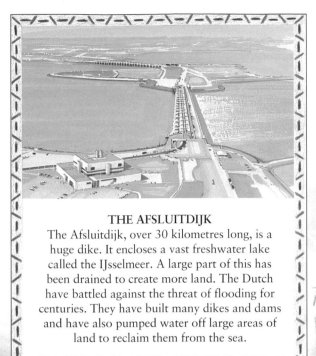

THE AFSLUITDIJK

The Afsluitdijk, over 30 kilometres long, is a huge dike. It encloses a vast freshwater lake called the IJsselmeer. A large part of this has been drained to create more land. The Dutch have battled against the threat of flooding for centuries. They have built many dikes and dams and have also pumped water off large areas of land to reclaim them from the sea.

▼ Houseboats line the canals in the centre of Amsterdam. The Dutch capital is filled with old churches, merchants' houses built during the 1600s and markets. Amsterdam is a centre of business and the arts. Its lively streets are popular with young people from all over Europe.

▲ Round, wax-covered cheeses are carried to market in Alkmaar, a popular destination for tourists. The Netherlands exports large amounts of cheese all over the world. Mature farmhouse varieties are mostly sold in local shops and markets.

LUXEMBOURG

Luxembourg lies between Belgium, Germany and France. The forested hills of the Ardennes extend into the north of the country and the Sauer and Moselle rivers form its eastern boundary. The south, with its green pastures and fertile farmlands, is known as the *Bon Pays* (Good Land).

Today industry is more important than agriculture in Luxembourg. Rich deposits of iron have made the country one of Europe's leading steel producers. Luxembourg City, perched high above the gorge of the Alzette River, is a centre of international banking and finance. The people of Luxembourg enjoy a very high standard of living with free social security and healthcare.

Luxembourg was founded by Siegfried, Count of Ardennes, in AD963. The country became a Duchy (ruled by a duke or duchess) in 1354. Over the centuries it was controlled by a variety of other countries including France, Spain, Austria and the Netherlands, but gained independence in 1867.

In 1948 Luxembourg joined Belgium and the Netherlands in an economic union known as Benelux. In 1957 it was a founder member of the European Economic Community, the forerunner of the European Union, and today Luxembourg plays an important role in European affairs.

▼ *A harvester tips grapes into a large container in the first stage of making Moselle wine, for which Luxembourg is famous. The grapes for this wine are grown on steep terraced hillsides beside the Moselle River.*

◄ *The beautiful old town of Esch-sur-Sûre is built on a spectacular bend in the river Sûre. This hilly northern district of Luxembourg is called the Oesling. Many holidaymakers go there every year to enjoy forest walks, fishing and camping.*

▲ Flags of the European Union fly outside
the administrative building of European institutions
in Luxembourg City. The capital is the seat of the
European Court of Justice and the Secretariat of
the European Parliament.

**SPEAK
LETZEBUERGESCH**

Hello – Moïen *(moy - en)*

Goodbye – Arwuer
(arv - wair)

Please – Wann ech gelift
(van esh g - lift)

Thank you – Merci
(mair - see)

Yes – Jo *(yoh)*

FACTS AND FIGURES

Area: 2,590 sq km
Population: 380,000
Capital: Luxembourg
City (76,000)
Other major city:
Esch-sur-Alzette
(24,000)
Highest point:
Buurgplatz (559 m)
Official languages:
French, German,
Letzebuergesch

Main religion:
Christianity
Currencies:
Euro, Luxembourg franc
Main exports: Iron, steel,
textiles, machinery,
chemicals, plastics
Government:
Constitutional monarchy
Per capita GNP:
US $35,260

SWITZERLAND

Switzerland is a land of towering, snowy mountains, high waterfalls and long, misty lakes. The Alps form a series of high ranges in the south and east, while rainy conifer forests of the Jura Mountains line the western border with France. Below these peaks alpine pastures provide summer grazing for cattle and goats. Very little Swiss land is suitable for growing crops, except for hay and other livestock fodder. Rushing rivers are dammed for hydroelectric power, but Switzerland has few other natural resources. Raw materials are imported and skilled craftspeople turn them into precision goods such as watches and electrical equipment.

More than 2,000 years ago the Romans conquered the Helvetii peoples who lived in this land and called it the province of Helvetia. The name Helvetia is still used on Swiss coins and stamps today. In 1291 the Swiss cantons, or provinces, began to fight for independence from the Holy Roman Empire. They waged several wars and independence was finally recognized in 1648.

Since 1815 the country has remained neutral, avoiding wars that have swept across Europe. Switzerland's neutrality has attracted many organizations that depend on international co-operation, such as the World Health Organization and the United Nations. The years of peace and stability have also helped the country to prosper as a world centre of banking.

FONDUE
Fondue is a famous Swiss dish made with melted cheese. Cheeses such as Gruyère and Emmental, produced on Swiss dairy farms, are heated in a pot and flavoured with garlic, pepper, white wine and kirsch (cherry liqueur). Fresh bread is dipped into the hot cheese using forks.

◄ *Gold bars are stored in the vaults of a Zurich bank. Swiss banks are probably the most secure in the world. All bank accounts kept in them are totally private.*

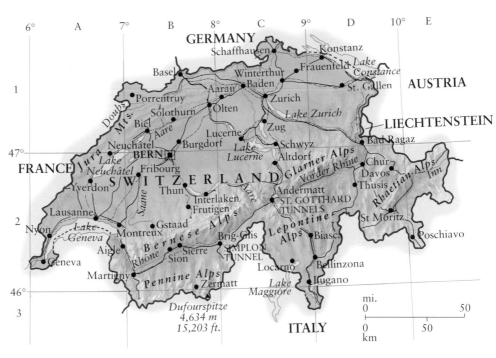

▲ A procession with lanterns marks the festival of Saint Nicholas in Küssnacht am Rigi, by Lake Lucerne. Saint Nicholas was the original Father Christmas. Swiss children are given presents after the parade on December 5th every year.

▼ Chalets nestle on the alpine pasture beneath one of Switzerland's highest peaks, the Jungfrau near Interlaken. The magnificent scenery attracts tourists and skiers throughout the year.

FACTS AND FIGURES

Area: 41,130 sq km

Population: 6,938,000

Capital: Bern (299,000)

Other major cities: Zurich (839,000), Geneva (389,000)

Highest point: Dufourspitze (4,634 m)

Official languages: German, French, Italian

Main religion: Christianity

Currency: Swiss franc

Main exports: Machinery, chemicals, clocks and watches, precision instruments, textiles, clothes, foods including chocolate

Government: Constitutional federal republic

Per capita GNP: US $36,230

AUSTRIA

Austria lies in mountainous Central Europe. About three quarters of the country is in the snow-capped, thickly forested Alps. Deer and small numbers of chamois live in these mountains. Austria has broad, green valleys, rushing rivers and deep mountain lakes. Cattle graze the high pastures, while barley, rye and potatoes are grown in the Vienna basin, the flat valley of the mighty river Danube. Much of the land is too rugged for agriculture, but by using modern farming methods Austria is able to produce three quarters of the food its people need. Grapes are grown for wine. Timber for wood pulp and paper is cut from forests that are replanted according to strict conservation laws. Austria is a highly industrialized country, though most of its population work in services such as retail, banking, tourism, healthcare and education.

The early inhabitants of this land mined and traded in iron and salt. Celtic peoples moved here around 400BC, then in 15BC Austria was conquered by the Romans. From the 1200s a powerful family called the Habsburgs ruled Austria, making it the centre of a vast empire that grew to include Spain, Hungary and the Netherlands. Austria began to lose power in the 1800s and by 1918 the Habsburg empire was finished. The country was torn apart during the two World Wars, but since the 1950s Austria has built up its economy and become politically stable. It joined the European Union in 1995.

ENDANGERED WORLD

White-tailed eagles are now rare due to hunting. Some may be seen over the Austrian Alps in winter.

▼ Sunlight catches the peak of Grossglockner. The village of Heiligenblut nestles below. Austria's magnificent scenery attracts many tourists, particularly for winter skiing holidays.

▲ Craftsmen cut glass at Rattenberg, in the Inn valley. Austria's highly valued craft skills also include wood carving and porcelain manufacture.

FACTS AND FIGURES

Area: 83,860 sq km
Population: 7,988,000
Capital: Vienna
(1,540,000)
Other major cities:
Graz (238,000),
Linz (203,000)
Highest point:
Grossglockner
(3,797 m)
Official language:
German

Main religion:
Christianity
Currencies: Euro,
Schilling
Main exports:
Machinery, timber, paper,
paper pulp, iron, steel,
textiles
Government:
Constitutional republic
Per capita GNP:
US $22,110

▼ *Vienna's Burgtheater was built in the late 1800s. At this time Austria's capital was one of the most important cultural centres in the world.*

▲ *The Kops-Stausee dam generates hydroelectricity for industry in western Austria. Hydroelectric schemes on Austria's lakes and rivers provide two thirds of the nation's electric power.*

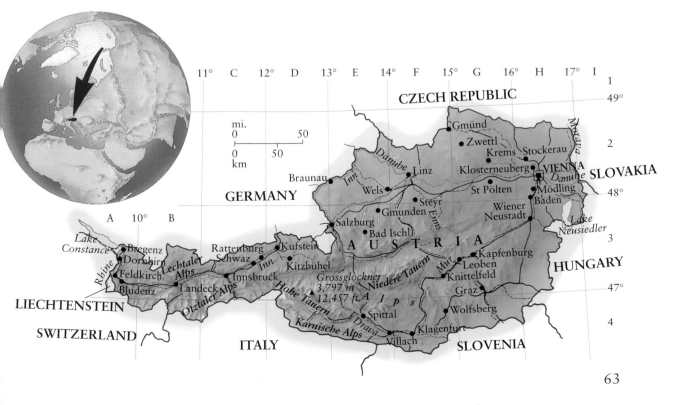

LIECHTENSTEIN

Liechtenstein's national population is no bigger than that of a small town. This small country has strong ties with neighbouring Switzerland and uses Swiss currency. Liechtenstein was formed in 1719 when Prince Johann-Adam Liechtenstein joined together the two small territories of Vaduz and Schellenberg, formerly parts of the Holy Roman Empire. His descendants still rule here, though laws are now passed by an elected parliament. Women in Liechtenstein did not gain the right to vote in elections until 1984.

The climate in this country is mild. The land rises from the valley of the river Rhine to the forested foothills and snow-capped peaks of the Alps. Dairy cattle graze the alpine pastures, while barley and fruit are grown in the valleys. However, only three percent of the population is employed in agriculture. Since the 1950s Liechtenstein has become an industrialized nation with one of the highest standards of living in the world. Banking and tourism are two of the country's main industries. The production of textiles, chemicals and pottery are also important. A great deal of money comes into the economy from the foreign businesses that have their headquarters here, attracted by Liechtenstein's low taxes.

FACTS AND FIGURES

Area: 160 sq km
Population: 28,000
Capital: Vaduz (5,000)
Highest point: Vorder-Grauspitz (2,599 m)
Official language: German
Main religion: Christianity
Currency: Swiss franc
Main exports: Machinery, chemical products, textiles, pottery, dental products, stamps
Government: Constitutional monarchy
Per capita GNP: Est. over US $8,000

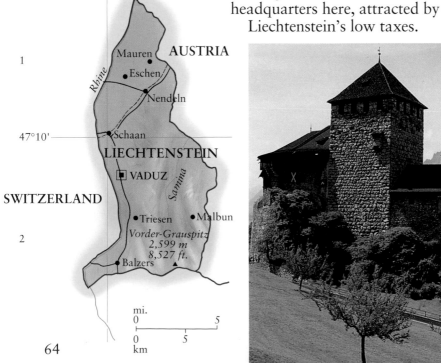

▼ *Vaduz castle is the home of the Prince of Liechtenstein. It overlooks a steep hillside, high above the country's capital. The castle's oldest fortifications date back to the 1500s.*

MONACO

Monaco is one of the world's smallest countries. It forms a narrow, steeply sloping strip along the Mediterranean Sea below the coastal hills of southeastern France. The whole country is a built-up area that takes in the towns of Monaco and Monte Carlo. There is also an industrial region called Fontvieille. Along the coastline land is being reclaimed from the sea to make more room for developments such as marinas, beaches and apartment blocks.

Monaco has been ruled by princes of the Grimaldi family since 1297. In 1793 it was taken over by France and did not regain full independence until 1861. Today Monaco is still ruled by a prince who makes laws on the advice of the National Council.

The combination of hot summers, mild winters and the blue waters of the Mediterranean Sea have brought tourists to Monaco from all over Europe since the 1800s. More recently many wealthy people have come to live in the country because it has low taxes. Monte Carlo is famed for its casino, where huge fortunes are won and lost on the roulette and other gaming tables. A law forbids the citizens of Monaco from gambling, which brings a large revenue to the country's government. Another of Monaco's attractions is motor racing. The Monaco Grand Prix and the Monte Carlo rally are held here every year.

FACTS AND FIGURES
Area: 1.9 sq km
Population: 28,000
Capital: Monaco (1,500)
Official language: French
Main religion: Christianity
Currency: French franc
Main products: Chemicals, pharmaceuticals, precision instruments
Government: Constitutional monarchy
Per capita GNP: Not available

▲ Monaco's harbour was once a fishing port, but today it is lined with luxury yachts from all over the world. Tourists visit Monaco for the nightclubs and gambling casinos, which bring great wealth into this small country.

FRANCE *Introduction*

France is the third largest country in Europe and one of the world's major economic and political powers. The French sometimes call their land *L'Hexagone* (The Hexagon) because of its six-sided shape. Seas or mountains form natural boundaries on all sides except the northeast. Within these boundaries is a country of varied and beautiful landscapes, modern industries, historic towns and great cities. It has helped to shape the history and culture of Western Europe, as well as many other parts of the world. France has produced great thinkers, politicians, writers, painters, musicians, architects, scientists, film-makers and fashion designers. It is also famous for its fine wines and food, which are often said to be the best in the world. Enjoyment of these is an important part of life for most French people and for many visitors to the country.

The French Revolution of 1789 made France one of the first European nations to overthrow its king and set up a republic. The monarchy was restored for a time during the 1800s, but a republic was established once more in 1871. Since then France has been a democratic republic almost continuously. The government is headed by a president, who appoints a prime minister.

France, which also includes the Mediterranean island of Corsica, is divided into 22 regions. These include Brittany, which juts out to the far northwest, and Burgundy, the region around Dijon. In the past the capital, Paris, has been at the centre of power. However, the regions have maintained strong individual identities and today they also have a greater say in how the country is run.

FACTS AND FIGURES
Area: 543,970 sq km
Population: 57,660,000
Capital: Paris (9,319,000)
Other major cities: Lyon (1,263,000), Marseille (1,231,000), Lille (960,000)
Highest point: Mont Blanc (4,807 m)
Official language: French
Main religions: Christianity, Islam
Currencies: Euro, French franc
Main exports: Wine, agricultural products, machinery, transport equipment, chemicals
Government: Constitutional republic
Per capita GNP: US $22,300

ENDANGERED WORLD

The Pyrenean Desman, a long-nosed water-mole, lives in the fast-flowing streams of the Pyrenees. Pollution is threatening its survival.

◀ *Orange trees and cypresses flourish above the blue Mediterranean Sea in the south. Tourists have been coming to resorts along this coast since the 1700s, attracted by the warm climate and spectacular scenery.*

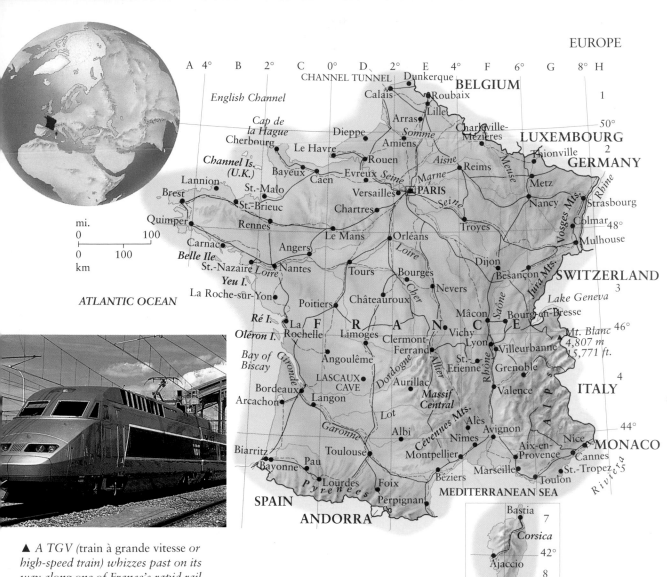

	A 4°	B 2°	C 0°	D 2°	E 4°	F 6°	G 8°	H

CHANNEL TUNNEL · Dunkerque
BELGIUM
Calais · Roubaix
English Channel
Arras · Lille
Cap de la Hague
Dieppe · Amiens · Charleville-Mézières
LUXEMBOURG
Cherbourg · Le Havre
Somme
Thionville
GERMANY
Channel Is. (U.K.)
Bayeux · Rouen · Aisne · Reims · Metz
Lannion
Caen · Evreux · Seine · Marne · Nancy · Strasbourg
Brest · St.-Malo
Versailles **PARIS**
Quimper · St.-Brieuc
Chartres · Seine · Troyes · Colmar 48°
Rennes
Le Mans · Orléans · Mulhouse
Carnac
Angers · Loire
SWITZERLAND
Belle Ile
Nantes · Tours · Bourges · Dijon · Besançon
St.-Nazaire · Loire
Cher · Nevers · Jura Mts.
Yeu I.
La Roche-sur-Yon · Poitiers · Châteauroux · Mâcon · Lake Geneva
Ré I.
La Rochelle **F R A N C E**
Oléron I.
Limoges · Vichy · Lyon · Mt. Blanc 46° 4,807 m 15,771 ft.
Bay of Biscay
Angoulême · Clermont-Ferrand · Villeurbanne
Bourg-en-Bresse
St.-Etienne · Grenoble
ITALY
LASCAUX CAVE · Dordogne · Aurillac · Valence
Bordeaux · Langon · Lot · Massif Central · Allier · Rhône · Alps
Arcachon
Garonne · Albi · Cévennes Mts. · Alès · Avignon · Nice
MONACO
Biarritz · Toulouse · Nîmes · Aix-en-Provence · Cannes
Bayonne · Pau · Montpellier · Marseille · St.-Tropez
Lourdes · Foix · Béziers · Toulon · Riviera
Pyrénées
SPAIN
Perpignan · **MEDITERRANEAN SEA**
ANDORRA

ATLANTIC OCEAN

mi.
0 — 100
0 — 100
km

Bastia 7
Corsica 42°
Ajaccio 8
I 9° J

▲ *A TGV (train à grande vitesse or high-speed train) whizzes past on its way along one of France's rapid rail routes. These trains can travel up to 500 kilometres per hour. They have made the French railway network the most advanced in Europe.*

▶ *The white domes of the church of Sacré Coeur rise above the square of Montmartre, the highest spot in Paris. During the 1800s famous artists such as Renoir and Toulouse-Lautrec worked there. Today painters still crowd the square and visitors often buy their pictures as souvenirs.*

FRANCE *Geography*

The wide range of landscapes found in France include rocky Atlantic headlands, broad river valleys, high, snow-capped mountains, rolling hills and sunny beaches beside the blue Mediterranean Sea. The climate is mild and rainy on the west coast, but hot summers and cold winters are common in the east.

Most of northern France is a large plain, crossed by rivers such as the Seine and Marne. This fertile farmland is bordered to the west by hills and cliffs. To the east, along the border with Belgium, are forested hills. These slopes continue southwards, rising to the Vosges Mountains above the Rhine valley and to the Jura range on the Swiss border.

The highlands of the Massif Central take up most of south-central France. This is a sparsely populated region of ancient volcanoes with poor soils mainly grazed by sheep, goats and cattle. To the southeast France's longest river, the Loire, begins in the Cévennes Mountains.

Southwestern France, around the river Garonne, includes the vineyards of Bordeaux, as well as an area of sand dunes and pine forest called the Landes. The mighty peaks of the Pyrenees mark France's border with Spain.

To the east of the Massif Central lie the broad, fertile valleys of the Saône and Rhône rivers. As the Rhône flows into the Mediterranean Sea it forms a wide delta where there are marshlands famous for their flamingos and wild, white horses. Along the Italian border lie the Alps, the highest peaks of Western Europe, where gleaming glaciers and walls of rock tower above mountain pastures.

▶ *The sunny slopes of the Beaujolais Mountains are planted with vineyards. This region extends northwards from Lyon and borders the Saône valley. It is famous for its light, fruity red wines, which are exported all over the world.*

◄ The valley of the Dordogne River is one of France's most popular holiday spots for visitors from abroad. The river rises in the mountains near Clermont-Ferrand and flows about 470 kilometres westwards through beautiful countryside. It meets the sea at the Gironde Estuary, north of Bordeaux.

► The volcanic crater of Puy de Dôme, in the Massif Central, is dormant today. Many thousands of years ago the landscape of this area was being shaped by lava flows and eruptions.

◄ Chalk cliffs and natural arches rise above this pebble beach at Etretat, north of Le Havre. One piece of rock forms a needle standing in the English Channel. The rock formations have been painted by famous French artists such as Matisse and Monet.

FRANCE *Economy*

▲ *The silver globe of this nuclear power station rises above the Vienne River at Chinon, near Tours. Nuclear power stations produce nearly three quarters of the country's electricity.*

A combination of rich farmland and a mild climate have made France an important agricultural nation for centuries. Wheat, sugar beet, vegetables and apples are grown in the north. Dairy cattle graze the lush pastures of the northwest, producing creamy butters and cheeses. Vines growing grapes for France's important wine industry flourish in large areas all over the country. In the south and southwest there are fields of sunflowers and maize, as well as orchards of peaches, plums and cherries.

Fishing is important along France's long coastline. There is also a large timber industry, based on the vast forests that cover about a quarter of the country.

France's natural resources include bauxite (used to make aluminium), iron ore and coal. There are also reserves of oil in the southwest, between Bordeaux and Biarritz. The powerful flow of mountain streams, waterfalls and tidal rivers is used to generate hydroelectric energy. France exports electricity to neighbouring countries and has built more nuclear power stations than any other nation in Western Europe. It has also experimented with solar and tidal power. The huge power station at Odeillo in the Pyrenees harnesses the heat of the sun to make electricity.

Today industry is even more important than agriculture to the French economy. French factories produce chemicals, textiles, aircraft, spacecraft and electronic equipment, many of which are exported. In addition, about half of the French labour force works in service industries such as tourism, catering, finance, healthcare and education.

◄ *Nice is the chief resort of the famous French Riviera. This sunny coastal strip borders the Mediterranean Sea. Tourism, based on the beautiful beaches, water sports, camping and luxury hotels, is a major industry in the south of France.*

► *Pine logs are stacked in the Bordeaux region. The French timber industry manages large forests in the southwest, in the mountainous regions of the Massif Central and on the eastern borders. Much of this wood goes into the production of furniture, paper and pulp.*

▲ *Traders crowd the floor of the Paris stock exchange, which is called the Bourse. This is where people buy and sell stocks and shares. It is the centre of France's finance industry.*

ECONOMIC SURVEY

Farming: France is Western Europe's leading farming nation. Wheat, barley, oats, sugar beet, flax, fruit and vegetables are grown. Livestock includes dairy cattle and sheep. Cheeses and wines are exported worldwide.
Fishing: Catches include cod, crabs, lobsters, monkfish, scallops, tuna, oysters and mussels.
Mining: Coal, iron, natural gas and sulphur are extracted.

Industry: France makes chemicals, aerospace and communications equipment, electronic goods, machinery and vehicles. The country is the fourth largest car manufacturer in the world. Oil refining is also important.
France is the world's fourth ranking exporting nation. French perfumes, textiles and fashion goods are world-famous and important exports.

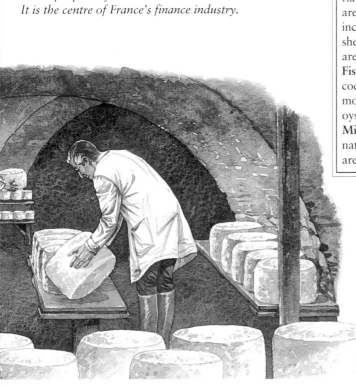

◄ *Round, creamy Camembert cheeses, produced in the northwest, are stored in a cellar to ripen. France makes and exports hundreds of different cheeses. Some are made from cows' milk, others from sheep or goats' milk. Brie, Roquefort and Port Salut are also famous French cheeses.*

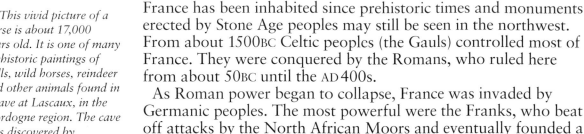

FRANCE *History*

▼ *This vivid picture of a horse is about 17,000 years old. It is one of many prehistoric paintings of bulls, wild horses, reindeer and other animals found in a cave at Lascaux, in the Dordogne region. The cave was discovered by schoolboys in 1940.*

France has been inhabited since prehistoric times and monuments erected by Stone Age peoples may still be seen in the northwest. From about 1500BC Celtic peoples (the Gauls) controlled most of France. They were conquered by the Romans, who ruled here from about 50BC until the AD400s.

As Roman power began to collapse, France was invaded by Germanic peoples. The most powerful were the Franks, who beat off attacks by the North African Moors and eventually founded a great empire under Charlemagne (AD742-814).

During the Middle Ages French civilization flourished in spite of a series of long wars with England. Then, in the late 1500s, a religious movement known as the Reformation spread Protestantism across Europe. In France, differences between Protestants and Roman Catholics led to more than 30 years of civil wars.

The French monarchy was at its most powerful during the reign of Louis XIV (1643-1715). However, resentment at the power and wealth of the king and the aristocracy was already growing. In 1789 this led to the French Revolution and the violent overthrow of royalty.

Napoleon Bonaparte emerged as the ruler of France from the chaos of the Revolution. He led victorious French armies across Europe before being defeated by the British and Prussians at Waterloo in 1815. During the 1800s France acquired a large empire in Africa and Asia, but the late 1800s and early 1900s were dominated by destructive wars with Germany. From the 1950s General Charles de Gaulle led the reconstruction of France after World War II. Both France and Germany helped to shape a new, more peaceful Europe with the founding of the European Economic Community, today's European Union.

◄ *The 275-metre Pont du Gard is a wonderfully preserved Roman aqueduct. It was built to carry fresh water to the city of Nîmes in southern France. The Romans built fine cities, theatres and roads during their long occupation of Gaul (modern France) from about 50BC until the AD400s.*

◄ The splendid château, or stately home, of Vaux-le-Vicomte was built for a minister of Louis XIV during the 1600s. Both French kings and their nobles built many fine châteaus during the 1500s and 1600s. The most famous is the magnificent royal palace of Versailles, just outside Paris.

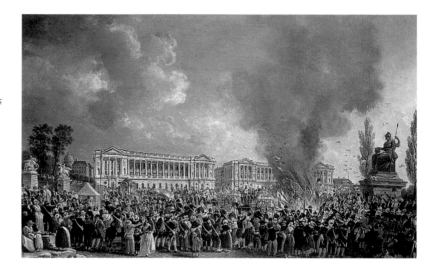

► Parisians burn the hated emblems of monarchy in the Place de la Concorde on August 10, 1793, during the French Revolution. Their ruler King Louis XVI had been executed in January of that year.

◄ General Charles de Gaulle leads Free French forces in a liberation parade through Paris in 1944, during World War II. France had been occupied by Germany for four terrible years. De Gaulle became president of France from 1958 to 1969.

SPAIN *Introduction*

▲ *Barcelona's most famous building is an unusual cathedral dedicated to* La Sagrada Familia *(The Holy Family). It was designed by the great Spanish architect and sculptor Antonio Gaudí. Building began in 1884, but the cathedral has still not been finished.*

Spain's historic cities and fine beaches make it one of the most visited countries in Europe. Tourism is vital to the economy because, for its size, Spain has few natural resources. Behind its rocky Atlantic and sandy Mediterranean coastlines most of the interior is a hot, dusty plateau broken by mountains. Good farmland is scarce and there is little rain, except in the north.

During the 1500s soldier-explorers called conquistadores (conquerors) created a huge empire in North and South America. Spain was one of the richest and most powerful countries in the world until wars with other countries and economic problems brought a slow decline that lasted until this century.

Today Spain is changing rapidly. From 1939 to 1975 a dictatorship under General Francisco Franco kept it isolated from other Western nations. However, democracy and membership of the European Union have brought the country closer to the rest of Europe. In 1992 Barcelona hosted the Olympic Games and Madrid was the European City of Culture. A world fair called Expo '92 was held in Seville in the same year.

Spain has had a monarchy since Franco's death in 1975, but political power lies with the government. Despite an attempt by army leaders to overthrow the government in 1981, the country has thrived under this form of democracy. People in different areas feel strongly about their regional identity and some parts have distinctive cultures and languages. This has led to campaigns for self-rule in northern areas such as the Basque region and Catalonia. There is also a great contrast between life in the modern cities and in the countryside, where much has stayed the same for centuries.

ENDANGERED WORLD

The tufted-eared Pardel lynx is in danger of extinction after centuries of hunting.

▶ *Crowds cross a busy street in Madrid to take the Metro (underground railway). Madrid became the capital city because it lies right in the centre of Spain. It is one of the country's main centres for industry and trade.*

FACTS AND FIGURES

Area: 504,750 sq km
Population: 39,143,000
Capital: Madrid
(2,910,000)
Other major cities:
Barcelona (1,626,000),
Valencia (753,000),
Seville (660,000)
Highest point:
Pico de Teide (3,718 m)
Official language:
Spanish
Main religion:
Christianity
Currencies:
Euro, Peseta
Main exports:
Vehicles, wine,
machinery, vegetables,
olive-oil, chemicals,
fruit, textiles, iron, steel
Government:
Constitutional
monarchy
Per capita GNP:
US $14,020

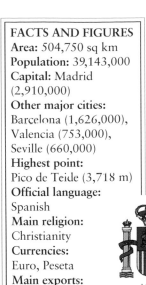

▲ *King Juan Carlos I and his wife, Queen Sophia, attend a state occasion. The Spanish monarchy was restored in 1975, after the country had been a dictatorship for nearly 40 years. Although the king is head of state, he does not play a direct role in governing the country.*

SPAIN *Geography*

Spain lies on the rugged Iberian Peninsula, the most westerly part of mainland Europe. To the northeast it is bordered by the snowy peaks of the Pyrenees Mountains. The beautiful north coast is made green by high rainfall. To the south, past forested mountains and gorges, stretches a huge plateau called the Meseta.

This name comes from the word mesa, which is used to describe flat-topped areas of land because it means table in Spanish. The plateau occupies most of inland Spain, where the climate is dry all year round, with blistering summers and cold winters. The Tagus and Guadalquivir rivers begin in the Meseta, while the Ebro River rises farther north. The Ebro carries water for irrigation across the plains of northeastern Spain.

The south is a land of red earth and shady olive groves. The landscape is green in spring, but soon becomes parched in the fierce summer sun. The great Sierra Nevada mountains drop to fertile plains along the sunny Mediterranean coast, which has warm seas and large tourist resorts. Spain's most southerly tip is just 13 kilometres from North Africa.

▲ *Warm seas wash the rocky northern coast of Tenerife, one of the Canary Islands. Cliffs along this coast rise to a steep ridge in the centre of the island. Tenerife's rocky landscape has been formed around a towering volcano called Pico de Teide.*

Spain also includes the Canary Islands and the Balearic Islands. The volcanic Canary Islands, which take in Tenerife, Lanzarote, Fuerteventura and Gran Canaria are in the Atlantic Ocean, off Africa's west coast. The Balearic Islands are in the Mediterranean. Of the three largest Balearics, Majorca is green and mountainous, Ibiza is hilly, while Minorca is mostly flat.

► *A pillar of eroded rock shimmers in the summer sun on the edge of the Meseta, Spain's central plateau. This harsh, dry landscape can be burning hot in summer and cold in winter. In spite of this, much of the Meseta is cultivated. Farmers there grow wheat and graze large herds of sheep and goats.*

◄ The farmland of Asturias, in the northwest of Spain, is kept green by rain-bearing breezes from the Atlantic Ocean. Asturias is a mountainous region cut by river valleys, with steep cliffs along its rocky coast.

► The southern part of Spain's central plateau forms a broad, dusty plain called Castile-La Mancha. It is famous for being the setting of Don Quixote, the story of a foolish landowner who sees himself as a brave knight. This novel was written in the early 1600s by the great Spanish writer Miguel de Cervantes.

► The remote Ordesa Valley lies in the heart of the Pyrenees Mountains in northeast Spain. It is a national park and a popular spot for visitors to go walking and climbing.

SPAIN *Economy*

ECONOMIC SURVEY
Farming: Although 79 percent of the Spanish people live in the country's towns and cities, agriculture is very important. Farms produce cereals, citrus fruits, olives, vegetables and rice. Sherry and other wines are also important products.
Fishing: Catches include anchovies, cod, hake, mussels, squid and tuna.
Mining: Spain has reserves of coal, lead, iron ore, copper, mercury and zinc.
Industry: The country manufactures textiles, chemicals, machinery and vehicles. Tourism is a major income-earner.

Until the 1950s Spain was one of the poorest European countries, but since then its economy has developed rapidly. The country is famous for its booming tourism industry based on beach resorts along the Mediterranean coast. Many new manufacturing industries have also been developed. Iron ore, Spain's most valuable mineral resource, is used to produce steel in northern regions. There are textile mills in the northwest and the country's chemicals industry is based around the cities of Bilbao, Madrid and Barcelona. These last two cities, along with Valencia and Saragossa, also manufacture motor vehicles. Spain is currently one of the largest car manufacturers in Europe.

Before the 1950s agriculture was the mainstay of the Spanish economy. It is still important, although it now employs less than 15 percent of the workforce. Today large areas of the Spanish countryside are owned by a small number of wealthy landowners, especially in the south. In the north cows graze on the green fields by the coast, while sheep and goats are herded in the drier areas. Much of the Iberian Peninsula has thin, dusty soil and the hot, dry climate makes it difficult to grow many crops. However, grain and vegetable crops thrive in some areas and the climate is ideal for growing olives, sunflowers, grapes, oranges and lemons. In the Canary Islands, even bananas can be grown.

Spanish wines are famous all around the world, especially sherry. Fish are another rich source of income for the country. Spain's large fishing fleet catches cod, sardines and anchovies in the waters of the Atlantic Ocean.

▲ *Spain is one of the world's largest exporters of citrus fruits. These include sweet mandarins, lemons and bitter oranges from Seville, which are used for making marmalade.*

▶ *Excavators extract iron ore from an opencast mine in the southwest. The ore is used to make steel for industries such as car manufacturing. Spain has been a centre of mining for thousands of years.*

◀ Strange towers provide a landmark in Barcelona's Park of Spanish Industry. This park occupies the site of an old textile mill. It was designed by a Basque architect called Luis Peña Ganchequi.

▲ Olive groves cover the silvery hills of the southwest. Several varieties of olives are grown in Spain. They may be pressed to make olive-oil or eaten whole. Spanish olives and olive-oil are exported all over the world.

▶ Tourists stroll through the resort of Benidorm, on Spain's Costa Blanca. High-rise hotels, bars and apartments line the beaches, which are packed with sun-seekers from northern Europe. Tourism employs ten percent of the Spanish workforce.

81

SPAIN *People*

PAELLA
Paella is rice flavoured with saffron, garlic and herbs. It is mixed with seafood, chicken or ham and vegetables. This popular dish is named after the large, shallow pan in which it is usually cooked. It comes from southwestern Spain.

Spain is a fascinating mixture of different traditions, ways of life and languages. The Basque people of northern Spain speak Euskara, a language that is not connected with any other in Europe. Galicians, who come from the far northwest, trace their history back to the ancient Celts. Their traditions include bagpipe playing and whirling dances to a drum accompaniment. In the south Moorish people from North Africa have left their mark on both the architecture and the farming methods. A Romany gypsy influence is obvious there too, in the strummed guitar music and spirited dancing. In the northeast the Catalans maintain their own language and culture.

In spite of such strong regional differences, many elements of the Spanish way of life are common to all its people. Castilian Spanish, the official language, is spoken throughout the country. Even though Spain no longer has an official religion, it is still strongly Roman Catholic. Religious festivals and processions take place everywhere, even in the smallest villages. There are also many fairs and fiestas. Most towns have a bull-ring where large crowds gather to watch bullfighting. Other popular sports include football and cycling.

Everyday life is affected by the climate. The fierce heat of the early afternoon makes a siesta (rest) necessary. Businesses and shops close in the middle of the day and do not reopen until late afternoon. After work people often enjoy a stroll outdoors to meet their friends, before dining late in the cool of the night.

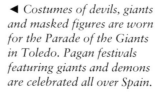

◄ *Costumes of devils, giants and masked figures are worn for the Parade of the Giants in Toledo. Pagan festivals featuring giants and demons are celebrated all over Spain.*

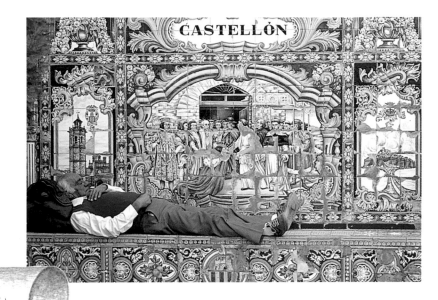

► A man takes his siesta (afternoon rest) under the cool arcades of the Plaza de España in Seville. This ornate palace, with its moats and fountains, was specially built for a large exhibition in 1929. The tiled walls show events from Spanish history.

SPEAK SPANISH

Hello – Hola *(oh - lah)*

Goodbye – Adiós
(ad - ee - oss)

Please – Por favor
(por fa - vor)

Thank you – Gracias
(gra - see - as)

Yes – Sí *(see)*

No – No *(no)*

▼ Shoppers look for fresh fruit and vegetables in the market hall at La Coruña on Spain's northwestern coast. Markets are at the centre of life in villages and towns throughout Spain. This is the place to buy onions, garlic, tomatoes or olives and to chat with friends.

◄ A man stamps and shouts while a woman struts to the sound of fiery flamenco music and castenets. Flamenco, from an area called Andalucia in southern Spain, includes singing, guitar music and a very passionate style of dancing.

SPAIN *History*

Cave paintings at Altamira in the north of the country show that Spain was settled in prehistoric times. About 5,000 years ago Iberians migrated to Spain from North Africa and mixed with the Celts who had settled in northern Spain. Other settlers included Phoenician and Greek traders. Spain was part of the Roman empire from around 200BC until AD475, when Visigoths invaded from the east.

During the early 700s Spain was conquered by the Moors from North Africa. During the later Middle Ages Christian kings gradually gained control of Spain and expelled the Moors. In 1512 it was united as a single Roman Catholic kingdom. Spain conquered lands in the Americas and became an extremely wealthy country. From the 1600s onwards its power began to weaken as a result of wars with other European countries. By the early 1800s it had lost most of its American possessions.

▲ *A young woman leads a communist parade in Madrid during the Spanish Civil War. Over 750,000 people died during the fighting, which lasted from 1936 to 1939. Communists, socialists and groups who supported the elected government fought against a rebel army led by General Franco.*

The early part of this century saw bitter political strife that led to civil war between 1936 and 1939. From then until 1975 Spain was a republic ruled by a harsh dictator, General Francisco Franco. After his death the monarchy was restored and democracy returned in 1978. In recent years Spain has given greater freedom to the peoples of certain regions, such as the northern Basques and Catalans.

▶ *Three small ships sail across the stormy Atlantic Ocean on a voyage of discovery. This is Christopher Columbus' fleet, which was sponsored by Queen Isabella of Spain. Columbus landed in the Bahamas in 1492, marking the start of Spain's conquest of the Americas.*

ANDORRA

FACTS AND FIGURES
Area: 450 sq km
Population: 48,000
Capital: Andorra la Vella (19,000)
Highest point: Coma Pedrosa (2,946 m)
Official language: Catalan
Main religion: Christianity
Currencies: French franc, Spanish peseta
Main exports: Clothes, mineral water, tobacco
Government: Principality
Per capita GNP: Est. US $3,000-8,000

This tiny country lies on the eastern slopes of the Pyrenees Mountains, between France and Spain. Crossed by the Valira River, it is a land of narrow gorges and mountain passes. Many people live by processing tobacco, grazing sheep or growing potatoes. Others work in the tourism trade, as large numbers of visitors come from all over Europe to ski, see the beautiful scenery and visit the old churches. They also come to buy cheap goods in the low-tax stores.

Legends say that the great Frankish emperor Charlemagne (AD742-814) founded Andorra. The Andorrans are believed to have helped Charlemagne defeat the Moors of North Africa. In 1278 a Spanish bishop and a French count became joint rulers of the country. Today Andorra still has two official heads of state – the Spanish Bishop of Urgel and the president of France. In this century many democratic reforms have been introduced, although women were not given the right to vote until 1971. In 1993 Andorrans voted to introduce a new parliamentary system of government which reduced the powers of the heads of state.

Native Andorrans are descended from a people called Catalans, who have their own language. Catalans also live in northern Spain and southern France. Many people here are French or Spanish immigrants and most non-Catalans speak Spanish.

► *The high peaks of the Pyrenees can be seen towering behind this hotel in Andorra la Vella, the capital. Many visitors come to Andorra for winter sports, making tourism very important to the economy.*

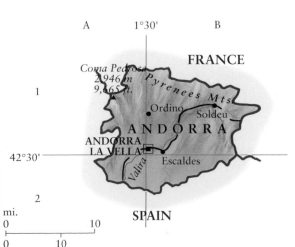

PORTUGAL

Portugal is part of the Iberian Peninsula, bordered to the north and east by Spain. The Azores and Madeira islands in the Atlantic are also Portuguese territories. Portugal is mainly a flat land broken up by rocky mountain ranges. On the broad coastal plains farmers grow a wide range of crops, including wheat, rice, almonds, olives and maize.

Three great rivers, the Douro, Tagus and Gaudiana, flow across the country. In their valleys vineyards produce Portugal's famous wines. Some grapes are still pressed in the traditional way, by treading underfoot in great vats. One third of the land is covered in forest, much of it valuable cork oak. Portugal's mountains are rich in deposits of coal and copper. The many streams that flow down from them are dammed to provide hydroelectric power.

Most Portuguese people live in rural villages, although increasing numbers are moving to the cities to find work. Along the Atlantic coast fishermen catch sardines and tuna. Others are involved in shipping or the tourism industry. Craftworkers produce lace, pottery and tiles that are prized all over the world.

The Iberians were the first known peoples to live in Portugal. They lived here about 5,000 years ago. Over the centuries Greeks, Romans and Moors from North Africa also settled. In the 1400s and 1500s Portuguese explorers sailed to the Far East and to South America, claiming a vast empire. The largest colony was Brazil. Portugal's power started to decline from the late 1500s and it was ruled by Spain from 1586 to 1646. Gradually its colonies broke away and became independent. Dictators ruled Portugal from 1926 to 1976, when a revolution brought democracy. Today Portugal is a member of the European Union.

▲ *This Monument to the Discoveries was built in Lisbon in 1960. It celebrates the Portuguese explorers of the 1400s. Their voyages were made possible by the work of Portugal's Prince Henry, who founded the world's first school of navigation.*

◀ *A woman cuts cork in the hot sun. This thick, lightweight bark is taken from cork oak trees. The cork is dried and made into wine bottle stoppers, floats, notice boards and floor tiles. Portugal is one of the world's major producers of cork.*

▲ The Santa Justa Lift connects the centre of Lisbon to the old part of the town at the top of the hill. This intriguing structure was built by Gustave Eiffel, the architect of Paris's famous Eiffel Tower.

◀ A cooper (barrel-maker) cuts staves for the big wooden barrels used to store port. This dark and sweet drink is stronger than ordinary wine. It is usually drunk after dinner and it is one of Portugal's best known exports.

FACTS AND FIGURES
Area: 91,830 sq km
Population: 9,860,000
Capital: Lisbon (831,000)
Other major city: Porto (350,000)
Highest point: Estrela (1,993 m)
Official language: Portuguese
Main religion: Christianity
Currencies: Euro, Escudo
Main exports: Clothes, textiles, cork, port and other wine, machinery, footwear, paper, timber, canned fish
Government: Constitutional republic
Per capita GNP: US $7,450

87

ITALY *Introduction*

Italy has played a major role in shaping the history and culture of Western Europe. Two thousand years ago this land was the heart of the Roman empire. It ruled much of Western Europe as well as territories all around the Mediterranean Sea. The Romans' language, Latin, is at the root of several modern European languages – not only Italian, but also French, Spanish, Portuguese and Romanian. The influence of Roman architecture, laws, literature and road-building can be seen right across Europe today.

During the 1400s and 1500s Italy was at the centre of a movement called the Renaissance. It was a time when artists and scientists experimented with many new ideas. Italian painters, sculptors, architects and writers were among the most influential in Europe. The towns and cities that the Italians built around this time are filled with world-famous paintings and sculptures.

Italy is also famous for the beauty and variety of its landscape. This ranges from the snowy peaks of the Alps to the green vineyards of Tuscany, an area northwest of Rome. Steep cliffs in the south overlook the island of Sicily, where a rugged landscape surrounds Etna, one of the largest active volcanoes in the world.

Italy became a united nation in 1861. Before that it was a collection of many different states. Rome became the capital and last state to join in 1871. Until then it had been ruled by the Pope. Modern Italy is a democratic republic and a founder-member of the European Community. It is famous for its industrial design, fashion, food, cinema and opera.

▼ *The river Tiber flows through the heart of Rome, Italy's capital. Rome is a busy modern city, where traffic swirls around some of the world's most famous ancient buildings.*

ENDANGERED WORLD

The grey wolf lives in the Apennine Mountains. It is hunted for its fur and has become very rare.

◄ *Women in traditional costume carry religious banners through the streets of Cagliari on the island of Sardinia. They are celebrating the feast day of a local saint, Saint Effisio. Nine out of ten Italians are Roman Catholics and saints' days are widely celebrated.*

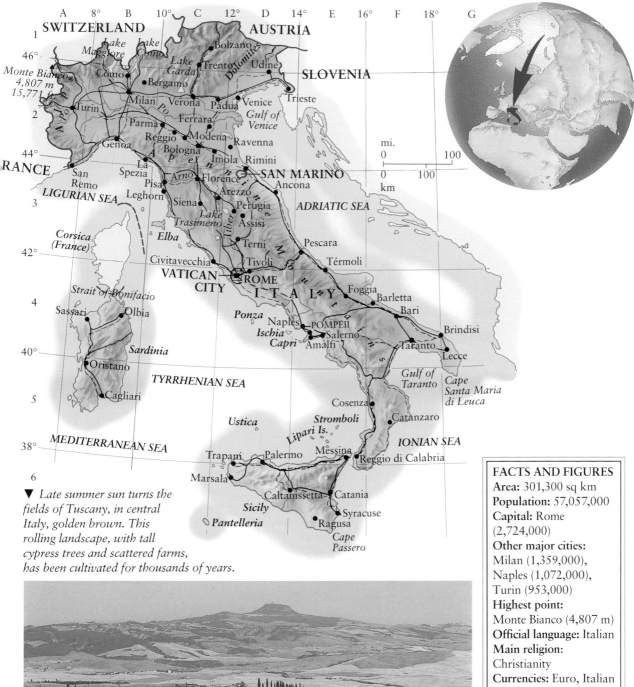

A 8° B 10° C 12° D 14° E 16° F 18° G

SWITZERLAND

1

46°

Lake Maggiore *Lake Como* Bolzano

AUSTRIA

Lake Garda Trento Udine

Monte Bianco 4,807 m 15,771 ft

Como Bergamo Verona Padua Venice

Milan *Gulf of Venice*

SLOVENIA

Trieste

Turin

2

Po

Parma Ferrara

Reggio Modena

Genoa Bologna Imola Ravenna

44°

RANCE San Remo La Spezia *A p e n n i n e s* Rimini

Pisa *Arno* Florence Arezzo

LIGURIAN SEA Leghorn Siena Perugia Ancona

SAN MARINO

3

Corsica (France) *Lake Trasimeno* Assisi

ADRIATIC SEA

Elba *Tiber*

42° Terni Pescara

Civitavecchia Tivoli Térmoli

VATICAN CITY **ROME**

I T A L Y Foggia

4

Ponza Naples POMPEII Barletta

Sassari Olbia *Ischia* Salerno Bari

Capri Amalfi Taranto Brindisi

Sardinia *M o u n t a i n s* Lecce

40° Oristano

Strait of Bonifacio *Gulf of Taranto* *Cape Santa Maria di Leuca*

TYRRHENIAN SEA

5 Cagliari Cosenza

Strómboli Catanzaro

Ustica *Lipari Is.*

38° **MEDITERRANEAN SEA** **IONIAN SEA**

6 Trapani Palermo Messina

Marsala Reggio di Calabria

Caltanissetta Catania

Sicily Syracuse

Pantelleria Ragusa

Cape Passero

mi. 0 100

km 0 100

▼ *Late summer sun turns the fields of Tuscany, in central Italy, golden brown. This rolling landscape, with tall cypress trees and scattered farms, has been cultivated for thousands of years.*

FACTS AND FIGURES

Area: 301,300 sq km

Population: 57,057,000

Capital: Rome (2,724,000)

Other major cities: Milan (1,359,000), Naples (1,072,000), Turin (953,000)

Highest point: Monte Bianco (4,807 m)

Official language: Italian

Main religion: Christianity

Currencies: Euro, Italian lira

Main exports: Wine, machinery, footwear, clothes, olive-oil, textiles, mineral products

Government: Constitutional republic

Per capita GNP: US $20,510

89

ITALY *Geography*

Italy is a peninsula on the edge of southern Europe. It is often said to be shaped like a boot. The country also includes Sicily, Sardinia and a number of smaller islands. Most of Italy enjoys mild, moist winters, but its hills and mountains can be cold and snowy. The summers are warm all over the country, with the southern and coastal plains becoming extremely hot and dusty.

The Alps rise on Italy's northern border, with snowfields and glaciers high above conifer forests and deep, green valleys. The mountains surround calm, blue lakes. South of the Alps lies the fertile north Italian plain, crossed by the Po River. This flat landscape is wealthy farming country and the most densely populated area in Italy. The smaller Adriatic Plain lies to the east, bordered by Slovenia and the Adriatic Sea. Italy has a long, rocky backbone in the form of the Apennine mountain chain. Parts of these forested peaks are still wild, the home of buzzards and wild boar. They descend to rolling countryside of farmland and vineyards. The coastal plains of the west, bordering the Tyrrhenian Sea, are very fertile. They are crossed by the Arno and Tiber rivers, which begin in the Apennines.

The hot, dry southeastern plains are filled with olive groves. In the southwest mountains plunge down to the sea, creating beautiful coastal scenery. Mount Vesuvius, one of Europe's most famous active volcanoes, dominates the Bay of Naples. The fertile island of Sicily is also volcanic. Lava and gases often roll down the slopes of Mount Etna, in the northeast of the island, which has erupted several times this century. Sardinia is a typical Mediterranean island with highlands covered in dry scrub and lowlands used for farming.

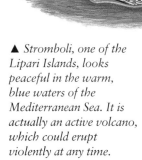

▲ *Stromboli, one of the Lipari Islands, looks peaceful in the warm, blue waters of the Mediterranean Sea. It is actually an active volcano, which could erupt violently at any time.*

◀ *Vines grow on the southern uplands of Emilia Romagna, a region bordered by the Po River to the north and the Apennines to the south. Northern Emilia Romagna is a fertile plain, watered by the Po and other rivers. It is intensively farmed and is one of Italy's major agricultural areas.*

◀ *The jagged limestone peaks of the Dolomites look like fantastic cathedral spires. This northeastern mountain range, which rises to more than 3,300 metres, is a branch of the Alps. Its sheer rockfaces and wonderful views attract rock climbers, walkers and tourists.*

▶ *Poppies turn a wheatfield scarlet on a hillside in northern Tuscany. This beautiful region of central Italy stretches from the Apennines westwards to the coast. The landscape ranges from forested mountains to gently rolling hills covered with vineyards, olive groves and wheatfields. In the south is a marshy coastal plain called the Maremma.*

▶ *Scrub covers the rugged hills of the Sila Massif in central Calabria. This region of the far south, lying between the Tyrrhenian and Ionian seas, is hot and barren. Its coarse grasses and mountain shrubs are grazed by sheep and goats.*

ITALY *Economy*

ECONOMIC SURVEY

Farming: Many Italian farms are small. Crops include barley, wheat, rice, fruit, tomatoes, artichokes, grapes, olives, sugar beet, tobacco and vegetables. Sheep, pigs, goats and cattle are reared.

Fishing: Italy has a large fishing fleet. Catches have recently been affected by pollution and shrinking fish stocks.

Industry: Italy is a major manufacturer of cars and other types of vehicles, machinery, office and household equipment, clothing and shoes, chemicals and electronics. It is world-famous as a producer of pasta, Parmesan cheese and Parma ham.

Italy was once a nation of farmers, but since the 1950s fewer and fewer people have been employed in agriculture. Although agriculture has become less important to the economy, grapes are still one of Italy's most important crops. The country is currently the world's leading wine-maker. It is also a major producer and exporter of olives and olive-oil.

Italy has few natural resources so it has to import oil and minerals. Even so, northern Italy has become one of the richest and most advanced industrial regions in Europe, hosting many major international trade fairs. Cars, textiles, processed foods and chemicals are all important exports. Milan is an internationally famous fashion centre and Italian clothes, shoes and leather goods are exported all over the world. Unfortunately, industry, traffic and agricultural chemicals have harmed the environment in northern Italy. The Italian government is attempting to deal with city pollution by restricting traffic flows in their crowded centres.

Goods for export overseas pass through the major ports of Genoa and Trieste. Italy has a large fleet of merchant ships as well as many fishing fleets, which catch tuna and sardines in the Mediterranean Sea. Over half of Italy's trade is with member states of the European Union. Italy helped to start the process of uniting Europe and was one of the original members of the European Economic Community in 1957.

The most important part of the Italian economy is made up of those industries that provide services rather than manufactured goods. These include tourism, education, healthcare, legal services, finance, insurance and administration.

► *Holidaymakers crowd a beach in the tourist resort of Amalfi. Millions of tourists go to Italy every year in search of sunny beaches, mountain lakes and historical buildings.*

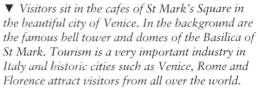

▼ Visitors sit in the cafes of St Mark's Square in the beautiful city of Venice. In the background are the famous bell tower and domes of the Basilica of St Mark. Tourism is a very important industry in Italy and historic cities such as Venice, Rome and Florence attract visitors from all over the world.

▲ A worker on the production line tightens bolts at Fiat's tractor assembly plant in Modena. Fiat is also known for its range of cars, including small hatchbacks that are ideal for parking in Italy's crowded cities.

◄ Motorways lead into the bustling city of Genoa, one of the major seaports of the Mediterranean. Genoa exports wine, olive-oil and textiles. It is also a centre of shipbuilding and oil refining. Iron and steel products are manufactured there too.

► Grapes used in Chianti wine ripen in north-central Italy. This strong red table wine is one of the best known in Italy. Italy produces more wine than any other country in the world. Barolo and Orvieto wines are also world-famous. Barolo is a red wine from Piedmont, a region in the northwest, while Orvieto is a white wine from the centre of the country.

ITALY *People*

Modern Italy was not united until 1861. Before then it was a collection of small states, each with its own culture, traditions and language or dialect. Even today many Italian people think of themselves as Romans, Venetians or Sicilians first, and as Italians second. Regional differences are strong in everything from food to local customs. The way of life in wealthy northern cities such as Milan, Turin, Bologna and Genoa is also very different from that of poor farming communities in the south.

Almost all the people of Italy speak the Italian language, but in the north there are small groups of French, German and Slovenian speakers. The Sards of Sardinia speak a dialect that is close to the Latin language of ancient Rome. Sicily, closer in distance to North Africa than to northern Italy, has its own traditions.

In spite of their differences Italians have many things in common. In all parts of Italy people have been moving away from the countryside to the cities since the 1950s. Many, especially from southern Italy, have emigrated overseas. Today the majority of the population lives in towns or cities, working mainly in service and manufacturing industries. Only nine percent still works in agriculture and in rural areas many farmhouses have been turned into holiday homes for both Italians and visitors from abroad. The Roman Catholic Church and large, close-knit families have traditionally been a major part of Italian society. However, these influences are weakening. The number of people practising their religion is falling all the time and families are getting smaller.

Throughout the country communities are brought together by customs such as the evening *passeggiata* (promenade), when families stroll together through the centre of the town or village. A love of good food and sport, especially football, is common to many Italians, as is a keen interest in fashion.

▲ *Beautiful masks, gowns and cloaks are worn by carnival-goers in Venice, an elegant city of islands and canals. The annual Venice carnival was at its grandest in the 1700s. Many of the costumes are based on designs from that period.*

◄ *Statues of Christ and the Virgin Mary are carried through the streets in a Sardinian Holy Week procession. Roman Catholic festivals are important in the lives of many Italians. Processions such as this take place all over Italy at Easter.*

▲ *Flags and scarves go on sale outside the football stadium in Turin. Football is the most popular spectator sport in Italy. This country is home to some of the world's best football teams, such as AC Milan and Juventus.*

SPEAK ITALIAN

Hello – Ciao *(chow)*

Goodbye – Arrivederci
*(a - ree - vah - **dair** - chee)*

Please – Per favore
*(pair fa - **vor** - ay)*

Thank you – Grazie
*(**grat** - see - ah)*

Yes – Si *(see)*

No – No *(no)*

SPAGHETTI BOLOGNESE
This dish from Bologna mixes spaghetti with a meat and tomato sauce. Spaghetti is just one form of pasta. Each region of Italy has its own favourite type of pasta and its own special sauces.

▶ *Horse-riders wearing medieval costumes gallop bareback around the main square of Siena each summer. This spectacular and dangerous race is known in Italy as the Palio. The custom goes back to the 1400s.*

95

ITALY *History*

▼ *Decorated walls and alcoves may still be seen in ancient Roman houses at Pompeii. In AD79 the city was buried in ashes when the volcano Mount Vesuvius erupted. Pompeii was rediscovered in 1748.*

The ancient Greeks founded colonies in many parts of the Italian peninsula from about 800BC. Their civilization influenced the Etruscans, a people who ruled in central Italy around 500BC.

One of the cities controlled by the Etruscans was Rome. In 509BC the Romans rebelled against the Etruscan kings. They went on to conquer the other peoples of Italy and then to defeat the powerful Carthaginian empire of North Africa. The Romans were highly skilled soldiers, engineers, writers and thinkers. By the AD100s their empire stretched from Spain to the Caspian Sea and from Britain to Egypt. The empire finally collapsed in AD476 after repeated invasions by northern peoples such as the Vandals. The Italian peninsula split into a collection of cities and small states, although the city of Rome remained powerful as the centre of the Roman Catholic Church. During the Middle Ages many independent cities in northern and central areas of the country grew wealthy through trade and banking. They became centres of art and science during the Renaissance, a time when new ideas swept through Europe.

From the 1500s some parts of Italy were ruled by French, Spanish and Austrian monarchs. Others were controlled by the Pope. After wars with Austria, France and Spain the states of modern Italy united as an independent kingdom in 1861. Giuseppe Mazzini and Giuseppe Garibaldi were leading figures in the fight for independence. In 1922 a fascist dictator, Benito Mussolini, came to power. He led Italy into a series of foreign wars and then into World War II. Since 1947 Italy has been a democratic republic and rapid economic growth has made it a major industrial country.

◄ *The Leaning Tower of Pisa is one of the most famous buildings in Italy. The marble bell tower was built on sinking ground between 1173 and the 1360s. It already leans five metres out of line and needs engineering work to stop it from collapsing.*

▶ *Florence is a magnificent city that reached its peak during the 1400s. It was home to many of the great artists, architects, writers and scientists of the Renaissance – the time of many new ideas in art and learning.*

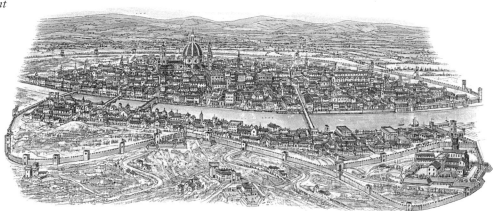

◀ *Milan's splendid cathedral, built of white marble, is one of the largest cathedrals in Europe. It was started in 1386 and not finished until the 1800s. Milan, Italy's second city, became wealthy during the Middle Ages because it controlled trading routes northwards across the Alps.*

▶ *This glass bottle was made on the island of Murano, Venice, in the mid-1400s. Glassware has been made in Venice since the 900s. The skills and techniques developed there were much sought after throughout Europe.*

▶ *The Italian hero Giuseppe Garibaldi leads the fight against French forces at Rome in 1849. Garibaldi and his followers fought tirelessly for an independent, united Italy. Their struggles were finally rewarded in 1861.*

VATICAN CITY AND SAN MARINO

VATICAN CITY, the world's smallest independent country, is a city within a city. It is completely surrounded by Rome, the capital of Italy. Vatican City is the world headquarters of the Roman Catholic Church, headed by the Pope. The tiny population is made up almost entirely of religious officials and people who work in the Papal Palace, the Vatican library and the museums. Vatican City is all that remains of the Papal States, a large area of Italy once ruled by the Roman Catholic Church. Its independence within modern Italy was agreed in 1929.

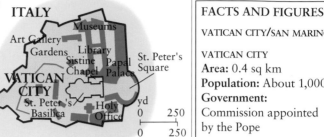

ITALY
Museums
Art Gallery
Gardens Library
Sistine Papal
Chapel Palace St. Peter's
VATICAN Square
CITY
St. Peter's Holy
Basilica Office
yd
0   250
0   250
m

San Marino

Vatican City

FACTS AND FIGURES

VATICAN CITY/SAN MARINO

VATICAN CITY
Area: 0.4 sq km
Population: About 1,000
Government: Commission appointed by the Pope

SAN MARINO
Area: 61 sq km
Population: 23,000
Capital: San Marino (4,500)
Main religion: Christianity
Currency: Italian lira
Main exports: Wine, machinery, chemicals
Government: Constitutional republic
Per capita GNP: Est. over US $8,000

◀ *Vatican City's buildings include the great St Peter's Basilica, which was built between 1506 and 1614. Next to it stands the Papal Palace.*

A   12°30'   B
mi.
0   2
ITALY
Falciano
Serravalle
0   2
km
1
Acquaviva SAN Domagnano
Borgo Maggiore Mt. Titano
SAN MARINO 755 m Faetano
2,478 ft.
43°55' MARINO
Monte Giardino
Chiesanuova Fiorentino
ITALY

SAN MARINO is another tiny independent country surrounded on all sides by Italy. It is the oldest republic in the world. San Marino is said to have been founded in the AD300s by a stonecutter called Marinus, who became a Christian saint. In 1631 the Pope in Rome, who had control over the area surrounding San Marino, formally agreed to the country's independence. This was confirmed by a treaty with Italy in 1862.

San Marino lies on the slopes of Mount Titano in the Apennine Mountains. The capital has houses built in the 1300s, lining winding cobblestone streets. Revenue is brought by tourists who come to watch San Marino's colourful festivals. Another important source of income is the sale of San Marino's postage stamps, which are collected throughout the world.

▶ *Fortress walls dating from the Middle Ages and beautiful views of the Apennine Mountains attract many visitors to the tiny country of San Marino.*

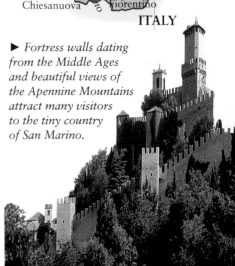

MALTA

This chain of islands lies to the far south of mainland Europe between Sicily and North Africa. The coastlines are ragged with many rocky inlets forming natural harbours, steep cliffs and sandy coves.

The three inhabited islands are Malta, Gozo and Comino. Malta has no rivers and poor soil. The island is heavily populated and much of its food has to be imported, but farmers manage to grow grain and vegetables on terraced fields, alongside sun-loving fruits such as grapes and figs.

The Maltese archipelago is positioned on the sea routes of the central Mediterranean and has many sheltered harbours. As a result invaders from many different parts of the world have occupied this country. It became a British colony in 1814 and suffered heavy bombing as a British naval base during World War II. Britain gave the islands independence in 1964 and the Maltese turned the naval base into dockyards for merchant shipping. Malta's stormy history means that its people are of Arab, Italian or English descent and their culture is filled with different influences. Today most work at the dockyards, in shipbuilding or in the construction industry. Tourism has become increasingly important to the country's economy.

▼ *Valletta, Malta's chief port and its capital, is built on a rocky headland between two fine natural harbours. The skyline is dominated by the Roman Catholic Cathedral of St John, built in the 1500s.*

FACTS AND FIGURES

Area: 310 sq km
Population: 361,000
Capital: Valletta (102,000)
Other major city: Birkirkara (21,000)
Highest point: On Malta Island (253 m)
Official languages: Maltese, English
Main religion: Christianity
Currency: Maltese lira
Main exports: Machinery, clothes, textiles, transport equipment, ships, beverages, tobacco
Government: Constitutional republic
Per capita GNP: US $6,850

ALBANIA

This rugged country lies beside the Adriatic Sea. In the Albanian language its name means eagle, after the majestic eagles that soar over Albania's lakes and high mountains. On the coastal plain farmers grow maize, fruit and tobacco. They raise cattle, sheep and goats on the high pastures.

Historians believe that the Albanians are descended from an ancient people called the Illyrians, whose kingdom covered this area around 300BC. The Illyrians intermarried with the Romans, Venetians, Normans and Serbs, who settled in Albania over the centuries. From 1468 until independence in 1912, Albania was part of the Turkish Ottoman empire. In 1946 the country became a communist republic under the leadership of Enver Hoxha. Fearing outside influence, the communist government forbade Albanians to travel abroad or own televisions. It also banned religious worship. Businesses and farms were taken into state ownership. When Hoxha died in 1985 the country remained communist, but Albanians called for reform. As a result the government gradually started to increase freedoms for ordinary people. The first democratic elections were held in 1991 and in 1992 the communists fell from power.

The new government no longer controlled wages and prices, so the cost of living rose. Many Albanians struggled against poverty, others emigrated. To improve the economy the government introduced projects to turn coastal lowlands into rich farmland. It also returned land and factories to private ownership. Albania's rich deposits of iron, oil and natural gas have brought new wealth to the country.

FACTS AND FIGURES

Area: 28,750 sq km
Population: 3,338,000
Capital: Tirane (251,000)
Other major cities: Durres (87,000), Shkoder (84,000), Elbasan (84,000)
Highest point: Mt Jezerce (2,693 m)
Official language: Albanian
Main religions: Christianity, Islam
Currency: Lek
Main exports: Iron ore, natural gas, oil, chrome, bitumen, nickel, copper, fruit and vegetables
Government: Multi-party republic
Per capita GNP: Est. $700-3,000

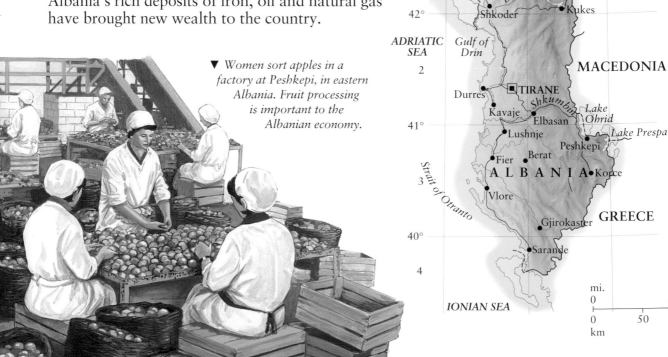

▼ Women sort apples in a factory at Peshkepi, in eastern Albania. Fruit processing is important to the Albanian economy.

BULGARIA

FACTS AND FIGURES
Area: 110,990 sq km
Population: 8,469,000
Capital: Sofia
(1,142,000)
Other major cities:
Plovdiv (379,000),
Varna (315,000),
Burgas (205,000)
Highest point:
Musala (2,925 m)
Official language:
Bulgarian
Main religions:
Christianity, Islam
Currency: Lev
Main exports:
Machinery, food, wine,
tobacco, fuels and raw
materials, footwear,
iron, steel, textiles
Government:
Multi-party republic
Per capita GNP:
US $1,330

In the north of Bulgaria is a fertile plateau that stretches from the river Danube towards the Balkan Mountains. It is an important farming region where grain, fruit and vegetables are grown. Beyond these mountains are rolling lowlands, rising to the Rhodope Mountains along the Greek border.

This land was once called Thrace. The Thracians were a people who originally settled here in about 1000BC. After AD500 Slavs poured into the region from the north and a century later an Asian people called the Bulgars invaded from the east. Modern Bulgarians are descended from these peoples. Bulgaria spent nearly 500 years (1396-1878) under Turkish rule. Then in 1944 it was occupied by the communist forces of the Soviet Union, which helped the Bulgarian communists gain power. Under communism ordinary people lost many personal freedoms. Those who criticized the government were often killed or put in harsh work camps. The communists built many factories, but most Bulgarians lived in rural areas where poverty was common. Communism collapsed in Bulgaria in 1990 and the country held its first democratic elections.

Today two thirds of Bulgarians live in cities, many working in industries such as textiles, food processing and the manufacture of machinery. Living standards have gone up since 1990, but jobs and housing are still in short supply. To improve its economy Bulgaria is encouraging international trade and tourism. Visitors are attracted to its beautiful churches and colourful festivals. People come from all over Europe to holiday resorts along the Black Sea coast.

Albania

Bulgaria

A 22°30'   B   24°   C   25°30'   D   27°   E   28°30'

1
44°   Vidin
ROMANIA   Silistra
Lom
Ruse
Danube
Pleven   Svishtov   Razgrad
2   Mikhaylovgrad   Vratsa   Lovech   Shumen   Dobrich
GOSLAVIA   43°   Veliko Turnovo   Varna
Balkan Mts. Kazanluk   Sliven   Kamchiya   BLACK SEA
SOFIA
Pernik   B U L G A R I A   Burgas
3   Kyustendil   mi.
Pazardzhik   Stara Zagora   0   50
Musala   Plovdiv   Maritsa
42°   Blagoevgrad   2,925 m   Khaskovo   0   50
ACEDONIA   9,596 ft.   Rhodope Mts.   TURKEY   km
4   Smolyan   Kurdzhali

41°   GREECE
5

▲ *Dancers celebrate the Festival of Roses in Kazanluk. It is held annually, one day before the rose picking begins. The sweet-scented petals are crushed to make attar of roses, an oil used in perfume-making.*

GREECE *Introduction*

FACTS AND FIGURES
Area: 131,960 sq km
Population: 10,350,000
Capital: Athens
(3,097,000)
Other major city:
Thessaloniki (378,000)
Highest point:
Mt Olympus (2,917 m)
Official language:
Greek
Main religion:
Christianity
Currency: Drachma
Main exports:
Clothes, olive-
oil, petroleum
products,
fruit, tobacco
Government:
Constitutional
republic
Per capita GNP:
US $7,180

▼ *The Acropolis is a rocky fortress on a hill above Athens. On its highest point is the Parthenon, a temple that was built around 438BC in honour of the city's goddess, Athene.*

Greece occupies the southern part of the Balkan Peninsula. It includes hundreds of beautiful islands scattered in the deep blue Aegean and Ionian seas. The largest Greek island is Crete, which lies farther south in the Mediterranean Sea.

Greece has natural harbours, mountains and deep valleys. It is a rocky land of limestone covered in scrub and scented wild herbs, grazed by flocks of sheep and goats. The earth is carpeted with wild flowers in the spring, but baked brown and dusty during the hot summer months. Olive groves and wheatfields surround peaceful, whitewashed villages. However, Greece's cities, with their mix of ancient and modern buildings, are busy with people and traffic. Air pollution in Athens is threatening health and eating away at the many ancient monuments. Controls have been placed on industry and traffic movement in the capital city.

Four thousand years ago the people of ancient Greece created a highly civilized society. They made great advances in science, philosophy, art, literature, the theatre and sport. Their great philosophers included Aristotle, Plato and Socrates. It was the ancient Greeks who developed the idea of democracy, or rule by the people. The term comes from the Greek words *demos*, which means people, and *kratia*, which means authority. They also believed in gods and goddesses who lived on Mount Olympus and created all kinds of myths about them.

Greece's main natural resources are its scenery and warm sunny climate, which attract thousands of tourists every year. Natural gas and oil have been discovered under the Aegean Sea and the country has potential for hydroelectric power in the rivers of the Pindus Mountains.

ENDANGERED WORLD

Hermann's tortoise is threatened because people have collected it for the pet trade. Rapidly increasing road traffic is another danger.

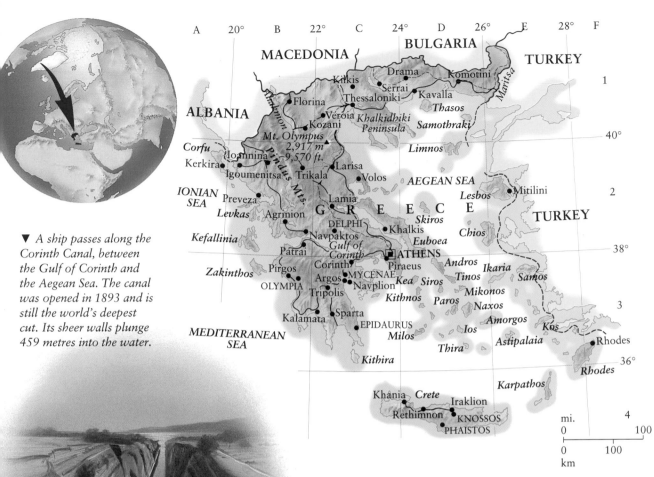

A ship passes along the Corinth Canal, between the Gulf of Corinth and the Aegean Sea. The canal was opened in 1893 and is still the world's deepest cut. Its sheer walls plunge 459 metres into the water.

▶ Houses on the island of Thira are typically Greek. They have thick walls and small windows to keep out the summer heat. The domed buildings are Greek Orthodox churches – over 90 percent of the Greek people belong to this religion.

103

GREECE *People and History*

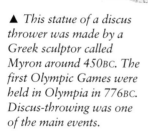

The first great European civilization began in Greece. From about 2500BC the Minoans flourished on the island of Crete. They lived in rich cities and traded all round the Mediterranean. Their civilization collapsed around 1400BC and was taken over by the Myceneans from the mainland. From about 1000BC peoples from the north began to invade Greece. They established independent city states, such as Athens and Sparta. For centuries the city states were immensely powerful and often fought wars with each other, only uniting to defeat their enemy Persia (now Iran). In 338BC the states were conquered by Macedonia and Alexander the Great set up a huge Greek empire in the Middle East. Eventually ancient Greece crumbled, becoming part of the Roman empire in 146BC. From AD330 Greece was part of the Byzantine empire until it was conquered by the Turks in 1453 and became part of the Ottoman empire. Greece gained its independence from Turkey in 1829, but years of political upheaval and military rule followed. The modern democratic republic of Greece was founded in 1975.

Today two thirds of Greece's population lives in urban areas. Many people work in cement or chemical factories or process foods for export. Greece has one of the biggest merchant fleets in the world and many are employed in the tourism industry, running hotels and restaurants. In rural areas farming and traditional crafts such as pottery and weaving are important.

▲ *This statue of a discus thrower was made by a Greek sculptor called Myron around 450BC. The first Olympic Games were held in Olympia in 776BC. Discus-throwing was one of the main events.*

▶ *Passengers board a ferry on the island of Naxos. The ferries are used by local people and tourists. In summer most passengers are holidaymakers, island-hopping their way around Greece. Many Greeks work in tourism, one of the country's major sources of income.*

► The ruins of the city of Mistras lie near Sparta, amid rolling hills covered in olive groves. Mistras was built in the 1300s and 1400s, when Turkey ruled Greece. It has a cathedral where the last of the Byzantine emperors was crowned.

GREEK SALAD
Greek salad is made with tomatoes, cucumber, black olives and cubes of feta (a crumbly white goats' cheese). It is sprinkled with herbs and olive-oil. Crusty bread and a Greek wine called retsina often accompany this dish.

► This silver owl coin was issued in Athens in 479BC, when the Greeks defeated Persia (modern Iran). An owl was the emblem of the city's goddess, Athene. The coin was widely used in trade and was accepted all over Greece, Turkey and Italy.

► On the island of Tinos, secondary school pupils join a parade to celebrate Greek independence. These boys are dressed as Evzones, the soldiers of the national guard. It was these soldiers who defeated Greece's Turkish rulers in 1829 to win independence for the country.

105

ROMANIA

The beautiful Carpathian Mountains and the Transylvanian Alps curve right across Romania. South and east of the mountains the land drops down to plains that form large areas of fertile farmland. The southern area is called Walachia and the region to the east is Moldavia. Holiday resorts have grown up along the sandy beaches of Romania's Black Sea coast. Inland the marshes of the Danube Delta form a major habitat for many birds and fish.

This area of Europe became part of the Roman empire in AD106 and the country takes its name from the Romans who occupied it. From the late 200s until the mid-1800s a variety of peoples, including the Ottoman Turks and the Russians, ruled here. Then in 1856 the states of Moldavia and Walachia united to form an independent kingdom – Romania.

Romania gained Transylvania and other regions when the Austro-Hungarian empire broke up in 1918. During the 1940s the country became communist and was strongly influenced by the Soviet Union. In the 1960s, under President Nicolae Ceausescu, it began to break away from the Soviet Union. Ceausescu tried to develop industry and many Romanians were forced from their villages into the towns and cities to provide a workforce. Living standards were low and the population had little freedom. In 1989 the people rebelled. They overthrew the government and Ceausescu was executed. Democratic elections were held in 1990 and 1992, when a huge effort to rebuild the country began.

ENDANGERED WORLD

Dalmatian pelicans fish in the Danube Delta. Drainage of wetlands and hunting have greatly reduced their numbers.

FACTS AND FIGURES
Area: 237,500 sq km
Population: 22,755,000
Capital: Bucharest (2,351,000)
Other major city: Constanta (351,000)
Highest point: Moldoveanu (2,543 m)
Official language: Romanian
Main religion: Christianity
Currency: Leu
Main exports: Petroleum products, oilfield equipment, cement, chemical factory equipment
Government: Multi-party republic
Per capita GNP: US $1,090

▼ *This aerial view of Bucharest, Romania's capital and largest city, shows a typical mixture of old and new buildings. In 1977 Bucharest was badly damaged by an earthquake, but rebuilding was rapid.*

SPEAK ROMANIAN

Hello – Salut
(*sah - loot*)

Goodbye – La revedere
(*lah reh - veh - dair - ay*)

Please – Vă rog
(*veh - rog*)

Thank You – Mulţumesc
(*mool - tsoo - mesk*)

Yes – Da (*dah*)

▲ *Ski slopes and wooded scenery attract tourists to the Transylvanian region. These dense forests are also famous as the source of vampire legends. The character of the vampire Count Dracula is said to have been based on a prince of the Middle Ages called Vlad the Impaler.*

▲ *A plough pulled by oxen prepares a field for sowing near Sibiu in central Romania. Grains such as maize and wheat are the most important crops in most parts of Romania. The country is also an important wine producer.*

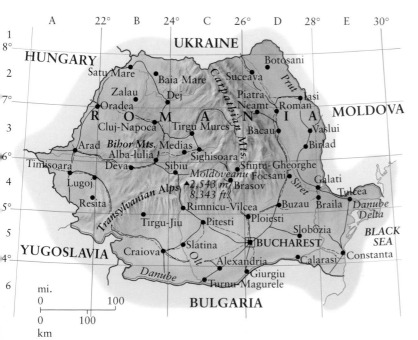

107

MOLDOVA

Moldova is a land of wide plains, forested hills and many rivers. Fertile, black soil covers much of the country, which has warm summers and mild winters. This makes the land suitable for farming and agriculture is very important to Moldova's economy. More than half its people live in rural areas, most working on farms. They grow sunflowers (for vegetable oil), maize, wheat, tobacco and root vegetables. Fruits are grown for the canning industry and vineyards produce wine. Food processing is a major industry. Other industries include the manufacture of tractors, household appliances and clothes.

Moldova lies on the edge of the steppes (plains) that stretch all the way to central Asia. This position has made it vulnerable to many invaders. In the Middle Ages an independent state called Moldavia was founded here. This included present-day Moldova, then called Bessarabia, and what is now eastern Romania. The Ottoman Turks ruled the area from the early 1500s until 1812, when Russia gained control of Bessarabia. The region then passed from Russia (later the Soviet Union) to Romania and back again several times before it finally became part of the Soviet Union in 1944.

Moldova gained independence in 1991. However, the unity of the new nation was threatened when non-Moldovan peoples living in southern and eastern regions attempted to form separate states. Fighting broke out in 1991, but peace was restored the following year.

▶ *Marchers in traditional costume celebrate the first anniversary of Moldovan independence in 1992. As the Republic of Moldavia, the country had been part of the Soviet Union since 1944. After independence, Moldovan (which is similar to Romanian) replaced Russian as the country's official language.*

FACTS AND FIGURES

Area: 33,700 sq km
Population: 4,356,000
Capital: Chisinau (753,000)
Other major cities: Tiraspol (182,000), Beltsy (159,000), Bendery (130,000)
Highest point: Mt Balaneshty (429 m)
Official language: Moldovan
Main religion: Christianity
Currency: Leu
Main exports: Chemicals, food, wine, machinery, textiles, tobacco
Government: Republic
Per capita GNP: US $1,260

BELARUS

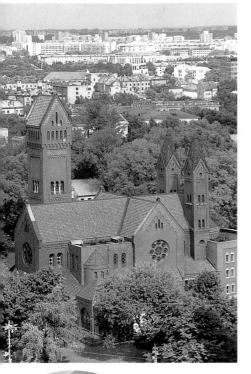

Most of Belarus is one large plain, broken by a central range of low-lying hills. It is crossed by rivers and there are many areas of marsh and woodland.

The Behlovezha forest, which stretches across the border with Poland, is managed jointly by the two countries. It is one of the few remaining parts of the vast forest that covered northern Europe in prehistoric times. The wildlife living there includes the last surviving herd of wisent, or European bison.

Belarussians are a Slavic people whose ancestors settled in the region 1,500 years ago. In the early Middle Ages they were part of Kievan Rus, a state that was centred on Kiev in neighbouring Ukraine. They united with Lithuania in the 1300s, then with Poland in the 1500s. Russia ruled from the 1700s. In 1922 Byelorussia, as it was then known, became part of the Soviet Union. When the Soviet Union collapsed in 1991, Belarus gained independence and became the headquarters of the Commonwealth of Independent States, an alliance of former Soviet states.

Industry and agriculture are both important to the country's economy. Most Belarussians are city-dwellers, but about a third work on large private or state-run farms.

▲ *A Polish Roman Catholic church rises against the Minsk skyline. Few old buildings remain in the city, which was badly damaged in World War II.*

FACTS AND FIGURES
Area: 207,600 sq km
Population: 10,313,000
Capital: Minsk (1,634,000)
Other major city: Gomel (504,000)
Highest point: Dzerzhinskaya Gora (346 m)
Official language: Belarussian
Main religion: Christianity
Currency: Rouble
Main exports: Machinery, transport equipment, petroleum, natural gas, chemicals, petrochemicals, metal goods, food
Government: Republic
Per capita GNP: US $2,910

UKRAINE

Ukraine is a country of steppes – wide, grassy plains with rich soil that is ideal for farming. The land yields grains and supports cattle. The forested Carpathian Mountains rise along the Ukraine's western borders. Two great rivers, the Dnepr and the Dnestr, flow into the warm waters of the Black Sea. Ukrainian industry is concentrated in the east, where there are large deposits of coal. Factories produce steel, ships and machinery.

Around 3,500 years ago this region was inhabited by nomadic herders. During the AD800s a Slavic state called Kievan Rus grew up around Kiev. From the 1300s Ukraine lost its independence, first to Poland and Lithuania, then to Russia. In 1922 it became one of the Soviet Union's four original republics. Under Soviet rule the religion, language and culture of Ukraine were suppressed and the country underwent a programme of intensive industrialization. When the Soviet Union collapsed in 1991 Ukraine declared itself independent. That same year it joined the Commonwealth of Independent States, an alliance with other former Soviet republics.

Today two thirds of the Ukrainian population lives in the country's crowded cities. Many people work in steel, chemical and processed food industries. Large numbers are also employed in the service sector. The industrial boom of the last few decades has caused severe pollution problems, which are currently being tackled by environmental groups.

FACTS AND FIGURES
Area: 603,700 sq km
Population: 52,179,000
Capital: Kiev (2,651,000)
Other major cities: Kharkiv (1,622,000), Dnipropetrovsk (1,190,000), Donetsk (1,121,000), Odessa (1,096,000)
Highest point: Mt Goverla (2,061 m)
Official language: Ukrainian
Main religion: Christianity
Currency: Hryvna
Main exports: Metals, machinery, food, chemicals, textiles
Government: Republic
Per capita GNP: US $1,670

▼ *Traders lay out their wares in Kiev's Bessarabian Market. City markets sell a variety of foodstuffs as well as the embroidered blouses and decorated Easter eggs that are popular souvenirs for visitors.*

▼ Molten iron is poured out at a mill in the city of Dnipropetrovsk. Metal-working is one of the country's main industries, making use of rich coal and iron ore deposits. Heavy industries were developed during the years of Soviet rule, from 1922 to 1991.

BELARUS

RUSSIA

POLAND

SLOVAKIA

HUNGARY

ROMANIA

MOLDOVA

Kovel
Rovno
Zhitomir
Lvov
Chernovtsy
Vinnitsa
Odessa
Kherson
Nikolayev
Kirovograd
Krivoy Rog
Zaporozhye
Melitopol
Sevastopol
Yalta
Simferopol
Crimea
Kerch

Chernobyl
Sumy
KIEV
Kharkiv
Poltava
Cherkassy
Kremenchug
Dnipropetrovsk
Donetsk
Mariupol
Lugansk

Desna
Dnepr
Dnestr
Southern Bug

Carpathian Mts.
Mt. Goverla
2,061 m
6,762 ft.

U K R A I N E

SEA OF AZOV

BLACK SEA

A 25°   B   35°   C

1
50°
2
45°
3

mi.
0   200
0   200
km

▼ Delegates meet at a conference centre in Kiev. The conference marked the first anniversary of Ukraine's independence. Ukraine became a multi-party, democratic republic in 1991. Since then, the it has faced many economic problems as well as political and military disputes with Russia.

▼ Ukraine's nuclear power stations generate 27 percent of the country's electricity. The world's worst-ever nuclear accident occurred in Chernobyl, north of Kiev, in 1986. Many Ukrainians now oppose the use of nuclear power.

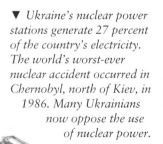

HUNGARY

Hungary lies in Central Europe. It is a land of plains, gentle hills and low mountains. The country's farmland is its chief resource. Crops of maize, wheat, potatoes and sugar beet grow well in its rich, black soil, particularly in the southeast. Grapes are grown for making wine and fruits are used to make jams for export. Most of Hungary's farms are collectives, owned and run by several families.

Most Hungarians are ethnic Magyars, a people who have lived in this land since the AD800s. Magyar kings ruled from 1000 to 1526, when the country was conquered by the Turks. In the 1600s the Turks were driven out by the Habsburgs, the rulers of Austria. After the defeat of Austria-Hungary in World War I, Hungary declared itself independent. Communists took over the Hungarian government in 1948 and began a programme of intensive industrialization. They restricted personal freedom and controlled wages and prices. When the Hungarians revolted in 1956, tanks rolled in from the communist Soviet Union to support the government and crush the rebellion. Many were killed or imprisoned and thousands fled as refugees. The government gradually relaxed restrictions and democratic elections were held in 1990.

Today most Hungarians live in towns or cities, working in factories set up by the communists, in engineering or in service industries. The government is working to clear up pollution from old-fashioned factories and to replant forests that have been depleted for fuel.

GOULASH
Goulash is Hungary's national dish. This rich, warming stew is made with meat, onions and potatoes. It is often served with noodles and thick slices of black bread. Goulash is flavoured with paprika (a spicy red pepper). Soured cream, mushrooms, cabbage or peas may be added according to the preference of the cook.

◄ *Crops are grown in northern Hungary in traditional strip or ribbon fields. Each year the crops are planted in a different strip. This method of farming is called rotation. It ensures that the soil keeps a healthy balance of nutrients.*

FACTS AND FIGURES

Area: 93,030 sq km
Population: 10,294,000
Capital: Budapest (2,000,000)
Other major city: Debrecen (217,000)
Highest point: Mt Kekes (1,015 m)
Official language: Hungarian
Main religion: Christianity
Currency: Forint
Main exports: Consumer goods, raw materials, agricultural products, machinery, transport equipment
Government: Multi-party democracy
Per capita GNP: US $3,010

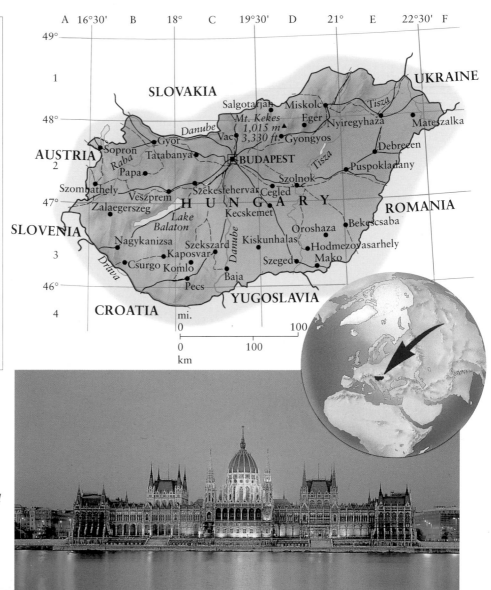

► Hungary's magnificent Houses of Parliament stand on the river Danube in the capital, Budapest. There are 88 statues outside this building and many beautiful wall paintings inside.

◄ Bathers enjoy the natural, hot springs in caves near the northern city of Miskolc. The water can reach 30 degrees centigrade and the steam is said to help sufferers from complaints such as asthma. Hungary has many popular health resorts such as this.

CZECH REPUBLIC

The Czech Republic lies at the heart of Central Europe, between the rugged Sudetes Mountains and the wooded hills of the Bohemian Forest. The fertile northwest is crossed by the great Elbe and Vltava rivers. In the northwest and south-central regions there are many farms and thriving industrial centres.

In the AD900s the Czechs, a Slavic people, founded a powerful kingdom called Bohemia in this area. Its capital, Prague, became a centre of art and learning. In 1526 the throne passed to the Austrian royal family, the Habsburgs. Apart from a short period of independence in the 1600s, Austria continued to rule until 1918. In 1918 Bohemia was united with neighbouring Slovakia in an independent republic, Czechoslovakia. From 1948 until 1989 it was ruled by communist governments under Soviet influence. The Soviets invaded in 1968, when reforms made by the leader Alexander Dubcek looked as though they might weaken communism. After democratic elections in 1990 Slovaks began to demand independence for their region. In 1993 Czechoslovakia split peacefully into two separate states – the Czech Republic and Slovakia.

The Czech Republic includes most of former Czechoslovakia's important industrial areas. Its factories produce steel, machinery, paper, glass and ceramics. Beer is a major product. Over two thirds of its people live in towns or cities and many are employed in these industries.

▼ *The picturesque town of Cesky Krumlov stands amid wooded hills in the southwest. It was founded in 1200s and still looks much as it did during the Middle Ages. The town became wealthy through silver mining. Its fine buildings include a castle, a church and a theatre.*

◄ *This worker is employed at the Kladno steel works, west of Prague. Heavy industries, such as steel and machinery manufacture, are important to the Czech economy. The town of Kladno is one of the Czech Republic's most important centres of steel production.*

▼ Flowers and flags fill Prague's Wenceslas Square. People leave them there as a tribute to those who struggled to help Czechoslovakia break away from Soviet control between 1948 and 1989.

FACTS AND FIGURES
Area: 78,860 sq km
Population: 10,328,000
Capital: Prague
(1,215,000)
Other major cities:
Brno (391,000),
Ostrava (331,000)
Highest point:
Snezka (1,602 m)
Official language: Czech
Main religion:
Christianity
Currency: Koruna
Main exports:
Machinery, transport
equipment, chemicals,
iron, steel, glass
Government:
Multi-party republic
Per capita GNP:
US $2,440

▼ Crowds gather to hear an open-air concert in Prague's Old Town Square. This is part of the city's International Spring Festival. The Czechs are known for their love of music. Famous Czech composers include Bedřich Smetana (1824-84) and Antonín Dvořák (1841-1904).

SLOVAKIA

Slovakia is a land of rugged mountains, lakes and forests. It is home to wild boars, lynx and bears.

This area was first settled thousands of years ago. The Slavs, ancestors of today's inhabitants, arrived in the AD400s. In the AD800s their land was taken into Greater Moravia, an empire that covered much of Central Europe. The Magyars from Hungary took over in AD906 and ruled for the next 1,000 years. In 1918 the Slovaks joined with their neighbours, the Czechs, to form a new country called Czechoslovakia. Communists, supported by the Soviet Union, governed Czechoslovakia from 1948. Czechoslovak communists demanded political reform in 1968, but their protest was squashed by Soviet troops. Then in 1989 a general strike triggered democratic elections. In 1993 Czechoslovakia was peacefully divided into two new independent countries – Slovakia and the Czech Republic.

At first Slovakia faced economic problems because it had little manufacturing industry. Czechoslovakia's industry had been concentrated in the area that became the Czech Republic. Slovakia's natural resources are timber, iron ore and the rich farmland around the river Danube, where farmers grow cereal crops and rear pigs. Around 40 percent of Slovaks work in industry, which is centred on Bratislava and Kosice. During the communist era most factories produced heavy machinery, but today more are producing consumer goods.

▲ A Slovak musician plays a zither. The strings are plucked with a plectrum, a pick attached to a ring on the musician's thumb. Traditional folk songs are extremely popular throughout Slovakia.

◄ Orthodox churches are often richly decorated with icons (religious paintings) and candles. When the communists came to power in 1948 religious worship was discouraged. However, in 1990 the government lifted restrictions and people were free to practise their religious beliefs.

◄ *The Tatra Mountains are a spectacular natural wilderness. They contain national parks where the environment is protected and hikers may spot chamois, sousliks and eagles.*

FACTS AND FIGURES

Area: 49,040 sq km
Population: 5,318,000
Capital: Bratislava (441,000)
Other major city: Kosice (236,000)
Highest point: Gerlachovsky Stit (2,656 m)
Official language: Slovak
Main religion: Christianity
Currency: Koruna
Main exports: Iron ore, chemicals, petroleum products, steel, weapons
Government: Multi-party republic
Per capita GNP: US $1,920

▼ *Bratislava castle overlooks the majestic river Danube. Built in the Middle Ages, the castle was home to the ruling emperors and empresses of Hungary. Hungarian rule lasted from AD906 to 1918.*

117

POLAND

Much of Poland is covered by the vast, open plains and the rolling hills that stretch eastwards from Germany and on into Russia. Potatoes and rye are grown in the plains of central Poland. The most fertile land, on the hills of the south, produces wheat and maize. Cattle and sheep graze the southern pastures. In the far south of the country are forested mountains, which are home to bears and wolves. The Baltic coastal region to the north has thousands of lakes and is dotted with peat bogs.

The Poles are a Slavic people who founded a powerful state in central Europe in the AD800s. From the 1300s to the 1600s this state became the centre of a great empire. The empire declined and was divided between Russia, Prussia and Austria in 1795. Independence was won back in 1918, but Poland disappeared from the map again during World War II. It was overrun by the Soviet Union and Nazi Germany. Nazi rule was brutal and millions of Poles were murdered. From 1947 Poland was governed by communists. During the 1970s and 1980s workers protested against bad living conditions with strikes and riots, demanding better pay and political reform. In 1989 democratic elections were won by Solidarity, the workers' party. The change from communism to democracy increased people's freedom, but at first it also brought unemployment and high prices.

Up until the 1940s Poland's economy was mainly based on agriculture and most people lived and worked in rural areas. Today the majority live in the cities. They work in service industries such as healthcare, education, finance and administration, or in heavy industries that produce coal, steel and machinery.

FACTS AND FIGURES
Area: 312,680 sq km
Population: 38,459,000
Capital: Warsaw (1,655,000)
Other major cities: Lodz (852,000), Krakow (748,000)
Highest point: Rysy Peak (2,499 m)
Official language: Polish
Main religion: Christianity
Currency: Zloty
Main exports: Copper, coal, machinery, vehicles, footwear
Government: Multi-party republic
Per capita GNP: US $1,960

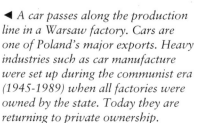

◀ *A car passes along the production line in a Warsaw factory. Cars are one of Poland's major exports. Heavy industries such as car manufacture were set up during the communist era (1945-1989) when all factories were owned by the state. Today they are returning to private ownership.*

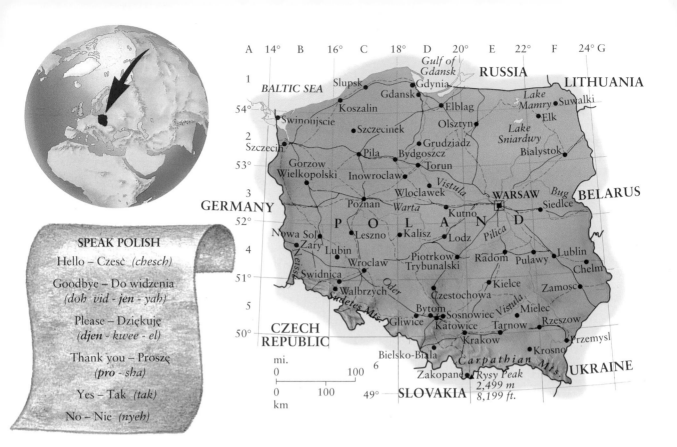

A 14° B 16° C 18° D 20° E 22° F 24° G

BALTIC SEA

RUSSIA

LITHUANIA

Gulf of Gdansk

Slupsk

Gdynia

Gdansk

Elblag

Lake Mamry

Suwalki

54°

Swinoujscie

Koszalin

Olsztyn

Elk

Szczecinek

Lake Sniardwy

Szczecin

Grudziadz

Bialystok

Pila

Bydgoszcz

Torun

GERMANY

Gorzow Wielkopolski

Inowroclaw

Vistula

Bug

BELARUS

Wloclawek

WARSAW

53°

Poznan

Warta

Siedlce

P O L A N D

52°

Nowa Sol

Leszno

Kalisz

Lodz

Pilica

Zary

Lubin

Radom

Pulawy

Lublin

Wroclaw

Piotrkow Trybunalski

Chelm

51°

Swidnica

Oder

Kielce

Zamosc

Walbrzych

Czestochowa

Sudetes Mts.

Bytom

Sosnowiec

Vistula

Mielec

Gliwice

Katowice

Tarnow

Rzeszow

50°

CZECH REPUBLIC

Krakow

Przemysl

Bielsko-Biala

Carpathian Mts.

UKRAINE

mi.

0   100

Zakopane

Rysy Peak 2,499 m 8,199 ft.

0   100

km

49°

SLOVAKIA

SPEAK POLISH

Hello – Czesć *(chesch)*

Goodbye – Do widzenia
(doh vid - jen - yah)

Please – Dziękuję
(djen - kwee - el)

Thank you – Proszę
(pro - sha)

Yes – Tak *(tak)*

No – Nie *(nyeh)*

▼ *The coastal plains of northern Poland are dotted with thousands of lakes connected by streams and rivers. Many Poles go there for windsurfing, fishing, yachting and canoeing.*

► *St Mary's church stands at the centre of the historic city of Krakow, in the main market square. This city has always been a busy centre for trade and culture. Today it is a very popular tourist spot.*

SLOVENIA

▼ *Long stalactites are illuminated for tourists visiting the Postojna Cave, 50 kilometres from Ljubljana. Western Slovenia's limestone rocks have been eroded into many extraordinary ridges, gorges and caverns.*

Slovenia lies on the main road and rail routes between western Europe and the Balkan countries. This has helped trade between Slovenia and countries such as Austria, Italy, France and Germany. Manufactured goods including steel, glass, chemicals, paper and textiles are produced in Slovenia. The country's mines provide brown coal, lead and mercury. Crops including wheat, tobacco, potatoes, sugar beet and grapes are grown in the fertile valleys. Tourism is also important in this land of forested mountains and plateaus. Visitors are attracted to the ski resorts, beautiful lakes and sunny beaches.

Throughout its history Slovenia has belonged to several empires, including Rome and Austria-Hungary. It has also been ruled by Bavaria. In 1918 Slovenia was united with Croatia and Serbia in an independent kingdom called the Kingdom of the Serbs, Croats and Slovenes. This union changed its name to Yugoslavia in 1929. Yugoslavia was torn apart during World War II, but was reunited as a communist country in 1945. In 1991 Slovenia broke away from Yugoslavia and became independent.

Most of the people of Slovenia are Slovenes. Their ancestors were part of a group of people called the South Slavs who settled much of the Balkan Peninsula in the AD500s. The country has no powerful minority groups. This has helped Slovenia to avoid the bloodshed that is still occurring in many other former Yugoslavian countries.

▶ *The capital's skyline includes ancient churches, museums and fine old public buildings. These stand side by side with modern high-rise offices and flats. Ljubljana is also an important industrial city, with factories that produce chemicals, soap, leather, paper and textiles.*

FACTS AND FIGURES
Area: 20,250 sq km
Population: 1,990,000
Capital: Ljubljana
(268,000)
Other major city:
Maribor (106,000)
Highest point:
Mt Triglav (2,863 m)
Official language:
Slovenian
Main religion:
Christianity
Currency: Tolar
Main exports:
Machinery, transport
equipment, raw
materials, food
Government:
Republic
Per capita GNP:
US $6,330

▲ *Smoke rises from factory chimneys at Jesenice, a major steel-making centre in the mountains of northwestern Slovenia. Air pollution from industry is a serious problem in Slovenia, as it is in many other parts of central Europe and the Balkans.*

► *Dark conifer forests and limestone cliffs rise to Alpine peaks at Podkoren in the far northwest. Forests like these cover half of Slovenia. They are felled for the country's timber and paper industries.*

CROATIA

Croatia's rocky coastline takes in many islands and headlands. Inland the craggy Dinaric Alps fall to the Pannonian Plains in the northeast. This is the country's main farming region.

From around 300BC this land was part of the powerful Roman empire. Croatia became an independent kingdom in the early Middle Ages and united with Hungary in 1102. It was later divided between Turkish and Austrian rule.

In 1918 Croatia joined a union of states that became communist Yugoslavia in 1945. Yugoslavia split up in 1990 and Croatia declared independence in 1991. However, neighbouring Serbia objected and a war followed. The Serbs seized one third of Croatia's territory and many Croats were killed or fled their villages to seek refuge in the towns. The war ended in 1992, but a United Nations peacekeeping force continued to supervise the frontier between Croatia and Serbia.

Before this war about half the country's population lived in rural areas. There was an important tourism industry centred on the Croatian coast, which brought in revenue. The Croatian economy was devastated by the war, but the country is now working to rebuild its factories, homes and historic cities.

► *The medieval town of Korcula overlooks the Adriatic Sea. Korcula is also the name of the island on which the town stands. It is famous for its stonemasons, who work the local white marble.*

FACTS AND FIGURES

Area: 56,540 sq km

Population: 4,789,000

Capital: Zagreb (727,000)

Other major cities: Split (190,000), Rijeka (168,000), Osijek (105,000)

Highest point: Mt Troglav (1,913 m)

Official language: Serbo-Croatian

Main religion: Christianity

Currency: Croatian dinar

Main exports: Chemicals, clothes, food, machinery

Government: Republic

Per capita GNP: Est. $700-3,000

◄ Bomb damage has left gaping holes in this wine factory near Dubrovnik. Despite the 1991-1992 war, Croats have continued to produce wine. Croatian wines are widely exported and are known for good quality and reasonable prices.

► The central square in Croatia's capital, Zagreb, is reserved for pedestrians and trams. Zagreb, a town built in Roman times, is the country's main centre of industry and business. It also has a university and several theatres.

◄ The huge amphitheatre at Pula was built by the Romans in AD80. It seated a crowd of 23,000, who came to watch gladiators and wild animals fighting to the death.

BOSNIA-HERZEGOVINA

FACTS AND FIGURES
Area: 51,130 sq km
Population: 4,366,000
Capital: Sarajevo
(526,000)
Other major city:
Banja Luka (143,000)
Highest point:
Mt Maglic (2,386 m)
Official language:
Serbo-Croatian
Main religions:
Islam, Christianity
Currency: New
Dinar
Main exports:
Clothes,
chemicals,
machinery
Government:
Republic
Per capita GNP:
Est. under US $700

The full name of this country, Bosnia-Herzegovina, is taken from its two main regions. Bosnia, in the north, is a land of high, forested mountains. Herzegovina, in the south, drops to rugged hills and flat farmland. Both have large iron and coal reserves.

In 11BC this region became part of the Roman empire. In the AD600s it was settled by the Slavs. From the 1100s there were long years of rule by a series of highly powerful empires, first Hungary, then Turkey, followed by Austria-Hungary. The Turks brought the religion of Islam with them and many Bosnians became Muslim. In 1918 Bosnia joined with Croatia, Serbia and Slovenia to form a federation (union) of states. They became known as Yugoslavia. The country was governed by communists from 1945. Communism collapsed in 1990 and Yugoslavia broke up into separate states.

When Bosnia declared independence in 1992 the Serbs living in Bosnia objected and began a brutal civil war. Forces from neighbouring republics of the former Yugoslavia became involved and thousands were killed or forced to flee their homes. The United Nations sent peacekeeping forces, food and medical aid. Peace talks were held in an attempt to resolve the conflict through new divisions of territory. However, Bosnians and Serbs became scattered throughout Bosnia, making any land division extremely difficult.

◀ *An elderly Bosnian woman waits at a refugee camp in Croatia in 1992. The Christian Serbs drove many thousands of Bosnian Muslims from their homes and villages. The bitter fight for land centred on religious and ethnic differences.*

MACEDONIA

FACTS AND FIGURES
Area: 25,710 sq km
Population: 2,173,000
Capital: Skopje
(449,000)
Other major city:
Bitola (84,000)
Highest point:
Mt Korabit (2,751 m)
Official language:
Macedonian
Main religions:
Christianity, Islam
Currency: Denar
Main exports:
Chemicals, clothes,
footwear, machinery,
transport equipment,
food, textiles
Government:
Republic
Per capita GNP:
Est. US $700-3,000

Macedonia is a land of rushing rivers and high mountains, many clad with forests of beech, oak and pine. The country is part of a larger historic region also called Macedonia, which was fought over in the Balkan Wars of 1912 and 1913. As a result of these wars most of its territory was taken by Serbia. In 1918 Serbian Macedonia joined Croatia, Serbia and Slovenia to form a federation of states. They called themselves Yugoslavia in 1929. When communist Yugoslavia broke up in 1990, Macedonians called for democratic elections. The country declared independence as the Republic of Macedonia in 1991. Greece was angered by this name. Ancient Macedonia had been part of the Greek world and the northern region of Greece was still called Macedonia. Some Greeks feared that the new republic would eventually try to include Greek territory. However, Macedonia insisted this was not the case and the name became generally accepted.

Most of the people are Slavs, another large group are Albanians. About half the population lives in rural areas. Many are involved in farming, growing tobacco and maize, or in logging. Four out of ten people work in industry, producing cement, steel or cotton goods. Some are employed in mining copper, lead, zinc and chromite. Most factories and businesses were the property of the state during the communist era and are still owned by the government. Much of the industry centres on the capital, which was destroyed by an earthquake in 1963, but was rapidly rebuilt.

► *The church of St John at Caneo overlooks beautiful Lake Ohrid. It was built in the 1200s. In 1964 restoration work led to the discovery of frescoes (wall paintings) in its dome.*

YUGOSLAVIA *Introduction*

Until the early 1990s present-day Yugoslavia was part of a larger country, also called Yugoslavia, which covered much of the Balkan Peninsula. The name dates back to 1929, when it was adopted by a kingdom that united the Balkan states of Croatia, Bosnia-Herzegovina, Dalmatia, Montenegro, Serbia and Slovenia. These states had formerly been ruled by either Austria-Hungary or the Ottoman empire. During World War II Yugoslavia was torn apart by fighting, but was recreated in 1945 under a communist government led by President Josip Brod Tito.

During 1991 and 1992 long-standing tensions between different ethnic groups in the country caused Yugoslavia to break up into separate nations. Serbia and Montenegro formed the new, smaller country of Yugoslavia. In 1992 Serbs living in both Yugoslavia and neighbouring Bosnia claimed parts of Bosnia for themselves. A bitter war began against the largely Muslim, Bosnian government. Thousands of innocent men, women and children were killed, wounded or lost their homes. Peacekeeping efforts by United Nations troops were unable to put a stop to the fighting, which continued into the mid-1990s. International trade sanctions against Yugoslavia were brought in and these severely disrupted the Yugoslav economy.

Although industries such as mining, chemicals, iron and steel have been developed in Yugoslavia since the 1950s, many people still work in agriculture. Farms in Serbia produce maize, wheat, potatoes and tobacco, while Montenegro is noted for its plums and cherries. The country also has forests and rich mineral resources. In peaceful times its beautiful mountain and coastal scenery attracted many tourists.

FACTS AND FIGURES
Area: 102,170 sq km
Population: 10,485,000
Capital: Belgrade (1,169,000)
Other major cities: Novi Sad (180,000), Nis (176,000), Kragujevac (148,000)
Highest point: Mt Daravica (2,656 m)
Official language: Serbo-Croatian
Main religions: Christianity, Islam
Currency: Dinar
Main exports: Textiles, chemicals, clothes, food, iron, steel, machinery, transport equipment, manufactured goods
Government: Republic
Per capita GNP: Est. US $700-3,000

▼ *Shoppers walk through the capital city. Belgrade was also the capital of the old Yugoslavia. It is a centre of communications, trade and industry and has been an important river port since the* AD*100s.*

ENDANGERED WORLD

The olm, a blind, cave-dwelling salamander is at risk from water pollution.

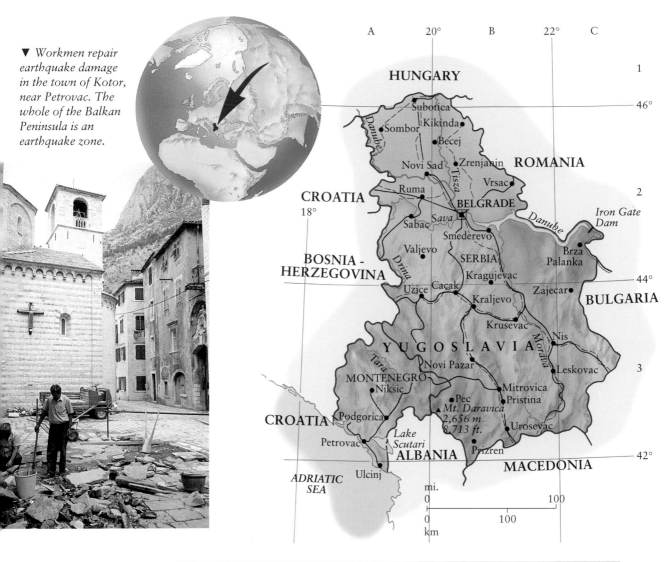

▼ Workmen repair earthquake damage in the town of Kotor, near Petrovac. The whole of the Balkan Peninsula is an earthquake zone.

► The blue waters of the Adriatic Sea shimmer in the hot summer sunshine beneath rugged mountains. Before civil war broke out in Croatia and Bosnia in 1991 Yugoslavia's Adriatic coast attracted many visitors. This tourism industry was an important part of the economy.

YUGOSLAVIA *People and History*

▲ *Stefan Dušan led the Serbs to victories over Bulgaria, Macedonia and Albania during the 1300s, making Serbia the leading power on the Balkan Peninsula. He died while marching on Constantinople, the capital of the Byzantine empire.*

Yugoslavia means 'Land of the South Slavs'. The country was named after the South Slav peoples – Serbs, Slovenes and Croats – who invaded the Balkan Peninsula in the AD500s. From about AD900 Serbia became the most powerful state in the Balkans, but in 1459 the area was invaded by the Turks of the Ottoman empire. Serbia did not regain its independence until 1878.

Serbia's neighbouring states, Slovenia, Croatia and Bosnia-Herzegovina, were ruled by the Austria-Hungary empire in the 1800s. During this period a movement for South Slav unity gathered force. World War I began in 1914 after Gavrilo Princip, a Bosnian Serb, assassinated the Austrian archduke, Franz Ferdinand. Austria-Hungary declared war on Serbia, which it blamed for the killing. At the end of the war in 1918 Austria-Hungary broke up and the Kingdom of the Serbs, Croats and Slovenes, later called Yugoslavia, was formed.

Different ethnic and religious groups were unable to live side by side peacefully and in the early 1990s Yugoslavia split into separate nations. Today two thirds of the people of modern-day Yugoslavia (former Serbia and Montenegro) are ethnic Serbs and Montenegrins, except in Kosovo, a province on the Albanian border. There, most people are of Albanian descent. The Serbo-Croatian language is spoken by the majority of Yugoslavs and many Serbs and Montenegrins are members of the Serbian Orthodox Church.

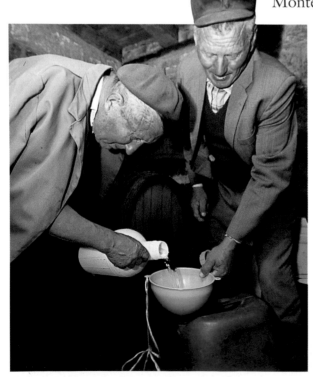

◀ *Spirits are distilled in Kopljar, a village to the south of Belgrade. The Balkan lands are famous for their fiery spirits, which are made from fruits such as plums, cherries and apricots. The most famous of these alcoholic drinks is a fiery plum brandy known as slivovitz. This is often served with spicy meats and sausages.*

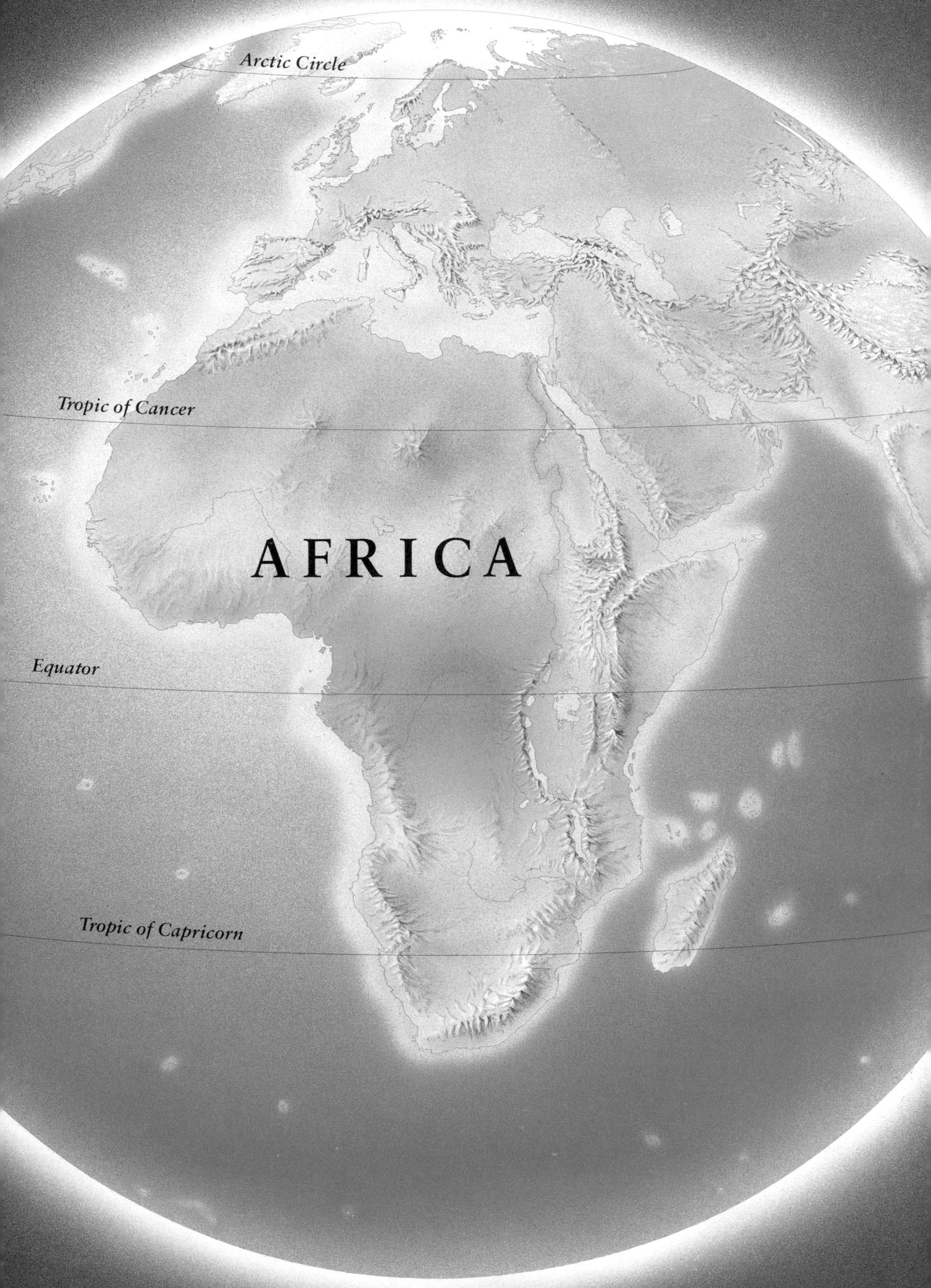

Arctic Circle

Tropic of Cancer

AFRICA

Equator

Tropic of Capricorn

AFRICA *Geography*

Africa is the world's second largest continent after Asia, covering about one fifth of the Earth's total land area. Only the artificial divide of the Suez Canal, in Egypt, separates it from the vast landmass of Europe and Asia. The west African coast curves out into the stormy waters of the Atlantic Ocean, while the east African coast is bordered by the Red Sea and the Indian Ocean.

The fertile Mediterranean coast gives way to the ranges of the Atlas Mountains in the northwest and the scorching wilderness of the Sahara, which is the world's biggest desert. The river Nile, carrying water from central Africa, has provided a lifeline through the deserts of Egypt for thousands of years.

To the south of the Sahara Desert, thin pasture and scrub give way to savanna (grassland dotted with trees). The humid region around the Equator and the vast basin of the river Zaire (Congo) are covered in one of the world's last great rainforests.

East Africa is dominated by a series of cracks in the Earth's crust. The Great Rift Valley runs from north to south and it has flooded in places to form a series of long, deep lakes. There are spectacular mountain ranges, too, from the Ethiopian Plateau to Mount Kenya, Mount Kilimanjaro and the snow-capped Ruwenzori Range.

Southern Africa also has its savanna regions and the dusty deserts of the Kalahari and Namib. The southern high plateau grasslands, known as veld, end in the sheer cliffs of the Drakensberg Mountains. Further mountain ranges descend in the southwest to Cape Agulhas, the southern tip of the continent.

▲ At the Victoria Falls, between Zimbabwe and Zambia, the Zambezi River plunges headlong over a towering cliff. A great cloud of spray rises in the air.

▼ The steep, craggy cliffs of the Great Rift Valley are called escarpments. The valley has some of Africa's most spectacular lakes and volcanoes.

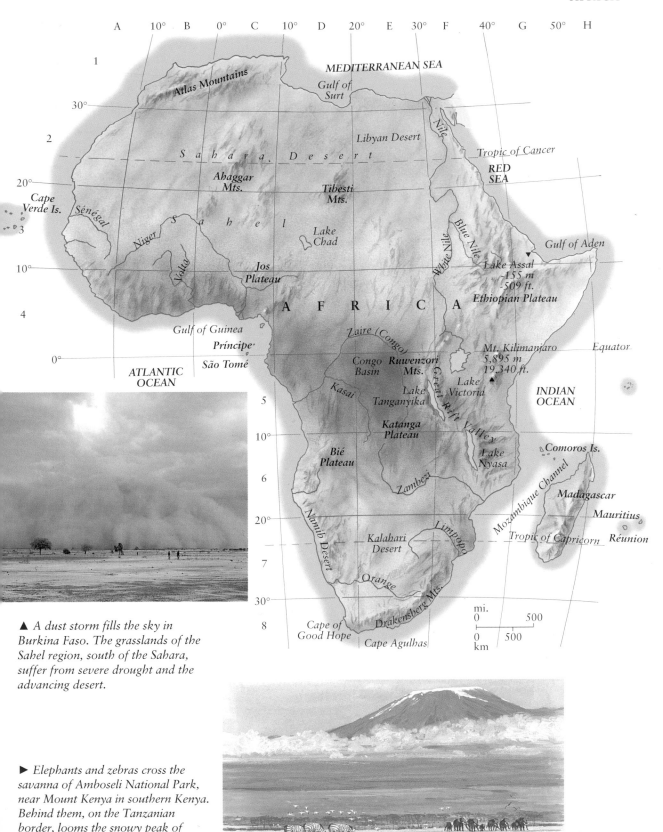

A B C D E F G H
10° 0° 10° 20° 30° 40° 50°

1

MEDITERRANEAN SEA

Atlas Mountains

Gulf of Surt

30°

Nile

2

Libyan Desert

S a h a r a   D e s e r t

Tropic of Cancer

20°

RED SEA

Ahaggar Mts.

Tibesti Mts.

Cape Verde Is.

Sénégal

3

S a h e l

Niger

Lake Chad

White Nile

Blue Nile

Gulf of Aden

10°

Volta

Jos Plateau

Lake Assal
155 m
-509 ft.

Ethiopian Plateau

Gulf of Guinea

4

A F R I C A

Príncipe

São Tomé

Zaire (Congo)

Congo Basin

Ruwenzori Mts.

Mt. Kilimanjaro
5,895 m
19,340 ft.

Equator

ATLANTIC OCEAN

0°

Kasai

Lake Tanganyika

Lake Victoria

INDIAN OCEAN

5

Great Rift Valley

Katanga Plateau

10°

Comoros Is.

Bié Plateau

Lake Nyasa

6

Zambezi

Madagascar

Mauritius

Namib Desert

20°

Kalahari Desert

Limpopo

Mozambique Channel

Tropic of Capricorn

Réunion

7

Orange

Drakensberg Mts.

mi.
0   500

30°

8

Cape of Good Hope

Cape Agulhas

0   500
km

▲ A dust storm fills the sky in Burkina Faso. The grasslands of the Sahel region, south of the Sahara, suffer from severe drought and the advancing desert.

▶ Elephants and zebras cross the savanna of Amboseli National Park, near Mount Kenya in southern Kenya. Behind them, on the Tanzanian border, looms the snowy peak of Mount Kilimanjaro. At 5,895 metres it is the highest mountain in Africa.

131

AFRICA *Political*

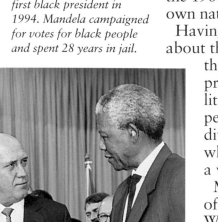

▼ *FW de Klerk hands over power to Nelson Mandela, who became South Africa's first black president in 1994. Mandela campaigned for votes for black people and spent 28 years in jail.*

The map of Africa shows over 50 countries, large and small. Just 50 years ago most were ruled by powerful European nations, which became rich from mining and farming their colonies. From the 1960s onwards African people once again began to rule their own nations, many of which have ancient histories.

Having gained independence, African leaders tried to bring about the new world they had dreamed of for so long. However, the years of foreign rule had left the continent with huge problems. Most of its people were poor and had received little education or training. Colonial rule had often set one people against another and traditional homelands had been divided by new national borders. Trying to unite nations where people spoke many different languages and followed a variety of different religions was a very hard task.

Many countries suffered years of dictatorship and millions of people became refugees from war, drought and famine. White South Africans refused to give the vote to the black people who made up most of this nation's population.

Tragic news still came from many African countries, including Rwanda, Somalia and Sudan. However, in 1994 hope was brought to the continent when Nelson Mandela became South Africa's first black president. In the 1990s many African countries started holding democratic elections and the world was reminded of the energy, goodwill and idealism of millions of ordinary African people.

Fossils found in the Great Rift Valley in Tanzania tell us that the human race had its origins in this continent. We all share Africa's past and we must all hope for its future.

► *The Presidential Palace in Dakar, the capital of Senegal, is a reminder of Africa's colonial era. Senegal was ruled by France for over 200 years. Most African countries had a period of European rule.*

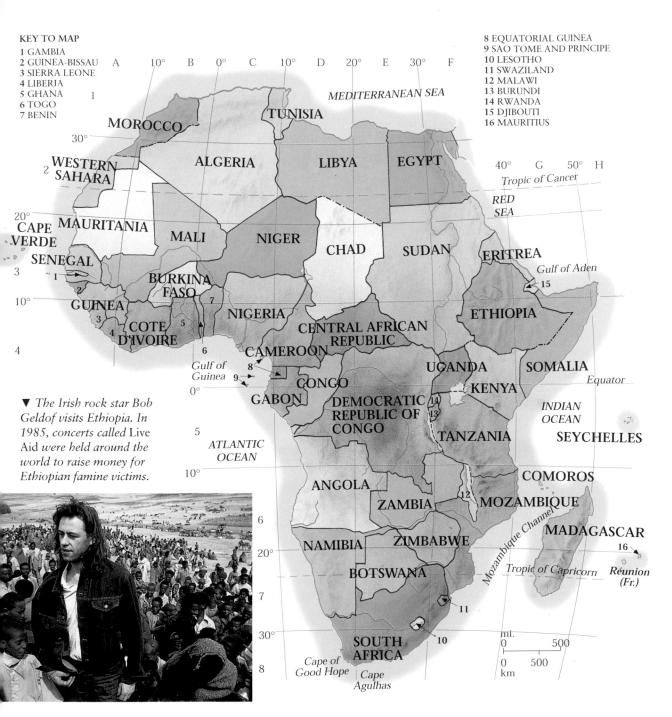

KEY TO MAP
1 GAMBIA
2 GUINEA-BISSAU
3 SIERRA LEONE
4 LIBERIA
5 GHANA
6 TOGO
7 BENIN

8 EQUATORIAL GUINEA
9 SAO TOME AND PRINCIPE
10 LESOTHO
11 SWAZILAND
12 MALAWI
13 BURUNDI
14 RWANDA
15 DJIBOUTI
16 MAURITIUS

MEDITERRANEAN SEA

MOROCCO
TUNISIA
WESTERN SAHARA
ALGERIA
LIBYA
EGYPT
Tropic of Cancer
RED SEA
CAPE VERDE
MAURITANIA
MALI
NIGER
CHAD
SUDAN
ERITREA
Gulf of Aden
SENEGAL
BURKINA FASO
GUINEA
COTE D'IVOIRE
NIGERIA
CENTRAL AFRICAN REPUBLIC
ETHIOPIA
Gulf of Guinea
CAMEROON
UGANDA
SOMALIA
Equator
GABON
CONGO
DEMOCRATIC REPUBLIC OF CONGO
KENYA
INDIAN OCEAN
ATLANTIC OCEAN
TANZANIA
SEYCHELLES
ANGOLA
COMOROS
ZAMBIA
MOZAMBIQUE
MADAGASCAR
NAMIBIA
ZIMBABWE
Réunion (Fr.)
BOTSWANA
Mozambique Channel
Tropic of Capricorn
SOUTH AFRICA
Cape of Good Hope
Cape Agulhas

mi.
0   500
0   500
km

▼ The Irish rock star Bob Geldof visits Ethiopia. In 1985, concerts called Live Aid were held around the world to raise money for Ethiopian famine victims.

► Somalis celebrate independence in 1960. During its colonial period Somalia was ruled by Britain and Italy. Like other countries in modern Africa it has faced many problems since independence. These include border wars, guerrilla fighting and the entry into the country of more than a million refugees.

AFRICA *Plants and Animals*

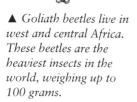

Africa is one of the last places in the world where great herds of wild animals can still be seen migrating in their thousands across the plains. In the savanna you can hear the loud trumpeting of a bull elephant and the roar of a lion at the kill. Deep in the equatorial rainforest are families of gorillas, the immensely powerful yet gentle great apes. Dangerous crocodiles lurk in the rivers and swamps.

Africa's plant life is rich and varied. In the parched scrub of southern Africa are stone plants that look like pebbles. There is also the strange welwitschia, a plant that can grow for a thousand years. Bright gourds swell on the desert sands, growing from a mass of tangled stems. In the steaming tropical forests are tall bamboos, majestic hardwood trees and oil-palms.

Tragically, wildlife is under threat all over the African continent. Many creatures have already been hunted to extinction. Their habitats are destroyed and their migratory routes are blocked by new roads and cities. Precious forests are cut down for timber as well as to clear land for farming. Without tree roots to anchor it, the soil is blown or washed away by tropical storms. The land becomes poor and gradually turns to desert.

The solutions are not simple. Conservation can be expensive and the interests of wildlife protection often conflict with those of local people, who need to graze their cattle and make a living. However, many African countries now protect their wild animals in national parks. Some countries are also beginning to restock rivers and lakes with fish and plant new forests. Africa's wildlife is one of the greatest treasures on Earth. We must find new ways of living with nature without destroying it.

▲ *Goliath beetles live in west and central Africa. These beetles are the heaviest insects in the world, weighing up to 100 grams.*

▼ *The chameleon lives in most of Africa's forests. It changes colour to camouflage itself by blending in with its surroundings. It turns dark when angry and pale when afraid. It has swivelling eyes and a long sticky tongue for catching insects.*

▲ *A male lion lazes in the shady bush in southern Africa. Lions are the largest cats in Africa. They were once cruelly hunted for sport. Today tourists' cameras have mostly taken the place of guns.*

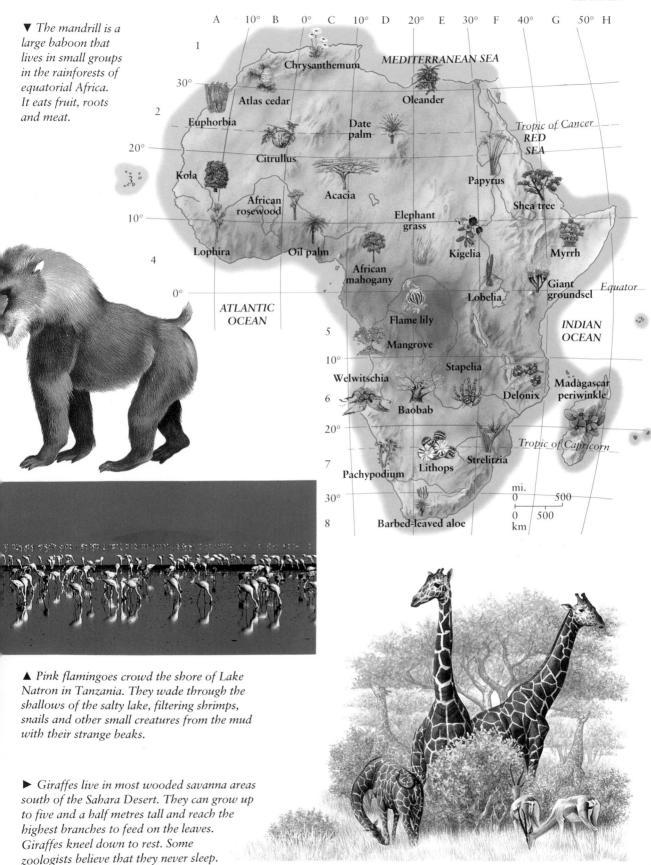

▼ The mandrill is a large baboon that lives in small groups in the rainforests of equatorial Africa. It eats fruit, roots and meat.

▲ Pink flamingoes crowd the shore of Lake Natron in Tanzania. They wade through the shallows of the salty lake, filtering shrimps, snails and other small creatures from the mud with their strange beaks.

► Giraffes live in most wooded savanna areas south of the Sahara Desert. They can grow up to five and a half metres tall and reach the highest branches to feed on the leaves. Giraffes kneel down to rest. Some zoologists believe that they never sleep.

MOROCCO AND WESTERN SAHARA *Introduction*

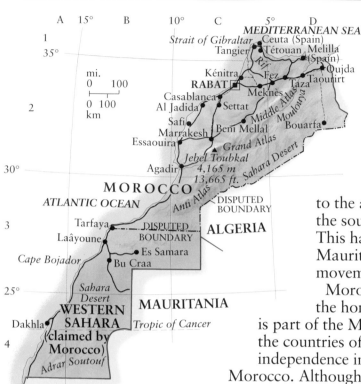

The coast of Morocco reaches up towards Spain at the Strait of Gibraltar. There, at the mouth of the Mediterranean, only 13 kilometres of blue sea separate Africa from Europe. Morocco's fertile plains stretch along its Mediterranean and Atlantic coasts. Behind them are the green valleys and dense forests of the Atlas Mountains, which drop south to the arid wastes of the Sahara Desert. To the south of Morocco lies the Western Sahara. This has been claimed by Morocco and Mauritania, as well as a Western Saharan movement called the Polisario Front.

Morocco is an ancient Islamic kingdom and the homeland of Berber and Arab peoples. It is part of the Maghreb, a term that is used to describe the countries of northwest Africa. From 1912 until independence in 1956 France and Spain ruled most of Morocco. Although the country is now self-governing, Spain still controls the ports of Ceuta and Melilla. The economy is based on mining and agriculture. Almost half the population are herders or farmers who use traditional methods and simple tools.

▶ *The sun sets behind the minaret of Koutoubia Mosque in Marrakesh. Lights are switched on to illuminate a colourful street bazaar. Goods and handicrafts on sale include leather, brassware and the rich handwoven carpets that have made these markets famous over the centuries.*

FACTS AND FIGURES

MOROCCO
Area: 458,730 sq km
Population: 26,069,000
Capital: Rabat
(519,000)
Other major city:
Casablanca (2,140,000)
Highest point:
Jebel Toubkal (4,165 m)
Official language:
Arabic
Main religion: Islam
Currency: Dirham
Main exports:
Phosphates, fertilizers,
mineral products,
dates, figs, canned fish,
tobacco
Government:
Constitutional
monarchy
Per capita GNP:
US $1,040

WESTERN SAHARA
Area: 252,120 sq km
Population: 261,000

▲ *A Berber water-seller*
is a familiar sight in
Morocco. He offers
passers-by a cool drink
from his goatskin bag.

THE GREAT KING HASSAN II MOSQUE
The King Hassan Mosque is the
biggest mosque in the world, holding
100,000 worshippers. It towers over the sea
and surrounding buildings of the city of
Casablanca. A laser beam on top of its
176-metre-high minaret can be seen
50 kilometres away. The mosque opened in
1993. It took 2,500 construction workers and
10,000 artists and craftsmen six years to
build. It will be the burial place of Hassan II,
king of Morocco since 1961.

◄ *Camel-riders in Western*
Sahara fly the Polisario
flag. These desert lands
have been at the centre of a
bitter political struggle for
many years.

137

MOROCCO AND WESTERN SAHARA *Geography and Economy*

Morocco's farmland lies on its coastal lowlands and in the fertile valleys of the snowcapped Atlas Mountains. More than a third of the farmland is owned by a few very rich people. It yields good crops of wheat, citrus fruits, tomatoes, beans and olives. Most farmers are poor and own small plots of land on which they graze sheep, cattle and goats. Many Moroccans make their living from fishing off the coast.

The Moroccan desert and Western Sahara form a landscape of sweltering sand-dunes and rocks. They are dotted with occasional, oases where date palms and fig trees can grow. Nomads wander across the parched land in search of grass to feed their herds. Beneath the sand of these remote regions lie nearly three quarters of the world's reserves of phosphates. There are also deposits of iron ore, silver, lead and copper. The Moroccan government controls mining, which brings in a large amount of money but employs relatively few workers. Manufacturing provides more jobs, especially in the great industrial centre of Casablanca. Morocco also refines oil and produces plastics and various chemicals. Since 1989 it has formed close economic ties with the other Arabic-speaking countries of northwest Africa.

▲ *A village lies under steep cliffs in the Jebel Sahro region of the Grand Atlas Mountains. Villagers are self-sufficient, living by herding sheep and goats or growing crops. However, many country-dwellers have now moved to the big towns in an attempt to find work.*

▶ *Workers arrive at a phosphate plant. Up to 20 million tonnes of phosphates are exported from Morocco each year. The wealth of Morocco and Western Sahara relies heavily on phosphates, which are used in international chemical and fertilizer industries.*

◄ *In this ancient town in the Atlas Mountains the houses have thick mud walls and small windows, which keep them cool inside. The roofs are flat because there is little or no rain to be drained off.*

▼ *Goat skins are dyed in deep vats at this tannery in the ancient city of Fez. They are made into the leather for which Morocco is famous.*

▲ *Fishing boats tie up along the waterfront at Casablanca. Their catch includes mackerel, sardines and tuna. The fish may be canned or turned into fish-meal fertilizers for export.*

MOROCCO AND WESTERN SAHARA *People and History*

▲ *This mosaic floor lies in the Roman ruins of Volubilis, near Meknès. It is a reminder that Morocco was once part of the Roman empire.*

The Berber people were Morocco's original inhabitants. The Arabs invaded in the AD600s and brought the religion of Islam with them. In the Middle Ages Moroccans (who were also called Moors) ruled large areas of North Africa, Spain and Portugal. They were famed for being great warriors, scholars and architects.

By the 1500s the Moors had been driven out of Europe and Spain and Portugal began to seize Moroccan ports. Despite decades of warfare Morocco stayed independent. In the 1800s many European countries tried to control this country. Part of it came under French rule and part under Spanish. From the 1920s Moroccans began to demand self-rule and there was widespread unrest. Morocco was finally granted independence in 1956.

In recent times Morocco has been in dispute over its border with the former Spanish province of Western Sahara. Morocco and Mauritania each claimed part of the area and both fought the Polisario Front (the Saharan independence movement). Mauritania gave up its claim in 1979 and in the 1990s Morocco and the Polisario Front entered into discussions about ownership of the land.

Most Moroccans are descended from Berbers and Arabs. Around half live in rural regions and half in rapidly growing cities. It is traditional for several generations of a family to live together in both rural and urban areas.

TAGINE OF LAMB
To make a *tagine*, lamb is stewed gently with pumpkin, raisins and chillies. This is served with either rice or couscous (tiny grains of wheat). Sugar and fruit, as well as strongly flavoured spices, are added to many Moroccan meat dishes.

▼ *Spectacular demonstrations of warrior skills, called* fantasias, *are a popular Moroccan tradition. Horsemen on richly decorated mounts race across the sand firing rifles in the air.*

MAURITANIA

◀ *Village shops sell locally grown foods such as millet, beans and rice. Many other foods have to be imported.*

FACTS AND FIGURES
Area: 1,030,700 sq km
Population: 2,206,000
Capital: Nouakchott (394,000)
Highest point: Kediet Ijill (915 m)
Official languages: Arabic, French
Main religion: Islam
Currency: Ouguiya
Main exports: Fish, iron ore, gypsum
Government: Islamic republic
Per capita GNP: US $530

Although much of Mauritania is made up of the parched Sahara Desert, most people depend on the land for their livelihood. In the south, along the Sénégal River, hardy crops such as sorghum, millet and peanuts are grown. During the 1980s widespread famine struck when drought killed livestock and crops, forcing many people to move to the towns and cities. Today the fishing and mining industries are being developed. There are plentiful stocks of fish off the coast and the land is rich in iron ore.

People of Arab and Berber origin (called Moors), make up about three quarters of the population in Mauritania. There is also a large group of black Africans. Some Moors are nomads, who herd animals across the country in search of pasture. Others live in cities or farm the land.

From 1903 until 1960, the country was ruled by France. After independence Mauritania claimed part of Western Sahara, but later withdrew its claim.

◀ *Adults are taught to read and write as part of a programme to improve education throughout Mauritania.*

141

ALGERIA *Introduction*

Algeria is part of the region known as the Maghreb, the countries of northwest Africa. It extends from the shores of the Mediterranean Sea all the way south to Mali and Niger. Most of this vast area is empty desert – a harsh landscape of rock, gravel and sand. The people live mainly in the north, where the land is green and the climate more bearable. The northern cities are linked by roads, while desert tracks cross the interior. The main routes southwards are being improved to form a trans-Sahara highway.

The hardship of a life spent herding animals in the arid regions has forced many rural people into the coastal towns to find work. Over half of all Algerians are now city-dwellers. Some live in smart, new apartment blocks, others in shacks and rambling slums. Algeria's growing economy is based on the rich oilfields of the eastern Sahara. With profits from oil the government has built new factories, but as yet there are not enough jobs to go round. Many people have gone abroad to work, especially to France, which ruled Algeria for 130 years and so has close ties with the country.

Since independence in 1962 Algeria has moved away from European influences. Arabic is the language of the courts and schools. Writers and artists are returning to the traditions of the Arab and Berber peoples.

▲ Sticks of bread are sold from the baker's cart. Algeria was once a French colony and many people still speak French and bake bread in the French style.

▼ At Taghit, underground water has created an oasis where plants grow in an otherwise barren landscape. For centuries desert travellers have relied on oases for their survival.

ENDANGERED WORLD

The sand cat (about 50 centimetres in length) is often caught and kept as a pet, but rarely survives. It is also shot for sport.

▶ *The limestone buildings of Ghardaia date back to the 1500s. This town has a fine mosque and is built on a hill in the Wadi Mzab region in the northern Sahara. It lies at the top of the main route south to Mali.*

FACTS AND FIGURES

Area: 2,381,740 sq km
Population: 27,070,000
Capital: Algiers (1,507,000)
Other major cities: Oran (664,000), Constantine (449,000), Annaba (349,000)
Highest point: Mt Tahat (2,918 m)
Official language: Arabic
Main religion: Islam
Currency: Algerian dinar
Main exports: Oil, natural gas, olive-oil, wine, machinery
Government: Republic
Per capita GNP: US $1,830

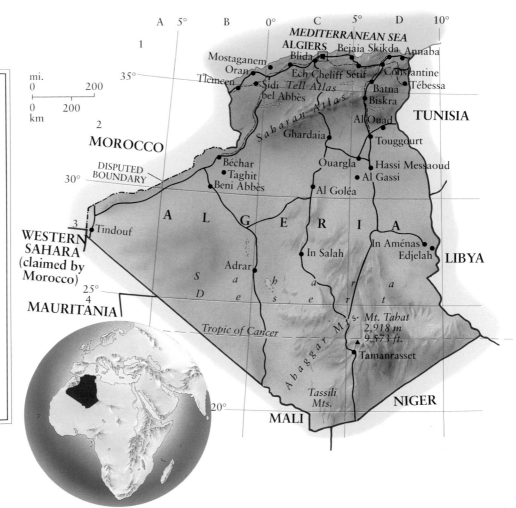

ALGERIA *Geography and Economy*

The Sahara Desert takes up the southern four fifths of Algeria, where temperatures can climb to 49 degrees centigrade. High sand-dunes shift with the wind. A wind called the Sirocco sometimes carries desert sand northwards across the Mediterranean Sea and far into Europe. In the southern desert, on the main route to Niger, an upland area called the Ahaggar bakes by day and freezes by night. The Sahara Desert is a barren wilderness, yet it provides most of the country's wealth. Beneath the sands are large reserves of oil and natural gas, which are piped north for processing and export. The desert also yields valuable phosphates and iron ore.

The coastal cities are important centres of Algerian industry, producing construction materials and textiles. They lie in a region of wooded hills and fertile plains where farmers grow wheat, citrus fruits and vegetables to feed their families. The Atlas Mountains divide the coastal region from the desert. In the high mountain plateaus, herders settle with their cattle, goats and sheep for most of the year, but leave their villages in search of fresh pasture when grazing becomes scarce. There is little rainfall and only undrinkable salt water collects in marshy depressions called chotts. The climate is hot, but less extreme than in the desert to the south.

▲ *Women pick the harvest in an olive grove on the coastal plains. Olives are eaten or pressed to produce fine oil. Olive trees also provide food and shelter for many birds and insects.*

▶ *In the kasbah customers and traders haggle over the price of vegetables, oranges, spices, dates, olives, cloth, pottery and souvenirs. The kasbah is an area of narrow alleys and street markets at the heart of old Algerian towns.*

◄ 'The forest is a place of entertainment,' says the poster, 'it should be looked after'. The small but precious forests of cedar and cork oak in Algeria are currently threatened. People cut them down for firewood and farmers clear forest land for grazing.

▼ Container ships and oil-tankers lie at anchor off Algiers. The national capital is one of the chief ports of the North African coast and a major centre for industry, business and communications.

► Snow covers sheer slopes in the Grande Kabylie region, which is in the Sahara's Atlas Mountains. Algeria's mountain ranges protect the coastal farmland from the worst of the harsh desert winds.

ALGERIA *People and History*

▲ *About 8,000 years ago this scene was painted on sandstone rock in mountains north of the Ahaggar range. It shows hunters and wild animals, providing a startling reminder that the Sahara was once lush grassland. A combination of climatic change and over-farming turned the region into a barren desert.*

Most Algerians are of mixed Berber and Arab descent. The Berber people have lived in this region for thousands of years. Arab conquerors invaded in the AD600s and converted the Berbers to Islam. Over the centuries many Arabs and Berbers intermarried, but they still form separate cultural groups, each with its own style of dress and language.

In the 1500s control of Algiers fell to fierce Turkish sea captains called the *Barbarossas* (Red Beards). Algeria became a Turkish province and prospered for many years as a centre of piracy. In 1830 it was invaded by France and passed into French hands.

Forts were built across the Sahara by the French Foreign Legion, a famously tough division of the French army that included mercenary (paid) soldiers from many countries. French colonists settled in the coastal cities.

In 1954 the Algerian National Liberation Front, which totally opposed French rule, began the long and violent War of Independence. When Algeria finally won its independence in 1962, most of the French colonists returned to France. The first president, Ahmed Ben Bella, was overthrown by Houari Boumedienne, whose rule began to bring prosperity to Algeria in the 1970s. The country's recent history has seen violent conflict between a political party called the FIS, whose members are extremely strict Muslims, and the ruling regime.

◄ *Ruined columns at Djemula, near Sétif, date back 2,000 years. At this time Algeria formed part of the fertile Roman province of Numidia. The fabulous ruined city now lies in semi-desert.*

◄ *A photograph from 1949 shows the French Foreign Legion going on truck patrol in the desert. Five years later open warfare had broken out between the Algerians and their French rulers.*

SPEAK BERBER

Hello –
Sallamou âllaykoum
(sa - lam al - a - khoom)

Goodbye – Vka allakhir
(vkha a - la - khair)

Please – Lâanayak
(la - ha - na - yek)

▼ *Nomadic Tuareg people live in the southern Sahara Desert by trading and herding camels and goats. By night they sleep in tents of animal hide. Their name means 'the veiled ones'. This is because Tuareg men wear traditional dress of black or dark blue cotton and they wind long scarves around their heads.*

► *Women vote for the first time after Algeria's independence from France in 1962. Women can now train to be teachers or lawyers and wear Western dress if they wish. However, very rigid followers of Islam want women to go back to a more traditional way of life.*

TUNISIA *Introduction*

Tunisia is the most northerly nation in the African continent. It lies at the eastern end of the Atlas Mountains, which drop down to grassy hills and plateaus grazed by sheep and goats. Wheat, oranges and olives are grown in the northern valleys or on the rich farmland of the Mediterranean coast. Towards the south of the country, however, the climate and landscape are more hostile. Salt lakes called chotts and desert sands bake in the fierce sun. But the south is productive in its own way. Its oil and phosphates make up half of Tunisia's exports.

Modern luxury hotels fringe the Mediterranean beaches and islands of Tunisia, attracting large numbers of tourists every year. Some travel south to see the desert sand-dunes. Unlike its neighbours this small country has few areas that are really remote.

Tunisia forms a link between three totally different cultures. The rest of the great continent of Africa lies to the south and Europe lies across the Mediterranean Sea to the north. It is also part of the Maghreb (the northwestern countries of Africa).

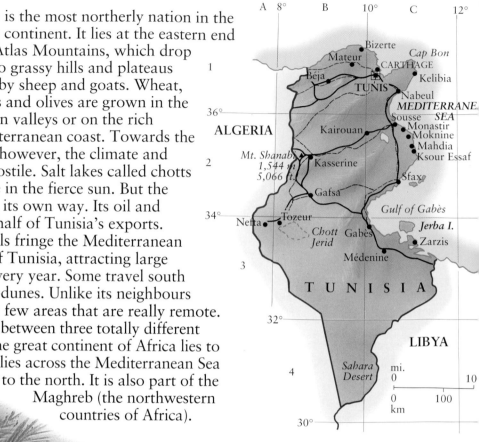

◄ *Date pickers reach the tops of the date palm tree by attaching themselves to the trunk with rope. Once picked, the dates are mostly dried and packed in boxes, or pressed into blocks for use in cooking.*

▶ *These masks were made by the Phoenicians, an ancient people from the eastern Mediterranean. They colonized the region that we now know as Tunisia about 3,000 years ago.*

FACTS AND FIGURES

Area: 164,150 sq km	**Currency:**
Population: 8,579,000	Tunisian dinar
Capital: Tunis (597,000)	**Main exports:**
Other major cities:	Crude oil, fertilizers,
Sfax (232,000),	phosphates, olive oil,
Bizerte (95,000)	textiles, fruit, fish
Highest point:	products, machinery
Mt Shanabi (1,544 m)	**Government:**
Official language:	Multi-party republic
Arabic	**Per capita GNP:**
Main religion: Islam	US $1,740

▲ *Sunbaked folds of mountains and slabs of rock are typical of the mountainous areas in western parts of Tunisia. This picture was taken near Tozeur.*

▼ *An old fort guards the Gulf of Hammamet, just south of Nabeul. The lovely resort of Hammamet has attracted artists since the 1800s.*

TUNISIA *People and History*

◄ Jewish pilgrims study the scriptures at the El Ehriba synagogue on Jerba Island. The country's Jewish community has been a part of Tunisian life for many centuries.

COUSCOUS
Tunisia is famous for its couscous dishes. Couscous is made from wheat that has been pounded into fine grains. It is steamed until fluffy and served with either stewed lamb or vegetables. The Arabic name for it (*kuskus*) comes from the word *kaskasa*, which means 'to pound' or 'to pulverize'.

Early settlers in this region included the Berber and Phoenician peoples, who built the great city of Carthage. The Romans destroyed Carthage and made the region a province of Rome. In AD439 Tunisia was conquered by a group of people called Vandals, who invaded from Spain. It then passed into the hands of Christian soldiers from Byzantium (now Istanbul, in Turkey).

Arab armies swept into Tunisia in the AD600s and the Muslim culture flourished. There were clashes with desert peoples and with warships from Christian Europe. In 1574 the Turks installed a ruler, but by the 1880s Tunisia was under French control. The struggle for independence was not won until 1956 and Tunisia became a republic the following year. Habib Bourguiba dominated political life from 1934 until 1987. Zine Ben Ali was elected president in 1989.

▼ These famous cave-dwellings are in Matmata, in central Tunisia. In this village, people live in homes that have been hollowed out of the barren, rocky ground.

Today over half the population lives in cities, which are a mix of ancient and modern buildings. Most Tunisians are of Arab descent and in rural areas many people still wear the long gown that is traditional Arab clothing. The standard of education is improving steadily. The country has been able to develop schools and colleges because its varied natural resources and close ties with Europe have made it wealthier than many African countries.

◄ The ruined colosseum of El Jem, south of Mahdia, is a spectacular reminder that ancient Tunisia was part of the Roman empire. In those days people flocked here to see chariot races and fights between people and wild beasts.

◄ Beautifully tiled buildings are a feature of the medina (old town centre) of Kairouan. This maze of narrow streets is circled by ancient city walls. Founded in AD671, the city is a centre of the Muslim faith.

► In the souk (market) richly coloured spices, vegetables and dried fruit are on display. Nearby shops sell rugs and carpets, baskets, pottery, brass and copperware.

LIBYA *Introduction*

About 70 percent of Libyans live in the large coastal cities of Tripoli, Misratah and Benghazi. Many moved there in the 1970s to seek work when oil production was booming. The government used profits from oil to improve farmland and to pipe water supplies across the country. New industries were developed, including mining and food processing. In the 1990s the world price of oil fell and Libya's economic progress slowed down. Faced with possible discontent from a disappointed people, Libya's government worked to build up trade with neighbouring countries.

This is a very hot land. The highest temperature ever recorded on Earth – 58 degrees centigrade in the shade – was reached in Libya in 1922. About 90 percent of Libya consists of the dunes of the Sahara Desert. The eastern section of the Sahara, which crosses into Egypt and Sudan, is called the Libyan Desert. There are scattered oases there. At the large oasis of Al Kufrah a huge underground water supply lies beneath the desert rock.

The semi-desert regions provide sparse grazing for sheep, goats and cattle. The only natural farmland is along the Mediterranean coast. On the northwestern plains and the northeastern highlands farmers use mainly traditional methods to grow oranges, wheat, olives, almonds and grapes.

▲ *Mosques rise above the skyline of old Tripoli. Since the 1970s the capital has grown to accommodate workers coming in from the countryside. Today traditional extended families crowd into high-rise flats.*

▼ *Burn-off flares light up a Saharan oilfield. Pipelines carry precious crude oil northwards to the Mediterranean coast. Oil and natural gas make up over 99 percent of the country's exports and form the base of its petrochemicals industry.*

◀ *In spring, rainfall transforms the desert fields of Cyrenaica, in eastern Libya, into a carpet of wild flowers.*

ENDANGERED WORLD

The Mediterranean monk seal is in danger from fishing, pollution and sea traffic.

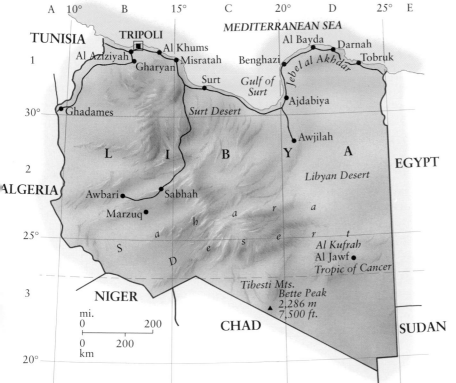

FACTS AND FIGURES

Area: 1,759,540 sq km
Population: 4,700,000
Capital: Tripoli (858,000)
Other major cities: Benghazi (368,000), Misratah (117,000)
Highest point: Bette Peak (2,286 m)
Official language: Arabic
Main religion: Islam
Currency: Libyan dinar
Main exports: Petroleum
Government: Socialist jamahiriya
Per capita GNP: Est. US $3,000-8,000

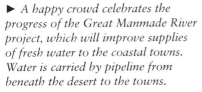

▶ *A happy crowd celebrates the progress of the Great Manmade River project, which will improve supplies of fresh water to the coastal towns. Water is carried by pipeline from beneath the desert to the towns.*

LIBYA *People and History*

▲ *These Roman baths are part of the ruins of Leptis Magna, which is 140 kilometres east of Tripoli. The site also has ruined market places, temples and a harbour. Leptis Magna was founded by the Phoenicians, but rose to importance about 1,800 years ago under the rule of the Romans.*

The Berber people were the original inhabitants of this land and today almost all Libyans are of Berber and Arab descent. In ancient times trading ships and war galleys brought Mediterranean peoples to Libya. The Phoenicians settled in the northwest and the Greeks in the east. The Romans conquered the whole coast, shipping wheat and fruit back to Italy from their African estates.

The Arabs invaded in the AD600s, bringing Islam to North Africa. For a long period the country was split between Tunisia and Egypt. In the 1500s it became part of the Turkish empire, but Arab rulers still had local power. Italy seized control and ruled the country from 1911 until 1943. During World War II, Britain defeated Italian and German armies in the Libyan Desert. As a result Britain and France briefly shared control of Libya.

Libya gained independence in 1951 and Idris I became king. In 1959 oil was discovered and brought sudden riches. However, this wealth was controlled by the ruling classes, which caused widespread discontent. In 1969 King Idris was overthrown by the army, under the leadership of Colonel Muammar el Qadhafi. Qadhafi strengthened the economy, but he made many enemies. He opposed Arab peace with Israel and raised oil prices for Israel's supporters in the West. Qadhafi's regime backed the Palestine Liberation Organization in its fight against Israel for a homeland and helped rebellions in Chad and Morocco. It also funded terrorist campaigns abroad. In 1986 the United States of America bombed Libya after an alleged Libyan bomb killed a US soldier in a nightclub. The United Nations imposed sanctions on Libya in the 1990s when it refused to surrender alleged terrorists for trial.

◀ *With flags and pennants fluttering, horses wheel around the race track in Libya's capital, Tripoli. The Arab nations have a long tradition of horse-breeding and great riding skills.*

▲ *A piper from Ghadames wears festival costume. Both folk music and pop music in North Africa show the influence of Arab traditions.*

▲ *The Libyan leader Qadhafi inspects a military parade. Conscripts, who are called up into the Libyan army, have to serve for three to four years.*

◄ *This ruined, fortress-like building was once used for storing grain. Many of the traditional buildings in Saharan parts of Africa are built of mud and crushed stone. They are strengthened by long wooden beams.*

155

EGYPT *Introduction*

Most of Egypt is a burning, sandy desert that stretches south and west into the vast wastes of the Sahara. The river Nile flows northwards from Sudan through the baking cliffs, depressions and sand-dunes of the Libyan Desert and the Arabian Desert. Its course is marked by a narrow green strip, the result of thousands of years of flooding and irrigation.

To the north the Nile spills across a coastal plain, forming a broad, fertile delta. Ships from all over the world lie at anchor in the great port of Alexandria. This is Egypt's second city, founded by the Greeks in 32BC. Its long waterfront and wide streets are cooled by sea breezes. Egypt has two other historic seaports. These are Suez, on the Red Sea coast, and Port Said, on the Mediterranean. They are linked by the Suez Canal. The country's eastern border, across the wilderness of the Sinai Peninsula, is with Israel.

Egypt's towns and cities, ancient and modern, all depend on the Nile. Cairo, the capital, is the largest city in Africa. Thousands of people go there to trade, worship or study. It is a bustling, dusty city full of hooting taxis and hurrying crowds. In the shaded bazaars and cafés people meet to talk, play backgammon and drink sweet black coffee or tea. Modern hotels and office blocks rise up next to beautiful old mosques and basic housing where the city's poor people live.

▲ *Wooden boats called feluccas carry goods and passengers up and down the river Nile. They have graceful, triangular sails. Boats have been sailing these waters for around five thousand years.*

◄ *The Nile winds its way past Luxor. The ancient Egyptians called the Nile Valley the 'Black Land', because river floods left rich, black mud behind each year. This soil is ideal for growing crops.*

▲ In this view of the crowded Cairo skyline, the minarets (towers) of the Sultan Hassan and Rifai mosques rise above the rooftops. In the distance is a haze caused by dust and traffic pollution.

◄ The famous pyramids at Giza are on the edge of the Libyan Desert. These are the huge tombs of the pharaohs (kings) who ruled here over 4,000 years ago.

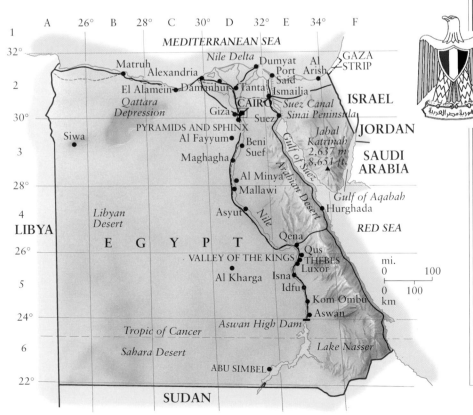

FACTS AND FIGURES
Area: 1,001,450 sq km
Population: 56,488,000
Capital: Cairo (6,452,000)
Other major cities: Alexandria (3,170,000), Giza (2,156,000), Port Said (461,000)
Highest point: Jabal Katrinah (2,637 m)
Official language: Arabic
Main religions: Islam, Christianity
Currency: Egyptian pound
Main exports: Crude and refined oil, cotton and other textiles, fruit
Government: Republic
Per capita GNP: US $630

EGYPT *Geography and Economy*

▼ *Farmers visit a busy livestock market on the outskirts of Luxor, the site of the magnificent ancient city of Thebes.*

Egypt's population is the second largest on the African continent, but nearly all of its inhabitants are crowded into the narrow strip of land that is watered by the river Nile. This is the only part of the country where the soil is fertile enough to be farmed and it covers less than six percent of Egypt's total territory.

There is an increasing need to make the deserts produce crops in order to feed the country's rapidly expanding population. Underground water already seeps to the surface in the desert oases, where dates are produced. Water has been drawn from the river Nile and channelled into irrigation ditches for thousands of years. The precious water allows villagers to grow a variety of crops along the banks of the river. These include rice, maize, sorghum, wheat, sugar-cane, beans, oranges and tomatoes. Hydroelectric power and water for larger irrigation schemes is provided by the Aswan High Dam in the southeast, which opened in 1970.

Egypt has the oldest tourism industry in the world. Over 2,000 years ago Greeks and Romans travelled here to marvel at the country's ancient temples and tombs. They even left graffiti behind. Today over two million tourists visit Egypt each year to enjoy wonders such as the Great Sphinx and the towering pyramids of the pharaohs. As a result, valuable revenue is brought into the country.

▼ *Simple tools and traditional methods are used to harvest a crop of sugar-cane. Although over one third of all Egyptians work in agriculture, the country has to import a great deal of its food.*

◀ *Women work in a clothes factory. Women workers play a vital role in the economy of modern Egypt, where cotton and clothing are major exports. They wear headscarves or veils, a tradition of the Islamic religion.*

▼ *Strangely eroded rocks, sand and salts shimmer in the hot sun at an oasis in the Libyan Desert. This harsh and arid landscape extends westwards into Libya and south to the empty wasteland of the Sahara Desert.*

▶ *Water surges through the Aswan High Dam. This amazing piece of engineering was built to control the floodwaters of the river Nile and provide hydroelectricity. However, the dam has also brought problems for the environment. The changes that it has made to the river's flow have led to the erosion of Egypt's Mediterranean coast.*

EGYPT *People and History*

Today's Egyptians are partly descended from the people of ancient Egypt, but also from the many other peoples who invaded or settled the region in later years. The early history of Egypt is remarkable. From around 3100BC until 1085BC, one of the world's greatest civilizations developed in the Nile Valley. The ancient Egyptians built huge temples, tombs and towns.

They traded far and wide. These people studied the stars, worshipped many different gods and believed in life after death, which led them to preserve the bodies of their dead as mummies.

This way of life was shattered by waves of invaders, including the Persians, Greeks and Romans. The Arabs brought the Islamic religion in AD638. Arab rule lasted many centuries and then passed to a people called the Mamluks, who had been the Arabs' slaves. In 1805, under Muhammad Ali, Egypt began a process of modernization and work started on the Suez Canal. Britain bought shares in the canal and took control of Egypt in 1882. Egypt became independent in 1922. By the 1950s the country had become a republic under President Gamal Abdel Nasser.

In recent times Egypt has fought wars with its neighbour, Israel. Peace finally came in 1977 under President Sadat. Egypt continues to strengthen its ties with the other Arab nations and helped to defend Saudi Arabia when Iraq invaded Kuwait in 1990.

▲ *This is the gold mask of Tutankhamun, a young pharaoh (king) who died around 1340BC. It was one of the treasures discovered by the British archaeologists Howard Carter and Lord Carnarvon in 1922.*

SPEAK ARABIC

Hello – أهلا (*eh - lun*)

Goodbye – مع السلامة (*mah el - sal - eh mah*)

Please – من فضلك (*min fud - lak*)

Thank you – شكرا (*shok - run*)

Yes – نعم (*nahm*)

◄ *St Catherine's monastery is in the arid wastes of the Sinai region. It is said to mark the site where Moses saw the burning bush. Christianity, Judaism and Islam all developed in the deserts of the east.*

▲ *These women are students at Cairo University. Egypt has one of the oldest universities in the world, which was founded over a thousand years ago. Today the country has 12 universities.*

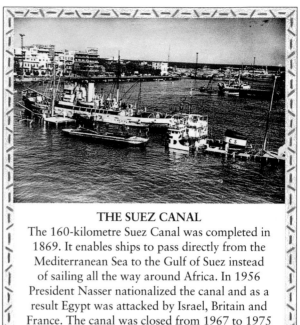

THE SUEZ CANAL
The 160-kilometre Suez Canal was completed in 1869. It enables ships to pass directly from the Mediterranean Sea to the Gulf of Suez instead of sailing all the way around Africa. In 1956 President Nasser nationalized the canal and as a result Egypt was attacked by Israel, Britain and France. The canal was closed from 1967 to 1975 because of further wars with Israel. Today Egypt is enlarging the canal to take big oil-tankers.

◄ *The Egyptians invented this ancient form of writing using picture symbols called hieroglyphs. Each picture stood for a sound, idea or object. Later the Egyptians used forms that could be written more quickly.*

► *A Bedouin woman spins while her husband makes music. Many Bedouin still follow the traditional nomadic lifestyle. They move across the sparse desert scrub in search of pasture for their herds of goats, sheep and camels. Tents are pitched at night. Other Bedowin have settled in towns or work in the oilfields.*

161

SUDAN *Introduction*

Sudan is the largest country in the whole of Africa. Its vast area contains all kinds of landscapes. Fiercely hot desert extends across much of the north and covers almost a third of the country. In this region there are flat-roofed houses. In central Sudan villages of round, thatched huts nestle on the wide and grassy plains. The river Nile and its various branches loop all over the country. A maze of waterways passes through tangled banks and steamy rainforests in the south.

Branches of the Nile divide the three cities that form the heart of Sudan's economy. Khartoum has broad streets, foreign embassies and government offices. Khartoum North is the centre of industry, with factories producing goods such as textiles and processed foods. The busy commercial town of Omdurman sprawls over the west bank of the White Nile.

Travelling around Sudan can be difficult. During the rainy season many of the dirt roads are washed away. There are rail links east to the Ethiopian border, west to the beautiful green highlands of the Jebel Marra and southwest, to the Democratic Republic of Congo. However, routes to the far south have been blocked due to years of civil war between northerners and southerners. For example, the journey up the White Nile from Kosti to Juba now takes about two weeks.

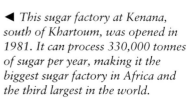

◄ *This sugar factory at Kenana, south of Khartoum, was opened in 1981. It can process 330,000 tonnes of sugar per year, making it the biggest sugar factory in Africa and the third largest in the world.*

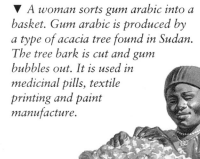

FACTS AND FIGURES

Area:
2,505,810 sq km
Population:
28,129,000
Capital: Khartoum
(477,000)
Other major cities:
Omdurman (527,000),
Khartoum North
(342,000),
Port Sudan (207,000)
Highest point:
Mt Kinyeti (3,187 m)

Official language: Arabic
Main religions: Islam,
traditional beliefs,
Christianity
Currency: Sudanese pound
Main exports: Cotton,
gum arabic, sesame seeds,
peanuts, sorghum
Government:
Military regime
Per capita GNP:
Est. under
US $700

▼ *A woman sorts gum arabic into a
basket. Gum arabic is produced by
a type of acacia tree found in Sudan.
The tree bark is cut and gum
bubbles out. It is used in
medicinal pills, textile
printing and paint
manufacture.*

▲ *Omdurman is a maze of narrow streets
clogged with hooting taxis. Men in white
robes and turbans pass on trotting donkeys.
Above this busy scene, the minarets
of mosques form a graceful skyline.*

▶ *A hut near Al Fasher
sells glasses of black tea,
which is hot, sweet and
highly refreshing after a
dry and dusty journey.
Wayside stalls like this
one are found in most
parts of Africa.*

SUDAN *People and History*

▼ *Many Sudanese live by herding sheep, goats, camels and cattle. These animals provide meat, milk, transport and hides, but years of drought have reduced their numbers.*

▼ *These ruined pyramids are at Meroë, east of Khartoum. Between 592BC and AD350 Meroë was a powerful kingdom. Carvings in stone show that the Meroites worshipped the gods of ancient Egypt.*

Vast areas of this blazing hot country are desert. Crops can be grown on just five percent of the land, yet two thirds of the people live by farming. Millet, sorghum and dates are the main crops. People work land that is watered by the Nile and its many tributaries. These rivers thread their way through the south of the country and provide rich supplies of fish. The drier north is home to nomads who herd camels and goats, while farther south farms are more common.

The Sudanese are descended from the Nubian people, who lived in ancient Egypt and from Arab traders, who settled in the region later. The north is the home of the Kababish and the Baqqara peoples, while the Nuer, Dinka and Shilluk live in the south.

In 1821 Egypt seized power in Sudan. In 1885 the Sudanese rebelled under their leader, the Mahdi. They captured Khartoum and killed the British general Charles George Gordon, who governed Sudan for the Egyptians. Two years later Britain and Egypt regained control of the country.

Sudan became independent from Britain and Egypt in 1956, but a bitter civil war followed. This war has continued for decades between Arabic-speaking Muslims from the north and southerners who follow Christianity or traditional religions. The country has also suffered from natural disasters. Around one and a half million people lost their homes in the floods of 1988.

▲ *A slave has her chains removed. During the 1800s, the British explorers Sir Samuel Baker and Florence Baker explored the Nile. One aim of their trips was to stop the slave trade in southern Sudan.*

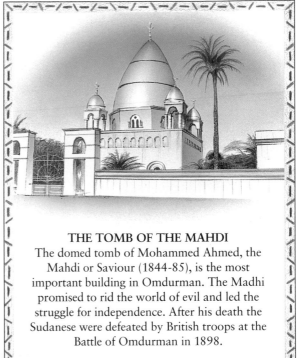

THE TOMB OF THE MAHDI

The domed tomb of Mohammed Ahmed, the Mahdi or Saviour (1844-85), is the most important building in Omdurman. The Madhi promised to rid the world of evil and led the struggle for independence. After his death the Sudanese were defeated by British troops at the Battle of Omdurman in 1898.

▲ *A river-boat sails down the Nile. These boats have shallow bottoms so that they can pass above the shifting sandbanks. They used to sail the length of Sudan, but travel to the south was disrupted by civil war.*

▶ *People from Eritrea share out water at a refugee camp in Sudan. During the 1980s refugees poured into Sudan from neighbouring lands that were suffering from severe drought and war.*

CHAD

Chad lies right at the heart of north Africa. Although it is completely surrounded by land, part of a huge lake lies within its borders. This is Lake Chad, which teems with a variety of fish and changes in size as it dries out or fills up with rain according to the season.

South of Lake Chad the country is moist and fertile with tropical forest and cotton plantations. This is the only area of the country that is able to support crops. A belt of dusty savanna spreads across the centre of Chad, providing sparse pasture for roaming cattle. In the north the landscape is dry and mostly barren. The Tibesti Mountains are bleak and temperatures in the Sahara Desert often reach 49 degrees centigrade. Arabs, Tuareg people and other nomads live in the northern areas and the Sara are the most numerous people of the south.

During Chad's early history the most powerful empire was Kanem-Bornu, which was established to the northeast of Lake Chad in the 1500s. The Kanem-Bornu people regularly plundered the south, seizing the Sara people who lived there and exporting them as slaves. The descendants of the Kanem-Bornu are today's Muslims of the north.

Chad was a French colony from 1920 to 1960. Since the 1960s, the clash between the north, which is Islamic, and the south, which mostly follows Christian or traditional African beliefs, has fuelled an almost continuous civil war.

▲ *A woman sells cornmeal at market. Farmers have to sell their crops locally because it is so difficult to transport produce across the country. There are no railways and only unpaved roads.*

ENDANGERED WORLD

The scimitar-horned oryx is on the edge of extinction because of drought and ruthless hunting.

▶ *Muslims in N'Djamena celebrate Chad's independence from France with an annual procession. Since independence Chad has suffered from conflict between northerners and southerners. Different political groups have also clashed.*

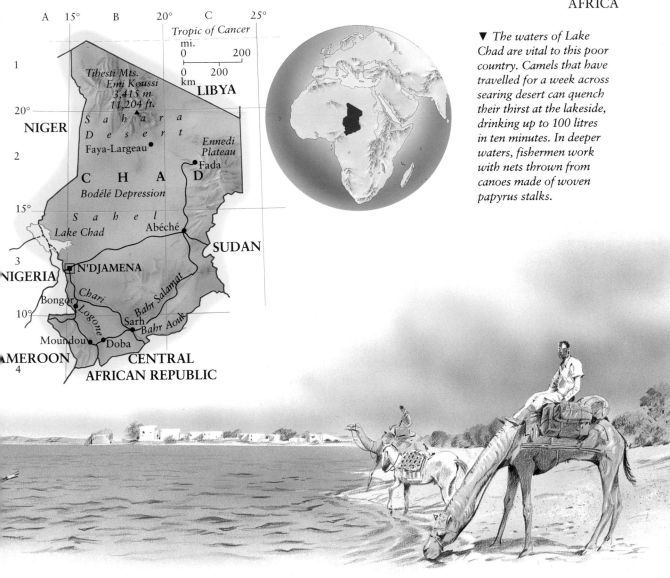

The map shows Chad with the following labels:

Tropic of Cancer

LIBYA

NIGER

Tibesti Mts.
Emi Koussi
3,415 m
11,204 ft.

Sahara Desert

Faya-Largeau

Ennedi Plateau

Fada

C H A D

Bodélé Depression

Sahel

Lake Chad

Abéché

SUDAN

NIGERIA

N'DJAMENA

Chari

Bongor

Logone

Bahr Salamat

Sarh

Bahr Aouk

Moundou

Doba

CAMEROON

CENTRAL
AFRICAN REPUBLIC

▼ *The waters of Lake Chad are vital to this poor country. Camels that have travelled for a week across searing desert can quench their thirst at the lakeside, drinking up to 100 litres in ten minutes. In deeper waters, fishermen work with nets thrown from canoes made of woven papyrus stalks.*

▼ *People driven from their homes by drought gather at a temporary settlement as a dust storm rages. Since the 1960s, a series of droughts has left much of the land unproductive and many families starving and homeless.*

FACTS AND FIGURES

Area: 1,284,000 sq km
Population: 6,098,000
Capital: N'Djamena (530,000)
Other major city: Moundou (282,000)
Highest point: Emi Koussi (3,415 m)

Official languages: Arabic, French
Main religions: Islam, Christianity, traditional beliefs
Currency: Franc CFA
Main exports: Raw cotton, livestock, meat, hides, fish, textiles
Government: Republic
Per capita GNP: US $220

NIGER

Over half the population of this land belongs to the Hausa, a people who have lived in West Africa for about a thousand years. The Hausa live in southern Niger and are farmers and traders. Other peoples include the Zarma, Kanuria, Tuareg and Teda. Most people live in rural areas to the south. Many of them keep camels, cattle, sheep and goats. In the southwest, where the land is watered by the river Niger, crops such as millet, sorghum, maize, cassava, sugar-cane and peanuts are grown. Fish are caught in the river Niger and in Lake Chad.

The scorched wastelands of the Sahara Desert and the Air Mountains stretch over two thirds of the country. In these areas temperatures can soar beyond 50 degrees centigrade. Only three percent of the land is fertile and forms a grassy plain that runs along Niger's southern border.

Long ago Hausa and Tuareg armies fought over Niger. From 1921 to 1960 it was colonized by France. After independence in 1960, Niger became a military republic, but in 1992 the people voted for multi-party elections. These elections were held in 1993 and brought Mahamane Ousmane to power.

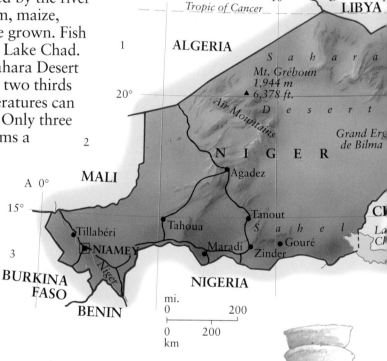

◀ These pupils attend a rural school, but many remote villages do not have any schools at all. Some nomadic groups in northern Niger have tent schools that move with the people as they travel in search of water and grazing land for their animals.

▶ A woman balances a stack of salt cakes on her head. This is a common way of carrying goods in many African countries.

◄ *Traders sell melons and squashes on the banks of the river Niger. The river has been an important trading route for centuries.*

FACTS AND FIGURES
Area: 1,267,000 sq km
Population: 8,361,000
Capital: Niamey (399,000)
Other major city: Zinder (121,000)
Highest point: Mt Gréboun (1,944 m)
Official language: French
Main religion: Islam
Currency: Franc CFA
Main exports: Uranium, livestock, vegetables
Government: Republic
Per capita GNP: US $300

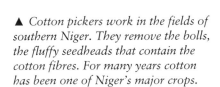

▲ *Cotton pickers work in the fields of southern Niger. They remove the bolls, the fluffy seedheads that contain the cotton fibres. For many years cotton has been one of Niger's major crops.*

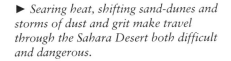

► *Searing heat, shifting sand-dunes and storms of dust and grit make travel through the Sahara Desert both difficult and dangerous.*

BURKINA FASO

Burkina Faso lies land-locked in western Africa. Its only link with the sea is a railway that runs south from Ouagadougou to the port of Abidjan in Côte d'Ivoire. The country was once called Upper Volta, because it contains the three main sources of the Volta River. In 1984 the government changed its name to Burkina Faso, which means 'land of honest people'.

This is mostly a dry and rocky land, which only becomes green during the summer rains. It has suffered from many severe droughts and basic foods have to be imported, even in years when there is rain.

Burkina Faso is home to a number of peoples. The largest group is the Mossi, whose kingdom dates back to the Middle Ages. The whole of this part of Africa was ruled by the French from 1896. Upper Volta became fully independent in 1960. Since then it has had both military and one-party rule. Multi-party elections were held in 1992 and were won by the Popular Front. In 1994 Roch Christian Kabore was appointed prime minister.

▼ *This government poster says, 'Now the word is for the peasants of Burkina'. Small farmers and peasants make up most of the population in Burkina Faso.*

FACTS AND FIGURES

Area: 274,400 sq km
Population: 9,682,000
Capital: Ouagadougou (443,000)
Other major cities: Bobo Dioulasso (232,000), Koudougou (52,000)
Highest point: Aiguille de Sindou (717 m)
Official language: French
Main religions: Islam, Christianity, traditional beliefs
Currency: Franc CFA
Main exports: Cotton, karite nuts, livestock, gold
Government: Multi-party republic
Per capita GNP: US $290

▲ *Village women work together to solve their problems. These women are discussing ways to stop locusts destroying their millet crops.*

▶ *Mopeds are assembled at a Peugeot factory. These light, cheap motor-cycles are ideal for travelling across the country's sandy tracks.*

▼ *Millet is carried to the stores in a farming village. This crop is an important source of food in many of the dry areas of Africa. The seeds are ground into flour for flat breads or used to make a type of porridge.*

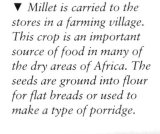

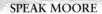

SPEAK MOORE

How are you? – Kebara
(kee - bah - ray)

Goodbye –
Win nā kond yindara
(win na kond yin - dah - ray)

Yes – Ōnhōw *(ong - hong)*

No – Ōnōnk *(hon - hon)*

Thank you – Barka
(bah - kah)

MALI

The powerful Ghana, Mali and Songhai empires flourished in this part of Africa during the Middle Ages. Their wealth came from trade in salt, gold, ivory and slaves. Camel caravans crossed the Sahara Desert and Timbuktu became a centre of Islamic learning. The Bambara and Malinke peoples still tell tales and sing songs that date back to the days of the Mali empire. Today the Bambara are the largest group of people in Mali.

By the 1800s the French were trying to seize control of this region. They finally took over as rulers in 1895 and named the country French Sudan. It stayed in French hands for many years, not gaining full independence until 1960 when it became the Republic of Mali. The military took over in 1968 and in 1979 Mali came under one-party rule. In the early 1990s there were demonstrations against one-party rule and military leaders took over once again. In 1992 there were moves towards a democratic government. Multi-party elections were held in this year and Alpha Oumar Konare became president.

Mali is far from the coast and has few roads. It relies on the great river Niger for transport, as well as the railway that runs from Bamako to the port of Dakar in Senegal. The Sahara covers the north of Mali. This desert is constantly edging its way southwards into the dusty scrub of the central region, which is called the Sahel. The south and far west are greener areas of grassland and forest, particularly when the river Niger floods and brings water. These southern and western areas are where most of Mali's many farmers live, growing cotton, sugar-cane, rice, millet and peanuts. The country also has deposits of iron ore, salt and phosphates.

▲ *Dogon villages have probably stayed the same for centuries. The Dogon people are thought to be among the earliest inhabitants of Mali.*

KYINKYINGA

Kyinkyinga are types of kebabs sold by street vendors right across West Africa. On the skewers are pieces of green pepper and meat flavoured with ginger and peanut sauce.

◄ *A masked stilt-dancer performs at a village festival in southern Mali. Stilt-walking began in West Africa as a way of passing more easily through swamps and tall grasses.*

▶ The Great Mosque is the centre of worship in the town of Djenné, between Mopti and San. Most Malians are Muslims. Mali was famed as a centre of Islam as early as AD1324, when its great ruler Mansa Musa travelled as a pilgrim to Mecca.

FACTS AND FIGURES
Area: 1,240,190 sq km
Population: 10,137,000
Capital: Bamako (740,000)
Other major cities: Ségou (99,000), Mopti (78,000)
Highest point: Hombori Tondo (1,155 m)
Official language: French
Main religions: Islam, traditional beliefs
Currency: Franc CFA
Main exports: Cotton, livestock, peanuts
Government: Republic
Per capita GNP: US $300

▼ Market traders lay out their wares. In Mali, as in many other parts of Africa, the open-air market is the centre of shopping and trade.

SENEGAL

Carved wooden masks, musical instruments made of large gourds, dancers, singers and storytellers are all part of Senegal's culture. This culture stretches back to the ancient Ghana, Mali and Songhai empires of West Africa, which thrived between the AD500s and the 1500s.

As these empires declined, smaller independent kingdoms grew up, such as those established by the Tukulor, Wolof and Serer peoples. Portuguese traders arrived in the 1400s and were soon joined by the British, Dutch and French. In 1895 Senegal officially became a French colony and the capital of the whole of French West Africa. In 1960 the country won independence and became the Republic of Senegal, although it still had strong trading links with France. Years of political instability and drought followed, as well as clashes with Mauritania over the border between the two countries. Talks were set up in 1992 to try to settle the dispute.

The country is a land of sandy plains giving way to forest in the southern Casamance region. During the summer, ocean winds bring tropical rains that turn the parched earth green. Most people live in rural areas and are relatively poor farmers or herders. They grow millet, cassava and rice for food. Cotton and peanuts are grown as cash crops. Senegal's cities, home to about a third of the population, show the country's modern face. They have blocks of flats, busy highways and factories. A variety of peoples mingle on the streets. Some Senegalese are wandering traders who travel to ports around the world in order to make some money before returning home.

FACTS AND FIGURES
Area: 197,160 sq km
Population: 7,736,000
Capital: Dakar (1,382,000)
Other major cities: Thiès (157,000), Kaolak (133,000)
Highest point: In the southeast (498 m)
Official language: French
Main religion: Islam
Currency: Franc CFA
Main exports: Fish products, peanuts, phosphates, chemicals
Government: Multi-party republic
Per capita GNP: US $780

ENDANGERED WORLD

The cheetah, the world's fastest animal on land, is now very scarce in West Africa. It is still hunted for its fur.

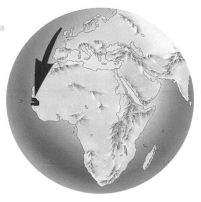

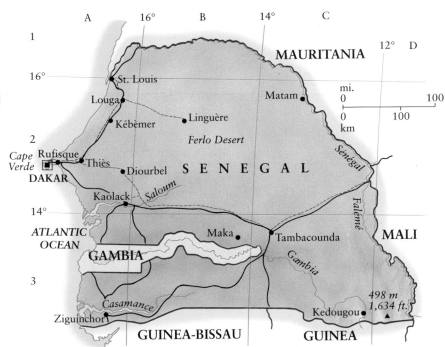

▼ Dakar is a busy, bustling capital. This great port on the southern coast of the Cape Verde peninsula is a centre of government, industry, commerce and communications.

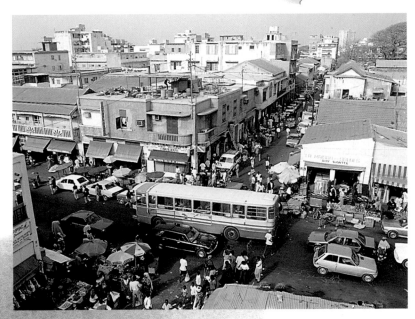

▼ This house for slaves at Gorée Island near Dakar stands as a grim reminder of the cruelty and misery of the slave trade. It was one of the coastal trading posts founded by the French in the 1600s.

◀ The peanut harvest is stacked high before being made into oil. Peanuts have been a major export since colonial times, but attempts are now being made to increase the harvest of other crops.

GAMBIA

The country of Gambia has an unusual shape. This is because its boundaries, which were drawn up in 1889, reflect years of squabbling between European countries over control of the area. During the Middle Ages, this region was part of the medieval empire of Mali. It was later divided into local kingdoms before being torn apart by European slave traders. By the 1600s the British were firmly established in the region. Britain and France fought over control of trade on the river Gambia, but all of Gambia was under British rule by the early 1900s.

At independence in 1965 many doubted whether this new country could survive. The soil was poor, the climate humid and the river Gambia, which often flooded, was lined with swamps and salt marshes. Nevertheless, peanuts and cotton were grown successfully and today most Gambians live by basic farming. Tourism is now helping to boost the economy.

Gambia has had its political problems. These include a rebellion in 1981, the failure of a close union with Senegal, which lasted from 1982 until 1989, and a military coup in 1994. However, it has been more peaceful than many other West African countries.

▲ The Gambian capital, Banjul, was called Bathurst in the colonial period. It is built on St Mary's Island, which lies in the mouth of the river Gambia.

▼ Women cultivate rice along the river Gambia. Rice grows well in river valleys, but it is not really grown as a commercial crop. Local women grow it to feed their own families.

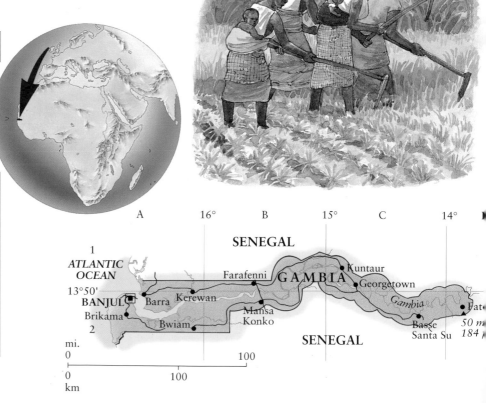

FACTS AND FIGURES
Area: 11,290 sq km
Population: 1,026,000
Capital: Banjul (45,000)
Other major city: Farafenni (11,000)
Highest point: In the east (50 m)
Official language: English
Main religion: Islam
Currency: Dalasi
Main exports: Peanuts and peanut products, fish and fish products, hides, palm-oil
Government: Military regime
Per capita GNP: US $390

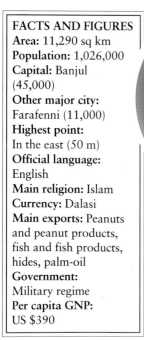

SENEGAL

ATLANTIC OCEAN

Farafenni   Kuntaur
GAMBIA   Georgetown
13°50'   Gambia
BANJUL   Barra   Kerewan
Brikama   Mansa   Basse
Bwiam   Konko   Santa Su

SENEGAL

A   16°   B   15°   C   14°

mi.
0   100

0   100
km

50 m
184

CAPE VERDE ISLANDS

▼ *Santa Antão Island has a rugged landscape and walking is the only way of getting about. Small, terraced fields are carved out of the steep mountainsides, where coffee, beans, maize and tomatoes are grown.*

This group of tropical islands rises steeply out of the Atlantic Ocean, about 500 kilometres off Senegal. The land is rocky, hot and dry and there is an active volcano on Fogo Island.

Nobody lived on the islands until the Portuguese arrived around 1460. They settled and established sugar and cotton plantations, which were worked by slaves brought from the African mainland. The islands grew rich from trading in slaves. Many slaves were trained in Cape Verde before being shipped to the Americas. When this trade declined, during the 1600s, Cape Verde sank into poverty and the islanders were left to scrape a living from fishing and farming.

Today the people are of mixed African and Portuguese descent. Most farm the land. Others mine volcanic rock for the cement industry or work in Praia, an important seaport. However, there is not enough work and many people have left to find jobs in Portugal or Brazil.

Cape Verde became independent from Portugal in 1975 and by 1981 was a one-party state. There were hopes for a union with Guinea-Bissau, but terms could not be agreed and the plan was dropped. In 1991 Cape Verde held its first multi-party elections and a party called the MPD won a majority.

SPEAK CRIOULO

Hello – Alo *(a - lo)*

Goodbye – Tchau *(chow)*

How are you? – C'me bo' sta? *(ca - ma bos - ta)?*

FACTS AND FIGURES
Area: 4,030 sq km
Population: 395,000
Capital: Praia (62,000)
Other major city:
Mindelo on São Tiago (47,000)
Highest point:
Pico (2,829 m)
Official language:
Portuguese
Main religion:
Christianity
Currency:
Cape Verde escudo
Main exports: Fish, salt, bananas
Government:
Multi-party republic
Per capita GNP:
US $850

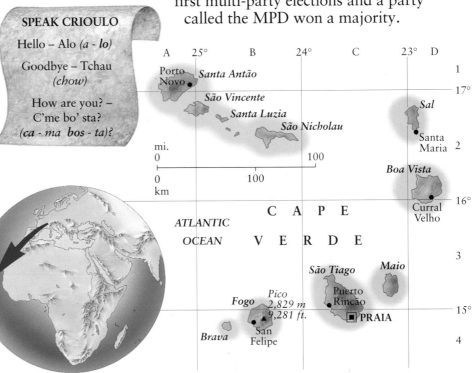

GUINEA-BISSAU

A ship approaching Guinea-Bissau from the Atlantic Ocean would first come to the Bijagós Archipelago, a chain of green islands covered in tropical forest. The curve of Africa's west coast would soon appear on the horizon, fringed with mangroves and mudflats and divided by wide river-mouths. The rivers Cacheu, Corubal and Geba lead into the interior, where coastal swamps and forests rise to open savanna, shimmering in the heat.

Various African peoples were living in this region for centuries before Europeans arrived in the 1400s and started to turn it into a base for trading in slaves. From 1879 the territory was ruled by Portugal, but the local people were fiercely independent and there were many wars. During the 1950s the fight for independence began in earnest.

The small population consists of 20 different ethnic groups, including the Balante, the Fulani and the Malinke. Some people are partly of Portuguese origin and Portuguese is the official language. Many people speak a dialect called *Crioulu* (a mix of local African languages and Portuguese).

Guinea-Bissau was declared an independent republic in 1974. This was a one-party socialist state, but in the 1990s the government approved the introduction of multi-party democracy.

▲ *Cotton plants grow well in Guinea-Bissau's tropical climate and heavy summer rains. The plants produce round bolls, which contain the soft white fibres used to make cotton fabric.*

▲ *Schoolchildren in Bissau, the capital, line up for a class picture. Educational facilities have improved since independence in 1974.*

FACTS AND FIGURES	
Area: 36,120 sq km	**Main religions:** Islam, Christianity, traditional beliefs
Population: 1,028,000	**Currency:** Guinea-Bissau peso
Capital: Bissau (125,000)	**Main exports:** Fish, peanuts, coconuts
Highest point: In southeast (123 m)	**Government:** Multi-party republic
Official language: Portuguese	**Per capita GNP:** US $210

GUINEA

FACTS AND FIGURES
Area: 245,860 sq km
Population: 6,306,000
Capital: Conakry (706,000)
Highest point: Mt Nimba (1,752 m)
Official language: French
Main religions: Islam, traditional beliefs
Currency: Guinean franc
Main exports: Bauxite, alumina, fruit, diamonds, coffee, hides
Government: Multi-party republic
Per capita GNP: US $510

"We prefer poverty in liberty to wealth in slavery," said Sékou Touré, who became the first president of an independent Guinea in 1958. Guinea remains poor, although huge reserves of bauxite and diamonds promise future wealth. Most Guineans are farmers. The largest group of people is the Fulani, who live on the dry central plateau. The Malinke people inhabit the savanna of Upper Guinea and the Susu people live on the swampy coast. Forest-clad mountains rise in the southeast.

People have lived in this region since prehistoric times. During the Middle Ages Guinea was ruled by various African empires. Europeans then began to arrive and by the 1600s were shipping Guineans off to the Americas as slaves. The country was governed by France from 1891 until 1958. Sékou Touré's presidency failed to improve living standards and a military government headed by Colonel Lansana Conté took over when Touré died in 1984. The first multi-party election was held in 1993 and returned Conté to power.

▲ A trader balances a tall stack of bread on her head. Most Guineans wear national dress. Cotton wraps are comfortable and cool in the steamy climate.

▼ Rural huts are made from readily available materials – sun-dried mud (adobe) and palm leaves. They are cheap to build and cool to live in.

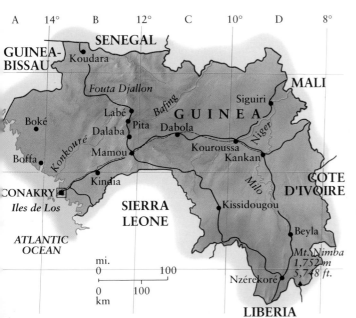

SIERRA LEONE

Sierra Leone means 'Lion Mountains'. Its harsh terrain and humid climate make farming difficult, yet the land holds priceless treasure. Huge deposits of valuable diamonds, bauxite and iron ore bring some wealth to this small independent country on Africa's west coast.

In the 1500s Europeans shipped many of the people who lived in the area to the Americas, for a brutal life working on plantations. In 1787 an Englishman called Granville Sharp founded Freetown, now Sierra Leone's capital, as a settlement for freed slaves. Britain made the trade in humans illegal in 1807 and many freed slaves returned from Europe and the Americas to settle here.

In 1808 the Sierra Leone peninsula became a British colony and soon British rule spread inland. The country became independent in 1961. The descendants of freed slaves, the Creoles, still live near Freetown and speak Krio, a dialect of English. They are far outnumbered by peoples who have always lived here, the Mende in the south and the Temne in the west. Since independence there have been periods of military and single-party rule.

▲ *A Mende woman sings to the rhythm of a traditional gourd rattle.*

FACTS AND FIGURES

Area: 73,330 sq km
Population: 4,494,000
Capital: Freetown (470,000)
Other major city: Bo (26,000)
Highest point: Loma Mansa (1,948 m)
Official language: English

Main religions: Traditional beliefs, Islam, Christianity
Currency: Leone
Main exports: Bauxite, rutile, cocoa, coffee, diamonds, ginger
Government: Single-party republic
Per capita GNP: US $170

◀ *The streets of Freetown present a typical West African scene. Beneath the mosque are market stalls, shared taxi wagons and colourfully dressed crowds.*

LIBERIA

A 10° B 8° C

GUINEA

SIERRA
LEONE

Moro Mano

Belle Yella

St. Paul

Bong Range

Totota

St. John

MONROVIA

Buchanan

Cess

L I B E R I A

COTE
D'IVOIRE

1,380 m
4,528 ft.

Cavally

Duobé

Putu Range

Dabwe

Cavally

mi.
0   50
ATLANTIC
OCEAN
0   50
km

Greenville

Harper

Sierra Leone

Liberia

SPEAK MENDE

Hello – Buwa
(boo - wah)

Goodbye – M'aalor
(ma - loh)

Please – Koneleh
(koh - na - lay)

▼ *Billboards in Monrovia
reflect a troubled history.
Liberia is torn by tensions
between rich and poor and
different ethnic groups.*

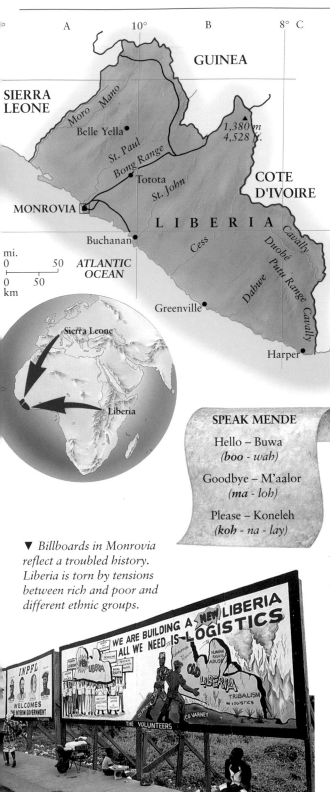

Liberia means 'Freed land'. Monrovia, now the capital of this country, was established in 1822 when the American Colonization Society began a settlement for freed slaves. The people that already lived in Liberia were probably descended from settlers who arrived from the north between the 1100s and 1500s. Trouble soon grew up between the descendants of the freed slaves, who became wealthy and powerful, and the larger and poorer native population. William Tubman, the president from 1944 to 1971, tried to resolve these tensions, but they led to a period of civil war that lasted from 1980 into the 1990s.

In this steamy country, the coastal plain rises to a mountainous interior covered in forest and crossed by rivers. Half the people live in villages of mud huts. The other half live in towns, in modern homes or in wooden houses with tin roofs. Many townswomen travel to rural areas each day to work on small farms growing cassava, rice and sugar-cane or raising poultry and pigs. Other people work with modern machinery on rubber plantations owned by foreign companies.

FACTS AND FIGURES

Area: 99,070 sq km
Population: 2,640,000
Capital: Monrovia (425,000)
Other major city: Buchanan (24,000)
Highest point: In the northeast (1,380 m)
Official language: English

Main religions: Christianity, Islam
Currency: Liberian dollar
Main exports: Iron ore, rubber, timber, coffee, cocoa, palm-oil, diamonds, gold
Government: Republic
Per capita GNP: Est. under US $700

COTE D'IVOIRE

Côte d'Ivoire (Ivory Coast) was named in the 1480s when sailors from France first came to the area to trade goods for ivory. They would have sailed past the cliffs of the western coast to the beaches and lagoons of the east. Inland lay tropical rainforests that stretched for hundreds of kilometres before rising to the central highlands and northern savanna. Today much of the country's landscape remains almost unchanged. The majority of the people still live in small villages and work the land, just as they have done for many centuries. Since the 1960s, however, an increasing number have moved to the towns and cities.

The ancient African kingdoms of peoples such as the Baoulé, Anyi, Dyula and Bambara had flourished in this area before the French arrived. Wars and the slave trade weakened the African peoples and in 1893 the region became a French colony. The French developed coffee and cocoa plantations, which helped Côte d'Ivoire to become the richest region in French West Africa.

The country's economy depended almost totally on coffee and cocoa exports until 1960, when Côte d'Ivoire became independent. Under Félix Houphouët-Boigny the range of exports widened and money poured into the country, making it the centre of business and industry that it is today. In the 1990s there were successful demands for a multi-party government and Houphouët-Boigny was elected president. He died in 1993 and was replaced by Henri Konan Bedié.

FACTS AND FIGURES
Area: 322,460 sq km
Population: 13,397,000
Capital: Abidjan (2,534,000)
Other major cities: Bouaké (390,000), Yamoussoukro (120,000)
Highest point: Mt Nimba (1,752 m)
Official language: French
Main religions: Islam, Christianity, traditional beliefs
Currency: Franc CFA
Main exports: Cocoa, coffee, petroleum products, timber, fruit
Government: Multi-party republic
Per capita GNP: US $670

ENDANGERED WORLD

African elephants are at risk because of the ivory trade.

◀ *Sticky latex oozes out of a rubber tree as the bark is slit. This process is called tapping. The liquid latex is collected and then processed to make natural rubber, one of Côte d'Ivoire's important products.*

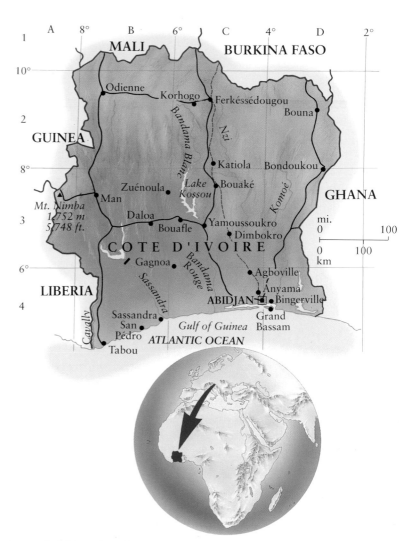

▲ *The capital's skyline rises beyond the palm-fringed pool of a luxury hotel. Abidjan has a successful tourism industry and is a prosperous trade centre.*

▼ *This 158-metre-high Roman Catholic cathedral is at Yamoussoukro. The Basilica of Our Lady of Peace was completed in 1989. Millions of dollars had been spent building it.*

GHANA

Ghana was called the 'Gold Coast' by the first European traders because they found so much gold here. Soon the Europeans were not just trading in gold, but in human lives. For hundreds of years countless Africans died in misery as they were sent to work as slaves in the Americas. When slavery came to an end in the 1800s the British took control of coastal trade and invaded the lands of the Ashanti people. There were fierce wars until the whole region came under British rule. The new rulers brought wealth to Ghana through cocoa exports. However, most native Ghanaians did not profit from this trade.

In 1957, after a rebellion, Ghana became independent. The new leader was Kwame Nkrumah, a man with a vision of a new, united Africa. Many thought he became too powerful and he was overthrown in 1966. Periods of both civilian and military rule followed. Having seized power during the 1970s and 1980s, Flight Lieutenant Jerry Rawlings was voted in as president in national elections in 1992.

Northern Ghana is a dusty grassland, where the dry season lasts from November until March. To the southwest rivers flow through rainforests to the hot, sticky coast on the Gulf of Guinea. Most Ghanaians live in the south and belong mainly to the Ashanti and Fante groups, who were among the earliest peoples to settle in Ghana.

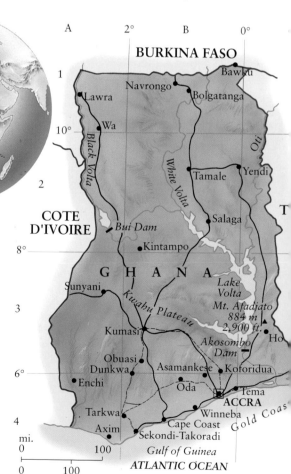

▲ *Small brass figures were made by Ashanti metalworkers in the 1700s. They were used for weighing gold. Other weights were decorated with bold patterns.*

FACTS AND FIGURES

Area: 238,537 sq km
Population: 16,446,000
Capital: Accra (868,000)
Other major cities: Kumasi (377,000), Sekondi-Takoradi (94,000)
Highest point: Mt Afadjato (884 m)
Official language: English

Main religions: Christianity, Islam, traditional beliefs
Currency: Cedi
Main exports: Cocoa, gold, timber, bauxite manganese, diamonds
Government: Military regime
Per capita GNP: US $450

◄ Many Ashanti traditions, such as this celebration, date back to the 1700s when their kingdom became powerful through trading in gold and slaves.

▼ Akosombo Dam on the river Volta has created Lake Volta, which spills across a vast area of central Ghana. The dam provides electricity for the countries of Togo and Benin as well as for Ghana.

OKRA STEW
Okra is a popular West African vegetable. When it is cooked in soups and stews it becomes smooth and sticky. In Ghana it is cooked with prawns, saltfish, meat and vegetables such as aubergines and tomatoes.

◄ Dense rainforest covers parts of southwestern Ghana. Here a termite mound towers above lush forest plants. Millions of termites may live in such a mound and can destroy crops. Other termites feed on wood and cause great damage to buildings.

185

TOGO

For 400 years, from when Portuguese explorers arrived in the 1400s until the 1800s, Togo was caught up in the slave trade and so earned the name 'Coast of Slaves'. German missionaries and traders arrived in the mid-1800s and Germany gradually took over Togo. During World War I the country was occupied by Britain and France. The area that Britain controlled was called British Togoland and became part of the Gold Coast (now Ghana) in 1956. French Togoland became independent Togo in 1960. The following years saw rivalry between the north and the south and periods of military rule. Multi-party elections held in 1993 were won by President Eyadéma, but his regime was soon replaced by opposition parties.

This small, narrow country stretches inland from the sweltering coast of the Gulf of Guinea. From the swamps and lagoons of the south, a plateau rises to the central mountains. Beyond these, lie dry grasslands, in the north.

About half of Togo's export wealth comes from mining phosphates, but most of the population works on small farms owned by groups of families. They grow yams, maize and cassava. The main peoples are the Ewe, Mina and Kabre. Many came to this region as long ago as the Middle Ages, fleeing from wars in neighbouring countries.

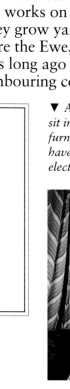

FACTS AND FIGURES

Area: 56,780 sq km
Population: 3,885,000
Capital: Lomé (500,000)
Highest point: Bauman Peak (983 m)
Official language: French

Main religions: Christianity, Islam, traditional beliefs
Currency: Franc CFA
Main exports: Phosphates, cotton, coffee, cocoa
Government: Multi-party republic
Per capita GNP: US $400

▼ A Togolese family sit in their simply furnished home. They have one luxury – an electric fan.

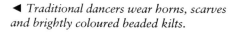

◄ Traditional dancers wear horns, scarves and brightly coloured beaded kilts.

BENIN

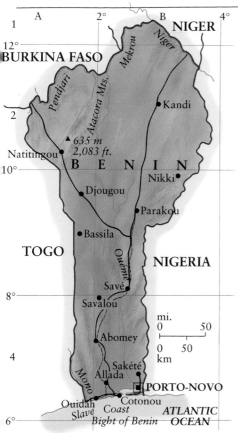

Togo's twin, on the great bulge of the West African coastline, is Benin (called Dahomey until 1975). Its new name was taken from a West African kingdom centred in the Nigerian rainforests during the 1500s. About 60 different peoples live there today.

Like Togo, Dahomey was ravaged by the slave trade from the 1600s onwards, when Europeans first arrived here. During the 1800s palm-oil became more important for trade than slaves and the French established coastal trading posts. Dahomey became a French colony in 1904 and France remains its main trading partner.

The years after independence in 1960 were chaotic, with control being tossed between civilian governments and the army. From 1972 Benin followed communist policies under the military leadership of Mathieu Kérékou. He was defeated by Nicéphore Soglo in the country's first ever democratic elections in 1991.

In the south, sandy beaches shield lagoons that give way to a highly populated belt of farmland called Terre de Barre, where much of the rainforest has been cleared. The central plateaus drain into the Ouémé River. In the northwest are the Atacora Mountains, where sheep and cattle are herded. The country has few natural resources, although there is offshore oil production. Cotton, palm-oil and cocoa are exported from Cotonou.

FACTS AND FIGURES
Area: 112,620 sq km
Population: 5,215,000
Capital: Porto-Novo (209,000)
Other major city: Cotonou (487,000)
Highest point: In the Atacora Mts (635 m)
Official language: French
Main religions: Traditional beliefs, Christianity, Islam
Currency: Franc CFA
Main exports: Petroleum, cotton, cocoa, sugar, palm-oil, peanuts, cement
Government: Multi-party republic
Per capita GNP: US $410

▲ *This bright wall hanging is in the traditional style. It shows a bull and local wildlife, including a chameleon, a snake and fruit bats.*

▶ *In the coastal lagoons villages of thatched huts may be built on stilts in the water. The fishermen and traders who live there travel to and fro in canoes.*

187

NIGERIA *Introduction*

▲ *This brass head is one of the treasures that have been found near Benin City. It is almost 500 years old.*

Among the small nations of the West African coast, Nigeria is a giant. More people live here than in any other African country. The profits from its huge oil reserves have helped to create large cities linked by a network of modern roads. In the 1970s the government decided to move its capital from Lagos, a sweltering, crowded seaport on the Bight of Benin, to a more central part of the country. The new capital was built at Abuja.

From ancient times Nigeria's position at the crossroads of Africa has made it a land of rich cultural heritage. Traders from the dry, central regions and the red, dusty plains of the north met the forest people that lived along the coast. They exchanged goods and ideas. Nigeria's archaeological treasures include Stone Age tools and sculptures from the Nok period (900BC-AD200).

Modern Nigeria also has a wide mix of very different peoples. There are over 250 ethnic groups, each with its own customs, traditions and languages. The government and schools use English, which was introduced during British rule. Most northerners are Muslims and most southerners are Christians, although others follow various traditional religions.

A land of so many varied cultures and peoples is never easy to unite. Nigeria has suffered from strife and civil war, corruption and many sudden changes of leadership. However, with its plentiful natural resources and the great energy of its people Nigeria has the basis for a bright future.

ENDANGERED WORLD

The African wild dog is in danger of being hunted to extinction in West Africa.

◄ *During the annual fishing festival at Argungu, north of Birnin Kebbi, fishermen armed with nets crowd into the river Rima to catch Nile perch.*

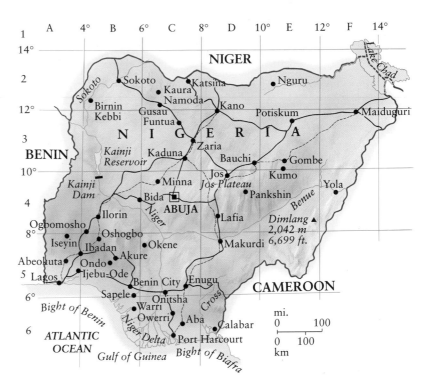

▲ The great river Niger winds through dense tropical forest before splitting up into a broad, swampy delta. It is Africa's third longest river.

▼ Kano is northern Nigeria's chief city. This sprawling town, with its baked mud buildings, is a centre for trading in hides and cotton.

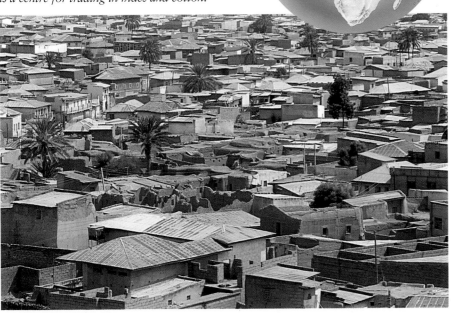

FACTS AND FIGURES
Area: 923,770 sq km
Population: 119,328,000
Capital: Abuja (306,000)
Other major cities: Lagos (1,347,000), Ibadan (1,295,000)
Highest point: Dimlang (2,042 m)
Official language: English
Main religions: Islam, Christianity, traditional beliefs
Currency: Naira
Main exports: Petroleum, cocoa, palm-oil, rubber, cotton, tin
Government: Military regime
Per capita GNP: US $320

NIGERIA *Geography and Economy*

Nigeria is one of the world's major oil producers. Its oilfields are operated by foreign companies, but Nigeria receives more than half the profits. Its wealth has risen and fallen along with world oil prices. Most of Nigeria's oil reserves lie in the south, where the mouths of the river Niger flow through an area of lagoons, creeks and mangrove swamps. Oil is refined at Port Harcourt, which also exports other major products, including palm-oil, peanuts and cacao. Factories and food processing plants are to be found in the big cities such as Ibadan and Lagos. Money from oil has been used to improve education, provide farmers with fertilizers and develop new industries. About half the population works in agriculture, using mainly traditional methods. Mining, especially for tin and coal, is the major growth industry.

▼ *At this market in Kano goats are sold for their milk, meat and skins. Many Nigerians make their living by herding goats, sheep or cattle.*

Two great rivers, the Niger and the Benue, carve a huge Y-shape through the country, which appears on Nigeria's national crest. They cross landscapes of immense variety, from swampy plains and lush palm forests to craggy rock. A band of flatlands stretches across the south, covered in steamy rainforest and rubber and cotton plantations. In the centre is the Jos Plateau, a high area of rocky outcrops and grasslands where cattle, goats and sheep graze. Branches of the river Niger, including the Sokoto, flow through the far northwest. Sometimes these rivers tumble from spectacular heights into deep gorges. During the rainy season they flood the land with fertile mud, occasionally washing away whole settlements of houses. In the far northeast lies the hot, sandy Chad basin, where long spells of drought allow only thorny scrub and spiky grass to grow.

▼ *Plantation workers use machetes to harvest the pods from cacao trees. Inside the pods are beans, which are roasted and husked, then processed to make cocoa and chocolate.*

▶ *Oil from fields such as this, in southern Nigeria, accounts for nearly all of the country's exports. Nigeria is investing in other industries, but oil will be its main source of wealth for many years.*

▲ The brown fruit of the oil-palm is processed at this plant. Palm-oil is exported for use in cooking and in making margarine and soap. The ripe fruits are pounded to remove the pulp. Then the palm kernels are pressed to extract the oil or soaked in vats so that the oil can be skimmed off.

▲ A community of mud huts roofed with palm thatch nestles on the Jos Plateau. This is an area of tin mining and dairy farming.

▶ Logs are lashed together for transportation down Nigeria's rivers. Forests of valuable tropical hardwoods cover about 15 percent of the country.

NIGERIA *People and History*

▼ *A vivid Yoruba painting conjures up several major aspects of Nigerian life – music, dance and the many creatures of the tropical forest.*

Nigeria is a country that is full of life. Each town has a busy market selling everything from soap powder to peanuts, while local pop music blares out in the background. Cycles and motor-bikes kick up dust along country roads and rutted tracks. Buses and taxis are jammed with passengers. Housing may be modern blocks of flats or traditional huts.

The ancestors of modern Nigerians have lived in this region for thousands of years. The three main peoples are the Hausa, Yoruba and Ibo. The Hausa live mainly in the north, farming and trading. The Yoruba, in the southwest, founded the port of Lagos hundreds of years ago and are mainly farmers or city workers. The Ibo, from the southeast, hold many of the jobs in business and government.

From around AD1000 powerful African states such as Benin, Kanem-Borno and Songhai ruled parts of Nigeria. Europeans first came to the coast about 500 years ago and traded in slaves until 1808. Then the British abolished slavery and began to trade in palm-oil. British traders seized more and more territory and by 1914 Nigeria had become a British colony. When independence came in 1960, conflict between Nigeria's ethnic groups erupted into rioting. From 1967 until 1970 a civil war was fought over the eastern part of the country, which had declared itself the independent Republic of Biafra. Recent decades have been dominated by military rule, although there have been strong moves towards democracy.

CHIN CHIN
Chin chin are small pastry balls flavoured with sugar and spices. Green or pink food colouring is sometimes added. They are a popular party snack, enjoyed with palm wine. *Chin chin* may also be served at weddings and birthday feasts.

▶ *This palace belongs to an emir, a Muslim leader. The emirs' power dates from the 1800s, when the north was mostly under Muslim rule.*

DJIBOUTI

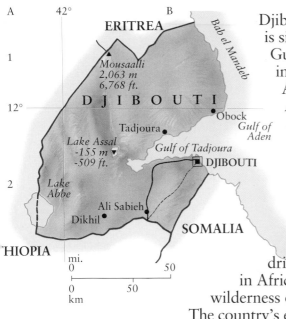

Djibouti is named after its capital city. This major port is situated on important shipping routes between the Gulf of Aden and the Red Sea. Before independence in 1977, the country was called the Territory of the Afars and Issa, after its two groups of peoples. The Afar people were converted to Islam in the AD800s and fought several wars against their Christian neighbour, Ethiopia. The Issa people, also Muslims, moved into the south of the Afars' territory from what is now Somalia.

In the past most of Djibouti's people were nomads, herding sheep, goats, camels and cattle in the deserts and mountains. Many still live this way, surviving in one of the hottest, driest and harshest landscapes in Africa. Djibouti is mainly a wilderness of scrub and rock. The country's economy is mostly dependent on shipping. Djibouti has been the chief port for trade with Ethiopia since it was built by French colonists in the 1800s. The hardships of nomadic life have encouraged increasing numbers of Afars and Issas to leave the countryside and seek work in the port. Many go even farther, finding jobs in countries such as Saudi Arabia.

FACTS AND FIGURES
Area: 23,200 sq km
Population: 481,000
Capital: Djibouti (317,000)
Highest point: Mousaalli (2,063 m)
Official languages: Arabic, French
Main religions: Islam, Christianity
Currency: Djibouti franc
Main exports: Hides, livestock, coffee in transit from Ethiopia
Government: Multi-party republic
Per capita GNP: Est. US $700-$3,000

◄ *A boat passes between islands made of salt on Lake Assal in central Djibouti, the lowest place in Africa. The islands form when the lake's salty water evaporates in the hot sun, leaving a salt crust.*

193

ETHIOPIA *Introduction*

Ethiopia is a hot and mountainous country with all kinds of wildlife, including giraffes, leopards, antelopes, elephants, rhinoceroses, lions and baboons. The central region consists of a high, rocky plateau which covers about two thirds of the country. It is mainly rich, fertile grassland rising to craggy peaks. This plateau is split in two by the Great Rift Valley, a long scar in the Earth's crust that stretches all the way from Syria southwards to Mozambique. The highlands are the coolest part of the country and this is where the majority of Ethiopia's farming takes place. The lowland regions that circle the plateau are hot and dry, giving way to scorching deserts along the Djibouti border.

Most Ethiopians are farmers in the highlands and live in round, wooden houses with conical, thatched roofs. They use wooden ploughs pulled by oxen to prepare the land for sorghum, teff and maize, which are the main food grains. Crops that are grown for sale or export include coffee, oil-seeds, pulses and sugar-cane. Many farmers struggle to survive because of the severe droughts that plague this hot, dusty country.

A number of different peoples live within Ethiopia's borders. Between them they speak about 80 different languages and dialects. The peoples fall into two main language groups. The Semites live in northern and central parts of the country and include the Amhara and Tigre. The Cushites live mainly in southern and eastern areas.

FACTS AND FIGURES
Area: 1,157,600 sq km
Population: 56,900,000
Capital: Addis Ababa (1,700,000)
Other major cities: Dire Dawa (99,000), Nazret (77,000)
Highest point: Ras Dashen (4,620 m)
Official language: Amharic
Main religions: Christianity, Islam, traditional beliefs
Currency: Ethiopian birr
Main exports: Coffee, hides, pulses, oil-seeds
Government: Republic
Per capita GNP: US $110

◀ *The Blue Nile thunders over Tisissat Falls, producing one of Africa's most dramatic sights. The Blue Nile is called river Abay in Ethiopia. It begins in Lake Tana and drains the western side of the central plateau, carving spectacular deep gorges into the rock.*

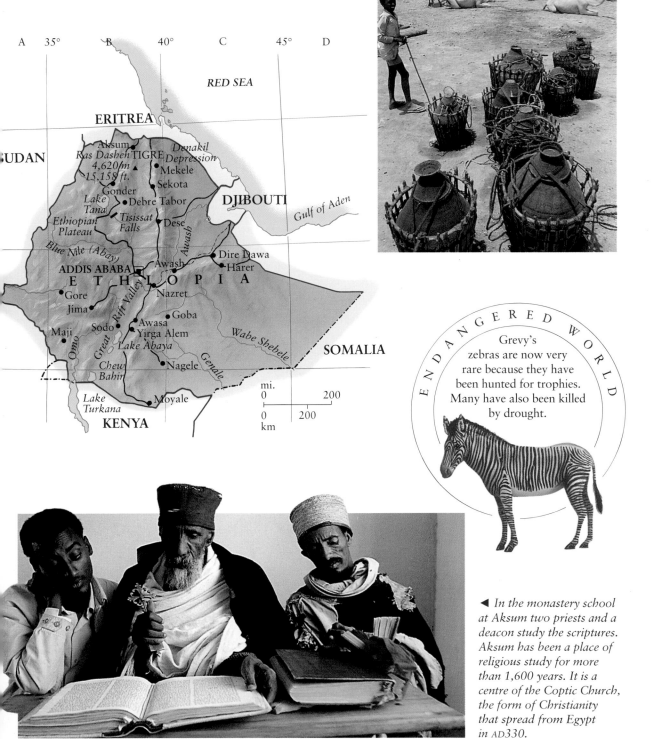

▶ A boy guards jars of precious water while the camels in the background remain thirsty. In this region of drought careful control of the water supply is vital.

RED SEA

ERITREA

SUDAN

Aksum
Ras Dashen TIGRE
4,620m ▲
15,158 ft.
Gonder
Lake Tana
Debre Tabor
Ethiopian Plateau
Tisissat Falls
Blue Nile (Abay)
ADDIS ABABA
E T H I O P I A
Gore
Jima
Maji
Sodo
Awasa
Yirga Alem
Lake Abaya
Chew Bahir
Lake Turkana
Omo
Great Rift Valley

Danakil Depression
Mekele
Sekota

DJIBOUTI
Gulf of Aden

Awash
Dire Dawa
Harer
Nazret
Goba
Wabe Shebele
Nagele
Genale

SOMALIA

Moyale

mi.
0   200

0   200
km

KENYA

ENDANGERED WORLD
Grevy's zebras are now very rare because they have been hunted for trophies. Many have also been killed by drought.

◀ In the monastery school at Aksum two priests and a deacon study the scriptures. Aksum has been a place of religious study for more than 1,600 years. It is a centre of the Coptic Church, the form of Christianity that spread from Egypt in AD330.

ETHIOPIA *People and History*

Ethiopia has one of the oldest civilizations in Africa. Legends say that Menelik, the son of King Solomon and the Queen of Sheba, ruled here around 1000BC. A powerful and prosperous Arab nation called Aksum had grown up by AD100. In AD330 it became Christian and from the Middle Ages onwards Ethiopia was ruled by Christian emperors. During the 1800s, while the rest of Africa was ruled by various other countries, Ethiopia managed to hold on to its independence. Although Italy succeeded in driving Emperor Haile Selassie out of Ethiopia in the 1930s, he later returned to become one of Africa's best known leaders.

By the 1970s Haile Selassie had become unpopular. People demanded better living conditions and accused the government of corruption. After an army mutiny, strikes and student demonstrations, Haile Selassie was overthrown in 1974. Years of military rule, uprisings and regional wars followed. While unrest spread across the country, Ethiopia suffered terrible droughts in which thousands died. The situation was made worse by refugees pouring into Ethiopia to escape civil war in southern Sudan. There were also rebel uprisings in the Ogaden and Eritrea, provinces that wanted independence from Ethiopia.

By the 1990s peace had been restored and the Ethiopians were able to grow their own food again. However, drought continued to be a problem and made many farmers desperately poor. Large numbers left rural areas for modern towns such as Addis Ababa to live in high-rise apartment buildings and work in factories producing cement, textiles or processed food.

BEG WOT

Beg wot is a thick stew made with red meat, tomatoes and chilli peppers. Here it is ringed with aubergine slices and served with green basil leaves on a bed of *injera* bread. This slightly sour tasting flat bread is used as both a food scoop and a communal plate.

▼ *Gonder's first palace was built for Emperor Fasilidas in 1633. Gonder was Ethiopia's capital from the early 1600s to 1892.*

ERITREA

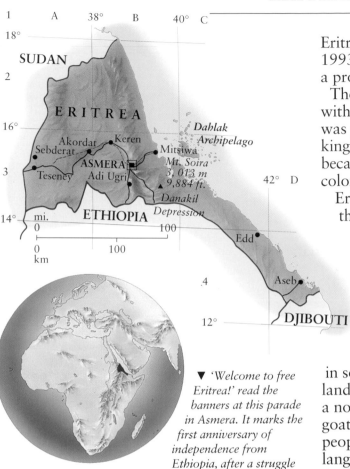

Eritrea became an independent country in 1993, after a long guerrilla war. It had been a province of neighbouring Ethiopia.

The history of this land has been linked with Ethiopia since the AD300s, when it was part of the powerful ancient Ethiopian kingdom of Aksum. More recently Eritrea became first an Italian and then a British colony, rejoining Ethiopia in 1952.

Eritrea is a small country on the coast of the Red Sea. Most of its land is covered in mountains and desert. The narrow coastal plain includes some of the hottest places on Earth. In the port city of Mitsiwa the average annual temperature is a scorching, hot 31 degrees centigrade. In this harsh landscape growing food is not easy, but irrigation projects have helped in some areas. Only five percent of the land is cultivated and many Eritreans live a nomadic life, herding sheep, cattle and goats. The country has a rich mix of peoples who speak several different languages, including Tigrinya and Saho. Arabic is also commonly spoken.

▼ 'Welcome to free Eritrea!' read the banners at this parade in Asmera. It marks the first anniversary of independence from Ethiopia, after a struggle that started in 1962.

FACTS AND FIGURES
Area: 93,680 sq km
Population: 3,500,000
Capital: Asmera (368,000)
Highest point: Mt Soira (3,013 m)
Principal language: Tigrinya
Main religions: Islam, Christianity
Main exports: Hides, cement, salt, gum arabic, citrus fruit
Government: Republic
Per capita GNP: Est. under US $700

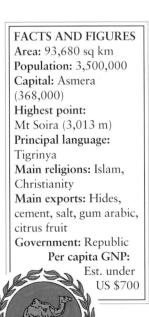

SOMALIA

Somalia is a hot, dry country. It lies on the Horn of Africa, the hook of land jutting out into the Gulf of Aden and the Indian Ocean. Most Somalis are nomads who live by herding camels, sheep and goats on the arid grasslands covering much of Somalia. In the south farmers grow crops such as bananas, citrus fruits and sugar-cane by the Jubba and Shabeelle rivers.

The country now called Somalia has a long history. It was on an important trading route between the Mediterranean Sea and the lands further east at the time of the ancient Egyptians. These people knew it as Punt. The northern part of the country was ruled by the British from 1884 and Italy controlled the southern part from 1905. These colonies were important because their ports lay on international shipping routes. They joined to become an independent single nation in 1960.

Somalia is a poor country and it suffered from severe drought in the 1970s and 1980s. Nomadic peoples faced starvation when their herds died and in 1974 the situation was made worse by war with Ethiopia. This war followed a rebellion by Somali-speaking Ethiopians in Ethiopia's Ogaden region. As different groups struggled to win political power, thousands of people were killed and wounded. Aid could no longer get through to people desperate for food. Between 1992 and 1995 United Nations troops attempted to restore order in Somalia, but unrest continued.

▲ *A Somali woman pours dough on to a griddle to make* anjeera. *This flat, unleavened bread is shaped like a pancake and eaten with stew.*

SPEAK SOMALI

Hello – Iska warran
(**skah** wah - **run**)

Goodbye – Nabad Galyo
(**nab** - ad **gal** - yoh)

Please – Fadlan (**fad** - lan)

Thank you – Mahadsanid
(**mah** - had - **san** - id)

Yes – Haa (**hah**)

No – Maya (**my** - ah)

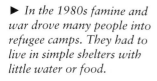

► *In the 1980s famine and war drove many people into refugee camps. They had to live in simple shelters with little water or food.*

◀ *Children study the Koran at Baardheere, a town on the Jubba River. Arab traders first brought Islam to Somalia during the 1000s and today most Somalis are Muslims.*

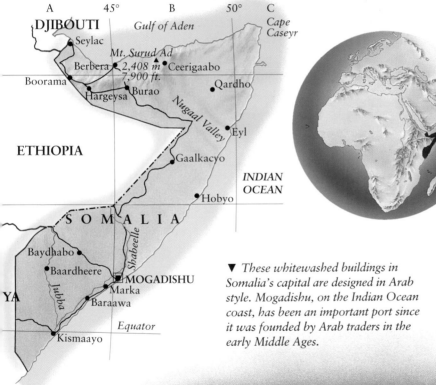

A   45°   B   50°   C

DJIBOUTI   Gulf of Aden   Cape Caseyr

Seylac

Mt. Surud Ad
Berbera 2,408 m Ceerigaabo
7,900 ft.
Boorama

Qardho

Hargeysa Burao

ETHIOPIA

Nugaal Valley

Eyl

Gaalkacyo

INDIAN
OCEAN

Hobyo

S O M A L I A

Baydhabo

Shabeelle

Baardheere

MOGADISHU

Marka

Jubba

Baraawa

Equator

YA

Kismaayo

200

200

▼ *These whitewashed buildings in Somalia's capital are designed in Arab style. Mogadishu, on the Indian Ocean coast, has been an important port since it was founded by Arab traders in the early Middle Ages.*

FACTS AND FIGURES

Area: 637,660 sq km
Population: 9,517,000
Capital: Mogadishu
(1,000,000)
Other major cities:
Hargeysa (400,000),
Kismaayo (200,000),
Marka (100,000)
Highest point:
Mt Surud Ad
(2,408 m)
Official languages:
Somali, Arabic
Main religion: Islam
Currency:
Somali shilling
Main exports: Bananas
and other fruit,
livestock, hides
Government:
Republic
Per capita GNP:
Est. under US $700

KENYA *Introduction*

▼ *Tourists on safari watch a family of elephants in one of Kenya's wildlife reserves. Many animal species have been hunted almost to extinction. The government is making an effort to protect them in several national parks.*

Visitors flying into Kenya's capital, Nairobi, find themselves in East Africa's most modern city. There are high-rise offices, rush-hour crowds and broad streets lined with jacaranda trees. Travellers who arrive in Kenya on a jolting truck from southern Sudan pass local Turkana people wearing traditional beads and waiting by desert truckstops. People who sail along the coast by dhow (a wooden boat with a triangular sail) can explore long beaches, mangrove swamps and ancient villages of white stone houses. By speeding into Kenya from Tanzania on a crowded *matutu* (minibus) travellers cross hot, rolling plains. Here and there are giraffes munching on the leaves of acacia trees, herds of elephants and galloping zebras. On a flight out of this country, Mount Kenya can be seen soaring above the clouds.

Kenya is one of the most beautiful countries in Africa. The low coastal plain with its thick tropical forests rises to a broad grassland plateau. In the north is a parched desert and to the west are the ancient volcanoes and craggy cliffs of the Great Rift Valley. Flocks of pink flamingoes wade through the shallows of Lake Turkana. Tourists are attracted by the wildlife and the scenery, the white beaches and the luxury hotels, but few see the other side of Kenya. There is very poor housing on the edge of Nairobi and labourers on coffee plantations and commercial farms are badly paid. Educational standards are high, but many people cannot find jobs. Unemployment increased when the country welcomed large numbers of refugees, who flooded in to escape the civil war in neighbouring Somalia.

▶ *Kenyan farmworkers lay out the sisal harvest to dry on racks in the sun. When dry, the fleshy leaves of the plant yield tough fibres that are used to make sacking, coarse rope, twine and matting.*

► *A worker picks tea leaves in the Kenyan highlands. The plateaus and hills in the southwest of the country have fertile soil. The relatively cool climate makes this area ideal for farming. Both tea and coffee are major export crops and are grown on large estates.*

FACTS AND FIGURES

Area: 582,650 sq km
Population: 28,113,000
Capital: Nairobi (1,104,000)
Other major cities: Mombasa (426,000), Kisumu (153,000), Nakuru (93,000)
Highest point: Mt Kenya (5,199 m)
Official language: Swahili
Main religions: Christianity, Islam, traditional beliefs
Currency: Kenya shilling
Main exports: Tea, coffee, fruit, vegetables, petroleum products
Government: Multi-party republic
Per capita GNP: US $330

► *The splendid Jamia Mosque is in the centre of Nairobi. Only six percent of the population is Muslim. However, there have been followers of the Islamic faith in Kenya since the AD700s, when Arab traders settled along the coast.*

201

KENYA *People and History*

The story of Kenya stretches back over millions of years. Some of the most ancient fossil remains of human beings have been discovered in the Great Rift Valley.

From the earliest days of seafaring Kenya's coast attracted traders. The Greeks, Romans, Arabs and Portuguese all built settlements here. In the 1740s much of the coast came under the control of Zanzibar Island. The Sultan of Zanzibar leased land to the British in 1895 and soon their influence spread inland. Kenya became known as British East Africa. Many British and other Europeans moved in and settled the highlands. They seized the territories of the Kikuyu and the Luo peoples in order to plant tea and coffee. The British used cheap African labour to build a railway and tend their plantations.

Kenyan discontent erupted from 1952 to 1959 in the terrorist rebellion of the Mau Mau, a secret Nationalist society. Thousands of Africans died. The British agreed to grant Kenya independence in 1963. The first president was Jomo Kenyatta, a leading African Nationalist. He and his successor, Daniel Arap Moi, improved Kenya's economy and did much to unite its peoples. Today there are about 50 different ethnic groups in Kenya, including the Kikuyu, Kalenjin and Luo. Some are nomadic herders, others have small farms or live by fishing. About one fifth are city-dwellers, working in offices, factories, schools or hospitals, or on construction sites.

▲ *This bottle has been made by a Kikuyu craftsman out of a gourd, a plant like a pumpkin. Kenyans are famed for their artistic skills.*

SPEAK SWAHILI

Hello – Jambo (*jam - boh*)

Goodbye – Kwaheri (*kwa - hair - ee*)

Please – Tafadhali (*ta - fah - tha - lee*)

Thank you – Asante (*a - san - tay*)

Yes – Ndio (*ndee - oh*)

No – Hapana (*ha - pah - na*)

◄ *Masai women wear bright cloth and beaded collars for a ceremony where their sons will become junior elders. Traditionally the Masai are cattle herders and many still live a semi-nomadic life just like their ancestors.*

▼ Today Fort Jesus, at the port of Mombasa, is a museum of Kenyan history. The Portuguese built it in 1593. Its strong, high walls defended the coastline they had seized from Arab traders early in the 1500s. It has also been used as a prison.

▲ A Kikuyu wears traditional dress at a ceremonial gathering. The Kikuyu people are the largest ethnic group in Kenya. They led the Mau Mau rebellion in the fight for independence.

▶ Moses Kiptanui, one of the greatest athletes on the flat and over hurdles, practises steeplechasing at home in Kenya. Training at high altitudes, where there is not so much oxygen, gives Kenya's long-distance runners enormously powerful lungs. It helps to make them the best athletes in the world.

TANZANIA *Introduction*

The snow-covered mass of Mount Kilimanjaro – Africa's highest mountain – looms high above northern Tanzania, close to the country's border with Kenya. To the west of Kilimanjaro are other natural wonders such as the Ngorongoro Crater, the centre of an ancient volcano inhabited only by elephants, rhinoceroses, hyenas and other wild animals. Vast herds of zebras, antelopes, wildebeests and the lions and cheetahs that prey on them roam the Serengeti Plains. Also many fossils have been found in the Olduvai Gorge, including human bones and tools that date back over a million years.

Tanzania is the largest country in East Africa. Most of it is on the African mainland, but there are also several islands, including Pemba and Zanzibar. These two islands are famed for the production of cloves and other spices. Zanzibar is the biggest coral island off the African coast.

Much of mainland Tanzania is wide open plains. It is very hot and dry with sparse grassland or patches of thorn and woodland. Clouds of dust mark the passing of cattle and their Masai herders. The climate is cooler in the mountainous areas in the north and south of the country. The south also has the huge Selous Wildlife Reserve, one of the largest game reserves in the world.

Tanzania's economy is based on agriculture, although two thirds of the land cannot be farmed because of lack of water and swarms of disease-carrying tsetse flies. The coastal region is fertile, producing bananas, mangoes, sisal and sugar-cane. Other important crops are coffee, tea, tobacco and cotton.

FACTS AND FIGURES
Area: 945,040 sq km
Population: 28,783,000
Capital: Dodoma (204,000)
Other major cities: Dar es Salaam (1,361,000), Mwanza (223,000)
Highest point: Mt Kilimanjaro (5,895 m)
Official languages: Swahili, English
Main religions: Islam, Christianity, traditional beliefs
Currency: Tanzanian shilling
Main exports: Coffee, cotton, sisal, cloves
Government: Single-party republic
Per capita GNP: US $110

ENDANGERED WORLD

The spectacular Kilimanjaro swallowtail butterfly is threatened by collectors and the clearance of its forest habitat.

◄ *Tanzanian workers melt down old metal to forge steel. Most of the steel produced by Tanzania's steel industry is made from recycled metal.*

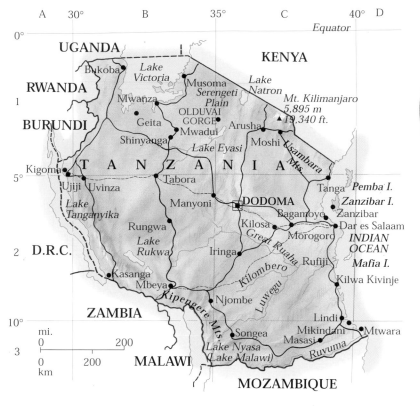

▼ Old stone houses, with beautifully carved doors, line the maze of narrow alleyways in the old town of Zanzibar. All the streets lead back to the waterfront, with its coconut palms and sailing dhows.

▲ The vast and impressive 2,878-metre volcano of Ol Doinyo Lengai rears up from the valley floor near Lake Natron in northern Tanzania. The volcano last erupted in 1967.

TANZANIA *People and History*

Tanzania is made up of two countries that joined together in 1964 – Tanganyika on the African mainland and the island country of Zanzibar. Its peoples are as varied as its scenery and wildlife. There are well over 100 ethnic groups. Although the different peoples have their own languages, most Tanzanians also speak Swahili.

During the early Middle Ages Arab traders settled along the coast of what is now Tanzania. They intermarried with the Africans who lived there, spreading the Muslim faith that is still practised by one third of Tanzania's people. The Swahili culture, a mixture of African and Arab traditions, was also developed. In the 1600s the sultans of Oman, a country on the Arabian peninsula, took control of Zanzibar. They planted cloves and traded in ivory and slaves brought from the east African interior.

Late in the 1800s Germany ruled Tanganyika, while Zanzibar came under British rule. After World War I the British governed both countries until the mainland gained independence in 1961. Zanzibar gained independence in 1963 and Tanzania was formed in 1964 by its first president, Julius Nyerere.

Unlike many other African countries, Tanzania has not suffered from ethnic violence. Although it is very poor, has undergone war with Uganda and endured serious economic problems, Tanzania has tried to solve the difficulties in its own way. Recently great efforts have been made to improve farming, healthcare and education. Today Tanzania has one of the highest literacy rates in Africa.

N'DIZI YA NA NYAMA
N'dizi ya na Nyama is a tasty stew made of beef, coconut milk, tomatoes and unripe bananas or plantains. A plantain is similar to a banana, but must be cooked before it is eaten. Bananas are widely grown in Tanzania and are often used in cooking.

◄ *Children celebrate at a Muslim wedding. Tanzanians follow Islam, Christianity and traditional African beliefs in about equal numbers.*

▶ *Porters carry fossilized brachiosaurus bones. They were among the 250 tonnes of dinosaur bones found at Tendaguru, just north of Lindi, between 1909 and 1913. The fossils were all shipped to the Berlin Museum in Germany.*

▲ *A Makonde carver works on a wooden sculpture. The Makonde people, who live on the coast and along the Mozambique border, are famed for their skill at wood carving.*

THE RUINS AT KILWA KISIWANI

The ruins of a mosque lie on the tiny island of Kilwa Kisiwani, near Kilwa Kivinje. Between the 1100s and the late 1400s this island was the most important Islamic centre on the Swahili coast. It was at the height of its power in the 1200s when Arab traders exported gold, ivory and hides to Arabia and India. The traders brought their Muslim faith and built beautiful mosques in the style typical of Arab architecture. The domes and arches were specially shaped so that the air inside the mosques remained cool and refreshing.

UGANDA

FACTS AND FIGURES
Area: 241,040 sq km
Population: 19,246,000
Capital: Kampala (774,000)
Other major cities:
Jinja (61,000),
Mbale (54,000),
Masaka (49,000)
Highest point:
Margherita Peak
(5,109 m)
Official language:
English
Main religions:
Christianity, Islam
Currency:
Uganda shilling
Main exports: Coffee,
cotton, tea, tobacco
Government:
Republic
Per capita GNP:
US $170

Most of Uganda is a large plateau stretching out between the highlands in the east and the Ruwenzori Mountains in the west. Its rich, red soil has been farmed for thousands of years and coffee, bananas, maize, millet and sweet potatoes all grow well in the equatorial climate. In regions where the land has not been cleared for farming there is thick, green forest. Only the northeast of the country is arid scrubland. Uganda is also a land of beautiful lakes, including Lake Victoria, the second largest freshwater lake in the world. From the lake various waterways feed into the great river system of the Nile.

Kingdoms such as Bunyoro and Buganda grew up on the Ugandan plateau from the 1300s onwards. Buganda became the richest and most powerful of these kingdoms and its people, the Ganda, are still the largest ethnic group in modern Uganda. In the late 1800s Buganda was united with Bunyoro, Ankole, Toro and Busoga as a British protectorate.

Since independence Uganda has had an unsettled history with many changes of government. The traditional kingdoms were abolished in 1967 and the country became a republic. Then, during the 1970s, General Idi Amin ruled Uganda as a dictator for nearly ten years. During this disastrous time Uganda's Asian community was expelled, businesses collapsed and Amin's political opponents were murdered. Amin was overthrown by an army of Tanzanians and Ugandan exiles in 1979. Since then a succession of civilian and military governments have worked to unite the country and repair its economy.

ENDANGERED WORLD
The forests where the mountain gorilla lives are being destroyed.

▶ *Giant lobelia plants grow high in the Ruwenzori Mountains, where snowy peaks rise from dense rainforests. The mountains lie on the Equator between Uganda and the Democratic Republic of Congo.*

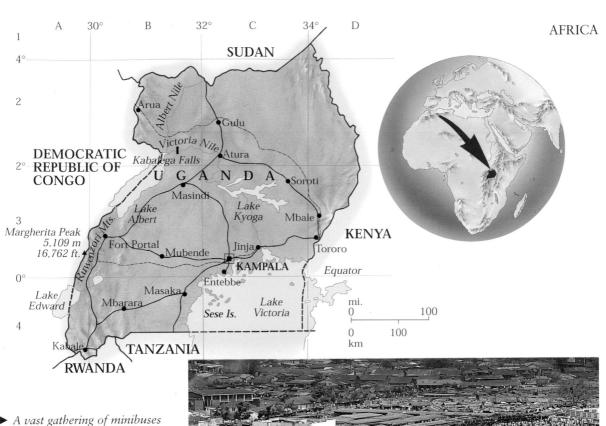

	A	30°	B	32°	C	34°	D

SUDAN

Arua

Albert Nile

Gulu

Victoria Nile

Kabalega Falls

Atura

U G A N D A

DEMOCRATIC
REPUBLIC OF
CONGO

Soroti

Masindi

Lake
Albert

Lake
Kyoga

Mbale

Margherita Peak
5,109 m
16,762 ft.

Fort Portal

Mubende

Jinja

KENYA

Tororo

KAMPALA

Equator

Ruwenzori Mts.

Entebbe

Lake
Edward

Mbarara

Masaka

Sese Is.

Lake
Victoria

mi.
0   100

0   100
km

Kabale

RWANDA

TANZANIA

► A vast gathering of minibuses parks in the market district of central Kampala, the capital of Uganda. These operate as shared taxis, taking passengers on local or long-distance rides. Now that the roads are being repaired after long years of war, they provide a better service than the railways.

◄ Cotton grown in Uganda is spun in a local factory. Uganda is developing its textile industry to increase the value of its exports. When sold abroad, the products of factories like this one will bring more money into the country than the raw cotton would have done.

RWANDA

Rwanda's villages cling to green, tropical hillsides. There are river valleys, grasslands and volcanoes with forested slopes. The country's forests are home to the rare mountain gorilla.

Most Rwandans belong to a group of people called the Hutu, but a minority of about ten percent are Tutsis. For hundreds of years the Tutsis held power while the Hutus were poor peasant farmers. In the late 1890s Ruanda-Urundi (Rwanda and its southern neighbour, Burundi) became first a German, then a Belgian colony.

When Rwanda became independent in 1962 the Hutus gained power and years of violence against the Tutsis followed. Many fled to neighbouring Burundi. There were also economic problems. Rwanda depended on its coffee exports and so it suffered in the 1980s when the world price of coffee fell sharply.

In 1994 the leaders of Rwanda and Burundi were killed in a plane crash, which was believed to have been caused by terrorists. Chaos followed as Hutu government troops fought the Tutsi rebels of the Rwandan Patriotic Front (RPF). By the time the RPF's victory ended the fighting, millions of innocent men, women and children had been killed and others had fled the country. A major international relief effort was needed to help the country recover from the effects of war.

▼ Rwandan refugees in Tanzania crowd around a water hole. This was the only source of water for 250,000 people who escaped the violence, but still risked hunger and disease.

FACTS AND FIGURES

Area: 26,340 sq km
Population: 7,789,000
Capital: Kigali (157,000)
Other major city: Butare (22,000)
Highest point: Mt Karisimbi (4,507 m)
Official languages: Kinyarwanda, French

Main religions: Christianity, Islam, traditional beliefs
Currency: Rwanda franc
Main exports: Coffee, tea, tin
Government: Military regime
Per capita GNP: US $250

BURUNDI

▲ *Tutsi dancers perform a ceremonial lion dance. Their plumed headdresses symbolize the lion's mane. The Tutsi people also live in Rwanda and Zaire.*

Most people in Burundi are farmers who herd goats and cattle or grow bananas, beans, maize and cassava. The country is small, but has a very large population for its size. Because of this, much of the land has been over-farmed. Heavy tropical rains have washed the soil from the mountain slopes, especially on the volcanic rocks of the west. In the centre and east are steep-sided plateaus rising from swamps. Burundi is close to the Equator, but its climate is cool and there are two wet seasons a year.

In colonial times Burundi and its neighbour Rwanda formed a single country called Ruanda-Urundi. Like Rwanda, Burundi has a Hutu majority and a Tutsi minority. The Tutsis have been the dominant group in Burundi since the 1400s. Another minority are the Twa, the country's earliest inhabitants. After Burundi became independent the Tutsis remained in control and there were Hutu uprisings. In 1993 democratic elections were held and Melchior Ndadaye, a Hutu, became president. Shortly afterwards he was assassinated. Violence broke out and thousands of refugees fled into Rwanda, Tanzania and Zaire. Politicians of all parties began to work towards a system that would protect the interests of all Burundi's people.

▶ *Red earth and lush, tropical plants form a typical central African landscape in Burundi's northwestern highlands. The fields belong to the small farms that crowd the country's mountain slopes.*

FACTS AND FIGURES

Area: 27,830 sq km
Population: 5,958,000
Capital: Bujumbura (236,000)
Highest point: Northeast of Bujumbura (2,700 m)
Official languages: Kirundi, French
Main religions: Christianity, traditional beliefs
Currency: Burundi franc
Main exports: Coffee, tea
Government: Military regime
Per capita GNP: US $210

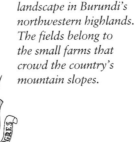

DEMOCRATIC REPUBLIC OF CONGO *Introduction*

From its narrow coastline on the Atlantic Ocean the Democratic Republic of Congo (DRC) broadens out into Africa's third largest country. It is crossed by the great river Congo, which forms the chief means of transport over the rugged terrain.

Northern DRC lies on the Equator. The humid, thundery climate supports the dense jungle of one of the world's last great rainforests and wildlife havens. Chimpanzees and monkeys chatter and swing among the trees. Colourful parrots flit through the high canopy of leaves. Crocodiles and hippopotamuses wallow in the rivers. The okapi, a forest animal related to the giraffe, is found only in DRC, and has become the country's national symbol. To the south lions, leopards and antelopes roam the open savannas. Large areas of land have been set aside by the DRC's government as national parks in which animals are protected. However, hunting has already endangered some species.

The raging river torrents in DRC's mountains offer massive hydroelectric potential, while the rocks conceal deposits of uranium and gold. DRC is a world leader in the production of copper, cobalt and industrial diamonds, but most people are subsistence farmers. Fish forms an important part of the people's diet, while pop music is one of the entertainments. The country's style of guitar playing, with singing in French or the Lingala language, has become world famous.

SPEAK LINGALA

Hello – Boni *(bo - nee)*

Goodbye – Kende malamu *(ken - day mal - a - moo)*

Please – Pardon *(par - don)*

Thank you – Botondi *(bo - ton - dee)*

Yes – Eh *(heh)*

No – Te *(tay)*

FACTS AND FIGURES
Area: 2,344,880 sq km
Population: 41,166,000
Capital: Kinshasa (2,796,000)
Other major cities: Lubumbashi (795,000), Mbuji-Mayi (625,000), Kananya (291,000)
Highest point: Margherita Peak (5,109 m)
Official language: French
Main religions: Christianity, Islam, traditional beliefs
Currency: Congo franc
Main exports: Copper, coffee, diamonds, cobalt, petroleum
Government: Single-party republic
Per capita GNP: Est. under US $700

◀ *From a bridge of tree trunks across the river Congo men fish with funnel-shaped traps. The traps are anchored to platforms on the riverbed.*

◀ *Hardwood trees grow in DRC's equatorial rainforest, which covers over half the country. It is so dense that little daylight reaches the forest floor.*

▶ *Women braid each other's hair into many tiny plaits, adding beads. These styles take hours to create. The tradition has spread to many other parts of the world.*

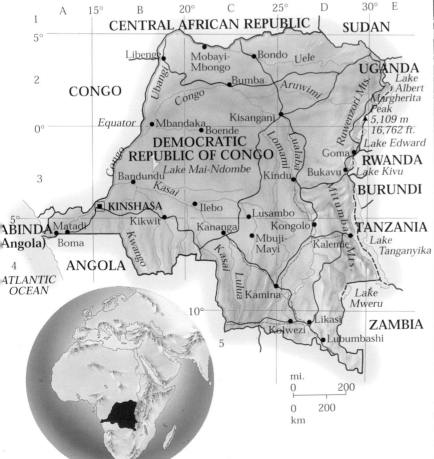

▲ *A roll of cloth is printed at a textile mill. Most women in the country wear a long cotton wrap decorated with bold patterns and bright colours or a blouse and long skirt.*

DEMOCRATIC REPUBLIC OF CONGO *People and History*

▲ *This carved mask is held over the face by Yaka boys during ceremonies that mark their passage to manhood. The Yaka people live in southern DRC.*

On some early European maps of Africa the centre of the continent, where DRC is, was left blank or marked with the words 'unknown land'. When European explorers eventually travelled up the river Congo in 1877 they found dense rainforest. Since prehistoric times the forest has been home to the Pygmies, who still live there today. The southern grassland was settled by ancestors of today's Kongo, Luba and Mongo peoples. These Bantu-speakers founded several powerful kingdoms. One of them, Kongo, was visited by Portuguese missionaries and explorers.

The Europeans saw this area as a source of wealth and many traders settled. They were followed by cruel slavers. In 1879 King Léopold II of Belgium declared the region his own personal property. International protests at the human misery caused by Léopold's rule led the Belgian government to take control. Belgium granted independence in 1960. This was followed by a violent struggle for power led by Patrice Lumumba. At the same time the rich southern copper-mining province of Katanga, now called Shaba, tried to break away from the new republic. The United Nations sent peace-keeping troops and the Belgians left.

In the 1970s, under President Mobutu, the country was named Zaire. Mobutu brought unity and a new national identity. Women began to find opportunities in jobs and education. However, Mobutu became corrupt and banned political opposition. In 1994 the country's economy was further burdened by a huge influx of refugees fleeing from the civil war in neighbouring Rwanda. In 1997, after years of civil war, Mobutu was deposed by rebels, who renamed the country the Democratic Republic of Congo.

▶ *Girls gather outside their missionary school in Kinshasa. Schools were set up by Roman Catholic missionaries during the 52 years of Belgian rule, but education did not become widespread until independence. Today around 75 percent of the country's children go to school.*

▼ The Mbuti Pygmies are forest dwellers and experts at hunting and gathering food. They call themselves bamiki ba'ndure, which means 'children of the forest'. Pygmies also work for neighbouring villages outside the forest and trade foods they have gathered for manufactured goods.

▲ A crowded river-boat travels down one of DRC's many waterways. This is the best way to cross DRC, a country with about 11,500 kilometres of navigable rivers. Roads are poor and often turn to mud in the rainy season.

▶ The former home of a Belgian colonialist falls into ruin. After independence in 1960 many Belgians stayed on as army officers and government officials. However, army mutinies and widespread violence finally forced them to flee the country.

CENTRAL AFRICAN REPUBLIC

Central African Republic (CAR) lies at the heart of the African continent. Its high plateau of grass and scattered trees rises to mountainous land on the Cameroon and Sudan borders. The northeast of the country is dry, but the forests of the southwest grow green and lush in the tropical rains.

In the rainy season roads often become a sea of mud, impassable to trucks. There are no railways, so rivers are used to transport goods. The main waterway is the river Ubangi, which flows south into the river Congo. All of CAR's borders are far from the sea, so exports bound for the coast must be taken through Congo by river-boat and train.

Diamonds are mined in CAR and there are some rubber and cotton plantations. The export of timbers, such as mahogany and obeche, is a recent development. Almost all the precious rainforest timber that is felled is used as fuel. Most people in CAR grow subsistence crops of cassava, bananas, maize and millet. Some supplement their diet by eating certain insects and caterpillars.

CAR's main trading partner is France, which ruled this part of equatorial Africa from the 1880s. In 1960 the country became independent. For 14 years it was ruled by Jean-Bedel Bokassa, who declared himself its emperor and lived in luxury while ordinary people went hungry. In 1979 he punished schoolchildren who did not wear expensive uniforms by throwing them into prison and having them killed. As a result he was removed from power. In 1993 the people chose a new leader in democratic elections.

FACTS AND FIGURES
Area: 622,440 sq km
Population: 3,258,000
Capital: Bangui (452,000)
Other major cities: Mbaiki (190,000), Bossangoa (120,000), Bouar (106,000)
Highest point: In the west (1,420 m)
Official language: French
Main religions: Christianity, traditional beliefs
Currency: Franc CFA
Main exports: Coffee, diamonds, timber, cotton, tobacco
Government: Multi-party republic
Per capita GNP: US $410

ENDANGERED WORLD

Chimpanzees are captured and exported to circuses, zoos and research laboratories all over the world.

▶ *At a busy market Sango people gather to sell tomatoes, peppers and okra (green pods with a sticky juice that are also called ladies' fingers). The market offers a chance to catch up with neighbours' news as well as to buy and sell home-grown produce.*

► Elisabeth Domitien, Central African Republic's (CAR's) first female prime minister greets President Giscard d'Estaing of France in 1975. Between them is Jean-Bedel Bokassa. Domitien was CAR's prime minister between 1975 and 1976.

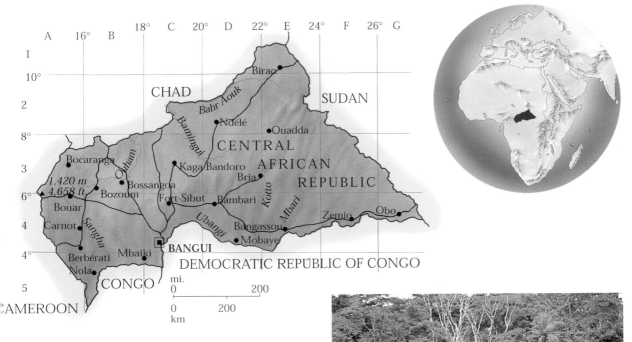

► A logger's truck travels the mud road that cuts through dense forest near Kongbo, north of Mobaye. Tree felling is a major industry in Central African Republic and the forests of the southwest are disappearing fast. There is, as yet, little awareness in this country of the threat that deforestation poses to the environment.

CAMEROON

A long arm of this West African country stretches right up to the marshes that border Lake Chad. To the south Cameroon broadens out, taking in savanna, tree-covered mountains, tropical forests and the palm-lined beaches of the Gulf of Guinea.

The people belong to many ethnic groups, including the Bamiléké, Fulani and Fang. Only a small proportion of the population works in industry. Most people make a living from farming. Maize, millet and yams are grown for home use and crops such as tobacco and peanuts are exported. As the population grows many rural families are moving to the cities, especially Yaoundé and Douala, in search of work.

In AD800 the Muslim empire of Kanem-Bornu was flourishing in this region. In the 1400s Portuguese explorers arrived and began to trade in ivory, rubber and slaves. They found crayfish in the Wouri River near Douala, but mistook them for shrimps. The country was named after the Portuguese word for shrimps, *camaroes*. Cameroon came under German rule in the late 1800s and early 1900s. From 1919 the French and British took control. Independence was gained in 1960 and the first multi-party elections were held in 1992.

▲ *Members of the Cameroon football team, stars of the 1990 World Cup competition, celebrate a goal scored against Italy. The highly skilled Cameroon team has become a favourite with international crowds.*

◀ *Cameroon's voodoo queens, who practise traditional spells and healing, sway during a ritual dance. Their faces are painted with clay. Belief in the spirit world is kept alive by many people in Cameroon.*

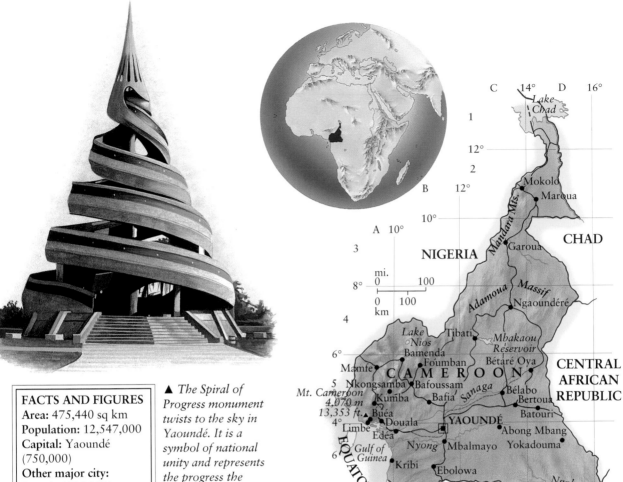

FACTS AND FIGURES

Area: 475,440 sq km
Population: 12,547,000
Capital: Yaoundé (750,000)
Other major city: Douala (884,000)
Highest point: Mt Cameroon (4,070 m)
Official languages: French, English
Main religions: Christianity, Islam, traditional beliefs
Currency: Franc CFA
Main exports: Crude oil, timber, cocoa, coffee, peanuts, bananas, cotton
Government: Single-party republic
Per capita GNP: US $820

▲ *The Spiral of Progress monument twists to the sky in Yaoundé. It is a symbol of national unity and represents the progress the nation has made since independence in 1960.*

▶ *The barren, lunar-like landscape of Roumsiki is in north Cameroon. Small volcanic eruptions formed the cones in the foreground. The eerie backdrop was created by weather erosion.*

EQUATORIAL GUINEA

Just north of the Equator, the Atlantic coast of Africa takes a great sweep westwards. This is the extremely hot and humid Gulf of Guinea. Its waters are fed by heavy rainstorms and muddy rivers. Equatorial Guinea consists of a mainland region called Mbini, where the majority of the people live, and five islands. By far the largest of the islands is Bioko. Here, near the volcanic slopes of Santa Isabel Mountain, is Equatorial Guinea's capital, Malabo.

Both Mbini and Bioko Island have coastal plains and dense rainforests. The country's main food crops are cassava, bananas and sweet potatoes. Most people live by fishing and farming. Life is hard because much of the soil is poor quality and harvests are often small.

It is likely that the first people to live in Equatorial Guinea were the Pygmies, who settled in the Mbini region. During the Middle Ages this area was invaded by various different peoples, including the Fang, the Benga and the Bubi. The Bubi were the first people to settle on Bioko Island. The Portuguese arrived in the 1470s and laid claim to large areas of territory. They were followed by the Spanish, who governed from the 1800s until the country became independent in 1968.

Political parties were officially made legal in Equatorial Guinea in 1992 and elections were held for the first time in 1993.

▲ A plantation worker cuts down bamboo. The canes are used to make furniture and poles for building.

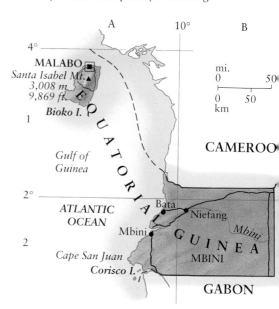

◀ This Spanish style church is a reminder of Equatorial Guinea's colonial past. Freedom to worship and other human rights were denied after independence.

FACTS AND FIGURES	
Area: 28,050 sq km	**Official language:** Spanish
Population: 379,000	
Capital: Malabo (10,000)	**Main religion:** Christianity
Other major city: Bata (17,000)	**Currency:** Franc CFA
Highest point: Santa Isabel Mt (3,008 m)	**Main exports:** Cocoa, timber, coffee
	Government: Republic
	Per capita GNP: US $330

SAO TOME AND PRINCIPE

The two islands of São Tomé and Príncipe lie in the Gulf of Guinea, about 200 kilometres west of Gabon. These islands are part of a group of extinct volcanoes. Mountain peaks, clad in dense forest, rise sharply on the western coasts, then the land slopes gently down to the east. The soil is mixed with volcanic ash, so it is very fertile. The climate is warm and humid.

When the Portuguese discovered these islands in 1470 there were no inhabitants. They soon established sugar plantations and shipped slaves from mainland Africa to work them. After periods of Dutch and French rule the Portuguese returned to power and planted the islands with cocoa. It remains the islands' chief crop, though coconuts, bananas and coffee are also grown.

Even after slavery was abolished in the 1800s Portuguese rule was often harsh. In 1953 hundreds of protesting workers were massacred. Independence came in 1975, but cultural and economic links with Portugal have remained strong. Around 70 percent of the inhabitants are of mixed Portuguese and African descent, called Creoles. Many are employed on large farms growing cash crops such as cocoa, while some work small farms of their own. Others are labourers or crew fishing boats. The islands are poor, depending on foreign aid to help them modernize farming and industry with new equipment.

▼ Workers' children play by old plantation buildings at a roca (a cocoa farm) in the highlands of São Tomé.

FACTS AND FIGURES
Area: 1,000 sq km
Population: 122,000
Capital: São Tomé (35,000)
Highest point: Pico de São Tomé (2,024 m)
Official language: Portuguese
Main religions: Christianity, traditional beliefs
Currency: Dobra
Main exports: Cocoa, copra, coffee, bananas, palm-oil
Government: Multi-party republic
Per capita GNP: US $370

GABON

The Equator cuts right across the sweltering country of Gabon. Beyond the surf and coconut palms of the Atlantic coast are swamps and lagoons. Further inland rolling hills are covered in dense tropical forest and drenched in heavy rain. Most of Gabon's rainfall drains into the Ogoué River. Along with the Trans-Gabon railway, which takes goods from the interior to the new port of Owendo, the Ogoué is a major transport route.

Gabon's natural resources make it one of Africa's richest countries. Oil from offshore rigs and minerals such as iron, uranium and manganese bring in most of the country's wealth. The forests provide valuable timber for sawmills – blackwood, mahogany and okoumé (a softwood used to make plywood). Today the government is preserving its forests by replanting. Most Gabonese live in villages on the coast or rivers and make their living by farming. They grow cassava, plantains and maize. Fishing is also important.

From the late 1400s Europeans plundered Gabon for slaves for hundreds of years. Then from 1919 until independence in 1960 it was ruled by France. French companies took over much of Gabon's foreign trade during this period and today links with France are still strong.

◄ The skyscrapers of Libreville provide a dramatic contrast with life in rural Gabon. The city was founded by freed slaves in 1849, near the site of a trading post set up by the French ten years earlier.

ALBERT SCHWEITZER

Albert Schweitzer (1875-1965) was a German musician and philosopher who became world famous as a doctor and missionary. He raised money to set up and run a hospital at Lambaréné and treated thousands of people during his lifetime. Since the 1960s, however, Schweitzer has been criticized for not allowing black people to train as doctors. His hospital is now a museum. A new hospital next to the old site has room for 600 families.

▼ *Gabonese women support the Gabonese Democratic Party (PDG) during the 1990 elections. A picture of Omar Bongo, the PDG leader, is printed on one woman's dress (left). Bongo had been in power since 1964 and defeated the opposition for the fourth time in 1990.*

FACTS AND FIGURES

Area: 267,670 sq km
Population: 1,012,000
Capital: Libreville (350,000)
Other major city: Port-Gentil (124,000)
Highest point: Mt Iboundji (1,575 m)
Official language: French
Main religions: Christianity, traditional beliefs
Currency: Franc CFA
Main exports: Oil, manganese, timber, uranium
Government: Multi-party republic
Per capita GNP: US $4,450

◄ *Oil is refined at Port-Gentil. Offshore oil reserves have helped Gabon escape from the poverty of the colonial period.*

CONGO

Congo lies to the west of the mighty river Congo and its main tributary, the Oubangui. The north of the country is forest-filled land and largely uninhabited. Most Congolese live in the south, either in Brazzaville, which is the industrial centre and capital, or on the coastal plain to the west.

The coastal plain is Congo's main farming area. However, the soil is poor because the rains that sweep across this humid, equatorial country wash away a lot of goodness. Just off the coast lie valuable reserves of oil, Congo's most precious mineral and major export. It is refined at the port of Pointe-Noire. Other important exports include timber, rubber, peanuts and coffee. The majority of the population, however, make a living by growing rice, bananas and maize to feed their families.

The Portuguese and other seafarers arrived in this area during the 1400s. They began 400 years of trading in slaves and ivory. From 1910 to 1960 the region was part of French Equatorial Africa, which is why French is still the official language in Congo today. After independence was declared in 1960 there were some years of political instability. Between 1970 and 1990 the country was a one-party socialist state. In 1992, the country became a democracy under President Pascal Lissouba. However, civil war broke out in 1997, Lissouba fled, and the military took power.

▼ *This wooden headrest, carved by people from the Congo region, shows two women wrestlers with traditional hairstyles. Woodworking skills have been passed down through generations and designs have changed little for hundreds of years.*

◄ *A group of Congolese ride on top of a truck bound for Brazzaville market. Bunches of green bananas, grain grown over the year and furniture made from the forest wood will be among the wares for sale.*

► *The gigantic Monument to Freedom outside Brazzaville railway station shows a slave bursting free of his chains. It reminds passers-by that they have escaped a history of slavery.*

FACTS AND FIGURES

Area: 342,000 sq km
Population: 2,441,000
Capital: Brazzaville (586,000)
Other major cities: Pointe-Noire (295,000), Louboumo (84,000)
Highest point: Mt de la Lékéti (1,040 m)
Official language: French
Main religions: Christianity, Islam, traditional beliefs
Currency: Franc CFA
Main exports: Petroleum, timber, coffee, cocoa
Government: Military regime
Per capita GNP: US $1,030

SPEAK KIKONGO

Hello – Ebue (*eb - way*)

Goodbye – Kuenda mbote (*kwen - dah **mboh** - tay*)

Please – dodokolo (***doh*** *- doh - koh - loh*)

Thank you – matondo (*ma - **ton** - doh*)

Yes – inga (***in*** *- gah*)

No – ve (*vay*)

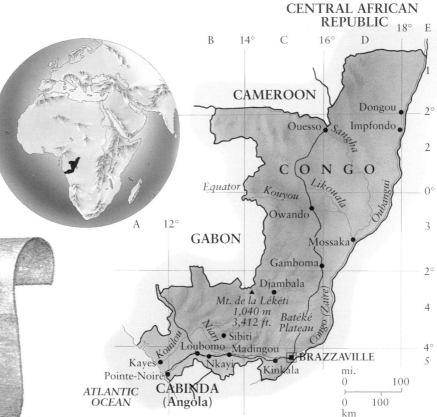

ANGOLA

Angola's narrow coastal plain rises to a vast plateau of sparse grassland with mountains in the centre. Tropical forests cover the north and the small territory of Cabinda, which is divided from the rest of Angola by the Democratic Republic of Congo. The south is desert. Only about three percent of this country is farmland, yet most Angolans grow sugar-cane or cassava for a living. Angola produces diamonds and offshore oil, but the nation's economy has been devastated by long years of civil war.

During the Stone Age hunter-gatherers lived in what is now Angola. Bantu-speaking peoples, who were skilled at making metal tools and weapons, settled here from about AD600. The Portuguese arrived in the 1400s and ruled Angola for 500 years.

In the 1960s guerrilla groups started a rebellion against their harsh regime. These were the MPLA (Popular Movement for Liberation of Angola), the FLNA (National Front for the Liberation of Angola) and UNITA (National Union for Total Independence of Angola). Independence came in 1975, but then the rebels fought each other for power to govern the country. In the early 1990s the United Nations supervised both elections and peace talks, but the war continued.

▲ *This Angolan child has been cared for by a Roman Catholic Mission. The civil war in Angola has left many children orphaned.*

FACTS AND FIGURES
Area: 1,246,700 sq km
Population: 10,276,000
Capital: Luanda (1,200,000)
Other major cities: Huambo (62,000), Lobito (60,000), Benguela (41,000)
Highest point: Moco (2,620 m)
Official language: Portuguese
Main religions: Christianity, traditional beliefs
Currency: Kwanza
Main exports: Crude oil, coffee, diamonds, fish products, sisal, maize, palm-oil
Government: Republic
Per capita GNP: Est. US $700-$3,000

► *A fading poster reads 'Angola and Cabinda united in revolution'. Cuba's Fidel Castro (right) supported Agostinho Neto (left) and the Communist MPLA in Angola's civil war. The MPLA was also backed by the Soviet Union and East Germany, while South Africa sent troops to help its rivals, UNITA and the FNLA. Foreign powers withdrew when peace was promised in the late 1980s, but the fighting went on.*

◄ *On the quayside at Lobito fish are packed into boxes. Fishing is important in Angola's coastal areas. Mackerel and sardines swim in the cool Atlantic waters and provide valuable food for Angola's people.*

▼ *Irrigation greens a dry landscape near Benguela, turning it into rice fields. Benguela is an important railway town, handling minerals on their way to the port of Lobito.*

NAMIBIA

Namibia is a dry land, largely taken up by a dusty plain dotted with trees and covered with sparse pasture for cattle, sheep and goats. Along the coast of the Atlantic Ocean are the sandy wastes of the Namib Desert, one of the driest places on Earth. In the east, spreading into Botswana, is another arid wilderness, the Kalahari Desert.

Droughts are common and Namibian farmers must struggle to grow crops of maize and millet in this harsh landscape. However, the terrain does conceal Namibia's vast natural wealth – its reserves of diamonds and uranium.

Cave paintings show that people lived in this region by hunting and gathering more than 25,000 years ago. The San people moved into the area around 2,000 years ago and their descendants still live in the east. Other Namibian peoples include the Ovambo, Herero and Damara.

German immigrants began to settle here in the 1860s and in 1884 it became a German colony. The Herero fought against foreign rule and around 60,000 of their number were brutally slaughtered between 1904 and 1907. In World War I South Africa invaded Namibia and in 1920 the League of Nations (forerunner of the United Nations) allowed South Africa to govern instead of Germany. When South Africa imposed its cruel apartheid laws on its new territory many countries around the world objected. The campaign for independence escalated into fighting. Independence was won in 1990 and Sam Nujoma was elected president.

FACTS AND FIGURES
Area: 824,270 sq km
Population: 1,584,000
Capital: Windhoek (125,000)
Other major cities: Swakopmund (16,000), Rundu (15,000), Rehoboth (15,000)
Highest point: Brandberg (2,580 m)
Official language: English
Main religion: Christianity
Currency: Namibian dollar
Main exports: Diamonds, uranium, fish products, meat products, livestock
Government: Multi-party republic
Per capita GNP: US $1,610

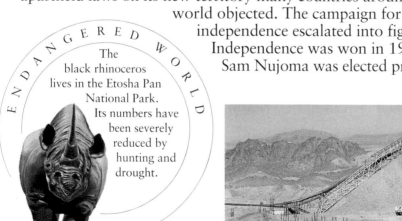

ENDANGERED WORLD
The black rhinoceros lives in the Etosha Pan National Park. Its numbers have been severely reduced by hunting and drought.

▶ *This mine in the Namib Desert produces uranium, a highly radioactive metal used in nuclear power stations. Namibia's uranium exports bring much needed wealth into the country.*

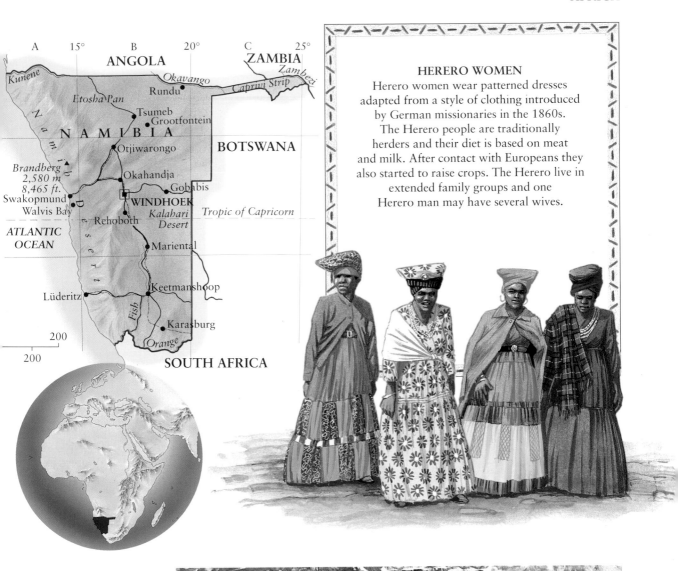

HERERO WOMEN

Herero women wear patterned dresses adapted from a style of clothing introduced by German missionaries in the 1860s. The Herero people are traditionally herders and their diet is based on meat and milk. After contact with Europeans they also started to raise crops. The Herero live in extended family groups and one Herero man may have several wives.

► *A wall painting celebrates an end to the long years of racism under South African rule and reflects hope for the future. The South West Africa People's Organization won independence for the country in 1990.*

AFTER "A LONG STRUGGLE" NAMIBIA IS FREE AT LAST.

SOUTH AFRICA *Introduction*

FACTS AND FIGURES

Area: 1,127,000 sq km
Population: 40,774,000
Capitals: Cape Town
[legislative] (2,351,000),
Pretoria [administrative]
(1,081,000),
Bloemfontein [judicial]
(301,000)
Other major city:
Johannesburg
(1,916,000)
Highest point:
Champagne Castle
(3,375 m)
Official languages:
Afrikaans, English,
Ndebele, North Sotho,
South Sotho, Swazi,
Tsonga, Tswana,
Venda, Xhosa, Zulu
Main religions:
Christianity, Hinduism,
Islam
Currency: Rand
Main exports: Gold,
metals, diamonds, food
products, machinery
Government:
Multi-party republic
Per capita GNP:
US $2,670

South Africa is a land of great scenic beauty with dramatic cloud-topped mountains, steep-sided valleys and vast, dusty plains. In its national parks endangered species such as elephants and rhinoceroses are actually increasing in number.
Along the east coast are sandy bays and above them pineapples, oranges and mangoes flourish in the warm, sunny climate. In the south are forests of cedar, while on the northwest borders parched scrub gives way to desert.
A wealth of minerals is buried in South Africa's rocks. It was the discovery of diamonds and gold that attracted a rush of European fortune-hunters in the 1800s. The Europeans conquered the African peoples, or bought their lands. They dug mines and made South Africa the richest and most highly developed country in the continent. Yet the wealth has benefited only a minority because in 1950 the white government brought into force the policy of apartheid. This separated blacks from whites and refused them equal rights. Almost the whole world spoke out against the cruelty of this regime, which left millions of people in grinding poverty. The democratic elections of 1994 gave South Africa a majority black government, which brought hope and a new sense of co-operation to all its ethnic groups.

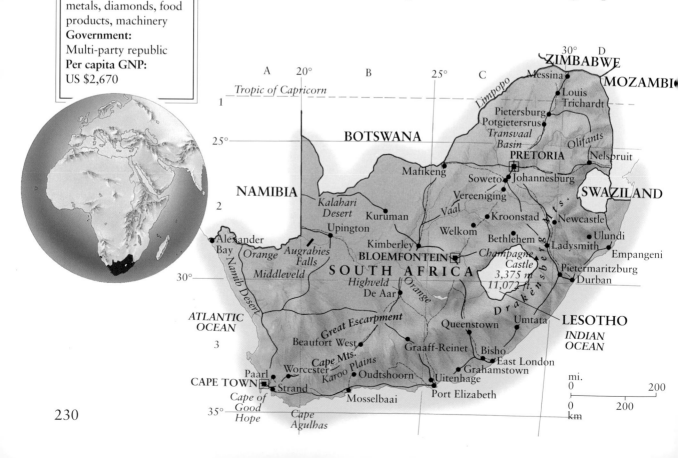

► *Striking designs decorate this Ndebele house, as well as the traditonal dress of the woman and child. The Ndebele people live in South Africa and Zimbabwe. Over 600,000 South Africans speak the Ndebele language.*

◄ *South Africa's parliament buildings, in Cape Town, date back to the 1880s. For over a century their doors opened only to whites, but since 1994 South Africa has been a multi-racial democracy.*

SPEAK ZULU

Hello – Sakubona
(*sa - koo - boh - na*)

Goodbye – Hamba kahle
(*ham - ba kah - la*)

Please – Ngicela
(*ngee - kay - la*)

Thank you – Ngiyabonga
(*ngee - ya - bon - ga*)

NELSON MANDELA

Nelson Rolihlahla Mandela was born in Umtata in 1918. He became a lawyer in Johannesburg and joined the African National Congress (ANC) in 1944. Mandela campaigned against the injustice of apartheid and was imprisoned for 28 years for his beliefs. Released in 1990, he negotiated a new constitution with the then president, FW de Klerk. Mandela was elected South Africa's first black president in 1994.

SOUTH AFRICA *Geography*

▼ *Giant's Castle is a towering section of the rugged Drakensberg Mountains on Lesotho's southern border. It is formed from volcanic rock.*

For many visitors the first sight of South Africa is the beautiful city of Cape Town. Right at the tip of the continent, it shimmers beneath the dramatic backdrop of Table Mountain. Most of the coast is overlooked by mountains, the towering Drakensberg range rising steeply in the east. The wilderness of the Namib Desert borders the misty northwest coast. In the north the Kalahari Desert stretches into neighbouring Botswana.

Central South Africa is a vast plateau, rimmed in the south by the cliffs of the Great Escarpment. The Highveld occupies most of this plateau. It is an area of coarse grassland with sparse trees, largely given over to mining and prairies of wheat and maize. In the northwest the Middleveld is more suited to livestock than crops. This is because it has poor soil, owing to erosion, and little rain. Large numbers of cattle and sheep are raised in the area. The northeast of the plateau is the Transvaal Basin, where farmers grow citrus fruits, maize and tobacco. Elephants, lions, leopards and great herds of antelopes and zebras live on Transvaal's thorny scrub and are protected in the Kruger National Park.

Many of South Africa's rivers run dry during the summer. This means they cannot be used for transport or hydroelectric power, but their water can be stored to provide irrigation for crops.

▼ *Bontebok, a rare species of antelope, graze in West Cape Province in the southwest. They are protected in the Bontebok National Park.*

◄ A quiver tree overlooks a barren landscape in the northwest. These unusual trees are also found in Namibia. They were named by the Khoisan people who used the branches of the tree to make quivers, or cases, for carrying arrows.

► A great sweep of ocean pounds Plettenberg Bay in West Cape Province on the south coast. The Cape divides the South Atlantic from the Indian Ocean. Sea and wind affect the climate, bringing rain to the east coast.

◄ God's Window is a viewing point in the Drakensberg Mountains. This gap in the mountain pass offers breathtaking views over fertile forest plantations and some of the most beautiful natural sites in Africa.

SOUTH AFRICA *Economy*

South Africa is one of the great driving forces of the continent's economy. It exports more diamonds than any other country on Earth and has the world's biggest goldfield in Witwatersrand, near Johannesburg. It also has vast reserves of other minerals including copper, iron ore and platinum. Enough grain and meat are produced to feed the nation and grapes from the Karoo plains behind Cape Town are exported around the globe. A quarter of the country's wealth comes from industries such as chemicals, textiles and machinery. Good communications, roads and railways also help to make South Africa a prosperous country.

However, the long years of apartheid meant that millions of blacks remained poor, without proper education, training or healthcare. In protest against South Africa's racist policies, other countries all over the world imposed sanctions (trading restrictions) that harmed its economy.

International relations were mended after the democratic elections of 1994, but the new democracy of South Africa faces enormous problems at home. Vast sums of money need to be spent on housing and schools, water and electricity supplies. Reform will take time and many people are impatient for change. Yet the country does have the natural wealth to make a bright future possible and improve the lives of all its people.

▲ *A miner in Witwatersrand drills into the rock for gold. Gold is also found in river water, from which it is removed by sieving or filtering. South Africa is the world's leading gold producer.*

▶ *Rows of vines grow in the warm sunshine beneath the mountains of the southwest. The soil and climate here are particularly suitable for growing grapes. This area is the centre of South Africa's successful wine industry.*

ECONOMIC SURVEY

Farming: Cattle, sheep, goats and pigs are raised. Wool is a major export. Fruit, tobacco, wines, grains and sugar-cane are important crops.
Forestry: Forests supply national needs for softwood and hardwood.
Fishing: A fleet of about 5,700 vessels. Anchovy are an important catch.

Mining: Major producer of gold, coal, copper, chromite, diamonds, iron ore, manganese, platinum and uranium.
Industry: Machinery, iron and steel, vehicles and processed food are the country's leading products. South Africa is Africa's most industrialized nation.

▼ *White farmers make deals at a busy sheep market in the southwest of the country. South African farmers also breed cattle, pigs and goats.*

▲ *Women check peaches on the conveyor belt at a canning factory. Farming produce and processed foods play an important part in the South African economy. Large numbers of black workers live below the poverty level. Trades unions are demanding a rapid improvement in rates of pay in the new South Africa.*

▶ *These homes in Kayelitsha, just north of Cape Town, are shacks made of planks and corrugated iron. Apartheid forced many blacks to live in sprawling slums called townships, without a proper water supply. Blacks were not allowed to live in rich white areas, except as servants.*

SOUTH AFRICA *People and History*

The first South Africans were the San and the Khoisan peoples. From about AD300, and for many centuries after, Bantu-speaking peoples such as the Zulu, Xhosa and Sesotho moved into the region. In 1652 Dutch seafarers settled Cape Town. Soon other Europeans were joining Dutch farmers (called Boers, or Afrikaners) in seizing land. When the Cape colony came under British rule in the 1800s, the Boers began the Great Trek northwards in ox-drawn wagons to claim new land. The late 1800s saw a series of bitter territorial wars between the British, the Boers and the Zulus. By the end of the 1800s all black South Africans had lost their independence.

From the 1950s South Africa's policies were dominated by the minority white government's rule of apartheid. This kept apart the main ethnic groups – the whites, the blacks and the coloureds (people of mixed descent and Asians). The government forced many blacks into small territories called homelands, to live on poor land with limited opportunities for work and education. Peaceful protests were met with violence and led to riots and massacres. In 1991 apartheid finally came to an end and Nelson Mandela became the nation's first black president in 1994. Inequality was still deeply rooted in South Africa, however, and Mandela's immediate priorities were to improve housing, education and job opportunities for black people.

▲ Zulus in national costume perform a traditional dance. Led by Chief Mangosuthu Buthelezi, the Zulus of the Inkatha Freedom Party have a powerful political voice within modern South Africa.

◄ The gleaming towers of Johannesburg's financial centre contrast with the dire poverty of Soweto, a sprawling black township on the outskirts of the city. Johannesburg was founded in 1886 when gold prospectors were arriving from Europe.

► In an engraving from the 1800s black workers extract diamonds from a mine. They are supervised by brutal whites (see front, left). Diamonds were discovered near Kimberley in 1868. Europeans settled the region and made their fortune while the blacks remained poor.

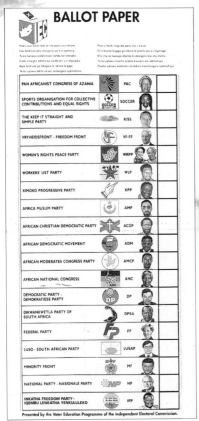

▼ An old building in Dutch style recalls the origins of the Afrikaner people. It was a Dutch naval surgeon called Jan van Riebeeck who began European colonization of southern Africa in 1652. He was originally sent by the Dutch East India Company to set up a halfway station between Holland and the East Indies.

◄ This ballot paper shows the 19 political parties that took part in the democratic elections of 1994. Black people were voting for the first time. People queued for many long hours to elect the African National Congress (ANC) led by Nelson Mandela.

237

SWAZILAND

FACTS AND FIGURES
Area: 17,360 sq km
Population: 814,000
Capital: Mbabane
(39,000)
Other major cities:
Manzini (18,000),
Big Bend (10,000),
Mhlume (7,000)
Highest point:
Mt Emlembe (1,862 m)
Official languages:
English, Swazi
Main religions:
Christianity,
traditional beliefs
Currency: Lilangeni
Main exports: Sugar,
wood and forest
products, canned fruit,
citrus fruit, asbestos
Government:
Monarchy
Per capita GNP:
US $1,080

Swaziland is one of the smallest countries on the African continent. It is completely surrounded by two other countries – South Africa and Mozambique. Central regions of rolling grassland make Swaziland a cattle-farming nation, with cash crops of sugar-cane, cotton and tobacco. It also has rich reserves of coal, iron ore, gold and tin, although large numbers of Swazi people work in gold mines over the border in South Africa.

Many of the farms, forestry plantations and mines are owned by foreign companies. This situation has grown since the 1800s, when British and Dutch settlers tricked the Swazi people into signing away their mining rights. This led to the country being overrun by white prospectors. Britain ruled Swaziland from 1902 until its independence in 1968.

When Mswati III became king in 1986 he faced a land divided between minority white people, who wanted to retain control, and majority black people, who wanted increased rights. The future of Swaziland will be greatly affected by the historic changes taking place across the border in South Africa, whose people elected their first black president, Nelson Mandela, in 1994.

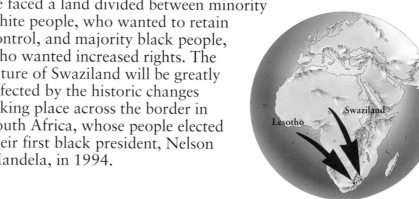

▼ *Women surge forward in a traditional folk dance. Swaziland maintains pride in its ancient customs and ceremonies. Costume includes brightly coloured textiles, animal skins and beadwork.*

LESOTHO

Lesotho is completely surrounded by South Africa. Its economy depends heavily on money sent home by labourers who work in South Africa. Those men who stay at home till the poor soil and herd sheep and goats, while the women tend the crops – maize, sorghum and beans. Boys help with the animals from a young age, so most schoolchildren in Lesotho are girls.

The snowy Drakensberg Mountains cover much of this country. The mountain climate is often cool and damp, so the national costume includes a warm, colourful blanket and a sturdy, broad-brimmed hat made from woven grasses.

Lesotho, once called Basutoland, has been caught up in the struggles of southern Africa since the 1700s. In the 1800s warriors, who had fled into the mountains of what would become Lesotho, came under the protection of Chief Moshoeshoe I and founded the new nation. They fought against newcomers, including the British and the Boers, and escaped inclusion within South Africa. In 1966 Lesotho became an independent kingdom.

Troubles in South Africa continued to spill over into Lesotho in recent years. However, the end of apartheid in South Africa and democratic elections in Lesotho may have helped to bring some stability to this country.

▼ *The waters of the Orange River cut through a rocky landscape in Lesotho's Maloti Mountains. The river continues flowing southwards and then westwards into South Africa and Namibia. Crops are grown on the valley floor.*

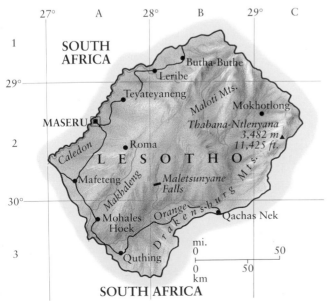

FACTS AND FIGURES

Area: 30,350 sq km
Population: 1,882,000
Capital: Maseru (110,000)
Other major city: Teyateyaneng (15,000)
Highest point: Thabana-Ntlenyana (3,482 m)
Official languages: Sesotho, English

Main religion: Christianity
Currency: Loti
Main exports: Wool, mohair, diamonds, wheat, vegetables, livestock
Government: Constitutional monarchy
Per capita GNP: US $590

BOTSWANA

Some of the earliest peoples of southern Africa, the San people, once lived right across the southern continent, including the area we now call Botswana. Around AD1000 the Tswana, from whom the country gets its name, moved in from the north and forced the San into the Kalahari Desert. Some still live in its dusty wastes by hunting and gathering in the tradition of their ancestors.

The Kalahari Desert covers most of Botswana, which is sparsely populated. It is a high plateau of bushes and tough grasses, with sand-dunes in the southwest. In the east there is enough rain to grow crops, so that is where most people live. They raise maize, millet and sorghum to feed their families. Cattle-breeding is very important, second only to diamond mining in the economy.

One of Botswana's main problems is unemployment, so large numbers of people work in South Africa for part of each year. To provide work at home, the government is currently developing the mining industry to exploit newly discovered deposits of coal and copper.

The British ruled this land from 1885 until 1966 and called it Bechuanaland. Since independence Botswana has formed closer ties with South Africa. In the 1980s there was tension between the two countries because Botswana criticized the unjust political system in South Africa. This problem was solved when South Africa held its first democratic elections in 1994.

FACTS AND FIGURES

Area: 581,730 sq km
Population: 1,143,000
Capital: Gaborone (139,000)
Other major cities: Mahalapye (105,000), Serowe (95,000)
Highest point: Otse Mt (1,489 m)
Official language: English
Main religions: Christianity, traditional beliefs
Currency: Pula
Main exports: Diamonds, copper, nickel, meat and meat products, hides, textiles
Government: Multi-party republic
Per capita GNP: US $2,790

▶ *A young girl bangs a tin can with a stick to make a racket. Her job is to scare greedy birds away from the ripening sorghum crop. The large flower-heads yield a glossy grain and the solid woody stems are used for hay. Syrup can also be made from sorghum.*

► *The Okavango Swamp is a vast area. In some years the floodwaters spill over and evaporate in the salt pans. The swamp teems with lions, crocodiles and buffaloes, but wildlife may be threatened by plans to develop the area for mining and farming.*

SPEAK TSWANA

Hello – Dumela
*(doo - **mail** - a)*

Goodbye – Go siame
*(ho see - **ah** - may)*

Please – Tswêê tswêê
(tsway tsway)

Thank you – Ke a leboga
*(kee a lay - **boo** - ha)*

▼ *A San man enjoys a sweet honeycomb. To get the honeycomb, which provides valuable nourishment in the winter, the San climb a tree and smoke out the bees. The bee grubs are considered the tastiest delicacy and are reserved for the elders.*

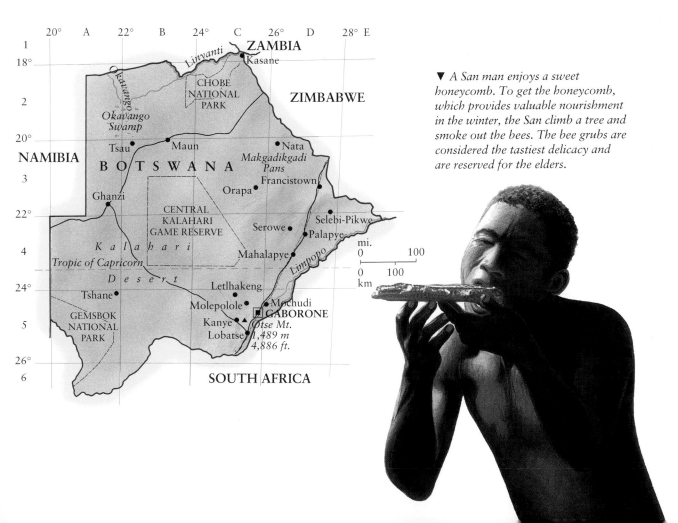

ZIMBABWE

Zimbabwe is a tropical country but has a mild climate because much of it lies on a high plateau. Water runs off the grassy veld into the Zambezi and Limpopo rivers, which are surrounded by thick forest. The veld is crossed by the Great Dyke, a rocky ridge with deposits of gold, nickel and chrome.

The people of Zimbabwe have lived by mining minerals and working metals since about AD800. In 1888 the Ndebele people granted mining rights to a British colonialist, Cecil Rhodes. Within seven years European prospectors had taken over completely. They had crushed uprisings of the Ndebele and the Shona peoples and named the country Rhodesia. In 1923 it became a British colony governed by its white settlers.

Wealth from mining and farming brought in more Europeans, who finally demanded independence. Britain refused, as the Rhodesians would not allow the Africans a share in government. Rhodesian leader Ian Smith declared independence in 1965 and the world reacted with sanctions that crippled the economy. After years of guerrilla warfare, majority rule and independence as the Republic of Zimbabwe finally came in 1980. Many whites emigrated and in 1990 the government made it possible for Africans to buy back most of their land. However, most black Africans still live in rural areas farming small plots of land while the largest landowners are white. The government is pressing ahead with land reform.

◀ *The Matopos National Park lies in wind-eroded granite hills, southwest of Bulawayo. The hills are famed for their ancient cave paintings. Animals including lions, zebras, elephants, buffaloes and hippopotamuses live in the park.*

◄ *These researchers are working in a microbiology laboratory at the University of Zimbabwe. Zimbabwe has one other university and a third is being built. Since independence the government has poured large sums of money into education. Standards in the country's schools and colleges have greatly improved.*

FRUITS OF THE LAND

Large rosy mangoes, small passion fruit with their perfumed pink flesh and edible pips, pineapples and avocado pears are four of the delicious fruits of Zimbabwe. The avocado is savoury and highly nutritious. The other fruits are prized for their juicy flesh.

FACTS AND FIGURES

Area: 390,580 sq km
Population: 10,898,000
Capital: Harare (657,000)
Other major city: Bulawayo (415,000)
Highest point: Mt Inyangani (2,595 m)
Official language: English

Main religions: Christianity, traditional beliefs
Currency: Zimbabwe dollar
Main exports: Tobacco, iron alloys, gold, nickel, cotton, steel
Government: Multi-party republic
Per capita GNP: US $570

► *The ancient city of Great Zimbabwe was settled around AD1000 and gave this country its name. The Shona people, and later traders known as the Rozwi, built walls of massive granite slabs. They can still be seen today at the ruins near Masvingo.*

ZAMBIA

Zambia is named after the great Zambezi River, Africa's fourth longest river. Winding its way through the west of the country, the Zambezi forms part of the southern border with Zimbabwe. There, the river plunges over the spectacular Victoria Falls. Below these falls the Zambezi is dammed to form Lake Kariba. Hydroelectricity produced by the Kariba Dam powers the country's all-important copper industry.

Today copper exports provide most of Zambia's income. Thousands of people have moved to mining towns to take up jobs in the copper industry. Most of those left in rural areas live in grass-roofed huts and farm the land. Maize is a major crop and one of the most popular dishes is a maize porridge called *nshima*.

The country lies on a plateau. Much of it consists of high, spreading plains of grassland and bush, giving way to mountains in the east. Because the land is high, the climate is cooler in Zambia than in many other African countries.

During the colonial period, from the early 1900s until the 1960s, what is now Zambia was known as Northern Rhodesia and was under British control. When Northern Rhodesia gained independence in 1964 it was named Zambia and Kenneth Kaunda became president. Up until 1990 only one political party was permitted by law. In 1991 Frederick Chiluba, head of the opposition party MMD (Movement for Multi-party Democracy), became president when he defeated Kaunda in the country's first multi-party elections.

▲ *A woman carries maize husks. Women do most of the farm labouring in Zambia. They grow crops such as millet, sorghum, cassava and maize on small plots to feed their families.*

◄ *Ivory, rhinoceros horns and poachers' weapons burn in a demonstration in 1992. This was to show that Zambia's government supported the international ban on hunting and trading in endangered animals.*

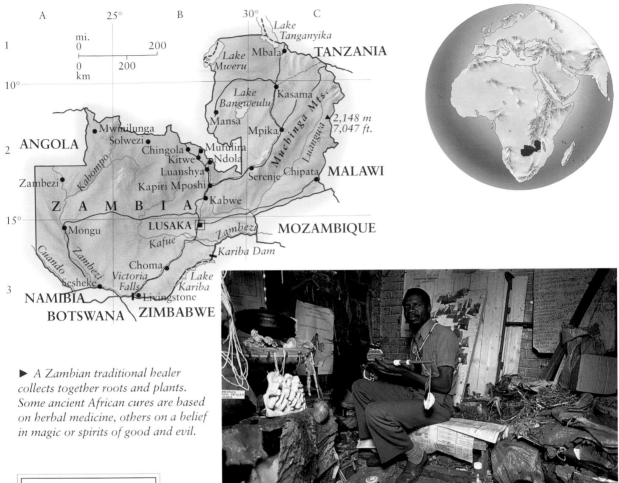

▶ A Zambian traditional healer collects together roots and plants. Some ancient African cures are based on herbal medicine, others on a belief in magic or spirits of good and evil.

FACTS AND FIGURES
Area: 752,610 sq km
Population: 8,885,000
Capital: Lusaka (921,000)
Other major cities: Kitwe (495,000), Ndola (467,000)
Highest point: In the Muchinga Mts (2,148 m)
Official language: English
Main religions: Christianity, traditional beliefs
Currency: Kwacha
Main exports: Copper, colbalt, zinc, emeralds, lead, tobacco
Government: Multi-party republic
Per capita GNP: US $290

▶ The Kariba Dam was completed in 1959. This hydroelectric scheme provides power for both Zambia and Zimbabwe.

MALAWI

Malawi lies along the shore of sparkling blue Lake Nyasa, the southernmost lake in the Great Rift Valley. The Shire River flows south from the lake, tumbling over waterfalls on its way to join the Zambezi River in Mozambique. From the humid lakeside the landscape rises westwards to cool plateaus and forested mountains dotted with tea plantations. Much of the country is covered in broad grasslands where antelopes and leopards roam, protected from hunters in Malawi's five national parks.

The people of Malawi mostly live in villages, in round houses of mud baked in the sun with roofs of sorghum thatch. In a traditional rural family the mother is head of the household. Women are in charge of planting and harvesting cassava, sorghum and maize to feed their families. The men look after livestock such as cattle and sheep, or go out hunting and fishing. Many also have jobs on tobacco or cotton plantations owned by Europeans.

The British first came here in the 1860s. They called the country Nyasaland and ruled it from 1891 until independence in 1964. In this year it took the African name Malawi and Hastings Kamuzu Banda became president. In 1994 Banda's one-party rule came to an end and Baliki Muluzi was elected the new ruler.

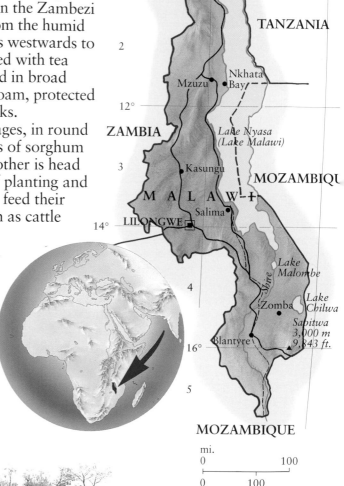

◄ A large class of pupils from the village in the background enjoys an outdoor lesson under the shade of a big tree. Less than half of the children in Malawi attend school because of a shortage of teachers and school buildings.

◀ *This is a cathedral window of Dr David Livingstone, the famous Scottish missionary. Livingstone explored Malawi in the 1850s, campaigning against slavery and opening Africa to the Europeans.*

▼ *Fishermen set off in canoes on Lake Nyasa. The government has promoted fishing to help make Malawi self-sufficient in food.*

FACTS AND FIGURES
Area: 118,480 sq km
Population: 9,135,000
Capital: Lilongwe
(234,000)
Other major cities:
Blantyre (332,000),
Mzuzu (45,000)
Highest point:
Sapitwa (3,000 m)
Official languages:
Chichewa, English
Main religions:
Christianity, Islam,
traditional beliefs
Currency: Kwacha
Main exports: Tobacco,
sugar, tea, cotton,
peanuts
Government:
Multi-party republic
Per capita GNP:
US $210

▶ *Forested mountains rise steeply above Zomba. This town was founded by European settlers in the 1880s and became the capital of British Nyasaland (the country's name between 1891 and 1964). After independence Zomba remained the capital of Malawi until 1975, when government offices were moved to Lilongwe.*

MOZAMBIQUE

FACTS AND FIGURES
Area: 799,380 sq km
Population: 15,322,000
Capital: Maputo
(1,098,000)
Other major cities:
Beira (300,000),
Nampula (203,000)
Highest point: Mt Binga
(2,436 m)
Official language:
Portuguese
Main religions:
Traditional beliefs,
Christianity, Islam
Currency: Metical
Main exports: Shrimps,
cashew nuts, sugar,
petroleum products,
copra, cotton
Government:
Multi-party republic
Per capita GNP:
US $60

Mozambique lies on the east coast of Africa opposite the island of Madagascar. It is a country of fine natural harbours. Sand-dunes and coastal swamps give way to a flat plain, which rises to a high plateau covered in grassland. Numerous rivers fringed by tropical forest flow down to the Indian Ocean. The land has several natural resources, including coal and diamonds. However, 80 percent of the people are farmers, growing cotton and cashew nuts for export, or cassava and wheat to feed their families.

For almost 500 years Mozambique's history was dominated by the Portuguese, who first arrived in 1498. They set up trading posts for slaves and fought off other nations that tried to take control. In the 1800s Portugal conquered the farming peoples of the interior, including the Makonde, Yao, Tete and Ronga, and made Mozambique a colony. Many Portuguese people came to live in the colony, but in 1962 a guerrilla army called Frelimo (Front for Liberation of Mozambique) began a long war to free the country from foreign rule. The Portuguese finally left in 1975.

Frelimo formed a Communist government, but the country faced many problems. The departure of skilled Portuguese workers weakened the economy. Mozambique also had to fight a war against National Resistance Movement (Renamo) guerrillas because it had offered support to the fight against white rule in South Africa. In addition, there were years of drought, disastrous floods and famine. Communist rule ended in 1990. A peace agreement and democratic elections followed in 1994.

► *Maputo has broad avenues, high-rise buildings and a thriving port. The capital's harbour and rail links are used by other countries, including South Africa, Zimbabwe and Swaziland.*

▲ Choirs and musicians celebrate the end of Mozambique's first year of peace in 1993. 'Never again war,' says the sign behind them. War and natural disasters such as drought, floods and famine have created devastation in Mozambique. A great deal needs to be done to build up the country's industry and repair its shattered economy.

◀ Women attending a cookery class are taught how to use cassava. This starchy root is a versatile source of food. It can be made into bread or pressed to yield bead-like grains of starch for tapioca puddings. Education in all fields is a top priority in Mozambique.

249

MADAGASCAR *Introduction*

E N D A N G E R E D   W O R L D

Lemurs are only found on Madagascar. Most species are now endangered. Ringtail lemurs have been hunted and shot as agricultural pests.

The island of Madagascar lies in the Indian Ocean, about 400 kilometres off the coast of Mozambique. In the east, forested mountain slopes rise from a narrow coastal strip fringed with rocks and reefs. Inland are cool, high plateaus which, in many places, have been stripped bare of natural vegetation. Precious hardwood trees have been felled for fuel and to clear land for farming. The hot and humid western lowlands give way to arid scrub in the south. Most people live in the island's central region or along the east coast. The coastal areas often suffer from destructive cyclones.

Madagascar separated from the African mainland about 160 million years ago and many of the island's animals evolved into species seen nowhere else on Earth. Tragically, human settlement and the loss of the island's forests mean that today its soil is the most eroded in the world and no fewer than 127 of Madagascar's animal species are considered to be endangered.

Most of the people depend on agriculture, though only five percent of the land can be farmed. Madagascans grow rice, sweet potatoes and cassava for food. They raise cattle in the west of the island and fish the rivers and lakes as well as the sea. Factory workers pack meat, brew beer and refine sugar. Madagascar has rich deposits of graphite, chromite and semi-precious stones such as beryl and garnet. Offshore reserves of oil may point to a more prosperous future, but so far have not proved to be worth exploiting commercially.

FACTS AND FIGURES

Area: 587,040 sq km
Population: 13,259,000
Capital: Antananarivo (804,000)
Other major cities: Fianarantsoa (125,000), Mahajanga (122,000)
Highest point: Maromokotro (2,876 m)
Official languages: Malagasy, French
Main religions: Traditional beliefs, Christianity
Currency: Malagasy franc
Main exports: Coffee, cloves, vanilla, sugar, sisal, shrimps
Government: Republic
Per capita GNP: US $230

► *Madagascar's capital, Antananarivo, is the centre of the island's food processing industry. It is a beautiful city built on hills, with palaces, churches and many houses that were built in the 1800s.*

◄ The huge baobab tree has a bottle-shaped trunk. The fibres inside it are swollen with moisture drawn from the ground. This store of water helps it to survive the drought.

◄ Soil on much of Madagascar's central plateau has been badly eroded. Almost all the island's natural forests have been destroyed. With no tree roots to hold down the red clay, tropical rains wash it away. Reforestation is now a government policy.

251

MADAGASCAR *People and History*

The first Madagascans came from Indonesia around 2,000 years ago, sailing via India and East Africa in double-hulled canoes. People from mainland Africa settled later and today's population is of mixed descent. Their language, Malagasy, is closely related to the Indonesian language Malay. Customs and beliefs, including ancestor worship, are a mixture of Indonesian and African.

In 1500 Portuguese seafarers became the first Europeans to discover Madagascar. The British and French arrived later and European missionaries converted many of the island's people to Christianity. In the 1800s the Merina kingdom of the plateau conquered most of the island. In 1895 the French took over and Madagascar was a French colony until it became independent in 1960.

After a peaceful decade under a pro-French government, recent history has been stormy. President Didier Ratsiraka came to power in 1975 as a virtual dictator and pursued a socialist, anti-Western policy. His government took over many of the country's businesses, including those owned by foreigners. In 1991 strikes and demonstrations compelled him to accept a more democratic constitution and in 1993 elections brought a new government to power under President Albert Zafy.

▼ *Cloves are spread out on the ground to dry in the sun, filling the air with their heavy scent. Madagascar is one of the world's leading producers of cloves, which are the dried flower buds of an evergreen tree. Cloves are used to flavour many types of food.*

◄ *In central Madagascar groups of musicians, dancers and singers perform at weddings, circumcisions and funerals as well as on national holidays. Their songs are made up specially for the occasion and the costume designs date from the 1800s.*

► *Villagers have brought lumps of quartz to a European trader. Quartz is found near rivers. It is carved into ornaments such as chess pieces and marbles on the island, or exported as a raw material.*

A HAUNT OF PIRATES

During the 1600s and 1700s the coast of Madagascar became the haunt of European pirates. One of the most notorious was Scottish-born William Kidd. In 1698 Captain Kidd joined the pirates based on St Mary's Island (now called Nosy Boraha). Three years later he was hanged in chains in London, England.

▼ *The formerly sacred village of Ambohimanga is a few kilometres north of Antananarivo. It was the home of Madagascar's most famous king, Andiranampoinimerina (1787-1810).*

COMOROS

The volcanic Comoros islands are fringed with mangrove swamps. They lie at the northern end of the Mozambique Channel, the part of the Indian Ocean that separates Madagascar from the African mainland.

From the 1400s to the 1800s the islands were controlled by Muslim sultans. The French invaded in 1843 and by 1886 owned the four main islands – Mayotte, Anjouan, Grande Comore and Moheli. The latter three voted for independence as Comoros in 1974 and the islands' names were changed to Nzwani, Njazidja and Mwali. Mayotte opted for continued French rule.

The islanders are descended from Arabs, mainland Africans and southeast Asian peoples. The archipelago has no major industry and no minerals, so about 85 percent of the people live by farming crops such as coconuts, bananas, rice and cassava. Spices and ylang-ylang (a perfume oil that comes from a tree of the same name) are produced for export. Though the islanders depend on agriculture there is a shortage of farmland. This is because the cutting down of natural forests to clear land has led to soil erosion by the tropical rains. Poverty is widespread and the years since independence have been marked by political strife and violence.

FACTS AND FIGURES
Area: 1,862 sq km
Population: 607,000
Capital: Moroni (22,000)
Other major city: Mutsamudu (14,000)
Highest point: Mont Kartala (2,361 m)
Official languages: French, Arabic
Main religion: Islam
Currency: Comorian franc
Main exports: Vanilla, cloves, ylang-ylang, copra, coffee
Government: Federal Islamic single-party republic
Per capita GNP: US $510

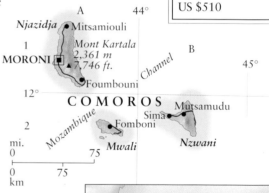

◄ Comoron women sometimes wear white make-up. This is made from wood ground against coral, which is mixed to a pulp with water. It protects the skin against the sun and cleanses it like a mud-pack.

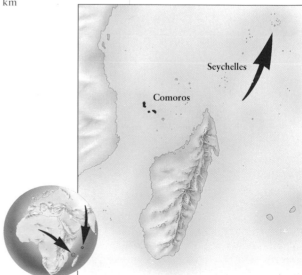

SEYCHELLES

FACTS AND FIGURES
Area: 455 sq km
Population: 72,000
Capital: Victoria
(25,000)
Highest point: Morne
Seychellois (905 m)
Official languages:
Creole, English, French
Main religion:
Christianity
Currency:
Seychelles rupee
Main exports: Copra,
fish, cinnamon
Government:
Multi-party republic
Per capita GNP:
US $5,480

These beautiful islands lie in the Indian Ocean, about 1,200 kilometres off the coast of East Africa. There are about 100 islands in the archipelago. The northern islands are shown below. Mahé Island is mountainous with granite rocks, streams and white, sandy beaches. The southern islands are low-lying atolls with rings of coral reef around lagoons. They have no fresh water and are largely uninhabited. Aldabra Island, about 400 kilometres northwest of Madagascar, is known for its unique giant Aldabra tortoise.

The islands were discovered by Portuguese sailors in the 1500s and for many years were the hiding place of European pirates and outlaws. The first permanent settlers arrived in 1756 when the French brought slaves from mainland Africa and planted sugar-cane. The British captured the islands in 1794 and more workers were moved in from Asia. Today's population is of mixed descent.

The Seychelles gained independence in 1976. The islands' beautiful beaches and sunshine attract many visitors from all over the world.

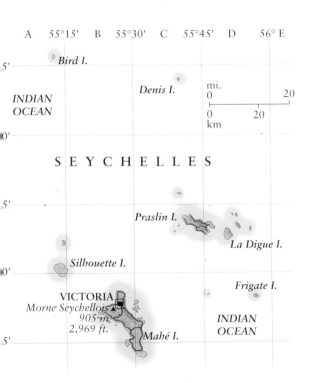

A 55°15' B 55°30' C 55°45' D 56° E

Bird I.

INDIAN
OCEAN

Denis I.

mi.
0   20
0   20
km

S E Y C H E L L E S

Praslin I.

La Digue I.

Silhouette I.

Frigate I.

VICTORIA
Morne Seychellois
905 m
2,969 ft.
Mahé I.

INDIAN
OCEAN

▶ *Mahé is the largest of the Seychelles and home to over 80 percent of the population. Lush vegetation sprawls across this fertile island, where tall cinnamon trees and coconut palms sway in the gentle breeze.*

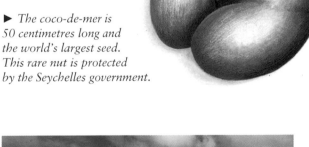

▶ *The coco-de-mer is 50 centimetres long and the world's largest seed. This rare nut is protected by the Seychelles government.*

MAURITIUS

All kinds of animals have lived on the rocky island of Mauritius over the years, but many have become extinct, including a large bird called the dodo. Animal extinction has been caused by centuries of settlement, plantation and hunting.

Mauritius is the largest island in a group that makes up the country of the same name. It is an expanse of black volcanic rock lying in the Indian Ocean. No people were living here when Arab seafarers discovered it 1000 years ago. The island was visited by Portuguese sailors and then settled in 1598 by the Dutch, who named it after Prince Maurice of Nassau. Then the French came, calling it Ile de France and shipping in slaves to plant sugar-cane. In the early 1800s the island was colonized by the British, who brought Indian labourers to work the huge sugar plantations. Independence came in 1968 and Mauritius became a republic in 1992.

The country has always depended on sugar, molasses (syrup squeezed from sugar-cane) and rum (alcohol made from sugar-cane) for its wealth. When world sugar prices plummeted in the 1980s the Mauritians began to develop new industries such as textiles, fertilizers and tourism.

▼ *A group of children from a fishing community show the mix of different peoples who live in Mauritius. They are the descendants of European settlers, Chinese and Indian traders and African slaves.*

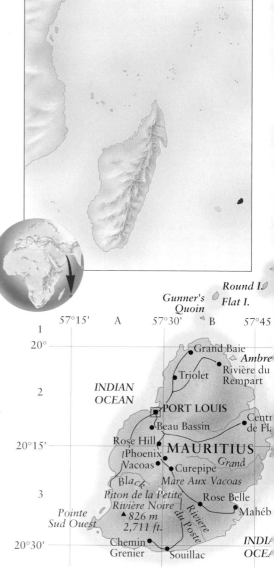

FACTS AND FIGURES

Area: 2,040 sq km
Population: 1,098,000
Capital: Port Louis (144,000)
Other major city: Curepipe (76,000)
Highest point: Piton de la Petite Rivière Noire (826 m)
Official language: English

Main religions: Christianity, Hinduism, Islam
Currency: Mauritius rupee
Main exports: Sugar, clothing, tea, toys, games
Government: Republic
Per capita GNP: US $2,700

NORTH
AMERICA

Arctic Circle

Tropic of Cancer

Equator

Tropic of Capricorn

NORTH AMERICA *Geography*

North America has a total land area of over 24 million square kilometres, making it the third largest continent after Asia and Africa. It is shaped like a giant triangle, narrowing at the base to form a thin strip of land that joins the continent to South America. This strip contains the countries of Central America. The North American continent also includes Greenland and many islands dotted across the Caribbean Sea.

The far north extends well above the Arctic Circle and is a frozen, treeless land. The continent's highest point, Mount McKinley, lies to the north in Alaska. The extreme south has both dry deserts and lush rainforests, with tropical vegetation covering many of the Caribbean islands. In between lie the forests of Canada and the northern United States of America. To the east the five Great Lakes form part of the continent's water drainage system. Prairies span the centre of North America.

Constant movement of the Earth's crust causes earthquakes from time to time. California's Death Valley, the lowest point in North America, lies in an earthquake zone. This movement of the crust has also shaped the great mountain ranges that run down the western side of the continent. It is still shaping them today.

▲ *Shimmering white sand stretches away behind a coconut palm on Tobago. This is one of the Windward Islands of the southeast Caribbean. Like most Caribbean islands, it enjoys a tropical climate.*

▲ *Rainforest covers much of Central America's eastern lowlands. Sea breezes from the northeast blow moisture in off the Atlantic Ocean, encouraging trees and plants to grow.*

▲ *Clear lakes surrounded by forests are typical of the mountain scenery of northwestern USA and western Canada.*

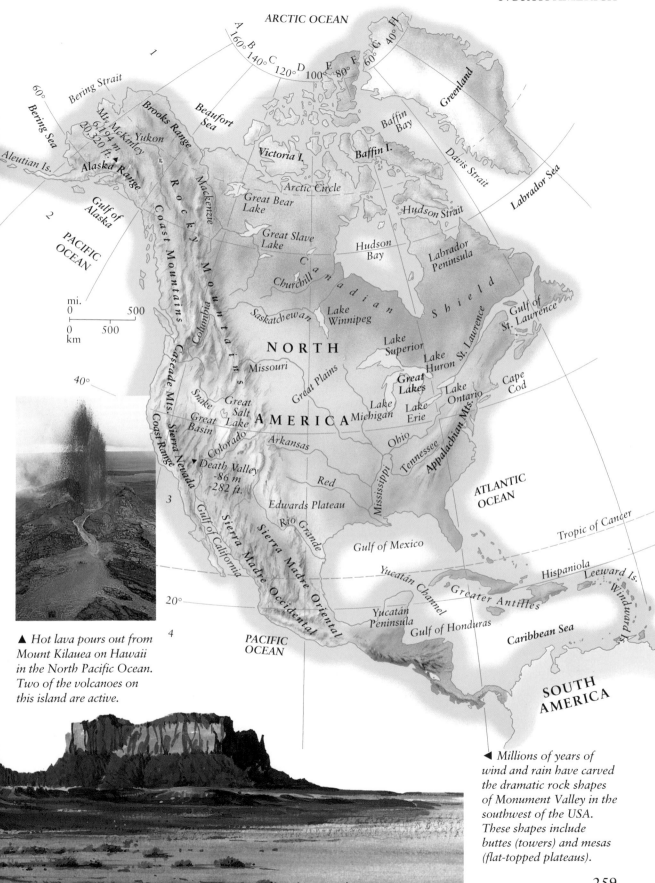

ARCTIC OCEAN

1

A 160° B C 120° D 100° E 80° F 60° G 40° H

60°

Bering Strait

Beaufort Sea

Greenland

Bering Sea

Brooks Range

Mt. McKinley 6,194 m 20,320 ft.

Yukon

Alaska Range

Aleutian Is.

Baffin Bay

Victoria I.

Baffin I.

Davis Strait

Labrador Sea

2

Gulf of Alaska

PACIFIC OCEAN

Coast Mountains

Mackenzie

Arctic Circle

Great Bear Lake

Great Slave Lake

Hudson Strait

Rocky Mountains

Churchill

Canadian

Hudson Bay

Labrador Peninsula

Shield

Gulf of St. Lawrence

mi.
0   500

0   500
km

Saskatchewan

Lake Winnipeg

Lake Superior

St. Lawrence

Columbia

Cascade Mts.

NORTH

Missouri

Great Plains

Lake Huron

Great Lakes

Lake Michigan

Lake Ontario

Cape Cod

40°

Snake

Great Salt Lake

Great Basin

AMERICA

Lake Erie

Sierra Nevada

Colorado

Arkansas

Ohio

Tennessee

Appalachian Mts.

ATLANTIC OCEAN

Coast Range

▲ Death Valley -86 m -282 ft.

Red

Mississippi

3

Edwards Plateau

Rio Grande

Gulf of Mexico

Tropic of Cancer

Hispaniola

Leeward Is.

20°

Gulf of California

Sierra Madre Occidental

Sierra Madre Oriental

Yucatán Channel

Greater Antilles

Windward Is.

4

Yucatán Peninsula

Gulf of Honduras

Caribbean Sea

PACIFIC OCEAN

SOUTH AMERICA

▲ Hot lava pours out from Mount Kilauea on Hawaii in the North Pacific Ocean. Two of the volcanoes on this island are active.

◄ Millions of years of wind and rain have carved the dramatic rock shapes of Monument Valley in the southwest of the USA. These shapes include buttes (towers) and mesas (flat-topped plateaus).

259

NORTH AMERICA *Political*

The enormous North American continent includes countries with all kinds of cultures, languages and economies. These very different countries have one thing in common – they were all controlled by a European power at one time. The countries of the North American mainland are now independent, but European links continue on some islands. Greenland is still officially part of Denmark and the islands of St Pierre and Miquelon, off Canada's east coast, are French. Britain, France and the Netherlands lay claim to a number of the Caribbean islands.

▲ *The White House in the city of Washington DC is the official residence of the President of the USA. Many of the people who live in the city work for the US government.*

The United States of America (USA) has the largest population and the most developed economy of any North American country. Canada has the next strongest economy, followed by Mexico. In 1994 the North American Free Trade Agreement came into operation between these three countries. This created the world's largest area of free trade (countries trading with each other without restrictions).

Most other Central American and Caribbean countries are much poorer, with a small number of people often controlling what wealth there is. This situation has frequently led to periods of revolution and war. In some cases countries have been controlled by the army. Over the years millions of people have left Central and South America, as well as the Caribbean, and moved to the USA or Canada. Large numbers still enter these countries, often illegally. The fastest-growing regions of the USA are the southern states that receive most of these immigrants, although these states are popular anyway because of their warm climate.

▲ *Nicaraguans attend a rally held by the National Opposition Union. This was the political party that defeated the socialists in the 1990 elections.*

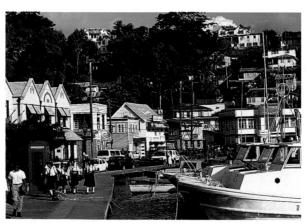

◀ *The peaceful dock area of St George's, the capital and main port of Grenada, was once overrun with soldiers. In 1983 Grenada's political system was upset when rebels killed the prime minister. Soldiers from the USA and other Caribbean islands helped to restore law and order.*

ARCTIC OCEAN

A B C D E F G H
160° 140° 120° 100° 80° 60° 40°

GREENLAND
(Denmark)

1

60°

Bering Sea

Beaufort
Sea

Aleutian Is.

U.S.A.

Labrador Sea

Arctic Circle

2

Gulf of
Alaska

PACIFIC
OCEAN

mi.
0   500

0   500
km

CANADA

40°

UNITED STATES OF AMERICA

KEY TO MAP
1 GUATEMALA
2 BELIZE
3 EL SALVADOR
4 HONDURAS
5 NICARAGUA
6 COSTA RICA
7 PANAMA
8 HAITI
9 DOMINICAN REPUBLIC
10 PUERTO RICO
11 ST CHRISTOPHER-NEVIS
12 ANTIGUA AND BARBUDA
13 DOMINICA
14 ST LUCIA
15 ST VINCENT AND THE
    GRENADINES
16 GRENADA
17 BARBADOS
18 TRINIDAD AND TOBAGO

3

Gulf of California

MEXICO

20°

4

PACIFIC
OCEAN

ATLANTIC
OCEAN

BAHAMAS   Tropic of Cancer

Gulf of Mexico

CUBA

8 9

JAMAICA

10   11 12

13

14
15
16

17

18

Caribbean Sea

2
1
4
3   5
6   7

◀ Toronto's dramatic
skyline looks out over
Lake Ontario. It is the
capital of the province
of Ontario and
Canada's leading
commercial centre.

261

NORTH AMERICA *Plants and Animals*

▲ *The monarch butterfly, with its distinctive orange, black and white markings, is common in most parts of North America.*

The wide range of climates on this continent means that it is home to numerous types of plants and animals. Only the far north is too cold to support much in the way of plant life, although polar bears, arctic wolves and various rodents survive in the snowy surroundings.

Thick forests cover much of Canada and the northern United States of America (USA). Animals such as raccoons and skunks are unique to the North American woodlands. Redwoods, the world's tallest trees, grow in California and can reach up to 110 metres in height. California is also home to one of the oldest living trees – a bristlecone pine that is 4,600 years old.

The prairies (grasslands) form the heart of the continent and animals such as prairie dogs, coyotes, badgers, pronghorns and gophers live there. Cacti, yuccas, jojoba shrubs and other hardy plants thrive in the deserts covering the southwestern USA and northern Mexico. The deserts also support lizards, jackrabbits, small rodents and various kinds of poisonous rattlesnake.

The Central American coast and Caribbean islands have lush tropical vegetation. This region is home to brilliantly coloured birds and spectacular insects, such as the Saint Vincent Amazon parrot and the Mexican sister butterfly.

▲ *Rattlesnakes eat birds and small rodents. They live in desert regions and hunt mostly at night, killing prey by injecting venom from their fangs.*

▼ *Millions of bison used to roam the continent's central prairies. They were nearly hunted to extinction in the 1800s, but are now protected.*

▼ *Flamingos gather on the coasts of Caribbean islands. Their long legs raise them high above the shallow waters that they sift constantly for food.*

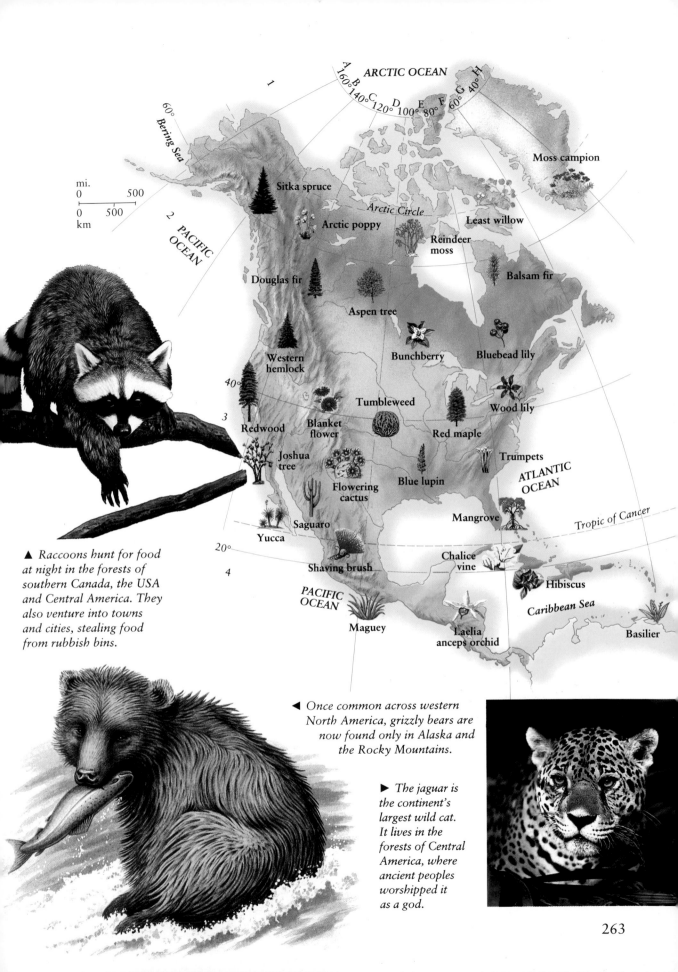

ARCTIC OCEAN

A B C D E F G H
160° 140° 120° 100° 80° 60° 40°

60°

Bering Sea

mi.
0   500
0   500
km

PACIFIC OCEAN

Arctic Circle

Sitka spruce

Arctic poppy

Least willow

Reindeer moss

Moss campion

Douglas fir

Balsam fir

Aspen tree

Bunchberry

Bluebead lily

Western hemlock

40°

Tumbleweed

Wood lily

Redwood

Blanket flower

Red maple

Trumpets

Joshua tree

ATLANTIC OCEAN

Flowering cactus

Blue lupin

Saguaro

Mangrove

Tropic of Cancer

Yucca

20°

Chalice vine

Hibiscus

Shaving brush

Caribbean Sea

PACIFIC OCEAN

Maguey

Laelia anceps orchid

Basilier

▲ Raccoons hunt for food at night in the forests of southern Canada, the USA and Central America. They also venture into towns and cities, stealing food from rubbish bins.

◄ Once common across western North America, grizzly bears are now found only in Alaska and the Rocky Mountains.

► The jaguar is the continent's largest wild cat. It lives in the forests of Central America, where ancient peoples worshipped it as a god.

263

GREENLAND

▲ *Kayaks have been used by the Inuit for thousands of years. An animal skin cover is stretched over a wooden framework.*

▼ *Viking swords have been found among the ruins of coastal settlements. These valued weapons were often richly decorated.*

Greenland is the largest island in the world. Geographically this remote country is part of North America, but it is actually a self-governing province of Denmark. Although 50 times larger than Denmark, Greenland has no more people than a big town. This is because it is so cold. Most of the island is covered by an ice sheet up to three kilometres thick. The mountainous coastline is broken up by fiords (narrow valleys deepened by glaciers) that were formed thousands of years ago.

Almost everyone lives on the southwest coast because the climate is mildest there. Most islanders are descendants of Inuit (Eskimos) and Danes. They speak Greenlandic, an Inuit language. Many also speak Danish.

The Inuit were the first people to settle on Greenland. Vikings from Norway and Iceland arrived in about AD985 and named the ice-covered island Greenland in order to attract more settlers. There have been periods of Danish rule since 1380, but in 1979 Denmark granted the island home rule. This means that Greenland now has control over its internal affairs.

▼ *Some hunters cross the snowy land on traditional sleds. The husky dogs provide company for the hunters, whose lives are often hard and lonely.*

◀ *Bright lights twinkle against the snow at the fishing village of Angmagssalik on the east coast. Much of Greenland does not see natural daylight for several months in the winter because it lies north of the Arctic Circle.*

FACTS AND FIGURES
Area: 2,175,600 sq km
Population: 55,000
Capital: Godthaab
(13,000)
Highest point:
Mt Gunnbjorn
(3,700 m)
Official languages:
Danish, Greenlandic
Main religion:
Christianity
Currency: Danish krone
Main exports:
Fish, lead, zinc
Government:
Self-governing part
of Denmark
Per capita GNP:
Est. over US $8,000

◀ *An Inuit girl and boy greet each other with a rub of the nose. Their trousers are made from animal skins to protect against the extreme cold.*

ARCTIC OCEAN

LINCOLN SEA

WANDEL SEA

Nord

GREENLAND
(Denmark)

GREENLAND SEA

Thule

Dundas

Danborg

Baffin Bay

Greenland Icecap

Upernavik

Scoresbysund

Umanak

Disko I.
Godhavn

Mt. Gunnbjorn
3,700 m
12,139 ft.

Egedesminde

Holsteinsborg

Sondre
Stromfiord

Denmark Strait

Davis Strait

Arctic Circle

Angmagssalik

ATLANTIC OCEAN

GODTHAAB ▣

mi.
0   200

0   200
km

Frederikshaab

LABRADOR SEA

Ivigtut
Julianehaab

Nanortalik

Cape
Farewell

CANADA *Introduction*

Canada is the second largest country in the world after Russia. Its northern lands reach deep into the frozen Arctic, but the majority of the population lives in the south, close to the border with the United States of America.

The country consists of ten provinces and two territories. It is full of contrasts, from fishing villages scattered along the Atlantic coast to major centres such as the French-speaking city of Montreal. The central plains form an immense grain-growing area, while rain-washed forests border the Pacific Ocean.

Canada was once a farming nation. Agriculture is still important, but now the country is highly industrialized and produces all kinds of manufactured goods.

The name Canada probably comes from *kanata*, a Native American word for village or community. The country itself has become a collection of different communities. Many people are of British or French origin and the country is officially bilingual (both English and French are spoken and written). Europeans, Asians and Native Americans, including the Inuit (Eskimos), also live here.

▲ *Road signs across Canada are printed in English and French. Most French-speaking Canadians live in the eastern province of Quebec.*

▶ *Canada's Houses of Parliament are in the capital, Ottawa, in the province of Ontario. The style of these buildings, and Canada's system of government, is based on the British parliament.*

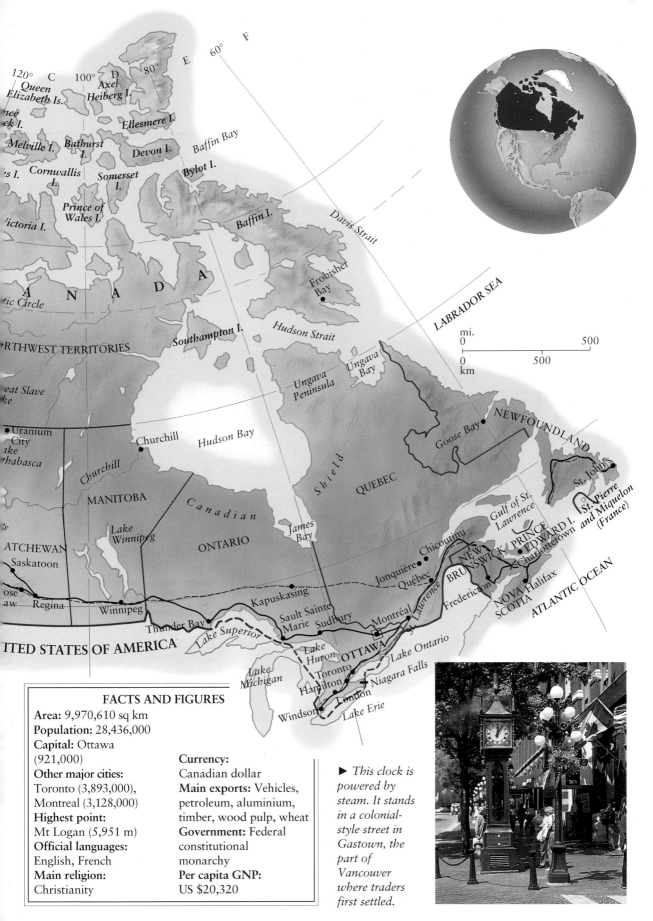

120° C 100° D 80° E 60° F

Queen
Elizabeth Is.

Axel
Heiberg I.

nce
ck I.

Ellesmere I.

Melville I.

Bathurst
I.

Devon I.

Baffin Bay

s I.

Cornwallis
I.

Somerset
I.

Bylot I.

Prince of
Wales I.

Victoria I.

Baffin I.

Davis Strait

C A N A D A

LABRADOR SEA

Frobisher
Bay

ic Circle

RTHWEST TERRITORIES

Southampton I.

Hudson Strait

mi.
0   500

0   500
km

eat Slave
ke

Ungava
Peninsula

Ungava
Bay

Uranium
City
ke
habasca

Churchill

Hudson Bay

Goose Bay

NEWFOUNDLAND

Churchill

S h i e l d

QUEBEC

St. John's

MANITOBA

C a n a d i a n

QUEBEC

Gulf of St.
Lawrence

St. Pierre
and Miquelon
(France)

Lake
Winnipeg

James
Bay

ONTARIO

Chicoutimi

PRINCE
EDWARD I.
Charlottetown

ATCHEWAN

Jonquière

Québec

NEW
BRUNSWICK

Saskatoon

Fredericton

NOVA
SCOTIA
Halifax

ATLANTIC OCEAN

ose
aw Regina

Winnipeg

Kapuskasing

Sault Sainte
Marie Sudbury

Montréal

St. Lawrence

Thunder Bay

Lake Superior

Lake
Huron

OTTAWA

Lake Ontario

UNITED STATES OF AMERICA

Lake
Michigan

Toronto

Niagara Falls

Hamilton

London

Windsor

Lake Erie

FACTS AND FIGURES

Area: 9,970,610 sq km
Population: 28,436,000
Capital: Ottawa
(921,000)
Other major cities:
Toronto (3,893,000),
Montreal (3,128,000)
Highest point:
Mt Logan (5,951 m)
Official languages:
English, French
Main religion:
Christianity

Currency:
Canadian dollar
Main exports: Vehicles,
petroleum, aluminium,
timber, wood pulp, wheat
Government: Federal
constitutional
monarchy
Per capita GNP:
US $20,320

► *This clock is
powered by
steam. It stands
in a colonial-
style street in
Gastown, the
part of
Vancouver
where traders
first settled.*

267

CANADA *Geography*

Canada has more lakes and inland waters than any other country in the world. It is well known for the extensive forests that cover almost half the country's total land area. Mountains dominate western Canada. The Coast Mountains follow its Pacific coastline and farther inland lie the snow-capped Rocky Mountains. The massive Rockies are split here and there by narrow river gorges and are part of the same range that runs all the way south to Mexico.

Beyond the Rockies the landscape softens into the Great Plains, with evergreen forests in the north and prairies further south. Bordering the plains is a gigantic, U-shaped region called the Canadian Shield, which surrounds Hudson Bay. It is made up of a rocky plateau of lakes and low hills. The Shield covers about half of Canada and is formed from some of the world's oldest rocks.

Canada extends into the Arctic, so icy winds keep winter temperatures well below freezing over much of the country. Only the south and the western province of British Columbia have a milder climate. Warm winds from the Gulf of Mexico can bring hot summers to southern regions, including south Ontario and areas along the St Lawrence River. It is rainy on the west coast.

▲ *The spectacular Athabasca Glacier is part of Jasper National Park, high up in the Rocky Mountains in Alberta.*

▼ *The famous Niagara Falls are two waterfalls on the Niagara River. They are on the border between Canada and the USA. Horseshoe Falls (front) are in Canada and the American Falls (behind) are in the USA.*

◄ *Wheat is grown in the prairie provinces. Once these western plains were wild, rolling grassland. Now the provinces of Alberta, Manitoba and Saskatchewan produce most of Canada's supply of wheat.*

▼ *Peggy's Cove is one of many tiny fishing villages nestled among the cliffs and bays of the Atlantic coast. People there have made a living from fishing for hundreds of years.*

▶ *The sea ice around Ellesmere Island, Canada's most northerly point, breaks up for a few weeks around June. There is 24-hour sunlight during this time and the waters become a rich feeding ground for migrating whales and seabirds.*

269

CANADA *Economy*

Canada is a rich country. Most of its wealth comes from developing what occurs naturally – trees, fish, oil, natural gas, minerals and water. It is the world's largest exporter of timber, paper and other forest products. Nearly 900,000 jobs depend on the forest industry. As well as being rich in all kinds of fish, Canada's huge lakes and rivers are dammed to provide electricity.

Oil and natural gas were found in the prairie provinces of Alberta, Saskatchewan and Manitoba in the 1940s and petroleum is now one of Canada's main exports. These provinces also provide fertile land for farming.

Canada has a highly modernized manufacturing industry, producing everything from cars to canned fruit. Most of the workforce, however, is employed in service industries such as education, healthcare, tourism and finance. Montreal and Toronto are the main financial centres.

Nearly 75 percent of Canada's trade is with its neighbour, the United States of America. The two countries signed an agreement in 1989 that aimed to abolish many trade barriers by 1999. Japan, the United Kingdom and Germany are also important trading partners.

▼ *Skilled workers assemble part of a jet engine. Canada has promoted and developed many high-tech manufacturing industries. Most of these goods are exported to other countries.*

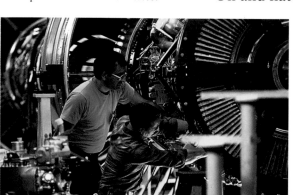

◄ *Helicopters are sometimes used to transport trunks to the sawmill from the steep forests where they grow in British Columbia. With over two and a half million square kilometres of forest, Canada is one of the world's leading producers of paper and its main ingredient, pulp.*

◀ *Grain warehouses stretch along the railway line in the tiny village of Viscount, Saskatchewan. The grain stored in them is easily loaded onto goods trains bound for eastern Canada.*

ECONOMIC SURVEY

Farming: Wheat and barley, fruit, vegetables, flax, rape, beef and dairy produce are important.
Forestry: Large amounts of timber, wood pulp and paper are produced.
Fishing: Cod is caught in the Atlantic, salmon in the Pacific. The lakes provide perch.

Mining: Petroleum, natural gas, copper, gold, iron ore, zinc, nickel and uranium are produced. Hydroelectric schemes provide about 60 percent of Canada's electricity.
Industry: Factories make processed food, vehicles, aircraft, machinery, steel, paper and chemicals.

THE ST LAWRENCE SEAWAY

The St Lawrence Seaway *(above)* is the waterway linking the heart of North America with the Atlantic Ocean. A network of 15 locks and canals overcome the 175-metre drop from the highest level of the Great Lakes to the St Lawrence River at Montreal. The Seaway, which opened in 1959, was built jointly by Canada and the USA. It remains a symbol of co-operation between the two nations.

▶ *The* Canadarm *is a robotic arm used on space shuttles. This one is lifting an astronaut safely out of the shuttle to work on a satellite. Canada has a thriving industry specializing in supplying goods for space travel.*

CANADA *People*

▲ *Today most Inuit children wear clothes made from modern fabrics instead of traditional animal skins.*

▼ *A woodcutter in north Quebec cuts a pine tree for firewood. The Native Americans only chop down as much wood as they need.*

For the last 350 years immigrants have flooded into Canada, mostly from Europe. By the 1800s many of these settlers were living in the cities of eastern Canada, while others pushed farther and farther westwards to set up farming communities on the prairies. Thousands of people have continued to arrive in recent decades.

Today most of the country's population lives in towns or cities. Almost half the people have either British or Irish ancestors. The other half are descended from the French or people who came from other European countries. The eastern province of Quebec is the centre of French culture – over 75 percent of its population are French Canadians. Across the country, on the west coast, the province of British Columbia is home to large numbers of British descendants as well as people who originally came from China, India, Pakistan, France, Germany and Scandinavia.

About two percent of Canadians are descended from the country's first inhabitants, the Native Americans. These include the Inuit (Eskimo) and Iroquois peoples. Most Inuit live in small communities in the colder, more northerly regions. Many of them still fish and hunt animals, but their traditional igloos and skin tents have now been replaced by modern housing. In 1992 Canada's Northwest Territories voted to create a self-governing homeland called Nunavut for the Inuit people, which will come into being in 1999.

▶ *Popular street cafes in the city of Quebec reflect the French lifestyle that dominates this part of Canada.*

WINTER SPORTS

Canada is a sports-loving nation and the country's long, cold winters are a time for outdoor fun. Ice hockey is Canada's most popular sport. Many boys and girls begin playing when they are only seven years old. Some professional players, who are now national heroes, began playing on frozen ponds as children. Canadians also enjoy skiing, skating, tobogganing and ice fishing. Canada was the host of the 1988 Winter Olympics.

◄ *A Nova Scotian boy learns to play the bagpipes. Nova Scotia means 'New Scotland' and many of its people preserve the old Scottish ways.*

▼ *The Calgary Stampede, a rodeo festival held each year, keeps alive the spirit of the Canadian Wild West. The Stampede is one of Alberta's leading events for tourists.*

CANADA *History*

The first people to make their homes here crossed over from Asia about 40,000 years ago. Thousands of years later the Inuit people (Eskimos) settled in the freezing north. The descendents of these early inhabitants are called Native Americans. The first Europeans to arrive, around AD1000, were probably Vikings from Iceland and Greenland.

In the 1400s and 1500s the French and British came. They laid claim to lands in the east, attracted by rich fishing grounds. There was also the chance to trade in furs. Bitter struggles erupted between the colonists during the 1700s. Britain took most of the French land and created two colonies, one English-speaking, the other French-speaking. These colonies were united under the Dominion of Canada in 1867, which created four provinces – Quebec, Ontario, Nova Scotia and New Brunswick. When the Canadian-Pacific Railroad was opened in 1885, new settlements were established in the far west.

Since World War II Canada has strengthened its political and economic ties with other countries. As part of the Commonwealth it also recognizes the British monarch. In recent decades many French Canadians, who want Quebec to become a separate nation, have caused tensions within the country. In 1994 provincial elections were held in Quebec. They were won by the Québecois party, which supports independence for Quebec.

▲ *Characters from Native American folklore are represented on traditional totem poles carved out of wood.*

▲ *This map of the Gulf of St Lawrence shows the first French settlers landing in Canada in 1534, led by the navigator, Jacques Cartier.*

▶ *During the American Revolutionary War (1775-1783) thousands of British loyalists fled the USA and went to Canada.*

◄ *The last spike is ceremonially driven home at the completion of the Canadian-Pacific Railroad in 1885. This railway linked Canada from coast to coast and was an engineering triumph. It cut through dense forests and vast regions of solid rock.*

▼ *A Mohawk demonstrator photographs the scene at a land dispute in Quebec in 1990. Many Native Americans are calling for more control over their ancestral lands.*

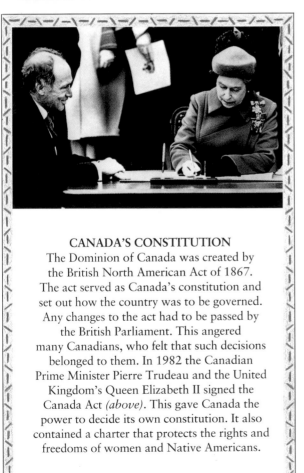

CANADA'S CONSTITUTION

The Dominion of Canada was created by the British North American Act of 1867. The act served as Canada's constitution and set out how the country was to be governed. Any changes to the act had to be passed by the British Parliament. This angered many Canadians, who felt that such decisions belonged to them. In 1982 the Canadian Prime Minister Pierre Trudeau and the United Kingdom's Queen Elizabeth II signed the Canada Act *(above)*. This gave Canada the power to decide its own constitution. It also contained a charter that protects the rights and freedoms of women and Native Americans.

UNITED STATES OF AMERICA *Introduction*

The United States of America (USA) is the world's fourth largest country. Its territory stretches a third of the way around the Earth, from the Atlantic Ocean to the Pacific Ocean, crossing eight time zones.

The country is divided into 50 states. Two of these are isolated from the rest – Alaska, which is on Canada's western edge, and Hawaii, a chain of tropical islands in the Pacific Ocean. The USA is ruled according to its famous Constitution, a document setting out how the country is governed. It allows individual states to make some of their own laws. This helps to give each state its own special character.

No other country in the world contains so much variety within its borders, from the icebound lands of Alaska and scorched deserts of the southwest, to the wide plains in the Midwest and subtropical forests of the southeast.

The population is no less varied. People from all over the world have made their homes in this country, bringing with them many different religions, customs and languages. Most American people enjoy a standard of living that is one of the highest in the world.

KEY TO MAP
NJ – NEW JER
VT – VERMON
DE – DELAWA
CT – CONNEC
RI – RHODE IS
PA – PENNSYLV
MA – MASSACHU
NH – NEW HAMPS
WV – WEST VIRGINIA

◀ *The Statue of Liberty was a gift from France in 1886. It towers over New York Harbor and represents freedom for the American people.*

FACTS AND FIGURES

Area: 9,158,960 sq km
Population: 258,233,000
Capital: Washington DC (607,000)
Other major cities: New York City (7,323,000), Los Angeles (3,486,000), Chicago (2,784,000)
Highest point: Mt McKinley (6,194 m)
Official language: English

Main religions: Christianity, Judaism, Islam
Currency: US dollar
Main exports: Aircraft, vehicles, chemicals, coal, machinery, maize, oil, soya beans, wheat
Government: Federal republic
Per capita GNP: US $23,120

F 110° G 100° H 90° I mi. 80° J 70° K

CANADA

MONTANA
Missouri
Helena
Yellowstone
IDAHO
Boise
Snake
Rocky Mountains
WYOMING
Great Salt Lake
Great Plains
NORTH DAKOTA
Bismarck
SOUTH DAKOTA
Pierre
MINNESOTA
St. Paul
Madison
Lake Superior
Lake Michigan
Lake Huron
WISCONSIN
Milwaukee
Chicago
MICHIGAN
Lansing
Detroit
Lake Ontario
Lake Erie
Niagara Falls
NEW YORK
Cleveland
PA
MAINE
Bangor
Augusta
Montpelier
VT NH Portland
Concord
Boston
MA Providence
Albany
Hartford
CT RI
Harrisburg
New York City
Trenton
NJ

UTAH
Great Salt Lake
Salt Lake City
Cheyenne
NEBRASKA
Platte
Colorado
COLORADO
Denver
Des Moines
IOWA
Davenport
Lincoln
Mississippi
Missouri
ILLINOIS
Springfield
INDIANA
Indianapolis
OHIO
Columbus
Philadelphia
WASHINGTON D.C.
WV Dover DE
Annapolis
MARYLAND

UNITED STATES
Arkansas
KANSAS
Topeka
Kansas City
Jefferson City
St. Louis
MISSOURI
Ohio
Frankfort
Charleston
KENTUCKY
VIRGINIA
Richmond
Raleigh
NORTH CAROLINA
NORTH ATLANTIC OCEAN

OF AMERICA
OKLAHOMA
Santa Fe
Canadian
Red
Oklahoma City
ARKANSAS
Little Rock
Memphis
TENNESSEE
Nashville
Tennessee
Appalachian Mts
Columbia
Atlanta
SOUTH CAROLINA

ARIZONA
NEW MEXICO
Phoenix
Tucson
El Paso
Rio Grande
Fort Worth
Dallas
TEXAS
Austin
San Antonio
Houston
Jackson
LOUISIANA
MISSISSIPPI
Baton Rouge
New Orleans
ALABAMA
Montgomery
GEORGIA
Tallahassee
Jacksonville
FLORIDA
Cape Canaveral
Tampa
Lake Okeechobee
Everglades
Miami
Florida Keys

MEXICO

Gulf of Mexico

◄ The bald eagle is the national symbol of the USA. It is found only in North America, where it is now a protected species.

► The Golden Gate Bridge spans San Francisco Bay in California. It is one of the world's most impressive suspension bridges.

UNITED STATES OF AMERICA *Geography*

▲ *Mangroves thrive in the tropical coastal swamps of Florida and other southeastern states. Tangled roots help to anchor these trees as the tide sweeps in and out. Mangrove swamps are home to alligators, turtles and several types of poisonous snake.*

Two great mountain chains dominate the east and west of the United States of America. In the east the Appalachian Mountains are low and covered with forest. To the west the Rocky Mountains are much higher, with many peaks reaching over 4,000 metres high.

Between these two ranges massive plains extend across the centre of the country. The northern and central parts of the plains are known as the Midwest. Drought is a problem in the north of this region. However, much of the area is fertile farmland, watered by major rivers such as the Mississippi, Missouri and Ohio. These rivers are part of a water drainage system that includes the five Great Lakes in the northeast. Forests cross much of the northern regions, covering parts of the Pacific northwest, the Midwest, the northeast and Alaska. Almost a third of Alaska lies north of the Arctic Circle and some of this land is permanently frozen, with temperatures falling to minus 60 degrees centigrade in the winter. Glaciers are common even in the southern parts of Alaska.

The Midwest experiences floods and fierce tornadoes. All the southern states have hot summers and mild, or even warm, winters. In the southeast the climate is humid, with storms along the coast. However, there is little rainfall in the southwest, where deserts cover much of the land. In the state of Hawaii, far out in the Pacific Ocean, the tropical climate hardly changes throughout the year.

◄ *Old Faithful is a regularly erupting geyser in Yellowstone National Park, in the Rocky Mountains. Set up in 1872, this was the world's first national park.*

▼ *Portland Lighthouse, in the northeastern state of Maine, was built in 1791. It is one of a chain of lighthouses that protects ships from the perils of Maine's choppy waters.*

◀ *Young wheat grows on the lowlands of western Washington. This state is famous for its breathtaking scenery – not only lush lowlands, but abundant evergreen forests and rugged mountain ranges.*

▼ *Mount McKinley is part of Denali National Park in Alaska. Denali, meaning 'the great one', is the Native American name for this mountain.*

THE GRAND CANYON

The Grand Canyon, in northwestern Arizona, is one of the most spectacular river valleys in the world. The waters of the Colorado River have carved this valley from the desert rock over the past six million years. The Grand Canyon is over one and a half kilometres deep in places. The world's tallest skyscraper (Sears Tower in Chicago) would fit into the deepest parts nearly four times over.

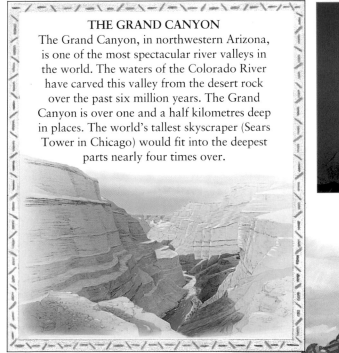

▶ *Plants must be very hardy to survive in the southwestern deserts, where temperatures can soar to 50 degrees centigrade. The roots of the saguaro cactus (right) can store up to eight tonnes of water, collected during the very brief periods of rain.*

UNITED STATES OF AMERICA *Economy*

▲ *The Trans-Alaska Pipeline carries huge amounts of oil from north Alaska to the state's southern coast.*

▼ *Cameras roll on a set in Hollywood, the centre of the film world. The film industry employs thousands of people in the Los Angeles area.*

"The business of America is business," President Calvin Coolidge said in 1925. He could have said exactly the same today. The United States of America (USA) has enormous economic power and it leads the world in the production of manufactured goods. Despite this, service industries (providing services rather than goods) are now the largest part of the economy of the USA. These include property, finance, insurance, entertainment and healthcare.

The country's enormous size has always been a great advantage. The land yields large amounts of natural resources such as mineral deposits and fresh water. Vast forests meet most of the country's timber needs and many of its large rivers have been dammed to provide hydroelectric power.

Agriculture earns much less income than manufacturing and service industries, but it is still carried out on a grand scale. Unlike countries that have to import food to feed their population, the USA is almost self-sufficient. The Midwestern plains are the most important farming regions. Kansas has earned the nickname 'breadbasket of America' because it produces so much wheat.

The country's economy is largely based on a free market system. Companies are encouraged to compete against each other to win trade.

ECONOMIC SURVEY
Farming: Large farms have made the USA the world's leading food producer. Major farm products include beef, dairy foods, pigs, chickens, turkeys, cereals including maize and wheat, soya beans, cotton, tobacco, fruit and vegetables.
Forestry: Timber is produced, plus pulp for paper making.
Fishing: Three fishing grounds – the Atlantic, the Gulf of Mexico and the Pacific – yield more than five million tonnes of fish a year.
Mining: Petroleum, natural gas, coal (the USA is the largest coal producer in the world), gold, copper, iron ore, silver and uranium are mined.
Industry: Products include aircraft, electronic goods, cars, chemicals and foods. Service industries are very important, generating over 70 percent of the GNP.

▲ *Computer components, such as microprocessors, are major exports. The two main high-tech regions are Silicon Valley in California and along Route 128, a road in Massachusetts.*

▼ *Building cars and trucks is big business in the USA. The major production centre is Detroit in Michigan.*

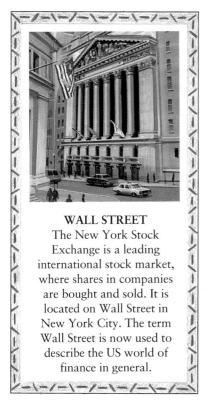

WALL STREET
The New York Stock Exchange is a leading international stock market, where shares in companies are bought and sold. It is located on Wall Street in New York City. The term Wall Street is now used to describe the US world of finance in general.

▶ *A combine harvester sweeps across a wheatfield in the Midwest. The USA began its history as an agricultural nation and today teams of combine harvesters travel the length of the country, working to get the harvest in on time.*

UNITED STATES OF AMERICA *People*

The United States of America (USA) has often been described as a melting pot, a place where people from all over the world have mixed together to make one nation. The people came from many different places, including Europe, Africa and Asia. Some are descended from the Native American peoples.

Many people of the USA have a strong sense of being American, yet wish to preserve the traditions of the countries they originally came from. As a result whole sections of cities mirror the way of life of particular nationalities.

Although most people speak English, Spanish is now the second most common language. About one in ten Americans comes from a Spanish-speaking country such as Mexico or Puerto Rico.

Three quarters of the population lives in large, sprawling cities. Many cities are continuing to expand, especially in the south and west.

Americans are free to worship as they please. The freedom of religion, along with the freedom of speech, is written down in the law of the land, which is called the Constitution. This law also sets out how the country is governed. Each state sends representatives and senators to Congress in Washington DC. Congress makes the laws, but the President of the USA can overrule some of them if he has the support of enough members of Congress.

▲ *Jazz is often seen as the one true American type of music. It grew up around 1900 in the southern city of New Orleans, which is still a centre for jazz music.*

◀ *This Puerto Rican police officer, on duty in a US city, reflects the importance of the Spanish-speaking population.*

▶ *The cowboy has long been a legendary American figure. Modern cowboys work on cattle ranches. They also display their skills at shows called rodeos.*

▲ *A class photograph shows how successful the USA has been in bringing people of all nationalities together.*

▲ *Most large cities in the USA have a neighbourhood with an Italian culture, such as New York's Little Italy.*

NATIVE AMERICANS

European explorers in the 1400s and 1500s thought that North America was India, so they called the local population Indians. Today the term Native American is considered a more accurate way of describing the original inhabitants of the continent and their descendants. Native Americans include the Inuit (Eskimo), Iroquois, Cherokee, Sioux and Apache peoples.

UNITED STATES OF AMERICA *History*

The first inhabitants of the United States of America (USA) were the Native Americans. They had lived here for around 40,000 years before Europeans arrived in the 1500s.

By the 1700s British settlers had established 13 colonies on the east coast, which were ruled from Britain. When the colonies objected to British control and taxes, the American Revolutionary War (1775-1783) broke out with Britain. The colonies won this war and became known as states. The USA was born. In 1787 the law of the land was drawn up. It was called the Constitution and still applies today.

During the early 1800s thousands of settlers pushed westwards and the country grew rapidly. Tensions developed between the industrial north and the agricultural south. The south wanted individual states to have more power and the right to use African slaves. From 1861 to 1865 a Civil War raged between the southern and northern states. The north won and slavery was finally abolished.

▲ *These homes in New Mexico were built by the Anasazi people about 2,000 years ago.*

By 1900 people from all over the world had settled in every part of the country. Since then the steady growth of the population has helped to make the USA a very powerful country.

▼ *Cherokees leave their lands near the Atlantic coast to travel west during the winter of 1838. Forced to leave by the US government, thousands of Cherokees died on the 2,000 kilometre journey. It became known as the 'Trail of Tears'.*

▲ *Molly Pitcher, the wife of an American soldier, loads a cannon in the American Revolutionary War (1775-1783). She became a national heroine as a result of her bravery.*

CIVIL RIGHTS MOVEMENT

Civil rights are rights, such as freedom of speech, that are given by law to a member of the community.

The enslavement of African Americans became illegal in 1865. However, many were still denied the right to get an education, a job, or to vote a hundred years later.

During the 1950s and 1960s people such as Martin Luther King led peaceful protests to press for rights for African Americans.

In 1964 the government of the USA approved the Civil Rights Act. This protected not only racial groups, but also disabled people and women.

► *Over half a million people died in the Civil War (1861-1865) between the Union (northern states) and the Confederacy (southern states).*

► *Huge aircraft carriers have helped the USA to continue growing as a massive military power.*

▼ *A space shuttle lifts off from the launch pad at Cape Canaveral on Florida's east coast. The journey into space has been a major achievement of the twentieth century. On 20 July 1969 the USA became the first country to put people on the Moon.*

IMMIGRANTS TO THE USA
Almost 38 million people arrived in the USA between 1820 and 1930. Many of them passed through Ellis Island *(above)*, the main reception centre for immigrants, in New York Harbor. This was their first glimpse of North America. Most of these immigrants, who came from all over the world, were eventually given US citizenship.

285

UNITED STATES OF AMERICA *Way of Life*

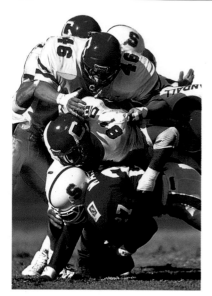

▲ *American football players wear shoulder and thigh pads to prevent injury. Each year the 28 professional teams of the National Football League compete to reach the championship, called the Superbowl.*

The United States of America (USA) has given the world the hamburger, Mickey Mouse, jeans, jazz music and cowboy films. Although each of the 50 states has its own identity, Americans have many things in common and take a great pride in the country in which they live.

Bringing friends and family together for celebrations plays a large role in the American way of life. One of the most popular holidays is Independence Day, on 4 July, when Americans celebrate the day they became independent from Britain. Another important date is Thanksgiving Day, a type of harvest festival that takes place in late Autumn. Both holidays are celebrated in true American style, which includes food, drink, parades and firework displays.

Families spend their leisure time in many ways, such as attending inner-city street festivals and state fairs, enjoying picnics and barbecues, or going to the cinema.

Many people live in the big suburbs that surround most American cities. Highways connect these areas to the city centres, where large numbers of suburban dwellers work.

All kinds of sports are extremely popular. Baseball, basketball and American football rank among the favourites. Some top sports personalities are the highest-paid people in the USA.

JAMBALAYA
Made up of leftovers, *jambalaya* mixes ingredients such as rice, prawns, green peppers and fiery spices. It is a recipe from New Orleans that blends French and African cookery.

◄ *Bright neon lights welcome thousands of visitors to the casinos and nightclubs of Las Vegas in the Nevada desert. This famous tourist resort is a gambler's paradise.*

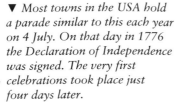

▼ *Most towns in the USA hold a parade similar to this each year on 4 July. On that day in 1776 the Declaration of Independence was signed. The very first celebrations took place just four days later.*

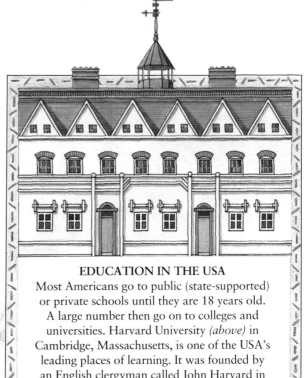

EDUCATION IN THE USA

Most Americans go to public (state-supported) or private schools until they are 18 years old. A large number then go on to colleges and universities. Harvard University *(above)* in Cambridge, Massachusetts, is one of the USA's leading places of learning. It was founded by an English clergyman called John Harvard in 1636 and is the oldest college in the country.

▲ *Yellow taxis are a common sight on the streets of New York City. Many New Yorkers leave their cars at home and take taxis and buses instead.*

◄ *The licence plate of an American car indicates which state it comes from. Each state has a different message on its licence plate.*

MEXICO *Introduction*

Mexico has been influenced by a rich mixture of traditions and cultures. These range from the country's own early civilizations, such as the Mayan, Toltec and Aztec, to Spanish and modern American ways of life. Over 90 percent of today's population belongs to the Roman Catholic Church, which the Spanish introduced in the 1500s. Also Spanish is the country's official language. The Mexicans' love of baseball reflects the influence of its neighbour, the United States of America (USA).

Mexico's landscape is unusually varied. Within very short distances of one another there are tropical coastal lowlands, high mountains, volcanoes and parched deserts. A great river in the north, the Rio Grande, forms over half the border between Mexico and the USA. Large numbers of Mexican people go to the USA in search of work and cross this river to get there.

Many young people from rural areas have moved to Mexico City to find work. As a result some villages now stand empty and the capital is growing rapidly. Over 21 million people live in and around this city today. It is growing too fast to provide for all of its population, so many people live in slums and have no work. However, a lot of new factories are springing up along Mexico's border with the USA, creating jobs for workers in the car and electronics industries.

▲ *This model celebrates Mexico's Day of the Dead fiesta, which takes place in November each year. It is a time when people remember friends and relatives who have died.*

◄ *The large cement factory in the background and the cramped houses show how industrialized Mexico City is. The football pitch nearby reveals the Mexicans' love of this sport. Mexico City has twice hosted the World Cup finals.*

FACTS AND FIGURES

Area: 1,967,180 sq km
Population: 91,261,000
Capital: Mexico City
(15,048,000)
Other major city:
Guadalajara (1,651,000)
Highest point:
Citlaltépetl (5,700 m)
Official language:
Spanish
Main religion:
Christianity

Currency:
Mexican peso
Main exports:
Petroleum and
petroleum products,
vehicles, engines, cotton,
machinery, coffee, fish,
fertilizers, minerals
Government:
Federal republic
Per capita GNP:
US $3,470

▲ Busy highways lead to
Mexico City. The capital's
growing population means
that the roads are becoming
increasingly crowded.

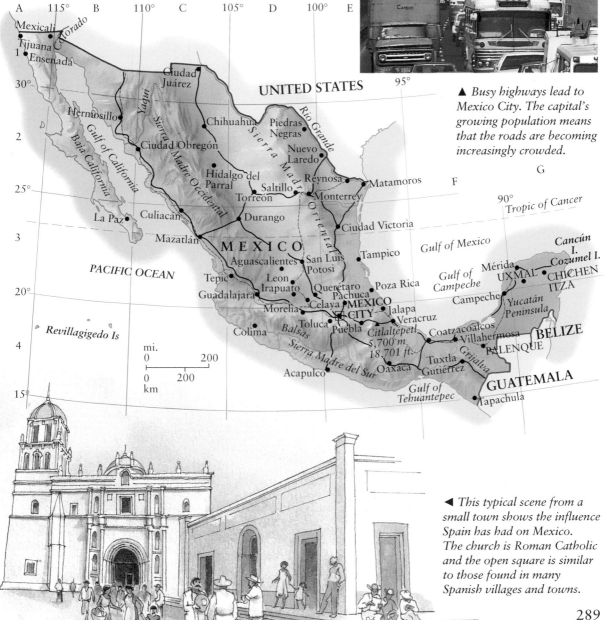

◄ This typical scene from a
small town shows the influence
Spain has had on Mexico.
The church is Roman Catholic
and the open square is similar
to those found in many
Spanish villages and towns.

MEXICO *Geography and Economy*

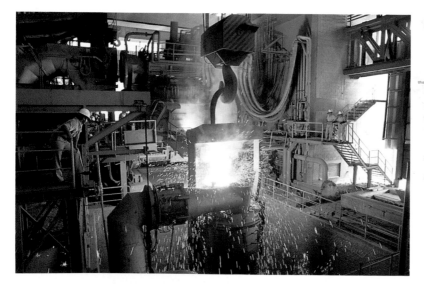

Mexico is dominated by a vast central plateau. Two rugged mountain ranges, the Sierra Madre Oriental and the Sierra Madre Occidental, tower either side of it. In places the plateau reaches heights of nearly 3,000 metres above sea level. Much of its northern region is like a desert, but the Valley of Mexico, on the plateau's southern edge, is more fertile. This has brought most of the population and industry to the valley, despite the threat of earthquakes and eruptions from nearby volcanoes.

Tropical lowlands lie around the Gulf of Mexico and along parts of the Pacific coast. To the west Baja California is a mountainous, 1,200-kilometre peninsula, filled with desert plants such as cacti.

Much of Mexico's economy depends on rapidly growing industry around the capital and trade with the United States of America (USA). The economy will probably be greatly improved by the North American Free Trade Agreement between Mexico, the USA and Canada, which came into being in 1994. Mexico was once a farming nation, but now only one in four workers is employed on farms. Its main products are manufactured goods and oil. Tourism also provides an income. Foreign visitors stay in resorts and visit the ruins of Mayan cities.

▲ *The inhospitable mountains of the Sierra Madre Occidental range run through the northern state of Chihuahua. Poor soil and dry conditions mean that few people live there. Large parts of these mountains are so wild that they have never been explored on foot.*

◀ *Steel production is one of Mexico's main manufacturing industries. Many of the country's steelworks are located around Monterrey, which is near Mexico's border with the USA.*

◀ *High above the waters of the Gulf of Mexico, an oil worker examines a drilling platform. Most of Mexico's extensive oil reserves lie offshore and were only discovered in the 1970s. Since then money earned from oil has helped to improve the country's economy.*

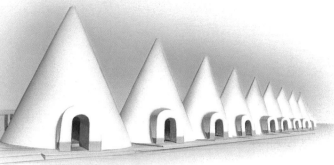

▲ *Cone-shaped silos store a year's maize harvest. The Mayans were growing maize as their main food crop in Mexico around 7,000 years ago. Today it is just as important a source of food, forming the basis of many Mexican dishes. More land is devoted to growing maize than to any other crop.*

▼ *Ox-drawn carts and ploughs are still common on many small farms. About half of the country's farmland consists of* ejidos *(areas of land owned jointly by members of local communities). Land passed into the hands of ordinary people after political reforms in 1917. Before this most farmers worked for a few powerful landowners on large estates called haciendas.*

MEXICO *People and History*

▲ *This Aztec shield, decorated with brightly coloured feathers, was used for ceremonies only. Fierce Aztec warriors would fight to enlarge their empire and take prisoners to sacrifice for the gods.*

Mexico's early history is one of great empires. Along the Gulf coast the Olmec people established Mexico's first advanced civilization by 1200BC. In southeast Mexico the Mayans prospered from AD250 to 850, building great cities and temples where they worshipped the Sun and Moon. Then a people called the Toltecs spread over the centre and south, creating an empire that lasted from the 900s to the 1200s. The powerful Aztec civilization flourished from the mid-1400s and stretched from coast to coast, with its capital at Tenochtitlán (now Mexico City).

In 1519 Spanish conquerors started a bloody war in the Gulf of Mexico. They conquered the Aztecs and Spain ruled for the next 300 years. Mexico became independent in 1821, but war with the United States of America (USA) followed and Mexico lost much of its land. This troubled period ended in 1917 and a new system of laws was adopted. Since then much has been done to try and improve conditions for ordinary people in Mexico.

The majority of Mexicans are mestizos (a mixture of Spanish and Native American). Many villagers still speak one of the Native American languages and the country's festivals reflect traditions that are 5,000 years old. Now most Mexicans live in large cities where influences from the USA and Europe are transforming everyday life.

▼ *The great pyramid of El Castillo, a sacred temple, lies behind an astronomical observatory at Chichén Itzà. Many Mayan ruins are found on the Yucatán Peninsula.*

▲ *The church, El Triunfo on Baja California, shows just how much Spanish rule has influenced Mexico's religion and architecture. Churches and public buildings all over the country are Spanish in style.*

► *Striking headdresses and colourful hand-woven clothes such as these would have been seen at many Toltec markets over a thousand years ago. Today Mexicans take great pride in keeping their Native American history alive.*

TORTILLAS

Tortillas have been a basic food for the majority of Mexicans since before the time of the Aztec civilization. These thin pancakes are made from maize or wheat flour. They can be eaten plain or as part of tacos (a fried tortilla stuffed with a meat or cheese filling). They are also served as enchiladas (rolled tacos covered with a hot sauce).

▼ *Stall-holders prepare for a market in Oaxaca. Mexican farmers have grown a wide variety of crops for thousands of years. As far back as 7000BC they became some of the very first people to grow maize, tomatoes, avocados, peppers and many types of beans.*

GUATEMALA

Guatemala has Central America's biggest population, largest city (Guatemala City) and highest peak (Volcan Tajumulco). Tropical rainforests lie to the north of this mountainous country and there are cool highlands in the centre. Most people live in the southern highlands where the chief crop, coffee, is grown. Agriculture is the main source of income and many farms lie in the Pacific lowlands. A mild climate, fertile soil and plentiful rainfall should make this a prosperous country, but it remains poor. This is mainly because of its violent history.

Civilized cultures flourished here 3,000 years ago. Spain invaded in 1523, conquered the local population and ruled until 1821. In 1839 the country became an independent republic, but power remained largely in the hands of the Spanish. From the 1950s onwards there was much fighting and the army took control for periods of time. An elected government has ruled since 1986.

Guatemala is famous for its spectacular ancient ruins, lively fiestas and marimba music, which is played on an instrument like a xylophone. About half the people are descended from the ancient Mayans and are poor farmers. Most other Guatemalans are *ladinos* (a mix of Native American and Spanish). The *ladinos* control the government and economy today.

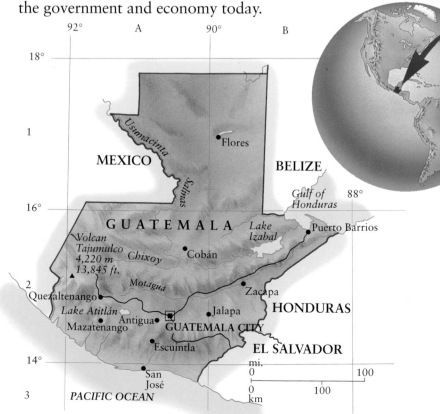

▲ The quetzal, with its spectacular green and scarlet plumage, is the national bird of Guatemala. Some of its tail feathers are up to 90 centimetres long and were used by Mayan chiefs as symbols of power. After centuries of hunting, the quetzal is now extremely rare.

◄ *Villagers carry fresh water from beautiful Lake Atitlán. A number of volcanoes are dotted around this lake, which itself has been formed from the crater of an extinct volcano.*

FACTS AND FIGURES
Area: 108,890 sq km
Population: 10,029,000
Capital: Guatemala City
(2,000,000)
Other major city:
Quezaltenango (246,000)
Highest point:
Volcan Tajumulco
(4,220 m)
Official language:
Spanish
Main religion:
Christianity
Currency: Quetzal
Main exports: Coffee,
sugar, bananas, cotton,
beef, cardamom
Government:
Multi-party republic
Per capita GNP:
US $980

▶ *Statues have been unearthed of the all-powerful gods worshipped by the ancient Mayans. Their faces combine babies' features with those of animals such as the jaguar, a traditional Mayan symbol of courage and strength.*

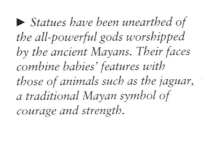

▶ *Horse races form part of the riotous celebrations for the fiesta of All Saints' Day. Fiestas are a mixture of very old traditions.*

BELIZE

Belize is a hot, humid land of mountain forests and coastal mangrove swamps. It is the most thinly populated country in Central America. The majority of its people live along the coast and are descendants of African slaves, Mayan people, European settlers, or a mixture of these groups.

Belize relies on agriculture for much of its income. Sugar-cane is grown on plantations and small farms produce maize, beans, fruit and vegetables. The timber industry has stripped large areas of forest. However, Belize has now set up national parks and conservation projects to preserve its land and wildlife.

The Mayan civilization flourished here from about AD300 to AD900. Little is known about life in Belize from that time until the 1520s, when Spain claimed the area as part of Guatemala. Shipwrecked British sailors settled a century later and Britain gained control of Belize, naming it British Honduras. This colony became self-governing in 1964, changed its name to Belize in 1973 and gained full independence in 1981. British armed forces were brought in to protect Belize from attacks by Guatemala, which only recognized Belize's independence in 1991.

ENDANGERED WORLD

The black howler monkey is at risk because the loss of forests is threatening its habitat.

FACTS AND FIGURES
Area: 22,960 sq km
Population: 205,000
Capital: Belmopan (5,300)
Other major city: Belize City (44,000)
Highest point: Victoria Peak (1,122 m)
Official language: English
Main religion: Christianity
Currency: Belize dollar
Main exports: Timber, sugar, fish products, clothes, fruit
Government: Constitutional monarchy
Per capita GNP: US $2,210

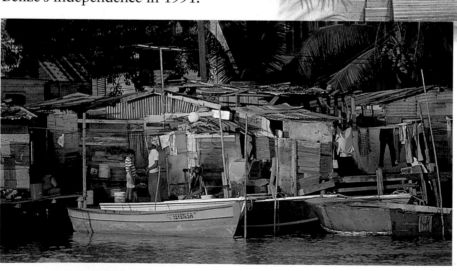

▲ *Altun Ha is one of many important Mayan sites in Belize. The Mayan people lived in this area of Central America for over 600 years, up until about AD900.*

◄ *Houses stretch right down to the water's edge in Belize City, which lies at the mouth of the Belize River.*

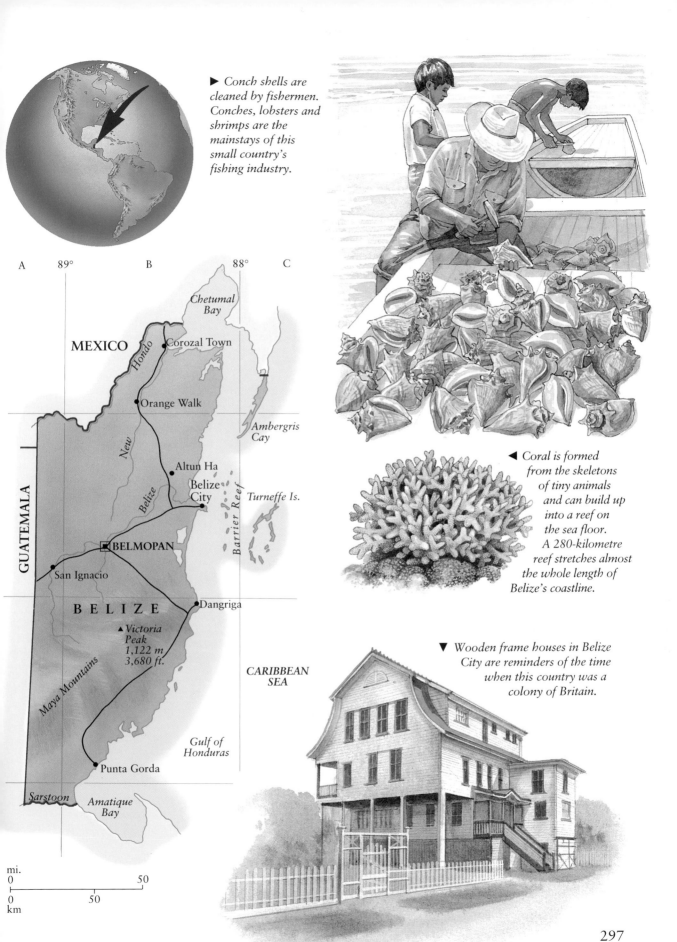

► Conch shells are cleaned by fishermen. Conches, lobsters and shrimps are the mainstays of this small country's fishing industry.

A   89°   B   88°   C

Chetumal Bay

MEXICO   Corozal Town

Hondo

Orange Walk

Ambergris Cay

New

Altun Ha

Belize City

Belize

Turneffe Is.

GUATEMALA

Barrier Reef

■ BELMOPAN

San Ignacio

B E L I Z E   Dangriga

▲Victoria Peak
1,122 m
3,680 ft.

Maya Mountains

CARIBBEAN SEA

Gulf of Honduras

Punta Gorda

Sarstoon   Amatique Bay

mi.
0   50
0   50
km

◄ Coral is formed from the skeletons of tiny animals and can build up into a reef on the sea floor. A 280-kilometre reef stretches almost the whole length of Belize's coastline.

▼ Wooden frame houses in Belize City are reminders of the time when this country was a colony of Britain.

297

EL SALVADOR

When Spanish soldiers conquered this region in 1524, they founded the city of San Salvador. It was named after a Roman Catholic festival, San Salvador del Mundo, which means Holy Saviour of the World. Later the whole country was named after the city.

El Salvador is Central America's smallest and most densely populated country. The majority of the people are descended from Native Americans and Spanish settlers. Many live on farms or in small towns, but the larger towns are growing rapidly and overcrowding is a serious problem.

Most people live in the fertile central highlands, an area of coffee plantations, small farms and forests of oak and pine trees. The climate is tropical. During the rainy season, which lasts from May to October, it pours each afternoon. The Lempa is El Salvador's main waterway and hydroelectricity plants on this river provide over half the country's electricity.

After El Salvador gained its independence from Spain in 1821, the country became violent and unstable. Wealthy landowners gained control in the early 1900s and since 1950 there have been periods when the army has held control. Civil war broke out in 1979 between government troops and rebel guerrillas. Riots continued through the 1980s, when 75,000 people died. A peace agreement in 1992 finally ended the years of fighting.

▲ *The country's grand churches were built by powerful Spanish landowners who wanted to show off their wealth.*

◄ *Many poor people in El Savador work small plots of land, with little or no machinery. Their wattle houses have walls made from branches covered with mud.*

▶ *Pedestrians crowd a busy street in San Salvador. About one quarter of El Salvador's rapidly growing population lives in the capital. Women carry goods on their heads and traders sell wares on the streets, just as people do in any small village in El Salvador.*

GUATEMALA

Monte Cristo
2,418 m
7,933 ft.
Metapán

HONDURAS

Chalatenango

Ahuachapán
Santa Ana
Lake Coatepeque
EL SALVADOR
Sensuntepeque

San Francisco
Gotera

Sonsonate
Cojutepeque
San Vicente

SAN SALVADOR
Lake Ilopango

Acajutla
Nueva San Salvador
La Libertad
Zacatecoluca
San Miguel

Usulután
Jiquilisco
Rio Grande de St. Miguel
La Unión

PACIFIC OCEAN

Gulf of Fonseca

▼ *A political poster in San Salvador welcomes peace after the country's lengthy civil war. The message on the right proclaims 'El Salvador para todos' (El Salvador for everyone).*

FACTS AND FIGURES

Area: 21,040 sq km
Population: 5,517,000
Capital: San Salvador (1,523,000)
Other major cities: Santa Ana (203,000), San Miguel (183,000)
Highest point: Monte Cristo (2,418 m)
Official language: Spanish

Main religion: Christianity
Currency: Colón
Main exports: Coffee, sugar-cane, shrimps, flowers, textiles, maize, cotton
Government: Republic
Per capita GNP: US $1,170

HONDURAS

▲ *An intricately carved statue peers out from a building at Copán near Santa Rosa. This Mayan city was built between 1000BC and AD800. By the time the Spanish arrived it was in ruins and the Mayan civilization had collapsed. No one knows why.*

Honduras is the Spanish word for depths. Named after the deep Caribbean waters that wash its northern coast, this small country is the poorest in Central America. Much of the interior is covered by forested mountains and mountain rivers flow into the southern plains near the Gulf of Fonseca.

Along the northern shores the Honduran people grow their main product, bananas, on which they rely heavily for income. In the early 1900s US companies owned all the banana plantations, which gave them great power over Honduras' weak government. This earned the country, and other countries like it, the nickname 'banana republic'.

Most of the Honduran people are mestizos (a mixture of Native American and Spanish). They live in villages and work either on large banana plantations or on their own small farms, growing mainly coffee or maize.

A Mayan city was established centuries before the explorer Christopher Columbus claimed this land for Spain in 1502. The Spanish ruled for more than 300 years and Honduras did not get full independence until 1838. Dictators came and went throughout the 1800s and early 1900s, when there were many rebellions. After 1948 the army and landowners controlled the country, but since 1981 there have been several elected presidents.

ENDANGERED WORLD

The pig-like tapir is at risk because many of the rainforests where it lives are being cut down.

▶ *Labourers harvest bananas in northern Honduras. Bananas are the country's main crop, but in recent years the government has encouraged farmers to grow other crops, such as coffee and sugar-cane.*

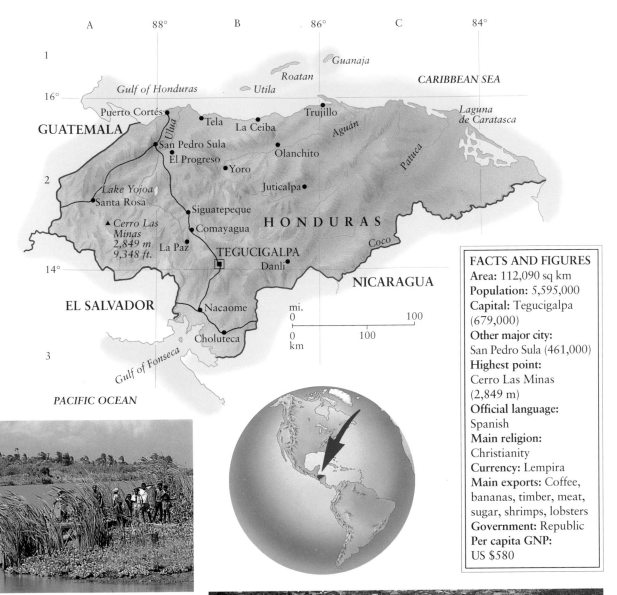

A 88° B 86° C 84°

1

Guanaja

Roatan

CARIBBEAN SEA

16° Gulf of Honduras Utila

Puerto Cortés Trujillo Laguna
de Caratasca

GUATEMALA •Tela La Ceiba

San Pedro Sula Aguán

El Progreso •Olanchito

•Yoro Patuca

2 Lake Yojoa •Juticalpa

Santa Rosa Siguatepeque H O N D U R A S

▲Cerro Las •Comayagua
Minas Coco
2,849 m La Paz
9,348 ft.

14° TEGUCIGALPA NICARAGUA
•Danlí

EL SALVADOR •Nacaome mi.
0 100

Choluteca 0 100
km

3

Gulf of Fonseca

PACIFIC OCEAN

FACTS AND FIGURES
Area: 112,090 sq km
Population: 5,595,000
Capital: Tegucigalpa
(679,000)
Other major city:
San Pedro Sula (461,000)
Highest point:
Cerro Las Minas
(2,849 m)
Official language:
Spanish
Main religion:
Christianity
Currency: Lempira
Main exports: Coffee,
bananas, timber, meat,
sugar, shrimps, lobsters
Government: Republic
Per capita GNP:
US $580

▲ *Boys play by a river at Santa
Rosa. Boats are an important
form of transport in Honduras
because of the lack of good roads
and railways. Some of these
children will stay in Santa Rosa all
their lives and never travel more
than 50 kilometres from home.*

▶ *The city of Tegucigalpa is
growing rapidly, but it has few
industries that provide work. Many
people are unemployed and live in
the overcrowded shantytowns that
line the surrounding hillsides.*

NICARAGUA

Nicaragua is the largest country in Central America. Most people live on the west coast, where the land is flat in the north but rises to include tall mountains in the south. Several volcanoes are found in this region. The mountainous centre of the country has steep, forested valleys. Eastern Nicaragua is flat and humid with rainforests, grassy plains and pine woodlands.

The Nicaraguan people are mainly descended from Europeans and Native Americans. They work on small farms or large plantations. Rich landowners built the plantations, but the government now owns many of them. In 1502 Christopher Columbus claimed the region for the Spanish, who ruled until Nicaragua became independent in 1821. Civil war then divided the country for nearly a century. In 1912 troops from the United States of America (USA) became involved and stayed for 20 years. The military leader Anastasio Somoza gained control in 1936. His family ruled as dictators until 1979, when left-wing rebels called Sandinistas took over. Groups known as the *contras* (which means against) disagreed with the Sandinistas over how the country should be run and fought them, supported by the USA. The Sandinistas were defeated in the 1990 elections and a new government finally ended the fighting.

▲ A worker turns coffee beans over with a rake to make sure they dry evenly in the hot sun. High-quality coffee is grown in the central highlands of Nicaragua.

◀ This elegant building in Granada is owned by one of the many rich people who live there. Granada is Nicaragua's oldest city.

▲ Bullet holes pepper a left-wing wall-painting. During the 1980s political groups fought each other for the right to run the country.

◀ Houses on stilts are common in eastern Nicaragua because of heavy flooding. Winds from the Caribbean bring over 400 centimetres of rain to the east each year.

FACTS AND FIGURES
Area: 130,680 sq km
Population: 4,265,000
Capital: Managua (683,000)
Other major city: León (101,000)
Highest point: In Cordillera Isabelia (2,438 m)
Official language: Spanish
Main religion: Christianity
Currency: Córdoba
Main exports: Coffee, cotton, sugar, chemical products, meat, bananas
Government: Republic
Per capita GNP: US $410

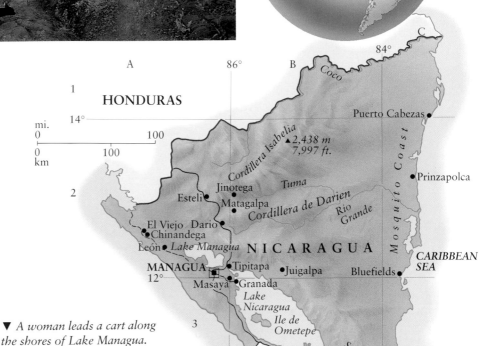

HONDURAS

Coco

1

14°

mi.
0   100

0   100
km

A   86°   B   84°   C

Puerto Cabezas

Cordillera Isabelia
▲ 2,438 m
7,997 ft.

2

Jinotega   Tuma

Esteli   Matagalpa

Prinzapolca

Cordillera de Darien

El Viejo Dario   Rio
Chinandega   Grande
León Lake Managua   N I C A R A G U A

MANAGUA   Tipitapa   CARIBBEAN
12°   Juigalpa   Bluefields   SEA
Masaya Granada

Lake
Nicaragua
3   Ile de
Ometepe

San Juan

COSTA RICA

Mosquito Coast

▼ A woman leads a cart along the shores of Lake Managua. Ox-drawn carts are frequently used because they cope well with the country's poor roads.

COSTA RICA

Costa Rica's original inhabitants were Native American farmers and hunters. In the 1500s the Spanish arrived and tried to enslave them, but the Native Americans fought back and kept their freedom. Today almost all Costa Ricans are of mixed Native American and Spanish descent.

The Spanish named this land Costa Rica (rich coast) because they mistakenly believed there was gold here. In fact its riches lie in the fertile volcanic soil of the central highlands, where some of the world's finest coffee beans are grown. Today about three quarters of the people live in this region, many working on coffee plantations. Either side of the highlands lie tropical lowlands. The Caribbean lowlands are swampy, but the Pacific plains are ideal for growing fruit.

In 1821 Costa Rica broke its ties with Spain and chose to become part of Mexico's empire. It became independent in 1838. There were power struggles until 1919, but since then it has become an oasis of calm in troubled Central America.

◄ Crowds watch a procession at a Roman Catholic feast day. About 90 percent of Costa Ricans are Roman Catholic.

◄ A cattle rancher leads his herd to pasture. Nearly two million cattle graze on the rich grasses of Costa Rica's central highlands.

FACTS AND FIGURES
Area: 51,100 sq km
Population: 3,199,000
Capital: San José (297,000)
Other major city: Limón (68,000)
Highest point: Chirripó Grande (3,819 m)
Official language: Spanish
Main religion: Christianity
Currency: Costa Rican colón
Main exports: Coffee, textiles, bananas, sugar, cocoa
Government: Multi-party republic
Per capita GNP: US $2,000

PANAMA

Panama is the thin sliver of land that leads from Central to South America. Its most famous feature is the Panama Canal, which is one of the world's busiest shipping routes. This important link between the Atlantic and Pacific oceans brings the country its wealth. Most people work at the canal or in the west, farming the rich soil of the highland valleys and the Atlantic lowlands. Steaming swamps and jungles cover the region lying to the east of the canal.

Spanish explorers landed in the 1500s and conquered the Native Americans. As a result, the modern people of Panama are mestizos (a mix of Native American and Spanish). In 1821 Panama became a province of Colombia, but with help from the United States of America (USA) it broke free in 1903. The USA took charge of central Panama and built the canal, which opened in 1914. It handed back the land around the canal to Panama in 1979 and Panama will take over the canal itself in the year 2000.

▲ *On the east coast local people use a small boat to transport bananas to the nearest market.*

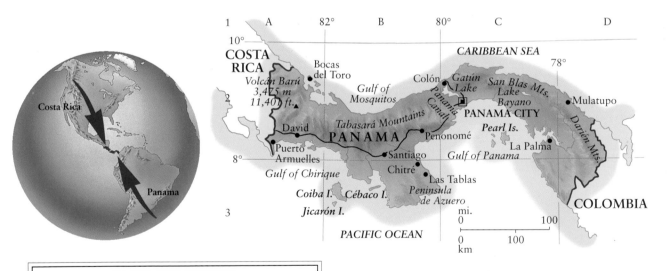

► *This stretch of the Panama Canal, called the Gaillard Cut, was cut out of rock.*

FACTS AND FIGURES

Area: 77,080 sq km
Population: 2,515,000
Capital: Panama City (585,000)
Other major city: Colón (141,000)
Highest point: Volcán Barú (3,475 m)
Official language: Spanish

Main religion: Christianity
Currency: Balboa
Main exports: Bananas, shrimps, coffee, sugar, textiles, petroleum products
Government: Republic
Per capita GNP: US $2,440

CUBA

Cuba includes the largest island in the Caribbean and over 1,500 smaller islands. Much of the island of Cuba consists of fertile plains and gentle hills. Thick forests cover the mountainous areas in the southeast.

Most Cubans are descended from Spanish settlers or African slaves. Many share a love of sport, music and dancing. Popular Cuban dances include the mambo, the rumba and the cha-cha-cha.

In 1492 Christopher Columbus claimed Cuba for Spain, which stayed in control until 1898. After years of unrest Fulgencio Batista seized control in 1933 and ruled as a dictator during the 1940s and 1950s. In 1959 he was overthrown by the communist rebel, Fidel Castro. Since this time Cuba and the United States of America (which lies only 140 kilometres across the water) have clashed bitterly over Cuba's policies. Castro's government relied heavily on aid from the Soviet Union until it broke up in 1991. Since then Cuba has become even poorer, but trade links are being established with Europe and Asia.

▲ *A worker hand rolls a Havana cigar, Cuba's most famous export. The best cigar tobacco comes from the northwest.*

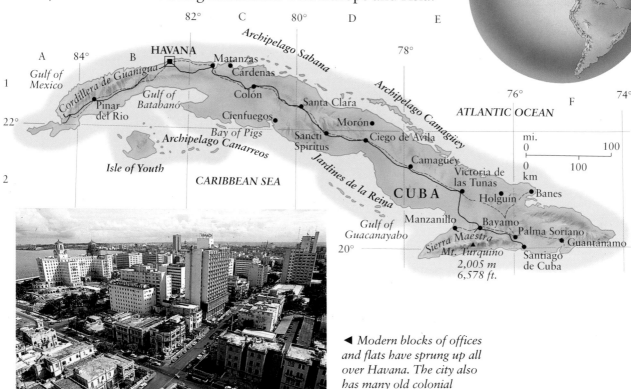

◄ *Modern blocks of offices and flats have sprung up all over Havana. The city also has many old colonial buildings. Some parts of the city date back as far as 1538.*

FACTS AND FIGURES

Area: 110,860 sq km
Population: 10,905,000
Capital: Havana
(2,015,000)
Other major cities:
Santiago de Cuba
(359,000),
Camagüey (261,000)
Highest point:
Mt Turquino (2,005 m)

Official language:
Spanish
Main religion:
Christianity
Currency: Cuban peso
Main exports: Sugar,
minerals, fruit, fish, coffee
Government:
Socialist republic
Per capita GNP:
Est. US $700-$3,000

▶ *Crowds gather to support the communist rebel Fidel Castro at a rally in 1965. On the building in the background are pictures of two heroes of the former Soviet Union, Karl Marx and Vladimir Lenin.*

▼ *Sugar harvesters work by hand using large, sharp knives called machetes to cut the sugar-cane. Sugar is Cuba's main crop.*

JAMAICA

PATOIS
Many Jamaicans speak a dialect called Patois. It is basically English, but also includes Portuguese, West African and Spanish words.

Christopher Columbus described Jamaica as "the fairest island that eyes have beheld". Sandy beaches lined with palm trees lead to fertile, low-lying coastal plains. Mountains, with cooler temperatures, cover most of the island and the northwest has limestone highlands. The only things that spoil this image of paradise are the hurricanes which can cause terrible damage.

Spain conquered this island in 1494. The Spanish treated the native Arawak people so badly that most of them died. In the 1600s the British arrived, seized control and turned Jamaica into a huge slave market. Slavery was abolished in 1838, but friction grew between workers and plantation owners. British troops stopped a revolt in 1865 and Jamaica was made a British crown colony. By the 1940s the island had won some independence and it became fully independent in 1962. Since then Jamaica has set up its own parliament and everyone over the age of 18 can vote.

Most Jamaicans are descendants of African slaves brought to the island by the Spanish and the British. Others are descended from white Europeans, Asians or Middle Eastern traders. Nearly two thirds of the islanders now live in cities, often in overcrowded slums. The economy relies heavily on agriculture and mining. Tourism is also important. Every year over 850,000 tourists visit Jamaica, attracted by the warm climate and beautiful scenery.

▼ *The Dunn's River Falls are a major attraction on the island, which is crossed by many free-flowing streams and rivers. Even the name Jamaica comes from a Native American word meaning 'island of springs'.*

▶ *Cricket is a popular sport in Jamaica. It is played and watched by young and old alike. The game was originally brought to Jamaica by the British. Nowadays Jamaicans regularly play for the West Indies' cricket team.*

▲ Fashionable Montego Bay is a popular stopping-off point for cruise ships.

▲ Rastafarians are Jamaicans who look to Africa as their homeland. Many wear their hair in long dreadlocks.

CARIBBEAN SEA

18°30'

1

A   78°

B   77°30'   C   77°

Montego Bay   Falmouth

St. Ann's Bay

The Cockpit Country

Browns Town   Ocho Rios

D   76°30'   E

JAMAICA

Negril   Savanna la Mar

2

Minho   Cobre

Blue Mountains   Port Antonio

Blue Mt. Peak
2,256 m
7,402ft.

Black River   Mandeville

18°

May Pen   Spanish Town   KINGSTON

CARIBBEAN SEA

Port Royal   Port Morant

Morant Point

3

Portland Bight
Portland Point

mi.
0   25
0   25
km

FACTS AND FIGURES

Area: 11,430 sq km
Population: 2,495,000
Capital: Kingston (588,000)
Other major city: Spanish Town (93,000)
Highest point: Blue Mt Peak (2,256 m)

Official language: English
Main religion: Christianity
Currency: Jamaican dollar
Main exports: Sugar, bauxite, alumina, bananas, fruit
Government: Constitutional monarchy
Per capita GNP: US $1,340

309

HAITI

Haiti occupies the western part of the island of Hispaniola. It is the Caribbean's most mountainous country and also one of the poorest in the world. The word Haiti means 'high ground' in the language of the Arawak people, the region's first inhabitants.

Most Haitians are farmers. Many are descended from the African slaves who were brought to the island by the French in the 1700s. African traditions have had a lasting influence. Voodoo was first developed in Haiti and is still widely practised.

Christopher Columbus landed on the island in 1492 and claimed it for Spain. The French took control of the western part in 1697. They made it a rich colony before a revolution, led by Toussaint L'Ouverture, resulted in Haiti becoming the first black republic in 1804.

From 1957 the dictator Papa Doc Duvalier and his son held power through the use of the army and secret police. Since military rule was declared in 1988, there has been continuing unrest.

▲ *Trading begins early in the markets of Port-au-Prince, Haiti's capital. The stalls are packed with a wide range of vegetables and spices.*

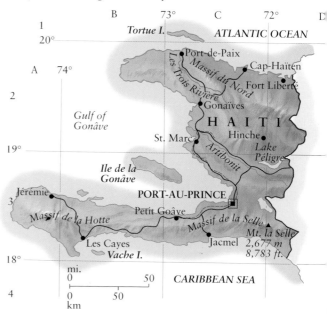

▲ *A former slave called Toussaint L'Ouverture leads a slave army to power in 1791. France, then Haiti's ruler, was forced to recognize its independence in 1804.*

FACTS AND FIGURES

Area: 27,750 sq km
Population: 6,903,000
Capital: Port-au-Prince (1,402,000)
Other major city: Les Cayes (251,000)
Highest point: Mt la Selle (2,677 m)
Official languages: French, Creole
Main religions: Christianity, Voodoo (a blend of Christianity and traditional African beliefs)
Currency: Gourde
Main exports: Assembled goods, coffee, sugar, sisal
Government: Republic
Per capita GNP: US $370

DOMINICAN REPUBLIC

This is the land of the merengue, a rhythmic dance mixing the sound of African drums with Spanish maracas. Most Dominicans are descended from African slaves and Spanish colonists. They enjoy a far higher standard of living than their neighbours, the Haitians.

▼ *Santo Domingo, the capital of the Dominican Republic, was founded in 1496. It is the oldest European settlement in the North American continent.*

The country is dominated by forest-covered mountains. Fertile land to the north of the Cordillera Central Mountains is farmed intensively and the flat eastern parts are ideal for growing sugar-cane.

Columbus claimed the island of Hispaniola for Spain in 1492 and some believe he is buried in Santa Domingo Cathedral. In 1697 Spain lost the western part of the island (now Haiti) to France, but kept control of the eastern two thirds. The Haitians took over the whole island in 1801 and again in 1822, but the Dominicans revolted and won independence in 1844. Years of unrest lay ahead. In 1930 Trujillo Molina began a 30-year dictatorship and communist rebels tried unsuccessfully to seize power in 1965. Since then a succession of elected presidents have helped to restore order.

FACTS AND FIGURES

Area: 48,440 sq km
Population: 7,608,000
Capital: Santo Domingo (1,314,000)
Other major city: Santiago (279,000)
Highest point: Pico Duarte (3,175 m)
Official language: Spanish
Main religion: Christianity
Currency: Peso
Main exports: Sugar, molasses, ferro-nickel, gold, cocoa, coffee
Government: Multi-party republic
Per capita GNP: US $1,040

▶ *Coffee plants are grown in the tree-covered foothills of the mountains.*

PUERTO RICO

The people of Puerto Rico are actually citizens of the United States of America (USA) because the island is a commonwealth. This means it is partially ruled by the USA. Puerto Rico has strong trade links with the USA and many Puerto Ricans have moved there in search of better living conditions.

Shaped like a rectangle, this is one of the largest islands in the Caribbean. It is a fertile country with mountains and foothills covering three quarters of the island. Coffee and tobacco are grown in the highlands and sugar-cane flourishes in the coastal plains and valleys. Manufacturing industries making chemicals, machinery and clothing are well-developed, but tourism is more important to the economy. Visitors are attracted by the year-round warm temperatures and colourful religious festivals.

Spain ruled the country from the early 1500s until 1898 when the USA took control. Puerto Rico means 'rich port' in Spanish, which shows how important the island was to Spain. Most Puerto Ricans are descended from Spanish settlers and Spanish is the country's main language.

ENDANGERED WORLD

Manatees are hunted for their meat and skins. They are also threatened by pollution.

▼ *This pineapple plantation uses a mobile conveyor belt at harvest time. Puerto Rican farms are the most advanced in the Caribbean.*

FACTS AND FIGURES

Area: 8,900 sq km
Population: 3,620,000
Capital: San Juan (438,000)
Other major city: Bayamon (221,000)
Highest point: Cerro de Punta (1,338 m)
Official language: Spanish

Main religion: Christianity
Currency: US dollar
Main exports: Sugar, coffee, chemicals, electronic equipment
Government: US Commonwealth
Per capita GNP: US $6,610

FAVOURITE FOODS
As well as American food, Puerto Ricans enjoy Spanish meals, such as traditional seafood paella. This is a mixture of rice, prawns, mussels and tomatoes all cooked together.

PUERTO RICO (U.S.)

A 67° B 66° C

ATLANTIC OCEAN

1

SAN JUAN
Puerto Rico
Bayamon
Isla de Culebra
Carolina
Mayaguez
Cerro de 1,338 m
Punta 4,389 ft.
Cordillera Central
Caguas
Isla de Mona
18°
Ponce
Isla de Vieques

mi.
0   50
0   50
km

2

CARIBBEAN SEA

BAHAMAS

FACTS AND FIGURES

Area: 13,860 sq km
Population: 269,000
Capital: Nassau
(136,000)
Other major city:
Freeport (25,000)
Highest point:
On Cat Island (63 m)
Official language:
English
Main religion:
Christianity
Currency:
Bahamian dollar
Main exports: Mineral
fuels, chemicals, cement,
crayfish, rum
Government:
Constitutional monarchy
Per capita GNP:
US $12,020

The Commonwealth of the Bahamas is a chain of about 2,000 coral islands and rocks that lie between Florida and Haiti. Sea breezes cool the islands during the summer months.

Christopher Columbus took his first steps in the Americas on one of the islands of the Bahamas. He landed on San Salvador Island in 1492 and claimed it for Spain. The Spanish sent many of the original Arawak inhabitants away as slaves to work in gold mines on nearby Cuba and the island of Hispaniola. The rest died out. During the 1600s Britain began to settle the islands and they became a British colony in 1717. The Bahamas finally gained independence in 1973 and since the early 1980s people from Haiti have fled here to escape poverty and political unrest.

Most people live on either Grand Bahama or New Providence and are descended from African slaves and British colonists. The Bahamas have a thriving tourism industry and many banks and foreign companies have branches here because of the favourable tax laws.

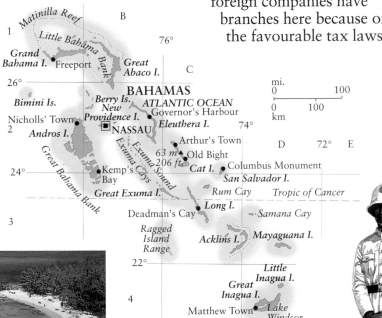

◀ The Bahamas' unspoilt beaches attract more than one million visitors each year.

▶ Police uniforms in the Bahamas have not changed much since British colonial days.

313

ANTIGUA AND BARBUDA

Antigua and Barbuda is a country in the eastern Caribbean. It is made up of three small islands. Almost all the people live on the largest island, Antigua, which is mainly flat with beaches of white sand. Coral reefs fringe its northern coast.

Most of Barbuda, a low-lying coral island, is a nature reserve. It is a haven for many birds, lizards and tortoises that face extinction on more developed Caribbean islands. No one lives on the smallest island, Redonda.

Antigua's tropical climate and cool sea breezes attract many visitors. Tourism is the island's main industry, although sugar-cane remains an important crop.

Stone Age settlers came to Antigua from South America about 4,000 years ago. When Christopher Columbus landed there in 1493, he was the first European that the native Arawak people had ever seen. The British established a colony in 1632 and the famous admiral, Lord Nelson, based his fleet at Antigua in the 1700s. The British also set up large sugar plantations, using mainly African slave labour. Most Antiguans are descended from these Africans. Slavery ended in 1834 and the islands gradually became more independent, gaining full independence in 1981.

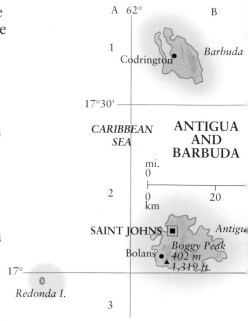

▼ Fishermen prepare their traps before setting off. Fresh fish and lobster are major parts of the local diet.

▼ Fried chicken is sold at a beach festival on the island of Antigua. Many tourists come each year to enjoy the warm hospitality and hot weather.

FACTS AND FIGURES

Area: 440 sq km
Population: 67,000
Capital: Saint Johns (30,000)
Highest point: Boggy Peak (402 m)
Official language: English
Main religion: Christianity

Currency: East Caribbean dollar
Main exports: Cotton, sugar, fruit, clothes, manufactured goods
Government: Constitutional monarchy
Per capita GNP: US $4,870

ST CHRISTOPHER (ST KITTS)-NEVIS

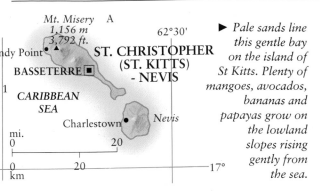

▶ *Pale sands line this gentle bay on the island of St Kitts. Plenty of mangoes, avocados, bananas and papayas grow on the lowland slopes rising gently from the sea.*

FACTS AND FIGURES

Area: 260 sq km
Population: 42,000
Capital: Basseterre (15,000)
Highest point: Mt Misery (1,156 m)
Official language: English
Main religion: Christianity

Currency: East Caribbean dollar
Main exports: Sugar, cotton, electronics
Government: Constitutional monarchy
Per capita GNP: US $3,990

The country of St Christopher-Nevis consists of two islands. They are the tips of volcanic mountains that lie beneath the Caribbean Sea. St Christopher, usually called St Kitts, is the larger island and most of the people live there. Nevis lies just three kilometres to the southeast. Both islands have central peaks and coastlines fringed by narrow fertile plains. Some beaches have black volcanic sand.

Nearly all the islanders are descended from African slaves. Most live along the coast and work in either the tourism or sugar industries. The fertile volcanic soil is ideal for sugar-cane.

France and Britain established settlements in the 1600s. They killed the original Arawak inhabitants and brought African slaves to work on their sugar plantations. Britain gained control in 1713 and ruled the islands as a single colony. St Christopher-Nevis became independent in 1983.

▼ *A carnival is held each year in St Kitts just after Christmas. Visitors are encouraged to join the local people's parties.*

DOMINICA

Dominica is the largest of the Windward Islands in the eastern Caribbean. Lush forests climb its steep volcanic slopes and dramatic waterfalls tumble through deep valleys. Heavy rainfall feeds the countless streams and Dominica sometimes exports its surplus water to other islands.

Most Dominicans are villagers who can trace their roots back to African slaves or British and French settlers. Dominica also has a population of about 3,000 Caribs (the Native American people after whom the Caribbean is named).

The Carib people defeated the original Arawak inhabitants in about AD900. On Sunday, 3 November 1493, Christopher Columbus sighted the island and named it Dominica, which is the Latin word for Sunday. French and British settlers soon arrived and began a long struggle against the Caribs. The British gained control in 1763 and started to bring in African slaves to work on their farms. From the 1930s onwards Dominica gradually gained more control and declared its independence in 1978.

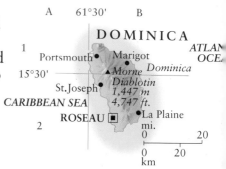

FACTS AND FIGURES

Area: 750 sq km
Population: 72,000
Capital: Roseau (9,000)
Highest point: Morne Diablotin (1,447 m)
Official language: English
Main religion: Christianity

Currency: East Caribbean dollar
Main exports: Bananas, coconuts, fruit juices, essential oils
Government: Republic
Per capita GNP: US $2,520

▲ Dense vegetation rises behind a harbour in south Dominica. The country is now promoted as the Caribbean's Nature Island.

▼ Cargo ships are loaded with bananas. Dominica relies heavily on the export of bananas which provide over half of the island's income.

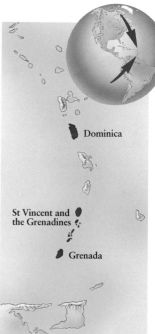

ST VINCENT AND THE GRENADINES
GRENADA

▲ *The people of St Vincent and the Grenadines rely on ferries to travel between the many islands.*

ST VINCENT AND THE GRENADINES is a country in the southeastern Caribbean. It is made up of the island of St Vincent and about 100 small islands of the Grenadine chain, including Bequia, Mustique and Union. Mountainous St Vincent is the country's largest island and its highest point, Mount Soufrière, is an active volcano.

Most of the islanders are poor and work on farms. Many are descended from African slaves or European settlers. A few are descendants of the Caribs who came from South America in about 1300. Both the French and British arrived in the 1600s, but Britain won control in 1783. The British brought African slaves to work on their farms. During the 1900s St Vincent and the Grenadines gradually gained more freedom from Britain, becoming fully independent in 1979.

GRENADA is a leading producer of spices, such as cinnamon and mace, so is nicknamed the 'Spice Island'. It is a land of forest-covered mountains and waterfalls. The country of Grenada consists of the islands of Grenada, Carriacou and several other tiny islands.

Most people are descended from African slaves. Farming is the main industry, but the tourism trade is growing. Under British control since 1783, Grenada became independent in 1974. Rebels overthrew the government in 1983, but troops from the United States of America and other Caribbean countries restored law and order. A new government and prime minister were elected in 1984.

FACTS AND FIGURES

ST VINCENT AND THE GRENADINES / GRENADA

Official language:
English

Currency:
East Caribbean dollar

ST VINCENT AND THE GRENADINES

Area: 390 sq km
Population: 111,000
Capital: Kingstown (27,000)

GRENADA
Area: 345 sq km
Population: 92,000
Capital: St George's (36,000)

Map labels

A 61°30' B
Soufrière
1,234 m
4,048 ft.
Chateaubelair Georgetown
KINGSTOWN St. Vincent
ST. VINCENT AND THE GRENADINES
13°
Bequia
CARIBBEAN SEA
Mustique
Grenadine Is.
2
Canouan
Union I.
12°30'
Carriacou
mi.
0   20
0   20
km
Ronde I.
3
GRENADA
Victoria Mt. St. Catherine
840 m
▲ 2,756 ft.
Grenada Grenville
ST. GEORGE'S
ATLANTIC OCEAN

▶ *Grenadan women separate the husks from the seeds of the nutmeg plant to produce the spices nutmeg and mace.*

ST LUCIA

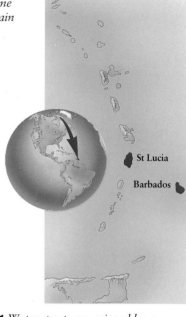

◀ St Lucia has some spectacular mountain scenery, especially near the coast in the southwest.

◀ Water sports are enjoyed by a growing number of tourists drawn to this island by its golden beaches, secluded bays and tropical climate.

St Lucia is a small, volcanic island-country in the eastern Caribbean. It is dominated by mountains, wide valleys and rainforest. The scenery is especially impressive around Soufrière, the island's first town that was built by French settlers. They named it after nearby sulphur springs. (*Soufre* is French for sulphur.)

Most people are descended from African slaves brought by British and French settlers to work on huge banana plantations. About ten percent of the population are of British or French descent. French influence is reflected in the French dialect spoken by some islanders and the creole cuisine, which uses a mixture of French and Caribbean recipes. Farming is the main industry, although money earned from tourism now exceeds the total earnings of all farm exports.

Britain gained control of St Lucia in 1814, after 200 years of struggle against the French and native Carib people. St Lucia gradually became more independent during the 1900s and fully independent in 1979.

FACTS AND FIGURES

Area: 620 sq km
Population: 139,000
Capital: Castries (54,000)
Other major city: Vieux Fort (14,000)
Highest point: Mount Gimie (959 m)
Official language: English

Main religion: Christianity
Currency: East Caribbean dollar
Main exports: Bananas, coconuts, cocoa
Government: Constitutional monarchy
Per capita GNP: US $2,900

BARBADOS

▲ *Mangoes are sold on a market stall. Barbadians are famous for their variety of cooking styles, using hot sauces, fresh fish and all kinds of tropical fruit.*

Barbados is the easternmost island in the Caribbean Sea. It is one of the most densely populated countries in the world. Its western coast borders the warm Caribbean Sea, but its eastern coast faces the Atlantic Ocean and so has a cooler climate with refreshing sea breezes. This low-lying island is mostly flat. It is covered with coral and ringed by pink coral reefs.

Barbados was uninhabited when the first British settlers arrived in 1627. It remained a British colony until independence in 1966. Today Barbadians, or Bajans as they are known, enjoy a higher standard of living than most of their Caribbean neighbours. The majority of the population are descendants of African slaves who were brought to work on British sugar plantations. A few are of European, mostly British, descent. All over Barbados there are constant reminders of the island's strong historical links with Britain. Old colonial buildings have been preserved, cars are driven on the left-hand side of the road and cricket is the national sport.

Sugar-cane has been an important way of making money for three centuries and is exported as refined sugar, molasses or rum. However, tourism is now the chief industry. The sandy beaches and sunny weather have attracted visitors for over 200 years. Today many resorts are clustered along the sandy beaches on the western and southwestern shores.

FACTS AND FIGURES
Area: 430 sq km
Population: 260,000
Capital: Bridgetown (7,000)
Highest point: Mount Hillaby (340 m)
Official language: English
Main religion: Christianity
Currency: Barbados dollar
Main exports: Sugar, chemicals, clothes, electronic equipment
Government: Constitutional monarchy
Per capita GNP: US $6,530

▶ *This fishing village on the south coast holds a two day festival at Easter. Displays of fishing skills, boat racing and fish-boning are accompanied by music and dancing.*

A   59°30'   B

BARBADOS

Mount Hillaby
340 m
1,115 ft.

1   Speightstown

CARIBBEAN
SEA

Bathsheba

ATLANTIC
OCEAN

BRIDGETOWN ◼

Barbados

mi.
0   20

0   20
km

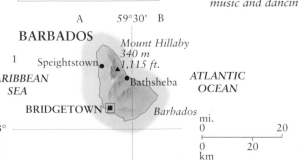

TRINIDAD AND TOBAGO

The country of Trinidad and Tobago, which lies off the coast of Venezuela, consists of two main islands and 21 smaller islands. Trinidad, the largest island, is famous for its calypso music and beaches. Forest-covered mountains and fertile plains cross its northern and central areas. The hilly island of Tobago is ringed with coral reefs. Its tropical woodland is home to many rare plants and birds.

Most of the islanders are descendants of slaves from Africa or plantation workers from India. The rest of the population are European, Chinese or of mixed descent.

Oil is the biggest industry. In southwest Trinidad oil has oozed up through rocks to create Pitch Lake, an 87-metre-deep tar lake that is the world's main source of asphalt.

▲ *Steel bands play at the famous Trinidad Carnival, which is held each year.*

Columbus landed on Trinidad in 1498. Spanish and French settlers destroyed the original Carib and Arawak peoples and developed the sugar industry using African slaves. Britain gained control of Trinidad and Tobago in 1889, but the country gained its independence in 1962. It became a republic in 1976.

▲ *Fishermen empty their nets at Store Bay on the west coast. Many Tobagans earn a living by fishing.*

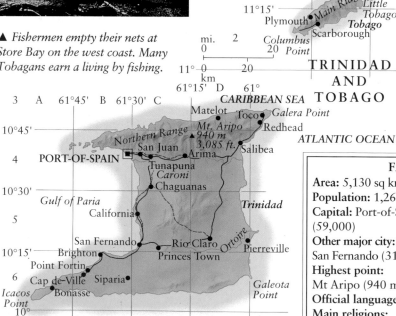

FACTS AND FIGURES	
Area: 5,130 sq km	Christianity, Hinduism
Population: 1,260,000	**Currency:** Trinidad and
Capital: Port-of-Spain	Tobago dollar
(59,000)	**Main exports:** Petroleum
Other major city:	and petroleum products,
San Fernando (31,000)	chemicals, rum, sugar
Highest point:	**Government:**
Mt Aripo (940 m)	Multi-party republic
Official language: English	**Per capita GNP:**
Main religions:	US $3,940

Tropic of Cancer

Equator

SOUTH
AMERICA

Tropic of Capricorn

Antarctic Circle

SOUTH AMERICA *Geography*

South America is the fourth largest continent. It stretches from the tropical warmth of the Caribbean Sea, off the coast of Colombia and Venezuela, to the icy and stormy tip of Tierra del Fuego, which is shared by Argentina and Chile. Between these two points are landscapes and climates of immense variety. The hot, dusty grasslands of the Pampas stretch through the cattle-ranching countries of Argentina and Uruguay. In the west are the soaring Andes Mountains, with cool, fertile valleys where coffee grows. The parched Atacama Desert of northern Chile is one of the driest places in the world. In Brazil the Amazon Basin teems with lush, green jungle. South America also has towering waterfalls, vast lakes and rugged islands.

The Andes, the longest mountain range on Earth, form the backbone of South America. They run 7,250 kilometres down almost the whole length of the continent. Even close to the Equator, snow stays on the highest peaks all year round. There are many volcanoes in the Andes. Occasionally they erupt, sending molten lava spewing over the landscape. Movement way below the surface of the Earth also causes the earthquakes that frequently rock this region. The Andes have rich deposits of gold, copper and tin. In parts of Colombia there are emeralds.

The world's second largest river begins in the Andes. The Amazon River crosses virtually the entire continent, with a network of smaller rivers feeding into it. This vast area of well-watered land is covered with the world's largest rainforest. Even today parts of the Amazon Basin have never been properly explored.

▼ *The Iguaçu Falls are a string of 275 waterfalls on the border between Argentina and Brazil, close to Paraguay. The water of the Iguaçu River cascades down drops of up to 70 metres.*

▼ *Flat-topped table mountains called tepuis reach up to the clouds in Gran Sabana, southeast Venezuela. Their sides are sheer and hard to climb.*

◄ *The highest mountain in the Andes range is Aconcagua (6,959 metres). Its peak lies in western Argentina, about 100 kilometres from Santiago in Chile.*

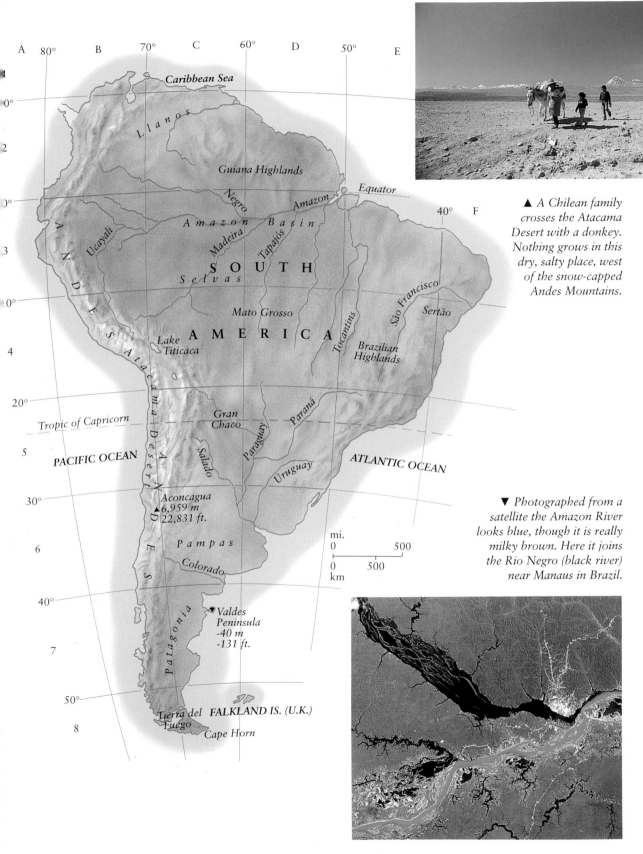

A ▲ *A Chilean family crosses the Atacama Desert with a donkey. Nothing grows in this dry, salty place, west of the snow-capped Andes Mountains.*

▼ *Photographed from a satellite the Amazon River looks blue, though it is really milky brown. Here it joins the Rio Negro (black river) near Manaus in Brazil.*

Caribbean Sea

A 80° B 70° C 60° D 50° E

Llanos

Guiana Highlands

Negro

Amazon

Equator

40° F

Amazon Basin

Ucayali

Madeira

Tapajós

SOUTH

Selvas

Mato Grosso

São Francisco

Sertão

A M E R I C A

Lake Titicaca

Tocantins

Brazilian Highlands

ANDES Atacama Desert

Tropic of Capricorn

Gran Chaco

Paraguay

Paraná

PACIFIC OCEAN

Salado

Uruguay

ATLANTIC OCEAN

Aconcagua
6,959 m
▲ 22,831 ft.

mi.
0   500

0   500
km

Pampas

Colorado

Patagonia

▼ Valdes Peninsula
-40 m
-131 ft.

Tierra del Fuego

FALKLAND IS. (U.K.)

Cape Horn

323

SOUTH AMERICA *Political*

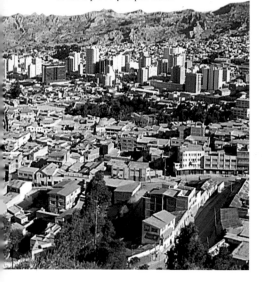

▼ *La Paz, Bolivia's seat of government, has a wealthy, modern centre surrounded by a jumble of shantytowns where poor people live.*

The Native Americans settled in this continent at least 11,000 years ago. They probably came from North America, but originated in Asia. In the Andes some of them developed sophisticated civilizations. The last and most brilliant of these were the Incas. Their civilization was destroyed in the early 1500s by conquerors from Spain. Many of the Native American peoples were killed or were wiped out by European diseases. Their lands were taken over, mainly as Spanish and Portuguese colonies. Millions of new settlers, from Italy as well as from Spain and Portugal, flooded into the continent.

In the 1820s the settlers began to break away from the rule of Spain and Portugal in a series of bloody wars of independence. During the 1800s many of the new nations prospered, but usually the settlers' descendants profited while the Native Americans stayed poor. The gap between rich and poor widened. Poverty increased after 1929, when the world economy went into decline. Strikes, riots, civil wars, corruption and greed led armies to seize power and rule by dictatorship in almost all the countries of South America at some point.

In recent decades more and more South American governments have been democratically elected. There has been a general concern to preserve political stability and improve basic living conditions. The continent has a great wealth of natural resources, but earning money from them often upsets the delicate balance of nature.

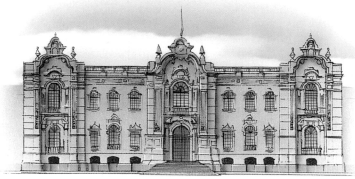

▲ *The Presidential Palace of Lima, the capital of Peru, is built in grand Spanish style. Many of South America's great buildings reveal its colonial past.*

▶ *The ceremonial guard parades in Santiago, the capital of Chile. This country was under a military dictatorship until 1989, when it became a democracy.*

A 80° B 70° C 60° D 50° E 40°

1

Caribbean Sea

10°

VENEZUELA

2

1

COLOMBIA

2

3

0° *Equator*

ECUADOR

3

PERU

BRAZIL

10°

BOLIVIA

4

20°

Tropic of Capricorn

4

5

PACIFIC OCEAN

ATLANTIC OCEAN

30°

ARGENTINA

5

6

CHILE

40°

mi.
0   500
0   500
km

7

50°

FALKLAND IS. (U.K.)

8

Cape Horn

KEY TO MAP
1 GUYANA
2 SURINAM
3 FRENCH GUIANA
4 PARAGUAY
5 URUGUAY

▼ *The Global Forum on Environment, held in 1992 in Rio de Janeiro, Brazil, is declared open. Environmental protection is one of South America's most pressing concerns.*

SOUTH AMERICA *Plants and Animals*

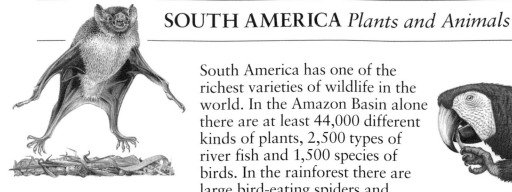

▲ *Vampire bats live in tropical South America. They feed off the blood of sleeping mammals such as horses and cows.*

South America has one of the richest varieties of wildlife in the world. In the Amazon Basin alone there are at least 44,000 different kinds of plants, 2,500 types of river fish and 1,500 species of birds. In the rainforest there are large bird-eating spiders and mammals include armadillos, jaguars and sloths. In the rivers are manatees, freshwater dolphins, giant catfish and electric eels. Of the thousands of forest insects, many have yet to be identified and studied.

The Andes are home to the alpaca and vicuña, which are distant relatives of the camel. They are prized for their wool, as is the rabbit-like mountain chinchilla. The rhea, a large flightless bird similar to an ostrich, lives on the grasslands of the Pampas. In the colder regions of the far south there are penguins and seals. Off the coast of Ecuador, the Galapagos Islands have spectacular forms of wildlife such as the famous giant tortoise.

Plants grow in rich profusion on the fertile soil. South America is the home of the spiny monkey-puzzle tree, the rubber tree and the potato. Many common houseplants, such as the monstera (cheeseplant), originated here.

Nature is under threat in South America. As people clear the forests to create mines, roads and farmland, the natural habitats of all kinds of animals disappear, making it impossible for them to survive. Plants of incalculable value are lost, as scientists are only just discovering the medicinal drugs they contain.

▲ *The scarlet macaw is the brightest of the parrot family. Macaws live in the high canopies of forest trees and crack nuts with their beaks.*

◄ *Arrow-poison frogs of the rainforest are so-called because Native American hunters tip arrows with their poison. The frogs' vivid colours warn other animals of their poisonous nature.*

▲ *A bull sea-lion guards a group of cows and pups. Sea-lions live in the cool South Atlantic. They come ashore on the coast of southern Argentina to breed each spring.*

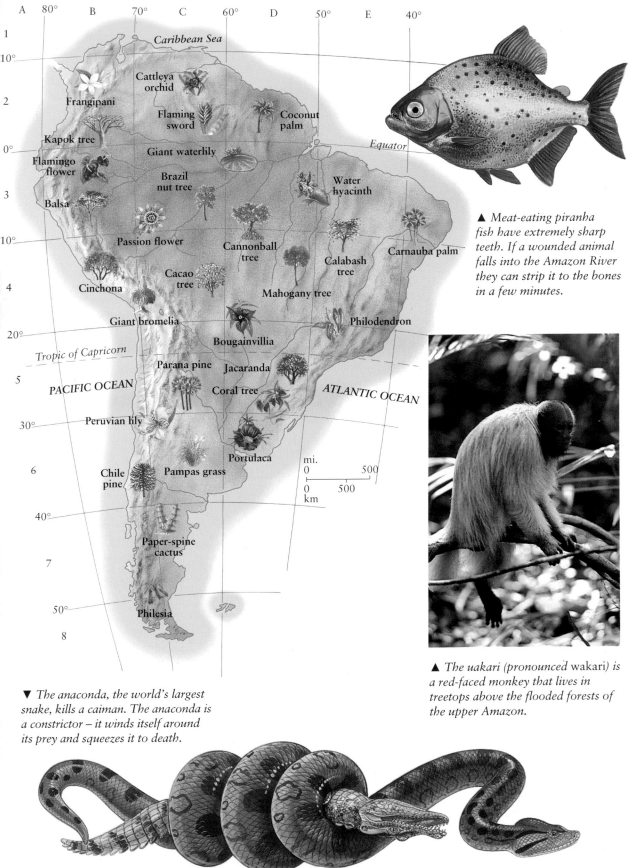

A 80°   B   70°   C   60°   D   50°   E   40°

1

10°

Caribbean Sea

Cattleya
orchid

Frangipani

Flaming
sword

Coconut
palm

2

0°

Kapok tree

Giant waterlily

Equator

Flamingo
flower

Brazil
nut tree

Water
hyacinth

Balsa

3

10°

Passion flower

Cannonball
tree

Calabash
tree

Carnauba palm

Cinchona

Cacao
tree

Mahogany tree

4

Giant bromelia

Philodendron

20°

Bougainvillia

Tropic of Capricorn

Parana pine

Jacaranda

5

PACIFIC OCEAN

Coral tree

ATLANTIC OCEAN

30°

Peruvian lily

Portulaca

6

Chile
pine

Pampas grass

mi.
0   500

0   500
km

40°

Paper-spine
cactus

7

50°

Philesia

8

▲ Meat-eating piranha
fish have extremely sharp
teeth. If a wounded animal
falls into the Amazon River
they can strip it to the bones
in a few minutes.

▲ The uakari (pronounced wakari) is
a red-faced monkey that lives in
treetops above the flooded forests of
the upper Amazon.

▼ The anaconda, the world's largest
snake, kills a caiman. The anaconda is
a constrictor – it winds itself around
its prey and squeezes it to death.

327

VENEZUELA *Introduction*

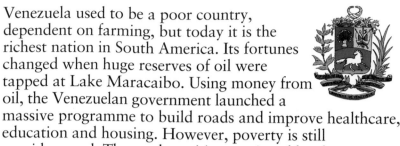

▼ *The stately Capitolio Nacional in Caracas was built in 1872 as a monument to Venezuela's independence. Today it is a government building where the Venezuelan Congress sits. Inside the building is an urn in which the original Declaration of Independence of 1811 is kept.*

Venezuela used to be a poor country, dependent on farming, but today it is the richest nation in South America. Its fortunes changed when huge reserves of oil were tapped at Lake Maracaibo. Using money from oil, the Venezuelan government launched a massive programme to build roads and improve healthcare, education and housing. However, poverty is still widespread. The modern cities are ringed by shantytowns that continue to sprawl as thousands of poor people flock in from the countryside to find work.

Meanwhile, vast areas of Venezuela remain unexplored. The remote southwest is densely cloaked in dripping rainforest, known only to the Native Americans who hunt and fish there. These people's lives are barely touched by the modern world. In the southeast there are great tables of sheer rock called *tepuis* that have never been climbed.

In the far north, tourists and foreigners are drawn to the white, sandy beaches of the Caribbean. In the centre, cattle-ranchers and farmers make a living on the Llanos Plains. To the west, coffee is grown in the high Merida valleys.

Spain colonized this area of South America in the 1500s, crushing the Native Americans. Today most Venezuelans are of mixed race and their main language is Spanish. The Venezuelan calendar is full of fiestas, at which people traditionally dance to the pulsating rhythms of maracas and the four-stringed cuadra guitar.

◄ *The Angel Falls tumble 979 metres into lush green forest. They are the highest falls in the world.*

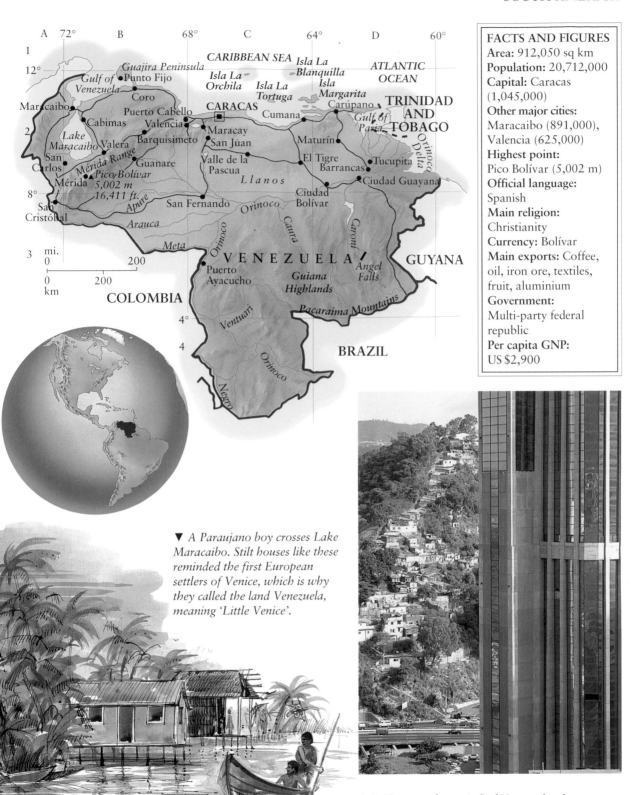

A   72°   B   68°   C   64°   D   60°

1

12°   CARIBBEAN SEA   Isla La

Guajira Peninsula   Isla La   Blanquilla   ATLANTIC
Gulf of   Punto Fijo   Orchila   Isla   OCEAN
Venezuela   Isla La   Margarita
Coro   Tortuga   Carúpano   TRINIDAD
Maracaibo   CARACAS   Cumana   Gulf of   AND
Puerto Cabello   Paria   TOBAGO
Cabimas   Maracay
Valencia   Maturín
Lake   Valera   Barquisimeto   San Juan
Maracaibo   Guanare   Valle de la   El Tigre
San   Mérida Range   Pascua   Barrancas   Tucupita
Carlos   Pico Bolívar   Llanos   Ciudad Guayana
Mérida   5,002 m   Ciudad
16,411 ft.   Apure   Bolívar
San   Arauca   San Fernando   Orinoco
Cristóbal   Meta   VENEZUELA   GUYANA
mi.   Orinoco   Angel
0   200   Puerto   Guiana   Falls
Ayacucho   Highlands
0   200   COLOMBIA   Pacaraima Mountains
km
Ventuari   BRAZIL
Orinoco

Negro

FACTS AND FIGURES

Area: 912,050 sq km
Population: 20,712,000
Capital: Caracas
(1,045,000)
Other major cities:
Maracaibo (891,000),
Valencia (625,000)
Highest point:
Pico Bolívar (5,002 m)
Official language:
Spanish
Main religion:
Christianity
Currency: Bolívar
Main exports: Coffee,
oil, iron ore, textiles,
fruit, aluminium
Government:
Multi-party federal
republic
Per capita GNP:
US $2,900

▼ *A Paraujano boy crosses Lake
Maracaibo. Stilt houses like these
reminded the first European
settlers of Venice, which is why
they called the land Venezuela,
meaning 'Little Venice'.*

▲ *In Caracas, the capital of Venezuela, the poor
live on the doorsteps of the rich. High-rise
apartment blocks occupy the low-lying centre of the
city, while slums called barrios creep up the steep
mountain slopes beyond.*

329

VENEZUELA *Geography and Economy*

▲ *Farmers work their small fields, hoeing between rows of coffee plants. A huge variety of crops, including cacao, maize and yams, grow well in the fertile soil and the cool climate of the high Merida valleys. Stone walls guard against soil erosion.*

Venezuela's rich reserves of oil are its most important product. Oil exports earn about three quarters of Venezuela's income. Industry is centred in cities on the coastal strip, including Caracas, Maracaibo, Valencia and Maracay, where products range from cars to medicines. Most Venezuelans live in and around these cities.

The Merida Mountains in the west have the highest peaks in Venezuela. The longest cable-car ride in the world is at Mérida, in the heart of Venezuela's coffee plantations. The cool, fertile landscape of the mountains drops east to the Llanos Plains. This hot and dusty world of grasslands and cattle-ranches stretches right across the country from the Colombian border to the delta of the mighty Orinoco River. The Orinoco snakes its way north from the border with Brazil in a grand clockwise curve through a thick mat of tropical forests. The mosquito-infested Casiquiare Channel links it to the great rivers of Brazil.

In the southeast are the remote mountains of the Guiana Highlands. This inhospitable region is cloaked in cloud and has valuable deposits of bauxite and manganese. There are thriving new aluminium and steel works at Ciudad Guayana. Fast-flowing rivers cut deep channels through the rock. The Angel Falls crash spectacularly over Mount Auyantepui and the Caroní River is dammed to produce three quarters of Venezuela's electricity.

◀ *An oil transporter makes its way to a refinery on the shore of Lake Maracaibo. The lake is really a huge inlet from the sea. It is rich in wildlife and has large flocks of scarlet ibises. However, the wildlife is threatened by pollution from oil installations, including more than 10,000 derricks through which the oil is extracted.*

▶ *Nothing grows on the shifting sand-dunes in the northwest of the country. Venezuela lies just north of the Equator, so its low-lying areas are very hot. Where there is little rain, vegetation cannot survive and the land becomes desert.*

▼ *Skilled cowboys called llaneros use horses and lassos to round up cattle on the Llanos Plains. Their cattle are mainly humpbacked zebu, which originated in India. The llaneros play an important part in the folklore of Venezuela.*

▼ *Venezuela's Caribbean coast has white, sandy beaches fringed with palms. It attracts tourists from abroad who contribute to the country's income, as well as holidaymakers from Venezuela's cities. On the horizon is the large island and popular resort, Margarita.*

VENEZUELA *People and History*

▲ *This statue in Caracas commemorates Simón Bolívar (1783-1830). Named 'The Great Liberator', he led the revolution that freed Venezuela, Colombia, Peru, Ecuador and Bolivia from Spanish control in the early 1800s.*

Native American groups, such as the Carib and the Arawak, lived all over Venezuela until the early 1500s. They used the land for sowing crops, hunting and fishing. In 1498 Christopher Columbus arrived from Spain, opening the way for Spanish fortune-hunters. Many Native Americans were killed, while others became slaves. However, unlike other South American countries, such as Peru, Colombia and Bolivia, Venezuela had little gold. It remained a poor country of farmers, ranchers and traders. The Spanish brought more slaves from Africa to work on the plantations. Gradually the Africans, Native Americans and Spanish intermarried. Today three quarters of Venezuelans are mestizos (of mixed ancestry).

By the late 1700s the settlers wanted independence. Under the leadership of Simón Bolívar, they fought a bitter war against their Spanish rulers that lasted for 15 years. Venezuela declared independence in 1811, but only finally broke free in 1821. Then the country plunged into years of bloody strife and civil war, passing through a series of military dictatorships.

In 1958 Venezuela held its first democratic elections and Rómulo Betancourt became president. He used profits from Venezuela's oil industry to improve standards of living. A new middle class of business people, government officials and professionals grew up in the cities. However, the value of oil began to fall in the early 1980s. Because Venezuela depended so heavily on this industry, the country's economy suffered. The government recognized the need to diversify and is now working to develop new industries, such as steel and textiles, to provide jobs and maintain economic stability.

◄ *Venezuelans enjoy a game of* bolas, *a traditional form of bowling played in the open air. The first ball to be thrown is the small target called the* mingo. *Then players aim to get their ball to land as close to it as possible.*

◀ *Children in the Llanos area wait for school to begin. Venezuela has a large proportion of young people – about a third of its population is under 15 years old. Education is a high priority and free for all. The government spends nearly a quarter of its budget on schools. Almost all Venezuelans can read and write.*

▼ *A Guajira woman rides her donkey through a desert camp, west of Lake Maracaibo. Long robes and black face-paint protect her skin from the sun and salty coastal air.*

HALLACAS

Hallacas is a traditional Christmas pasty. It is a stew of different meats inside an envelope of maize flour pastry. The pasty is wrapped up in plantain leaves, then cooked in boiling water. It is usually eaten with ham and bread *(right)*.

▶ *Travelling across the congested city of Caracas has been made much easier by the new underground railway, or Metro. The first line was opened in 1989. New lines and stations are currently being planned and built.*

GUYANA

Guyana is the only South American country where English is the main language. Once known as British Guiana, it was ruled by Britain for over 150 years until it became independent in 1966. Today British traditions such as playing cricket still survive. As a result the country often seems to have more in common with the English-speaking Caribbean islands than with the rest of South America.

Guyana's original inhabitants were the Carib people, some of whom still live in forests in the south. The Dutch arrived in the late 1500s, followed by the French and British. They brought slaves from Africa to work on sugar plantations. After slavery was abolished in 1834, labourers came from Portugal, China and India. The descendants of people from India now form the largest population group and run many of the businesses.

Sugar-cane is still the most important crop. It is grown on the fertile plains near the coast, like many of Guyana's crops. This is also where most people live. To the south are rugged hills, cloaked in the tropical rainforest that covers over three quarters of the country and provides Guyana with valuable timber. Large deposits of bauxite, manganese and gold are mined in the country. Mining is a major economic activity and Guyana is one of the world's largest producers of bauxite.

▲ *This is City Hall in Georgetown, Guyana's capital. It is typical of the days of British rule, when many public buildings in the city were built from wood.*

▲ *Sugar-cane arrives by barge at a factory. It will be unloaded by crane and made into sugar syrup and raw sugar. The brown sugar called demerara is named after the Demerara River in Guyana.*

▶ *Children wear cool, cotton uniforms to school. The education system begins with nursery school and ends with college or university.*

▲ In a sheet of water about 90 metres across, the Kaiteur Falls on the Potaro River drop 226 metres. Guyana's native peoples consider these falls to be sacred. The Potaro River is one of dozens of rivers that cross the country. The name Guyana means 'land of many rivers'.

FACTS AND FIGURES

Area: 214,970 sq km
Population: 816,000
Capital: Georgetown (188,000)
Highest Point: Mt Roraima (2,772 m)
Official language: English
Main religions: Christianity, Hinduism, Islam
Currency: Guyana dollar
Main Exports: Gold, aluminium, sugar, rice, rum, bauxite, timber
Government: Co-operative republic
Per capita GNP: US $330

▼ Bauxite is extracted from open mines before being shipped abroad and made into aluminium. This mineral is an important export.

SURINAM

The original inhabitants of this land, the Arawak, Carib and Warrau peoples, were forced into slavery when the Dutch arrived in the early 1600s. The Dutch established sugar-cane and cotton plantations. They brought more slaves from Africa. For three centuries, until its independence in 1975, Surinam was ruled by the Netherlands and called Dutch Guiana. When the Netherlands abolished slavery in 1863, thousands of workers from India and the old Dutch colony of Indonesia were encouraged to settle in the country to work on the plantations. As a result modern Surinam has a great mix of peoples. Most are Asians or creoles (of mixed African and Native American descent). Others are European. The official language is Dutch, but Sranan Tongo, a combination of African languages, Dutch and English, is more widely used.

Most people live on the hot, wet coastal strip, where they grow rice, sugar, cocoa and bananas. The interior has barren dunes, dry grasslands and vast mountainous areas of tropical rainforest. Cutting down valuable forest timber has driven Surinam's Native Americans deeper into the remote rainforest areas.

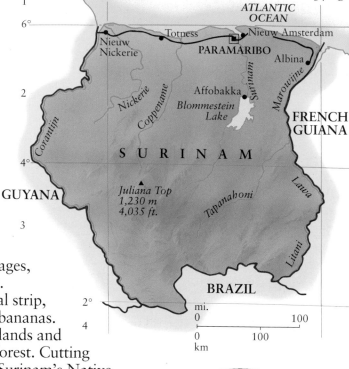

◄ The Marowijne River is one of many rivers running through the dense rainforests of Surinam's interior. These rivers provide the principal means of transport beyond the flat plains that line the coast.

◀ Almost half the population of Surinam lives in the capital, Paramaribo. It is the country's main seaport and lies on the estuary of the Surinam River. The busy main streets are lined with shops and some Dutch-style buildings, as well as mosques, churches and temples.

▼ Descendants of the Javanese people who came to live in Surinam keep their heritage alive by performing a traditional horse dance. During this ritual the dancers wear ceremonial headdresses and imagine they are possessed by the spirits of horses.

FACTS AND FIGURES
Area: 163,820 sq km
Population: 446,000
Capital: Paramaribo
(201,000)
Highest point:
Juliana Top (1,230 m)
Official language: Dutch
Main religions:
Christianity, Hinduism, Islam
Currency:
Surinam guilder
Main exports:
Alumina, bauxite, aluminium, shrimps, rice, bananas, timber
Government:
Multi-party republic
Per capita GNP:
US $3,700

◀ An aluminium freighter docks in a loading bay in Paramaribo harbour. Surinam has large reserves of bauxite. This is either exported raw or smelted into aluminium. The aluminium industry is extremely important to Surinam, producing about three quarters of the income that the country earns from exports.

FRENCH GUIANA

French Guiana is not an independent country, but has belonged to France since 1667. For about 150 years it was used as a penal colony, a place where dangerous prisoners were sent. Today representatives from French Guiana have seats in the parliament in France.

This hot land lies just north of the Equator. A plateau spreads across the centre of the country, with a plain to the north and mountains to the south. Much of French Guiana is covered in steamy rainforest, cut through with numerous rivers flowing to the Atlantic Ocean.

The majority of the population lives on the coast, especially in Cayenne, which is the only large town. Most people are descended from African slaves who were brought to the country to work on French banana plantations. There are also Europeans, Chinese, Lebanese, Syrians and Haitians. Many people are employed by the government. Others work in agriculture, growing yams, maize and pineapples. A small number of Native Americans continue to lead a traditional life in rainforest areas.

At present this is not a wealthy country and it depends heavily on the money that it receives from France. French Guiana has large reserves of bauxite, as well as some gold. There are plans to strengthen the economy by developing the mining industry and exploiting timber from the forests.

ENDANGERED WORLD

The black spider monkey's noisy habits make it an easy target for hunters.

▶ *Devil's Island, which is just north of Kourou, was one of several extremely harsh French prison colonies. The prison was closed in 1945 and the island is now a tourist resort.*

338

◀ *Boats moor on one of the country's canals. Water travel is vital because dense forest and heavy rain make road-building difficult.*

▼ *Chilli peppers are used to make Cayenne pepper. This fiery spice is named after the capital and has been an export for around 200 years.*

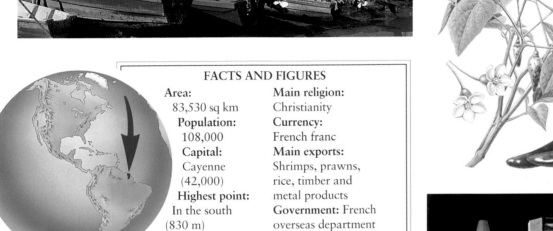

FACTS AND FIGURES

Area: 83,530 sq km	**Main religion:** Christianity
Population: 108,000	**Currency:** French franc
Capital: Cayenne (42,000)	**Main exports:** Shrimps, prawns, rice, timber and metal products
Highest point: In the south (830 m)	**Government:** French overseas department
Official language: French	**Per capita GNP:** Est. US $3,000-8,000

▲ *An Ariane rocket lifts off from the European Space Agency station at Kourou. Rockets launched from here often carry satellites into space.*

◀ *Rice plants are laid out to dry. Rice is grown beside the many rivers that run through the coastal regions.*

BRAZIL *Introduction*

Brazil is the largest country in South America and occupies almost half the continent. The country's first inhabitants were native peoples such as the Arawak. When Portuguese fleet commander Pedro Alvares Cabral landed on Brazil's shores in 1500, he claimed the land for his country. Centuries of Portuguese influence followed and today Brazil is the largest Portuguese-speaking nation on Earth.

The country's culture is a mix of traditions from all kinds of peoples, particularly Europeans, Africans and Native Americans. Everyone joins in when the most famous carnival in the world takes place each year. All over Brazil the streets come alive with colourful parades, music and dancing. Carnival is especially spectacular in Rio de Janeiro, the second largest city. This city also shows the huge gap between rich and poor people in Brazil. Shantytown slums exist just a short distance away from modern, high-rise buildings and sophisticated nightclubs.

Brazil is filled with natural wonders. The brown, sluggish waters of the great Amazon River snake their way across the north of the country. The river passes through the world's largest area of dense, steamy rainforest, which teems with wildlife. Brazil also has rich mineral resources and fertile soils where timber, coffee, cocoa and sugar-cane grow. This should bring great wealth but, like much of South America, Brazil suffers from economic problems. There is widespread poverty among its ever-growing population, so a lot of people have moved inland in search of new farmland. As a result huge areas of the Amazon rainforest are being destroyed. This has become an environmental issue of worldwide concern.

FACTS AND FIGURES
Area: 8,512,000 sq km
Population: 151,534,000
Capital: Brasília (1,597,000)
Other major cities: São Paulo (15,200,000), Rio de Janeiro (9,601,000)
Highest point: Neblina (3,014 m)
Official language: Portuguese
Main religion: Christianity
Currency: Cruzeiro real
Main exports: Iron ore, coffee, fruit, timber, sugar, vehicles, beef
Government: Multi-party federal republic
Per capita GNP: US $2,770

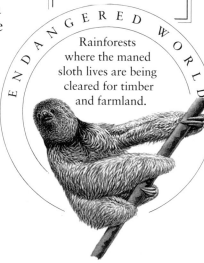

ENDANGERED WORLD

Rainforests where the maned sloth lives are being cleared for timber and farmland.

◄ *The vast slum areas around the edge of Rio de Janeiro are called favelas. These homes belong to poor Brazilians who have come to the city in search of work. Sugar Loaf Mountain in the background* (left) *earned its name in the days when sugar was sold in pointed, solid blocks.*

SOUTH AMERICA

ATLANTIC OCEAN

VENEZUELA
GUYANA
SURINAM
FRENCH GUIANA
COLOMBIA
PERU
BOLIVIA
PARAGUAY
ARGENTINA
URUGUAY

Guiana Highlands
Neblina 3,014 m 9,888 ft.
Japurá
Negro
Branco
Manaus
Amazon Basin
Macapá
Marajó Island
Belém
São Luis
Tucuruí Reservoir
Teresina
Fortaleza
Natal
João Pessoa
Campina Grande
Recife
Maceió
Aracajú
Salvador
Feira de Santana
Brazilian Highlands
São Francisco
Yavari
Purus
Madeira
TRANS AMAZONIAN HIGHWAY
Tapajós
Xingu
Araguaia
Tocantins
Pôrto Velho
B R A Z I L
Mato Grosso
Cuiabá
Goiânia
BRASILIA
Uberlândia
Uberaba
Belo Horizonte
Governador Valadares
Vitória
Campo Grande
São José do Rio Prêto
Riberão Prêto
Juiz de Fora
Campos
Niterói
Campinas
Rio de Janeiro
Londrina
Sorocaba
São Paulo
Ponta Grossa
Santos
Iguaçu Falls
Curitiba
Joinville
Paraná
Uruguay
Florianópolis
Santa Maria
Caxias do Sul
Pôrto Alegre
Patos Lagoon
Pelotas
Rio Grande
Mirim Lake

Equator
Tropic of Capricorn

mi. 0 — 500
km 0 — 500

▲ Modern government buildings dominate the skyline in Brasília. This city was built in the late 1950s and replaced Rio de Janeiro as the capital in 1960.

▶ Different races mixing freely with each other is part of everyday life. Settlers from all over the world have come here – farmers from Portugal, slaves from Africa, traders from the Middle East, pepper-growers from Japan and factory workers from eastern Europe.

341

BRAZIL *Geography*

Over one third of this large country is occupied by the Amazon Basin, which consists of the Amazon River itself and more than 200 rivers that feed into it. This enormous drainage basin carries about one fifth of all the water found in the world's rivers.

Around the Amazon the land is very flat. The river and its tributaries flow slowly, often spilling over their banks during the rainy season and flooding large areas of forest. On higher land rainforest trees create lofty canopies that block out much of the sunlight from the ground below. Few plants can grow in this semi-darkness, so it is easy to walk through many of these forests.

Towards the northeastern tip of Brazil rainforest gives way to desert-like areas and thorny scrub, but most of the Atlantic coast has plenty of rain and rich vegetation. The coastal strip between Pôrto Alegre, in the south and Salvador, in the east is only about 100 kilometres wide before it rises sharply into the central and southern plateaus. Half of the population lives in the cities along this strip and on the fertile plateaus inland, where coffee is grown. Cattle are raised on the grasslands of the far south, on the border with Uruguay.

The north of the country lies across the Equator and Rio de Janeiro is just north of the Tropic of Capricorn, so Brazil's weather is mostly very warm. In the hot, humid Amazon Basin temperatures hover constantly around 27 degrees centigrade.

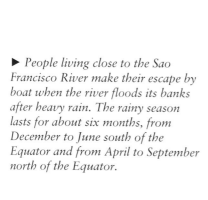

▲ *Forest stretches right down to the sea on some parts of the Atlantic coast. The warm, rainy climate means that much of the country is covered by lush vegetation.*

▶ *People living close to the Sao Francisco River make their escape by boat when the river floods its banks after heavy rain. The rainy season lasts for about six months, from December to June south of the Equator and from April to September north of the Equator.*

◄ Large expanses of rainforest are burned off to open up areas for farming, but the land cleared in this way is not very fertile and soon becomes useless. If forest clearing continues at the current rate, there may be no rainforest left in the Amazon Basin within 100 years.

▼ The Amazon winds its way through low-lying land. A Spanish explorer named the river after female warriors called Amazons, who appear in Greek mythology. Sailing down the Amazon in 1542, he thought at one point that he was being attacked by women warriors.

THE ITAIPU DAM
The Itaipú Dam straddles the Paraná River on the border with Paraguay. This is one of the largest dams in the world. It is also one of the world's most powerful hydroelectric plants, capable of producing 12,600 million megawatts of electricity. The lake formed by the dam drowned one of the world's great waterfalls, the Guairá Falls.

◄ Only hardy plants such as cacti and tough grasses grow in the dry Sertão region. Farmers here can raise few crops and live in basic huts. This area covers much of the inland part of northeast Brazil. It is one of the poorest regions in the country.

343

BRAZIL *Economy*

Brazil is South America's leading industrial nation, with a wide range of different industries. These industries cluster around the country's major cities, particularly São Paulo. Brazil is the world's largest producer of coffee and sugar-cane. It is also one of the largest exporters of agricultural products. There are enormous reserves of iron ore and the country's mines yield everything from tin to gold and diamonds. Large deposits of oil have been found in the Amazon Basin.

These statistics sound impressive, but Brazil remains a relatively poor country. It cannot meet the needs of the huge population and so has to import all kinds of goods, including food. To pay for this and for projects designed to develop the economy in the long term, Brazil has borrowed heavily from other countries and has trouble repaying its massive debts.

One answer to these problems is to try to earn more money from the Amazon Basin. Roads have been built that go deep into remote parts of the forest so that fresh reserves of minerals can be mined, more trees torn down for timber and extra land cleared to create farmland and cattle ranches. However, there is strong pressure worldwide to stop destroying the forests and the economic benefits have often proved disappointing.

> **ECONOMIC SURVEY**
> **Farming:** Brazil is the leading producer of sugar-cane, coffee, cassava, oranges and papayas. Cattle, poultry, pigs, horses and sheep are reared.
> **Forestry:** Brazil is also a major producer of forest products such as timber, nuts, resins, rubber, oils and medicines.
> **Fishing:** Major catches are lobsters, shrimps and bony fish.
> **Mining:** Minerals include quartz, chrome, diamonds, gold, lead, copper, iron ore, manganese, mica and oil.
> **Industry:** The major products are vehicles, aircraft, cement, chemicals, machinery, textiles, foods and pharmaceuticals.

◄ *Making cars is one of Brazil's major industries. Brazil assembles vehicles for several leading companies. It also produces car parts for assembly in other countries around the world.*

▼ *Manaus is the main port on the Amazon River. Although it is 1,600 kilometres from the sea, the river is deep enough for large ocean-going ships to reach the city.*

◀ Prospectors dig for gold at Serra Pelada, turning it into a landscape of muddy hillocks. Vast quantities of gold have been found in this area, which is about 500 kilometres south of Macapá.

▼ Large areas of cleared forest are now grassland, where beef cattle are raised. Beef is a vital export and much is used to make beefburgers for multinational companies.

▼ Coffee beans are grown and sorted on large plantations called fazendas, which are mainly in the southern part of the country. About two million tonnes of coffee are produced in Brazil every year.

▼ Brazil nuts come from trees found in the Amazon rainforest. Many nut trees are being cut down to create new farmland. However, just one tree can produce a larger quantity of nutritious food than the land that is cleared when it is felled.

345

BRAZIL *People*

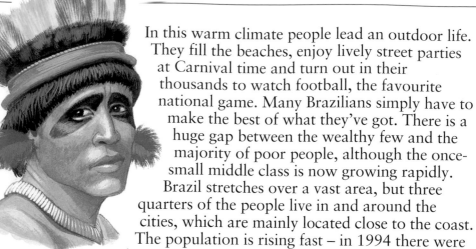

► *The Kamayura are just one of the many native peoples living in the rainforests. The men wear earrings and headdresses made from the colourful feathers of forest birds.*

In this warm climate people lead an outdoor life. They fill the beaches, enjoy lively street parties at Carnival time and turn out in their thousands to watch football, the favourite national game. Many Brazilians simply have to make the best of what they've got. There is a huge gap between the wealthy few and the majority of poor people, although the once-small middle class is now growing rapidly. Brazil stretches over a vast area, but three quarters of the people live in and around the cities, which are mainly located close to the coast. The population is rising fast – in 1994 there were four times as many people as there were in 1940. As a result half the population is under 25 years old, so Brazilian culture tends to be youthful and exuberant. Many of the people are descendants of several ethnic groups. Popular food – a spicy blend of European, African and Asian cooking – reflects this varied ancestry.

The first inhabitants were Native Americans. Unlike the city-building peoples of the Andes, the native peoples of the Amazon Basin continued to live by hunting and fishing, relying on the natural products of the forest. The way of life for many of these people remained unchanged for thousands of years until this century. Today their numbers are falling fast because of disease and destruction of the forest. Many are also moving to the towns.

▲ *Some people have to scrape a living by recovering what they can find on city rubbish heaps. Widespread poverty is a serious problem in Brazil.*

► *Day after day of sun brings good business for the beach hatseller. Brazil has some of the world's best beaches, such as the famous Copacabana Beach in Rio de Janeiro.*

346

▲ Carnival-goers in breathtaking costumes take to the streets of Rio de Janeiro. Carnival marks the start of Lent, 40 days before Easter. It is a five-day party of floats, feasting and dancing to samba music.

▼ Brazilians who follow a religion called Candomblé take part in a ceremony on a beach in Salvador. Candomblé combines parts of Roman Catholicism with African-based religions brought by slaves in the early 1600s. Each individual is personally attached to one of the religion's many spirit gods, who are known as orixás.

► Pelé, the world-famous football player, holds the World Cup after a Brazilian victory in 1970. Brazil is the only nation to have reached every final since the World Cup began in 1930. It has also won more times than any other country, adding a fourth victory in 1994.

BRAZIL *History*

▲ *This European map, from the 1500s, shows the location of some native settlements. There are few details because Europeans had not explored much of Brazil at this point. All the early European settlements were along the coast.*

▼ *Xingu headmen gather to protest against the building of a dam in their region of central Brazil. Over the years the rainforest peoples have seen their homelands dramatically reduced by forest clearing and development projects.*

Native peoples were well established in Brazil when the explorer Pedro Alvares Cabral landed on its shores in 1500. This was the start of many years of Portuguese rule. Settlers from Portugal gradually built up towns along the coast, then further inland. They created large plantations where sugar-cane was grown, bringing in African slaves to work them. In two centuries a total of about four million African slaves were transported to Brazil.

In 1808 Napoleon led his French armies into Portugal. The Portuguese king, João VI, fled to Brazil, where he established the Portuguese empire. He returned home in 1821, leaving Brazil in the hands of his son, Pedro. The following year Pedro declared the Brazilian empire to be an independent nation. In 1889 the royal family were forced to flee after they brought about the abolition of slavery, which was vigorously opposed by Brazil's wealthy landowners.

The Brazilian republic, founded in 1889, thrived for 40 years. Its prosperity ended when a worldwide economic crisis occurred in 1929. Since then there have been mostly unstable governments and military regimes. The last military government left office in 1985 and civilian rule returned. In the same year legislation was passed which meant that future presidents would be elected by the people. Economic difficulties have continued and now pose an enormous challenge for the country's government.

▼ *This magnificent opera house was opened in 1896 in Manaus, a river port buried deep in the rainforest. It was built by wealthy barons who controlled Brazil's highly profitable rubber trade.*

▲ A painting of gardens in Rio de Janeiro, by W Havell (1782-1857), shows the elegant life led by some people during the Brazilian empire. This lifestyle was all too often the result of greed, violence and slavery.

▼ Demonstrators voice support for Tancredo Neves during the 1985 elections. He became the first non-military president for 20 years.

▲ One of several colonial-style churches found in the old quarter of Salvador. This city lies close to the spot where Pedro Alvares Cabral landed in 1500. It was the first city in Brazil and served as its capital until 1763.

COLOMBIA *Introduction*

Situated in the northwest corner of the continent, Colombia joins North America at its border with Panama. One of its coasts looks over the Pacific Ocean, while the other is washed by the warm Caribbean Sea. It was from the Caribbean that the Spanish arrived in the 1530s. They named the country after Christopher Columbus, the European who first discovered it. The Spanish killed many of the native peoples and more died as slaves, while digging for emeralds and gold in the mines. Today most Colombians are partly Native American and partly Spanish in origin. Their Spanish past lives on in Colombia's grand colonial architecture, while popular music, dancing and food have a Native American flavour.

Colombia has many extremes of landscape and climate. Along the coasts are sweltering swamps, humid forests, arid deserts and sugar plantations. Most Colombians live in cities in the Andes Mountains, working in mines or factories. Some grow coffee in the valleys. The eastern plains are vast, hot and dusty. The south is clad in dense rainforest, which is home to pumas, sloths, tapirs and caimans. Colombia has some 1,500 species of birds, from tiny hummingbirds to enormous harpy eagles.

(Map of Colombia showing cities including Riohacha, Santa Marta, Barranquilla, Cartagena, Cienaga, Sincelejo, Monteria, Cúcuta, Bucaramanga, Barrancabermeja, Medellín, Quibdó, Muzo, Tunja, Pereira, Ibague, Bogotá, Villavicencio, Tulua, Cali, Neiva, Buenaventura, San Augustín, Pasto, Tumaco; features Pico Cristóbal Colón 5,775 m 18,947 ft, Cordillera Occidental, Cordillera Central, Cordillera Oriental, Magdalena, Cauca, Llanos, Meta, Orinoco, Guaviare, Selvas, Caquetá, Putumayo, Amazon; bordering PANAMA, VENEZUELA, ECUADOR, PERU, BRAZIL; Caribbean Sea, Pacific Ocean, Gulf of Venezuela, Punta Gallinas)

mi.
0   200

0   200
km

E N D A N G E R E D W O R L D

Fewer nesting areas are available to the green turtle as beaches are developed for tourists.

FACTS AND FIGURES

Area: 1,141,750 sq km
Population: 33,951,000
Capital: Bogotá (4,922,000)
Other major city: Medellín (1,582,000)
Highest point: Pico Cristóbal Colón (5,775 m)
Official language: Spanish

Main religion: Christianity
Currency: Colombian peso
Main exports: Coffee, emeralds, petroleum, coal, flowers, meat
Government: Multi-party republic
Per capita GNP: US $1,290

▼ *This gold model shows El Dorado (The Golden Man) receiving a sacrifice on his raft. The legendary Native American king was said to be so rich that he covered himself in gold dust. Tales of El Dorado encouraged the Spanish conquerors to look for gold in the 1500s.*

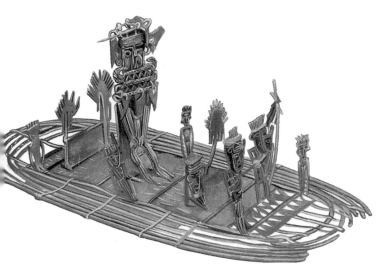

▲ *Large hauls of captured cocaine are burned by the police. Although illegal, cocaine is Colombia's most valuable export. The Colombian government, assisted by the USA, is trying to stamp out cocaine production.*

▶ *Colombia's capital, Bogotá, is a bustling city. Its modern centre is surrounded by large suburbs and the shantytowns where the poor live. In the heart of the city is the bullring (right). Bullfighting is popular in much of South America, a reminder of its historic links with Spain.*

COLOMBIA *Geography and Economy*

The Equator runs through south Colombia, so the weather is very hot and sticky in the low-lying coastal regions. There are areas of scorching desert, but where enough rain falls crops such as cotton grow well. To the east, bordering Venezuela, lie the dusty Llanos Plains, where cattle are raised on huge, remote ranches. Further south numerous rivers rush through thick, lush rainforests on their way to meet the mighty Amazon River in Brazil.

Most of Colombia's activities are focused on the mountains in the west of the country. The weather is cooler there and abundant rain falls. A wide range of crops are grown on the fertile hillsides and there are cattle farms on the lush, rolling grasslands. The Andes fan out into three long fingers pointing north. Perched in their valleys are the main cities and towns. Bogotá, Medellín, Cali and the old university town of Popayán, near San Augustín, are also the industrial centres. Factories produce a wide range of goods, from steel and machinery to clothing. In Medellín market gardens specialize in exotic orchids for export worldwide. Mines in the Andes yield coal and salt as well as gold and emeralds. The mountains are the source of Colombia's wealth, but they can also be dangerous. Occasionally there are earthquakes. In 1985 a volcanic eruption triggered a massive mudslide that engulfed the city of Amero, northwest of Bogotá, and killed 25,000 people.

▲ *In the early morning market traders set out their home-grown wares as crowds jostle to buy. The fertile Andean land and temperate weather help farmers to grow a variety of fruit and vegetables.*

◄ *In the far north of Colombia, near the Caribbean Sea, the Sierra Nevada de Santa Marta forms a cluster of rugged mountains. They include Colombia's highest peak, Cristóbal Colón. These mountains are the northern outpost of the Andes, which stretch the length of South America.*

EMERALDS

Colombia produces about half of the world's emeralds. These brilliant green gemstones are used to make valuable jewellery. Raw emeralds are found in the Andes, particularly at Muzo, north of Bogotá. They have to be carefully cut to make them into sparkling gems. Sometimes, huge, high-quality emeralds weighing as much as 1.4 kilograms have been found in Colombia's mines.

▲ *A coffee farmer works on his small plot of land. After the beans are harvested, they are washed and fermented, then left to dry in the sun. The dried beans are roasted and ground into coffee.*

▶ *A trapper sells animal skins from his van in the town of Villa de Llera, near Tunja. He offers ocelot skins for sale, even though trading in endangered animals is illegal.*

◀ *A freight train cuts through the Andes. It is taking a load of coal to a port on the Caribbean coast. Colombia is the largest producer of coal in the South American continent.*

353

COLOMBIA *People and History*

This land was originally home to many groups of Native Americans. Some communities lived in rainforest settlements or, like the Guajira, wandered the open plains in search of food. Another group, the Chibcha, established an advanced civilization in the Andes. They traded gold and emeralds for Guajira salt and cotton. Gold was their most common metal and the Chibcha used it to make needles and fish-hooks, as well as beautiful jewellery and ornaments. Over 25,000 such historic golden objects are preserved in Bogotá's Gold Museum.

The Spanish conquered the Chibcha in the 1530s and plundered their land in a feverish search for gold. They brought slaves from Africa to work alongside Chibcha survivors on sugar-cane plantations. Many groups of Native Americans were destroyed or killed by disease. Only a few Guajira communities still lead traditional lifestyles today.

Colombia won independence from Spain in 1819, but freedom did not bring peace. Disagreements over government erupted into a full-scale civil war known as the War of a Thousand Days (1899-1902). Disputes rumbled on, then flared again into a period of civil strife called The Violence (1948-1958).

Today wealth and power are held by a relatively small number of people. Although the middle class is growing, the majority of Colombians are very poor. Some of the wealthiest individuals are those who control huge exports of cocaine and other drugs. Since the mid 1980s the government has been campaigning vigorously to stop this illegal trade, but it has met violent resistance from the drug barons. Despite this turmoil Colombia has maintained its fragile hold on democracy.

▲ *This is one of over 300 stone statues that have been found in the hills near San Augustín. They are at least 1,000 years old and appear to mark burial sites.*

◄ *The Kogi Mama people live in remote parts of the Andes. They wear strings of coca leaves around their necks. These leaves have been chewed as a stimulant by the Native American peoples of Colombia for thousands of years.*

► *All sorts of services are offered in a modern square in Cartagena. Three men wash a car in the background. A chair is ready for the shoe-shiner and his client (left). The man in the foreground prepares to cook savoury snacks for passers-by.*

▼ *Cartagena was founded in 1533, when the Spanish built a fortress as a base for their conquest of South America. Masses of silver and gold objects collected by the Spanish conquerors were exported to Spain from Cartagena. It became a rich city.*

▼ *These Tukano children live in the rainforests southeast of Colombia. The Tukano live in family groups of 20 or 30, sharing longhouses called* halocas.

ECUADOR *Introduction*

The Equator passes through the north of this country, so when the Spanish conquered it in the 1500s they called it Ecuador, the Spanish word for Equator. The Spanish destroyed the great Inca civilization they found here, killing many of the Native American peoples and seizing their gold. Today some descendants of the original peoples survive in the remote eastern rainforests on the border with Peru. However, their future is not secure because both Ecuador and Peru lay claim to this forest, intending to exploit its valuable timber and rich reserves of oil.

The Andes Mountains run through the centre of Ecuador, with snow-capped peaks that are often cloaked in cloud. Among these there are 30 active volcanoes that occasionally erupt. Earthquakes have long posed threats to this country. In 1942 Ecuador's largest city, Guayaquil, was severely damaged.

About half the population lives in the Andes, farming the fertile mountain valleys and plateaus. Most of the rest live on the humid coastal strip west of the Andes, where the weather is ideal for growing bananas, coffee, cocoa and sugar-cane. These are some of the products shipped from Guayaquil, which manufactures goods ranging from cement to chemicals. Fishing is another major source of income. The Pacific yields large catches of herring, mackerel and tuna.

FACTS AND FIGURES
Area: 283,560 sq km, Galápagos Islands 7,844 sq km
Population: 10,981,000
Capital: Quito (1,101,000)
Other major cities: Guayaquil (1,509,000), Cuenca (195,000)
Highest point: Chimborazo (6,267 m)
Official language: Spanish
Main religion: Christianity
Currency: Sucre
Main exports: Bananas, petroleum, shrimps, coffee, cocoa, sugar
Government: Republic
Per capita GNP: US $1,070

▲ *On the Pacific coast large fields are cleared and flooded to make shrimp farms. Shrimps are one of Ecuador's most important exports.*

◄ *Snow-capped Mount Cotopaxi lies close to the Equator and is one of the highest active volcanoes in the world, rising to 5,896 metres. It last erupted in 1877, destroying a large area of farmland. The boulder in the foreground is a lump of volcanic lava that is now overgrown with lichen.*

▶ *Two men operate an oil drill in Oriente, the vast low-lying rainforest of eastern Ecuador. Oil was first discovered in 1967 and is now Ecuador's main export.*

▲ *Saraguro is a small town built high on a plain in the Andes Mountains. The houses are built of adobe (sun-dried mud brick) and have terracotta-tiled roofs. The church is in Spanish colonial style.*

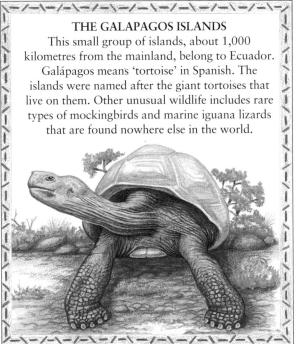

THE GALAPAGOS ISLANDS

This small group of islands, about 1,000 kilometres from the mainland, belong to Ecuador. Galápagos means 'tortoise' in Spanish. The islands were named after the giant tortoises that live on them. Other unusual wildlife includes rare types of mockingbirds and marine iguana lizards that are found nowhere else in the world.

ECUADOR *People and History*

▲ *A Waorani man prepares a poison-tipped arrow to shoot through a blow-pipe. The Waorani live in the rainforest and hunt monkeys, sloths and tapirs.*

▼ *These school children come from Ingapirca, near Cuenca. Ecuadorians attend school until they are 14.*

Almost half the population of Ecuador is made up of Native American peoples. Some groups lead nomadic lives deep in the Ecuadorian rainforests. They clear land to build villages of thatched huts, grow small amounts of crops, then move on after harvest to hunt and fish. Most Native Americans live in eastern Ecuador, but one group, the Colorados, lives on the coast. They are the only rainforest people in South America to live west of the Andes Mountains.

Other Native American groups live high in the Andes, farming tiny plots of land and selling crafts. The ancestors of these peoples were part of the Inca empire, which spread north from Peru during the 1400s and covered much of the central Andes. The Spanish conquered the Incas in the 1530s and used them as slaves. They brought more slaves from Africa to work with the Incas on the sugar plantations along the coast. Today much of the population is of mixed descent, part Native American, part Spanish, part African. Spanish is the official language, but many of the Native Americans speak the old Inca language of Quechua.

Ecuador won its independence from Spain in the 1820s, but the people of Spanish descent have always remained the richest and most powerful group, while many of the native peoples live in poverty. In modern times the politics of Ecuador have been unstable, with a long line of military takeovers and violent upheavals. Since 1979 the government has been democratically elected, but the problem of poverty remains unsolved.

► *A Native American family from Zumbahua in the Andes Mountains returns home from church. More than 90 percent of Ecuadorians belong to the Roman Catholic Church. Members of this family are carrying palm leaves from a Palm Sunday mass.*

◄ *This cathedral is in Cuenca, a city founded by the Spanish conquerors in 1557. Throughout the 1800s the Church had considerable power over the Ecuadorian government, but this ended in 1896 when the Liberals seized control.*

PANAMA HATS

Ecuadorian women hand-weave traditional Panama hats. Though they originated in Ecuador, Panama hats were first exported from Panama, which is how they got their name. Made of straw from the jipijapa plant, Panama hats are light and strong, so ideally suited for wearing in the tropics. Good Panama hats are very flexible. They bounce back into shape even if sat upon. They can be rolled up and stored in a tube when not in use and it is in tubes that these hats are exported all over the world.

◄ *Ecuadorians get ready to ride on a* lanchero, *a bus converted from a lorry. Some sit on top, where there are no seats but a handrail to hold on to.*

359

PERU *Introduction*

Peru was the homeland of the Incas, who ruled over an impressive empire in the mountains and fertile valleys of the Andes some 600 years ago. The Inca civilization was destroyed by Spanish conquerors and today most Peruvians are mestizos (of mixed race). Descendants of the Incas still farm the ancient terraces on the steep mountain ridges. Llamas loaded with baggage tread old Inca trails and condors, the elegant vultures of the Andes, glide through the clear air overhead. To the west of the Andes the country's main cities lie on the coastal plains. To the east a vast, remote region of tropical forest stretches towards the Amazon Basin. The Amazon begins its immense journey in Peru's mountains, just 190 kilometres from the Pacific coast. At the port of Iquitos the river is deep enough to receive ocean-going vessels from the other side of the continent.

Peru is rich in mining, fishing and agriculture, yet it remains a poor country troubled by violent unrest. In the early 1990s Maoist guerrillas called the *Sendero Luminoso* (Shining Path) controlled large parts of Peru. Thousands of farming families were caught up in the troubles, while struggling simply to survive.

▲ *In Chincheros, in the Andes, Native American people keep their heritage alive with traditional costumes and dancing. Peru's Native Americans make up almost half of the total population.*

▲ Soldiers guard the Government Palace at Lima. Behind them stands the Roman Catholic Cathedral, built in the Spanish colonial years.

E N D A N G E R E D   W O R L D

Drainage and pollution are destroying the rivers and lakes where black caimans live and breed. These animals are also hunted for their skins.

▲ The terraced ruins of Machu Picchu, an Inca city, perch on a ridge high in the Andes near the old Inca capital of Cusco. The Spanish conquerors of Peru did not find this city and no one knows why the Incas abandoned it. Its ruins were discovered in 1911.

◀ A Native American musician, wearing a traditional embroidered hat and cape, plays a haunting tune on the rondador or pan-pipes. The notes are produced by blowing across the tops of a series of hollow tubes made of wood, bamboo or reeds.

FACTS AND FIGURES

Area: 1,244,280 sq km
Population: 22,454,000
Capital: Lima (5,760,000)
Other major cities: Callao (638,000), Arequipa (621,000)
Highest point: Huascarán (6,768 m)
Official languages: Spanish, Quechua
Main religion: Christianity
Currency: Nuevo sol
Main exports: Copper, lead, fish products, iron, zinc, oil, coffee, llama and alpaca wool, cotton, sugar
Government: Multi-party republic
Per capita GNP: US $950

PERU *Geography and Economy*

Peru is a farming nation. High in the Andes Mountains, the backbone of the country, farmers work small plots of land to grow maize, wheat and beans. They also grow potatoes, which are believed to have originated here. Guinea-pigs are reared for food. Chickens, sheep and llamas are raised for their produce.

The majority of the population lives along the narrow strip of land lining the Pacific coast. The landscape there is dusty and dry, streaked by fertile, green river valleys planted with cotton and sugar, which are among Peru's most important exports.

Lima, the capital, lies right in the middle of Peru's coastline, spread out under a cloud of smog. The Peruvian Current, a cold ocean current from the Antarctic, dramatically reduces the rainfall that could help to clear the severe pollution in this area.

The country's economy is plagued by inflation and unemployment. Peru's resources were once in the hands of a few wealthy families. Ordinary people were allowed to buy shares in their workplaces during the 1960s, but the 1980s saw a return to private ownership. Neither of these situations provided the answers to Peru's continuing economic problems.

▼ *Foundry workers pour liquid iron into moulds. Before this the iron ore is separated from the earth and rock in which it was mined by smelting at high temperatures. Metal processing is a major industry in Peru.*

▼ *On an island in Lake Titicaca, Native American women weave colourful shawls, blankets and wall-hangings for the tourist market. They use horizontal looms placed on the ground. Weaving is a traditional craft that brings extra income to the poor farming families.*

▲ *The Peruvian Andes reach up to a series of impressive, snow-capped peaks. The highest mountain in the country is Huascarán (6,768 metres), an extinct volcano. It is part of Huascarán National Park, which includes 20 mountains over 6,000 metres.*

◄ A copper mine near the southern city of Arequipa. Where metal ores lie close to the surface, they can be extracted in an open-cast mine, a vast, open pit. Circular steps spiral upwards from a central point in the valley where the operation starts. The machinery moves along the roadways, cutting ore from the side of each step. As the rock is cut, so the mine spreads outwards, creating this characteristic whirlpool formation.

▲ High in the Andes at Colca Canyon, farming still takes place on terraces carved out of the mountainside by the Incas some 500 years ago. By creating a series of steps, farmers are able to prevent soil from eroding away and can control the irrigation of their crops.

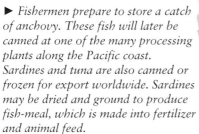

► Fishermen prepare to store a catch of anchovy. These fish will later be canned at one of the many processing plants along the Pacific coast. Sardines and tuna are also canned or frozen for export worldwide. Sardines may be dried and ground to produce fish-meal, which is made into fertilizer and animal feed.

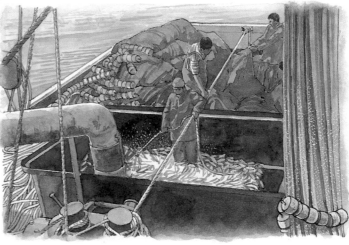

PERU *People and History*

▶ *Dating back some 700 years to the Chimu period, this ornate dagger is made of gold and studded with the semi-precious stone turquoise. It shows a nobleman wearing an extravagant headdress and large golden earrings. It may have been used by priests to perform sacrifices.*

The Incas came to power in the 1400s. They followed the Huari and the Chimu peoples in a series of civilizations that first developed in Peru about 3,000 years ago. The Inca period was famous for its monumental architecture and for beautifully crafted gold and pottery. The Incas used precious metals freely because they were readily available. Careful organization and a good network of roads enabled them to hold together a vast empire that covered all the central Andes.

In 1532 the conqueror Francisco Pizarro arrived to find two Inca leaders, Atahualpa and Huascar, quarrelling over who should be king. Attracted by the enormous quantities of gold and silver that they possessed, Pizarro took advantage of the dispute and set about destroying their empire.

During the 300 years that Spain ruled Peru, thousands of Spanish settlers arrived, bringing their language and religion. Today most Peruvians are Roman Catholic. Both Spanish and Quechua, the old Inca language, are widely spoken. The immigrants also brought slavery and disease, which killed a large proportion of the Native American population. There is still a deep division between the Native Americans and Spanish descendants today.

In the 1820s Peru won its independence in a series of battles led by José de San Martin of Argentina and Simón Bolívar of Venezuela. Since then Peru has suffered many setbacks, including the War of the Pacific (1879-1883), when it lost part of its coast to Chile. The president, Alberto Fujimoro, who was elected in 1990, inherited a country where recent history had been clouded by violence, military takeovers and armed rebellion.

◀ *Traders in traditional dress display their wares at a lively market north of Cusco. Market day is a social occasion as well as a chance to do business.*

SPEAK QUECHUA

How are you? – Imaynalla?
*(ee - mie - **nal** - ya)*

Fine – Allinmi
*(al - **yeen** - mee)*

Do come in – Yaykurimuy
*(yie - koo - **ree** - mwee)*

Yes – Arí *(a - **ree**)*

No – Mana *(**ma** - na)*

◄ This painting, by José Effio (1840-1917), commemorates the founding of Lima by Francisco Pizarro in 1535. It shows Pizarro as an heroic conqueror, although he destroyed the Inca empire through savagery and greed. In 1541 violence caught up with Pizarro and he was murdered by rivals in Lima.

▲ The Uru people, living around Lake Titicaca, build their boats and houses out of reeds. Clusters of houses stand on floating rafts, which are also made of reeds.

► Crowds watch descendants of the Inca people celebrate the Festival of the Sun from the walls of an Inca fortress at Sacsahuaman, near Cusco. How these huge stone building blocks were moved from the quarries remains a mystery.

CHILE *Introduction*

Chile is the longest, thinnest country in the world. Like a long ribbon, it stretches from the tropics in the north to the cold, windswept seas around Cape Horn in the south.

The country has a spectacular mixture of landscapes. The fertile central region is filled with orchards, vineyards, wheatfields and green pastures where cattle and sheep are raised. The summers are warm and sunny and the winters mild. This is where the main cities are and where most people live. To the north is the arid expanse of the Atacama Desert, one of the world's driest areas. The far south is a land of islands, forests, mountains and glaciers.

Eastern Chile is hemmed in by the majestic Andes Mountains. These mark a fault in the Earth's crust, which causes volcanic eruptions and earthquakes. Both Santiago and Valparaiso have been devastated by earthquakes. Some way off the coast at Valparaiso lie the Juan Fernandez Islands, owned by Chile. Alexander Falkirk was shipwrecked there in the early 1700s, which gave Daniel Defoe the idea for his famous tale, *Robinson Crusoe*.

Oil and natural gas have been found among the southern islands and the country is also rich in minerals. Chile's large fishing fleet trawls the waters of the southern Pacific for mackerel, sardines and tuna.

► *The jagged mountains and lakes of the Torres del Paine region, near Punta Arenas, are typical of the dramatic scenery of the far south. This area has been made one of Chile's 30 national parks, in order to protect its natural beauty.*

◀ Old and new exist side by side in Santiago, seen here from a local viewpoint called Santa Lucia Hill. A fort was built on the hill by Chile's Spanish conquerors, who founded the city in 1541. Santiago is Chile's largest city and one of the main industrial cities of the central region.

▼ Clouds of smoke and earth fill the air as explosives are used to expose a new seam of copper at Chuquicamata, in the north. This is one of the largest open-cast copper mines in the world.

FACTS AND FIGURES
Area: 736,900 sq km
Population: 13,813,000
Capital: Santiago (4,859,000)
Other major cities: Vina del Mar (298,000), Concepción (295,000)
Highest point: Ojos del Salado (6,880 m)
Official language: Spanish
Main religion: Christianity
Currency: Chilean peso
Main exports: Copper, iron, fruit, wood pulp
Government: Republic
Per capita GNP: US $2,730

▲ Wine is sampled carefully to see if it has matured properly. Chile has been producing wine since the 1500s and today exports it to countries all over the world.

▶ Valparaiso is Chile's main port. It serves Santiago, lying 100 kilometres inland. Its industries include iron, steel, textiles and chemicals.

CHILE *People and History*

Native American peoples, including the Incas in the north, were living in Chile when the Spanish conquerors arrived in the 1530s. The Spanish forced them to work on farms and many died of diseases brought by the invaders. Over time the Spanish and Native Americans intermarried and today about three quarters of the population is of mixed descent.

The country broke away from Spain in 1818, after a revolution led by the Irish-Chilean Bernardo O'Higgins. During the 1800s economic booms were followed by collapses. Chile was gripped by war with Bolivia and Peru, as well as civil war at home. In the early 1970s economic problems led to a takeover of government by the armed forces. General Pinochet's military regime lasted until 1990, when a democratically elected government was restored.

Until recent years most of Chile's farmland was owned by a few wealthy Europeans. Government land reforms from the mid 1960s broke up many of the big estates and about a fifth of Chile's workers are currently employed in agriculture. Most Chileans, especially the middle class, live and work in the country's towns and cities.

▲ *About 600 strange stone heads were left behind on Easter Island by early Polynesian settlers. This island, lying nearly 4,000 kilometres off its western shores, is owned by Chile. These statues, or* moai, *were sculpted around 1,000 years ago and were thought to have magical powers.*

◄ *This photograph, taken in 1903, shows nuns teaching Chilean women to spin. Roman Catholic missionaries converted many Native Americans to Christianity during the 1800s. They encouraged the women to pursue traditional crafts and to sell what they produced.*

◀ The brightly coloured traditional dress of the Araucanian people includes huge pieces of silver jewellery. The Araucanians, or Mapuche, are part of the largest group of Native Americans in Chile. They resisted the Spanish vigorously for 300 years, but were gradually pushed back into the Los Lagos region, near Puerto Montt. Many have tried to keep up their traditions, living in small villages and farming.

▶ A woman flicks a handkerchief gracefully at her partner as she takes part in the Cueca, Chile's national dance. Most festivities in Chile include dancing and a band playing lively music. Traditional singing and dancing is accompanied by guitar, accordion, harp and drums.

◀ General Pinochet inspects his troops. Pinochet seized control from the democratically elected socialist leader Salvador Allende in 1973. While Pinochet was in power thousands of people who opposed his government left Chile, died in the civil war or were imprisoned. Others disappeared or were tortured. A democratically elected government replaced Pinochet in 1990, but he remained head of the armed forces.

BOLIVIA *Introduction*

▼ *A miner works in one of Bolivia's underground tin mines in the Andes. Working conditions are hard and often dangerous for the extraction of this valuable metal. Other metal deposits in the Andes Mountains include copper, lead, silver, tungsten, antimony and lead.*

About one third of Bolivia lies high in the Andes Mountains, on a dusty plateau called the Altiplano. The weather there is bright, cool and mainly dry. The highest mountain peaks are capped with snow throughout the year. Bolivia has two capitals, La Paz and Sucre. La Paz, the largest city and the centre of government, is considered to be the main capital. It stands on the Altiplano plain at a height of about 3,660 metres. This makes it the world's highest capital and visitors arriving from lower lands often feel quite breathless and dizzy in its thin air. Sucre is the legal capital, where the country's main law courts are.

To the east the weather is warm and humid. There, the Andes drop away through tropical rainforests to the Amazon Basin. In the well-watered river valleys farmers grow tropical crops such as coffee, cocoa, sugar-cane, pineapples, bananas and avocados. Coca, the plant from which the drug cocaine is made, is also grown. The country's forests supply large quantities of timber, such as mahogany and balsa wood, as well as rubber (which comes from tree sap) and brazil nuts. The bark of the chinchona tree yields quinine, which is used to treat the disease malaria and is an ingredient of tonic water.

In the southeast of Bolivia lies the Gran Chaco, a vast area of swamps, tangled scrub and dry grasslands where herds of cattle graze. The oil and natural gas found in this area are sent by pipeline to Argentina and Chile. Natural gas is one of Bolivia's most valuable exports.

▶ *Perched on the steep, terraced mountains to the west, farmers harvest potatoes. Potatoes originally came from South America and were introduced to Europe by Spaniards in the 1500s. Potatoes are still one of Bolivia's main crops.*

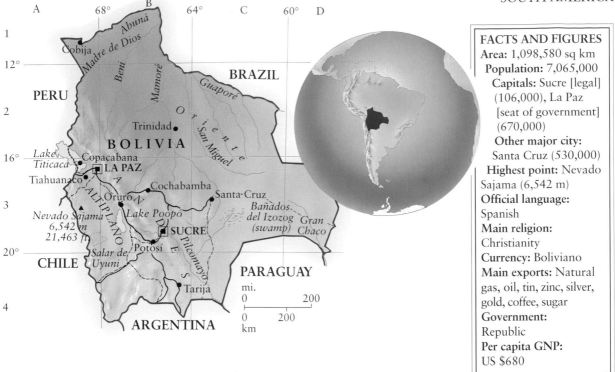

BOLIVIA

FACTS AND FIGURES
Area: 1,098,580 sq km
Population: 7,065,000
Capitals: Sucre [legal]
(106,000), La Paz
[seat of government]
(670,000)
Other major city:
Santa Cruz (530,000)
Highest point: Nevado
Sajama (6,542 m)
Official language:
Spanish
Main religion:
Christianity
Currency: Boliviano
Main exports: Natural
gas, oil, tin, zinc, silver,
gold, coffee, sugar
Government:
Republic
Per capita GNP:
US $680

◄ *Llamas graze high up in the Andes,
where they are kept for their leather
and meat. These animals are
distant relatives of the camel.*

ENDANGERED WORLD

The giant anteater
is declining in numbers
as more and more of its
grassland habitat is fenced off
for cattle-grazing.

▼ *One of many anti-government demonstrations
takes place in La Paz. These are often led by the
miners, who form a powerful
political group.*

BOLIVIA *People and History*

Bolivia was home to the Tiahuanacos, one of the first great civilizations of the Andes. This civilization centred on the city of Tiahuanaco and lasted until about AD1000. By the 1400s the region had been controlled first by the Aymara people and then by the Incas. Conquerors from Spain swept aside the Incas during the 1530s and began over 200 years of Spanish rule. Spanish settlers broke free from Spain in 1825 and named their country after the great hero of the South American wars of independence, the Venezuelan Simón Bolívar.

Since independence Bolivia has had a troubled history of war, unrest and military rule. It lost its only stretch of coast to Chile in the 1880s and a large part of the Gran Chaco region to Paraguay in the 1930s. Years of economic difficulties lie behind many of Bolivia's problems. It is one of the poorest countries on the South American continent.

People in rural areas tend to live in small communities, raising just enough crops and animals to feed their families. Some women make pottery or weave textiles to earn extra money. In the city most people work in factories and live in sprawling areas of poor housing called barrios, which surround the city centres. In contrast, the wealthy few live in modern houses or apartments and often own large areas of land.

Bolivia is unusual because over half of its people are Native Americans, mostly the Quechua and Aymara. The rest are mainly of Spanish origin or of mixed parentage. Spanish is the official language, but only about one third of the population speaks it.

▲ *This man is selling traditional wares such as woollen shawls, blankets, ponchos and knitted caps with earflaps to keep out the mountain cold. The Native Americans make many of these things for their own use, as well as to sell to tourists.*

◄ *The gleaming, ornate interior of the shrine of the Dark Virgin in Copacabana. As in almost all the countries of South America, the majority of the people are Roman Catholic. As well as holding Christian beliefs, many Bolivians also worship the various gods and goddesses of Native American religions.*

▶ A bus queue stretches across the square in La Paz. Very few people can afford a car. There are railway lines, but most people use buses. These provide services in the towns and cities. They also travel over the rough roads that spread throughout the country.

SPEAK AYMARA

How are you? – Kamisasktas?
(ka - mee - sask - tass)

Fine – Walikiwa
(wa - lee - kee - wa)

Do come in – Mantama
(man - ta - ma)

Yes – Jisa *(hee - sa)*

No – Janiwa *(ha - nee - wa)*

▶ This is one of the towering stone sculptures found at the once-great ruined city of Tiahuanaco, close to Lake Titicaca. The largest statue found so far at this site is over seven metres high.

▲ Women gather to chat on the steps of San Francisco Monastery, one of the finest Spanish colonial buildings in La Paz. Many women still wear traditional clothes, including these highly distinctive hats.

373

PARAGUAY

Paraguay lies landlocked in the centre of South America. It is a hot and humid country, divided in two by the Paraguay River. To the east are lush grasslands and thick forests. Almost all the people live there, mainly ranching cattle and farming sugar-cane, rice, coffee and soya beans. To the west the Gran Chaco is a vast plain of salt marshes, thorny scrub and sparse grass.

Native Americans called the Guaraní lived peaceably in this region until the 1500s, when Spanish explorers arrived on their way to Peru to seek gold. The Spanish founded Asunción, now Paraguay's capital, and ruled the country for 300 years, putting the Guaraní to work on their estates. Today almost all Paraguayans are mestizos (of mixed descent).

Paraguay won independence from Spain in 1811, but there followed more years of bitter war with its neighbours and political unrest under military dictators. It remains a poor country, but Paraguay's fertile farmlands and potential for hydroelectric power may well provide a brighter future.

▲ The Paraná River, coloured by sediment, runs through dense tropical rainforests on its way to the Atlantic Ocean. It is big enough to carry ships, so is used to transport large quantities of goods to the sea for export abroad.

◄ A lacemaker works at a bedspread in traditional Guaraní style. Flowers, birds, animals and decorative patterns are created out of the lace, which is called ñandutí, the Guaraní word for spider's web.

374

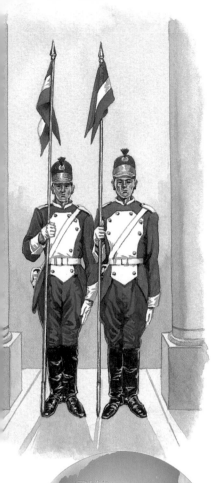

► *Thriving Ciudad del Este is on the Paraná River. It used to be called Puerto Presidente Stroessner, after the military dictator who ruled Paraguay for 35 years from 1954 to 1989.*

◄ *Soldiers guard the Pantheon of the Heroes in Asunción. This monument commemorates the death of more than 300,000 Paraguayans in the border wars with Brazil, Argentina and Uruguay (1865-1870).*

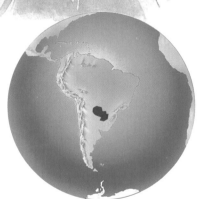

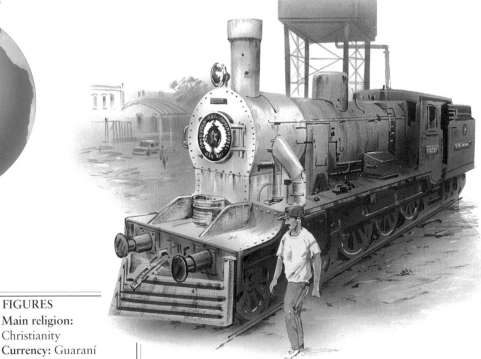

FACTS AND FIGURES

Area: 406,750 sq km
Population: 4,643,000
Capital: Asunción (945,000)
Other major city: Ciudad del Este (134,000)
Highest point: Near Villarrica (680 m)
Official language: Spanish

Main religion: Christianity
Currency: Guaraní
Main exports: Cotton, soya beans, timber, meat, vegetable oil
Government: Multi-party republic
Per capita GNP: US $1,340

REPUBLICA DEL PARAGUAY

▲ *This old steam train is used to transport tropical hardwood. The timber is a valuable resource, but its harvest is wiping out large areas of rainforest.*

375

URUGUAY

By South American standards Uruguay is a small country, which is further dwarfed by its giant neighbours, Argentina and Brazil. The majority of the population lives along the south coast, which overlooks the wide estuary of the Río de la Plata (Plate River) and the Atlantic Ocean. In summer large numbers of tourists flock to the sandy beaches of this long coastline. Just inland begin fertile, low-lying plains, where crops such as rice, oranges, tangerines, peaches and grapes grow through the hot summers and mild winters, watered by regular rainfall.

Beyond the plains lie rich pastures with huge farms called estancias, where gauchos (cowboys) raise cattle and sheep. Leather, wool and meat products are a vital source of income. A great deal of meat is eaten in the country itself. A Uruguayan's favourite meal will almost always include beef.

Most Uruguayans are descended from early Spanish colonists or from European immigrants, especially Italians, who came to Uruguay in the 1800s. The Spanish arrived in 1726 and ruled the country from the early 1800s, until settlers formed an army to fight for independence. This was finally won in 1828, after 17 bitter years of war.

Uruguay enjoyed prosperity and democratic rule in the early 1900s. However, by the 1960s the situation had changed and the country suffered economic problems, unrest and military dictatorships. Since 1985 Uruguay has had a democratically elected civilian government, which is trying to rebuild the country's troubled economy.

▲ A local enjoys a sip of mate, a hot, slightly bitter drink that is popular throughout much of southern South America. It is made from the leaves of the mate tree and is traditionally drunk from a gourd, through a metal tube.

▼ Children play football, a national passion, from an early age. Uruguay won the first ever World Cup, held here in 1930.

▲ This brightly painted building houses a meat packing factory. Beef, lamb and pork have to be specially packed for export in refrigerated ships and so factories such as this one play an important role in the economy.

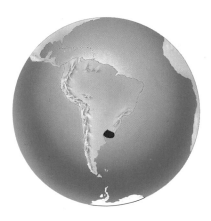

▲ An elaborate bronze statue in Montevideo celebrates the early Spanish settlers. They crossed the country with ox-drawn carts to build farms and towns inland.

▼ The harbour of the capital, Montevideo, lies on the broad mouth of the Río de la Plata (Plate River). About half of the country's total population lives in this city.

FACTS AND FIGURES
Area: 176,210 sq km
Population: 3,149,000
Capital: Montevideo (1,384,000)
Other major city: Salto (81,000)
Highest point: Mirador Nacional (501 m)
Official language: Spanish
Main religion: Christianity
Currency: Uruguayan peso
Main exports: Meat, leather, hides, wool, fish, textiles
Government: Republic
Per capita GNP: US $3,340

ARGENTINA *Introduction*

▼ *The Congress Building in Buenos Aires is built in a French style. The city is often referred to as the 'Paris of South America'.*

Argentina is the second largest South American country after Brazil. Its huge area includes semi-tropical regions in the north, the icy southern tip of the continent and open plateaus and grasslands in-between.

Native Americans were the first inhabitants. They were forced into slavery or killed by the Spanish, who arrived and claimed the land as their own in the 1500s. It was the Spanish who named this land Argentina, from *argentum*, the Latin word for silver. They believed that they would find rich deposits of silver here, but they were wrong. As it turned out, Argentina's greatest treasures were not metals, but lush, green pasture and fertile soil. This is largely an agricultural country, relying heavily on cattle and sheep farming, wheat, fruit and wine. Enticed by opportunity, millions of immigrants have come to settle in Argentina over the years so the towns and cities contain people of many nationalities.

Argentina has suffered severe political troubles. In 1982 the country went to war with Britain over ownership of the Falkland Islands and Argentina was defeated. Although economic problems continued, the 1980s and 1990s saw a more stable political situation.

ENDANGERED WORLD

The maned wolf, which lives in the Pampas, has been hunted almost to extinction.

▶ *A couple tango in the street. The tango is the most famous dance to come from South America. It is now seen in ballrooms all over the world, but it is said that only Argentinians know how to tango with true passion.*

◄ *People stand on a public viewing platform in Patagonia to witness the end of a glacier. Having come down from the high Andes, this is the point at which the glacier melts and the water begins to flow as a river.*

FACTS AND FIGURES

Area: 2,780,090 sq km
Population: 33,778,000
Capital: Buenos Aires (9,928,000)
Other major city: Córdoba (982,000)
Highest point: Aconcagua (6,959 m)
Official language: Spanish
Main religion: Christianity
Currency: Peso
Main exports: Wheat, maize, meat, hides, wool, tannin, linseed oil, minerals, peanuts
Government: Federal republic
Per capita GNP: US $6,050

▼ *Buenos Aires' waterfront is lined with skyscrapers. Founded originally as a port, the name means favourable winds.*

ARGENTINA *Geography and Economy*

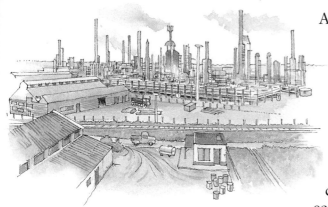

▲ *This oil refinery in La Plata is linked by a pipeline to nearby Buenos Aires. Argentina has almost enough reserves of oil and natural gas to meet its own industrial and domestic needs.*

▼ *A Patagonian child holds a lamb that has lost its mother. Sheep thrive on scrubby terrain in conditions too harsh for planting crops.*

Argentina has two vast areas of natural grassland, the Pampas and Patagonia. Patagonia is a high, windswept plateau that covers much of the south. This rocky, scrubby land suffers blistering heat in summer and bitter cold in winter. Most of Argentina's sheep are farmed there for lamb and wool, which are major exports. The rolling pastures of the Pampas occupy the central plains. This is a land of endless wheat prairies and remote, sprawling cattle ranches called estancias. Argentina's economy was founded on the meat and leather industry in the 1800s. Beef was preserved in salt water, then canned and sold as corned beef. Since the invention of refrigeration Argentina has exported huge quantities of fresh and frozen meat.

In the sweltering far north the Pampas runs into the Gran Chaco, a region of vast swamps and scrub forest where cattle-ranching gives way to cotton farming. To the east the border with Brazil is marked by the spectacular Iguaçu Falls. To the west the towering Andes form Argentina's border with Chile. In the warm foothills of the Andes are olive groves, citrus orchards and vineyards. The fertile region around Mendoza is called the Garden of the Andes. Agriculture produces about three quarters of the country's exports, but Argentina also manufactures cars, televisions, aircraft, electrical goods, textiles and leather products.

▲ *Ushuaia, capital of Argentine Tierra del Fuego, is the most southerly town in the world. In 1520 the Portuguese navigator Ferdinand Magellan saw small fires lit along the shore by Native Americans as he sailed close by. He named this land Tierra del Fuego (Land of Fire).*

◄ At Antonio de Areco, near Rosario, grain stores are emptied into trucks ready for export. Wheat, maize, rye, barley and sorghum are grown on the drier eastern Pampas. Argentina is the fifth largest exporter of wheat in the world.

► Skilled Argentine cowboys called gauchos herd cattle into pens for a cattle fair in Entre Rios in the far northeast. Gauchos still wear the traditional high boots with spurs, baggy trousers and round felt hats.

▼ The Pampas covers an area larger than the countries of Spain and Portugal put together. It is generally flat, with few trees. The weather is usually mild, with a fair amount of rain. The term Pampas comes from a Spanish word meaning 'a plain'.

ARGENTINA *People*

Around 500 years ago there were probably some 300,000 Native Americans living in Argentina, from the Guaraní in the sub-tropical northeast to the Guajira communities in the far south of Patagonia and Tierra del Fuego. Then in the 1500s the Spanish arrived and began to take control of the country. Gradually the indigenous peoples fell victim to European diseases, died in slavery, or were killed in wars and massacres. Today Argentina has only small numbers of Native Americans, who live in remote areas. Most Argentinians are descended from European immigrants, though about 15 percent are mestizos (of mixed descent).

▲ *Girls from the Spanish community and a family of Welsh origin wear traditional dress and join in national celebrations on Independence Day. Several groups of Welsh people came to Patagonia after 1865 to preserve their traditional way of life and language, which they felt were being destroyed in Wales.*

As centuries passed, more waves of immigrants flooded into Argentina. The Italians and British followed the Spanish. Another huge influx after World War II included Germans, Dutch, Poles, Hungarians and Lebanese. Today, while Spanish is spoken everywhere, Argentina is proud of being a multicultural land. Its people usually mix freely and also keep their original languages, food, festivities and traditions.

Most Argentinians live in towns and about one third of the population lives in or around Buenos Aires. About half are scattered across the Pampas, but large areas of the country have no inhabitants because of their harsh climate and difficult terrain. Nevertheless, Argentina is one of the most modern countries in South America. It has trading contacts around the world and a high standard of education, which is provided free to everyone.

◄ *Traditions of skilled horse-riding have made Argentina one of the world's leading countries in the sport of polo. Football, rugby, boating and car racing are also popular sports in this country. The national game is* pato, *a form of basketball played on horseback.*

▼ *La Boca is the artists' quarter of Buenos Aires. La Boca was settled by Italians from Genoa in the 1800s. The colourful houses are a reminder of their Mediterranean origins.*

▲ *The ornately carved cathedral in Salta is part of Argentina's Spanish heritage. Spanish colonists introduced the Roman Catholic religion to this country in the 1500s. Today most Argentinians belong to the Roman Catholic Church, but all religions are tolerated.*

◄ *Gauchos enjoy music before a barbecue or asado. Whole lambs or sides of beef are split open, skewered on stakes, then propped up around an open fire. This feast is often associated with Christmas.*

383

ARGENTINA *History*

▲ *Eva (Evita) Perón, the second wife of President Juan Perón, waves to adoring crowds from the balcony of Government House in Buenos Aires. She became immensely popular, but died of cancer in 1952 aged just 33. The whole nation mourned.*

Native Americans had set up farming communities in Argentina long before a Spanish explorer named Juan Díaz de Solís first set foot in the country in 1516.

Centuries of Spanish control followed. Early settlers from Spain crossed over the Andes from Peru and established Buenos Aires in 1580. By the early 1800s the settlers were unhappy with Spanish rule. They fought a war of independence and gained freedom in 1816, but the fighting turned into civil war. A strong government was finally established in 1861.

Argentina prospered, but by the late 1920s it was in economic and political crisis and a series of military governments began. Colonel Juan Perón became president in 1946. He backed social reforms, but again there were economic problems and he was overthrown. He returned to power in 1973 and after he died his wife Isabel took over. Again the Peróns were brought down and many people died under the new military government. In 1982 claims to the Falkland Islands, known in Argentina as Las Malvinas, led to war with Britain. Argentina surrendered, but did not give up its claims. The military dictatorship ended the following year, when a democratically elected government came to power.

▼ *Ruins of the church of San Ignacio stand in the province of Misiones in the far northeast. The province was named after the Jesuits, who came to the region in the 1600s to convert the Guaraní peoples.*

▲ *This statue in Buenos Aires commemorates José de San Martin (1778-1850), Argentina's celebrated revolutionary leader. He helped to free Chile and Peru, as well as his homeland, from Spanish rule.*

ASIA

Arctic Circle

Tropic of Cancer

Equator

Tropic of Capricorn

ASIA *Geography*

Asia is the largest continent in the world, covering almost one third of the Earth's total land surface. It is part of the same landmass as Europe and stretches from Africa and Europe in the west to the Pacific Ocean in the east. Chains of volcanic islands mark the continent's eastern border, which is a danger zone for earthquakes.

Asia's northwestern borders are formed by the steep crags of the Ural and Caucasus mountains. Lands in the far north extend above the Arctic Circle, where much of the region is tundra – a frozen, treeless wilderness that is locked in ice for many months each year. Farther south lies a broad belt of evergreen forest known as taiga, which in turn gives way to open, fertile grasslands in the west and east. However, few rain-bearing winds reach Central Asia, so deserts have formed in this region. Little grows on the sandy wastes and barren, rocky plateaus where it is bitterly cold in winter and as hot as a furnace in summer.

The great triangular peninsula of India stretches south into the warm Indian Ocean. The world's highest mountain ranges, the Himalayas and Karakorams, form a barrier of ice and snow in the north. South of the mountains the snow melts into rivers that run through broad plains. These rivers often flood and deposit fertile soil over a wide area.

Asia's sunny southwestern coastline is washed by the Red Sea and the Mediterranean, but the lands and islands of southern Asia have a tropical climate. There, it is hot and dry for part of the year, but drenched by rain during the summer months. At this time stormy winds called monsoons gather up moisture from the southern oceans and shed it over the land.

▼ *The world's highest peak is Mount Everest* (left). *This snowy giant is in the Himalaya Mountains, which lie along the border between China and Nepal.*

◄ *Rice has been grown on these irrigated hillside terraces in the Philippines for 2,000 years. It thrives in the hot, monsoon climate of Southeast Asia and is the continent's most important food crop.*

A 40° B 60° C 80° D 100° E F 120° F G 140° H 160° 180° I

I

Arctic Circle

KARA SEA

Taymyr Peninsula

LAPTEV SEA

EAST SIBERIAN SEA

Bering Strait

Eastern Siberia

Kamchatka Peninsula

BERING SEA

Ural Mts.

Ob

Yenisey

West Siberian Plain

Central Siberian Plateau

Lena

SEA OF OKHOTSK

Sakhalin

Hokkaido

ARAL SEA

Lake Balkhash

Irtysh

Ob

Altai

Lake Baikal

Plateau of Mongolia

Amur

A S I A

PACIFIC OCEAN

Pamir Mts.

Tian Shan

Gobi Desert

SEA OF JAPAN

Honshu

Hindu Kush

Karakoram

Kunlun Shan

Huang He

YELLOW SEA

EAST CHINA SEA

Indus

Plateau of Tibet

Himalaya Mts.

▲Mt. Everest 8,848 m 29,028 ft.

Chang Jiang (Yangtze)

Tropic of Cancer

Thar Desert

Ganges

Ayeyarwady

Red

Taiwan

AN

Deccan Plateau

Mekong

Hainan

Luzon

Godavari

SOUTH CHINA SEA

PHILIPPINE SEA

Bay of Bengal

Gulf of Thailand

Mindanao

Sri Lanka

Borneo

CELEBES SEA

New Guinea

Maldive Is.

INDIAN OCEAN

0° Equator

5

JAVA SEA

Sumatra

Sulawesi

Timor

TIMOR SEA

1000

1000

Java

▼ *Mount Bromo is an active volcano on the Indonesian island of Java. It is one of a chain of volcanoes called 'The Ring of Fire' that surrounds the Pacific Ocean.*

► *The Rub al Khali (Empty Quarter) is a sandy waste stretching across Saudi Arabia. The sand has been shaped into rippled hills, called dunes, by the wind. These dunes change their shape as the wind blows.*

ASIA *Political*

Some of the world's first great civilizations sprang up in Asia from 3500BC onwards. Their riches attracted trade and conquering armies. Over the centuries peoples such as the Mongols and the Turks built up and then lost vast empires. From the 1800s much of Asia was colonized by European countries. These new rulers took away wealth, but did not help the colonies develop their industries.

Great social changes have taken place in Asia during this century. Many colonies freed themselves from their European rulers, creating independent nations such as India and Jordan. In countries where a large majority of poor people were ruled by a wealthy few, communism seemed to be the answer. Communist governments set prices for goods and labour. They also owned all property. The idea was that people would share the profits as well as the work. However, the spread of communism often caused wars with capitalist countries where individuals were able to own property and to set all prices. In 1991 the Soviet Union abandoned communism and, as it broke up, republics such as Kazakhstan and Uzbekistan became independent countries. Some Asian countries still have communist governments, although a number have recently held democratic elections for the first time.

Many Asian governments are now improving the economies of their countries by creating new industries and improving old ones. They are using both government money and foreign aid.

mi.
0 _____ 1000
0 _____ 1000
km

▲ Mikhail Gorbachev was the leader of the communist Soviet Union. He brought in many reforms before the Soviet Union collapsed and he lost power in 1991. Since then the republics of the Soviet Union have become independent nations.

► Election posters line the streets of Lahore in Pakistan. After long periods of military rule Pakistan has become a democracy. The people now vote to choose a government.

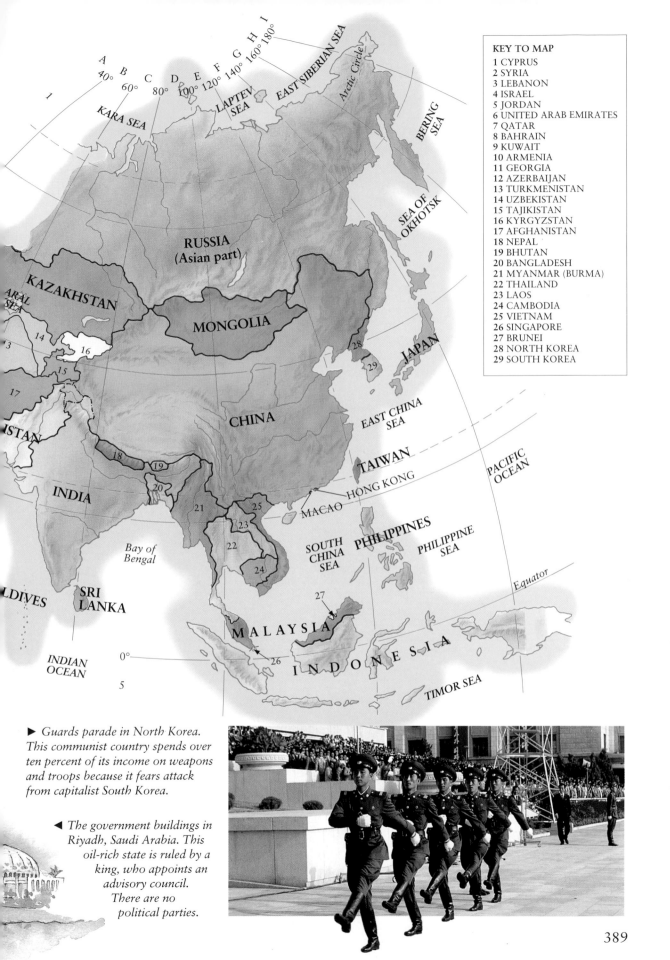

KEY TO MAP

1 CYPRUS
2 SYRIA
3 LEBANON
4 ISRAEL
5 JORDAN
6 UNITED ARAB EMIRATES
7 QATAR
8 BAHRAIN
9 KUWAIT
10 ARMENIA
11 GEORGIA
12 AZERBAIJAN
13 TURKMENISTAN
14 UZBEKISTAN
15 TAJIKISTAN
16 KYRGYZSTAN
17 AFGHANISTAN
18 NEPAL
19 BHUTAN
20 BANGLADESH
21 MYANMAR (BURMA)
22 THAILAND
23 LAOS
24 CAMBODIA
25 VIETNAM
26 SINGAPORE
27 BRUNEI
28 NORTH KOREA
29 SOUTH KOREA

▶ *Guards parade in North Korea. This communist country spends over ten percent of its income on weapons and troops because it fears attack from capitalist South Korea.*

◀ *The government buildings in Riyadh, Saudi Arabia. This oil-rich state is ruled by a king, who appoints an advisory council. There are no political parties.*

389

ASIA *Plants and Animals*

Thousands of the world's most beautiful plant species originally came from Asia, including tulips from Turkey and rhododendrons from the Himalayas. Other Asian plants have become valuable food crops. Rice was once a wild grass that grew in many of the continent's flooded river valleys.

Animals of all shapes and sizes are found throughout Asia. They include the Asian elephant, the Bactrian camel and the giant panda. The world's largest and smallest bats are also found on this continent. The tiny Kitti's hog-nosed bat lives in caves in Thailand, while the large Bismark flying fox is found in Indonesia. In the waters off southern Japan lurks the giant spider crab with a massive claw span of up to four metres.

Some of the most densely populated areas on Earth are found in Asia. To make room for fast-growing cities and industries, forests have been cleared, swamps drained and rivers dammed. This has often caused great damage to the nearby countryside. There has also been serious pollution, over-hunting and over-fishing. Some traditional Asian medicines include ingredients such as powdered rhinoceros horn and gall bladders of bears, so many animals have been killed to supply the trade. However, great efforts are now being made to ensure that no more animals are put in danger.

▲ *The caracal is a medium-sized desert cat related to the lynx. It was once found over large areas of the Middle East and India, but has become increasingly scarce.*

▶ *The male peacock fans out his tail to impress the female, a peahen. Peafowl are native to India, Sri Lanka and Southeast Asia.*

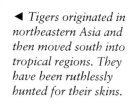

◀ *Tigers originated in northeastern Asia and then moved south into tropical regions. They have been ruthlessly hunted for their skins.*

▶ *The Arctic hare lives in the far north. In winter its brown or grey summer coat turns white to conceal it against the snow.*

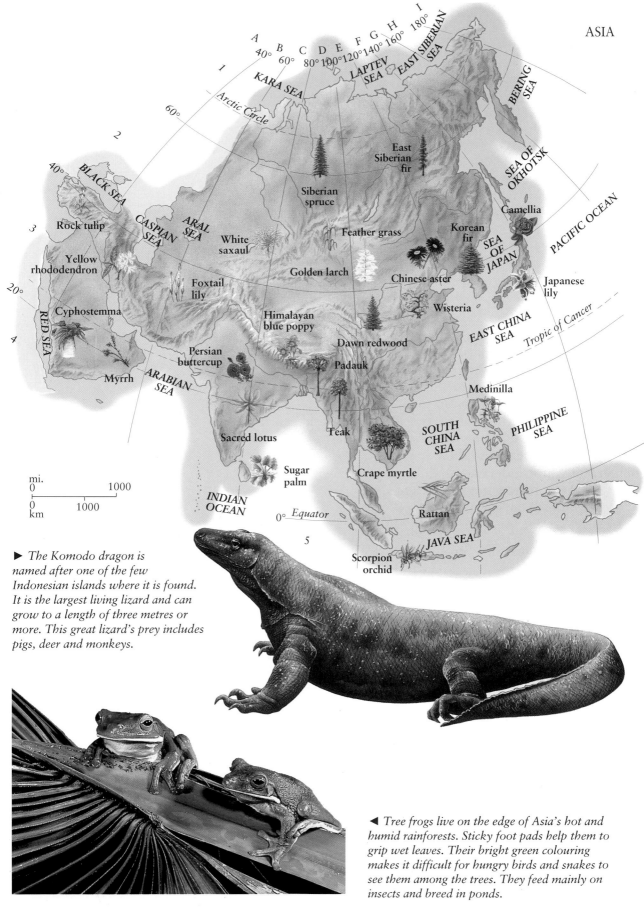

A **B** **C** **D** **E** **F** **G** **H** **I**
40° 60° 80° 100° 120° 140° 160° 180°

1

KARA SEA

LAPTEV SEA

EAST SIBERIAN SEA

BERING SEA

Arctic Circle

60°

2

60°

East Siberian fir

SEA OF OKHOTSK

BLACK SEA

40°

40°

Siberian spruce

PACIFIC OCEAN

3

Rock tulip

CASPIAN SEA

ARAL SEA

White saxaul

Feather grass

Korean fir

Camellia

SEA OF JAPAN

Yellow rhododendron

Golden larch

Chinese aster

Japanese lily

20°

Foxtail lily

Wisteria

EAST CHINA SEA

Tropic of Cancer

Cyphostemma

RED SEA

Himalayan blue poppy

Dawn redwood

4

Persian buttercup

Padauk

Medinilla

Myrrh

ARABIAN SEA

Teak

SOUTH CHINA SEA

PHILIPPINE SEA

Sacred lotus

Sugar palm

Crape myrtle

mi.
0   1000

0   1000
km

INDIAN OCEAN

0° Equator

Rattan

JAVA SEA

5

Scorpion orchid

► The Komodo dragon is named after one of the few Indonesian islands where it is found. It is the largest living lizard and can grow to a length of three metres or more. This great lizard's prey includes pigs, deer and monkeys.

◄ Tree frogs live on the edge of Asia's hot and humid rainforests. Sticky foot pads help them to grip wet leaves. Their bright green colouring makes it difficult for hungry birds and snakes to see them among the trees. They feed mainly on insects and breed in ponds.

RUSSIA *Introduction*

Russia is the largest country in the world. It covers over 17 million square kilometres, borders 14 other countries and crosses eight time zones. Extending north to the frozen wastes that lie above the Arctic Circle, its expanses also take in vast forests, high mountains and wide plains. Russia has long, bitter winters and short summers. Snow can cover more than half of the country for six months a year, so it can be difficult to make the most of the many natural resources available. These resources include large regions of farmland and plentiful reserves of timber, oil, coal, natural gas and minerals.

For centuries Russia was a vast empire ruled by emperors called tsars. However, a workers' revolution in 1917 eventually ended the reign of the tsars and brought the Bolsheviks (later called the Russian Communist Party) to power. Russia became a republic and in 1922 joined with three smaller republics to form the Union of Soviet Socialist Republics (USSR), also known as the Soviet Union.

By the 1940s the four original republics had been further subdivided and there were 16 republics in the Union. Over the next 40 years individual republics made increasing demands for independence. The USSR eventually broke up in 1991 and communism collapsed.

ENDANGERED WORLD

The musk deer is hunted because the male secretes musk, a scent that is used in the perfume trade. It lives in the forests of Siberia.

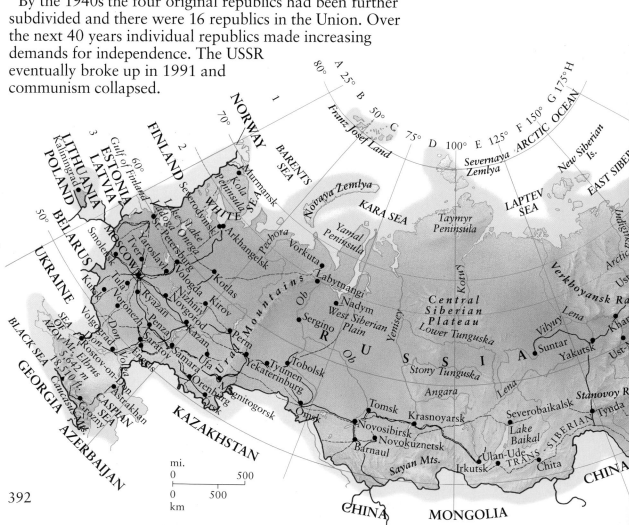

FACTS AND FIGURES
Area: 17,075,000 sq km
Population:
148,366,000
Capital: Moscow
(8,957,000)
Other major cities:
St Petersburg
(5,004,000),
Novosibirsk
(1,446,000)
Highest point:
Mt Elbrus
(5,642 m)
Official language:
Russian
Main religions:
Christianity, Islam,
Judaism
Currency: Rouble
Main exports: Natural
gas, petroleum,
chemicals, machinery,
timber, coal, food
Government: Federal
republic (transitional)
Per capita GNP:
US $2,680

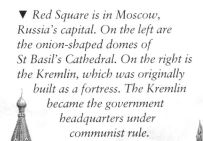

▲ *Kolominskye village is on the West Siberian plain. Despite Siberia's large reserves of oil and gold, few people live in this vast region because of its bitterly cold and long winters.*

▼ *Red Square is in Moscow, Russia's capital. On the left are the onion-shaped domes of St Basil's Cathedral. On the right is the Kremlin, which was originally built as a fortress. The Kremlin became the government headquarters under communist rule.*

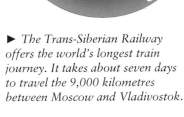

► *The Trans-Siberian Railway offers the world's longest train journey. It takes about seven days to travel the 9,000 kilometres between Moscow and Vladivostok.*

RUSSIA *Geography*

Most of this enormous country lies on the Asian continent, but western Russia is in Europe. The Ural Mountains are usually considered by geographers to form the dividing line between European Russia and Asian Russia.

Russia's climate includes great extremes, growing steadily hotter towards the south and colder and drier towards the east and north. As the climate changes, so does the landscape. Tundra covers much of the most northerly region. Little grows on this frozen plain and relatively few people live there. Only hardy animals such as reindeer and Arctic foxes can survive the bitterly cold temperatures.

Below this region a belt of dense forest sprawls across the country. Taiga, which is the name for forest made up of coniferous trees, makes up the northern part of the belt. The soil is mainly too poor to grow crops. Farther south the forest becomes a mixture of coniferous and deciduous trees. The climate in this region is milder and some areas can be farmed.

Rolling plains known as steppes start below the forests. Meadows and wooded plains make up the northern steppes. The southern steppes are mainly treeless, but their rich soil makes this some of the best farmland in the whole country.

The Caucasus Mountains and the shores of the Caspian Sea form Russia's southernmost area. The slopes of the Caucasus Mountains have lush, green, fertile meadows, while the Urals contain important deposits of iron and copper.

▼ *An ice-breaker works a passage through the floes on the Kara Sea. These vessels play an important role in a country where sea and river transportation is hampered by ice for much of each year.*

◀ *Lake Baikal is the deepest lake on Earth and contains more fresh water than any other. There are many species of plants and animals, including the Baikal seal, that are unique to the lake and its surrounding area.*

◀ The Indigirka River runs through the Russian taiga. This is a belt of spruce, fir, larch and pine forest that stretches across northern Russia. The region is also home to bears, elks and wolves. Under the trees is a scrubby growth of bushes that include crowberry, cowberry and bilberry.

▶ The Caucasus Mountains stretch from the Black Sea to the Caspian Sea. Spectacular glaciers and volcanic formations are found throughout the range. The Caucasus region is rich in mineral resources. There are oilfields and rich deposits of manganese.

◀ Hot water springs called geysers send up clouds of steam in Geyser Valley on the Kamchatka Peninsula. This region of active volcanoes juts out between the Sea of Okhotsk and the Bering Sea.

395

RUSSIA *Economy*

When communism ended here, with the break-up of the Soviet Union in 1991, Russia's economy had to make the huge and very difficult change from communism to capitalism. The word soviet means a council elected by the people and the basis of communism was that everybody should share both the work and the profits. Communist law stated that the government of the Soviet Union owned all the country's factories and farms as well as controlling everyone's wages and the prices of goods. Any profits were shared by the people and no one was allowed to run a private business. From the 1920s onwards communist Russia became a heavily industrialized nation. The government set up large factories and mines all over the country. Huge state farms were created and farming practices were modernized with the use of pesticides and fertilizers to increase yields.

After communism collapsed government price controls were lifted. Producers could suddenly charge what they liked for goods and prices soared dramatically. However, incomes remained very low and this caused great economic problems. Shortages were just as common as they had been under communism, partly because of the lifting of price controls. Today heavy industry, farming and mining are still extremely important and new ways are being found to exploit Russia's mineral resources. Service industries are also being developed.

▲ *Shoppers jostle each other to buy goods on the black (illegal) market. Under communist rule buying and selling was strictly controlled, but people with money were able to deal privately.*

▼ *Fishermen lift their catch out of the water. Ice covers many Russian lakes in winter. Holes are cut into the ice for fishing nets and the fish are carried home by sled.*

▲ *Combine harvesters work the fields on a collective farm. Under communism a collective farm is government-owned, but worked by people who share the profits. Though the growing season is short and rain is scarce, Russia's vast areas of farmland make it one of the world's major grain producers.*

▲ *A worker in Siberia checks oil-extracting machinery. Russia has large reserves of both oil and natural gas in Siberia and new fields are still being opened up. However, outdated equipment means that oil production is far less efficient than it could be and new investment in this industry is badly needed.*

ECONOMIC SURVEY

Farming: Most land is still government-owned, but private farms are being set up. Major crops are barley, flax, fruits, oats, potatoes, rye, sunflower seeds, wheat, sugar beet and vegetables. Forestry and fishing are important.

Mining: Russia has huge reserves of coal, oil and natural gas. It is also a major producer of gold, iron ore, lead, nickel, manganese, tungsten, tin and zinc.

Industry: Under communism the government owned all manufacturing plants and heavy industry took priority. Since 1991 consumer goods have increased in importance. The government is also working to convert the country's government-owned properties to private ownership.

RUSSIA *People*

The majority of Russians are descended from a people called Slavs, but there are small numbers of about 100 other ethnic groups. These include Ukrainians, Jews, Belarussians and Armenians. Most Russians live in European Russia, in the west of the country. Inuits are among the groups in the frozen far north. People in different areas feel strongly about their own identity. Some former Russian republics became independent in 1991 and there are still people in parts of Russia who would like total independence. One such area is Chechnya, with its capital at Grozny, where a revolt broke out in 1994.

Three quarters of the population lives in towns and cities. Russian cities have huge populations, so many people live in crowded, high-rise apartment blocks. Moscow has one of the highest population counts in the world – over eight million people have made their homes here.

During the years of communism education was made a top priority by the government, but religious worship and freedom of speech were severely restricted. With the end of communism Russians began to worship more openly.

Russia's strong artistic tradition has produced many famous writers, composers, artists and musicians. From the 1800s onwards the country was a world leader in literature, drama, music, ballet and other arts. It has also become a leading medal-winner in the world of sport. This is actively encouraged by the government, which provides a wide range of sports facilities such as stadiums, recreational centres and athletics clubs.

BORSCHT
Borscht is a classic Russian soup. There are many different recipes, but one brightly coloured favourite has beetroot as its main ingredient. This dish is eaten cold in summer and hot in winter. Sometimes meat or wild mushrooms are added. Barley is also used to thicken it.

▼ *In Siberia these Yakut and Khant women are making traditional clothes. Today these are worn only by rural people on special occasions.*

SPEAK RUSSIAN

Hello – Здравствуйте
(*zdras - vid - ye*)

Goodbye – До свидания
(*dah svee - dahn - ya*)

Please – Пожалуйста
(*pah - zahl - sta*)

Thank you – Спасибо
(*spa - see - ba*)

Yes – Да (*dah*)

◄ *These buildings are part of Moscow University. It was founded in 1755 and is Russia's oldest and largest university. Many teenagers go on to higher education. There are about three million students at the country's 500 colleges and universities.*

► *Stars of Moscow's Bolshoi ballet dance in a scene from* Swan Lake. *Russian ballet became internationally famous in the 1800s and the Bolshoi is still famed for its performances of the great Imperial Russian ballets of that era, such as* Sleeping Beauty *and* The Nutcracker.

◄ *These beautifully painted wooden dolls are traditional Russian toys. They are called matruschka (little mother) dolls and each one contains a series of smaller dolls inside it.*

RUSSIA *History*

Balkan people were living in Russia around 1200BC and by the AD800s Slavs had settled here. Mongols invaded in 1237 and Russia was part of the Mongol empire for 200 years until a long line of Russian rulers called tsars began their reign. From the 1600s to the 1800s discontent with the tsars erupted into revolts. By the early 1900s revolutionary groups had emerged and in 1917 a group called the Bolsheviks led a revolution, under Vladimir Ilyich Lenin. Tsar Nicholas II was killed and Lenin set up a communist government, forming the Union of Soviet Socialist Republics (USSR).

Lenin's successor, Joseph Stalin, ruled by terror from 1929 until 1953. He was followed by less oppressive leaders such as Khrushchev, Brezhnev and Kosygin. The 1940s to the 1980s marked a period of distrust between the West and communist countries in the East, which is often called The Cold War. When Mikhail Gorbachev became president in the 1980s he introduced reforms that gave the people greater freedom. At this time some republics began to demand independence. By the early 1990s most of the republics were part of a Commonwealth of Independent States. Boris Yeltsin became Russia's new president.

YURI GAGARIN
The Soviet astronaut Yuri Gagarin became the first man to travel in space in 1961, when he orbited Earth in the satellite *Vostok I*.
The orbit took 89 minutes and was a triumph for the Soviet Union. It had beaten the United States of America in the race between the two countries to be first to put a man in space.
In 1963 the Soviet Union also put the first woman in space, Valentina Tereshkova.

◀ *Women march banging empty pots in protest against food shortages. After the collapse of the Soviet Union in 1991 state subsidies were stopped so the price of food went up. The end of communism has not brought improvements for everyone.*

► *Russia's president, Boris Yeltsin, came to power after Gorbachev resigned in 1991. Under Yeltsin's leadership most of the former members of the Soviet Union formed the Commonwealth of Independent States (CIS). The CIS is a group of independent countries with economic and defence interests in common.*

▼ *The Winter Palace in St Petersburg, built in 1732, was the winter home of the tsars. In 1905 thousands of striking workers marched to the palace to demand reforms from Tsar Nicholas II. Hundreds were killed by the Tsar's troops and the event became known as Bloody Sunday.*

◄ *A Palm Sunday Parade gathers in front of St Basil's Cathedral (left) in Moscow. The cathedral was built during the 1550s by Tsar Ivan IV, famous for his fearsome temper, brutal behaviour and absolute power over the Russian people.*

GEORGIA

FACTS AND FIGURES

Area: 69,700 sq km
Population: 5,471,000
Capital: Tbilisi
(1,283,000)
Other major city:
Kutaisi (235,000)
Highest point:
Mt Shkhara (5,201 m)
Official language:
Georgian
Main religions:
Christianity, Islam
Currency: Lari
Main exports: Food,
chemicals, machinery,
metal products
Government:
Republic
Per capita GNP:
US $850

▼ *Georgia's ancient
capital, Tbilisi, is also its
largest city. The swift
current of the river Kura
provides the region with
hydroelectric power.*

Although most of this country is in Asia, part of northern Georgia is in Europe. Forested mountains cover much of the land and snow stays on the highest peaks all year round. However, near the Black Sea the mountains' lower slopes are lush and fertile. These areas, along with the coastal lowlands, have a mild climate and plenty of rain, enabling farmers to grow citrus fruits, tea and tobacco. Farther inland cereals and vegetables are grown, as well as grapes for Georgia's famous wines. Georgia is noted for its food and hospitality and for the health resorts along its Black Sea coast.

Georgia was established as a separate region around 500BC, at a time when the ancient Greeks had settled here. It has been fought over by the Romans, the Persians, the Arabs and the Turks, but enjoyed a golden age of science and art under Queen Tamara (1184-1213). Since then arts such as music, opera and poetry have continued to flourish. The country also has its own language and alphabet. Georgia gradually became part of the Russian empire during the 1800s. In 1936 it joined the Soviet Union. Georgia became independent in 1991 and the early 1990s saw conflict between the country's different ethnic groups. In 1993 Georgia joined the Commonwealth of Independent States, the group of former Soviet Republics.

More than half of Georgia's people live in urban areas and many work in food processing, the country's main industry. Most of the population are Christian and belong to the Georgian Orthodox Church.

► *This church at Ananuri, just east of Tskhinvali, was built in 1689. The fortifications protected it from the Turks and Iranians, who were fighting over Georgia at the time. Christianity came to Georgia in the AD300s.*

▼ *For centuries shaggy sheepskin hats have been worn by Georgian shepherds and other rural people. They are said to keep the wearer's head cool in summer as well as warm in winter.*

◄ *Georgian horsemen play a form of polo known as* tskhenburi. *The game of polo originated in Persia in about the 500BC and was brought to Georgia by Persian invaders. Polo is still a very popular sport and most towns in Georgia sponsor a polo team.*

ARMENIA

Armenia is a rugged country in the Little Caucasus Mountains, with deep gorges, lakes and rushing rivers. The earliest peoples were probably farming the land around 6000BC. Ancient Armenia was once a powerful independent kingdom. After defeat by the Romans in about 55BC it became part of the Roman empire. Later it was conquered by Arabs and Turks. Between the 1890s and the end of World War I the Turks massacred more than half a million Armenians and others were deported or fled. Over the years people from Armenia have settled in many other countries. Today there are millions of Armenians living all over the world.

Modern Armenia is only the northeastern part of the old kingdom of Armenia. The Russians captured this area from the Turks in the 1820s and it later became a republic of the Soviet Union. Armenia gained independence in 1991. The rest of historic Armenia is now largely part of Turkey. From the late 1980s there has been a dispute between Armenia and its neighbour Azerbaijan over the ownership of Nagorno-Karabakh. This area, in the southeast of Azerbaijan, is inhabited mainly by Armenians.

Most Armenians were farmers or herders until ruled by the Soviets. The Soviets set up copper mines and factories and many Armenians moved to the cities to work. Today only a third of the population is rural, keeping sheep or cattle and growing fruit and vegetables. Most people speak the Armenian language, which is unlike any other and has its own alphabet. The country also has a strong artistic tradition that includes religious music and the making of decorative stone carvings called *khatchkars*.

FACTS AND FIGURES
Area: 29,800 sq km
Population: 3,732,000
Capital: Yerevan (1,283,000)
Other major city: Gyumri (120,000)
Highest point: Mt Aragats (4,090 m)
Official language: Armenian
Main religion: Christianity
Currency: Dram (rouble also still in use)
Main exports: Chemicals, food products, machinery, transport equipment, metal goods
Government: Republic
Per capita GNP: US $780

◀ *Geghard Church perches against a rock in the gorge of the Garny River, southeast of Yerevan. Armenia was the first country in the world to make Christianity its official religion.*

AZERBAIJAN

In Azerbaijan the lofty Caucasus Mountains sweep down to the Caspian Sea. The small area of the country north of the Caucasus is considered to be part of Europe, but the remainder of Azerbaijan is in Asia. In the southwest a corridor of Armenian territory separates one section of Azerbaijan, called Nakhichevan, from the rest. Much of the land is mountainous and through the broad valleys run the Kura and Aras rivers, which provide hydroelectric power for industry and irrigation for farming.

The people, called Azeris, are descended from a mix of Turkic peoples and Persians that were living in this area around AD1200. By the 1800s Russia was in control and Azerbaijan was part of the Soviet Union until the Union broke up in 1991. The Russians brought industrialization and today the economy is based on Azerbaijan's large reserves of oil and natural gas. There are also many factories and over half the people live and work in towns and cities. In rural areas farmers grow cotton, fruit, tobacco and tea. Sheep, cattle and goats are herded on the mountain slopes.

Ownership of the Nagorno-Karabakh region has been challenged by Armenia and there has been bitter fighting since the late 1980s.

▲ Baku, the capital, is Azerbaijan's major trading port and the centre of the oil refining industry.

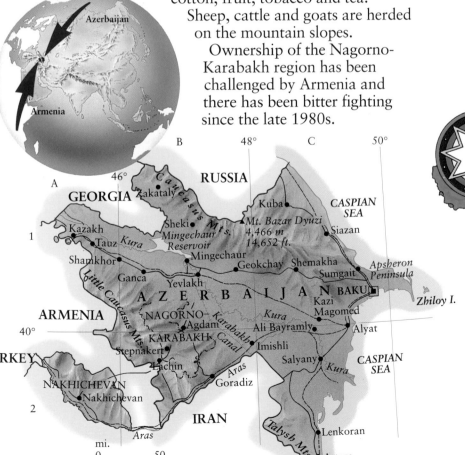

FACTS AND FIGURES
Area: 86,600 sq km
Population: 7,392,000
Capital: Baku (1,081,000)
Other major city: Ganca (283,000)
Highest point: Mt Bazar Dyuzi (4,466 m)
Official language: Azeri
Main religions: Islam, Christianity
Currency: Manat (rouble also still in use)
Main exports: Chemicals, food, machinery, oilfield equipment, petroleum, natural gas, textiles
Government: Federal republic
Per capita GNP: US $870

KAZAKHSTAN

From west to east, the country of Kazakhstan stretches from the salty Caspian Sea to the soaring Altai Mountains. In the north are high, grassy plains called steppes and in the south there are arid, sandy deserts. Kazakhstan has bitterly cold winters and long, hot summers.

The Kazakh people are descended from the Turkic and Mongol invaders of the past. For centuries they were nomads, roaming the plains with their herds of camels, horses, sheep and cattle. The animals provided meat, milk, wool and even an alcoholic drink called kumis, made from fermented mare's milk.

This traditional way of life began to change when Russia conquered Kazakhstan about 100 years ago. Thousands of Russians settled here and today over a third of the population is of Russian origin. The Russians began to mine iron and lead. They also planted the Kazakhs' grazing lands with wheat. This process continued after Kazakhstan became part of the Soviet Union and rapid industrial development also took place. Many Kazakhs left their nomadic way of life and settled in villages, although a few still live in the old way. Traditional livestock herding continues, but many people now work on modern farms and their produce contributes greatly to the country's economy.

The years of industrialization and intensive farming have left pollution problems and many people in rural areas still live without electricity or running water. However, the discovery of oil in the Caspian Sea promises wealth and independence in 1991 brought a new sense of pride in the Kazakh language and traditions.

ENDANGERED WORLD

The snow leopard has been hunted almost to extinction for its fur and only survives high in the mountains.

FACTS AND FIGURES
Area: 2,717,300 sq km
Population: 16,956,000
Capital: Akmola (300,000)
Other major cities: Almaty (1,151,000) Qaraghandy (609,000), Shymkent (439,000),
Highest point: Mt Tengri (6,398 m)
Official language: Kazakh
Main religion: Islam
Currency: Tenge
Main exports: Oil, metals, chemicals, grain, wool
Government: Republic
Per capita GNP: US $1,680

► *Women on horseback look after their flocks of sheep. The tent, called a yurt, is traditionally used by Kazakh nomads. Some Kazakh villagers live in yurts today and herd livestock as their ancestors have done for generations.*

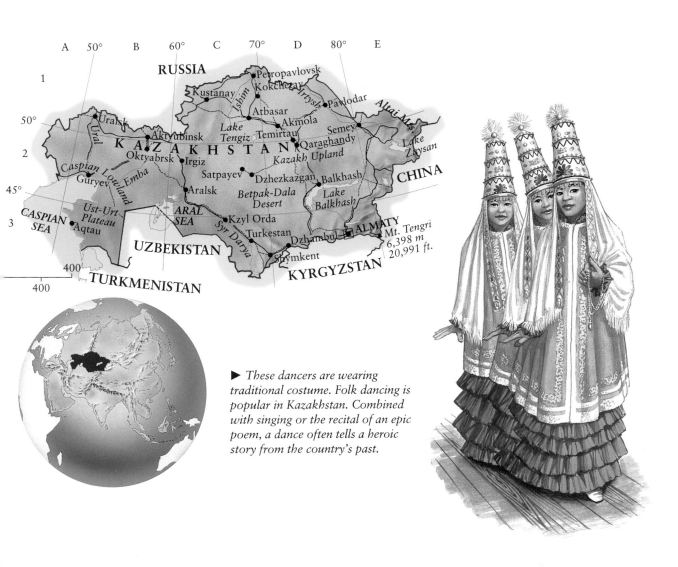

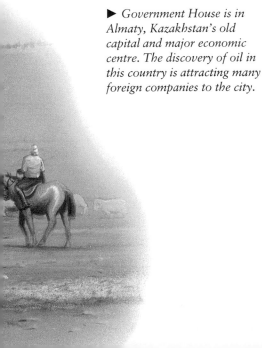

▶ These dancers are wearing traditional costume. Folk dancing is popular in Kazakhstan. Combined with singing or the recital of an epic poem, a dance often tells a heroic story from the country's past.

▶ Government House is in Almaty, Kazakhstan's old capital and major economic centre. The discovery of oil in this country is attracting many foreign companies to the city.

TURKMENISTAN

Few people live in the arid desert region of Karakum that covers most of Turkmenistan. The inhabited areas of the country are mainly along the foothills of the Kopet Mountains in the south and in the river valleys of the southeast. Half the population of Turkmenistan makes its living from farming, which would be impossible without the canals that bring water from the rivers to irrigate the land. The most important crop is cotton, but grain, potatoes and grapes are also grown. Thoroughbred Turkomen horses and karakul sheep are reared and some farmers also breed silkworms. Wool is woven into the highly colourful carpets for which this country is famous.

The very first people to have lived in Turkmenistan may have wandered the deserts with livestock or farmed the more fertile areas. Turkic peoples made their home here around AD900 and controlled all or part of the area on and off until the 1800s. Russia invaded in the 1870s and from 1924 to 1991 Turkmenistan was a republic of the Soviet Union.

About 70 percent of the country's present population are ethnic Turkmen. They are Sunni Muslims and are descended from the first Turkic settlers. Family life is important to these people and several generations of a family often live together.

◀ *A Turkmen woman works at the loom, weaving a carpet. Turkmen carpets are known for their strong colours and bold designs.*

FACTS AND FIGURES
Area: 488,100 sq km
Population: 3,809,000
Capital: Ashkhabad (411,000)
Other major citiy: Charjew (166,000)
Highest point: In the east (3,137 m)
Official language: Turkmen
Main religion: Islam
Currency: Manat
Main exports: Consumer goods, food, machinery, metals, oil, natural gas, cotton, textiles, chemicals
Government: Republic
Per capita GNP: US $1,270

UZBEKISTAN

Much of Uzbekistan is a land of rolling plains and barren deserts, with the huge desert of Kyzylkum at its centre. Streams flowing from Kyrgyzstan's mighty Tian Shan Mountains water the fertile, heavily populated valley that contains the town of Fergana.

Uzbekistan is on the ancient Silk Road. For over four centuries, up until the 1400s, this was an important trade route from China to the Middle East. In about 300BC the region was conquered by the Greeks under Alexander the Great. By the AD600s the Arabs had invaded, bringing their religion of Islam. They were followed by the Mongols in the early 1200s.

Most of the people are Uzbeks, who are descended from a mixture of Turkic groups and other peoples including Mongols. There are also several minority groups, the largest being Russians. Russia conquered Uzbekistan during the 1800s, then in the 1920s the country became a republic of the Soviet Union. Uzbeks are nomadic herders by tradition, but the Soviet Union turned much of the country's grazing land into cotton plantations and the Uzbek people began to work on these. When the Soviet Union broke up in 1991 Uzbekistan became independent. It then joined the Commonwealth of Independent States, the association of former Soviet republics.

FACTS AND FIGURES

Area: 447,400 sq km
Population: 21,207,000
Capital: Tashkent (2,120,000)
Other major city: Samarkand (395,000)
Highest point: In the south (4,643 m)
Official language: Uzbek
Main religion: Islam
Currency: Som (rouble also still in use)
Main exports: Cotton, chemicals, food, metals, minerals, machinery, textiles, gold
Government: Republic (transitional)
Per capita GNP: US $860

▼ *The dramatic skyline of the ancient town of Khiva. The view is dominated by soaring minarets and the dome of a mausoleum for the khans (Uzbek rulers) of the area.*

TAJIKISTAN

Tajikistan is a mountainous country, prone to earthquakes. In the Pamir Mountains snow makes the few roads impassable for more than six months a year. Yet in the fertile river valleys, where most people live, the summers are long and hot. The Tajiks are descended from the Persians, who first settled here thousands of years ago. The country has been invaded many times since and Islam was introduced by Arab conquerors in the AD600s. Today most Tajiks are Sunni Muslims. Minority groups include Uzbeks and Russians.

About two thirds of the population lives in rural areas, mostly along the rivers and in oases. Villagers grow mainly cotton, grain, vegetables, olives, figs and citrus fruits. Cattle breeding is important on the rich pasture lands. More and more rural people are moving to the cities to find jobs in Tajikistan's textile factories, steel works or other industries.

Tajikistan was controlled by the Soviet Union from the early 1920s. The Soviets brought many changes, such as building roads and schools, putting industry and agriculture under state control and discouraging religion. Opposition to their government reached a climax in the 1980s and Tajikistan gained independence in 1991. It then became a member of the Commonwealth of Independent States.

FACTS AND FIGURES
Area: 143,100 sq km
Population: 5,514,000
Capital: Dushanbe (592,000)
Other major city: Khudzhand (164,000)
Highest point: Communism Peak (7,495 m)
Official language: Tajik
Main religion: Islam
Currency: Rouble
Main exports: Cotton, food, metals, textiles, fruit, vegetables
Government: Republic
Per capita GNP: US $480

▲ Snow stays on Moskva Peak in the rugged Pamir Mountains all year round. The nomads who wander this vast range call it the 'roof of the world'.

▶ At an open market in rural Tajikistan shoppers come to buy melons grown in the fierce summer heat. The men wear traditional embroidered skull caps.

410

KYRGYZSTAN

The early settlers of this mountainous country were nomadic peoples, who reared animals in the high valleys and took them down to graze in the warmer foothills during the bitterly cold winters.

Today only about half the population is rural, herding sheep, cattle, goats and pigs or growing cotton and tobacco. Most rural people are ethnic Kyrgyz and live in large clans, each with its own leader. A minority live in yurts. These wooden-framed, felt tents are traditional Kyrgyz homes, but today there might be a modern car parked outside them. About one fifth of the population is Russian in origin. These people live mainly in concrete apartment blocks in the cities and work in industry.

Turkic peoples came here between the AD500s and 1100s. There were periods of Mongol and Chinese rule before the Russians took over in the 1870s. Russia brought farm workers from other countries into the region, which left the nomads with fewer grazing grounds. In 1916 the Kyrgyz rebelled against Russian rule, but failed. Many thousands were killed, while thousands more fled to China. In 1922 the country came under Soviet rule. There were controls over the ways in which industry was run and land was used. The Soviets also banned the teaching of religion. In the late 1980s, however, they began to allow greater freedom and in 1991 Kyrgyzstan became an independent country.

FACTS AND FIGURES

Area: 198,500 sq km
Population: 4,528,000
Capital: Bishkek (642,000)
Other major city: Osh (239,000)
Highest point: Peak Pobedy (7,439 m)
Official language: Kyrgyz
Main religion: Islam
Currency: Som
Main exports: Food, machinery, manufactured products, wool, chemicals, metals
Government: Republic
Per capita GNP: US $810

▶ *The Naryn, one of Kyrgyzstan's main rivers, runs through dramatic mountain scenery.*

AFGHANISTAN

FACTS AND FIGURES
Area: 652,090 sq km
Population: 20,547,000
Capital: Kabul
(2,00,000)
Other major city:
Qandahar (179,000)
Highest point:
Nowshak (7,485 m)
Official languages:
Pashto, Dari
Main religion: Islam
Currency: Afghani
Main exports: Karakul
skins, raw cotton,
fruit and nuts,
natural gas, carpets
Government:
Single-party republic
Per capita GNP:
Est. under US $700

Afghanistan is a rugged country with many mountains. Its climate ranges from extreme heat to biting cold as the land rises from scorching deserts to towering, snow-capped peaks. A narrow corridor through the mountains, the Khyber Pass, links the country with Pakistan.

About 20 different ethnic groups live in Afghanistan, each with its own language and traditions. Some Afghans are semi-nomadic. In summer they roam the grasslands beneath the mountain peaks with their herds and sleep in tents made of felted goat hair. In winter they settle down to farm in the fertile valleys, where most people live. Only about ten percent of the population lives in towns and cities. These are mostly craftspeople who work at home. Afghanistan has relatively little industry.

Arabs swept into the region in the AD600s bringing their religion, Islam, with them. Over the following centuries Mongols, Iranians and native Afghans held power and Britain and Russia fought for control during the 1800s. By the 1970s Afghanistan was an independent country, but the Soviet Union had a great deal of power over the government because they supplied financial and military aid. Many of Afghanistan's Muslims believed that Soviet communist teachings went against their own traditions. A Muslim rebellion broke out and Soviet troops invaded in 1979, killing over one million Afghans. Ten years of civil war devastated the country and one quarter of the people fled the fighting. Many are still refugees in Pakistan and Iran. Soviet troops withdrew from Afghanistan in 1989, but conflict continued over who should govern the country and between different ethnic and religious groups.

▼ *A Kyrgyz girl wears brightly coloured traditional dress and jewellery. The semi-nomadic Kyrgyz are one of the smallest of Afghanistan's ethnic groups. They live in the far northeast.*

► *Shepherds with their flock of karakul sheep. Wool and sheepskins are some of Afghanistan's most important products. The curly fleece of young karakul lambs is highly prized for making coats and hats.*

► *A carpet seller spreads out his wares in an Afghan market. Brightly coloured woollen carpets like these, hand-woven in both traditional and modern designs, are now a major export.*

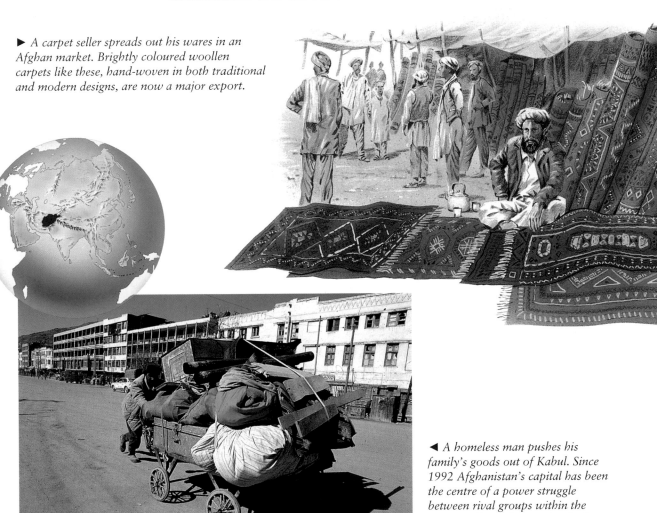

◄ *A homeless man pushes his family's goods out of Kabul. Since 1992 Afghanistan's capital has been the centre of a power struggle between rival groups within the country. Many thousands of refugees have fled the city because of destruction caused by the fighting.*

CYPRUS

The fertile island of Cyprus lies in the east of the Mediterranean Sea. Four fifths of its people are of Greek descent, while the rest are Turkish. Disagreements between the two groups have caused serious political problems. In 1974 a Turkish army invaded northern Cyprus and forced 200,000 Greek Cypriots to flee to the southern part of the island, where they still live today. The island remains divided although northern Cyprus is only recognized as an independent country by Turkey, where it is known as the Turkish Republic of Northern Cyprus.

Cyprus has played an important part in the history of the Mediterranean region and many peoples have contributed to its culture, including the Greeks, Egyptians, Romans, Byzantines, Venetians, French and Turks. Britain controlled the island from 1878 until its independence in 1960.

Today the rugged beauty of Cyprus, its historic sites, hilltop castles, sandy beaches and mild climate, have made tourism a major industry. Although many Cypriots now find work in the towns, agriculture is important. On the broad plain between the country's two mountain ranges farmers grow grapes, olives, potatoes and citrus fruits. There is also increasing industrial development, especially in the south.

▼ *Modern yachts and traditional fishing boats moor in Kyrenia harbour, northern Cyprus. Kyrenia has a long history as a port. In the town's Shipwreck Museum are the remains and cargo of a ship that sank just outside the harbour in about 300BC.*

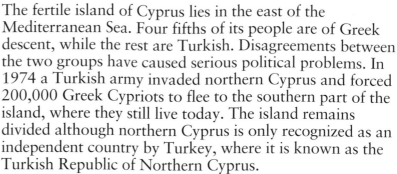

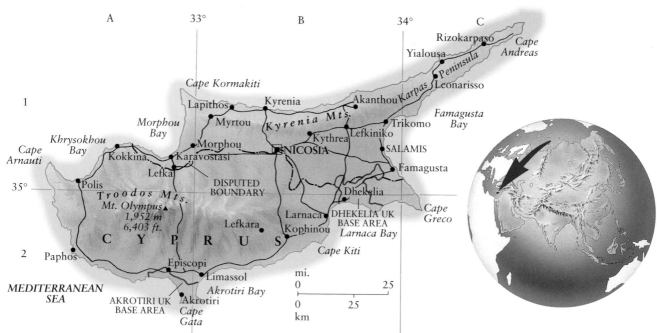

▶ *Villagers play* tavala *(the Cypriot name for backgammon). This dice game originated in Turkey and is popular throughout Turkish Cyprus, where men gather to play in local cafés.*

▼ *Village houses cluster round a church on a steep hillside in the Troodos Mountains. The mountains, protected by the state, are forested with dwarf oak, cypress and cedar and watered by swift-flowing streams. Copper has been mined in this part of Cyprus since Roman times.*

FACTS AND FIGURES
Area: 9,250 sq km
Population: 723,000
Capital: Nicosia (167,000)
Other major city: Limassol (130,000)
Highest point: Mt Olympus (1,952 m)
Official languages: Greek, Turkish
Main religions: Christianity, Islam
Currency: Cyprus pound
Main exports: Clothes, shoes, wine, potatoes, citrus fruit
Government: Constitutional republic
Per capita GNP: US $9,820

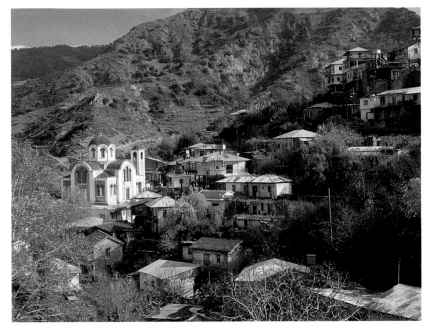

◀ *Folk dancing plays an important part in Cypriot life. People may dress in national costume to dance at religious feasts, weddings and other important occasions.*

TURKEY *Introduction*

Turkey has land in two continents, Asia and Europe. It commands an important waterway, the Bosporus, which joins the Black Sea to the Mediterranean. The land west of the Bosporus is European Turkey, while to the east lies the much larger Asian part of Turkey. Along the Black Sea coast are plains where farmers keep animals and cultivate fruit, nuts and tobacco. The most productive farmland is in the west. Wheat and maize are grown in the broad valleys and along the hot Mediterranean coast there are olive groves, orange trees and fields of cotton. Bears and wolves roam Turkey's mountains and forests. In farming areas sheep and goats graze around farmhouses made of stone or sun-dried brick.

A vast plateau extends across the centre of Turkey. Rimmed with mountains, this plateau has especially hot summers and cold winters. Turkey is also a land of lakes and rivers. Lake Van and Tuz Lake are large saltwater lakes and there are smaller freshwater lakes in the southwest. Many of the country's rivers dry up in the summer, but become fast-flowing torrents every spring, when they are used for hydroelectric power and irrigation.

About half the population lives in large towns. Some people work in coal and chromium mines, others in factories producing iron, steel, machinery and processed foods. People working in traditional cottage industries make carpets and pottery. Tourism is growing fast, particularly along the Mediterranean coast, where many holiday resorts are being built.

FACTS AND FIGURES
Area: 779,450 sq km
Population: 58,775,000
Capital: Ankara (3,023,000)
Other major cities: Istanbul (6,408,000), Izmir (2,666,000)
Highest point: Mt Ararat (5,123 m)
Official language: Turkish
Main religion: Islam
Currency: Turkish lira
Main exports: Textiles, iron, steel, tobacco, fruit, leather clothing, chemical products
Government: Multi-party republic
Per capita GNP: US $1,950

◄ *Hagia Sophia is a museum and one of Istanbul's most famous landmarks. It was built as a cathedral in the AD500s and was converted into a mosque in the 1400s.*

ENDANGERED WORLD

The loggerhead turtle breeds on beaches. Numbers are declining because of increasing tourism.

► In Cappadocia, a region west of Kayseri, some people live in buildings carved out of the cliffs. The yellow and pink volcanic rock has also been eroded by the weather into odd shapes.

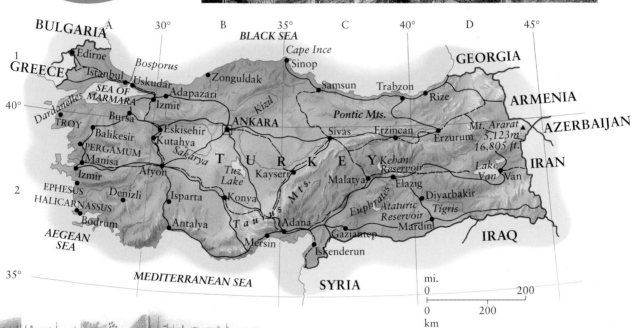

BULGARIA

GREECE

BLACK SEA

Cape Ince

GEORGIA

ARMENIA

AZERBAIJAN

IRAN

IRAQ

SYRIA

MEDITERRANEAN SEA

AEGEAN SEA

Edirne
Istanbul
Uskudar
Bosporus
Adapazari
Zonguldak
Sinop
Samsun
Trabzon
Rize
Izmit
Bursa
Dardanelles
SEA OF MARMARA
TROY
Balikesir
PERGAMUM
Eskisehir
Kutahya
Manisa
Izmir
Afyon
Sakarya
ANKARA
Pontic Mts.
Sivas
Erzincan
Erzurum
Mt. Ararat
5,123m
16,805 ft.
Kizil
EPHESUS
HALICARNASSUS
Denizli
Isparta
Tuz Lake
Kayseri
Konya
Taurus Mts.
Keban Reservoir
Malatya
Lake Van
Van
Elazig
Diyarbakir
Tigris
Euphrates
Ataturic Reservoir
Mardin
Bodrum
Antalya
Adana
Gaziantep
Mersin
Iskenderun

30°
35°
40°
45°
40°
35°

A   B   C   D
1

2

mi.
0   200
0   200
km

◄ Whirling dervishes are members of a Muslim sect who whirl and dance as part of their worship. Through the whirling, they enter a trance-like state in which they concentrate totally on spiritual matters.

417

TURKEY *People and History*

▲ *These Turkish women are spinning wool in the traditional way, using short sticks called spindles. By spinning the wool the fibres are twisted together to make a strong thread or yarn.*

Standing at the crossroads of two continents, Turkey has been a prized possession of some of the world's greatest empires. A people called the Hittites established themselves in the area around 1500BC and were followed by Persians and Greeks. By the AD400s this region was part of the mighty Byzantine empire, which was the eastern half of the Roman empire. The Byzantine capital was at Constantinople, now Istanbul. Seljuks, who were Muslims from central Asia, won control in the AD1000s and established Islam and the Turkish language. In the 1400s the Ottoman Turks made this region the centre of their empire and rapidly conquered the surrounding lands. The Ottoman empire, under its greatest sultan (ruler) Suleiman I, stretched from Hungary to Egypt and its navy controlled the Mediterranean Sea.

By 1600 the empire was in decline, although it did not finally break up until 1920. War against foreign powers in the early 1920s brought independence and Turkey became a republic in 1923. A military leader, Mustafa Kemal, became president and set out to make Turkey a modern, secular (non-religious) state. Kemal's reforms gained him the name Atatürk (Father of the Turks). He abolished Muslim schools and the Islamic legal system. Kemal also gave women the vote. Today Kemal's picture hangs in public buildings everywhere and his face is on all the banknotes.

SPEAK TURKISH

Hello – Merhaba
(*mer* - hah - ba)

Goodbye – Hoşça kalm
(*hosh* - ja kal)

Please – Lütfen (*lewt* - fen)

Thank you – Teşekkür ederim
(tesh - e - *kewr* ed - e - rim)

Yes – Evet (eh - *vet*)

No – Hayir (hie - *yerh*)

◄ Inside the magnificent Blue Mosque in Istanbul worshippers kneel to pray. They are facing Mecca, the holiest shrine in Islam. Although Turkey has no official state religion, most Turks are Muslims.

▼ This portrait of the Emperor Justinian is made of mosaic (coloured glass cubes set in plaster). Justinian ruled the Byzantine empire during the AD500s. He was famed for fair laws and for making the empire a centre of arts and learning.

◄ The Celsus Library, thought to date from AD110, is one of many fascinating ruins in the ancient city of Ephesus, founded by the Greeks. In AD262 the Goths destroyed much of Ephesus and it began a long decline.

SYRIA

Many thousands of years ago a Middle Eastern people called the Semites created a string of city states across what is now Syria. The ancient fortresses and mosques seen everywhere show that this is a country rich in history. Several of its cities are among the oldest in the world and the very first alphabet was developed here around 1500BC.

Ancient civilizations including the Persians, Romans and Ottoman Turks have all ruled this area. Muslim Arabs first settled during the AD600s, establishing Islam and the Arabic language. Today most people are Muslim Arabs. In this century first Turkey and then France took control. Since independence in 1946 Syria has been one of the leaders of Arab opposition to its Jewish neighbour Israel. Part of Syria, called the Golan Heights, has been occupied by Israel since 1967. Syria has also sent troops into Lebanon, where its army tried and failed to prevent civil war.

Syria is rapidly becoming more industrial. Many people are moving to the towns and cities from rural areas in search of jobs in the developing textile and chemical industries. About half the population still lives in farming villages along the coast, in the fertile river valleys and on the grassy western plains. These places have probably been cultivated since about 4000BC. A variety of other landscapes are found in this country, from arid deserts to snow-tipped mountains and pine and oak forests.

FACTS AND FIGURES

Area: 185,180 sq km
Population: 13,393,000
Capital: Damascus (1,497,000)
Other major cities: Aleppo (1,494,000), Homs (537,000), Latakia (293,000)
Highest point: Mt Hermon (2,814 m)
Official language: Arabic
Main religion: Islam
Currency: Syrian pound
Main exports: Petroleum and petroleum products, cotton, natural phosphate, fruit and vegetables
Government: Multi-party republic
Per capita GNP: Est. US $700-3,000

◄ These Syrian girls are wearing military cadet uniform. All Syrians between the ages of 15 and 18 have military training at school. Adult males over 18 years of age have to go on to do a further 30 months of military training when they leave school.

▼ Much of the city of Damascus now looks modern, but this is thought to be the oldest city in the world. Some ancient parts still exist, with narrow streets and markets.

HUMMUS

Hummus is a spread made from crushed, shelled chickpeas. The spread is often mixed with tahini, a toasted sesame seed paste. Flavoured with garlic, lemon juice and salt, hummus with tahini has a delicious nutty taste. Syrians eat it with flat bread and olives.

▼ This castle, called Krak des Chevaliers, was built by the Crusaders in the early 1200s. The Crusades were a series of wars fought during the early Middle Ages. The Christian Crusaders from Europe were trying to recapture the Holy Land (Palestine) from the Muslim Arabs.

LEBANON

A   36°   B

MEDITERRANEAN SEA

Kebir
Halba
Tripoli
Al Hirmil
Qurnat as Sawda
▲3,083 m
10,115 ft.
Al Batrun   Bsharri
1
L E B A N O N
Baalbek
34°   Juniyah
BEIRUT
Zahlah   Riyaq
Alayh
SYRIA
Sidon   Jazzin   Rashayya
2
Marj Uyun
Tyre
Bint Jubayl   mi.
0   20
33°
ISRAEL   0   20
km

Lebanon Mountains
Anti-Lebanon Mts.
Litani Bekaa Valley
Hasbani

Lebanon is dominated by two mountain ranges, which run from north to south. The fertile farmlands of the Bekaa Valley lie sandwiched between them. Around 2500BC the seafaring Phoenicians became the first people to establish a civilization in this part of the world. Many centuries on, in the 1920s, the French were in control. Total independence from France came in 1946 and today most of the people are Arabs who have settled in the country's towns and cities. One quarter of the population lives in or around the capital. Some of the Arab population are Palestinians who believe that lands owned by Israel are rightfully theirs. The Palestine Liberation Organization (PLO) has been in conflict with Israel for many years and between 1969 and 1991 used Lebanon as a base for attacks on Israel. The country's Muslims and Christians have also had long-standing political differences which, combined with the Palestine-Israel dispute, led to the outbreak of civil war in 1975. The PLO supported the Muslims in this war. Troops from both Syria and Israel became involved and fighting continued until 1991. Some Israeli troops remained in the south and Syrian troops stayed in the Bekaa Valley to protect Muslim interests.

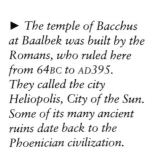

► *The temple of Bacchus at Baalbek was built by the Romans, who ruled here from 64BC to AD395. They called the city Heliopolis, City of the Sun. Some of its many ancient ruins date back to the Phoenician civilization.*

◄ *A United Nations water truck heads into war-damaged Beirut in 1993. The United Nations sent a peacekeeping force to Lebanon in 1978, but fighting and terrorist bombings drove them out in 1984. The conflict ended in 1991 and much of Beirut was quickly rebuilt. Today the city is promoted as a tourist destination.*

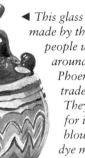

◄ *This glass perfume bottle was made by the Phoenicians, a people who lived here from around 2500BC. The Phoenicians were great traders and explorers. They were also famous for inventing glass blowing and a purple dye made from shellfish.*

FACTS AND FIGURES

Area: 10,450 sq km
Population: 2,901,000
Capital: Beirut
(1,500,000)
Other major cities:
Tripoli (160,000),
Zahlah (45,000)
Highest point:
Qurnat as Sawda
(3,083 m)
Official language: Arabic

Main religions:
Islam,
Christianity
Currency:
Lebanese pound
Main exports: Clothes,
jewellery, fruit
Government:
Multi-party republic
Per capita GNP:
Est. US $700-3,000

► *These splendid cedars are found to the north of Baalbek. Cedars once covered the mountains of Lebanon, but were cut down for timber. Today these ancient trees are protected. Lebanese nurseries are also growing millions of seedlings to replant the forests.*

ISRAEL *Introduction*

Israel was founded in 1948 as a home for Jews from all over the world. During the following years, many immigrants have brought all kinds of skills to the country. New industries, technologies and farming techniques have been developed and the standard of living is high. Along the coast is a fertile plain. This is the country's most important farming and industrial region. Hills run down the centre of Israel from north to south. Here, there are farms in the valleys, but much of the land is used for grazing. Some northern and eastern parts of Israel were once infertile, as was the arid Negev Desert. Since the 1950s, however, water has been pumped from the Sea of Galilee to irrigate the land. Now olives grow in dry northern parts, while potatoes and tomatoes flourish in the Negev.

Israel's capital, Jerusalem, is a holy city for Jews, Christians and Muslims. For Christians it is the site of Christ's burial place. For Jews it has the Western Wall, all that remains of the holy Temple of biblical times. Its main Muslim shrine is the Dome of the Rock, believed to be the place from which Muhammad rose to heaven.

Since Israel was created in 1948, there have been years of bitter fighting between the Jews and their Arab neighbours. The Arabs believe that Israel is occupying lands that should belong to their people. In 1994 peace agreements between Israel, the Palestine Liberation Organization and Jordan brought hopes that co-operation would replace warfare.

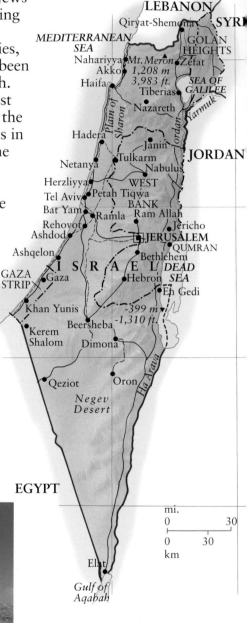

◄ *The Dead Sea is the world's lowest body of water. It is so salty that swimmers can float with ease. Few plants and no fish live there. The hot sun evaporates the water, leaving strange salt formations behind.*

SPEAK HEBREW

Hello – שָׁלוֹם
(sha - lom)

Goodbye – שָׁלוֹם
(sha - lom)

Please – בְּבַקָּשָׁה
(bee - vak - a - shah)

Thank you – תּוֹדָה
(toh - dah)

▲ *Wadi Farah lies between Nabulus and the river Jordan. This area was arid and infertile until it was irrigated by the National Water Carrier. This is a system of canals, pipelines and tunnels that pumps water from the Sea of Galilee and the river Jordan. Fruit trees and vegetables can now be grown in the desert.*

FELAFEL
Felafel are little round patties made of chickpeas. They are deep-fried to a crisp golden brown. Israelis often eat them on their own as a snack. Alternatively they can form part of a meal, stuffed into pitta bread with a crunchy salad of cucumber, lettuce, tomato and hot chilli pepper. Felafel are sold from barrows on many busy Israeli streets.

FACTS AND FIGURES

Area: 21,950 sq km
Population: 5,256,000
Capital: Jerusalem (557,000)
Other major cities:
Tel Aviv (357,000),
Haifa (250,000),
Petah Tiqwa (151,000),
Bat Yam (146,000)
Highest point:
Mt Meron (1,208 m)
Official languages:
Hebrew, Arabic

Main religions:
Judaism, Islam,
Christianity
Currency: Shekel
Main exports:
Fruit, vegetables,
oil products, chemical
products, diamonds,
machinery, fertilizers
Government:
Multi-party republic
Per capita GNP:
US $13,230

ISRAEL *People and History*

▲ *A Jewish man blows on a shofar, a ram's horn fitted with a reed. The shofar is one of the world's oldest musical instruments and is blown on Jewish High Holy days. The woven prayer shawl is called a tallith.*

Israel is part of a historic land called Palestine. Today the word Palestine refers to most of Israel, although ancient Palestine extended farther east. Palestine is also known as the Holy Land, where both the Jewish and Christian faiths began. By about 1000BC the Hebrew people (also called Israelites) had founded the kingdom of Israel here. Israel grew powerful under its great kings, David and Solomon, but after Solomon's death in 922BC it divided. The northern part was called Israel and the southern part Judah. Judah is the origin of the name Jew, by which the Hebrews came to be known. In about 500BC Judah was captured by the Babylonians and many Jews were exiled. Although some returned later, this was the start of the Diaspora – the scattering of Jews from their homeland to settle all over Europe and Asia. The process continued after the Roman conquest of 63BC. During the AD600s Palestine was conquered by the Muslim Arabs. In 1516 it became part of the Ottoman empire. By this time many people in Palestine were Muslim Arabs, although a Jewish community remained.

In the late 1800s Jews abroad started Zionism, a movement to establish a Jewish state in Palestine. Jews began to immigrate to Palestine, causing tensions with Palestinian Arabs. In 1948 the Jewish state of Israel declared itself independent and was immediately attacked by its Arab neighbours. A ceasefire in 1949 was followed by more Arab-Israeli wars. In the 1960s Israel occupied Arab land on the Gaza Strip, the West Bank, the Golan Heights and the Sinai Peninsula. Egypt and Israel signed an agreement in the 1970s and by 1994 Jews and Arabs were working together to establish peace.

◀ *Arab students study at a Palestinian school in the Gaza Strip. This was Israeli-occupied territory from 1967 to 1993, when the Palestinians were given partial control of the area.*

426

► *The Western Wall is in the foreground of this view of Jerusalem. This is the western wall of the holy Temple, which was used in biblical times. Today many Jews go on a pilgrimage to pray there. Behind the wall is the Dome of the Rock, sacred to Muslims.*

▲ *Workers pick oranges on a kibbutz, a collective farm where work and profits are shared. The famous Jaffa oranges are named after Tel Aviv's old town, which is known as Jaffa. They are grown on the fertile Plain of Sharon.*

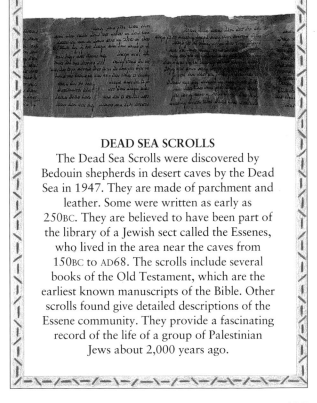

DEAD SEA SCROLLS

The Dead Sea Scrolls were discovered by Bedouin shepherds in desert caves by the Dead Sea in 1947. They are made of parchment and leather. Some were written as early as 250BC. They are believed to have been part of the library of a Jewish sect called the Essenes, who lived in the area near the caves from 150BC to AD68. The scrolls include several books of the Old Testament, which are the earliest known manuscripts of the Bible. Other scrolls found give detailed descriptions of the Essene community. They provide a fascinating record of the life of a group of Palestinian Jews about 2,000 years ago.

JORDAN

Jordan is an Arab nation in the heart of the Middle East. It is a hot, dry country of deserts, mountains, deep valleys and scrubby plains. Jordan's long history has left it with many spectacular monuments, the remains of ancient cities built by the peoples who once ruled here, such as the Nabateans, Greeks, Romans and Ottoman Turks.

After a brief period of British control, from 1921 to 1946, Jordan gained complete independence. The country then became involved in the Palestinian conflict. When the new state of Israel was set up in Palestine in 1948, Jordan and Israel's other Arab neighbours attacked it. Jordan took control of some of the former Palestinian territory including the West Bank. During the Six-Day War of 1967 Jordan lost the West Bank to Israel and refugees poured into Jordan. Many of them joined the Palestine Liberation Organization (PLO), which organized terrorist attacks on Israel from bases in Jordan and other Arab countries. Conflict between the PLO and the Jordanian government of King Hussein led to a civil war in 1970. King Hussein's government was defeated within a month, but fighting continued between various groups. In 1994 Jordan signed a peace treaty with Israel.

The majority of the population in this Muslim country are Jordanian Arabs. There are also a large number of Palestinians, mostly refugees from the Arab-Israeli wars. Around ten percent still live in refugee camps, but most Jordanians live in towns and cities. Many work for the government or in service industries such as finance, trade and tourism. Much of the land is infertile, so there is little large-scale agriculture. However, vegetables and citrus fruits are grown in the Jordan river valley.

▲ *The buildings of ancient Petra have been carved out of solid rock. This beautiful city was built in about 400BC as the capital of the Nabateans, an Arab people. It is sometimes called the 'rose-red city' because of the colour of the rock from which it is built.*

FACTS AND FIGURES

Area: 91,880 sq km
Population: 4,440,000
Capital: Amman (1,272,000)
Other major city: Az Zarqa (605,000)
Highest point: Jabal Ramm (1,754 m)
Official language: Arabic

Main religion: Islam
Currency: Jordan dinar
Main exports: Phosphate, potash, fertilizers, fruit and vegetables
Government: Constitutional monarchy
Per capita GNP: US $1,120

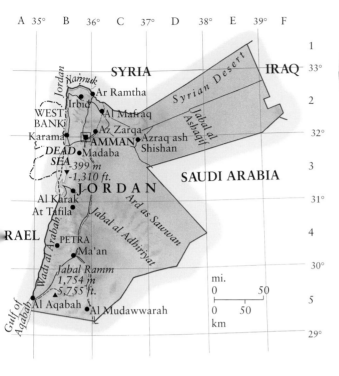

▼ These men are members of the Jordanian army's famous Desert Patrol. The Desert Patrol was set up in 1931 to police the border with Saudi Arabia. Its members' distinctive uniform was designed for practical wear in the extreme temperatures of the desert.

◄ A boy sells oranges outside the Abu Darwish mosque in Amman as people go in to pray. Arab conquerors brought Islam to Jordan in the AD600s. Since then it has been on an important pilgrimage route to the Muslim holy city of Mecca in Saudi Arabia.

IRAQ *Introduction*

Iraq is an Arab state at the top of the Persian Gulf. In the west and southwest are wide expanses of desert. The only people who live there are Bedouins, moving with their camels between oases fringed with date-palms. In the northeast rugged mountains form the border with Iran and Turkey. This region also provides scrubby pasture for goats and sheep.

The foothills of these mountains are home to many Kurds, semi-nomadic people who make up about 20 percent of Iraq's population. At the heart of the country lies the capital Baghdad, which is one of the largest cities in the Middle East.

South of Baghdad a green and fertile plain opens up between the Tigris and Euphrates rivers. It is part of an area once called Mesopotamia, meaning 'the land between the rivers'. The world's earliest known civilization, ancient Sumer, developed there about 3500BC. Today most of Iraq's population lives on the plain, which has become the centre of the country's agriculture and industry. There are oil and sugar refineries, tanneries and factories producing cotton and cement. In the southeast are wetlands, a haven for kingfishers and storks, wild boar and ibis. For at least five thousand years this wetland region has been home to a people called the Marsh Arabs, who fish and farm using complicated systems of irrigation and drainage.

Iraq's economy is built on oil reserves, which are especially vast in the south. In 1990 Iraq invaded Kuwait. This led to the Gulf War, which Iraq lost. The United Nations banned Iraq from selling oil until it had paid Kuwait for the devastation caused by the war. This was a severe blow to the Iraqi economy, already badly damaged by eight years of war with Iran in the 1980s.

FACTS AND FIGURES
Area: 438,320 sq km
Population: 19,918,000
Capital: Baghdad (3,850,000)
Other major cities: Al Basrah (617,000), Mosul (571,000), Kirkuk (570,000), Irbil (334,000)
Highest point: In the Zagros Mountains (3,608 m)
Official language: Arabic
Main religion: Islam
Currency: Iraqi dinar
Main exports: Petroleum, wool, dates
Government: Single-party republic
Per capita GNP: Est. US $700-3,000

◀ *The Ramadan mosque stands in an area of Baghdad that was swiftly rebuilt soon after the destruction of the 1991 Gulf War. Although reconstruction is a major industry in Iraq, many homes are still without water or drainage.*

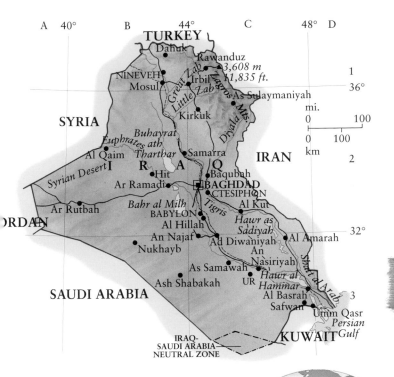

▲ *This brick minaret, with its spiral ramp, belongs to the Great Mosque of Samarra. Built around AD850, it is one of the world's largest mosques.*

▼ *People in the industrial centre of Mosul show their support for Iraq's president, Saddam Hussein. Two disastrous wars under Hussein's leadership caused hardship and the deaths of millions, but he remained popular with many Iraqis.*

KLAICHA

Klaicha, small pastries stuffed with dates and dusted with sugar, are a popular food in Iraq. Date-palms are widely grown here. Dates are not just used in sweet dishes. Various Iraqi foods combine dates or some other fruit with meat.

431

IRAQ *People and History*

By about 3000BC the Sumerian people were establishing a great civilization in this region. It was the Sumerians who invented the art of writing, using wedge-shaped symbols scratched onto wet clay tablets. Archaeologists have dug up many Sumerian tablets and the earliest inscriptions found so far were discovered in southeastern Iraq. The Sumerian civilization declined towards 2000BC. Then other ancient civilizations – Assyria and Babylonia – grew up in Mesopotamia. From about 500BC its conquerors included the Persians, Greeks and Arabs. The Arabs brought the Islamic religion and made Baghdad the capital of their empire.

The Ottoman Turks were a force in the area for many centuries, after invading Mesopotamia in 1534. By the start of this century their glory had waned. Britain then took some control and Iraq did not gain independence until 1932. After 1950 the country's oil industry brought prosperity. However, Iraq was shattered by war under Saddam Hussein, who became president in 1979. First he invaded Iran, starting a war that lasted from 1980 until 1988. Hussein then invaded Kuwait, sparking the Gulf War of 1991.

The majority of Iraqis live in towns and cities, working in business, government, factories or the oilfields. Both the Kurdish people and the Marsh Arabs have been persecuted by the Iraqi government and many have fled the country. The Kurds have long been fighting for self-rule and the Marsh Arabs are Shiite Muslims who do not support Saddam Hussein, a Sunni Muslim. Life is difficult for most other Iraqis because war has destroyed homes and jobs. Also sanctions (international trade restrictions) have caused shortages of food and medicine.

▲ *This gold pendant was found in a grave at Ur, once the capital of the Sumerian civilization. It is thought that when royalty died their servants were killed and buried alongside them. Both royalty and servants were buried still wearing their jewellery.*

◀ *Craftsmen work on brass trays, beating out their shape and design with hammers. Fine metalwork has been a tradition in Iraq for many thousands of years. Pitchers, pots and trays are among the country's specialities.*

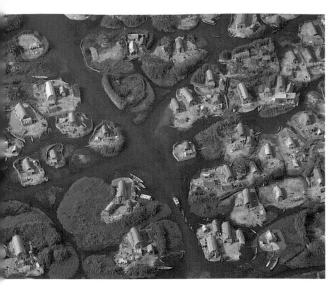

◄ *The houses of the Marsh Arabs are built from reeds. They are often constructed on floating platforms woven from the tips of reeds still growing up out of the swamp. The people travel about the swamp by canoe. The Marsh Arabs' lifestyle is threatened by drainage projects that are taking water from the swamps, causing them to dry up.*

▶ *The palace at Ctesiphon dates from the AD500s. The arch is the remains of an enormous hall with a vaulted ceiling (a ceiling held up by curved ribs). Ctesiphon was the capital city of the Parthian empire. It was also occupied by the Greeks and Romans, but was abandoned when the Arabs came and founded nearby Baghdad around AD765.*

◄ *Kurdish refugees take a rest on their journey to Iran. In 1991 the Kurds rebelled against Saddam Hussein, demanding self-rule. Hussein replied with a massacre. Thousands were killed or died of starvation or disease. More than two million fled into the mountains bordering Iran and Turkey.*

IRAN *Introduction*

Iran is a country of mountains, deserts and fertile valleys. About 70 percent of the land is sparsely populated. The centre of Iran, a vast plateau, is an empty desert of salt, sand and gravel. To the north the Elburz Mountains slope down to the land-locked Caspian Sea. In these warm waters sturgeon are fished for their eggs, known as caviar. The coastal plain and valleys are green and productive. Farmers living in scattered villages grow tobacco, cotton and tea, while nomads travel with herds of donkeys and sleep in round tents of black felt, called yurts.

In the southeast the Khuzestan Plain is an important agricultural area. It is also the site of Iran's major oilfields. Iran is one of the world's leading oil producers, although revolution and war have caused its output to drop since 1979. Oil is also drilled in the Iranian waters of the Persian Gulf. There is a big oil terminal just off the coast at Kharg Island.

In rural areas many Iranian men wear the traditional long coat and black, baggy trousers. In the towns and cities, however, men usually wear Western dress. Most city women are cloaked in a black robe called a chadar. Some Islamic religious teachings tell women to cover themselves like this. About half the population of Iran lives in cities, often working in manufacturing or service industries. In the traditional parts of towns and cities Iranians shop in the bazaar, a market with tiny passageways under domed brick roofs. The stalls sell crafts such as jewellery, pottery, metalware and the rugs for which the country is famous.

▼ *The Madrasa-i Chahar Bagh is in Isfahan. It was built in the 1700s as a college for religious studies. Isfahan has some of the most beautiful examples of Islamic architecture in Iran.*

◄ *The city of Teheran is at the foot of the Elburz Mountains. It is Iran's largest city and its capital. There are modern schools, hospitals, offices and apartment blocks alongside traditional homes built of mud bricks. Teheran has been the capital of Iran since the late 1700s.*

A 45° B 50° C 55° D 60° E

1 40°

AZERBAIJAN
ARMENIA
TURKEY
TURKMENISTAN

Lake Urmia
Orumiyeh
Tabriz
Ardabil
CASPIAN SEA

2 35°

Rasht
Zanjan
Qazvin
Elburz Mountains
Mt. Damavand
5,604 m
18,386 ft.
Meshed

Sanandaj
TEHERAN
Rey
Hamadan
Qom
Bakhtaran
Borujerd
Arak
Daryacheh-ye Namak
Dasht-e Kavir

Khorramabad
Dezful
Isfahan
Birjand

IRAQ
Zagros Mts.
Yazd
Dasht-e Lut

3 30°

Shatt al Arab Waterway
Ahvaz
Khuzestan Plain
Zabol

Khorramshahr
Abadan
Kharg I.
PERSEPOLIS
Kerman
Zahedan
AFGHANISTAN
PAKISTAN

KUWAIT
Shiraz

Bushehr
Persian Gulf

4

Bandar-e Abbas
Qeshm
Bashakerd Mts.
Strait of Hormuz 25°
Chah Bahar

mi.
0   200
0   200
km

IRAN

ENDANGERED WORLD
Farming has driven the Persian onager into the desert where survivial is difficult.

▼ *Farm workers sieve wheat in the foothills of the Elburz Mountains. The wheat will be pounded into flour and then made into flat bread. Most Iranians eat bread with every meal.*

FACTS AND FIGURES

Area: 1,648,000 sq km
Population: 63,180,000
Capital: Teheran (6,043,000)
Other major cities: Meshed (1,464,000), Isfahan (987,000), Tabriz (972,000)
Highest point: Mt Damavand (5,604 m)
Official language: Farsi (Persian)
Main religion: Islam

Currency: Rial
Main exports: Petroleum, carpets, fruit, cotton, textiles, metalwork
Government: Islamic republic
Per capita GNP: US $2,190

435

IRAN *People and History*

▼ *Iran's religious leader, Ayatollah Khamenei, makes a speech in 1994. The picture is of his predecessor, Ayatollah Khomeini, who died in 1989. The country's religious leader also holds enormous political power.*

Iran used to be called Persia. Its first civilized society probably established itself over five thousand years ago. Most Iranians are descendants of migrants from central Asia, who first settled the area around 1500BC. Arab conquerors brought Islam to Persia about AD600 and the arts and sciences flourished for several centuries. The Mongols, led by Genghis Khan, invaded in 1220. By the early 1500s they had been replaced by the dynasty of the Safavids. During the 1800s the British and Russian empires struggled over control of Iranian territory.

Reza Pahlavi, an officer in the Iranian cavalry, became shah (king) in 1925. He was succeeded by his son, Mohammed Reza Pahlavi. Large oilfields had been discovered in Iran in the early 1900s and both shahs used the profits from Iran's new oil industry to modernize the country. They made social and economic improvements, but ruled Iran as dictators.

The Muslim leader, Ayatollah Khomeini, led a revolution that overthrew the shah in 1979. He made Iran an Islamic republic, governed by strict religious law. Freedom of speech and other civil rights, especially women's rights, were taken away. Modernization was stopped and the economy suffered. In 1980 war broke out with Iraq. It was started by a dispute over the Shatt al Arab Waterway, the important oil route that divides the two countries. The eight-year war killed thousands, destroyed factories and cut oil exports. A new government came to power in the early 1990s and set about finding solutions to the economic problems caused by the war.

▶ *Iranian women weave a rug in the traditional way. Made of wool or silk, the rugs are prized for their rich colours and intricate patterns. In some Iranian homes the rug serves as table, chair and bed.*

STUFFED QUINCES

These quinces are stuffed with minced meat and spiced with cinnamon. Apples are sometimes used instead of quinces. Fruit and meat are often eaten together in Iran. Mixing sweet and sour flavours started with the Persians.

SPEAK FARSI

Hello – سلام
(sa - lahm)

Goodbye – خدا حافظ
(kho - da ha - fez)

Please – خواهش میکنم
(kha - hesh mee - ko - nam)

Thank you – متشکرم
(moo - te - sha - ke - ram)

▼ This Persian miniature painting shows King Bahram Gur killing two lions. The story is told in Farsi script at the top. The Persians were famous for their detailed and brilliantly coloured miniatures. They often illustrated scenes from traditional poems.

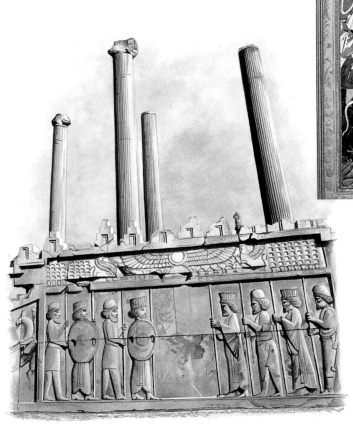

◄ The ruins of the great city of Persepolis are still a magnificent sight. The capital of King Darius I of Persia was built on a spectacular mountain site around 520BC. Its palaces and administrative buildings were decorated with splendid sculptures of people and animals, carved in limestone.

437

KUWAIT

Kuwait is a small desert country at the top of the Persian Gulf. There are no lakes or rivers, so distilled seawater is the main source of fresh water. Kuwait has large oilfields and the vast profits made from exporting oil have turned it into one of the richest countries in the world.

Until the early 1700s the area that is now Kuwait was almost uninhabited. Then Arabs of the Anaza peoples settled in Kuwait Bay and built a port there. This became Kuwait City, which is now the country's capital. In 1899 the ruler of Kuwait appealed to Britain for protection against the Turks, who had tried to take control of the country. Britain was responsible for Kuwait's defence until it became fully independent in 1961. After 1946 Kuwait began to export oil on a large-scale and the once-poor country was transformed. Today it has free education and healthcare. There is no income tax and the government subsidizes food, transport and services. It is investing profits from oil in irrigation projects so that crops can be grown in some desert areas. The government is also trying to develop other industries to increase employment opportunities.

In 1990 Kuwait was invaded by Iraq. In 1991 Allied forces, including troops from the United Kingdom and the United States of America, drove out the Iraqis. The Iraqis retaliated with bombs, setting hundreds of oil wells on fire. Kuwait's economy was badly damaged and the land and sea polluted. However, after the war rebuilding of the damaged areas was rapid.

▲ *Spectacular water towers dominate the skyline of Kuwait City. The water towers are part of desalination plants that turn seawater into fresh water by removing the salt. Fresh water is scarce in Kuwait and these plants are its main source.*

◄ *These women were among the first female oil workers in Kuwait. Few Kuwaiti women were educated or had jobs outside the home before 1960. Now increasing numbers study at Kuwait University and work in business and industry.*

FACTS AND FIGURES

Area: 17,820 sq km
Population: 1,433,000
Capital: Kuwait City (32,000)
Other major city: As Salimiyah (117,000)
Highest point: In the west (283 m)
Official language: Arabic
Main religion: Islam
Currency: Kuwaiti dinar
Main exports: Petroleum
Government: Monarchy (emir is head of state)
Per capita GNP: Est. over US $9,000

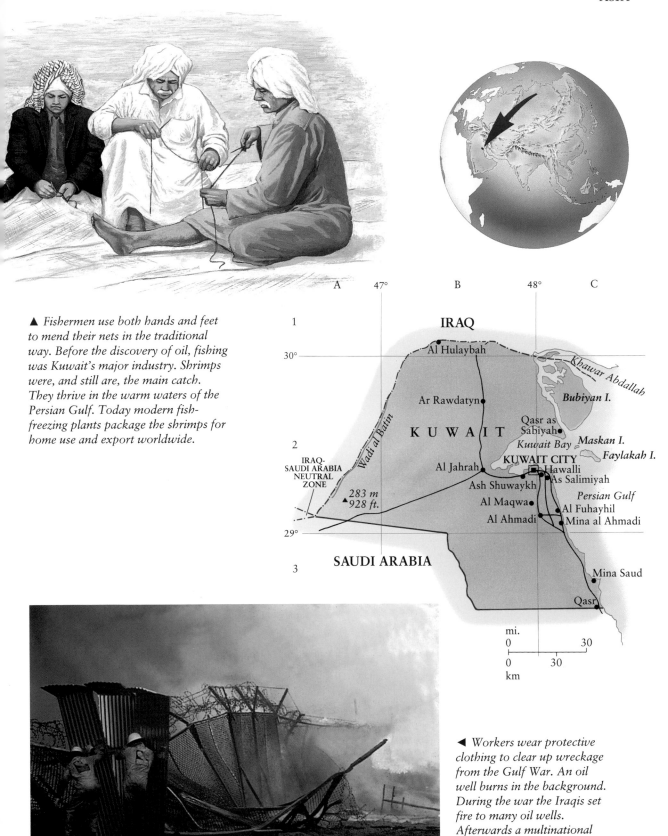

▲ Fishermen use both hands and feet to mend their nets in the traditional way. Before the discovery of oil, fishing was Kuwait's major industry. Shrimps were, and still are, the main catch. They thrive in the warm waters of the Persian Gulf. Today modern fish-freezing plants package the shrimps for home use and export worldwide.

◄ Workers wear protective clothing to clear up wreckage from the Gulf War. An oil well burns in the background. During the war the Iraqis set fire to many oil wells. Afterwards a multinational effort went into restoring Kuwait's environment.

439

SAUDI ARABIA *Introduction*

Saudi Arabia occupies most of the huge barren waste of the Arabian Peninsula. It has no permanent rivers or lakes, only wadis (valleys where rain collects, then drains away or dries out in the sun). This desert kingdom is enormously wealthy because it has the biggest oil deposits in the world. It is one of the world's leading producers of petroleum.

In the middle of Saudi Arabia is the Central Plateau. Here, under the fierce heat of the scorching sun, nomads may be found wandering in search of grass for their herds of goats, sheep and camels. To the south lies a huge desert called the Rub al Khali (Empty Quarter). There are no landmarks in this area to guide travellers because winds whip up terrific sandstorms that make the dunes change their shapes. To the north is more desert of rock, sand and gravel.

In the west, bordering the Red Sea, are low, rocky mountains. Their slopes are Saudi Arabia's most fertile area. Farmers grow wheat, melons and dates on small terraced fields. They also keep chickens outside their houses of stone or baked mud.

The oil industry is based in the eastern lowlands on the Persian Gulf. There, modern cities such as Dhahran have sprung up. Cars share roads with camels and apartment blocks tower above huts of mud. The Saudis are developing new industries and expanding agricultural production to keep the economy stable after oil resources run out.

FACTS AND FIGURES
Area: 2,200,000 sq km
Population: 16,472,000
Capital: Riyadh (1,500,000)
Other major cities: Jiddah (1,400,000), Mecca (618,000), Medina (500,000)
Highest point: Jabal Sawda (3,207 m)
Official language: Arabic
Main religion: Islam
Currency: Riyal
Main exports: Petroleum and petroleum products, wheat and dates
Government: Monarchy
Per capita GNP: US $7,940

PRAWN BALLS
Prawn balls are flavoured with the spices coriander and turmeric. They are eaten with a tamarind sauce, which is both bitter and sweet. Delicate, spicy foods like this have a cooling effect in the searing heat of Saudi Arabia. The prawn balls are served with rice, which is eaten at most Saudi meals.

▼ *The Saudi royal family enjoy a day out at the races in Riyadh. The Saud dynasty (ruling family) has reigned over much of the Arabian Peninsula since the late 1700s.*

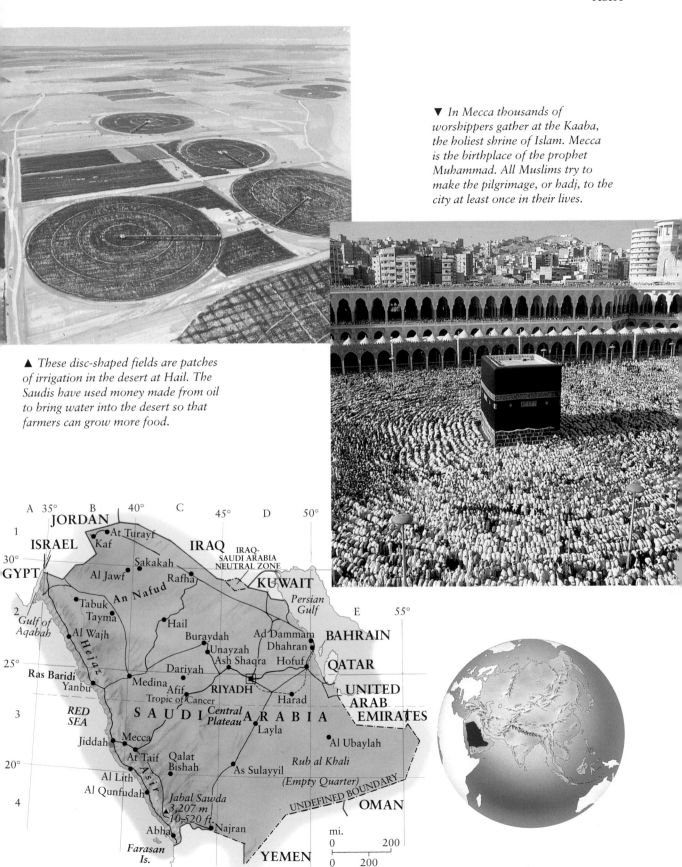

▼ *In Mecca thousands of worshippers gather at the Kaaba, the holiest shrine of Islam. Mecca is the birthplace of the prophet Muhammad. All Muslims try to make the pilgrimage, or hadj, to the city at least once in their lives.*

▲ *These disc-shaped fields are patches of irrigation in the desert at Hail. The Saudis have used money made from oil to bring water into the desert so that farmers can grow more food.*

JORDAN
ISRAEL
EGYPT
IRAQ
IRAQ-SAUDI ARABIA NEUTRAL ZONE
KUWAIT
BAHRAIN
QATAR
UNITED ARAB EMIRATES
OMAN
YEMEN

At Turayf
Kaf
Sakakah
Al Jawf
Rafha
Tabuk
Tayma
An Nafud
Hail
Al Wajh
Buraydah
Unayzah
Ad Dammam
Dhahran
Ash Shaqra
Hofuf
Dariyah
Ras Baridi
Yanbu
Medina
Afif
RIYADH
Harad
Hejaz
SAUDI ARABIA
Central Plateau
Tropic of Cancer
RED SEA
Mecca
Layla
Al Ubaylah
Jiddah
At Taif
Qalat Bishah
As Sulayyil
Rub al Khali
(Empty Quarter)
Al Lith
Al Qunfudah
Asir
Jabal Sawda
▲ 3,207 m
10,520 ft.
Najran
Abha
Farasan Is.
UNDEFINED BOUNDARY

Gulf of Aqabah
Persian Gulf

mi.
0   200

0   200
km

441

SAUDI ARABIA *People and History*

Saudi Arabia is the home of Islam, the religion founded by Muhammad around AD600. Under Islamic law the king is also the imam (religious leader) and the prime minister. The royal family, including about five thousand princes, is the most important political group. The strict form of Islam practised by Saudis has a major influence on everyday life. Women, for example, have little freedom outside the home.

A large proportion of the population are descendants of traders who settled in the Arabian Peninsula more than two thousand years ago. There are also large numbers of Bedouin Arabs. Some Bedouins lead a traditional nomadic life that has changed little for centuries.

During the early 1800s the Saud family, rulers of a small area around Riyadh, expanded their territory by conquest to include most of what is now Saudi Arabia. Civil war and opposition from the Turks, who controlled large parts of the Arabian Peninsula from the 1500s, wiped out their gains. In the early 1900s the Turks' power faded and Saudi forces, led by Ibn Saud, recaptured the lost territory. By 1932 Saudi Arabia had become a kingdom with Ibn Saud as its first king.

From the 1940s oil wealth brought prosperity to Saudi Arabia and made it a leading power in the Middle East. The standard of living rose quickly with the development of modern healthcare, schools, housing and roads. Until the discovery of oil most Saudis lived in rural areas, but today three quarters of the population lives in cities. Many have come to Saudi Arabia from other countries in search of work.

▼ *This Bedouin family live in a tent made of animal skins. Many Bedouins still follow their traditional nomadic lives in the desert, but some have become farmers or work in the cities.*

▼ *These ruins are part of Dariyah, which was the capital city until the early 1800s. Dariyah was captured and destroyed by the Turks in 1819 and never rebuilt. Instead the capital was moved to nearby Riyadh.*

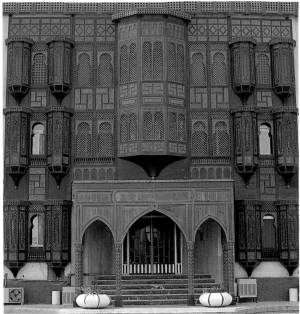

▲ *This municipal office building is in Jiddah, the second largest city in Saudi Arabia. It is built in traditional Islamic style with domed archways and latticed windows. Lattices (criss-cross strips of wood or metal) help to keep out the glare of the sun.*

ARAB HORSES

Horses approach the finish line in a race at Riyadh racecourse. Horse-racing is a popular sport in Saudi Arabia. The Arab horse is the ancestor of the modern thoroughbred racehorses seen in this picture. It is the oldest pure breed of horse in the world. Its beauty, speed and endurance have been famous for many centuries.

◀ *Saudi men relax, sitting cross-legged on the carpet to drink tea and play dominoes or cards. Islamic traditions mean that there are never any women at gatherings like this. Both men and women are forbidden entertainments such as going to the theatre and drinking alcohol.*

443

YEMEN

In the northeast of Yemen is a baking, stony desert where years can pass without rain. On the mountains between the desert and the coastal plain monsoon rains come every winter. In the steep valleys farmers grow coffee, cotton, fruit and vegetables on terraced fields. Other Yemenis make their living by fishing in the sea, while many are craftspeople whose work fills colourful bazaars.

Since oil was discovered in the 1980s it has become vital to the economy. The construction industry is also very important. However, there are not enough jobs and many Yemenis work in other countries, mainly Saudi Arabia.

Nomadic herders have lived in this region for thousands of years. From 1500BC the area prospered as camel caravans moved across it, trading between Africa and India in pearls and spices. Islam came to Yemen in the AD600s. By 1517 it had joined the Turkish empire and in northern Yemen Turkish rule lasted until 1924. Southern Yemen came under British control in 1839, only gaining independence in 1967. The south was reunited with the north as the Republic of Yemen in 1990, but civil war broke out between the two in 1994.

▲ *Sana is one of the most beautiful Arabian cities. Inside its ancient walls are mosques, palaces and bazaars of white stone and mud bricks.*

◄ *Curved daggers called* djambias *are carried by most Yemeni men. The daggers have ornately carved handles made of ivory or rhinoceros horn.*

FACTS AND FIGURES

Area: 531,000 sq km
Population: 12,302,000
Capital: Sana (500,000)
Other major city: Aden (418,000)
Highest point: Mt Hadur Shuayb (3,760 m)
Official language: Arabic
Main religion: Islam
Currencies: Yemeni dinar, riyal
Main exports: Petroleum products, cotton, fish
Government: Republic
Per capita GNP: Est. under US $700

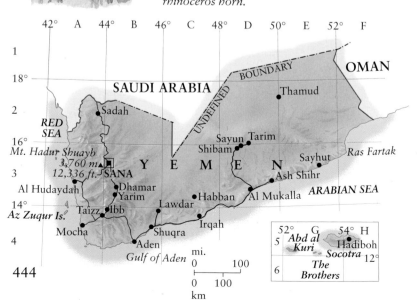

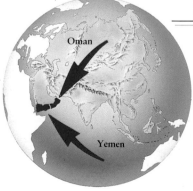

OMAN

▲ *An Omani Muslim woman follows religious custom by wearing a black mask to prevent her face from being seen. She is a desert woman – city women cover only the nose, mouth and cheeks.*

Much of Oman, which is one of the world's hottest countries, is desert. The land ranges from barren, rocky mountains in the north to the empty, rolling sands that cover the border with Saudi Arabia. Most Omanis live on the fertile coastal strip between the mountains and the sea in the north of the country and around the town of Salalah in the south. Oman also owns Musandam, the rocky peninsula overlooking busy shipping lanes between the Persian Gulf and the Arabian Sea.

Oman has an ancient sea-trading tradition and for centuries was famed for the export of frankincense, a scented gum from a desert shrub. Today many Omanis earn their living from fishing, farming or driving herds of camels, goats and horses through scrubby wasteland in search of pasture. All depend for their water on wells, some of which are fed from underground canals built hundreds of years ago.

Oman was a poor country until 1970, when Sultan Qaboos came to power. Under his rule Oman has exploited its considerable oil wealth. Some of the income from oil has been used to improve irrigation of the land and build roads, hospitals and schools.

FACTS AND FIGURES

Area: 309,500 sq km
Population: 1,697,000
Capital: Muscat (380,000)
Other major city: Nawza (63,000)
Highest point: Jabal Ash Sham (3,035 m)
Official language: Arabic

Main religion: Islam
Currency: Omani rial
Main exports: Petroleum, fish
Government: Monarchy with consultative council
Per capita GNP: US $6,490

► *A group of fishermen launch a hand-built wooden boat. Oman has long been famous for boat building. Its large wooden sailing ships once carried cargoes along the Persian Gulf and to East Africa and India.*

UNITED ARAB EMIRATES

In the early 1970s seven emirates (states ruled by emirs, or Arab princes) joined together to form the United Arab Emirates (UAE). The emirates are Abu Dhabi, Dubayy, Ash Shariqah, Ajman, Umm al Qaywayn, Ras al Khaymah and Al Fujayrah.

Until the 1900s the Arabs of this part of the Persian Gulf were seafarers. Some traded in perfumes and silk. Others were pirates and smugglers, fighting over shiploads of pearls, spices and slaves. In 1820 Britain, a strong trading power in the Persian Gulf, forced the emirates to sign a truce. They gave up warfare at sea in return for British protection. However, the emirates continued to fight each other over boundary disputes and fishing rights up until the mid-1900s, when oil brought wealth to the region.

The UAE is a barren expanse of sandy desert rising to rocky mountains in the east. Salt marshes and swamps line the coast. Before oil was discovered most people lived by diving for pearls, fishing, growing dates or herding camels. Today the majority of people live in cities and work in the oil and construction industries. Profits from oil have been used to build roads and improve healthcare and education.

▲ *Dubayy creek curves through the modern city. Dubayy is the most important commercial centre and port in the United Arab Emirates.*

FACTS AND FIGURES

Area: 83,660 sq km
Population: 1,206,000
Capital: Abu Dhabi (363,000)
Other major cities: Dubayy (585,000), Al Ayn (176,000)
Highest point: Jabal Yibir (1,527 m)

Official language: Arabic
Main religion: Islam
Currency: Dirham
Main export: Petroleum, natural gas, fish, dates
Government: Monarchy, union of emirates
Per capita GNP: US $22,220

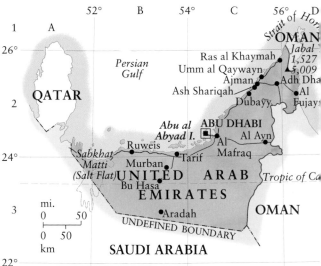

Map showing: Strait of Hormuz, OMAN, Jabal 1,527 5,009, Ras al Khaymah, Umm al Qaywayn, Ajman, Adh Dha, Ash Shariqah, Al, Dubayy, Fujay, Persian Gulf, QATAR, Abu al Abyad I., ABU DHABI, Al Ayn, Ruweis, Al Mafraq, Sabkhat Matti (Salt Flat), Murban, Tarif, UNITED ARAB EMIRATES, Bu Hasa, Tropic of Ca, OMAN, Aradah, UNDEFINED BOUNDARY, SAUDI ARABIA. Scales: mi. 0 50, km 0 50. Coordinates: 26°, 24°, 22°, 52° A B 54° C 56° D, 1, 2, 3

◀ *Jockeys, many of them young boys, urge their racing camels to run faster. Camel racing is a popular sport in the United Arab Emirates. Racing camels are specially bred for speed and are highly prized.*

QATAR

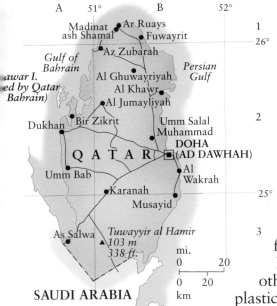

A 51° B 52°

Madinat ash Shamal · Ar Ruays
· Fuwayrit
· Az Zubarah

Gulf of Bahrain

awar I.
ed by Qatar
Bahrain)

Al Ghuwayriyah
Al Khawr

Persian Gulf

Al Jumayliyah

Dukhan · Bir Zikrit

Umm Salal Muhammad

Q A T A R

DOHA (AD DAWHAH)

Umm Bab

Al Wakrah

Karanah

Musayid

As Salwa

Tuwayyir al Hamir
▲*103 m*
338 ft.

mi.
0 — 20

0 — 20
km

SAUDI ARABIA

1
26°

2

25°

3

Qatar

United Arab Emirates

The small peninsula of Qatar sticks up like a thumb into the Persian Gulf. Qatar was protected first by its neighbour Bahrain and then by Britain before becoming an independent emirate (ruled by a prince) in 1971. It is mainly stony desert with barren salt flats in the south. Before oil was discovered in 1939 most people survived by pearl diving, fishing and camel herding. Today 90 percent of the population are city-dwellers. Most live in or near Doha, the capital, working in oil or related industries. Plentiful jobs and good pay have attracted workers from other Arab countries and from India and Pakistan. There are now three foreigners to every native Qatari.

Profits from oil in Qatar are being used to develop other industries such as fish-freezing, fertilizers and plastics. Oil money also provides free education, free healthcare and housing for the poor. Drinking water used to come from natural springs or wells, but now Qatar has built large desalination plants where seawater is distilled to remove the salt. The fresh water is then piped to homes and used to irrigate crops. The government also helps farmers to grow more vegetables, fruit and grain by supplying them with free seeds, pesticides and fertilizers.

▶ *Wooden slats in this wind tower catch the wind and funnel it down to the building below. This simple air conditioning system was developed in ancient times and is still used in modern Qatari buildings.*

FACTS AND FIGURES
Area: 11,440 sq km
Population: 559,000
Capital: Doha (236,000)
Other major city: Al Wakrah (26,000)
Highest point: Tuwayyir al Hamir (103 m)
Official language: Arabic
Main religion: Islam
Currency: Qatari riyal
Main exports: Petroleum, fertilizers
Government: Constitutional monarchy (emir is head of state)
Per capita GNP: US $16,240

447

BAHRAIN

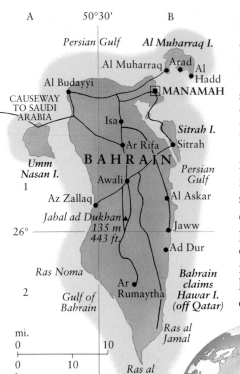

Bahrain consists of about 30 islands, most of which are uninhabited desert. The largest island, also called Bahrain, is rocky and barren in the south, but in the north plentiful springs have greened the land. Bridges join the main islands and a causeway links Bahrain Island to Saudi Arabia.

Most Bahrainis are Muslim Arabs and live in the fertile north of the largest island. Traditional occupations include fishing, pearl diving, tending animals and growing fruits such as pomegranates and figs on irrigated land. Since the discovery of oil in 1932 many people have taken jobs in the petroleum industry and live in or near the capital. About one fifth of the population are immigrant workers, mainly from Pakistan and India. Oil money provides free healthcare and education. It also finances the development of new industries such as aluminium processing.

Bahrain's position in the Persian Gulf made it an important trading nation in ancient times. Today it is a thriving financial centre. During its long history Bahrain has been invaded by the Portuguese, Persians and mainland Arabs. Britain handled the country's defence and foreign affairs from 1861 until 1971, when Bahrain became independent.

FACTS AND FIGURES
Area: 690 sq km
Population: 521,000
Capital: Manamah (152,000)
Other major city: Al Muharraq (78,000)
Highest point: Jabal ad Dukhan (135 m)
Official language: Arabic
Main religion: Islam
Currency: Bahraini dinar
Main exports: Petroleum, aluminium products, manufactured goods, machinery, transport equipment
Government: Monarchy (emir is head of state)
Per capita GNP: Est. US $3,000-8,000

► Burning gases from oil wells blacken the sky of Bahrain. The country has less oil than most Gulf states, but its oil refinery is one of the biggest and most modern in the world.

448

MALDIVES

The Maldives are a string of tiny tropical islands lying in the turquoise waters of the Indian Ocean. There are about 1,200 islands altogether, but only 200 are inhabited. They are low and flat, many only just sticking up above sea level. White sandy beaches line the shores and brilliantly coloured fish, such as the poisonous scorpion fish, dart among the corals of the clear blue lagoons. Some islands have no vegetation, but on most coconut palms and breadfruit trees grow in shallow soil. At dusk giant fruit bats called flying foxes glide between the trees.

Sinhalese people sailed west from Sri Lanka to settle the islands around 500BC. The Maldives became trading posts for the Portuguese and Dutch from the 1500s, then were ruled by the British from 1887 until independence in 1965. A major source of the islanders' income is fishing. Bonito, the main catch, and other fish are exported to Sri Lanka and Japan. Pineapples, pomegranates and yams are grown on the islands, but rice has to be imported.

Tourism is by far the fastest-growing industry. Many of the resorts are foreign-owned, but increasingly islanders are developing their own resorts. Local crafts, such as shell necklaces and carved wooden fish, are sold to tourists.

▼ *This aerial view shows that the Maldives are formed from coral reefs. Corals are tiny underwater animals, some of which live inside chalky skeleton-like structures. These structures build up into a rocky deposit. Sometimes they stick out above the water and form an island.*

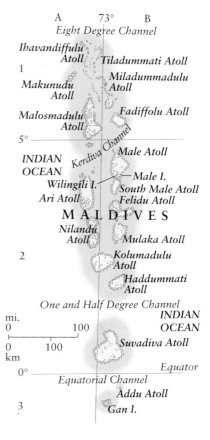

FACTS AND FIGURES	
Area: 300 sq km	**Official language:**
Population: 238,000	Divehi
Capital:	**Main religion:** Islam
Male, on Male Island	**Currency:** Rufiyaa
(56,000)	**Main export:** Fish
Highest point:	**Government:** Republic
On Wilingili Island	**Per capita GNP:**
(24 m)	US $500

PAKISTAN *Introduction*

Pakistan is an Islamic republic in southern Asia. Along its northeastern border with China the high peaks of the Karakoram range form a desolate barrier of ice and stone. In contrast, the neighbouring northern territory of Jammu and Kashmir is a beautiful land of lakes and mountains. Ownership of part of this region is disputed with Pakistan's neighbour, India. In the northwest the road climbs the lonely heights of the Khyber Pass, a narrow passage through the mountains to Afghanistan. To the west a dusty highway leads to southern Iran. In the southwest little grows on the dry and rocky Baluchistan Plateau, while the sandy wastes of the Thar Desert stretch into the southeast from India.

The centre of Pakistan is a great plain called the Punjab, which means five rivers. The plain is so-called because it is watered by the Indus River and its four major tributaries the Jhelum, Chenab, Ravi and Sutlej. The Punjab is extremely hot and dry, but a vast irrigation system allows the cultivation of wheat, rice, cotton and sugar-cane. During the occasional violent rainstorms that occur, the irrigation channels help to prevent serious flooding. They catch the water that might otherwise wash away the crops. The Punjab's rivers are also used to harness hydroelectric power at dams such as the Tarbela Dam on the Indus River.

Pakistan's many industries produce cotton, carpets, sugar and processed foods. These goods are transported between large cities such as Rawalpindi, Lahore and Karachi by road and rail.

FACTS AND FIGURES
Area: 796,100 sq km
Population: 122,802,000
Capital: Islamabad (201,000)
Other major cities: Karachi (5,103,000), Lahore (2,922,000), Faisalabad (1,092,000), Rawalpindi (928,000)
Highest point: K2 (8,611 m)
Official language: Urdu
Main religion: Islam
Currency: Pakistani rupee
Main exports: Cotton and cotton goods, rice, leather, carpets, fish
Government: Islamic republic
Per capita GNP: US $410

ENDANGERED WORLD
The Indus dolphin is endangered because dams on the Indus River have divided its breeding and fishing grounds.

► *Boats line the quayside in Karachi's fishing harbour. The Arabian Sea yields an immense array of fish, including sharks and several kinds of herring. Pakistan exports large quantities of fish and shellfish.*

► Irrigation brings water to the Punjab, the flat plain in the centre of Pakistan. This allows rice to be grown in flooded paddy-fields, which would otherwise be dusty and dry. Farmers also grow wheat and raise goats in this region. They use oxen to help them till the land.

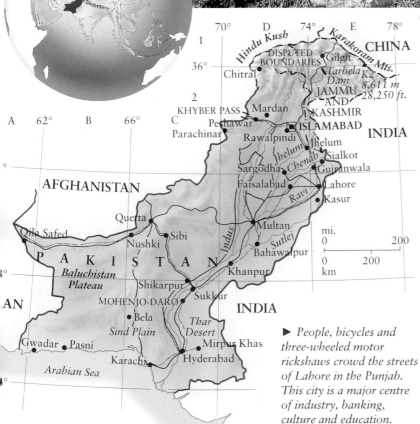

► People, bicycles and three-wheeled motor rickshaws crowd the streets of Lahore in the Punjab. This city is a major centre of industry, banking, culture and education.

451

PAKISTAN *People and History*

One of the world's first great civilizations flourished in this land around 2000BC. The peoples of the ancient Indus empire settled in the Indus Valley and produced fine architecture and pottery. Over the next 3,500 years the area was invaded by Arabs, Greeks, Persians and Turks. The British gradually took over India during the 1800s and, by 1900, this included all the lands that are now Pakistan. From the early 1900s, however, India wanted to be independent from Britain. At the same time tensions increased between the two main religious groups – Muslims and Hindus.

When India eventually won its independence in 1947, two separate Muslim areas in northwest and northeast India became the country of Pakistan (meaning Land of the Pure). Muslims from all over India moved to the new country while most Hindus stayed in India. In 1971 civil war broke out between East and West Pakistan. The eastern half renamed itself Bangladesh, while the western half became modern-day Pakistan.

Since the 1970s the army has repeatedly seized control of the country, but Pakistan has also had periods of democratic rule. In 1988 Benazir Bhutto was elected the Islamic world's first woman prime minister. However, many Pakistani women still do little work outside the home and are veiled in public. Some Pakistani men dress in Western-style clothes, others wear the traditional long shirt and baggy trousers called shalwar-kameez. Many are farmers who grow crops such as rice and sugar-cane.

▲ *A potter adds the finishing touches to a teapot in Peshawar, near the Afghan border. Pakistan has a long tradition of fine craftwork, which also includes carpet making, leather tooling and metalwork.*

◄ *This classroom is crowded with boys from the Sind Plain. There is no law in Pakistan that says children must be educated and few girls are sent to school. Most adults are unable to read or write, though the children of wealthier families may study at one of the country's 24 universities.*

◄ Worshippers crowd in front of the great Badshahi mosque in Lahore, built in 1674. The people of this land were converted to Islam by Arab invaders around AD700. Modern Pakistan is a strongly Muslim nation.

► Ruins of the city of Mohenjo-Daro show that it was one of the earliest examples of a planned city. The streets were laid out according to a grid and were well drained. It was an important centre of the Indus civilization, which flourished in Pakistan about 4000 years ago.

◄ Boys in Faisalabad get ready to ride on the roof of a crowded bus. Pakistanis take pride in decorating their buses, lorries and vans with pictures, mottoes and slogans, coloured lights and chains.

INDIA *Introduction*

ENDANGERED WORLD

The Indian python is threatened by hunters. Its beautifully patterned skin is used to make belts, wallets, handbags and shoes.

India is the seventh largest country in the world and it has the second largest number of people. This vast land contains contrasts of every possible kind – in its peoples, languages, customs, religions and landscapes. There are massive mountain ranges hidden permanently under ice and snow, vast plains crossed by broad rivers, a parched desert, dense tropical forests and palm-fringed beaches.

By air many of these places can be reached within hours. However, most travellers use the crowded buses or trains and journeys can take days. Passengers cram onto the seats, often sharing space with chickens, goats or other animals that are being taken to market.

About three quarters of India's vast population lives in rural areas, where most people are farmers. Crops of rice and wheat are grown in the fields and animals are kept on small plots of land. However, in recent years thousands of people have moved away from this traditional life to find work in the cities. Life is very different away from the countryside. Noisy crowds fill the city streets and rickshaws thread their way through the traffic. The larger cities are now major industrial centres as India continues to make great progress in science, technology and industry.

▲ *The Taj Mahal, near the city of Agra, is a tomb. It was built in memory of Mumtaz Mahal, the wife of the Muslim ruler Shah Jahan. The tomb was constructed from gleaming white marble. It took 20 years to build and was completed in 1653.*

FACTS AND FIGURES	
Area: 3,165,600 sq km	Sanskrit, Sindhi, Tamil,
Population: 896,567,000	Telugu, Urdu, Nepali
Capital: Delhi	**Main religions:**
(8,400,000)	Hinduism, Islam,
Other major cities:	Christianity, Sikhism
Bombay (12,596,000),	**Currency:**
Calcutta (11,022,000)	Indian rupee
Highest point:	**Main exports:** Gems
Kanchenjunga (8,598 m)	and jewellery, clothes,
Official languages:	cotton, textiles, tea,
Hindi, Assamese,	engineering goods
English, Bengali,	**Government:**
Gujarati, Kannarese,	Multi-party republic
Kashmiri, Malayalam,	**Per capita GNP:**
Marathi, Oriya, Punjabi,	US $310

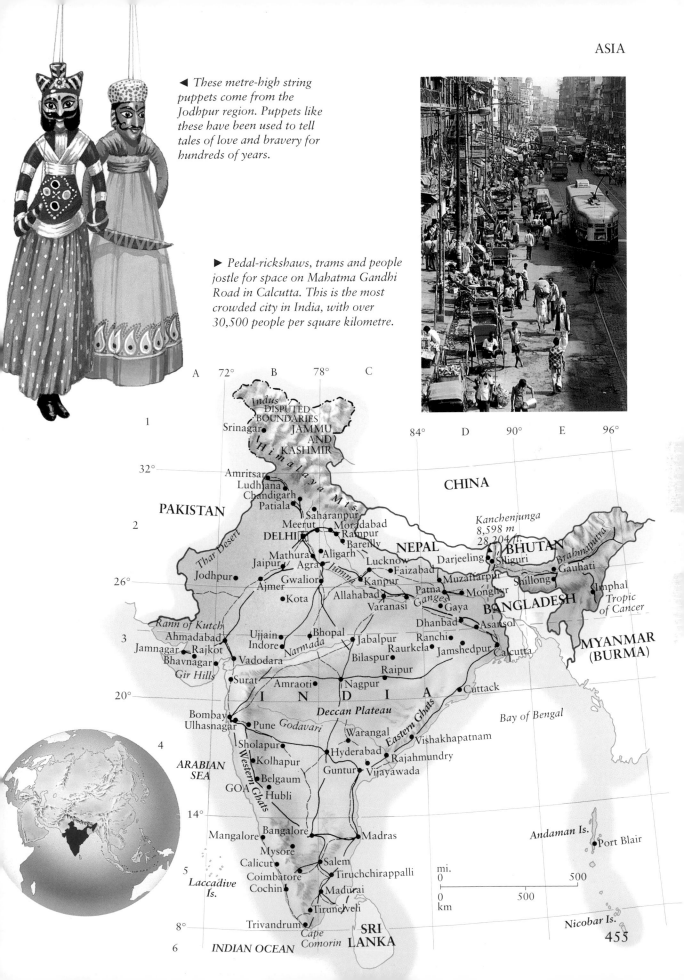

◄ *These metre-high string puppets come from the Jodhpur region. Puppets like these have been used to tell tales of love and bravery for hundreds of years.*

► *Pedal-rickshaws, trams and people jostle for space on Mahatma Gandhi Road in Calcutta. This is the most crowded city in India, with over 30,500 people per square kilometre.*

A 72° B 78° C

Indus
DISPUTED
BOUNDARIES
Srinagar JAMMU
AND
KASHMIR

32°
Amritsar
Ludhiana
Chandigarh
Patiala
Saharanpur
Meerut Moradabad
DELHI Rampur
Bareilly
Mathura Aligarh Lucknow
Jaipur Agra Faizabad
Jodhpur Gwalior *Jumna* Kanpur
Ajmer Allahabad Patna
Kota Varanasi *Ganges* Gaya

PAKISTAN

Thar Desert

CHINA

84° D 90° E 96°

Kanchenjunga
8,598 m
28,204 ft.
NEPAL BHUTAN
Darjeeling Siliguri
Muzaffarpur Gauhati
Monghyr Shillong
BANGLADESH Imphal
Tropic of Cancer

26°

Rann of Kutch
Ahmadabad Ujjain Bhopal
Jamnagar Rajkot Indore *Narmada* Jabalpur Dhanbad Asansol
Bhavnagar Vadodara Bilaspur Ranchi MYANMAR
Gir Hills Surat Raurkela Jamshedpur (BURMA)
Amraoti Raipur Calcutta
Nagpur Cuttack

I N D I A

3

20°

Deccan Plateau *Eastern Ghats*

Bombay
Ulhasnagar Pune *Godavari*
Warangal Vishakhapatnam
Sholapur Hyderabad
Kolhapur Rajahmundry
Belgaum Guntur Vijayawada
GOA Hubli

Bay of Bengal

ARABIAN
SEA

Western Ghats

4

14°

Mangalore Bangalore Madras
Mysore
Calicut Salem
Coimbatore Tiruchchirappalli
Cochin Madurai
Tirunelveli

Andaman Is.
Port Blair

Laccadive Is.

5

8°
Trivandrum
Cape Comorin SRI
LANKA

Nicobar Is.

mi.
0 500
0 500
km

455

6 INDIAN OCEAN

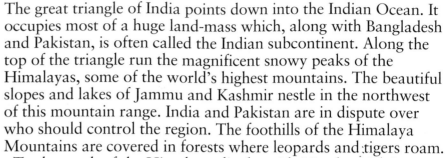

INDIA *Geography*

▼ *The towering Himalaya Mountains separate India from Central Asia and China. Melting snow from their ridges and glaciers feed the river Ganges. Both the mountains and the Ganges are sacred to the Hindus, who make up most of the population of India.*

The great triangle of India points down into the Indian Ocean. It occupies most of a huge land-mass which, along with Bangladesh and Pakistan, is often called the Indian subcontinent. Along the top of the triangle run the magnificent snowy peaks of the Himalayas, some of the world's highest mountains. The beautiful slopes and lakes of Jammu and Kashmir nestle in the northwest of this mountain range. India and Pakistan are in dispute over who should control the region. The foothills of the Himalaya Mountains are covered in forests where leopards and tigers roam.

To the south of the Himalayas lie the wide Northern Plains. The majority of the population lives there, in fertile areas such as the huge flood plain of the mighty river Ganges. The arid wastelands of the Thar Desert stretch away to the west.

Moving farther south, the third major region of the country is

the great plateau of the Deccan, which makes up most of central and southern India. This giant plateau includes farming and grazing land. It is also rich in mineral deposits. The Deccan is bordered on either side by the mountains and hills of the great Western and Eastern Ghats, which drop down to coastal plains. The Western Ghats are higher than the Eastern Ghats and large parts of the foothills are covered in tropical rainforest. The west of the country catches the full force of the summer winds each year, which bring heavy monsoon rains to the whole of India.

▶ *Wild elephants wade in the lake at the Periyar Wildlife Sanctuary in the south. The park also protects antelopes, monkeys, tigers, wild boars and large deer called sambars.*

► *Sandy beaches lined with coconut palms form the coastline of Goa, a popular tourist spot. Goa is India's smallest state. It is affected heavily by the monsoon rains, which sweep across the country from June to September each year.*

▼ *Camels make their way across the fiercely hot, empty sands of the Thar Desert. Little of this region can be cultivated, although crops such as millet, sorghum and maize grow on the irrigated edges of the desert.*

► *Tea grows on the hills of Darjeeling. The climate in these Himalayan foothills seems cool in comparison with the heat of the plains to the south.*

INDIA *Economy*

India is a land rich in natural resources. It produces vast quantities of food and manufactured goods. However, the rapid growth of its population means that there is still not enough food for everyone. Many of India's people remain extremely poor and natural disasters such as severe drought, earthquakes and floods often add to their hardship.

The country has huge expanses of farmland, but much of it is not naturally fertile. Since India gained its independence in 1947 a great deal has been done to modernize farming practices. Today agriculture contributes about one third of the country's income. Various irrigation projects have been developed to bring water to dry areas. Experiments with new types of seeds and fertilizers have also resulted in much bigger harvests. Despite this, most farms are too small for modern machinery and can produce only enough food to feed one family. Farms in India are getting smaller all the time. This is because, under Hindu law, land is divided equally among the children on their parents' death. Some Indian people want to reform this law so that farms can be much larger and more productive.

Since the 1950s industry has transformed India's cities. Heavy machinery and electrical goods are now manufactured alongside traditional products such as cotton and silk. Plentiful supplies of oil and coal provide power for the factories and generate more than half the country's electricity. Service industries are also growing in importance and more Indians are working in tourism, banking and communications.

> **ECONOMIC SURVEY**
> **Farming:** Most farms are small and grow food crops such as rice, millet, wheat and beans. Mangoes, nuts, tea, jute, sesame seeds, spices and betel nuts are produced. Sixty two percent of the population are farmers.
> **Forestry:** Cedar, teak and rosewood are felled for timber.
> **Fishing:** Mackerel, sardines and shrimps are caught in the sea. Carp and catfish are fished in the rivers.
> **Mining:** Iron, coal, oil, mica, manganese and diamonds are extracted.
> **Industry:** Textiles, iron and steel, machinery and electronic goods are produced. Craft products include leather, jewellery and carpets.

▼ *Traders crowd an alleyway as shoppers haggle over the prices of vegetables and spices in a typical Indian market.*

▲ *A potter shapes clay on the wheel in a scene that has changed little in thousands of years. Other traditional crafts include metalwork, weaving and fabric printing. These items are exported all over the world.*

◄ *Steel is processed at a mill in Jamshedpur. The metal is used in the manufacture of cars, trucks, buses, bicycles, industrial machinery, electrical goods and domestic appliances such as sewing machines.*

► *Women carry rubble from a building site. Much of the heavy work in cities and on farms is still carried out using muscle power rather than machines. Many of the hardest jobs tend to be done by the lowest caste (social class).*

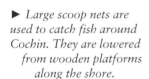

► *Large scoop nets are used to catch fish around Cochin. They are lowered from wooden platforms along the shore.*

INDIA *People*

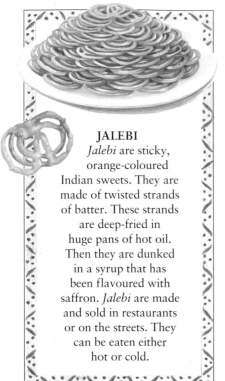

JALEBI
Jalebi are sticky, orange-coloured Indian sweets. They are made of twisted strands of batter. These strands are deep-fried in huge pans of hot oil. Then they are dunked in a syrup that has been flavoured with saffron. *Jalebi* are made and sold in restaurants or on the streets. They can be eaten either hot or cold.

India is a country with many different ethnic groups and around a thousand languages and dialects. There are also a large number of religious faiths, although more than four fifths of the population is Hindu. According to Hindu tradition, people are born into social classes called castes. Strict religious rules govern the food, clothing and jobs of each caste.

Family ties are very important in India and marriage is often seen more as a union between two families than a relationship between two people. It is the custom for parents to choose their children's marriage partners for them. Today some Indians are trying to break down these social rules by encouraging young people to pick their own husband or wife.

In India's many villages the way of life has not changed much in centuries. People fetch their water each day from the village well and light their homes with oil lamps. As the economy continues to grow, more villages have access to plumbing facilities and electricity.

In the cities large numbers of people live crowded together in slums, while many wealthier Indians choose to live in areas that show a strong Western influence. Some people wear Western clothes, while others prefer traditional dress, such as the brilliantly coloured saris worn by many Indian women. Indian social life centres on the marketplaces in the towns and cities. They are full of people exchanging news and views amid the blare of pop music, the hooting of car horns and the shouts of street sellers.

◄ *Hindu children stand covered in coloured water and dye as they celebrate the spring festival, Holi. During this festival people throw coloured powder everywhere. They also play tricks on each other in memory of the mischievous behaviour of Krishna, one of the Hindu gods.*

◄ Posters show popular Indian film stars. India's enormous film and video industry has gained a worldwide reputation. So many films are produced in Bombay that it has been given the nickname 'Bollywood'. Films are a favourite form of entertainment throughout the country and popular subjects include love stories and dramas.

SPEAK HINDI

Hello – नमस्ते
(*nah - mah - stay*)

Goodbye – अलविदा
(*al - vee - dah*)

Please – कृपया
(*crew - pah - ya*)

Thank you – धन्यवाद
(*dan - ya vad*)

Yes – हाँ (*hah*)

▼ Traditional costume is worn for kathakali dancing in southwestern India. The dances tell stories about the lives of Hindu gods and demons. They are accompanied by chanting and drumbeats.

▲ Poor people struggle to survive on the streets of Calcutta. Above their shelters a bank advertises pension schemes that none of them could ever afford. There is a huge gap between the rich and the poor in this country. Most Indians live in villages, but many have moved to large cities such as Calcutta, Bombay and Delhi in search of work that is not available.

461

INDIA *History*

One of the world's greatest ancient civilizations sprang up in the valley of the Indus River. There, from around 2500BC, the Dravidian peoples developed an advanced economy and system of government. The Aryan peoples invaded northern India and pushed the original inhabitants south around 1500BC. It is from these two peoples that Indians are mostly descended.

India has seen the rise and fall of various great empires founded on religion. From about 272 to 232BC Emperor Ashoka ruled most of India and encouraged the Buddhist faith. By AD400, under a family of rulers called the Guptas, Hinduism was enjoying a golden age. Muslim invaders conquered Delhi in 1192 and their rule spread across the north, while the powerful Hindu state of Vijayanagar flourished in the south. In 1526 a Muslim leader called Babur founded the empire of the Mughals (Mongols) in the north. The Mughal emperors became fabulously rich. Emperor Shah Jahan used some of his wealth to build the lavish Taj Mahal at Agra in the 1600s.

At this time European traders began to gain a foothold. By the 1800s the British East India Company controlled large areas and in 1858 India became part of the British empire. Demands for self-rule grew during the 1920s and 1930s with a peaceful campaign organized by Mahatma Gandhi. When India gained its independence in 1947, Muslim territories in the northeast and northwest became the new nation of Pakistan. Since then India has experienced conflicts over religion and language, but it has remained the largest democracy in the world.

▼ *A splendid procession makes its way through the streets of Delhi on Republic Day, January 26th. India became a republic in 1950. Independence from Britain is also celebrated each year on August 15th.*

◄ *Hindus gather at dawn to bathe in the holy waters of the river Ganges at Varanasi. Hinduism has shaped Indian society since ancient times. Its sacred scriptures are believed to date back over 4,000 years.*

► *The Golden Temple is in the city of Amritsar. It is the holy place of the Sikh religion, founded in the 1400s by Guru Nanak. He instructed his followers to live a good and simple life. Today there are about 14 million Sikhs, many of whom live in the northern state of Punjab.*

▼ *This model of a tiger eating a European was made for Tipu Sultan of Mysore in the late 1700s. He fought many battles against the British East India company.*

MAHATMA GANDHI
Mohandas Karamchand Gandhi was born in India in 1869. A believer in peaceful protest, he headed the successful campaign for Indian independence using marches and hunger strikes. Gandhi led a simple life and became known as Mahatma, which means wise and holy leader. He was assassinated in 1948.

NEPAL

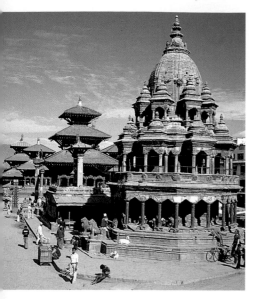

▼ *This is the temple of the Hindu god Krishna in Kathmandu. There are thousands of beautiful Buddhist and Hindu temples in this deeply religious country. The capital is especially famous for its temples.*

The Himalaya Mountains cover most of Nepal and form a snowy wall along the northern border with China. Their highest peak is Mount Everest, the tallest mountain in the world. Far below the icy peaks, rhododendrons cover the mountain passes of the Himalayan foothills. To the south of the mountains lie the humid and fertile Tarai Plains, where rhinoceroses and tigers roam.

Most of the people of Nepal are farmers, who use traditional methods to grow sugar-cane, rice, maize and wheat. Others herd sheep and yaks. Some work in tourism, as Nepal's spectacular landscape attracts mountaineers and trekkers from all over the world. Tourism has brought much needed money and development to this poor country. However, these changes are also threatening the local farmers' way of life and the environment. A cloud of pollution now hangs over Nepal's capital, Kathmandu. Also, more than one third of the forests have been cut down since the 1950s. Both locals and tourists use the timber for cooking and heating. Poster campaigns encourage everyone to conserve resources.

From the late 1700s to the start of the 1990s Nepal was ruled as a dictatorship, either by a monarch or by members of the powerful Rana family. In 1991 King Birendra gave up his powers. Elections were held, which brought in a democratic government.

FACTS AND FIGURES
Area: 147,180 sq km
Population:
(21,086,000)
Capital: Kathmandu
(419,000)
Other major city:
Biratnagar (131,000)
Highest point:
Mt Everest (8,848 m)
Official language:
Nepali
Main religions:
Hinduism, Buddhism
Currency:
Nepalese rupee
Main exports: Grains, jute, timber, oil-seeds, clarified butter, potatoes, herbs, hides
Government:
Constitutional monarchy
Per capita GNP:
US $170

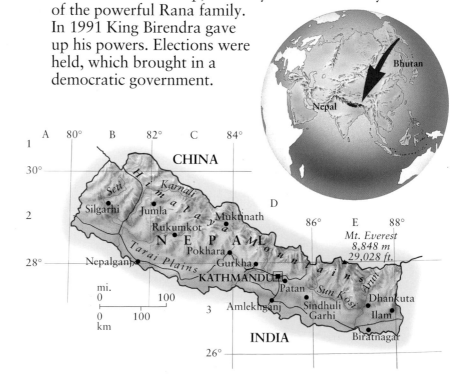

BHUTAN

This small country calls itself the 'Land of the Thunder Dragon', the mythical beast that appears on its flag. Bhutan is protective of its centuries-old cultural traditions. Television is banned and the people are required by law to wear national costume. Both tourism and mountaineering are limited. Most of the people of Bhutan are Buddhists of Tibetan descent. Another important group are Nepali-speaking Hindus.

This is a land of extremes. Bananas grow on the humid, southern plain that borders India and forests of oak cover the cool, central hills. In the north the rugged Himalaya Mountains lie permanently under ice and snow.

The country came under Tibetan rule in the 1500s. From the 1800s it was protected by Britain. In 1949 Bhutan became independent, although it placed the management of its foreign affairs in India's hands. India helped to build roads, develop hydroelectric power and mine coal. However, Bhutan remains a basically agricultural country. Long-haired oxen called yaks are herded in the high mountain ranges. Farmers grow crops such as potatoes, barley, citrus fruits, rice and wheat in the country's rich, fertile valleys.

FACTS AND FIGURES
Area: 46,500 sq km
Population: 1,650,000
Capital: Thimphu (31,000)
Highest point: Kula Kangri (7,554 m)
Official languages: Dzongkha, English, Nepali
Main religions: Buddhism, Hinduism
Currency: Ngultrum
Main exports: Timber and wood products, coal, rice, oranges and apples, distilled spirits, talc, cement
Government: Constitutional monarchy
Per capita GNP: US $180

▶ *In the capital, Thimphu, young monks watch the Tsetchu festival. It is held in honour of a Tibetan saint. Bhutan has many spectacular religious festivals and dances.*

◀ *Traditional farmhouses cling to the mountainside above irrigated terraced fields. Communities like this are often isolated because they are cut off by the steep mountains.*

465

BANGLADESH

FACTS AND FIGURES
Area: 148,390 sq km
Population:
122,210,000
Capital: Dhaka
(6,106,000)
Other major cities:
Chittagong (2,041,000),
Khulna (878,000),
Rajshahi (518,000)
Highest point:
Mt Keokradong
(1,230 m)
Official language:
Bengali
Main religions:
Islam, Hinduism
Currency: Taka
Main exports: Jute, tea,
hides, clothes, leather,
newsprint, fish
Government:
Multi-party republic
Per capita GNP:
US $220

Most of Bangladesh is flat, very low-lying land. Two great rivers, the Ganges and the Jamuna, join forces just west of the capital, Dhaka. The rivers spill into a maze of waterways along the Bay of Bengal and form the largest delta in the world. There are frequent floods in Bangladesh, which have drowned both livestock and people. The floods also wash away crops, causing famine. Some experts want to control these floods with various engineering schemes. Others recommend setting up local projects to help people survive, such as building platforms on stilts where people can escape from the floodwaters.

Most Bangladeshis use the traditional tools and methods of their ancestors to farm the fertile plain and fish its rivers. The males of the family plant and harvest rice, tea, sugar-cane or jute. The women and girls usually look after the home and garden, where they tend pumpkins or spices. Rural families live mostly in villages of bamboo houses built on embankments of mud. Travel between villages is often by canoe. Fewer than one fifth of Bangladeshis live in cities, as housing and factory jobs are scarce.

This land was once part of the Indian province of Bengal. By the late 1940s it had become the eastern half of Pakistan. In 1971 civil war broke out when East Pakistan fought to break away from the control of West Pakistan. India fought on the side of East Pakistan and helped it to become the new nation of Bangladesh. Since independence there have been periods of military rule, but today Bangladesh is governed by a democratically elected parliament.

▲ *River water has flooded these homes near Dhaka. Bangladesh is a land of rivers and when the torrential monsoon rains come, the rivers burst their banks. Over the years millions of people have been drowned or made homeless by heavy floods. Flooding is made worse by the cyclones that often strike Bangladesh.*

ENDANGERED WORLD
The gharial is a long, slender-snouted relative of the crocodile. It is hunted for its skin and its eggs are taken for food.

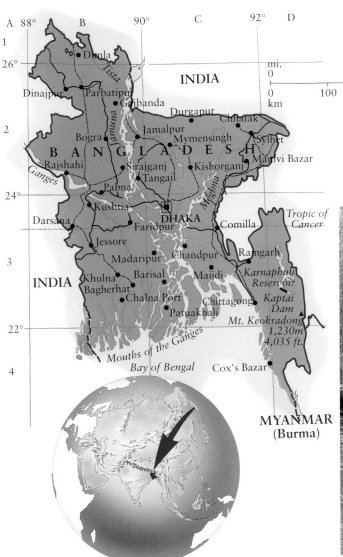

▼ Long stems of jute are harvested and bundled together. Its tough fibres are used to make rope, matting and sacking. Bangladesh grows the best quality jute in the world and it is the country's most important export.

◄ A Bangladeshi health worker holds a clinic for mothers and babies. As part of her job she may also advise villagers on using clean water, preparing food hygienically and immunizing children against disease. Health education is particularly important in areas devastated by flooding.

467

SRI LANKA

Sri Lanka is an island ringed with palm-fringed beaches. Inland is a fertile plain that rises through rolling hills, planted with tea bushes, to misty mountains. Rainforest covers the southwest.

In about 500BC a Sinhalese prince from India conquered the Vedda people who were living on the island and called the country Sinhala. Around AD200 it was invaded again from India, by Tamil kings. The Tamils drove the Sinhalese into the south. The two groups continued to struggle for control of the country until the Portuguese arrived in the 1500s. They were followed by the Dutch and then the British, who ruled from 1802. The British called the island Ceylon. It became independent in 1948 and changed its name to Sri Lanka in 1972.

In the 1980s and 1990s old tensions erupted again. The Hindu Tamils of the north resented being governed from the south by the Sinhalese Buddhists. Thousands were killed in guerrilla battles and many Tamils left for India. However, throughout these troubles Sri Lanka has held on to a basically democratic system of government. Peace talks in the early 1990s brought hopes of settling the situation.

About half of the population are farmers. Agriculture is the main economic activity, producing the important crops of coconuts, rubber, rice and tea.

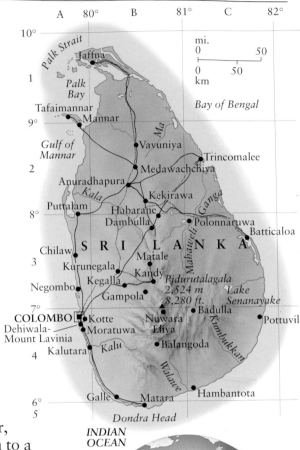

◄ *The paddy-fields of Balangoda are surrounded by coconut palms. Beyond them forested slopes rise into the clouds. The forests are home to monkeys, elephants and parakeets, while crocodiles lurk in the rivers. The rich beauty of this island inspired its name, Sri Lanka, which means shining land.*

FACTS AND FIGURES

Area: 65,610 sq km
Population: 17,619,000
Capital: Colombo (588,000)
Other major cities: Dehiwala-Mount Lavinia (174,000), Moratuwa (135,000)
Highest point: Pidurutalagala (2,524 m)
Official languages: Sinhalese, Tamil

Main religions: Buddhism, Hinduism, Christianity, Islam
Currency: Sri Lankan rupee
Main exports: Textiles, clothes, tea, gems, rubber, coconut products
Government: Multi-party republic
Per capita GNP: US $540

▲ At Polonnaruwa in central Sri Lanka an ancient statue of Buddha sits in calm meditation. The statue has been carved out of a single slab of granite. People leave flowers and rice cakes at its feet.

▲ A young woman goes shopping in the town of Jaffna. She wears the uniform of a Tamil Tiger, the guerrilla army that challenges the rule of the Sinhalese government.

▶ An elephant is dressed for a festival in Kandy. Elephants play an important part in Sri Lankan life. They take part in religious processions and work in timber yards, where they are trained to carry logs with their trunks.

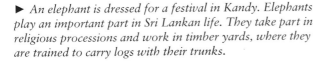

MYANMAR (BURMA)

▼ A Myanmar boy studies a holy book. Dressed in a monk's robe, he is one of many boys sent to monasteries to learn the teachings of the Buddha.

Myanmar was called Burma until 1989. It is rimmed by forest-clad mountains that surround the broad valley of the Ayeyarwady River. Most of the population lives in the delta of this great river, where the houses are built on stilts to protect them from floods and wild animals. The delta is covered with paddy-fields. Rice farming is the major occupation of the Myanmar people, but minority groups such as the Chin people live in the hills, where they survive by hunting and fishing.

The ancestors of today's population migrated down the Ayeyarwady River from Tibet and China, settling in the area from around 3000BC. Over the centuries various empires held power in these lands. In the 1800s the British moved in and from 1885 until 1937 Burma was part of Britain's Indian empire. Some years after full independence in 1948, the country began a period of military rule. The army closed Burma's borders to the outside world, taking over schools and the running of newspapers. When people protested, many were shot or imprisoned. Meanwhile, rural areas were overrun by guerrillas. Some were led by warlords who traded in the illegal drug opium. In 1990 the country was in crisis and an election was called. The opposition party won, but their leader, Aung San Suu Kyi, was imprisoned by the military who continued in power.

Myanmar has rich natural resources of oil, gas and precious gems and in the 1990s it began to open up to foreign trade. However, some nations still refuse to deal with a government that does not respect human rights.

HTAMIN LE THOKE
Htamin le thoke consists of small dishes of leftovers such as rice, onions, potatoes, noodles and spinach. Tamarind juice is poured over the top. This juice comes from the pods of the tamarind tree, which contain a reddish sweet and sour pulp.

► Ruined Buddhist temples rise from the plain at the ancient capital of Pagan. Founded in AD849, the City of a Thousand Temples covered a vast area. It was partially destroyed by a Mongol army in 1287.

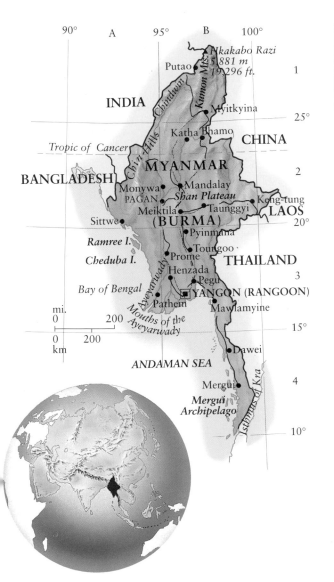

90° A 95° B 100°

Hkakabo Razi
5,881 m
Putao *19,296 ft.*

1

INDIA

Kumon Mts.

Myitkyina

25°

Chindwin

Katha Bhamo

Tropic of Cancer

CHINA

Chin Hills

MYANMAR

2

BANGLADESH

Monywa Mandalay
PAGAN *Shan Plateau*
Meiktila Taunggyi
Keng-tung

LAOS

Sittwe

(BURMA)

20°

Pyinmana

Ramree I.

Toungoo

Cheduba I.

Prome

Henzada

THAILAND

Bay of Bengal

Pegu

3

Ayeyarwady

Pathein YANGON (RANGOON)

mi.
0   200

Pathein

Mawlamyine

Mouths of the
Ayeyarwady

15°

0   200
km

ANDAMAN SEA

Dawei

Mergui

4

Mergui
Archipelago

10°

Isthmus of Kra

FACTS AND FIGURES

Area: 676,580 sq km	**Main religions:**
Population: 44,613,000	Buddhism, Christianity,
Capital: Yangon	Islam
(Rangoon) (2,459,000)	**Currency:** Kyat
Other major city:	**Main exports:** Teak, rice,
Mandalay (533,000)	pulses, beans, rubber
Highest point:	**Government:**
Hkakabo Razi (5,881 m)	Military regime
Official language:	**Per capita GNP:**
Myanmar	Est. under US $700

▲ *This floating market on Lake Inle, just south of Taunggyi, sells rice, fish, fruit and vegetables. The produce is grown by local farmers. Until 1990 all farming was controlled by the government. Today farmers are free to choose which crops they grow.*

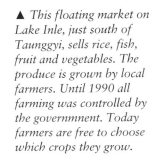

THAILAND

Thailand (formerly Siam) stretches eastwards from the fertile basin of the Ping Chao Phraya River across much of Southeast Asia. It is a land of paddy-fields, mountains and tropical beaches.

The Thais are descended from peoples who migrated from southern China between AD200 and 1100. From the 1300s to the 1500s Thailand fought wars with the Burmese, Malays and Cambodians, but unlike its neighbours it was never a colony of a European power. The Thais founded a kingdom with its capital at Bangkok in 1782. Descendants of the original royal family still rule today, but since 1932 real power has been with the government. Modern Thailand has seen periods of military rule and political unrest. An elected coalition government was set up in the 1990s.

Many Chinese, Indians and Malays live in Thailand as well as the native Thais. From 1970 to 1973 the country also became home to a million refugees from the Vietnam War.

Thailand's economy depends mostly on agriculture and many people live by fishing or farming. The forests produce valuable teak, but the government banned tree-felling in the late 1980s. This was because large-scale felling had led to mudslides that killed hundreds of people. Manufacturing thrives in the cities and industry is bringing increased wealth to Thailand. Tourism is also growing.

FACTS AND FIGURES
Area: 513,120 sq km
Population: 58,584,000
Capital: Bangkok (5,876,000)
Other major city: Chiang Mai (165,000)
Highest point: Inthanon Mt (2,595 m)
Official language: Thai
Main religions: Buddhism, Islam
Currency: Baht
Main exports: Rice, tapioca, manufactured products, machinery
Government: Monarchy, military rule
Per capita GNP: US $1,840

KICK BOXING
Kick boxing originated in Thailand and its popularity has now spread to other parts of the world. In this gruelling sport fighters use gloved hands, bare feet, elbows and knees. The loser often ends up unconscious. There are about 100,000 kick boxers in Thailand, both amateur and professional.

▼ *Strange limestone outcrops, like this one off Phuket Island, rise steeply from the waters around Thailand's coast.*

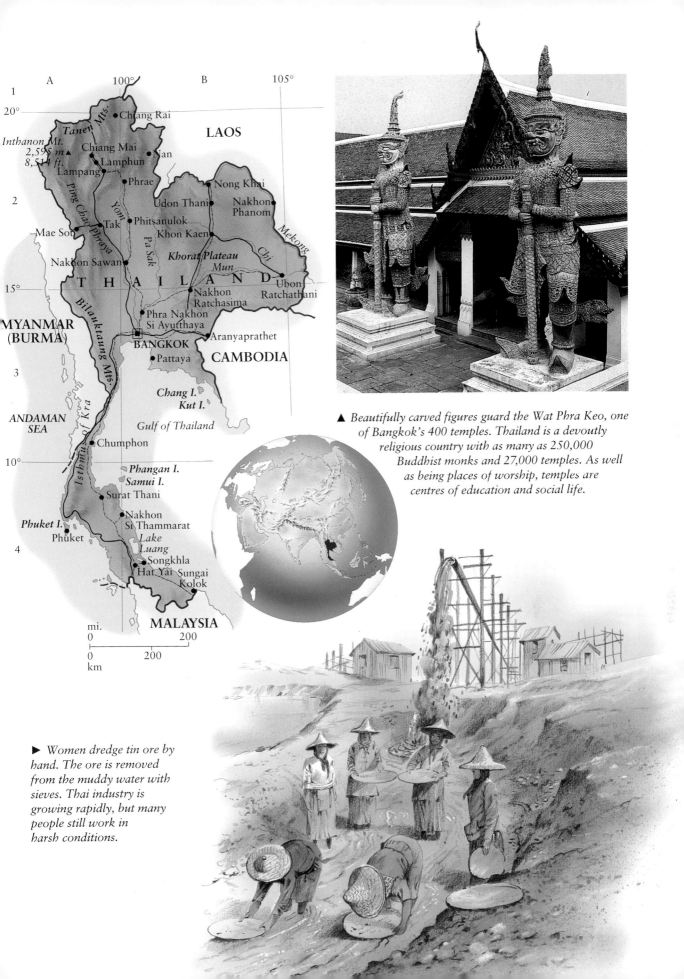

Map labels

1
A
100° B
105°
20°

Chiang Rai

Tanen Mts.

LAOS

Inthanon Mt.
2,595 m ▲
8,514 ft.
Chiang Mai
Nan
Lamphun
Lampang

Ping Chao Phraya
Phrae
Nong Khai

2
Udon Thani
Nakhon
Phanom

Yom
Tak
Phitsanulok

Mae Sot
Khon Kaen

Pa Sak
Mun
Chi

Nakhon Sawan
Khorat Plateau

T H A I L A N D

15°
Nakhon
Ratchasima
Ubon
Ratchathani

Phra Nakhon
Si Ayutthaya

MYANMAR
(BURMA)
Bilanktaung Mts.
BANGKOK
Pattaya
Aranyaprathet
CAMBODIA

3

Chang I.
Kut I.

ANDAMAN
SEA
Gulf of Thailand

Chumphon

10°
Phangan I.
Samui I.

Surat Thani

Phuket I.
Phuket
Nakhon
Si Thammarat
Lake
Luang

4
Songkhla
Hat Yai Sungai
Kolok

MALAYSIA

mi.
0   200
0   200
km

▲ Beautifully carved figures guard the Wat Phra Keo, one
of Bangkok's 400 temples. Thailand is a devoutly
religious country with as many as 250,000
Buddhist monks and 27,000 temples. As well
as being places of worship, temples are
centres of education and social life.

► Women dredge tin ore by
hand. The ore is removed
from the muddy water with
sieves. Thai industry is
growing rapidly, but many
people still work in
harsh conditions.

CAMBODIA

Cambodia is a land of low plains and forested hills. It has a warm, tropical climate, fertile soil and plentiful monsoon rains, which make it ideal rice-growing country. Most of Cambodia's population lives in farming villages and works in paddy-fields.

Nine out of ten Cambodians belong to the Khmer people. Between the 800s and the 1300s the Khmer built up a great empire across much of Southeast Asia, with its capital at Angkor. By the 1400s Khmer power had weakened and a Thai army captured Angkor in 1431. A small Khmer kingdom existed until the 1800s. Cambodia was ruled by the French from 1863 to 1953, apart from five years of Japanese occupation during World War II.

During the Vietnam War (1957-1975) Cambodia tried to remain neutral. However, bitter fighting between US troops and Vietnamese communists spilled across the border. There were years of fighting before the Khmer Rouge, a political party led by Pol Pot, seized power in 1975. This new dictatorship forced town-dwellers to farm the land and millions of people died of hunger and disease or were murdered. Both industry and farming collapsed.

In 1978 Vietnam invaded Cambodia and helped to overthrow the Khmer Rouge government. Unrest continued as the Khmer Rouge fought against the new Vietnamese-backed government. Democratic elections were held in 1993 and the monarchy was restored, but the Khmer Rouge continued their efforts to regain power.

FACTS AND FIGURES
Area: 181,040 sq km
Population: 9,308,000
Capital: Phnom Penh (800,000)
Other major city: Battambang (45,000)
Highest point: Phnom Aural (1,813 m)
Official language: Khmer
Main religions: Buddhism, Islam
Currency: Riel
Main exports: Rubber, rice, pepper, timber
Government: Constitutional monarchy
Per capita GNP: Est. under US $700

▼ *This poster was put up in Phnom Penh by the Khmer Rouge, who ruled the country from 1975 to 1978. It shows an ideal state with happy farm workers. In reality Khmer Rouge rule was very brutal.*

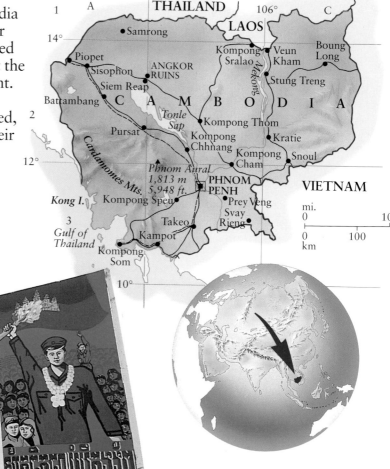

▲ These single-storey houses, at a village near Siem Reap, are typical rural homes. They are built on stilts because flooding is common across Cambodia. Their walls may be made of bamboo, timber planks or palm leaves.

▲ A smiling god looks out from the tower of the Bayon, a monument at the centre of the ancient capital of Angkor. This city was once the biggest in the world. Its temple, called a wat, is the largest religious building ever recorded.

◀ In the capital's rush hour traffic passengers are crowded onto a rickshaw drawn by a motorcycle. Bicycles and motorcycles are the most popular forms of transport. Few Cambodians can afford cars.

475

LAOS

Laos lies at the heart of Southeast Asia. Much of it is steep and rugged mountain country cloaked in dense forests. The majority of the population are farmers living along the fertile plains of the Mekong River. They cultivate maize, rice, coffee and tobacco. Others work in the forests, which yield valuable woods such as teak. Trained elephants are used in these forests to move tree trunks. The few industries in Laos include tin refining and making footwear. Another source of income is hydroelectric power, which is generated by a dam on the Mekong River and sold to Thailand.

From the 1400s to the 1700s Laos was a powerful state known as Lan Xang, the Kingdom of a Million Elephants. It later split into separate kingdoms. In 1893 the area came under French rule, joining with its neighbours to make up French Indo-China. During the 1950s French rule in Southeast Asia collapsed and northern Laos was invaded by communist rebels called the Pathet Lao. In the 1960s and 1970s the bitter fighting of the Vietnam War spilled over into Laos. When the Vietnam War ended in 1975 the Pathet Lao set up a new communist republic in Laos. Today the government of the country is strongly influenced by the policies of the Vietnamese communists.

FACTS AND FIGURES

Area: 236,800 sq km
Population: 4,605,000
Capital: Vientiane (378,000)
Other major cities: Savannakhet (51,000), Pakxé (45,000)
Highest point: Mt Bia (2,820 m)
Official language: Lao
Main religions: Buddhism, traditional beliefs
Currency: Kip
Main exports: Timber, electricity, coffee, tin
Government: People's republic
Per capita GNP: US $250

▼ *Buddha Park lies about 20 kilometres from the centre of Vientiane. The grounds contain many Hindu as well as Buddhist sculptures. This site was built in the 1950s to honour both of these religions and their philosophies.*

CHINA

MYANMAR (BURMA)

Phongsali

Ban Houayxay

Xam Nua

Mekong

Louangphrabang

Xieng Khouane

Mt. Bia
▲2,820 m
9,251 ft.

L A O S

Nape

VIENTIANE

THAILAND

VIETNAM

Muang Khammouan

Savannakhet

Saravan

Pakxé

Attopu

Khong

CAMBODIA

mi.
0 — 100
0 — 100
km

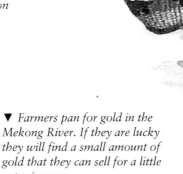

▼ A village woman carries baskets full of raw cotton. Cotton grows well in Laos's humid tropical climate and is one of the country's most important crops. Farmers either sell it or use it to make clothes for themselves.

▲ The small town and river port of Louangphrabang lies in the valley of the Mekong River. This region has an extremely dry climate. However, the land in the river valley is very fertile and crops such as rice and maize grow there. Louangphrabang has many Buddhist temples. One of these, on a hill called Phu Si, is said to have been built on the site of a footprint made by Buddha.

▼ Farmers pan for gold in the Mekong River. If they are lucky they will find a small amount of gold that they can sell for a little extra income.

477

VIETNAM

Most Vietnamese are rice farmers living in the deltas of the Red River and the Mekong River. There, and on the narrow coastal plain, the climate is hot and humid. It is cooler in the forested mountains inland, where bamboo and cinnamon are grown.

The French colonized Vietnam between the 1860s and 1880s. They developed rubber plantations and built factories in the cities. French rule ended in 1954 when communist guerrillas took over the north and the country was split into North Vietnam and South Vietnam. When communists tried to take over South Vietnam as well, North and South went to war. In 1965 the United States of America joined forces with the South against the communist North. The fighting got more intense and turned into a major war. The government of South Vietnam was overthrown in 1975. The US troops left and the country became one again in 1976. Vietnam's economy suffered greatly as a result of the war and the political isolation that the war caused. However, much has been done to repair the damage. Tourism has developed steadily, as has trade with countries such as Japan and Singapore.

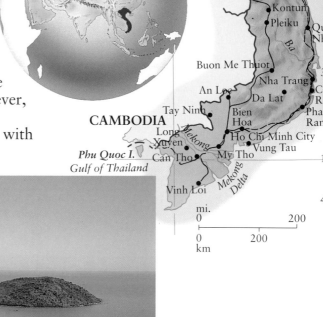

◄ This stretch of beautiful coastline near Da Nang will soon be lined with hotels. Many are being built with US money. Tourism is increasingly important and Vietnam is aiming to attract around three million tourists each year.

FACTS AND FIGURES

Area: 329,560 sq km

Population: 70,902,000

Capital: Hanoi (1,089,000)

Other major city: Ho Chi Minh City (3,170,000)

Highest point: Fan Si Pan (3,143 m)

Official language: Vietnamese

Main religions: Taoism, Buddhism, Christianity

Currency: Dong

Main exports: Coal, agricultural products including rice, rubber, iron

Government: One-party socialist republic

Per capita GNP: Est. under US $700

▼ *Farm workers wash carrots in the Mekong River. They wear traditional straw hats to shade themselves from the tropical sun.*

▲ *Followers of the Cao Dai religion celebrate mass in the Great Temple at Tay Ninh, southwest of An Loc. Their beliefs mix Islam, Christianity, Buddhism and Taoism. Cao Dai has its own saints, including Joan of Arc from France and the British statesman Sir Winston Churchill.*

◄ *A Vietnamese army officer opens a trap door leading to underground tunnels. During the Vietnam War (1957-1975) the communists dug this maze of secret tunnels. Over 16,000 communists lived underground and attacked the US troops from their hiding places.*

CHINA *Introduction*

China occupies about one fifth of the Asian continent. This colossal country has the largest population in the world. Each day about 50,000 babies are born here. In order to provide food for such large numbers of people, every scrap of fertile land has to be cultivated.

The river plains of eastern China have been farmed for thousands of years and great industrial cities have grown up in this region. Fewer people live in the more remote areas of the north and west, which include barren deserts and high mountains.

China has one of the world's greatest and most ancient civilizations, with a written history that stretches back 3,500 years. Among its many inventions are paper, silk and gunpowder.

In the course of this century China has experienced many changes. After more than 2,000 years as an empire, the country became a republic in 1911. Following an uprising in 1949, China became a communist state.

During the 1990s a transformation has taken place in China's major cities. Their narrow streets and low houses have been replaced by multi-lane highways and high-rise buildings. In contrast, life has altered little in many rural areas for centuries. Most people are farmers and use traditional methods to cultivate rice on the terraced paddy-fields.

▼ *The Imperial Palace is one of many palaces in the Imperial City at the centre of Beijing. In the days of the emperors ordinary Chinese people were not allowed to step inside its high walls. This is why it became known as the Forbidden City. Today many of the buildings are preserved as museums, which anyone can visit.*

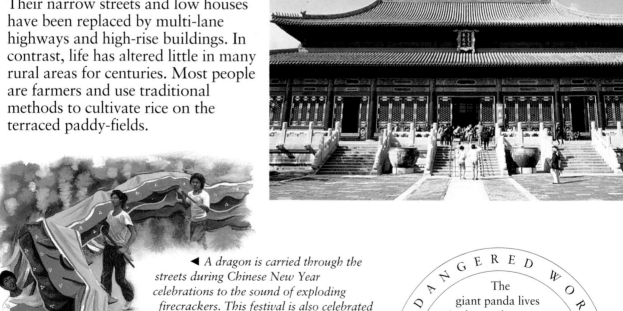

◄ *A dragon is carried through the streets during Chinese New Year celebrations to the sound of exploding firecrackers. This festival is also celebrated in many overseas cities where people of Chinese descent have settled.*

ENDANGERED WORLD

The giant panda lives in the southwestern bamboo forests. Its future is threatened by the loss of this habitat and poaching.

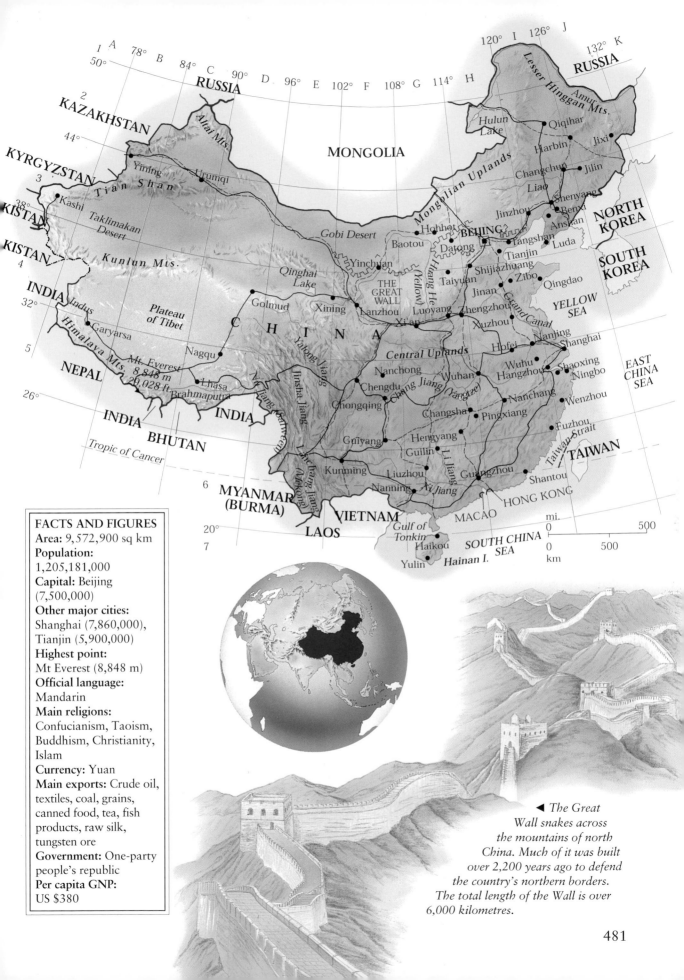

Map labels (longitude markers): 1 A, 78° B, 84° C, 90° D, 96° E, 102° F, 108° G, 114° H, 120° I, 126° J, 132° K

2, 44°, 3, 38°, 4, 32°, 5, 26°, 6, 20°, 7
50°

RUSSIA

KAZAKHSTAN

KYRGYZSTAN

Altai Mts.

Yining · Urumqi

MONGOLIA

RUSSIA

Lesser Hinggan Mts.

Amur

Hulun Lake · Qiqihar · Jixi

Harbin

Changchun · Jilin

Liao

Shenyang · Benxi

Jinzhou

NORTH KOREA

Anshan

Tian Shan

KISTAN

Kashi

Taklimakan Desert

Kunlun Mts.

INDIA

Indus

Himalaya Mts.

NEPAL

Garyarsa

Nagqu

Mt. Everest 8,848 m 29,028 ft

Lhasa

Brahmaputra

INDIA

BHUTAN

Tropic of Cancer

Gobi Desert

Mongolian Uplands

Hohhot

Baotou

Yinchuan

Qinghai Lake

Golmud

Xining

Plateau of Tibet

C H I N A

Yalong Jiang

Jinsha Jiang

Lancang Jiang (Mekong)

Nu Jiang (Salween)

MYANMAR (BURMA)

Beijing

Datong

THE GREAT WALL

Huang He (Yellow)

Taiyuan

Lanzhou

Xi'an

Luoyang

Zhengzhou

Tangshan

Tianjin

Shijiazhuang

Zibo

Jinan

Xuzhou

Grand Canal

Qingdao

YELLOW SEA

SOUTH KOREA

Luda

Central Uplands

Nanchong

Chengdu

Chongqing

Wuhan

Chang Jiang (Yangtze)

Hefei

Nanjing

Shanghai

Wuhu

Hangzhou

Shaoxing

Ningbo

Nanchang

Wenzhou

EAST CHINA SEA

Changsha

Pingxiang

Hengyang

Guiyang

Guilin

Li Jiang

Kunming

Liuzhou

Nanning

Xi Jiang

Guangzhou

Fuzhou

Taiwan Strait

TAIWAN

Shantou

HONG KONG

MACAO

VIETNAM

LAOS

Gulf of Tonkin

Haikou

Yulin

SOUTH CHINA SEA

Hainan I.

mi.
0 — 500
km
0 — 500

FACTS AND FIGURES

Area: 9,572,900 sq km

Population: 1,205,181,000

Capital: Beijing (7,500,000)

Other major cities: Shanghai (7,860,000), Tianjin (5,900,000)

Highest point: Mt Everest (8,848 m)

Official language: Mandarin

Main religions: Confucianism, Taoism, Buddhism, Christianity, Islam

Currency: Yuan

Main exports: Crude oil, textiles, coal, grains, canned food, tea, fish products, raw silk, tungsten ore

Government: One-party people's republic

Per capita GNP: US $380

◀ *The Great Wall snakes across the mountains of north China. Much of it was built over 2,200 years ago to defend the country's northern borders. The total length of the Wall is over 6,000 kilometres.*

481

CHINA *Geography*

China is the third largest country in the world after Canada and Russia. Its enormous landscape is full of contrasts and the climate also varies from region to region. The far northeast has long, frozen winters and short, very hot summers. The land there is forested and rich in minerals, including coal. Extreme temperatures are also typical of the northern areas where grasslands border the wilderness of the Gobi Desert. In the summer the desert's daytime temperatures may be as high as 38 degrees centigrade, but they can fall to minus 34 degrees centigrade at night.

The central northern provinces are crossed by the Huang He (Yellow River). This broad, winding waterway is greatly feared for its terrible floods. However, rich mud from the Huang He has also made this a fertile farming region. Another river, the Chang Jiang (Yangtze), cuts straight across the centre of the country. It is China's most important trade route and the world's third longest river, flowing 6,300 kilometres from the western mountains into the Yellow Sea.

China's western regions take in the high, bleak Plateau of Tibet, which has often been called the 'Roof of the World'. To the south, the country is bordered by the Himalayan mountain range. The world's highest mountain, Mount Everest, is found there. The Himalayas descend into foothills in southwest China, where the climate is warm for much of the year. Both southern China and the nearby island of Hainan are hot and humid, with monsoon winds bringing heavy rain from May to October each year.

▼ *Yellow fields of rape brighten the rocky landscape near Xining. This is an arid region with harsh winters. The land needs to be irrigated in order to give crops any chance of survival.*

▶ *The peaceful waters of Karakoli Lake may be seen from the Karakoram highway, a rough road that carves its way through the remote mountain ranges of the far west. The Karakoram highway links China with north Pakistan.*

◄ This Tibetan farming village lies on high ground, ringed by barren mountains. The summers here are short, but barley and vegetables can be grown before the winter sets in. Tibet is a remote region with an average of only two people per square kilometre.

► This village clings to a mountain peak in the Huangshan (Yellow Mountains), south of Wuhu. The misty summits, waterfalls and forests in this area attract walkers from all over China.

▼ Pillars of limestone rock rise from the Li Jiang at Yangshuo (Bright Moon), to the south of Guilin. This strange and beautiful landscape is a very popular destination for tourists.

CHINA *Economy*

So many people live in China and the country is so vast that it could have one of the most powerful economies in the world. It has rich resources in the form of coal, oil, iron, tungsten, timber, hydroelectric power and fisheries. Its fertile farmland could provide enough food for almost the whole population. China also has a centuries-old tradition of commerce, craft skills and invention. It was Chinese scientists who brought the world the compass, fine porcelain, printing and even banknotes.

Despite all these advantages, the country has always had economic problems and still does today. Many of its minerals are found only in remote, inaccessible regions. There are large areas of barren wilderness where it is too dry to grow crops without irrigation. Also, expanding cities and factories have tended to spread across precious farmland. The people of China provide a large workforce, but as the population continues to grow more resources are needed for food, healthcare and education.

China's farmers and workers had suffered centuries of injustice and poverty when the communists came to power in 1949 and attempted to improve their lives. In the 1950s and 1960s heavy industry was developed under state control. Farming was organized in units called communes, where villagers combined their land and farmed it together. From the 1980s free markets, private ownership and foreign investment were permitted. The economy boomed and Chinese goods were soon flooding into countries all over the world. Industrial modernization has continued and services such as up-to-date telecommunications networks have been developed.

▼ *Trees are felled in snowy Heilongjiang, China's northernmost province. Logging is a key industry in China and this province supplies timber to the rest of the nation. Heilongjiang also has reserves of oil, coal, iron ore and gold.*

▶ *Cotton is sorted at a farming village, while cobs of maize dry out in the sun. Before 1978 farming was organized by village groups called communes. Today farming families have to provide a certain amount of crops for state organizations, but they can sell any extra produce at the local market.*

ECONOMIC SURVEY

Farming: China is the world leader in rice and tobacco. Barley, cotton, peanuts, maize, millet, tea, sorghum and wheat are also grown in large quantities. More pigs are reared here than in any other country. Cattle, sheep, goats and camels are also kept.

Mining: Antimony, coal, iron ore, mercury, natural gas, oil, tin and tungsten are produced.

Industry: Iron and steel, clothes, machinery, fertilizers, vehicles, ships and toys are manufactured. Heavy industry has caused serious air and water pollution in some areas. Most industries are state-run, but foreign investment is now encouraged in special economic zones in the east of the country.

▶ *Paddy-fields have been carved into the hillside around the southern city of Guiyang. Rice is China's most important crop and it is mostly grown to the south of the Chang Jiang (Yangtze River).*

▶ *A woman weaves an elaborate design in silk on a hand loom. Beautiful silk like this has been produced in China for thousands of years. In ancient times the way in which silk thread was made from silk worms was a closely guarded secret.*

◀ *The iron and steel works in Baoshan, near the great port of Shanghai, is the most modern in China. It was completed in 1990 and produces high quality steel. China's steel industry is one of the largest and fastest growing in the world.*

CHINA *People*

CHOW MEIN

Chow Mein is a very popular main course in southern China. It consists of egg-noodles that are stir-fried with vegetables and shredded chicken or other meat. The dish is flavoured with sesame oil. Chinese cooking varies greatly from region to region, but noodles are eaten almost everywhere.

There have been many changes to Chinese life since this country became communist in 1949. The standard of living for most people has risen, especially for city-dwellers. Family life, traditionally very important to the Chinese, has altered greatly. Several generations once lived in the same household, but today families are much smaller. Religious practices have also changed. For centuries religion was a central part of Chinese life and many faiths existed side by side. When the communists came to power, however, religious belief was discouraged. This was especially true during the 1960s, a period known as the Cultural Revolution. Today the government is more tolerant and people are free to worship once more.

Like so many generations before them, more than three quarters of all Chinese people live in villages and farm the land. Wheat, maize and rice are the main crops in the north, while rice and tea are important in the south. Chinese farmers currently produce enough food for the country's growing population. However, the government is worried that there will soon be too many people to feed. Laws have been passed to try to reduce the birth rate. People are not allowed to marry until they are in their early twenties and couples are encouraged to have only one or two children.

Most people live in the crowded eastern part of the country where the land is suitable for growing crops. Over 90 percent of the population belongs to the Han group, who were originally a northern people. The rest is made up of over 50 other peoples including Mongols, Tibetans, Uygurs, Kazakhs and Koreans.

◄ *Performers wear beautiful silk costumes and colourful make-up to star in a Beijing opera. This is China's most popular form of drama and includes traditional stories of princes and princesses, heroes and villains. The stories are acted out with speech, songs and dances, while musicians play off-stage.*

◄ People crowd Nanjing Road in Shanghai, China's largest city. Scenes such as this are an everyday sight because of the huge population. Streets, apartment blocks and public transport are noisy and busy, day and night.

WUSHU

This girl is performing wushu, one of the ancient Chinese martial arts. Wushu is a traditional form of exercise that develops both the mind and the body. There are many different kinds of wushu, which may make use of bare hands, swords or sticks. The most well-known form is kung fu.

SPEAK MANDARIN

Hello – 你好
(*nee - how*)

Goodbye – 再见
(*dzeh - jien*)

Please – 请 (*ching*)

Thank you – 谢谢
(*shay - shay*)

Yes – 是 (*shi*)

No – 不是 (*boo - shi*)

► A Buddhist priest, or lama, chants from the scriptures during a funeral. The body is being cremated in the open air. Buddhism came to China from India before AD100. Over the centuries it has played an important part in Chinese history.

487

CHINA *History*

About 9,000 years ago Stone Age peoples were hunting and fishing along China's river valleys. By 5000BC rice was cultivated here. Great civilizations developed from about 2100BC. In 221BC Shi Huangdi, the first emperor of China and founder of the Qin dynasty, came to the throne.

Defended to the north by its Great Wall, China soon ruled a vast empire with trading links as far away as ancient Rome. Despite long wars during the Middle Ages, China also saw a golden age of the arts, technology and exploration. The Mongols invaded China in the AD1200s and brought a highly civilized way of life with them. Their leader, Kublai Khan, founded a new capital at Khanbalik (modern Beijing). The years of Mongol rule, known as the Yuan dynasty, were followed by the rule of the southern Chinese (the Ming) and by Manchus from the northeast (the Qing).

During the 1800s China's power was challenged by European trading nations such as Britain. This led to wars and civil unrest inside China. In 1841 the Treaty of Nanking gave Britain the island of Hong Kong, which became a major trading port. (Hong Kong returned to Chinese rule in 1997.) During the early part of this century the rule of the emperors collapsed. Years of chaos followed, marked by a struggle for power between communists and nationalists, as well as an invasion by Japan. By 1948 the communists, under Mao Zedong, controlled the whole country. After Mao's death in 1976 China began to make economic reforms and increase trade with foreign countries.

▼ *A Chinese scientist called Zhang Heng invented this seismograph (earthquake recorder) in* AD132. *When an earthquake took place, a bronze ball would drop into the mouth of one of the frogs. This showed the general direction of the earth tremor.*

▶ *In 1989 students gathered in Beijing's Tiananmen Square, demanding more freedom in China. This peaceful scene was soon shattered when troops fired into the crowd. Hundreds of demonstrators were killed. The protest movement was broken up and many of its leaders fled abroad. The political system did not change.*

TAIWAN

FACTS AND FIGURES

Area: 36,180 sq km
Population: 20,800,000
Capital: Taipei
(2,720,000)
Other major city:
Kaohsiung (1,400,000)
Highest point: Yu Shan
(3,997 m)
Official language:
Mandarin
Main religions: Taoism,
Buddhism
Currency:
New Taiwan dollar
Main exports: Electrical
equipment, machinery,
textiles, metal goods,
plastic goods
Government:
Multi-party republic
Per capita GNP:
Est. US $10,200

The island of Taiwan is separated from mainland China by the narrow Formosa Strait. Formosa, which means beautiful one, was the name given to Taiwan by Portuguese sailors in the 1500s.

Much of the island is mountainous and forested. There is lower ground in the west, where most people live. The moist, tropical climate enables farmers to grow crops such as rice and pineapples, although only about a quarter of Taiwan can be farmed. Tuna, shrimps and other fish are caught off the coast. Industry has become very important to the country's economy. Roughly one third of Taiwan's workers now have jobs in manufacturing and its factories export goods all over the world.

From the 1700s onwards the island was settled by China, but in 1895 it was taken over by Japan. Taiwan returned to Chinese rule in 1945 after the Japanese were defeated in World War II. In 1949 China became communist. The defeated leaders fled to Taiwan and set up a government there. Anti-communist Taiwan represented all of China at the United Nations (UN) until 1971. Communist China then became internationally recognized. Taiwan lost its membership of the UN in 1971 and now it has official diplomatic ties with only a few countries. Tensions between Taiwan and China lessened during the early 1990s.

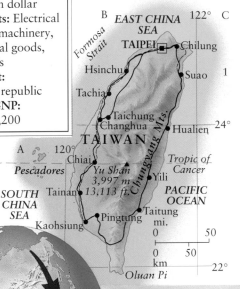

▶ *Dragon dancers celebrate Taiwan's Double Tenth National Day on October 10th each year. It is a national holiday and is marked by huge parades and firework displays.*

MONGOLIA

▼ *People celebrate May Day on the streets of the capital, Ulan Bator. Over a quarter of the population lives in this industrial town, which lies on the railway line from Moscow in Russia to Beijing in China.*

The mountains, plateaus and lakes of northern Mongolia give way to the Gobi Desert in the south, an empty wasteland of sand and gravel. Mongolia bakes in the summer and freezes under snow in the winter. By tradition the Mongolians are herders. Mounted on stocky ponies, they cross these bleak landscapes in search of pasture for their sheep, cattle and Bactrian camels. Today, encouraged by the government, many have settled to work on livestock farms. Others have jobs in factories or mining.

In the Middle Ages Mongolia built one of the largest empires the world has ever seen. Under their leader, Genghis Khan, Mongolian horsemen conquered land from Central Europe to the Far East. This empire soon fragmented and Mongolia was swallowed up by China. In 1924 most of it became a communist republic that was strongly influenced by the Soviet Union (SU). The communists took property away from the country's noble families and destroyed Buddhist monasteries. They also began to develop industry. With the collapse of the SU in 1991 Mongolia developed as a multi-party democracy. It faced economic problems without Soviet support. At the same time many Mongolians took new pride in their history and religious traditions, which had been suppressed since the 1920s.

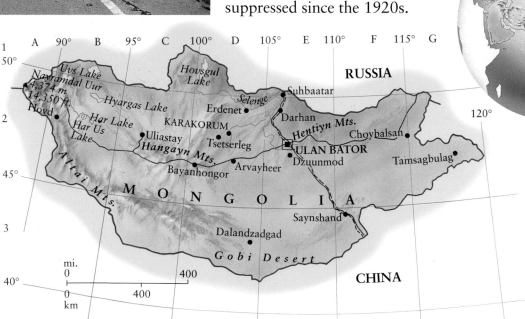

◀ Wrapped up warmly against the bitter winds, a Mongolian woman brings in the hay with a horse-drawn cart. The carts behind are hauled by Bactrian (two-humped) camels. Beyond the fields stretch the bare hills of this sparsely populated country. Very little land in Mongolia is suitable for cultivation. Even so, the government is encouraging farmers to grow grain, potatoes and vegetables to reduce imports of food.

FACTS AND FIGURES
Area: 1,566,500 sq km
Population: 2,371,000
Capital: Ulan Bator (575,000)
Other major cities: Darhan (87,000), Erdenet (59,000)
Highest point: Nayramdal Uur (4,374 m)
Official language: Mongolian
Main religion: Buddhism
Currency: Tugrik
Main exports: Minerals, meat, hides, wool, livestock, consumer goods
Government: Multi-party republic
Per capita GNP: Est. US $700-3,000

▶ In some areas of Mongolia people live in traditional gers. These round tents have a frame of wooden slats covered with thick felt. Some gers are set up permanently outside towns to solve local housing shortages.

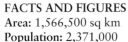

◀ Horse racing is popular throughout Mongolia. Boys and girls as young as five take part in races all over the country. There are large prizes of cash, silk cloth or household goods. Jockeys usually retire around the age of 12.

NORTH KOREA

North Korea is a communist country where all the factories and farms, even the cars, are owned by the government. The farms are collectives, which means that work and profits are shared. Until the 1950s most North Koreans worked as farmers, but today more than half the country's workers have jobs in factories. Most of them cycle to work, leaving their babies in state-run nurseries.

North Korea and South Korea formed a single country for hundreds of years, from the 1300s until this century. Between 1910 and 1945 Korea was occupied by Japan. This ended when Japan was defeated in World War II. After this the country divided into two, with troops from the United States of America (USA) occupying southern Korea and Soviet Union (SU) troops occupying the north. In 1950 North Korea, backed by the SU and China, attacked South Korea, which was supported by the USA. Millions were killed or made homeless. The war ended in 1953, but tensions between North and South Korea continued. This was despite peace talks from the 1970s onwards. Under communist rule, reunification with South Korea still appears unlikely in the short term.

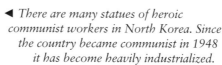

◄ *There are many statues of heroic communist workers in North Korea. Since the country became communist in 1948 it has become heavily industrialized.*

FACTS AND FIGURES

Area: 122,760 sq km
Population: 23,054,000
Capital: Pyongyang (2,640,000)
Other major cities: Hamhung (775,000), Chongjin (755,000)
Highest point: Paektu Mt (2,744 m)
Official language: Korean
Main religions: Traditional beliefs, Ch'ondogyo (combines elements of Roman Catholicism, Buddhism, Confucianism, Taoism, and Shamanism)
Currency: Won
Main exports: Coal, iron, copper, textiles
Government: Single-party republic
Per capita GNP: Est. US $700-3,000

SOUTH KOREA

FACTS AND FIGURES
Area: 99,270 sq km
Population: 44,056,000
Capital: Seoul
(10,628,000)
Other major city:
Pusan (3,798,000)
Highest point:
Halla Mt (1,950 m)
**Official
language:**
Korean
Main religions:
Buddhism,
Christianity
Currency: Won
Main exports:
Machinery and
electronic equipment,
transport equipment,
manufactured products,
textiles, steel
Government:
Multi-party republic
Per capita GNP:
US $6,790

South Korea has one of the world's fastest-growing economies. Its industry is highly developed, with factories producing computers and electrical goods, optical equipment and heavy machinery. The country's rapid industrial growth has taken place since the 1950s. Before this its economy was largely based on agriculture. Unlike North Korea, South Korea is not a communist country and most of its industry is privately owned.

In the south and west of South Korea cool, forested mountains descend to a fertile plain. Farmers grow rice in these humid coastal regions and fish are caught in the Yellow Sea.

South and North Korea were once a single country, but divided in 1945. At the end of World War II the United States of America took control of South Korea, while the Soviet Union held North Korea. From 1950 to 1953 war raged between the two. After the war South Korea saw political turmoil and harsh military rule. However, during the late 1980s this began to change. South Korea became a multi-party republic and held democratic elections.

▶ *This palace in Seoul was the centre of the Choson kingdom. Korea (North and South) was called Choson from 1392 until 1910, when it was invaded by Japan.*

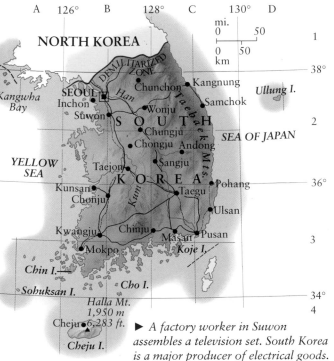

▶ *A factory worker in Suwon assembles a television set. South Korea is a major producer of electrical goods.*

JAPAN *Introduction*

The Japanese call their island country Nippon, meaning 'the source of the sun'. This ancient name explains the red disc on their national flag, which represents the rising sun.

For many centuries emperors have been heads of state in Japan. Until the 1900s Japanese emperors claimed to be divine, believing they were descended from the gods. The amount of power held by the emperor has varied greatly from one era to another. Today the emperor's role and duties are ceremonial only. The government of the nation is carried out by a democratic parliament called the Diet.

The Diet is made up of an elected House of Representatives and a House of Councillors. Political parties include socialists, liberals and communists, but since 1955 the most successful party has been the conservative Liberal Democratic Party.

Modern Japan is world-famous for its powerful business corporations and advanced electronic technology. However, this is still a land in which traditions and ancient customs are held in the highest respect. Among the busy streets and bright lights of the capital visitors can glimpse the past in the form of temples and shrines. They can also take part in chanoyu, a 500-year-old tea-drinking ceremony that honours courtesy and hospitality.

Most of the population lives in crowded cities on the coastal plains. Farther inland, much of the country is covered with forested hills and mountains. The land is both beautiful and unstable. There are many volcanoes and earthquakes are common throughout Japan.

FACTS AND FIGURES
Area: 377,730 sq km
Population: 124,959,000
Capital: Tokyo (7,976,000)
Other major cities: Yokohama (3,233,000), Osaka (2,506,000), Nagoya (2,098,000)
Highest point: Mt Fuji (3,776 m)
Official language: Japanese
Main religions: Shintoism, Buddhism
Currency: Yen
Main exports: Machinery, vehicles, ships, electronic equipment, steel, chemicals, textiles
Government: Constitutional monarchy
Per capita GNP: US $28,220

ENDANGERED WORLD

Hunting of the red-crowned Manchurian crane led to its near-extinction. Now it is protected.

▶ *The active volcano Sakurajima towers behind the modern city of Kagoshima. Over half a million people live in this sea port, which is on the southern island of Kyushu. It is famous for its textiles and pottery.*

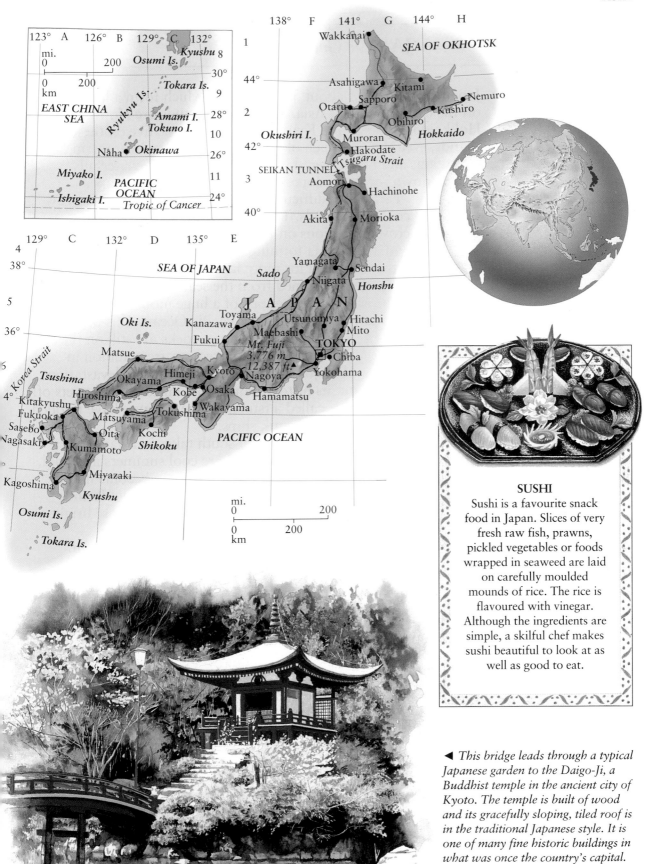

Inset map (East China Sea region):

123° A 126° B 129° C 132°

mi.
0   200
km
0   200

Kyushu 8

Osumi Is.

30°

Tokara Is. 9

Ryukyu Is.

EAST CHINA
SEA

Amami I. 28°
Tokuno I.

10

Naha • *Okinawa*

26°

Miyako I.

PACIFIC
OCEAN

11

Ishigaki I. 24°

Tropic of Cancer

Main map (Japan):

138° F   141° G   144° H

1   Wakkanai   SEA OF OKHOTSK

44°   Asahigawa   Kitami

Otaru Sapporo   Nemuro
2   Kushiro
Muroran Obihiro
42°   *Hokkaido*
Okushiri I.

Hakodate
SEIKAN TUNNEL   *Tsugaru Strait*
3   Aomori

Hachinohe

40°   Akita   Morioka

4   Yamagata   Sendai
38°   *Honshu*
SEA OF JAPAN   Niigata
Sado

5   J A P A N

Toyama   Utsunomiya Hitachi
Kanazawa   Mito
36°   Fukui Maebashi TOKYO
Mt. Fuji   Chiba
3,776 m Nagoya Yokohama
12,387 ft▲
Kyoto
Himeji Osaka Hamamatsu
Okayama Kobe
Hiroshima   Wakayama
Matsuyama Tokushima
Oita Kochi
Shikoku
Kumamoto   PACIFIC OCEAN
Miyazaki

Kyushu

129° C   132° D   135° E

Oki Is.

Matsue

Korea Strait
Tsushima

Kitakyushu
Fukuoka
Sasebo
Nagasaki

Kagoshima

Osumi Is.

Tokara Is.

mi.
0   200
km
0   200

SUSHI

Sushi is a favourite snack
food in Japan. Slices of very
fresh raw fish, prawns,
pickled vegetables or foods
wrapped in seaweed are laid
on carefully moulded
mounds of rice. The rice is
flavoured with vinegar.
Although the ingredients are
simple, a skilful chef makes
sushi beautiful to look at as
well as good to eat.

◀ *This bridge leads through a typical
Japanese garden to the Daigo-Ji, a
Buddhist temple in the ancient city of
Kyoto. The temple is built of wood
and its gracefully sloping, tiled roof is
in the traditional Japanese style. It is
one of many fine historic buildings in
what was once the country's capital.*

495

JAPAN *Geography*

▼ *Steam rises from hot springs at Beppu, near Oita on Kyushu. The waters are heated deep inside the volcanic rocks below. Hot springs are found all over Japan.*

Japan is made up of about 3,000 islands, which form a long chain off the eastern coast of Asia. The biggest islands are Honshu, Hokkaido, Shikoku and Kyushu. Most Japanese live on these four islands, even though much of the land is taken up by towering mountains and hills covered in forest. Streams and waterfalls tumble down the steep slopes in this spectacular landscape.

Farming is difficult everywhere except on the narrow coastal lowlands. These include some of the most crowded regions on Earth, with cities such as Tokyo and Yokohama forming huge urban areas. To help satisfy the need for more land, parts of the coastline have been reclaimed from the sea.

The islands are the tops of a huge mountain range that rises from the floor of the Pacific Ocean. This is a weak area of the Earth's crust and its rocks are still on the move. Volcanoes and earth tremors are common in Japan and major earthquakes have caused devastation throughout its history. Sometimes an earthquake sets off a huge wave called a tsunami. These waves have flooded coastal areas and sunk ships.

A journey from north to south takes in a variety of climates. In the north, there are cool summers and cold, snowy winters. Moving south, winters become milder and summers warm and humid. The Ryukyu Islands have a tropical climate. Autumn and spring are bright and sunny in much of Japan and in spring the countryside is filled with cherry and plum blossom.

▶ *Surveyors check earthquake damage to measure how far the rocks have shifted. A terrible earthquake destroyed Tokyo in 1923. During the massive earthquake of 1995 thousands died in the rubble of Japan's fifth largest city, Kobe.*

◄ *A family clears a path through a high snowdrift. Hokkaido and the northwestern part of Honshu receive heavy snowfalls in winter when bitter winds blow in from northern Russia across the Sea of Japan. Snow can last for more than six months in some areas.*

▼ *The snow-capped slopes of Mount Fuji look so peaceful that it is hard to believe this is a volcano. It last erupted in 1707. Japan's highest mountain has inspired artists for centuries. Its many shrines and temples are visited by pilgrims.*

► *Rocky headlands and stacks (pillars of rock) extend from the Oki Islands into the Sea of Japan. The Okis lie off the coast of Honshu, north of the town of Matsue. Air and sea routes link these islands to mainland Honshu.*

JAPAN *Economy*

▼ *Harvested rice is stacked for drying and threshing, as it has been for thousands of years. Modern machinery is now used to do jobs like this on many farms. Rice is the most important food in Japan and is eaten with almost every meal.*

Japan is a land of economic miracles. One miracle is the way in which land is used. Modern farming methods make it possible for the very small amount of land suitable for farming to produce large crops of rice, tea, potatoes, fruit, rapeseed and tobacco. These methods include growing specially developed strains of crops that give high yields and using fertilizers and pesticides. Modern equipment, such as specialized rice-planting machines, also means that far fewer people are needed to work the land.

Another miracle is how these small islands have become one of the world's greatest industrial powers. They have achieved this with hard work and investment in new technology. Japan has to import huge amounts of oil and raw materials for industry, but it produces more cars and colour televisions than any other country. Japanese firms have opened factories all over the world. However, they do face increasing competition from other Asian countries, such as South Korea.

Some people believe that Japan is so successful because the working conditions here promote hard work. Large companies often demand great loyalty from their staff. Employees may be expected to sing a special company song, wear the company uniform and join in physical exercise sessions each day. In return, many employers organize their workers' holidays, healthcare and housing.

▶ *A farm-worker drives a machine that sprays fruit trees with pesticides. This will help to produce a larger fruit crop. Japanese farms use modern technology to grow a large amount of food on a small area of land.*

◄ *These modern offices in Tokyo's Ginza district are typical of the city's many business buildings. Tokyo is the centre of the Japanese business world. It also has one of the world's leading stock exchanges. Twenty-six percent of the Japanese labour force work in finance and commerce.*

ECONOMIC SURVEY

Farming: Japanese farmers produce much of the nation's food, despite the shortage of farmland. About half the usable land is used for growing rice. Fruit and vegetables are also grown. Dairy production is increasing.

Fishing: Japan, with China and Russia, is one of the leading fishing nations. It accounts for about one tenth of the world catch.

Mining: Japan has only a small quantity of minerals. It has to import most raw materials and fuel.

Industry: Manufactured goods include electronic products, cameras, watches, machinery, cars, ships, silk and other textiles, plastics and ceramics. It is also a major producer of steel and chemicals.

▲ *Automated robotic machinery saves time and money on the car production line. Japanese firms were among the first to introduce modern methods of assembling vehicles. Manufacturers such as Nissan and Honda are famous all over the world.*

► *Octopuses are sold at the Tokyo fish market. Japan is one of the world's leading fishing nations and fish is an important part of the Japanese diet. Large catches include mackerel, herring and tuna.*

499

JAPAN *People*

The first inhabitants of Japan may have been the Ainu, who were pale-skinned people. Descendants of these people now live on Hokkaido and a few of Japan's northern islands. Some Ainu villages survive, but many Ainu have intermarried with the Japanese. Most of today's Japanese are descended from peoples who migrated to the country from the Asian mainland thousands of years ago. Minority groups include Koreans and Chinese.

Today the majority of the Japanese live in the crowded cities on Honshu Island. They may work in offices, banks, factories or department stores and usually travel to work by train.

Before 1945 most Japanese lived in rural villages. Family units were large with several generations often sharing the same household. Now smaller families are common and many city people live in small flats. However, the old way of life has not entirely disappeared. There are still traditional Japanese houses with sliding screens and floor mats called tatami. Also, the traditional silk robe, or kimono, is still worn by men and women on special occasions.

Complicated gadgets, arcade games, computers and televisions are all a vital part of life in modern Japan, but there is a very different side to the Japanese. For centuries this has shown itself in the simple beauty of Japanese architecture, gardens, art and ceramics. A love of nature is also important. This is reflected in the ancient religion of Shinto and in Japanese forms of Buddhism. Followers of Shinto, for example, worship the spirits of trees, rocks, mountains, rivers and other forces of nature.

▼ *Decorated boats take to the sea during a festival at Shiogama, northeast of Sendai. They are followed out by the local fishing fleet. Every summer the boats sail to a nearby island, where they give thanks for their catch.*

▼ *These girls are practising a custom called* nagashi-bina. *This takes place during the Shinto festival,* Hinamatsuri. *Paper dolls or flowers are floated down a river and this is believed to take a person's troubles away.*

KENDO
Kendo students attempt to score points by striking their opponent in a ritual contest. Kendo is a martial art that aims to develop self-control. It is a form of fencing that uses long bamboo staves instead of swords. The fighters wear long, black skirts, padded gloves, light armour and helmets. Kendo has its origins in the training of the samurai, the warriors of ancient Japan. The modern form was developed in the late 1700s.

▼ *The temple of the Golden Pavilion is one of the most famous buildings in Japan and stands amid beautiful landscaped gardens in the historic city of Kyoto. It was built in 1394 as a Buddhist temple. Today it contains a rich collection of art treasures and is more of a tourist attraction than a place of worship. Buddhism is the main religion in Japan with more than 90 million followers.*

▲ *This tiny sleeping space is a room in a Japanese invention called a capsule hotel. The sleeping capsules were designed to save space and are cheaper than rooms in ordinary city centre hotels. They are often used by business people on short city visits.*

SPEAK JAPANESE

Hello – こんにちは
(kon - nich - ee - wah)

Goodbye – さようなら
(sah - yoh - nah - rah)

Please – どうぞ
(doh - zoh)

Thank you – ありがとう
(a - ree - gah - toh)

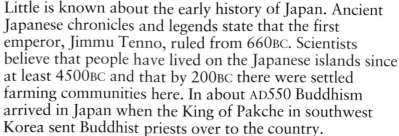

JAPAN *History*

▼ *A famous samurai (warrior) of the 1300s, called Shirafuji Hikoshichiro, watches enemy ships burning. Japanese samurai wore elaborate armour and helmets and carried some of the deadliest swords ever made. This picture, by Utagawa Kuniyoshi, was painted in about 1840.*

Little is known about the early history of Japan. Ancient Japanese chronicles and legends state that the first emperor, Jimmu Tenno, ruled from 660BC. Scientists believe that people have lived on the Japanese islands since at least 4500BC and that by 200BC there were settled farming communities here. In about AD550 Buddhism arrived in Japan when the King of Pakche in southwest Korea sent Buddhist priests over to the country.

The Middle Ages was a time of turmoil. Power passed from the emperors to warlords called shoguns. Sometimes there were civil wars between rival bands of warriors called samurai. In 1603 Tokugawa Ieyasu became shogun of a united Japan. By this time Portuguese traders and Christian priests had arrived, but Ieyasu expelled them. After this Japan closed its doors to the outside world until the 1850s. In 1867 the ruling shogan was overthrown and power returned to the royal family, with Mutsuhito as emperor. A period of rapid industrialization followed.

During the 1930s the Japanese army invaded China. Then, during World War II, it overran most of Southeast Asia and the Pacific islands. Japan was defeated in World War II and occupied by United States forces until 1952. Since the 1950s the war-damaged economy has grown rapidly and today Japan is a major world economic power.

▶ *Himeji castle was one of many splendid buildings erected by the samurai general Toyotomi Hideyoshi (1536-1598). Hideyoshi was the son of a humble woodcutter, but rose to fame as a ruthless warrior. For the last ten years of his life he was the most powerful man in Japan.*

◀ *Actors wearing traditional costume and make-up perform a Japanese kabuki play. Kabuki is a type of drama that was developed during the late 1600s. It is still performed in Japan today. Men play female roles as well as male parts and act out exciting historical stories to the sound of music and singing. Japanese forms of drama have existed for centuries and in modern times they have had an important influence on world theatre.*

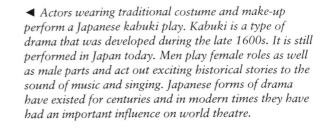

COMMODORE PERRY

On March 31, 1854 Commodore Matthew Perry, commander of a United States squadron, signed a treaty with the Japanese emperor. As a result Japanese ports were opened to Western traders for the first time in over 200 years. Many Japanese people disapproved of Western influences, but in 1868 the emperor decided to modernize Japan. Western ideas and technology were rapidly introduced. By the 1900s Japan had become a major world power.

◀ *This children's memorial stands in the Peace Park in Hiroshima. World War II ended in 1945 when the United States of America dropped atomic bombs on Hiroshima and Nagasaki. Both cities were utterly destroyed. Over 155,000 civilians were killed in Hiroshima alone.*

SINGAPORE

Over 50 islands make up the Republic of Singapore. The largest is linked by road across the Johor Strait to mainland Malaysia. Many of the smaller islands are uninhabited. Singapore lies just above the Equator, so the climate is hot and sticky. It is a country that cannot produce enough food for its overcrowded population and water supplies have to be piped in from Malaysia. Yet Singapore has become one of the richest countries in Southeast Asia. Almost all its rainforest has been cut down to make room for homes, businesses or parks and there is very little agricultural land. The country's wealth is based on shipping, banking, electronics manufacture and international trade.

▲ *Singapore City is a busy port built on the south coast of the largest island. More than 90 percent of the population lives in this crowded city of towering blocks of flats and gleaming high-rise offices.*

There is a legend that Singapore was founded by a Malay prince who landed on the island in 1299. Over the centuries many Chinese people have settled here to work and trade. Modern Singapore was founded in 1819 by Sir Stamford Raffles, who was a trader with the British East India Company. Britain ruled the country from 1858 until 1959. In 1963 Singapore became part of the Federation of Malaysia, but it withdrew to become a separate nation in 1965. The people live under very strict laws. Any religion can be practised, but gambling and even chewing gum are forbidden. There are also huge fines for dropping litter. Personal freedom is limited, but the crime rate is the lowest in the world.

FACTS AND FIGURES

Area: 640 sq km
Population: 2,874,000
Capital: Singapore City
Highest point:
Timah Hill (177 m)
Official languages:
English, Mandarin, Malay, Tamil
Main religions:
Buddhism, Taoism, Islam, Christianity, Hinduism
Currency:
Singaporean dollar
Main exports:
Machinery, vehicles, electronic equipment, petroleum products, rubber, chemicals, food, clothes
Government:
Multi-party republic
Per capita GNP:
US $15,750

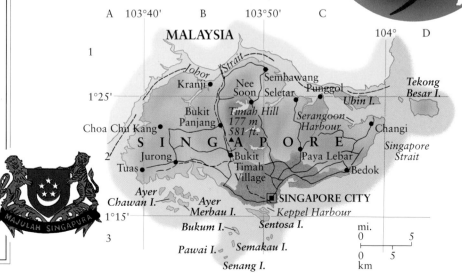

BRUNEI

The Sultan of Brunei is the richest ruler in the world. His small nation on the north coast of the island of Borneo has become vastly wealthy since oil was discovered here in the 1920s. Reserves of oil and natural gas are now beginning to run low, so the government is encouraging development of banana and rubber plantations as well as other private businesses.

Seventy percent of the mostly Malay and Chinese population lives in cities. Over half work for the government, some in the state-owned oil industry. Education and healthcare are paid for by the government from oil profits and the standard of living is high. Even those who choose to live in traditional longhouses (wooden buildings that house dozens of families) often own luxury cars. Others live in water villages called kampongs, where houses are built on stilts and boats ferry people around.

Brunei once ruled a large area of Borneo, but over the centuries its power was weakened by piracy and lawlessness. From the 1800s it was a protectorate of Britain, so Britain looked after its foreign affairs and defence in return for shipping rights. Brunei received full independence from Britain in 1984.

▲ Children celebrate Brunei's Independence Day by parading in colourful costumes and waving butterfly wands or paper flowers. Flag-waving crowds gather near the Royal Palace to greet the Sultan (king and ruler).

FACTS AND FIGURES

Area: 5,770 sq km
Population: 276,000
Capital: Bandar Seri Begawan (46,000)
Other major city: Seria (21,000)
Highest point: Pagon (1,850 m)
Official language: Malay
Main religions: Islam, Buddhism, Christianity
Currency: Bruneian dollar (ringgit)
Main exports: Crude oil, liquefied natural gas, petroleum products
Government: Absolute monarchy
Per capita GNP: Est. over US $8,000

► The Belait River winds through dense green tropical rainforest. Three quarters of Brunei is forested and home to large, brilliantly coloured butterflies, flying squirrels, hornbills, monkeys, wild pigs and deer.

A   115°   B

1 SOUTH CHINA SEA

Brunei Bay

Muara

Muara Besar I.

5°

BANDAR SERI BEGAWAN

Tutong

Brunei

Bangar

114°

Seria

Tutong

Temburong

Kuala Belait

Kampong Badas

B   R   U   N   E   I

Kampong Belai

Kampong Labi

Belait

2

Pagon 1,850 m 6,069 ft.

mi.
0   20

0   20
km

MALAYSIA

PHILIPPINES

The Philippines is a nation of more than 7,000 islands. The larger islands are mountainous, with over 30 active volcanoes. Much of the land is clad in forest where bamboo, orchids and a huge variety of trees grow. Unfortunately, the country's rich resources have been ruthlessly plundered. Logging companies have felled millions of hardwood trees, causing problems with soil erosion.

About half the population earn their living by farming, growing rice, sugar-cane, pineapples, bananas and coconuts. The economy is mainly based on agriculture and timber production. However, the manufacturing industry is expanding, producing clothing and processed foods. Fishing provides much of the islanders' food.

The Filipinos are descended from Malays who arrived around 3000BC. The Spanish colonized the islands in 1565 and named them after their king, Philip II. After the Spanish-American War of 1898 the United States of America (USA) bought the Philippines for 20 million dollars. Independence came in 1946 and under the military dictatorship of President Marcos the islands experienced censorship, corruption and poverty. Many left to work abroad. Marcos was overthrown in 1986 and fled to the USA. Today's government is working to solve the environmental and economic problems that he left behind.

▼ The rice terraces at Banawe in northern Luzon were dug out 2,000 years ago. Channels and pipes bring water to the seedlings. In the 1960s an organization based in the Philippines developed a new rice plant to double the grain yield. This has increased rice production, but the fertility of much of the land has been ruined by the new pesticides used.

◄ Workers make wicker furniture in a rattan factory. Masks are worn to protect them against the dust and splinters. Rattan is a cane that is taken from the stem of the rattan palm, a type of climbing plant. This palm is common throughout Southeast Asia. Because it is strong, flexible and long-lasting, rattan is ideal for a wide range of uses, from baskets to ships' cables.

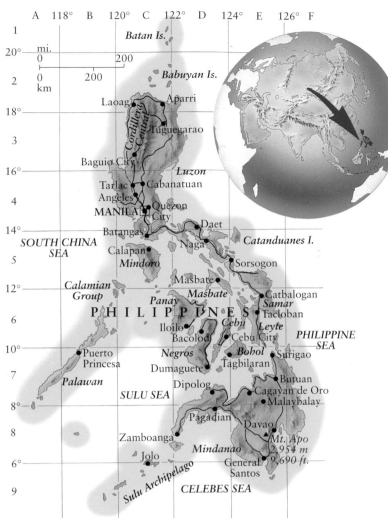

Batan Is.

mi.
0   200

0   200
km

Babuyan Is.

Laoag
Aparri

Túguegarao

Cordillera Central

Baguio City

Luzon

Tarlac
Cabanatuan

Angeles

Quezon
MANILA City

Batangas
Daet

Naga
Catanduanes I.

**SOUTH CHINA
SEA**

Calapan
Mindoro

Sorsogon

*Calamian
Group*

Masbate

Masbate
Catbalogan

Panay
Samar

P H I L I P P I N E S
Tacloban

Iloilo
Cebu
Leyte

Bacolod
Cebu City
**PHILIPPINE
SEA**

Puerto
Princesa
Negros
Bohol
Surigao

Dumaguete
Tagbilaran

Palawan
Dipolog
Butuan

Cagayan de Oro

SULU SEA
Malaybalay

Pagadian

Zamboanga
Davao

Mindanao
▲ *Mt. Apo
2,954 m
9,690 ft.*

Jolo
General
Santos

Sulu Archipelago
CELEBES SEA

FACTS AND FIGURES

Area: 300,000 sq km
Population: 65,649,000
Capital: Manila
(1,599,000)
Other major cities:
Quezon City
(1,667,000),
Davao (850,000)
Highest point:
Mt Apo (2,954 m)
Official languages:
Filipino, English
Main religions:
Christianity, Islam
Currency:
Philippino peso
Main exports: Clothes,
electronic equipment,
coconut oil, timber
Government:
Multi-party republic
Per capita GNP:
US $770

▼ *The streets of Manila are crowded
with jeepneys. These are jeeps fitted
with a long coach body, which is
painted and decorated in bright
colours. The jeepneys are used for
public transport.*

SPEAK FILIPINO

Hello – Kumusta
(koo - moos - tah)

Goodbye – Paalam
(pah - ah - lahm)

Please – Paki *(par - kee)*

Thank you – Salamat
(sah - lah - maht)

Yes – Oo *(o'o)*

No – Hindi *(hin - day)*

MALAYSIA

Malaysia is a green land with mountains cloaked in dripping rainforest, huge plantations of rubber and oil palms and sandy beaches. One thousand different orchids bloom in the tropical forests, which are home to many wild animals and plants. Wildlife such as tigers, leopards and rhinoceroses are protected in several national parks.

Many Malays live in farm villages strung out along the roads between paddy-fields and pineapple fields. Along the coast most people fish for a living. A large Chinese minority (35 percent of the population) lives mainly in the cities. This is an Islamic country, but all kinds of religions are practised. Malaysia is dotted with Buddhist and Taoist temples as well as Christian churches.

The ancestors of today's Malays came from China around 2000BC. Many made their living by fishing or piracy along the swampy coast of Sarawak. The Arabs, Portuguese and Dutch all occupied this area before the British seized control in the early 1800s. After the Japanese occupation, during World War II, communist guerrillas launched a terrorist campaign against the British. Independence came to Peninsular Malaysia in 1957 and by 1963 the eastern territories had joined the new nation.

Malaysia has a democratic system of government. Since independence it has achieved economic success with rubber, tin and oil. Timber-felling has laid waste great areas of forest, but is now controlled by the government.

CHICKEN SATAY
Small pieces of chicken or other meat are skewered and barbecued over glowing charcoal to make satay. The dish is flavoured with spices and served with a hot peanut sauce. It is often eaten with sliced cucumbers, onions and *ketupat* (boiled rice wrapped in palm leaves).

▼ *In the capital, Kuala Lumpur, modern architecture contrasts with the traditional Islamic style of the government buildings. This city is the centre of business and industry.*

SPEAK MALAYSIAN

Goodbye – Selamat tinggal
*(se - lah - mat **tin** – gahl)*

Please – Tolong *(**toh** - long)*

Thank you – Terima kasih
*(te - ree - mah **kah** – see)*

Yes – Ya *(yah)*

No – Tidak *(tee - **dak**)*

◀ Tea is grown in the Cameron Highlands, to the east of Ipoh. This cool hill country is surrounded by green mountains and sparkling waterfalls. The fertile soil supports fruit, vegetables and flowers, which are grown in large market gardens.

FACTS AND FIGURES

Area: 329,580 sq km
Population: 19,239,000
Capital: Kuala Lumpur (938,000)
Other major cities:
Ipoh (301,000),
George Town (251,000),
Johor Bahru (250,000)
Highest point:
Mt Kinabalu (4,094 m)
Official language:
Bahasa Malaysia
Main religions: Islam, Buddhism
Currency: Malaysian dollar (ringgit)
Main exports: Rubber, palm-oil, timber, petroleum, tin, electronic equipment
Government: Federal constitutional monarchy
Per capita GNP:
US $2,790

▶ A man practices kite-flying. This sport is a popular pastime among villagers in the east of the country. Competitions are held to see whose kite can fly the highest or stay in the air for the longest time.

INDONESIA *Introduction*

Indonesia is the world's biggest archipelago, a long chain of more than 13,600 mountainous islands. Their many active volcanoes form part of the danger zone that geologists call the Pacific Ring of Fire. Indonesia has seen some of the most violent volcanic eruptions ever recorded. However, people continue to live close to the smouldering volcanoes because their ash makes the soil rich and fertile.

The islands are watered by monsoon rains and warmed by humid, tropical heat. There are clear lakes, coastal mangrove swamps and some of the most spectacular rainforests on Earth. Rafflesia, the world's largest flower, blooms here. This bright orange flower is up to a metre across with an unpleasant stench that attracts insects. Many rare animals such as tigers and rhinoceroses roam through the forests, but logging companies are destroying their habitat to fell precious hardwoods such as teak and ebony.

The economy is based on agriculture, forestry and fishing. Indonesia has one of the world's largest fishing industries. Its seas yield plentiful supplies of mackerel, anchovies and tuna, as well as pearls and shells. Spices such as pepper, cloves and nutmeg once made this country an important destination for traders and pirates and they are still grown today. Other products include rubber, coffee, tobacco and petroleum. The country's mines yield copper, nickel and coal. Reserves of oil have been exploited since the 1960s and income from this has helped to boost the economy.

▼ *Men on the island of Bali perform the Hindu temple ceremony known as Kecak. The word* Kecak *means monkey. The men fall into a trance in which they believe they are possessed by the spirits of monkeys. This island is famous for its Hindu ceremonies and festivals.*

◄ *These distinctive wooden houses have curved roofs with tall gable ends that make them look like boats. The houses are built on stilts and are entered by carved steps and beautifully decorated doorways. They are the homes of the Toraja peoples, who live in central Sulawesi.*

FACTS AND FIGURES

Area: 1,919,440 sq km
Population:
189,136,000
Capital: Jakarta
(6,504,000)
Other major city:
Surabaya (2,028,000)
Highest point:
Puncak Jaya (5,030 m)
Official language:
Bahasa Indonesia
Main religions: Islam,
Christianity, Hinduism,
Buddhism
Currency: Rupiah
Main exports: Oil,
liquefied natural gas,
timber, rubber, coffee
Government:
Multi-party republic
Per capita GNP:
US $670

▶ *The bright lights of
Jakarta surround the
Independence Monument
on the densely populated
island of Java. Jakarta, the
capital of Indonesia, is the
centre of its industry,
government and business.*

◀ *Workers bundle dried
stems of rice into sheaves
during a harvest. Rice is
the main food crop in
Indonesia. The high levels
of production have made
it one of the world's
leading rice producers.*

E N D A N G E R E D W O R L D
Orang utans are
endangered because
people are destroying
the forests where they live.

511

INDONESIA *People and History*

The first people to live on these islands probably came from mainland Malaysia. From about AD700 the islands' wealth of spices and their position on important trade routes drew seafarers from many other nations. Indian merchants brought the Hindu religion and Arab traders brought Islam.

During the 1500s and 1600s the Portuguese and British struggled to control the islands, but it was the Dutch who succeeded in 1798. Under Dutch rule the islands developed a sense of unity. They fought for independence and declared Indonesia a republic in 1949. Since independence the army has been a powerful political force. It squashed a communist rebellion in 1965 and has occupied East Timor since a rebellion in 1975. Two leaders have dominated recent history. The independent nation's first president was Achmed Sukarno, who gave Indonesians a real feeling of national identity. A military coup led to a takeover by General Suharto, who has encouraged greater political and religious tolerance.

▲ *Schoolchildren play outside their classroom in Bali. Many learn English and Bahasa Indonesia, the national language, at school. Children usually speak their island's regional dialect at home.*

A fast-growing population means that poverty is a problem on the islands, even though the government has increased food production, industry and healthcare. Most Indonesians are farmers and some practise slash-and-burn agriculture, cutting down the forest and moving on once the soil is exhausted. Indonesian life is filled with ancient traditions drawn from Buddhist, Hindu and folk sources even though most people are Muslims. Each island follows its own customs.

◀ *This Buddhist temple, on the island of Java, has 72 bell-shaped structures that contain stone sculptures of Buddha. Buddhism was once an important religion on the islands, but few Indonesians follow it today.*

Tropic of Cancer

Equator

AUSTRALIA
AND THE
PACIFIC ISLANDS

Tropic of Capricorn

Antarctic Circle

AUSTRALIA AND THE PACIFIC ISLANDS *Geography*

Australia is the world's smallest continent as well as a country. Australia, New Guinea, New Zealand and thousands of smaller Pacific islands are sometimes known collectively as Oceania. This whole area includes vast parts of the Pacific Ocean. It stretches from the warm seas north of the Equator all the way south to the chilly waters around Antarctica.

Australia is a hot continent with a climate that changes from tropical in the north to temperate in the south. Low plateaus and plains, dotted with large expanses of dry scrub and desert, take up much of the land. The largest fertile regions lie close to the east coast where there are mountains and lush rainforests.

New Guinea is hot, rainy and mountainous with swampy plains along its coasts. New Zealand, which is made up of two main islands, is also mountainous. Parts of North Island are hot and wet, while South Island has a cool, wet climate. Clustered around South Island's peaks are a number of icy glaciers.

Most of the Pacific islands were formed by fierce volcanic activity, which continues today. Some islands, such as New Caledonia and the main islands of the Fiji, Samoa and Vanuatu groups, have steep, forested mountains. Others are low islands formed from corals, the tiny warm-water creatures that live inside chalky skeletons. Volcanoes that have collapsed into the water may be capped by a ring of coral growth called an atoll. This is made from coral remains that have built up around underwater mountains and ridges until they stick out above the sea. Both mountainous and low islands are often surrounded by coral reefs.

▼ *Uluru, also called Ayers Rock, is a huge single piece of sandstone that lies in Australia's Northern Territory. Iron in the rock has rusted to give an orange colour that glows in the setting sun.*

▼ *Water cascades down a sheer cliff at the Taura Falls in Samoa. Many of the larger Pacific islands are very mountainous, rising to steep, forested volcanic peaks.*

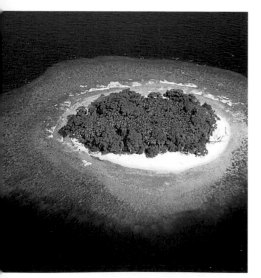

◀ *This little island is part of Papua New Guinea. It is typical of the many low-lying coral islands in the Pacific Ocean. Sand and soil support plants such as coconut palms on top of a coral reef. Colourful fish and seaweeds live in the warm waters around the reef.*

◄ *Melting snow from Mount Ruapehu, an active volcano, fills Crater Lake on the North Island of New Zealand. Like many other Pacific islands, New Zealand was formed by the movement of volcanoes under the sea.*

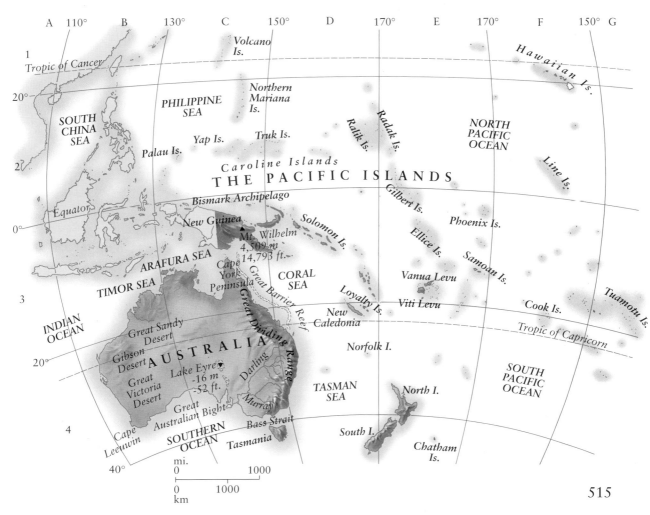

515

AUSTRALIA AND THE PACIFIC ISLANDS *Political*

▼ *Australia's Parliament House in Canberra was built in 1988. Australia is a federation of six states and two territories. It has a federal government that decides national issues and separate state governments.*

The countries bordering the Pacific Ocean and the island groups scattered across it are coping with rapid political and economic changes. The Melanesian, Micronesian and Polynesian peoples of the Pacific islands have recently founded independent states, although some islands and island groups remain overseas territories of France, the United States of America, Australia or New Zealand. In Australia, the Aboriginal peoples, who have lived there since ancient times, are demanding a right to lands that were taken from them by European settlers in the 1800s. The Maoris, a Polynesian people who were the first to settle New Zealand, are asking for similar rights.

Australia and New Zealand's traditional trading links with the United Kingdom have weakened and both countries have become important powers in the Pacific region. They are benefiting from a booming trade with Southeast Asia, Japan, China and the United States of America.

Many smaller island nations have had to rely on larger countries to help them develop. Years of colonial rule brought mining and the testing of nuclear weapons to some islands, causing serious environmental damage. Today tourism and industry create some wealth, but often disrupt the traditional, self-sufficent way of life based on fishing and farming. However, the modern communications that make tourism possible have also helped to bring together remote communities such as Pacific islanders, Australian farmers and villagers in the mountains of Papua New Guinea.

▶ *A French nuclear weapon is tested on Mururoa Atoll in the South Pacific in 1966. The United Kingdom and the United States of America have also carried out nuclear tests on South Pacific islands.*

◄ *Samoans celebrate independence day in Apia, the capital. Samoa gained independence from New Zealand in 1962. Other islands, such as Fiji and Tonga, have become independent since then.*

KEY TO MAP
1 NAURU
2 NEW CALEDONIA (France)
3 TONGA
4 AMERICAN SAMOA (USA)
5 SAMOA

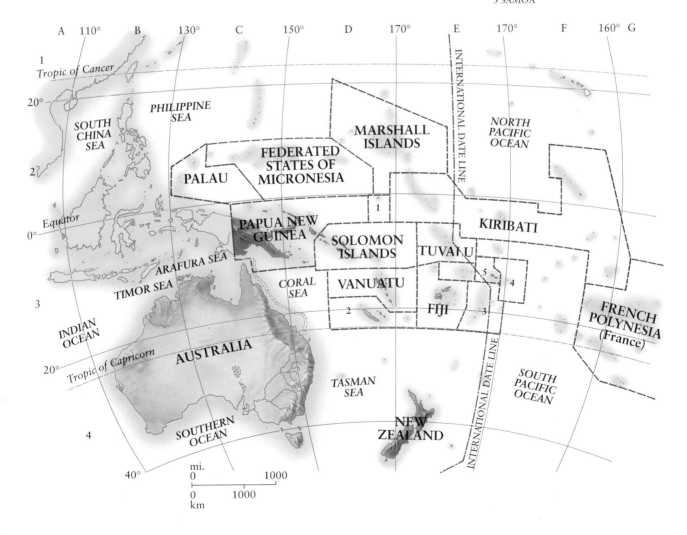

AUSTRALIA AND THE PACIFIC ISLANDS *Plants and Animals*

▼ *The tuatara is the only survivor of a group of lizard-like reptiles that lived on Earth millions of years ago. It is now found on just a few islands, which are part of New Zealand.*

The isolated position of Australia and the Pacific islands means that the wildlife is very different from the animals and plants found in Asia, Europe, Africa and the Americas. The only two mammals in the world that lay eggs, the duck-billed platypus and the echidna (a spiny anteater), are found in Australia and New Guinea. These countries are also the home of pouched animals called marsupials, which include kangaroos, wallabies, koala bears, bandicoots, possums, Tasmanian devils and wombats. Australia's many different habitats – desert, rainforest, eucalyptus woodland, muddy creeks and scrub – also provide homes for a wide range of insects, lizards, crocodiles and birds. New Zealand, however, has few native land mammals of its own. The country's varied climate and habitats support a large number of animals, such as cattle and rabbits, which have been introduced from other countries. There are numerous types of birds that are native to New Zealand, such as the flightless kakapo parrot.

Coconut groves and rainforest thrive on the Pacific islands. Turtles, crabs and seabirds from the Pacific Ocean visit the islands' coral reefs and sandy shores. All kinds of birds live on these islands, many of them known for their brilliant plumage, such as New Guinea's bird of paradise.

▼ *Kiwis leave their burrows by night to probe the forest floor for grubs and worms. To do this they have long, sensitive bills fringed with bristles. Although they are birds they cannot fly. Only three species survive and these are all in New Zealand. The government has made strict laws to protect the kiwi bird from extinction.*

▲ *The reefs of the Pacific form a magical underwater world for the diver. Reefs are home to many different types of marine life including flower-like corals. Colonies of these tiny creatures form the structure of the reef. Brightly coloured fish dart between plants, while deadly jellyfish lurk in the shadows of the corals.*

◄ *The funnel-web spider is found in Australia. As its name suggests, it spins a funnel-shaped web, which is where it lives. The bite of some funnel-webs can be fatal to humans.*

► *The Queen Alexandra's Birdwing is the largest butterfly in the world. Its wingspan can measure over 28 centimetres. These butterflies flutter in the treetops of Papua New Guinea.*

▲ *The koala is a marsupial, an animal carried in a pouch on its mother's body when very young. Koala cubs are carried on their mothers' backs after they leave the pouch.*

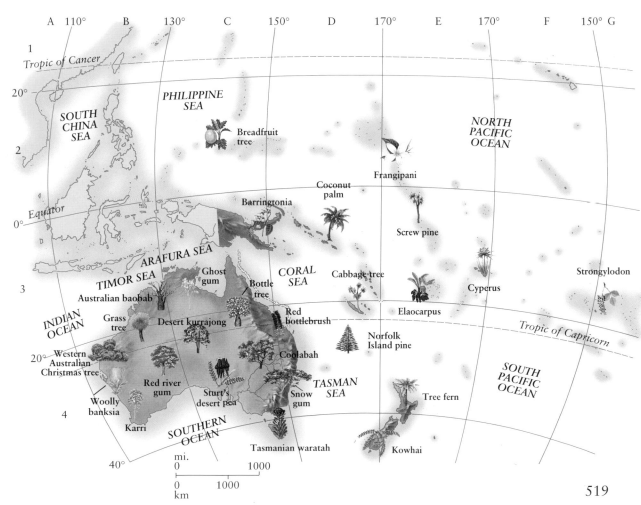

PAPUA NEW GUINEA

The country of Papua New Guinea lies on the eastern half of New Guinea, the second largest island in the world. The western half of the island is part of Indonesia. Papua New Guinea also includes many small islands, such as the Bismarck Archipelago and the northern Solomon Islands.

Papua New Guinea is a land of mountains, fast-flowing rivers and dense forests. Its fertile soils support vast plantations of coconuts, coffee, tea, palm-oil and rubber. Grassy lowlands and marshes are home to crocodiles and tortoises. Other wildlife includes giant butterflies, large flightless birds called cassowaries and marsupials such as possums.

Most people live in rural areas, often in remote valleys that are inaccessible by road. This has meant that a huge variety of customs and languages have developed – more than 700 languages are spoken. Over recent decades a network of airstrips has been built, making mountain towns and villages more accessible. Traditional ways of life are still strong in rural parts of the country, with communities growing their own food and hunting animals. However, life in the modern towns and on the huge plantations is more like urban life elsewhere in the world.

The earliest inhabitants probably reached Papua New Guinea from Asia at least 30,000 years ago. European explorers arrived in the 1500s and in the 1800s European traders and missionaries settled. Germany and Britain controlled parts of Papua New Guinea until 1920 when Australia took over. Independence came in 1975.

▲ *A villager from the Goroka area wears a mask to represent an evil spirit. These were first worn by warriors to scare enemies. Today they are worn at feasts or for tourists.*

SPEAK PIDGIN

Good morning – Moninnau
(*moh - nin - now*)

Goodbye – Lukim yu
(*look - im yoo*)

Please – Plis
(*pliss*)

Thank you – Tenku
(*tank - yoo*)

◄ *This large copper mine is on one of the islands in the Solomon group. There are extremely rich mineral deposits in Papua New Guinea. Mineral exports pay for nearly all of the country's many imports.*

FACTS AND FIGURES
Area: 462,840 sq km
Population: 3,922,000
Capital: Port Moresby
(194,000)
Other major city:
Lae (81,000)
Highest point:
Mt Wilhelm (4,509 m)
Official language:
English
Main religion:
Christianity
Currency: Kina
Main exports: Gold,
coffee, copper, timber,
cocoa, copra products
Government:
Constitutional
monarchy
Per capita GNP:
US $950

▲ *Village houses line a clearing in the forest between Port Moresby and Goroka. Villagers clear small plots of land around the village for crops such as sweet potatoes. When the soil is exhausted another plot is cultivated nearby, allowing the first patch to regain its fertility.*

UNU BONA BOROMA
Unu Bona Boroma is a dish consisting of boiled, sliced breadfruit in a sauce of fried bacon, onions and chicken stock. *Unu* means breadfruit, which is an extremely popular vegetable throughout the South Pacific.

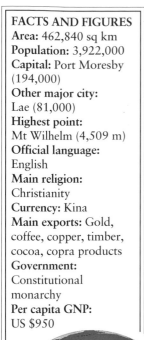

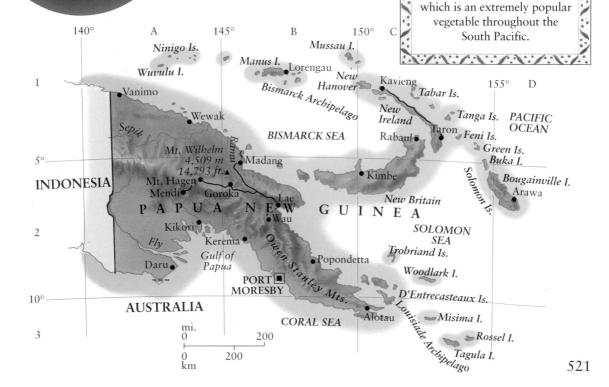

AUSTRALIA *Introduction*

FACTS AND FIGURES
Area: 7,682,300 sq km
Population: 17,662,000
Capital: Canberra
(279,000)
Other major cities:
Sydney (3,699,000),
Melbourne (3,154,000)
Highest point:
Mt Kosciusko (2,228 m)
**Official
language:**
English
Main religion:
Christianity
Currency:
Australian dollar
Main exports: Gold,
other metals and metal
ores, diamonds, coal,
meat, wool, cereals
Government:
Federal constitutional
monarchy
Per capita GNP:
US $17,070

Australia is a land of sunshine, open spaces and lively, modern cities. It is the sixth largest country in the world and the only country that is also a continent. Australia is divided into six states and two areas called territories. It includes the island of Tasmania. Each state has its own government, which controls aspects of daily life such as schools, hospitals and transport.

Despite Australia's vast size it has a relatively small population. Most Australians live on a narrow strip of land extending along the east and southeast coasts. The interior, known as the outback, is too dry and barren to support many people. Much of it is desert or scrubby grassland where it may not rain for years at a time. However, rich deposits of minerals and grazing for vast numbers of cattle and sheep make this region a major source of wealth for the country.

The first inhabitants of Australia were called the Aboriginal peoples, who originally came from Southeast Asia about 40,000 years ago. The country was discovered by Europeans in 1606, when a Dutch sea captain called Willem Jansz landed on its shores. It became a British colony in the 1700s and thousands of people who had committed crimes in Britain were given the choice of either going to prison or moving to Australia. As a result many Australians are of British ancestry and the country has maintained strong links with the United Kingdom. The head of state is the British monarch, who is represented in Australia by a governor-general. In recent years, however, a movement to make the country a republic has continued to gather strength.

ENDANGERED WORLD
The numbat lives in eucalyptus woodland in southwest Australia. It is threatened by the spread of human settlement.

▶ *The busy centre of Sydney borders its beautiful harbour. It is crossed by the steel arches of Harbour Bridge* (centre). *Sydney is Australia's largest city and an important port.*

◀ *An Aboriginal painter puts the finishing touches to a painting using the traditional materials of bark, coloured earth and charcoal. The Aboriginal peoples were the first to live in Australia and many of their paintings are influenced by ancient myths dating back 40,000 years. As well as animals and spirits, their art shows human activities such as hunting and fishing.*

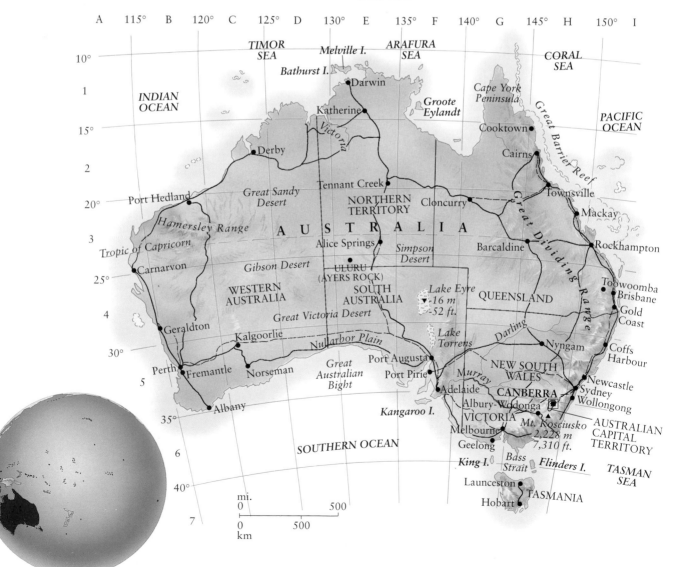

523

AUSTRALIA *Geography*

▼ *Mount Feathertop's snowy ridges and slopes rise above the peaks that stretch south from the Great Dividing Range. Much of this beautiful area is protected as a national park.*

The mostly flat country of Australia is completely surrounded by water. All the wettest, most fertile areas are concentrated along the coastline. The northern coast is tropical and humid, with lush rainforests and mangrove swamps. A narrow, fertile strip along the east and southeast coasts rises to the rocky Great Dividing Range. The highest peaks of this range are known as the Australian Alps. The Murray River begins there and winds slowly westwards for more than 2,500 kilometres.

West of the Great Dividing Range lie vast, rolling plains broken by occasional rocky hills or low mountains. The landscape includes scrub, sparse pasture and dried-out river-beds. Water from wells enables livestock to be grazed there. Beyond these plains a huge plateau covers the western two thirds of Australia. Much of this interior is harsh desert, a baking hot wilderness of sand, stone and cracked clay. However, the southwest coast enjoys warm, dry summers and moist winters. In the southeast the mountainous island of Tasmania lies about 250 kilometres off the mainland, across the stormy waters of the Bass Strait.

Australia's geographical remoteness from other countries means that a number of unique plants and animals have developed here. The best known Australian animals are the marsupials, which include kangaroos, wallabies and koalas. The commonest trees include the extremely tall evergreen eucalyptuses and the bright-flowered wattles.

▼ *Cattle graze peacefully against a backdrop of woodland and hills on the island of Tasmania. As well as rugged mountains and lakes, this island has lush forests because of the plentiful rainfall.*

◀ *Rounded domes of rock called the Olgas are found in the far south of Northern Territory. They form a cluster of about 30 boulders to the west of Uluru (Ayers Rock). These rocky outcrops tower above the sandy plain, rising to 540 metres in places.*

▶ *Partly submerged tree stumps are grouped in the shallows of the Murray River in South Australia. This extremely long waterway is fed by snow from mountains in the far southeast. It slowly winds its way through dry lands, creating creeks and lakes called billabongs. The Murray is one of the few rivers in Australia that rarely dries up.*

▶ *Australia's Great Barrier Reef is the largest coral reef in the world. It stretches for over 2,000 kilometres off the coast of Queensland. The reef has built up over millions of years. It is home to 350 different species of coral as well as thousands of fish and other marine creatures.*

AUSTRALIA *Economy*

▼ *Water is piped to the turbines that produce hydroelectric power at a power station in Victoria. This is part of the huge Snowy Mountains Scheme which harnesses water from mountain rivers to provide power and irrigation for crops.*

Most of Australia's wealth has come from farming and mining. Although much of the country is too dry for growing crops, the vast grasslands that spread across all the states are ideal for grazing large numbers of sheep and cattle. Crops such as wheat, sugar-cane and fruit are only grown on about five percent of the farmland, but this land is extremely productive because of modern farming methods. Australia's major farming exports include wool, meat and dairy products, as well as wines made from grapes grown in the south.

Since the 1800s Australia has exported large amounts of minerals, including gold, copper, silver and zinc, mainly to the United Kingdom (UK). In this century Australia has become one of the world's major mining countries. Huge deposits of bauxite (used to make aluminium), iron ore and coal were discovered in the 1950s and natural gas and oil were found in the 1960s. As well as processing minerals, Australian factories produce vehicles, textiles, chemicals and household goods. In recent years Japan and the United States of America have replaced the UK as Australia's main trading partners.

A large part of the Australian workforce is employed in service industries, such as banking, education or healthcare. The film industry is also expanding quickly and Australian television series and films have been sold around the world.

▶ *Aluminium is made at a metal-works near Gladstone, east of Port Pirie. Australia is one of the world's leading producers of bauxite, which is used in the manufacture of aluminium. The huge amounts of bauxite have helped Australia to become a rich country.*

◄ *Cattle and calves are herded into a pen at a Queensland cattle station. Queensland and New South Wales are centres of the beef cattle market. Large dairy herds are kept in Victoria.*

▼ *Workers offload sheep outside a station in the Australian outback (the interior of the country). Sheep are raised in all the states, but Western Australia and New South Wales are the main areas.*

ECONOMIC SURVEY

Farming: Farming, particularly stock rearing, is a major activity. However, it is less important than it once was in terms of employment and revenue. Australia is the world's leading wool producer, with more than 160 million sheep. It also produces lamb, beef, butter and cheese. Crops include sugar, wheat, barley, rice, bananas, apples, pineapples, oranges, grapes and vegetables.

Fishing: Main catches include shellfish, tuna, mullet and salmon.

Mining: There are large deposits of uranium, bauxite, diamonds, lead, iron ore, coal, tungsten, manganese, tin, oil and natural gas.

Industry: Service industries have grown in importance. Factory goods include steel, farm products, vehicles, chemicals, textiles and light engineering.

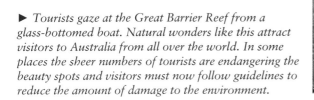

► *Tourists gaze at the Great Barrier Reef from a glass-bottomed boat. Natural wonders like this attract visitors to Australia from all over the world. In some places the sheer numbers of tourists are endangering the beauty spots and visitors must now follow guidelines to reduce the amount of damage to the environment.*

527

AUSTRALIA *People*

The Aboriginal peoples were the first to live in Australia. The word aboriginal means 'people who were there in the beginning'. They lived a nomadic life, travelling from place to place, hunting and gathering food wherever they went. Today only one and a half percent of Australia's population belongs to this ethnic group and very few live in the same way as their ancestors did. Some live in settlements in the outback while others have moved to the cities. In recent years some Aboriginal peoples have campaigned successfully for rights to the land that had been taken from them by European settlers.

Most Australians originally came from Europe. By far the greatest proportion of settlers came from Britain and Ireland, but large numbers of Greeks, Italians and Slavs also settled here. Until the 1950s the Australian way of life mirrored life in the United Kingdom. Since then it has been enriched by the traditions, customs and foods of other immigrant groups, including the Greeks and peoples of Southeast Asia and Japan. Cities such as Sydney now display an exciting mix of Asian and European cultures.

Wherever they originally came from, Australians have a strong sense of their national identity. They have also managed to keep elements of the pioneering spirit of the early European settlers alive, ensuring that Australia is an easy-going, self-reliant place. Although four out of five Australians live in towns, most people love the outdoor life. Sports are a popular leisure time activity, particularly cricket, football, rugby and all types of water sports.

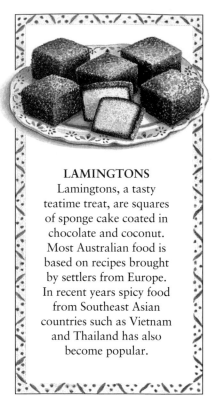

LAMINGTONS
Lamingtons, a tasty teatime treat, are squares of sponge cake coated in chocolate and coconut. Most Australian food is based on recipes brought by settlers from Europe. In recent years spicy food from Southeast Asian countries such as Vietnam and Thailand has also become popular.

◀ *Lifesavers row a surf boat through the crashing breakers at a beach in New South Wales. Popular water sports include surfing, sailing, water skiing and windsurfing.*

► An Australian firefighter tackles a serious bushfire. Fires are a major problem in Australia's hot, dry climate. A single spark, caused by human carelessness or even a bolt of lightning, may start a raging fire that quickly destroys vast areas of countryside.

◄ A child uses a two-way radio to study at home, tuning in to the School of the Air. Teachers broadcast lessons on the radio to children who live on farms and sheep stations that are often hundreds of kilometres from the nearest school.

► Trotting races are a highlight of Sydney's annual Royal Easter Show. Livestock and farm produce from all over Australia are judged there. Showjumping and driving contests are held, as well as craft displays and cattle auctions.

AUSTRALIA *History*

▲ *This Aboriginal rock painting shows a kangaroo, one of the animals once hunted by the Aboriginal peoples for food. Some rock paintings were painted in secret holy places where these peoples gathered to worship ancient spirits.*

Aboriginal peoples have lived in Australia for at least 40,000 years. They probably came from Southeast Asia. These peoples lived by gathering plants and insects, fishing and hunting. There were many different groups, each with their own language and lands. They were deeply religious.

Dutch explorers first mapped parts of the Australian coast in the 1600s. In 1770 the English explorer James Cook claimed the southeast coast for Britain, naming it New South Wales. The first British settlers arrived at Botany Bay, south of Sydney, in 1788. They were 700 convicts who had been sentenced to hard labour in Australia. Convicts continued to be transported from Britain until the mid-1800s, so many new colonies were founded. The settlers treated the Aboriginal peoples extremely badly.

During the early 1800s a number of settlers moved into Australia's interior. Sheep were brought over from South Africa and a wool industry established. After gold was discovered in 1851 a rush of new settlers arrived, eager to make their fortunes. In 1901 the Australian states united in the self-governing Commonwealth of Australia, but the British monarch remained head of state and links with Britain were still strong. Since 1945 large numbers of settlers have arrived from Europe and Southeast Asia. Australia is now a country of mixed cultures, where many people enjoy a high standard of living.

◄ *This painting shows Captain James Cook, the English explorer, studying a navigation chart. Cook sailed to Australia in a ship called* HMS Endeavour. *He landed in southeast Australia in 1770, naming it New South Wales.*

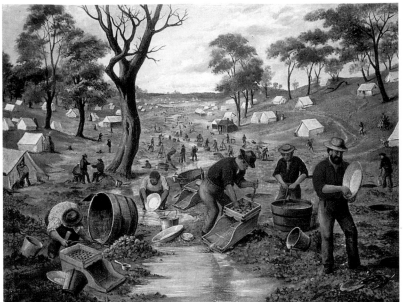

◄ Miners pan for gold in an Australian stream during the 1800s. Gold was discovered in New South Wales in 1851, then in Victoria. The discovery sparked a massive gold rush that brought many new settlers to Australia. Later gold was also found in Western Australia and Queensland.

◄ These ruins were once part of the penal colony at Port Arthur in southeast Tasmania. Convicts brought from Britain were imprisoned there between 1830 and 1877 when Australia was a British colony. Many had only committed minor crimes, but were treated with great brutality.

► Aboriginal peoples demonstrate in protest during Australia's bicentennial celebrations in 1988, which marked 200 years of European settlement. Many Aboriginal peoples protested at this time because the arrival of the Europeans had meant ill-treatment and loss of their traditional lands. As a result some of the lands were returned to them.

NEW ZEALAND *Introduction*

New Zealand is a beautiful country in the southwest Pacific Ocean. It is made up of two large islands called North Island and South Island and a number of smaller islands, some of which lie far away in the South Pacific. Its nearest large neighbour, Australia, lies about 1,600 kilometres away.

This spectacular land has towering mountain ranges, lush forests, rolling grasslands and long, sandy beaches. On North Island there are several active volcanoes and many hot springs and geysers. Unique species of birds, reptiles and plants have developed in New Zealand, cut off from the rest of the world by hundreds of kilometres of sea.

It is believed that the country was first settled by a people called the Maoris during the AD800s. They sailed here in large canoes from islands farther north, crossing vast distances of the Pacific Ocean. Europeans first visited New Zealand in 1642 and started to settle in the late 1700s. Between 1840 and 1907 this country was a British colony and today most of its people are of British descent.

New Zealand is now an independent country, although the British monarch remains head of state. It has a high standard of living and a strong tradition of equality. In 1893 it became the first country in the world to give women the vote.

A temperate climate and plentiful rainfall make New Zealand a good farming country. Although there is some industry, its economy is largely dependent on agriculture. The meat, wool and dairy products produced by sheep and cattle reared on New Zealand's green pastures are exported all over the world.

ENDANGERED WORLD

The yellow-eyed penguin nests in the coastal forests of South Island. It is threatened by the loss of its habitat to farming.

SPEAK MAORI

Hello – Tena koe
(*ten - a kway*)

Goodbye – Haera ra
(*hy - air - ay rah*)

Please – Whakawaireka
(*wak - a - wair - eh - kah*)

Thank you – Kia ora
(*Kee or - ah*)

Yes – Ae *(eye)*

◄ *Blue waters surround the modern buildings of Auckland on North Island. Auckland is built on a tongue of land between two large harbours. It is New Zealand's largest city and also the country's main port and industrial centre.*

▼ *Maori women in traditional costume gather below the carved roof of a wharerunanga (meeting house). The Maoris were the very first inhabitants of New Zealand and their descendants keep alive a rich culture of wood carving, weaving and dance.*

FACTS AND FIGURES

Area: 270,530 sq km
Population: 3,471,000
Capital: Wellington (326,000)
Other major city: Auckland (897,000)
Highest point: Aorangi-Mount Cook (3,754 m)
Official language: English
Main religion: Christianity
Currency: New Zealand dollar
Main exports: Meat, milk, butter, cheese, wool, fish, fruit
Government: Constitutional monarchy
Per capita GNP: US $12,060

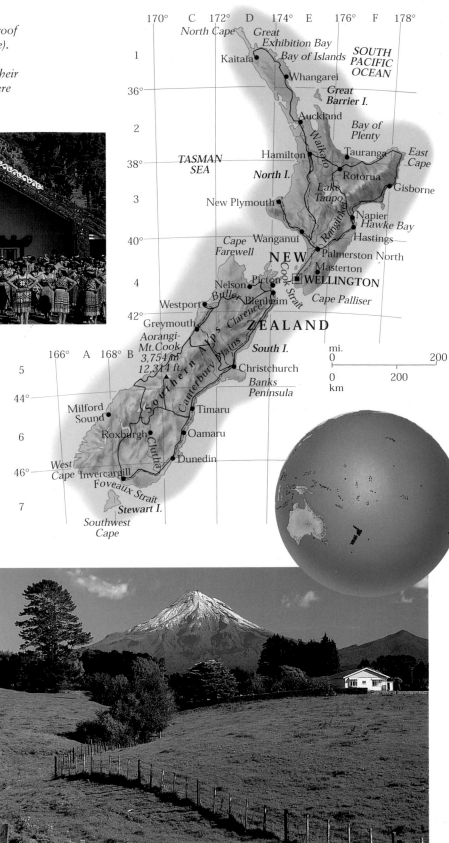

▶ *Snow covers the peak of 2,518-metre-high Mount Taranaki (Egmont), one of several volcanoes on North Island. Beautiful mountain scenery like this can be found in many parts of New Zealand.*

533

NEW ZEALAND *Geography*

On the two main islands of New Zealand no place lies more than 130 kilometres from the sea. Winds from the ocean keep the climate mild and wet, with especially heavy rainfall on the west coast. Northern New Zealand is hot and rainy. It is cooler in the south of the country and on high ground.

North Island has a very irregular coastline with several peninsulas projecting into the sea. Fertile lowlands rise to hills fringed by inlets and sandy beaches. The centre of North Island is a volcanic region. Four volcanoes are still active and there are many hot, bubbling springs and geysers. Earthquakes are common, but they are rarely severe. Farther south, rugged hills descend to plains and coastal lowlands.

South Island, which lies just 26 kilometres across the Cook Strait, is dominated by the soaring peaks of the Southern Alps with their snowfields and glaciers. Many beautiful lakes lying in thickly forested mountain valleys feed fast-flowing rivers. To the east of the Alps lie the fertile Canterbury Plains, New Zealand's largest area of flat land. In the far south spectacular fiords cut narrow gashes into the land.

New Zealand is home to many plants that are found nowhere else in the world, such as the scarlet-flowered pohutukawa and the kowhai with its bright yellow blossoms. The animal life is equally unique. The kiwi, a large bird that cannot fly, is the best known animal, although there are several other types of flightless birds. The tuatara, an ancient lizard-like reptile, is also only found in New Zealand. Many wildlife habitats throughout the islands are now protected as national parks.

▲ *Clouds of steam burst into the air from volcanic rock at Whakarewarewa, near Rotorua on North Island. New Zealand has many geysers and hot springs. They are the result of high temperatures deep inside the Earth.*

▶ *An island called Urapukapuka (centre) lies in the blue seas of the Bay of Islands, about 240 kilometres north of Auckland. It is just one of about 150 islands in this beautiful region. New Zealand's coastline has many inlets and small islands.*

▲ The cloud-covered pyramid of Mitre Peak
rises high above the waters of Milford Sound.
This stretch of water is the most spectacular
of many fiords (sea inlets) on the southwest
coast of South Island.

◀ The green and lush Canterbury Plains roll
gently for many kilometres on South Island.
These fertile lowlands are used for raising sheep
and cattle. Grain crops such as wheat and
barley are also grown there.

▶ Ridges of ice edge
down the Southern
Alps, forming the huge
Franz Josef Glacier. This
is one of over 360 glaciers
in New Zealand. It was first
explored in 1865 and today is
popular with hikers and tourists.

NEW ZEALAND *Economy*

New Zealand is a land of farms. For every person who lives here, it is estimated that there are about 20 farm animals. Sheep produce the famous lamb and wool that are exported around the world. Large herds of cattle are also raised for the country's other major exports – beef, milk, cheese and butter. Crops include wheat, maize, barley, peas and apples. There are increasing numbers of vineyards producing high-quality wines. New Zealand's native evergreen forests are mostly protected, but extensive plantations of conifer and eucalyptus trees supply sawmills and the paper industry. Fish such as hoki, snapper and barracuda are caught in New Zealand's waters and shellfish, including mussels, are farmed along the coast.

Industry is largely based on processing New Zealand's dairy produce, crops, meat and fish. Other industries include textiles, aluminium and plastics. New Zealand's main trading partners are Australia, Japan, the United States of America and member states of the European Union, especially the United Kingdom.

The country makes use of its natural resources, such as the swift-flowing rivers that are a source of hydroelectric power. There are also reserves of natural gas, oil, coal and gold. However, tourism has recently overtaken all other ways of making money. New Zealand's greatest natural resource is now its spectacular scenery, which attracts tourists from all over the world.

▼ *This dam at Roxburgh in Otago powers one of New Zealand's 30 hydroelectric schemes, which provide 75 percent of the country's electricity.*

◄ *The power station at Wairakei just north of Lake Taupo is one of ten that produce geothermal electricity in volcanic regions. Underground volcanic activity turns water into steam. This is used to drive the turbines that produce electric power.*

▶ A shepherd and his dogs
bring in a large herd of
sheep for shearing on the
plains below Aorangi-
Mount Cook. Farming is
an essential part of the
New Zealand economy.
Sheep, raised for meat and
wool, are the most
important livestock.

▶ Kiwi fruit are picked at a
farm near the Bay of Plenty, one
of the three main fruit growing
areas on North Island. They are
an important export for New
Zealand, which is now the world's
largest kiwi fruit producer.

◀ Steel girders are stacked and cut at a
factory in Christchurch, South Island.
Although New Zealand has some
heavy industry like this, it is not as
important as the timber trade or the
electronics industry. Most factories are
on North Island, around Auckland.

537

NEW ZEALAND *People and History*

▲ *For centuries the Maoris decorated themselves with tattoos for religious reasons and to scare enemies. Many aspects of their lives have changed little since their arrival in the AD800s. Since the 1800s the Maoris have been increasingly influenced by European ways of life.*

The majority of New Zealanders are descended from European settlers, mostly British, although more than 10 percent are Maori people. The Maoris originally came from the eastern Pacific. A large part of the population is also a mixture of Maori and European.

No one knows exactly when the first Maoris settled in New Zealand – it may have been during or even before the AD800s. The first European to discover the islands was the Dutch navigator, Abel Janszoon Tasman, in 1642. The next European visitor, Captain James Cook, did not arrive until 1769. British settlers founded Wellington, on North Island, in 1840 and New Zealand became a British colony. After gold was discovered on South Island in 1861 a rush of settlers arrived to try and make their fortunes. During the 1860s the settlers and the Maoris quarrelled over land and a number of fierce wars occurred. As a result the Maoris lost many of their ancestral lands and rights.

New Zealand became an independent nation in 1907, but kept its strong political and economic links with the United Kingdom. More recently the country has developed closer ties with Australia and other South Pacific nations. Following a period of Maori unrest in the 1970s, there is now a new interest in Maori culture and traditions.

▲ *The Round the Bays run attracts more than ten thousand joggers to the streets of Auckland every spring. Many New Zealanders enjoy the outdoor life, particularly activities such as running, hiking, climbing and sailing. Other popular sports include cricket, rugby, tennis, skiing and golf.*

BAKED KUMARAS
Kumaras (sweet potatoes) are a traditional Maori food. They are often baked in their jackets and taste delicious served with sizzling pork and apple or with lamb. Kumaras may also be boiled, roasted, fried or scalloped (sliced, seasoned and slowly cooked in milk).

NEW CALEDONIA

New Caledonia, in the southwest Pacific Ocean, is an overseas territory of France. It consists of the island of New Caledonia and several outlying islands, principally the Loyalty Islands, the Isle of Pines and the Bélep Islands. The island of New Caledonia, the largest in the group, is circled by one of the world's largest barrier reefs. Its landscape stretches across rugged mountains, forests and open grasslands.

The original inhabitants of New Caledonia were the Kanaks, a Melanesian people whose ancestors probably came from the islands of Papua New Guinea. The Melanesians still make up the largest group of people in the territory, but there are also many Europeans.

The French claimed the islands of New Caledonia as part of their overseas territory in the mid-1800s. Between 1864 and 1897 the French government used the territory as a penal colony.

European dominance has been a constant source of irritation to the Kanak people. In the 1980s they began a campaign to win independence for New Caledonia. Disputes broke out between the Kanaks and the French community in 1988. In the same year it was agreed that a vote on independence would be held in 1998.

▼ *Dancers from the island of New Caledonia wear traditional costumes. Dancing plays a large part in Melanesian life. People dance for entertainment and during traditional ceremonies.*

FACTS AND FIGURES

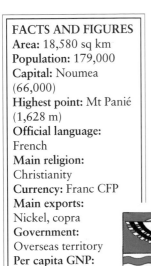

Area: 18,580 sq km
Population: 179,000
Capital: Noumea (66,000)
Highest point: Mt Panié (1,628 m)
Official language: French
Main religion: Christianity
Currency: Franc CFP
Main exports: Nickel, copra
Government: Overseas territory
Per capita GNP: Est. US$3,000-8,000

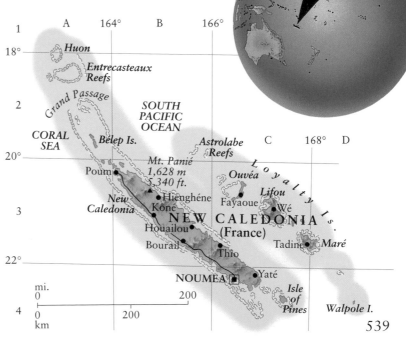

539

FEDERATED STATES OF MICRONESIA

FACTS AND FIGURES
Area: 700 sq km
Population: 114,000
Capital: Kolonia,
on Pohnpei (7,000)
Highest point: Totolom,
on Pohnpei (719 m)
Official language:
English
Main religion:
Christianity
Currency: US dollar
Main export: Copra
Government:
Federal republic
Per capita GNP:
Est. US $700-3,000

The Federated States of Micronesia are made up of all the islands of the Caroline group in the western Pacific, except for the Palau islands. The federation consists of four states – Kosrae and Pohnpei, which are both single islands, and the island groups of Yap and Chuuk. In all there are more than 600 islands. Scattered over 2,900 square kilometres of sea, they have a total land area of just 700 square kilometres.

Some of the islands are mountainous and forested. Others are low coral islands surrounded by reefs and lagoons. Rainfall is high and typhoons (fierce seasonal storms) may occur. The typhoons have very strong winds, often reaching speeds of 240 kilometres per hour, and can cause a great deal of destruction.

Most islanders grow just enough food for their own needs, but exports include copra (dried coconut kernels) and fish. Tourism also helps the economy of the islands.

Micronesian people probably started arriving here from Asia in about 2000BC. The islands were colonized by Spain in the 1600s and sold to Germany in 1899. When World War I broke out in 1914 control passed to Japan. From 1947 they were governed by the United States of America (USA) following an agreement with the United Nations. The Federated States became independent in 1990. The USA still controls foreign policy and defence, but each of Micronesia's four states has its own government for internal matters such as transport and education.

▲ *Houses line the beach on the island of Kosrae. These traditional homes are thatched with palm leaves and some have open sides to allow air to pass through.*

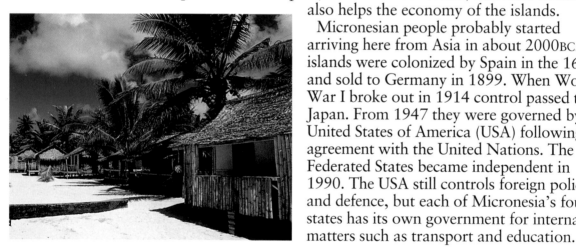

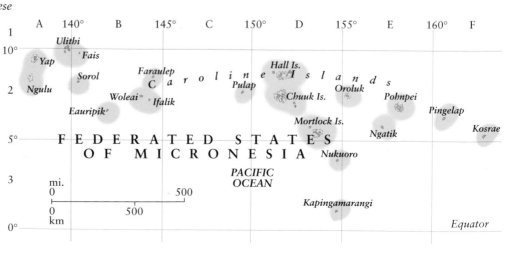

PALAU AND THE MARSHALL ISLANDS

FACTS AND FIGURES
Area: 490 sq km
Population: 16,000
Capital: Koror (10,000)
Official languages:
Palauan, English
Main religion:
Christianity
Government: Republic

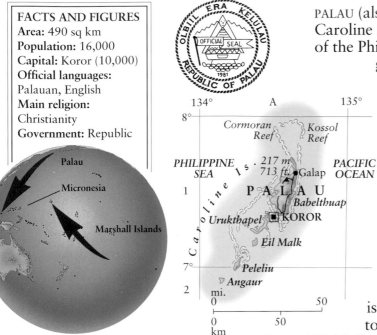

PALAU (also spelled Belau) lies in the Caroline islands, 800 kilometres to the east of the Philippines. The islands of the Palau group were probably the first to be settled in this area, many thousands of years ago.

Palau is made up of over 200 islands, but only eight are permanently inhabited. The forested islands of the north have been formed by volcanoes. Tapioca, coconuts, fruit and vegetables are grown in their fertile soil. Southern Palau is made up of low-lying coral islands. Palau's main exports are copra and tuna, but tourism is becoming increasingly important to the country's economy.

From 1886 Palau was ruled by Spain. It was sold to Germany in 1899 and passed into Japanese hands during World War I. After 1947 it was governed by the United States of America on behalf of the United Nations. It became an independent republic in 1994.

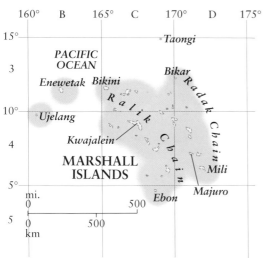

THE MARSHALL ISLANDS are named after the British sea-captain John Marshall, who landed here in the late 1700s. The group consists of the low-lying Radak (Sunrise) and Ralik (Sunset) chains, which contain 31 islands and atolls. Their resources include phosphate, which is used to make fertilizers, and beautiful beaches that attract tourists. The islanders are of Micronesian origin. They grow papaya, breadfruit and arrowroot (a starchy root). Coconut kernels are dried to make copra for export.

The Marshall Islands were colonized by Germany in the 1880s. Japan then took over in 1914. From 1947 they were ruled by the United States of America (USA) on behalf of the United Nations. The USA has kept some ties here following the islands' independence in 1991.

FACTS AND FIGURES
Area: 180 sq km	**Main religion:** Christianity
Population: 52,000	**Currency:** US dollar
Capital: Majuro (20,000)	**Government:** Republic
Official languages:	**Per capita GNP:**
Marshallese, English	Est. US $700-3,000

541

KIRIBATI

Kiribati, in the central Pacific, is made up of 33 coral islands. They include Banaba Island, the Gilbert Islands, the Phoenix Islands and eight of the eleven Line Islands. These islands have a small total land area, but they are scattered over five million square kilometres of ocean. The islanders live by fishing and growing coconuts, bananas and breadfruit. Pigs and chickens are also raised. Phosphate, mined on Banaba, was the country's main export until 1979 when the supply was exhausted.

Kiribati was probably settled by people from nearby islands, such as the Marshall Islands, between AD1000 and 1300. Spanish explorers visited the islands in the late 1500s. From 1916 they were part of a British colony that also included the Ellice Islands (now Tuvalu). During World War II Tarawa, Kiribati's main island, was the scene of fierce fighting between troops from Japan and the United States of America (USA). In the 1950s and 1960s the United Kingdom and the USA tested atom bombs on Kiritimati (Christmas) Island. Kiribati became independent in 1979. In 1983 the Kiribati government bought the islands of Teraine and Tabuaeran, resettling nearly 5,000 islanders there.

FACTS AND FIGURES
Area: 730 sq km
Population: 75,000
Capital: Bairiki, on Tarawa (25,000)
Highest point: Summit of Banaba, on Banaba Island (81 m)
Official language: English
Main religion: Christianity
Currency: Australian dollar
Main exports: Copra, fish
Government: Republic
Per capita GNP: US $700

▶ *Finely-woven mats are traditionally made from strips of dried palm leaf. Coconut palms also provide fresh coconut and copra (dried coconut) for export and leaves for roofing.*

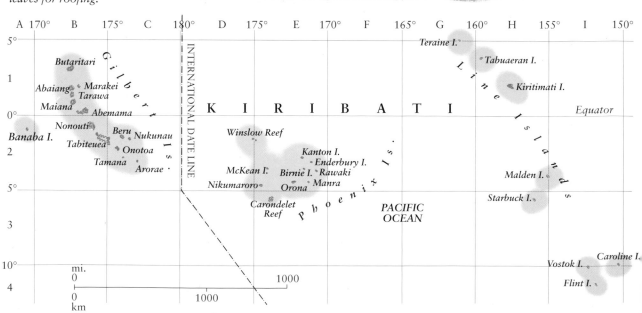

NAURU

FACTS AND FIGURES
Area: 20 sq km
Population: 10,000
Seat of government:
Yaren
Highest point: On west
of island (70 m)
Official language:
Nauruan
Main religion:
Christianity
Currency:
Australian dollar
Main export:
Phosphate
Government:
Republic
Per capita GNP:
Not available

Nauru is one of the world's smallest independent countries. It is a tiny coral island, lying just below the Equator in the southwest Pacific Ocean. Most of Nauru's people live along the coast where there is a strip of fertile land. Almost all the rest of the island consists of a plateau that once contained large deposits of phosphate rock, a valuable source of fertilizer.

Before the discovery of phosphate in the early 1900s the people of Nauru led a peaceful life, growing their own food and farming fish in the shallow lagoons. Since then nearly a hundred years of phosphate mining has reduced much of the island to desert and all Nauru's food now has to be imported. The Nauru government took over the phosphate industry from Australia, New Zealand and the United Kingdom (UK) in 1970. The wealth it generated has made Nauru's people among the richest in the Pacific, but there is now little phosphate left and the government is trying to develop other industries.

Until an English explorer arrived in 1798, the Nauruans believed that their island was the only place in the world. Germany governed Nauru from 1888 to 1914. After Japan's occupation during World War II the island was jointly ruled by Australia, New Zealand and the UK, gaining independence in 1968. Since then Nauru has claimed compensation from Australia for exploiting its phosphate resources. The country's government aims to restore the over-mined land so that it can be used for growing food again.

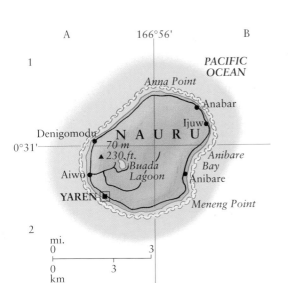

▲ *Phosphate rock is loaded into the hold of a ship. It is Nauru's only export and is used to make fertilizers. The phosphate was created by sea birds living on the island. Over millions of years their droppings built up to form the phosphate rock.*

SOLOMON ISLANDS

▼ *Bananas, cassava, yams, taros, sweet potatoes and coconuts are sold at a busy local market. Most Solomon Islanders grow just enough food for their own use, with a little spare to sell.*

The Solomon Islands form a 1,500-kilometre-long archipelago (island chain) in a hot and humid region of the southwest Pacific. The larger islands were formed by volcanoes and are covered in thick rainforests, which are home to several species of large birdwing butterflies. The smaller islands are low-lying coral reefs.

The northwest Solomon Islands belong to Papua New Guinea, but the southern ones make up an independent nation. The largest of the islands is Guadalcanal, where Honiara, the capital and largest city, is situated. The islanders live by fishing, growing root vegetables and raising pigs and chickens. Over 80 different dialects are spoken on the Solomon Islands, but most people also speak a version of English called Pidgin. The majority of inhabitants live in small, scattered villages along the coasts of the larger islands. Houses are often built on stilts to allow air to circulate and keep them cool.

The Solomon Islands were first settled about 6,000 years ago by people who came from Papua New Guinea, but they were not named until Spanish explorers arrived in the 1500s. Britain ruled the islands peacefully from 1893, although in World War II a number of fierce battles took place here between United States and Japanese forces. In 1978 the Solomon Islands became independent.

FACTS AND FIGURES

Area: 28,370 sq km
Population: 354,000
Capital: Honiara (34,000)
Highest point: Mt Popomanaseu (2,331 m)
Official language: English
Main religion: Christianity

Currency: Solomon Island dollar
Main exports: Fish products, timber, copra, cocoa beans, palm-oil products
Government: Constitutional monarchy
Per capita GNP: US $710

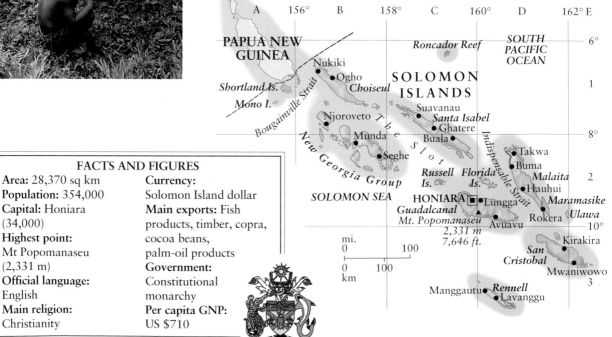

TUVALU

FACTS AND FIGURES
Area: 24 sq km
Population: 13,000
Capital: Funafuti, on
Funafuti Atoll (3,000)
Official languages:
Tuvaluan, English
Main religion:
Christianity
Currency:
Australian dollar
Main export:
Copra
Government:
Constitutional
monarchy
Per capita GNP:
US $970

Tuvalu, in the southwest Pacific, is made up of nine low-lying islands that form coral atolls around peaceful, blue lagoons. It is one of the smallest nations in the world. Eight of Tuvalu's islands are inhabited. They have the second highest population density in the Pacific, after Nauru.

The islands' soil is very poor and there are few natural resources. Islanders grow bananas and taro (a starchy root) to eat and keep chickens and pigs. Fishing is also important. Coconut palms grow everywhere and copra (dried coconut kernels) is exported along with handicrafts such as woven mats and baskets. Many young islanders try to find jobs on ocean ships to earn money. Another growing source of income for the people of Tuvalu is charging foreign ships money when they fish for tuna in the waters around the island chain. The sale of Tuvalu postage stamps to dealers also raises some income.

The ancestors of the Tuvaluan people probably came from Samoa hundreds of years ago. The islands, formerly known as the Ellice Islands, came under British rule in 1892. Together with the Gilbert Islands (now part of Kiribati), they became a British colony in 1916. The Ellice Islands eventually separated from the Gilbert Islands in 1975 and three years later became independent as Tuvalu.

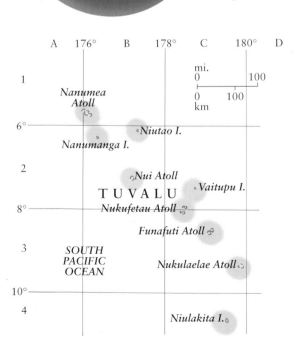

▲ *A woman prepares food for her family outside a palm-thatched village house. Most of the islanders of Tuvalu live in villages of open-sided, raised houses with steeply sloping roofs. The houses do not need thick walls because the climate is warm all year round.*

545

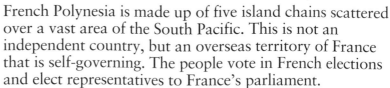

FRENCH POLYNESIA

▼ *A stone tiki (mythical figure) is carved on the island of Nuku Hiva in the Marquesas Island chain. Other traditional arts include wood carving and mat-weaving. French Polynesia has inspired many artists, including the French painter, Paul Gauguin, who produced beautiful pictures of Tahiti in the 1890s.*

French Polynesia is made up of five island chains scattered over a vast area of the South Pacific. This is not an independent country, but an overseas territory of France that is self-governing. The people vote in French elections and elect representatives to France's parliament.

There are around 130 islands in French Polynesia. Many were formed by volcanoes and have rugged, cloud-capped peaks. Rainforests thrive in the deep valleys, while coconut palms and fruit trees flourish on the coasts. Coral reefs shelter warm, sandy lagoons and they also form many low-lying island rings. Powerful ocean currents and strong winds in the region occasionally bring tropical typhoons.

The largest and most famous of French Polynesia's islands is Tahiti in the Society Islands. The majority of the territory's population lives there. Many people have moved from the outlying islands to Tahiti, where tourism is an increasingly important source of income. In the small coastal villages most people live by fishing and growing crops such as vanilla pods, pineapples and bananas.

The islanders' Polynesian ancestors arrived from Samoa around 2,000 years ago. By the 1700s Europeans had settled here and since 1842 France has ruled the region. Under the 1984 constitution the islands are governed by a council of ministers headed by a president, although France remains in overall control of the territory.

▶ *Shades of blue and white make up the spectacular coral-reef lagoon of Bora Bora, which is one of the Society Islands. A coral-reef lagoon is a sheltered stretch of warm water, separated from the sea by a necklace of coral.*

SPEAK TAHITIAN

Hello – Ia ora na
(ee - ah or - a nah)

Goodbye – Parahi
(pah - ra - ee)

Thank you – Mauruuru
(mah - oo - roo - oo - roo)

Yes – E *(ay)*

No – Aita
(eye - ee - tah)

▲ *Papeete, the main town on the island of Tahiti, is also the capital of French Polynesia. A centre for tourism and trade, this bustling port has many modern buildings.*

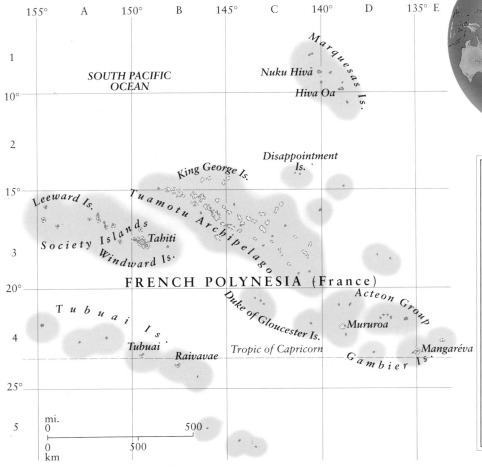

155°   A   150°   B   145°   C   140°   D   135° E

1

SOUTH PACIFIC OCEAN

Marquesas Is.

Nuku Hiva

10°

Hiva Oa

2

Disappointment Is.

King George Is.

15°

Leeward Is.

Tuamotu Archipelago

Society Islands

Tahiti

3

Windward Is.

FRENCH POLYNESIA (France)

20°

Tubuai Is.

Duke of Gloucester Is.

Acteon Group

4

Mururoa

Tubuai

Raivavae

Tropic of Capricorn

Mangaréva

Gambier Is.

25°

mi.
0   500

5

0   500
km

FACTS AND FIGURES
Area: 3,270 sq km
Population: 212,000
Capital: Papeete, on Tahiti (79,000)
Highest point: Mt Orohena, on Tahiti (2,241 m)
Official languages: French, Tahitian
Main religion: Christianity
Currency: Franc CFP
Main exports: Coconut-oil, cultured pearls
Government: French territory
Per capita GNP: Est. over US $8,000

FIJI

FACTS AND FIGURES

Area: 18,330 sq km
Population: 747,000
Capital: Suva (72,000)
Highest point:
Mt Tomanivi (1,323 m)
Official language:
English
Main religions:
Christianity, Hinduism,
Sikhism, Islam
Currency: Fiji dollar
Main exports:
Sugar, gold,
fish, clothes
Government:
Republic
Per capita GNP:
US $2,010

Only one in ten of the 800 islands that make up this nation is inhabited. The main islands are Viti Levu and Vanua Levu. Suva, on Viti Levu, is the biggest city in the South Pacific. Forest covers the mountain slopes of the larger islands, which are the tops of volcanoes. Heavy rains enable a variety of crops such as ginger and sugar-cane to be grown. The economy relies greatly on sugar and on the tourists who come to enjoy the coral reefs and beaches.

Fijians are a mixture of Melanesian people, who came here over 3,000 years ago, and Polynesians. About half the population is descended from people who were brought from India to work on British sugar-cane plantations in the 1800s. Europeans explored the islands during the 1600s and 1700s. In 1874 Fiji became a British colony. After independence in 1970 tension grew between Indians and native Fijians. In 1987 the Indian-dominated government was overthrown in a military coup. Civilian government returned, but in 1990 a new constitution ensured that the native Fijians kept political power.

◀ *Children make their way to school by canoe. This is the local equivalent of a school bus. There are over 800 schools in Fiji, spread over more than 50 islands. Languages spoken in the classrooms include English, Fijian and Hindi.*

SAMOA AND AMERICAN SAMOA

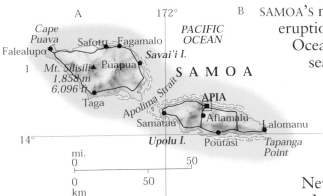

SAMOA'S mountainous islands were formed by the eruptions of volcanoes on the floor of the Pacific Ocean. They were settled by Polynesian seafarers around 2,000 years ago. A series of chiefs ruled these islands until they were united under the female leader Salamasina in the 1500s. By the 1800s Europeans were coming here to trade and in 1900 the islands came under German rule. From 1914 until independence in 1962 New Zealand governed Samoa.

Most Samoans live on the islands of Savai'i and Upolu. About 70 percent of the population are farmers. As well as growing food for their own needs, they export crops such as taro and coconut.

FACTS AND FIGURES

SAMOA
Area: 2,830 sq km
Population: 158,000
Capital: Apia (33,000)
Official languages:
Samoan, English
Currency: Tala
Per capita GNP:
US $940

AMERICAN SAMOA
Area: 200 sq km
Population: 38,000
Capital: Pago Pago
Official languages:
Samoan, English
Currency:
US dollar
Per capita GNP:
Est. US $3,000-8,000

◀ Tuna are offloaded on the quayside at Pago Pago harbour in American Samoa. Fishing is a major industry there, with large catches of tuna canned for export.

AMERICAN SAMOA is a group of seven islands lying east of Samoa. The largest is Tutuila, which has a fine natural harbour at Pago Pago. The humid climate is ideal for growing crops such as taro, pineapples, bananas and coconut. This tropical climate also attracts a growing number of tourists, which helps to boost the economy.

Polynesian people came to these islands over 2,000 years ago. By the late 1800s ships from the United States of America (USA) were using Pago Pago as a refuelling stop. The islanders granted trading rights to the USA, which took control of the islands in the early 1900s and still administers them today. However, the Samoans elect their own government and send a delegate to the US House of Representatives.

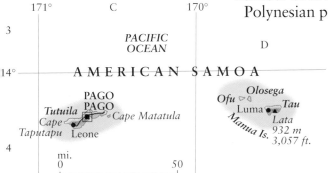

VANUATU

Eighty islands make up this Pacific nation. The largest is the mountainous island of Espiritu Santo. Port-Vila, the largest town and the national capital, is on Efate Island to the south. Many of the Vanuatu islands are the peaks of underwater mountains and some are active volcanoes. Others are coral islands with reefs and brilliant blue lagoons.

Vanuatu has a tropical climate with high rainfall and warm temperatures all year round. Bananas grow here as well as yams and cassava. All these are an important part of the islanders' diet. Crops such as copra and cocoa are major exports. Tourism also contributes to the economy and the islands are a particularly popular destination for visitors from Australia and New Zealand.

Nine out of every ten islanders are Melanesian people. Their ancestors came from Asia and probably began settling here from about 3000BC. When the English navigator James Cook mapped this region during the 1770s he named these rugged islands the New Hebrides because their landscape reminded him of the Scottish Hebrides. They were governed jointly by Britain and France from 1906 to 1980, when they became independent.

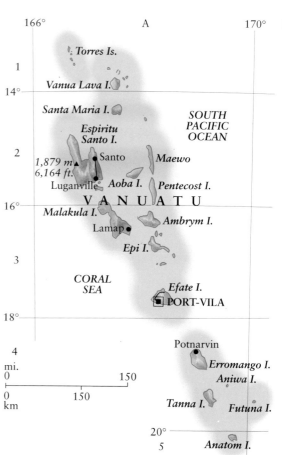

▲ Coastal fishermen paddle their canoes back to the beach. Shallow waters surround these islands. They soon give way to the deep expanses of the South Pacific, where tuna and poulet fish are caught.

FACTS AND FIGURES

Area: 12,190 sq km
Population: 156,000
Capital: Port-Vila (20,000)
Highest point: On Espiritu Santo Island (1,879 m)
Official languages: Bislama, English, French

Main religion: Christianity
Currency: Vatu
Main exports: Copra, beef, timber, cocoa
Government: Republic
Per capita GNP: US $1,220

TONGA

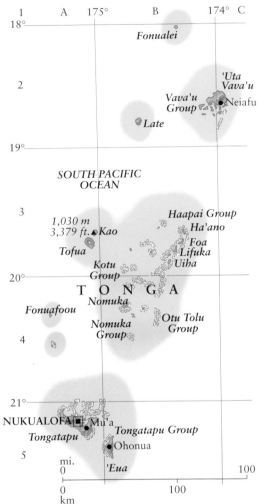

The kingdom of Tonga is made up of a number of island groups lying to the southeast of Fiji. Some of the 172 islands are steep and volcanic, while others are low platforms of coral. Most people live on the fertile Tongatapu islands, where coconut palms, banana trees and watermelons are grown. The islands export fruit and vegetables, copra (dried coconut) and coconut-oil, as well as vanilla pods for flavouring puddings and ice cream.

The Tongans are descended from Polynesian seafarers who had probably settled in this area by about 1000BC. European explorers discovered the islands in the 1600s and 1700s. Captain James Cook called them the Friendly Islands because he was welcomed by the inhabitants when he visited in 1773. During the 1800s civil war raged as various groups of islanders fought for control. These ended when the islands were united as a monarchy in 1845.

From 1900 to 1970 Tonga was governed by the British, although Tongan kings and queens still played an important part in home affairs. After independence Tonga remained a monarchy within the Commonwealth of Nations, the association of free countries that were once parts of the British empire. Recent years have seen improved communications between the islands and the development of tourism.

FACTS AND FIGURES

Area: 750 sq km
Population: 98,000
Capital: Nukualofa (29,000)
Highest point: On Kao (1,030 m)
Official languages: Tongan, English
Main religion: Christianity
Currency: Pa'anga
Main exports: Coconut products, copra, vanilla,
Government: Constitutional monarchy
Per capita GNP: US $1,350

SPEAK TONGAN

Hello – Malo e lelei
(mah - loh ay leh - lay)

Goodbye – 'Alu a
(ah - loo ah)

Yes – 'Io
(ee - oh)

▲ *Members of the Tongan royal family gather for a wedding photograph in December 1982. They are descended from Tonga's first monarch, King George Tupou I (1796-1893). He introduced written laws to the islands. The Tongan monarch is head of state and appoints the prime minister and cabinet.*

551

PACIFIC OCEAN *Introduction*

▼ *Pogonophora worms live on the seabed north of the Galapagos Islands. They feed on bacteria that thrive on hydrogen sulphide released through vents in the Earth's crust.*

The word Pacific means peaceful. This enormous ocean can certainly be tranquil, blue and beautiful, but it can also be stirred to a fury during wild storms or when underwater earthquakes strike. In fact, the whole of the ocean is ringed by major earthquake and volcano zones.

Pictures of Earth taken from Space reveal the sheer size of the Pacific. This is the largest ocean in the world, covering about one third of the planet's surface. Its waters stretch from eastern Asia and Australia to the Americas. The Pacific's shallowest waters average about 120 metres and wash over ledges of land called continental shelves. These are really flooded parts of the continents, which begin at the continents' shorelines and slope down as they extend into the ocean. The average depth of the Pacific Ocean is about 4,000 metres. A series of trenches in the west descend into the world's deepest, darkest waters at Challenger Deep in the Mariana Trench.

The Pacific Plate, a great section of the Earth's crust, is marked by ridges of high, underwater mountains. In places there are volcanic islands, such as Hawaii, the largest island of the Hawaiian group. Hawaii is where the world's largest island peak, Mauna Kea, is found. This is no longer volcanically active and measures about 10,000 metres from its base on the seabed. In contrast, there are also low-lying islands made of coral in the Pacific. These have built up over many thousands of years on top of underwater volcanic mountains.

This great ocean is home to many animal species, from the world's biggest fish (the whale shark) to flying fish, squid and sealions. Thousands of brightly coloured fish and plants live in the warm, shallow waters of the coral reefs. Far out into the ocean, in deeper, cooler waters, there are all kinds of fish, sea mammals, molluscs, crustaceans and other creatures.

▼ *Tetiaroa is one of the Society Islands in French Polynesia. Many of these islands are the tops of volcanoes that have risen up from the sea floor.*

FACTS AND FIGURES
Area: 180,000,000 sq km
Greatest width: 24,000 km
Average depth: 4,000 m
Deepest point: Challenger Deep in the Mariana Trench (-10,920 m ±10 m)
Mineral resources: Oil, natural gas
Living resources: Fish, shellfish, seals (skins), seaweed, oysters (pearls)
Largest island: New Guinea

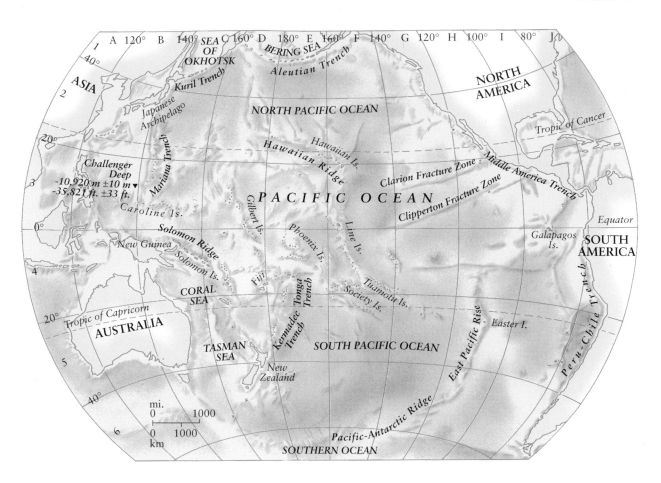

Map labels (Pacific Ocean map):

A 120° B 140° C 160° D 180° E 160° F 140° G 120° H 100° I 80° J

SEA OF OKHOTSK

BERING SEA

Aleutian Trench

ASIA

Kuril Trench

NORTH AMERICA

Japanese Archipelago

NORTH PACIFIC OCEAN

Mariana Trench

Challenger Deep
-10,920 m ±10 m ▼
-35,821 ft. ±33 ft.

Hawaiian Ridge

Hawaiian Is.

Tropic of Cancer

Clarion Fracture Zone

Middle America Trench

Caroline Is.

PACIFIC OCEAN

Clipperton Fracture Zone

Gilbert Is.

Galapagos Is.

SOUTH AMERICA

Equator

Solomon Ridge

New Guinea

Solomon Is.

Phoenix Is.

Line Is.

Fiji

Tuamotu Is.

Society Is.

CORAL SEA

Tonga Trench

Kermadec Trench

East Pacific Rise

Easter I.

Peru–Chile Trench

Tropic of Capricorn

AUSTRALIA

TASMAN SEA

New Zealand

SOUTH PACIFIC OCEAN

mi.
0   1000
0   1000
km

Pacific-Antarctic Ridge

SOUTHERN OCEAN

ENDANGERED WORLD

The giant clam is the world's largest shellfish, weighing up to 300 kilograms. It is collected for its meat and shell.

► A scuba diver explores Fiji's Rainbow Reef, which takes its name from multi-coloured soft corals, seaweeds and a dazzling array of small fish. Corals thrive in warm, tropical waters and some Pacific reefs have hundreds of different species.

PACIFIC OCEAN *People and History*

Some of the world's earliest sea journeys took place across the Pacific Ocean. Aboriginal peoples may have used canoes on these waters to leave New Guinea for Australia around 40,000 years ago. Centuries later, between about 1500BC and AD1000, Polynesian peoples ventured across huge stretches of water to colonize the Pacific islands. This proved to be one of the greatest achievements in seafaring history. Using special double-hulled canoes with sails made of matted leaves, Polynesian explorations eventually covered about 20 million square kilometres of open ocean. On the western side of the Pacific, the Chinese made great advances in navigation around the AD1100s. They were the first to use large ships with several masts, underwater rudders and compasses.

European exploration began in the 1600s when the Dutchman Abel Janszoon Tasman sailed around Australia and New Zealand. One of the most famous Pacific explorers was the English sea captain James Cook. He mapped New Zealand, the eastern coast of Australia and many of the Pacific islands between 1768 and 1779. In 1947 the Norwegian explorer Thor Heyerdahl travelled from Peru to the Tuamotu Islands in French Polynesia on his raft *Kon Tiki*. His trip showed that ancient native peoples from South America could have explored the Pacific on rafts.

In this century exploration has continued with the measurement of the Mariana trench and the discovery of new animal and plant species. Growing tourism, pollution and beach developments have threatened life in the Pacific, but environmental groups and some governments in the region are trying to minimize these problems.

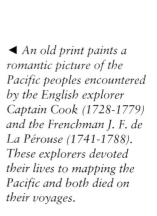

▼ *A Tahitian boy holds up a net containing a black pearl oyster. Young pearl oysters are collected from the seabed around French Polynesia and cultivated on floating farms.*

◄ *An old print paints a romantic picture of the Pacific peoples encountered by the English explorer Captain Cook (1728-1779) and the Frenchman J. F. de La Pérouse (1741-1788). These explorers devoted their lives to mapping the Pacific and both died on their voyages.*

◀ This painting shows a tsunami, a giant wave set off by an earthquake. The zone of volcanic and earthquake activity around the Pacific is called the Ring of Fire. For thousands of years islands and coasts in this zone have been swamped by tsunamis, which can travel at speeds of up to 800 kilometres per hour.

▶ Sails catch the wind off Auckland, in New Zealand, during the famous Whitbread round-the-world yacht race. The Pacific Ocean provides the setting for all kinds of watersport.

◀ In 1990, workers clean up oil that has been spilled from a tanker and washed ashore. The beach is Huntingdon Beach in California, on the United States' Pacific coast. Crude oil spills from huge supertankers have polluted many coasts in recent years. The oil seriously endangers seabirds, fish, seals and other marine life.

INDIAN OCEAN *Introduction*

▲ *Male Atoll is a low-lying coral island in the Maldives. Like other Indian Ocean islands it is thought that it may be submerged if the sea level rises because of global warming.*

The Indian Ocean is the third largest ocean in the world. It stretches from the shores of East Africa across to Indonesia and Australia and from India to the Antarctic. This vast body of water includes the Arabian Sea and the Bay of Bengal as well as the Persian Gulf and the Red Sea. It is linked to both the Atlantic and the Pacific oceans. The Suez Canal, at the northern end of the Red Sea, connects it with the Mediterranean Sea.

Large sections of the Earth's crust, the African Plate, the Antarctic Plate and the Indo-Australian Plate, meet underneath this great ocean. Movement of these plates causes frequent underwater earthquakes that set off enormous ocean waves called tsunamis. This movement has also caused a series of rocky ridges to rise up from the ocean floor. In places these form underwater mountains which break the surface of the water to create most of the islands that lie scattered across the Indian Ocean. In between the ridges lie deep-water basins. The Java Trench, for example, plunges to depths of about 7,450 metres.

The ocean waters support a rich variety of marine life, including corals, sharks, whales, turtles and jellyfish. Major currents move huge bodies of water across the Indian Ocean. The West Australian current brings cold Antarctic waters northwards to the tropics. Warm waters are circulated below the Equator by the Equatorial current, which moves anticlockwise. The northern currents vary with the monsoons, rain-bearing winds that change direction according to the time of year.

◀ *This yellow tube coral looks just like a flower. However, it is really a small animal with a tubular limestone cup that it can withdraw into. It catches small animals with its stinging tentacles. Corals are common in the warm waters of the Indian Ocean, where their stony skeletons or cups build up into reefs and atolls.*

▶ *The great white shark is found in the tropical and temperate waters of the Indian Ocean and in all the world's other oceans. It is the largest flesh-eating fish known and can reach 11 metres in length. The shark is famous for being extremely dangerous to humans. This hungry hunter usually feeds on fish, turtles and seals.*

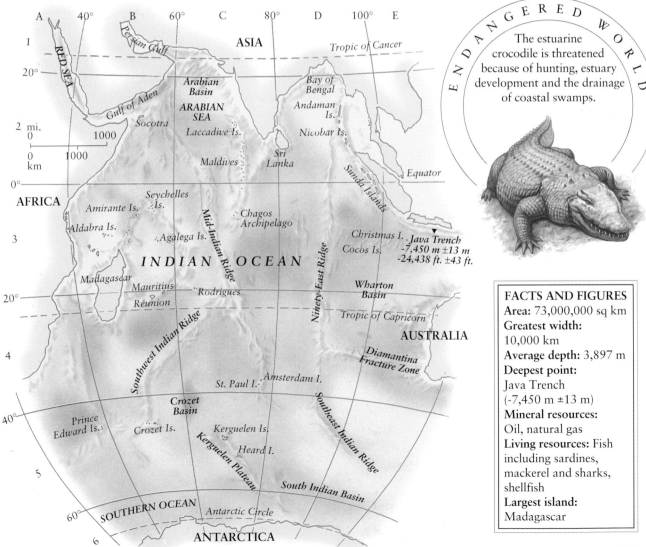

E N D A N G E R E D   W O R L D

The estuarine crocodile is threatened because of hunting, estuary development and the drainage of coastal swamps.

FACTS AND FIGURES
Area: 73,000,000 sq km
Greatest width:
10,000 km
Average depth: 3,897 m
Deepest point:
Java Trench
(-7,450 m ±13 m)
Mineral resources:
Oil, natural gas
Living resources: Fish including sardines, mackerel and sharks, shellfish
Largest island:
Madagascar

INDIAN OCEAN *People and History*

▲ *This map was drawn up by Europeans in the 1600s. It shows the western half of the Indian Ocean (labelled in Latin as* Mare Indicum). *The map was used to guide trading vessels to the coasts of Africa and southern Asia.*

The waters of the Indian Ocean were being navigated by explorers and traders many centuries ago. The ancient Egyptians, Phoenicians, Persians and Indians all criss-crossed this vital trade route. In the early Middle Ages settlers sailed to Southeast Asia from India and Sri Lanka, while Arabs founded trading settlements along the East African coast. For hundreds of years wooden ships called dhows sailed the Arabian Sea, carrying exotic spices, African ivory and bales of fine cloth.

During the 1400s the great Chinese navigator Zheng Ho led large exploration fleets across the Indian Ocean to Sri Lanka, India, Persia, Arabia and Africa. In 1497 the Portuguese seafarer Vasco da Gama became the first European to sail around southern Africa and cross from East Africa to India. He was followed by British, French and Dutch traders as the age of colonialism began.

Over the centuries the Indian Ocean islands and the peoples living on them were taken over by settlers, pirates and traders. Many of the islands' animals, which were not found anywhere else in the world, perished. For example the dodo, a goose-sized, flightless dove of Mauritius, was extinct by the late 1600s. The giant tortoises of Rodrigues had died out by 1800.

Exploration of the Indian Ocean continued through the 1800s and into this century, as scientists worked on the huge task of mapping the seabed. Today there are satellites in orbit above the Earth that are taking photographs of the ocean, measuring it and sending communications across it.

◀ *Fishermen perch on stilts in the surf at Matara on the south coast of Sri Lanka. The Indian Ocean has vast stocks of fish. Traditional fishing methods such as this do not seriously cut down their numbers, unlike fishing from modern factory trawlers.*

► *The Charlotte Louise takes tourists on a cruise around the beautiful Seychelles islands. The tourism trade is extremely important to the island groups of the Indian Ocean.*

◄ *The ruler of the southern Indian state of Calicut receives Portuguese explorer Vasco da Gama in the summer of 1498. Da Gama had left Lisbon with just four ships one year earlier. The Portuguese made claims to land and trading rights all over the Indian Ocean.*

► *A scuba diver feeds a huge moray eel. Many species of moray are found in the Indian Ocean. They hide in the nooks and crannies of coral reefs, waiting to dart out and devour their prey – other fish and molluscs.*

ATLANTIC OCEAN *Introduction*

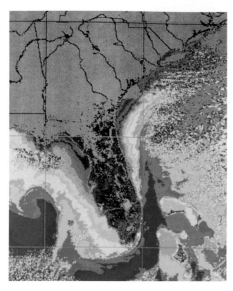

▲ *This computer image shows the source of the Gulf Stream, a warm ocean current that begins in the western Caribbean Sea. Grey represents the coolest areas (0°C) and the warmest are shown in red (26°C).*

The Atlantic is the second largest ocean in the world, with a total area of about 81,500,000 square kilometres. Arms of the Atlantic form the North, Baltic, Caribbean and Mediterranean seas. The Atlantic Ocean is bordered in the west by the Americas and in the east by Europe and Africa. The edges of these continents extend underwater and form gently sloping continental shelves at depths of up to 200 metres.

Beyond the continental shelves the ocean floor plunges to deep basins and trenches, where the water is thousands of metres deep. Running down the centre of the ocean bed is the Mid-Atlantic Ridge. This is one of the great cracks in the Earth's crust. The two sections, or plates, on either side of it are edging apart. As molten rock from deep inside the Earth oozes through and cools, it builds up into ridges of high underwater mountains. These break the surface to form volcanic islands such as St Helena and Tristan da Cunha.

The mixing of cold water from polar regions with warm waters from tropical regions causes powerful ocean currents in the Atlantic. Icy waters are brought from the Arctic by the Labrador and East Greenland currents, while the Benguela and Malvinas currents come from Antarctica. Tropical waters are dispersed by the Brazil Current, the Gulf Stream and the North Atlantic Drift.

The Atlantic Ocean is a treasure store of marine life. It is rich in plankton, which drift with the ocean currents. These tiny plants and animals support whales, seals, turtles, sea birds and thousands of species of fish.

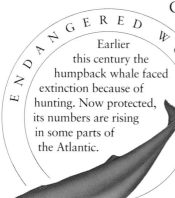

ENDANGERED WORLD

Earlier this century the humpback whale faced extinction because of hunting. Now protected, its numbers are rising in some parts of the Atlantic.

▶ *This picture shows part of the Mid-Atlantic Ridge. It was taken by sonar, which bounces sound waves off the seabed. The bright areas show where lava has welled up to form humps. Underwater mountains appear as round features and rock faults (cracks) as bright lines.*

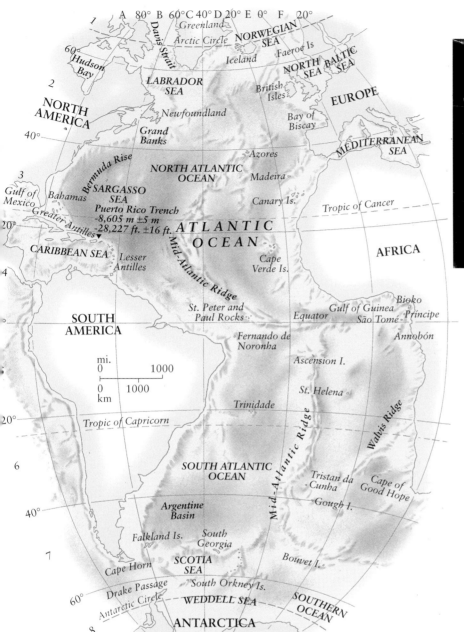

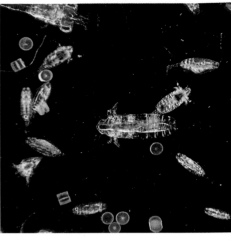

▲ *This is a microscope picture of plankton, the smallest living things in the ocean. Plankton include minute animals and plants, jelly-fish and the eggs and young of fish. They provide plentiful food for larger marine creatures such as fish and whales. Some plankton glow in the dark, making the ocean waves sparkle at night.*

◄ *Great clouds of gas and steam fill the sky as lava from an underwater volcano breaks the surface to form a new island. This volcano erupted off the coast of Iceland in the 1960s. The island that it created is called Surtsey.*

FACTS AND FIGURES
Area: 81,500,000 sq km
Greatest width:
6,700 km
Average depth: 3,600 m
Deepest point:
Puerto Rico Trench
(-8,605 m ±5 m)
Mineral resources:
Oil, natural gas
Living resources: Fish including cod, herring, plaice, flounder, haddock, mackerel and sardines, shellfish
Largest island:
Greenland

561

ATLANTIC OCEAN *People and History*

The Atlantic Ocean began to form about 150 million years ago when movements of the Earth's crust separated North and South America from Europe and Africa. It is the youngest of the world's oceans and takes its name from Atlas, a god that was worshipped by the ancient Greeks.

Early peoples such as the Phoenicians explored the waters of the Atlantic from about 700BC. However, it was not until the AD900s that the Vikings crossed from Europe to Greenland and North America. The great age of Atlantic exploration began with Christopher Columbus, an Italian navigator employed by the Spanish court. In 1492 he sailed to the Caribbean in a fleet of three small, storm-tossed ships. He thought he was sailing to the East Indies, but in fact he had discovered what became known as the New World – the Americas. He was soon followed by explorers from Portugal, Spain, England and France. Exploration of the Atlantic has continued into modern times. Today scientists use sonar (sound waves) to map the ocean floor.

The Atlantic is fished by the fleets of many nations. People have caught fish in these waters for thousands of years, but modern trawling methods have led to a decline in fish stocks. The shallow seas around the ocean's fringes have also been affected by pollution. The Atlantic continues to be a major meeting point for trade and its waters are crossed by many busy shipping routes.

▼ *Natural gas is produced from a drilling rig in the North Sea. Many rich mineral reserves lie underneath the Atlantic Ocean. There are large gas and oil fields beneath the North Sea, the Gulf of Mexico, the Caribbean and the Gulf of Guinea.*

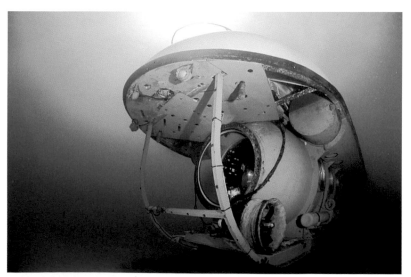

◄ *This vessel is a submersible (a non-military submarine). Submersibles like this are used by scientists to explore the ocean floor. They carry lights, cameras and a variety of recording equipment. Some can reach depths of more than 4,000 metres.*

▲ Survivors take to the lifeboats as the SS Titanic *is sunk by an iceberg in 1912. This great liner was designed to be unsinkable, but 1,513 passengers and crew were drowned on its first voyage. The Atlantic is a dangerous, stormy ocean and even today shipwrecks occur. Icebergs are still a potential threat, but aircraft belonging to the International Ice Patrol can now warn ships of their whereabouts.*

▲ *Activists from the environmental group Greenpeace protest against Norwegian whaling. During the first half of this century whale-hunting had a disastrous effect on many species, including the humpback and the bowhead. It has now been strictly limited by international treaties, but some slaughter continues.*

▶ *This map of the Atlantic Ocean was drawn in 1558. It shows the coastlines of Africa and America. The European explorers of the 1500s rushed greedily to exploit the resources of newly discovered lands. They killed or enslaved many Native Americans and Africans and committed acts of piracy against each other.*

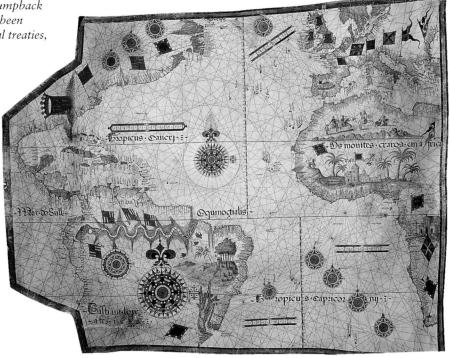

ANTARCTICA *Introduction*

This vast wilderness at the bottom of the world is almost entirely covered by a sheet of ice that is about 4,800 metres thick at its deepest point. Antarctica is the fifth largest continent and the coldest by far. The world's lowest-ever recorded temperature, minus 89·2 degrees centigrade, was measured at a Russian scientific base called Vostok Station in 1983.

The only ice-free land to be seen in Antarctica consists of a few mountain peaks and other barren, rocky areas. As ice sheets around the coasts melt during the southern summer, great sections break off as icebergs. These icebergs can measure up to 60 metres in height and many kilometres long. They are extremely dangerous to passing ships.

The Transantarctic Mountains cross this icy continent, dividing it into eastern and western regions. There is a high, ice-covered plateau in the east, while the western region consists of a group of mountainous islands joined by ice. There are some volcanoes there, including the continent's most active volcano, Mount Erebus. The western region also contains the continent's highest point, Vinson Massif, which measures 4,897 metres above sea level.

The cold Antarctic waters are rich with krill, small crustaceans (hard-shelled animals), fish, seals and whales. Seabirds such as skuas and albatrosses abound and there are eight types of penguins. Plant life is limited because of the bitter cold, but mosses and lichens are found around the coast. In 1994 scientists reported a rapid rise in the number of coastal plants, which seemed to support suggestions that the world's climate is getting warmer.

▲ *The aurora australis (southern lights) flash eerily across the sky. They may be seen when particles from the Sun stream into the Earth's atmosphere. Magnetic forces around the Earth pull the particles towards the North and South poles.*

◄ *A colony of Emperor penguins crowds a stretch of thick sea ice. The smaller grey birds are penguin chicks. The Emperor is one of two species of penguins that nest on the ice shelves of Antarctica. Six other species visit Antarctic waters, but nest on remote islands. Penguins cannot fly, but they are excellent swimmers.*

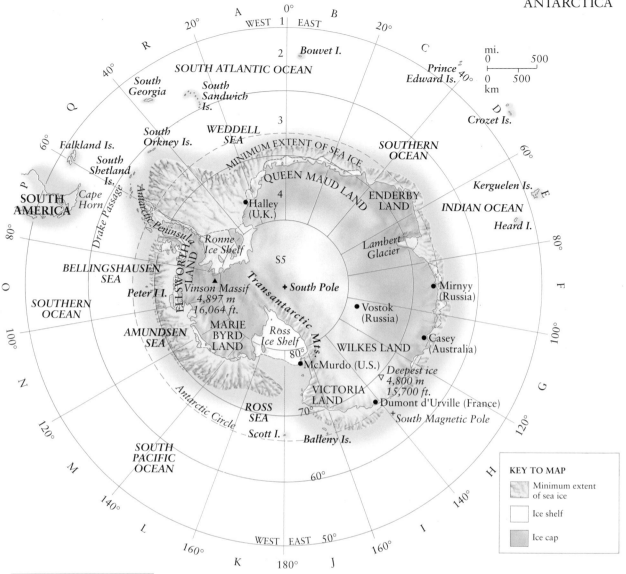

KEY TO MAP

Minimum extent of sea ice

Ice shelf

Ice cap

FACTS AND FIGURES
Area: 14,000,000 sq km
Population: No permanent population
Highest point: Vinson Massif (4,897 m)
Ice cover: Ice and snow cover 98 percent of Antarctica.
Average depth of ice: 2,000 m
Deepest ice: 4,800 m
Mineral resources: In 1991 commercial mining was banned in Antarctica for 50 years.
Living resources: Cod, icefish, krill

▶ *Taylor Valley is in the Transantarctic Mountains. It is one of Antarctica's dry valleys (places where glaciers have retreated to reveal the bare rock). These are among the driest places on Earth – Antarctica is really a frozen desert. Its air is too cold to contain much moisture and rain is almost unknown there.*

ANTARCTICA *People and History*

▲ *This fossil of a fern was found on Alexander Island, off the Antarctic Peninsula. Fossils such as this show that about 300 million years ago Antarctica was a much warmer place than it is today, covered with plants.*

Antarctica has such a harsh landscape and climate that people have never settled here permanently. Its only inhabitants are visiting scientists who carry out research projects.

The Antarctic Circle is an imaginary line around the world that marks the latitude of 66 degrees 30 minutes south. The first people to cross it were probably Maoris from New Zealand. In 1773 the English navigator James Cook visited the ice pack surrounding the continent. He was followed by British, Russian and French expeditions as well as seal hunters from many countries.

By the early part of this century the inland area of Antarctica was one of the last unexplored places on Earth. Robert Falcon Scott led an expedition from 1900 to 1904 and in 1909 Ernest Shackleton got to within 150 kilometres of the South Pole. The Pole was finally reached by the Norwegian Roald Amundsen in 1911. Another expedition led by Scott arrived at the Pole a month later, but all its members died on the return journey. Later expeditions made use of icebreaking ships, aircraft and tracked vehicles.

Antarctica is not owned by any country. However, it is rich in minerals and fish, so various nations have made claims here. Twelve nations signed a treaty in 1959 encouraging scientific research and peace in Antarctica. Thirty-eight countries now support this treaty. In 1991 mining was banned for 50 years as part of an effort to keep this wilderness unspoilt and unexploited by people.

◄ *Aircraft fitted with skis land on the ice, bringing much-needed supplies to the camp of an Antarctic expedition. Aircraft have been used for exploring Antarctica since the 1920s and are a vital link between scientists there and the outside world.*

◄ The Norwegian explorer, Roald Amundsen, plants his country's flag at the South Pole. Amundsen's expedition was the first to reach the Pole. It arrived on December 14, 1911. Amundsen's success was due to his wise choice of route and skilled use of sled dogs to pull supplies.

► This satellite picture shows ozone levels over Antarctica in 1994. Ozone is a gas, high in the Earth's atmosphere, that protects life on Earth from harmful rays. The ozone layer is being destroyed by the use of chemicals on Earth such as CFCs. A thinning of the layer has taken place over Antarctica. On this picture the thin area is coloured grey and pink.

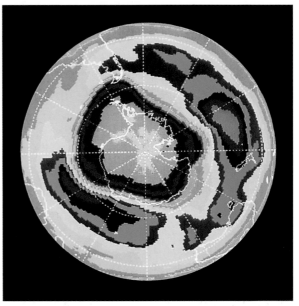

◄ A scientist takes measurements on Antarctica's ice. The scientific study of ice is called glaciology. Glaciologists go to Antarctica to find out how the world is affected by Ice Ages and climatic changes. Keeping Antarctica as an unspoilt area where scientists can carry out their studies could be vital to the future of the planet.

ARCTIC

▼ The aurora borealis (northern lights) form bands of coloured light in the Arctic sky. They are caused by a stream of particles from the Sun that are attracted to the poles by the Earth's magnetism.

The Arctic Circle is an imaginary line around the northern part of the globe. On maps it appears at the latitude of 66 degrees 30 minutes north. Within this desolate area lies the Arctic Ocean, which is frozen over for much of the year. When the ice breaks up in spring it forms huge floes (fields of ice). Parts of the ocean never melt, but create a great ice cap around the North Pole.

The Arctic Ocean is bordered by Greenland and the northern parts of Canada, Alaska, Russia and Scandinavia. The peoples of these snowy lands include the Inuit (Eskimos) of Greenland, North America and northeast Asia, the Aleuts of Alaska, the Lapps of Scandinavia and the Yakuts and Chukchee of Russia. Many follow a traditional way of life, hunting fish, seals and whales, or herding reindeer.

There are many islands here, some of them mountainous, and treeless plains called tundra cover a wide area. During the brief summer it is warm enough on the tundra for flowers to bloom and scrubby plants provide grazing for caribou and reindeer. There are also voles and lemmings, providing food for Arctic foxes and birds of prey such as owls. The Arctic Ocean is rich in plankton, which are devoured by whales. Fish such as cod and Arctic char are preyed on by walruses and seals, which in turn are hunted by polar bears.

Russians and Scandinavians were exploring the Arctic from the 1600s onwards, but the first person to reach the North Pole over the ice was Commander Robert Peary of the United States Navy in 1909.

FACTS AND FIGURES
Area (Arctic Ocean): 9,500,000 sq km
Area (land): The Arctic includes the northern parts of Europe, Asia and North America. Its southern boundary is the Arctic Circle.
Average depth of Arctic Ocean: 1,300 m
Deepest point: -5,450 m
Mineral resources: Oil, natural gas, coal
Living resources: Fish, seals

▶ The Scottish explorer Captain John Ross meets some of the peoples of the Arctic, the Inuit (Eskimo) of northern Greenland, in 1818. Captain Ross was searching for the Northwest Passage, a sea route around North America to China.

◄ In the bitter cold, an Inuit scientist uses alcohol to free his instruments from frost. His equipment is used to measure Arctic sunlight by focusing the rays of the Sun onto a card. Several countries have scientific research stations in the Arctic. Weather information collected here helps forecasters predict storms in some parts of the world.

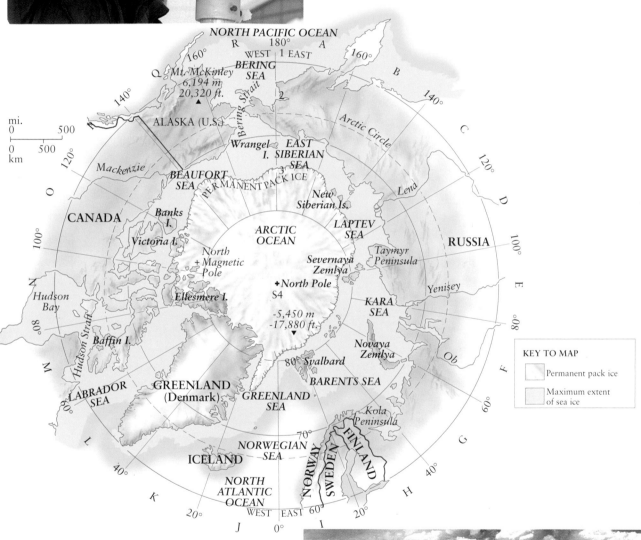

► A polar bear picks its way across an ice floe off the island of Spitzbergen in the Norwegian Arctic. Polar bears live all around the Arctic coasts. They are strong swimmers, with a thick layer of fat and dense fur to protect them against the icy waters. Camouflaged by this creamy fur, they can pounce on seals coming up to breathe though holes in the ice.

PLANET EARTH

Buried deep in the heart of our planet is a metal core of iron and nickel that is larger than the Moon and almost as hot as the surface of the Sun. The outer layer of the core is liquid metal, but at the centre enormous pressure has compressed it into a solid. When the Earth formed 4,600 million years ago, it glowed red hot and the molten metals sank to its centre while the lighter rocks floated to the surface.

Around the core is wrapped a thick layer of hot rock called the mantle. This acts like a heated blanket, holding in the warmth. Around the mantle is a third layer called the crust, which forms the rocky surface of the Earth on which we live. The thickest parts of the crust are about 60 kilometres deep, but if the Earth were compared to an apple, the crust would only be as thick as the apple's skin.

The mantle contains traces of radioactive uranium which steadily gives out heat. This warmth rises, creating a more fluid part of the mantle known as the asthenosphere. Above the asthenosphere lies the lithosphere, which includes the outermost mantle and the crust. The lithosphere is made up of massive plates which float on the fluid asthenosphere. These plates are constantly moving, causing the continents to drift apart, mountains to form, the ground to shake and volcanoes to erupt.

FACTS AND FIGURES
Diameter at the Equator: 12,756 km
Diameter at the poles: 12,713 km
Diameter of core: 7,000 km
Thickness of mantle: 2,900 km
Temperature of inner core: up to 7,000 °C
Mass of Earth: 5,900 billion billion tonnes
Average density: 5.5 tonnes/cu m
Land area: 149 million sq km
Ocean area: 361 million sq km
Volume of ocean: 1,321 million cu km
Age: 4,600 million years
Atmosphere: 78% nitrogen, 21% oxygen, 1% argon
Time to rotate on axis: 23 hours 56 minutes
Time to orbit the Sun: About 365 days 6 hours

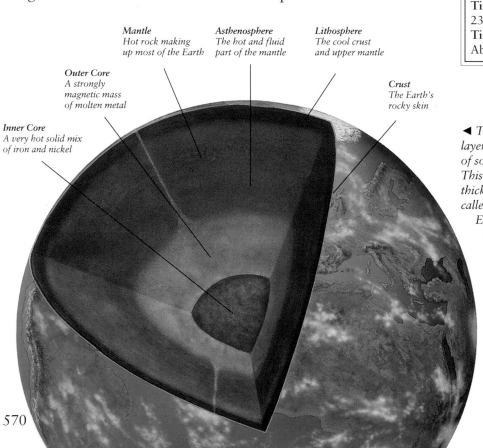

Mantle
Hot rock making up most of the Earth

Asthenosphere
The hot and fluid part of the mantle

Lithosphere
The cool crust and upper mantle

Outer Core
A strongly magnetic mass of molten metal

Crust
The Earth's rocky skin

Inner Core
A very hot solid mix of iron and nickel

◀ *The Earth is made up of layers. At its centre is a core of solid and liquid metal. This is surrounded by a thick layer of hot rock called the mantle. The Earth's surface is formed by a thin, hard crust.*

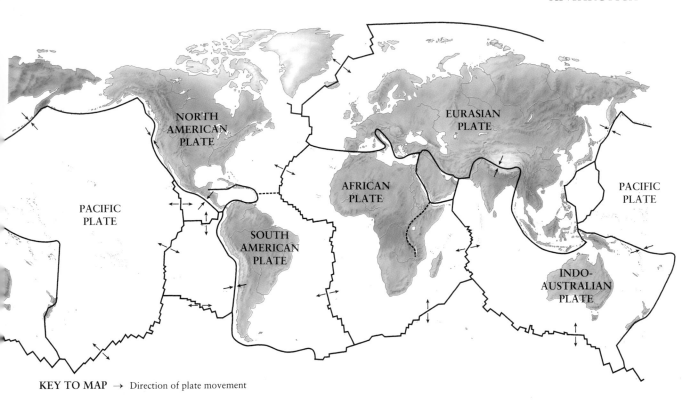

KEY TO MAP → Direction of plate movement

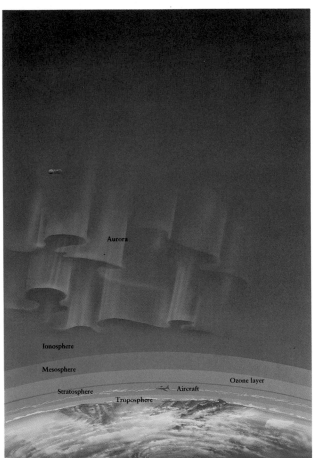

▲ The Earth's lithosphere (the crust and upper mantle) is broken up into huge pieces called plates. These plates are slowly moving. Where they collide with each other, mountain ranges rise. Where they move apart, hot rock wells up from below, creating new crust.

◄ The layers of the Earth's atmosphere form a blanket of air surrounding our planet. The atmosphere is mainly made up of the gases nitrogen and oxygen. The layer nearest the Earth, the troposphere, contains most of these gases. Above it aircraft fly in the stratosphere, which also contains the ozone layer, a protective barrier against harmful radiation from the Sun. High up in the ionosphere spectacular displays of coloured light, called auroras, are seen. Beyond about 1,000 kilometres from Earth the atmosphere fades into Space.

571

EARTH IN THE SOLAR SYSTEM

The Earth belongs to a family of nine planets, each of which is in orbit (travelling) around the Sun. Together they make up the Solar System, which also includes the moons orbiting around their planets, lumps of rock called asteroids and comets with their long tails of dust and gas.

The Sun, the star at the centre of the Solar System, is a burning hot ball of shining gas. Without its heat and light the Earth would be a frozen, dead world. Among the nine planets that orbit the Sun the Earth is unique. Only the Earth has water in its oceans and enough oxygen in its atmosphere to support animal life. Mercury, Venus, Mars and Pluto are rocky wastes. The giant planets Jupiter, Saturn, Uranus and Neptune are globes of gas and ice particles. The Earth is habitable because it is at just the right distance from the Sun. A little closer and it would resemble roasting Venus. A little farther away and it would be a permanently frozen waste.

However, the Earth has not always been how it is now. Soon after it formed, about 4,600 million years ago, this planet was a roasting cauldron. Over millions of years the surface cooled and the atmosphere, oceans and continents formed. Life began in the oceans about 3,500 million years ago with tiny, microscopic life-forms. Many scientists think that animals and plants started to live on the land about 400 million years ago.

Opposite are the nine planets in order of distance from the Sun. Pluto, normally the outermost planet, will be closer to the Sun than Neptune until 1999.

KEY

1 Mercury	6 Saturn
2 Venus	7 Uranus
3 Earth	8 Neptune
4 Mars	9 Pluto
5 Jupiter	

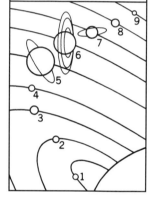

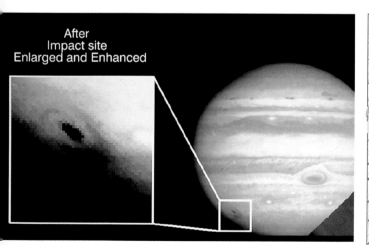

▲ *In July 1994, large pieces of the comet* Shoemaker-Levy 9 *collided with Jupiter, causing explosions like the one shown here. If this happened to the Earth the impact would throw up huge amounts of dust into the atmosphere. This would block out heat and light from the Sun, turning the Earth much colder.*

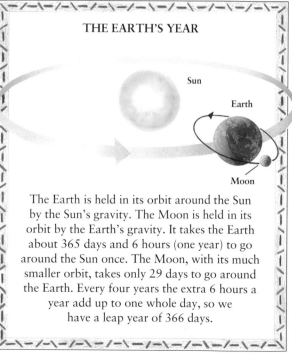

THE EARTH'S YEAR

The Earth is held in its orbit around the Sun by the Sun's gravity. The Moon is held in its orbit by the Earth's gravity. It takes the Earth about 365 days and 6 hours (one year) to go around the Sun once. The Moon, with its much smaller orbit, takes only 29 days to go around the Earth. Every four years the extra 6 hours a year add up to one whole day, so we have a leap year of 366 days.

HOW EARTH BEGAN

▲ *This huge cloud of dust and gas is the Orion Nebula. Inside it, stars are forming. About 4,600 million years ago the Sun and the planets were forming inside a nebula like this.*

Most scientists believe that the Sun and planets formed about 4,600 million years ago from a huge cloud of tiny, solid particles and gases called a nebula. The solid particles and some of the gas had been thrown out of earlier stars that had died. The nebula began to shrink and spin, collapsing inwards because of its own gravity. Soon, material near the centre was colliding at tremendous speeds and giving out so much heat that a glowing star, the Sun, was born. The rest of the nebula formed into a ring around the Sun and collisions inside this ring built up the planets. For a time the planets were very hot, but they never became hot enough to shine like stars.

All the planets were bombarded by other much smaller bodies, so that their surfaces became covered with craters like the ones still seen on the Moon today. On the Earth, however, wind and rain have gradually worn most of the craters away. The Earth's original atmosphere probably contained large amounts of carbon dioxide, a gas made up of carbon and oxygen. As plants developed on Earth they used the carbon dioxide to make food and released the oxygen on which all animal life depends.

The Sun will continue to shine for millions of years, but eventually it will burn up all its fuel and die. Then the Earth will be left as a cold, lifeless rock. This process is shown opposite.

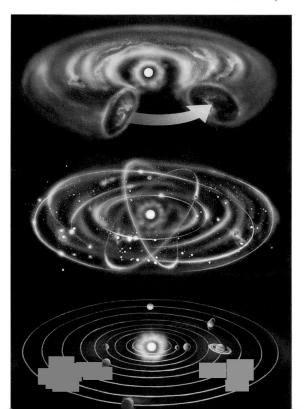

◄ *When the Solar System formed, about 4,600 million years ago, it could have looked like this. The young Sun was surrounded by a ring of gas and dust. Inside it the planets began to form.*

◄ *As the planets grew the force field around them became stronger. When small bodies passed by some were pulled in and began to orbit the planets. Others were flung out and became comets with long orbits around the Sun.*

◄ *After several million years the planets settled down to form the Solar System. They continued to be hit by smaller rocks and these impacts formed craters. As the Sun heated up any remaining gas and dust was blown into Space.*

◄ *Today the Sun shines on the Earth, producing heat and light by nuclear reactions deep inside its centre. The Sun is fuelled by hydrogen, a type of gas which it turns into helium, another gas. This releases energy as heat and light. The Sun will continue to shine like this for millions of years.*

► *Some astronomers believe that in about 5,000 million years the Sun will have used up all its hydrogen fuel and will start to die. It will grow brighter and hotter. The Earth's polar caps will melt and the oceans will turn to steam. All life on Earth will die in the stifling heat.*

◄ *The Sun will then expand into a giant red star. Its outer layers will blow out, becoming cooler and redder. The Earth's atmosphere will be stripped away, leaving a bare, rocky planet whose surface will be scorched by the Sun.*

► *After a few hundred million years the Sun will shrink to a tiny, white dwarf star. The daytime sky will be black, and the Sun's rays will be too weak to warm the Earth's dead, frozen landscape. Finally, it will cool to become an invisible, black dwarf star.*

THE SEARCH FOR OTHER EARTHS

The Sun belongs to a galaxy made up of many millions of stars. Some of these stars are much brighter than the Sun and some are much dimmer. Even so, there are probably millions of stars just like our own Sun. The formation of planets is thought to have been a natural part of the Sun's formation. This may mean that other stars in the galaxy have also formed planets. Some of these, like our Earth, may be able to support life. There are countless millions of other galaxies in the Universe, so many scientists believe that intelligent life must exist elsewhere. Some scientists hope to find other inhabited planets by picking up radio signals sent out by any alien civilizations that may exist. A project called the Search for Extra-Terrestrial Intelligence (SETI), has been trying to identify signals from space that sound artifical. So far it has been unsuccessful.

Other scientists have sent out radio messages from Earth. They hope that if there are alien civilizations, they will pick these up and reply. Some space probes have plaques on their sides showing the position of Earth and its people. Others have electronically encoded pictures, greetings and music. It is hoped that as they drift out of our Solar System and into others, alien spacecraft may intercept them because they want to find out about life on our planet.

▲ *Radio telescopes like this one at Parkes Observatory, Australia, are used to hunt for signals from other inhabited worlds. The search is difficult because nobody knows what kinds of signals they are looking for.*

▶ *This coded radio message was transmitted in 1974 by the world's largest radio telescope, at Arecibo in Puerto Rico. It was sent to the Hercules constellation and will arrive there in about the year 26,000.*

◀ *This is the Andromeda spiral galaxy, photographed through a telescope on Earth. Our galaxy, the Milky Way, would look something like this if seen from space. The Andromeda galaxy contains billions of stars, millions of which are like the Sun. Perhaps these stars have planets orbiting them too.*

MAP PROJECTIONS

GLOBE PROJECTIONS OF THE WORLD

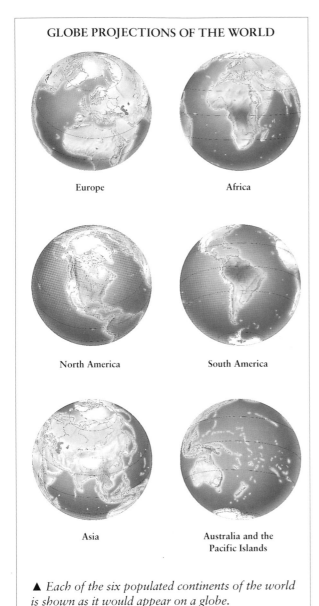

Europe

Africa

North America

South America

Asia

Australia and the
Pacific Islands

▲ *Each of the six populated continents of the world
is shown as it would appear on a globe.*

The only really accurate map of the world is a round model called a globe, because the Earth itself is round. Map-makers use a technique called projection to show the curved surface of the Earth on flat maps of continents and countries. It is impossible for all areas, shapes, distances and directions to be drawn accurately on a flat map, so map projections are worked out mathematically to preserve chosen features. For example, Mercator's projection distorts areas in order to maintain directions, so that it can be used for navigation.

Map-makers draw imaginary lines around the Earth in a grid to help the map-reader find places. These are lines of latitude and longitude. Lines of latitude run horizontally across the globe. The line where the Earth's circumference is at its greatest is called the Equator. Parallel lines of latitude are drawn north and south of the Equator.

Lines of longitude run vertically up and down the globe. The prime meridian (zero degrees longitude) runs through Greenwich in London, England. Other lines of longitude are drawn up to 180 degrees east and west of this line. They all start at the North pole and finish at the South pole.

Egyptian Sun disc

World map from 1600s

		BC30,000		8000		5000
	EUROPE	c.30,000 Cro-Magnon people living in Europe.		c.8000 End of last Ice Age, widespread floods.	c.6500 Farming in Southeast Europe.	c.5000 Rising sea levels isolate Britain.
	AFRICA	c.30,000 Stone Age peoples living in most of Africa.	8500 Rock paintings in Sahara, then rich grassland.		6000 Farming in Egypt.	
	THE AMERICAS	c.30,000 Native Americans living in North America.	c.10,000 Hunters spread over North and South America.	c.8000 End of last Ice Age. Floods cut off the Americas from Asia.	c.7000 Beans grown in Mexico.	c.5000 Llamas domesticated in Andes.
	ASIA	c.30,000 Stone Age peoples living across most of Asia.		c.8000 Farming in Southwest Asia. End of last Ice Age, widespread floods.		c.5000 Rice grown in China.
	AUSTRALIA AND THE PACIFIC ISLANDS	c.30,000 Aboriginal peoples living in Australia.				c.5000 Rising sea levels isol New Guinea and Tasmania.

c. = circa (around)

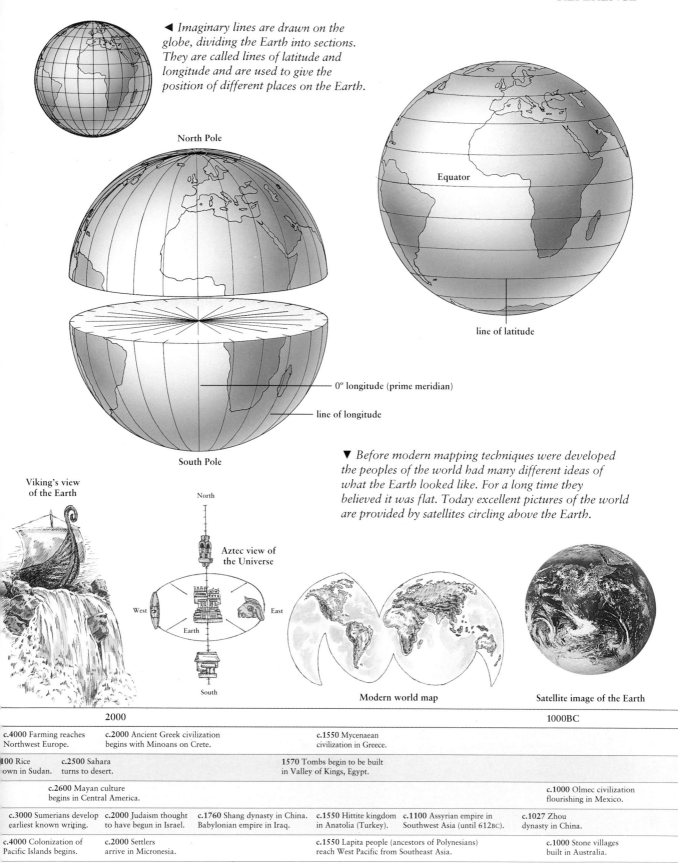

◄ *Imaginary lines are drawn on the globe, dividing the Earth into sections. They are called lines of latitude and longitude and are used to give the position of different places on the Earth.*

North Pole

Equator

line of latitude

0° longitude (prime meridian)

line of longitude

South Pole

Viking's view of the Earth

▼ *Before modern mapping techniques were developed the peoples of the world had many different ideas of what the Earth looked like. For a long time they believed it was flat. Today excellent pictures of the world are provided by satellites circling above the Earth.*

North

Aztec view of the Universe

West   East

Earth

South

Modern world map

Satellite image of the Earth

2000				1000BC
c.4000 Farming reaches Northwest Europe.	**c.2000** Ancient Greek civilization begins with Minoans on Crete.	**c.1550** Mycenaean civilization in Greece.		
100 Rice own in Sudan. **c.2500** Sahara turns to desert.		1570 Tombs begin to be built in Valley of Kings, Egypt.		
c.2600 Mayan culture begins in Central America.				**c.1000** Olmec civilization flourishing in Mexico.
c.3000 Sumerians develop earliest known writing.	**c.2000** Judaism thought to have begun in Israel.	**c.1760** Shang dynasty in China. Babylonian empire in Iraq. **c.1550** Hittite kingdom in Anatolia (Turkey).	**c.1100** Assyrian empire in Southwest Asia (until 612BC).	**c.1027** Zhou dynasty in China.
c.4000 Colonization of Pacific Islands begins.	**c.2000** Settlers arrive in Micronesia.	**c.1550** Lapita people (ancestors of Polynesians) reach West Pacific from Southeast Asia.		**c.1000** Stone villages built in Australia.

CONTINENTS C

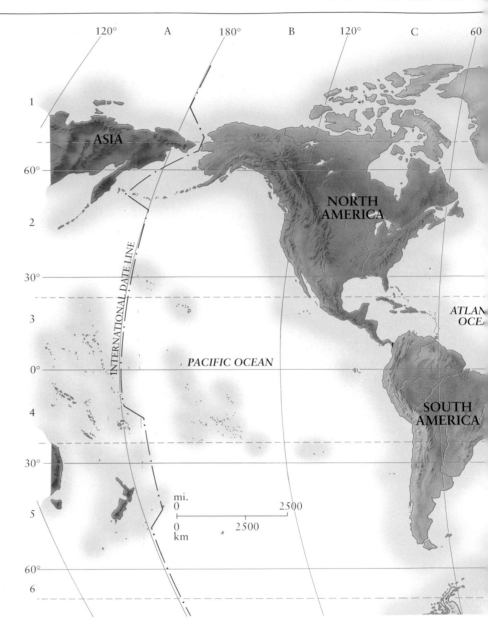

		900BC	800		600
	EUROPE		**c.800** Celtic Hallstatt culture flourishes in central Europe. Etruscan civilization begins in Italy.	**753** Rome founded.	
	AFRICA	**c.900** Kingdom of Kush founded, Nubia. Nok culture in West Africa (until AD200).	**814** Phoenicians colonize city of Carthage, North Africa (destroyed by Rome 146BC).		
	THE AMERICAS		**800** Intensive maize cultivation in the Amazon Basin.		
	ASIA		**800** Cities and farming flourishing in Ganges Valley, India.	**660** Jimmu Tenno becomes first emperor of Japan.	**c.600** Birth of Lao-Tzu, founder of Taoism, in Chi
	AUSTRALIA AND THE PACIFIC ISLANDS				**600** Development of Polynesian languages.

HE WORLD

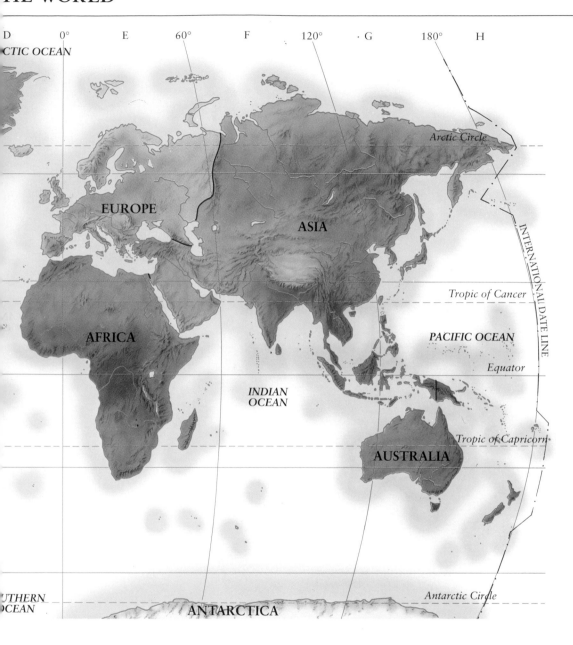

D　　0°　　　　E　　　60°　　　　F　　　120°　　·G　　　180°　　　H

CTIC OCEAN

Arctic Circle

EUROPE

ASIA

AFRICA

INTERNATIONAL DATE LINE

Tropic of Cancer

PACIFIC OCEAN

Equator

INDIAN
OCEAN

Tropic of Capricorn

AUSTRALIA

UTHERN
OCEAN

Antarctic Circle

ANTARCTICA

	550				BC 0 AD		AD150
		c.480 Celtic culture spreads across Europe. Greek civilization at its peak.		146 Greece conquered by Rome. Greek civilization ends.	50 Rome is largest city in the world (about one million people).		117 Roman empire at its greatest size.
				100 Bantu languages spread outwards from West Africa.	c.50 Kingdom of Aksum important in Ethiopia.		
			200 Nazca civilization flourishing in Peru.		50 Pyramid of the Sun built in Tenochtitlán, Mexico.		
563 Birth of autama Siddhartha.	551 Birth of Confucius.	c.550 Persian empire founded.	206 Han empire is vast in China.	c.5 Birth of Jesus Christ.	30 Crucifixion of Jesus Christ.	105 Paper is invented in China.	150 Buddhism reaches China.
			c.200 Lapita people settle on Marquesas Islands.		c.100 First settlers arrive in Tahiti, French Polynesia.		

PHYSICAL GEOGRAPH

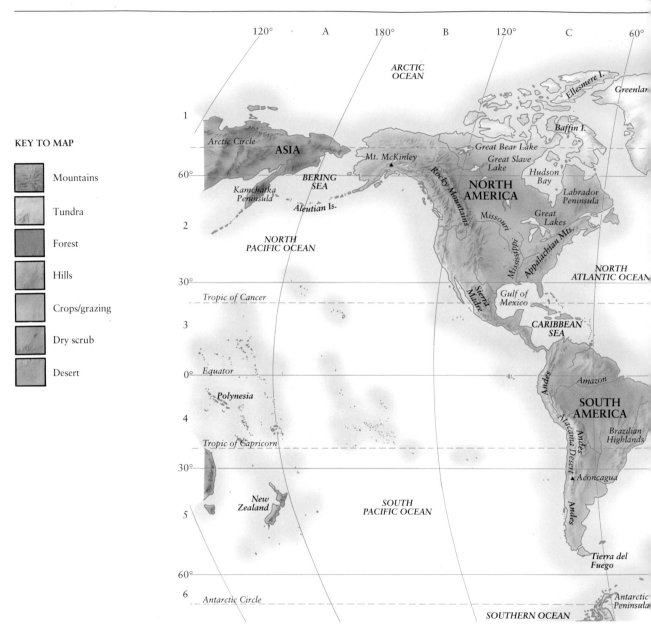

KEY TO MAP

Mountains

Tundra

Forest

Hills

Crops/grazing

Dry scrub

Desert

		AD200		400	500
	EUROPE		**285** Roman empire divided into eastern and western parts.	**313** Christianity allowed throughout Roman empire.	**476** Collapse of western part of Roman empire, eastern part continues as Byzantine empire.	**486** Foundation of Frankis kingdom in Western Europ
	AFRICA				**429** Vandals colonize North Africa.	**c.500** Bantu-speaking peoples in southern Afric
	THE AMERICAS		**c.250** Mayan culture dominates Central America (until 900).			**c.500** Farming settlemen in Mississippi Basin.
	ASIA			**320** Gupta empire starts in India (ends 500).	**400s** Hinduism flourishing in India.	**c.550** Buddhis reaches Japan
	AUSTRALIA AND THE PACIFIC ISLANDS	**c.200** Decline of Lapita culture in Pacific.			**c.400** Polynesians settle Easter Island.	

OF THE WORLD

0°   E   60°   F   120°   G   180°   H

ARCTIC OCEAN

Svalbard

Novaya Zemlya

Iceland

Siberia

Scandinavian Peninsula

Lake Onega

British Isles

NORTH SEA

Lake Ladoga

Volga

Ural Mountains

Kamchatka Peninsula

EUROPE

ASIA

Lake Baikal

NORTH PACIFIC OCEAN

Alps

BLACK SEA

CASPIAN SEA

Mt. Elbrus

ARAL SEA

Lake Balkhash

Gobi Desert

SEA OF JAPAN

Honshu

MEDITERRANEAN SEA

Plateau of Tibet

Atlas Mts.

Himalaya Mts.

Mt. Everest

Chang Jiang (Yangtze)

Sahara Desert

Nile

RED SEA

Rub al Khali

ARABIAN SEA

Bay of Bengal

SOUTH CHINA SEA

Sahel

Lake Chad

Sri Lanka

Borneo

Micronesia

AFRICA

Ethiopian Plateau

Gulf of Guinea

Lake Victoria

Sumatra

New Guinea

Mt. Wilhelm

Mt. Kilimanjaro

INDIAN OCEAN

Java

Lake Tanganyika

Melanesia

Lake Nyasa

SOUTH ATLANTIC OCEAN

Kalahari Desert

Madagascar

AUSTRALIA

CORAL SEA

Great Victoria Desert

SOUTH PACIFIC OCEAN

Darling

Cape Agulhas

Mt. Kosciusko

Murray

New Zealand

mi.
0   2500
0   2500
km

Tasmania

SOUTHERN OCEAN

ANTARCTICA

	700			AD800
	c.680 Bulgars invade Balkans.		711 Spain invaded by Moors. 787 Vikings start to raid Europe.	800 Charlemagne, king of the Franks, crowned Holy Roman Emperor.
	641 Arabs invade North Africa, bringing Islam.	c.700 Songhai empire founded in West Africa.	710 All North Africa occupied by Arabs.	800 Kanem-Bornu empire thriving in West Africa.
		c.700 Hohokam, Mogollon and Anasazi cultures flourish in southwestern North America.		
22 Muhammad in Medina. tart of Islamic calendar.	630s Islamic Arabs begin to conquer Middle East and spread Islamic faith.	700s Spices traded from islands in Southeast Asia.		c.800 Khmer empire established in Cambodia.
				c850 Polynesian ancestors of Maoris settle North Island, New Zealand.

GEOGRAPHICAL COMPARISONS

The surface of the Earth is made up of about 70 percent water and 30 percent land. It is divided into four oceans and seven continents. The largest ocean is the Pacific, which covers an area larger than all the land put together. The Pacific also contains the deepest point on Earth, Challenger Deep in the Mariana Trench. Asia is the largest continent. It is more than four times the size of Europe and covers nearly a third of the total land area.

Apart from ice-bound Antarctica, the continents share many geographical features. Mountains, which have been formed by movements of the Earth's crust and volcanoes, cover around a quarter of the landmass. Deserts, both hot and cold, cover about a fifth. The world's largest desert, the Sahara, stretches over nearly a third of the African continent.

The Earth's climate ranges from freezing cold at the North and South poles to the tropical heat and abundant rainfall commonly found in areas near the Equator. Climate plays an important part in influencing how and where people live. Most of the world's population is found in places where the soil is fertile and rainfall is plentiful. Regions that are too hot, cold or dry can support very little life.

▼ *Sulphur springs stain the ground yellow at Dallol in Ethiopia, one of the hottest places on Earth. The average yearly temperature recorded there is a scorching 34 degrees centigrade.*

► *A signpost marks the Earth's magnetic south pole near the South Pole in Antarctica. Permanently covered in ice, Antarctica is the world's coldest place. Temperatures there rarely rise above 0 degrees centigrade. Russian scientists have measured an incredibly low temperature of minus 89 degrees centigrade at Vostok research station (behind).*

		AD900		1000	
	EUROPE	896 Magyars invade Hungary.	930 World's first parliament, the Althing, founded in Iceland.		
	AFRICA	900 Swahili traders on East African coast.		1000 West African kingdoms prospering.	1056 Growth in powe of Berber people.
	THE AMERICAS	c.900 Arawaks conquered by Caribs in Caribbean (until 1300). Inuit Thule culture starts, North Alaska.	c.950 Toltec empire thriving in Mexico (until 1200).	c.1000 Vikings arrive in North America from Europe.	c.1050 Anasazi settlements in Chaco Canyon, North America
	ASIA		939 Vietnam independent.	960 Song dynasty starts in China (ends 1279). Growth of trade.	1050 Start of Muslim invasions of India.
	AUSTRALIA AND THE PACIFIC ISLANDS			c.1000 Huge stone heads raised on Easter Island. Polynesians are the most widespread people on Earth.	

▲ *Rain clouds gather on the hills above Cherrapunji in northeastern India, one of the wettest places in the world. Over 2,600 centimetres of rainfall was recorded there in one year. Mawsynram, about 16 kilometres from Cherrapunji, is the wettest place in the world. Over a 38-year-period scientists recorded an average annual rainfall of over 1,187 centimetres.*

FACTS AND FIGURES

Largest ocean: Pacific (180,000,000 sq km)
Smallest ocean: Arctic (9,500,000 sq km)
Largest sea: South China Sea (2,975,000 sq km)
Largest lake: Caspian Sea, Europe and Asia (371,000 sq km)
Largest freshwater lake: Lake Superior, North America (82,200 sq km)
Deepest lake: Lake Baikal, Asia (1,620 m)
Highest waterfall: Angel Falls, South America (979 m)
Longest river: Nile, Africa (6,670 km)
Largest river basin: Amazon, South America (7,045,000 sq km)
Largest river delta: Ganges-Brahmaputra, Asia (75,000 sq km)
Largest land gorge: Grand Canyon, USA (446 km long, up to 1.6 km deep)
Largest plateau: Tibetan plateau, Asia (1,850,000 sq km)
Highest point: Mt Everest, Asia (8,848 m)
Lowest point: Shoreline of the Dead Sea, Asia (399 m below sea level)
Largest desert: Sahara, Africa (9,200,000 sq km)
Longest coral reef: Great Barrier Reef, Australia (2,030 km)
Largest island: Greenland (2,175,600 sq km)

▶ *A plant struggles through a crack in the ground after a rare shower of rain in the Atacama Desert, Chile. The city of Arica in this desert is the driest place on Earth. At one time no rain fell there for 14 years. Although the Atacama Desert itself is almost barren of life, it contains many valuable minerals.*

1100		AD 1200	
1066 Normans from France conquer England and build castles.	1143 Portugal independent.		1236-41 Mongols invade Russia, Poland, Hungary and Bohemia.
	1100 Age of Great Zimbabwe flourishing in southeast Africa.		1240 Mali becomes most powerful state in West Africa (defeated by Songhai 1546).
		c.1200 Rise of new Maya culture in Mexico.	
1096 Crusades (holy wars) start between Muslims and European Christians (Crusades end 1291).	1192 Minamoto Yoritomo becomes first shogun of Japan.	1206 Genghis Khan and Mongols begin conquest of Asia.	1259 Kublai Khan becomes emperor of China. (His Yuan dynasty lasts until 1368.)
		c.1200 Tahitians migrate to Hawaii from Polynesia and win control over earlier settlers. Growing power of Polynesian chiefs.	

GEOGRAPHICAL COMPARISONS

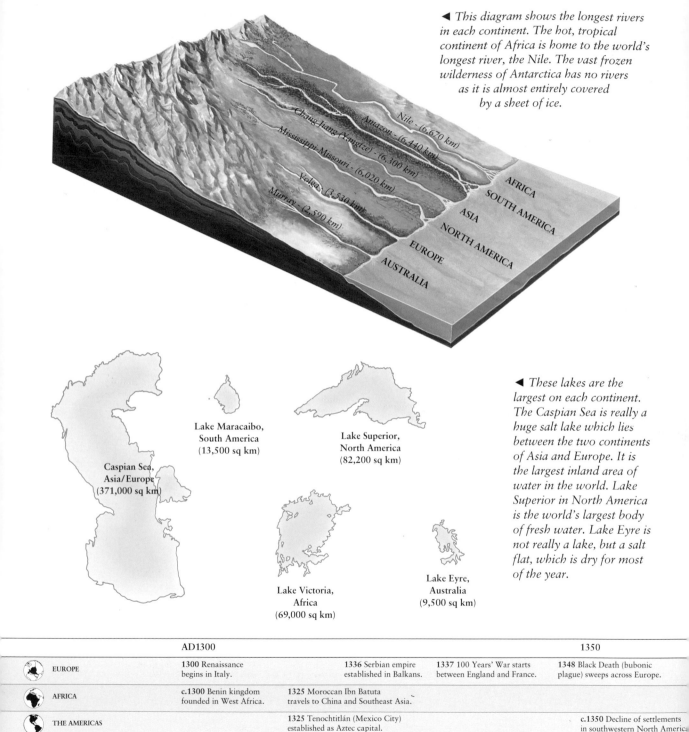

◄ *This diagram shows the longest rivers in each continent. The hot, tropical continent of Africa is home to the world's longest river, the Nile. The vast frozen wilderness of Antarctica has no rivers as it is almost entirely covered by a sheet of ice.*

Nile - (6,670 km)

Amazon - (6,440 km)

Chang Jiang (Yangtze) - (6,300 km)

Mississippi-Missouri - (6,020 km)

Volga - (3,530 km)

Murray - (2,590 km)

AFRICA

SOUTH AMERICA

ASIA

NORTH AMERICA

EUROPE

AUSTRALIA

Lake Maracaibo,
South America
(13,500 sq km)

Lake Superior,
North America
(82,200 sq km)

Caspian Sea,
Asia/Europe
(371,000 sq km)

Lake Victoria,
Africa
(69,000 sq km)

Lake Eyre,
Australia
(9,500 sq km)

◄ *These lakes are the largest on each continent. The Caspian Sea is really a huge salt lake which lies between the two continents of Asia and Europe. It is the largest inland area of water in the world. Lake Superior in North America is the world's largest body of fresh water. Lake Eyre is not really a lake, but a salt flat, which is dry for most of the year.*

		AD1300			1350
	EUROPE	**1300** Renaissance begins in Italy.	**1336** Serbian empire established in Balkans.	**1337** 100 Years' War starts between England and France.	**1348** Black Death (bubonic plague) sweeps across Europe.
	AFRICA	**c.1300** Benin kingdom founded in West Africa.	**1325** Moroccan Ibn Batuta travels to China and Southeast Asia.		
	THE AMERICAS		**1325** Tenochtitlán (Mexico City) established as Aztec capital.		**c.1350** Decline of settlements in southwestern North America
	ASIA	**1299** Ottoman empire founded in Turkey.	**1336** Vijayanagar kingdom founded, southern India.	**c.1341** Black Death (bubonic plague) sweeps across Asia.	**1350** Siam state founded in Thailand.
	AUSTRALIA AND THE PACIFIC ISLANDS	**1300s** Second wave of Polynesians (Maoris) migrate to New Zealand.			**c.1350** Maoris build fortifications in New Zealand.

CONTINENT	AREA (sq km)	% OF WORLD'S LAND AREA	LARGEST COUNTRY AND AREA
ASIA	44,000,000	29.4	RUSSIA[1] (12,766,000 sq km)
AFRICA	30,300,000	20.2	SUDAN (2,505,810 sq km)
NORTH AMERICA	25,300,000	16.9	CANADA (9,970,610 sq km)
SOUTH AMERICA	17,611,000	11.7	BRAZIL (8,512,000 sq km)
ANTARCTICA	13,300,000	8.9	not applicable[2]
EUROPE	10,500,000	7.0	UKRAINE (603,700 sq km)
AUSTRALIA	8,900,000	5.9	AUSTRALIA (7,682,300 sq km)

[1] Russia is in Europe and Asia. This figure is for the area of Russia in Asia.
[2] There are no countries in Antarctica, but several countries in the world claim sectors of the continent.

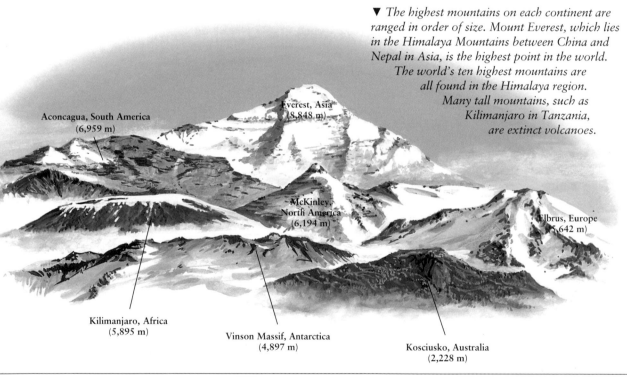

▼ The highest mountains on each continent are ranged in order of size. Mount Everest, which lies in the Himalaya Mountains between China and Nepal in Asia, is the highest point in the world. The world's ten highest mountains are all found in the Himalaya region. Many tall mountains, such as Kilimanjaro in Tanzania, are extinct volcanoes.

Aconcagua, South America (6,959 m)

Everest, Asia (8,848 m)

McKinley, North America (6,194 m)

Elbrus, Europe (5,642 m)

Kilimanjaro, Africa (5,895 m)

Vinson Massif, Antarctica (4,897 m)

Kosciusko, Australia (2,228 m)

1400		AD1450	
1397 Union of Kalmar unites Sweden, Norway and Denmark (until 1448).	1433 Portuguese exploration at its peak.	1438 Austrian Habsburg dynasty takes over Holy Roman Empire (until 1806).	
		1450 Songhai empire at its peak. Timbuktu is great centre of learning.	
	1428 Aztecs defeat neighbours in Mexico.	1438 Inca empire established in Andes.	
368 Ming dynasty begins in China.	1392 Korea independent.	1400s Laos powerful in Southeast Asia.	1453 Ottoman Turks capture Constantinople (Istanbul), ending Byzantine empire.
		c.1400 Malays visit northern coast of Australia.	

DEPENDENCIES

▲ *Captain Bligh arrives on the island of Timor, Indonesia, after his crew on* HMS Bounty *mutinied in 1789. The mutineers settled on Pitcairn Island in the Pacific Ocean. Pitcairn is now a British dependency and the mutineers' descendants live there today.*

Most countries of the world are independent, but there are around 40 states which are not. These states are controlled by other, more powerful nations and are known as dependencies or territories. Many dependencies govern themselves, but others are run directly by their controlling country.

Some dependencies were explored and colonized by the country which now governs them. For example, the island of Madeira was uninhabited until Portuguese explorers arrived there in the 1400s. A number of dependencies were gained through war, as when Britain took control of Gibraltar from Spain in the 1700s.

In the first half of this century there were more dependencies in the world than there are today. Since then, many have either gained their independence or continue to ask for it. For example, some New Caledonians have campaigned for independence from France since the 1980s.

States that remain dependent are often too small or too lacking in resources to survive alone. Other dependencies, however, are of military importance to the controlling country, such as Guam, a United States air and naval base in the Pacific Ocean.

On the next page is a chart of the world's inhabited dependencies that do not appear earlier in the encyclopedia.

◄ *Goonybirds nest around a rusting gun on Midway Island, a United States naval base in the Pacific Ocean. Countries often use their dependencies for military purposes. Several have also been used as sites for testing nuclear weapons, such as the Gambier Islands in French Polynesia.*

		AD1490			1520	
🌍	EUROPE	1479 Thrones of Aragon and Castile united in Spain.			1517 German priest Martin Luther starts Reformation, which establishes Protestantism in North Europe.	
🌍	AFRICA	1482 Portuguese set up trading posts in Ghana.	1492 Spanish invade North Africa.		c.1510 African slaves taken to the Americas by Europeans.	
🌎	THE AMERICAS		1492 Christopher Columbus reaches the Caribbean islands, claiming them for Spain.	1494 Treaty of Tordesillas divides Americas between Spain and Portugal.	1521 Spanish conquer Aztec empire.	1532 Spanish conquer Inca empire
🌏	ASIA	1483 Russians explore Siberia.	c.1490s Sikhism founded in India by Guru Nanak.			1526 Babur founds Mogul empire in India.
🌐	AUSTRALIA AND THE PACIFIC ISLANDS				1520 Portuguese Ferdinand Magellan sails into the ocean he names the Pacific.	

◀ Holidaymakers enjoy the silver sand and warm weather of Horseshoe Bay. This lies on the island of Bermuda, a British dependency in the Atlantic Ocean. Like many dependencies Bermuda relies on tourism for much of its income, but it is also an important banking and insurance centre.

▶ Skyscrapers cluster together on Hong Kong, a former British dependency. Hong Kong was loaned to Britain by China in 1842. It has since become an important centre for trade, manufacturing and finance. Hong Kong returned to its former ruler, China, in 1997.

AD1600			
1543 Polish Nicolaus Copernicus' book is published stating that the Earth moves around the Sun.	1562 Wars of Religion in France fought between Protestants and Catholics (until 1598).		1610 Golden age of art and trade in Netherlands.
	1574 Portuguese colonize Angola.	1600 Oyo empire flourishes in West Africa.	
534 French settlers nd in Canada.		1607 English settlers colonize Virginia, North America.	1608 Frenchman Samuel de Champlain founds Quebec, Canada.
	1547 Ivan IV (The Terrible) becomes first tsar of Russia.	1582 Hideyoshi unites Japan.	1603 Tokugawa Ieyasu becomes shogun (ruler) of a united Japan.

589

DEPENDENCY	LOCATION	AREA	POPULATION	CAPITAL OR CHIEF TOWN
Anguilla (UK)	In Caribbean Sea	155 sq km	9,000	The Valley
Aruba (Netherlands)	In West Indies	193 sq km	62,000	Oranjestad
Azores (Portugal)	In North Atlantic Ocean	2,247 sq km	238,000	Ponta Delgada
Bermuda (UK)	In North Atlantic Ocean	53 sq km	63,000	Hamilton
Cayman Islands (UK)	In Caribbean Sea	260 sq km	31,000	George Town
Channel Islands (UK)	In English Channel	194 sq km	144,000	St Helier, Jersey St Peter Port, Guernsey
Cook Islands (New Zealand)	In South Pacific Ocean	293 sq km	17,000	Avarua
Easter Island (Chile)	In South Pacific Ocean	118 sq km	2,000	Hanga-Roa
Faeroe Islands (Denmark)	In North Atlantic Ocean	1,339 sq km	47,000	Torshavn
Falkland Islands (UK)	In South Atlantic Ocean	1,815 sq km	2,000	Stanley
Gibraltar (UK)	On south coast of Spain	6.5 sq km	31,000	Gibraltar
Guadeloupe (France)	In West Indies	1,705 sq km	405,000	Basse-Terre
Guam (France)	In Pacific Ocean	541 sq km	141,000	Agana
Isle of Man (UK)	In Irish Sea	572 sq km	71,000	Douglas
Madeira Islands (Portugal)	In Atlantic Ocean	745 sq km	254,000	Funchal
Martinique (France)	In West Indies	1,079 sq km	371,000	Fort-de-France
Midway Island (USA)	In Pacific Ocean	5.2 sq km	450	None
Montserrat (UK)	In West Indies	106 sq km	11,000	Plymouth
Mayotte (France)	In Indian Ocean	373 sq km	101,000	Dzaoudzi
Netherlands Antilles (Netherlands)	In Caribbean Sea	800 sq km	175,000	Willemstad
Niue Island (New Zealand)	In South Pacific Ocean	258 sq km	2,000	Alofi
Norfolk Island (Australia)	In South Pacific Ocean	34 sq km	2,000	Kingston
Northern Mariana Islands (USA)	In West Pacific Ocean	477 sq km	47,000	Saipan
Pitcairn Islands Group (UK)	In South Pacific Islands	4.6 sq km	71,000	Adamstown
Réunion (France)	In Indian Ocean	2,512 sq km	634,000	Saint-Denis
St Helena Island Group (UK)	In South Atlantic Ocean	122 sq km	6,000	Jamestown
St Pierre & Miquelon (France)	Off southern coast of Newfoundland	242 sq km	6,000	St Pierre
Tokelau (New Zealand)	In southwest Pacific Ocean	10 sq km	1,600	None
Turks and Caicos Islands (UK)	In West Indies	430 sq km	13,000	Grand Turk
Virgin Islands (UK)	Between Atlantic Ocean and Caribbean Sea	130 sq km	18,000	Road Town
Virgin Islands (USA)	Between Atlantic Ocean and Caribbean Sea	342 sq km	107,000	Charlotte Amalie
Wake Island (USA)	In West-Central Pacific Ocean	8 sq km	300 (military personnel)	None
Wallis and Futuna Islands (France)	In South Pacific Ocean	240 sq km	14,000	Mata-Utu

		AD1620		1650
EUROPE		**1618** Thirty Years' War breaks out in Central Europe and Germany.	**1642** Outbreak of civil war in England, leading to overthrow of monarchy.	
AFRICA		**1618** West African companies founded by British and Dutch.	**1625** Kingdom of Dahomey, West Africa, established.	**1652** Dutch set up Cape Colony in South Africa.
THE AMERICAS		**1620** English Pilgrim Fathers settle New England.	**1626** Dutch settlers found New Amsterdam (New York City).	
ASIA			**1639** Shogun of Japan forbids foreigners to enter Japan (until 1853).	**1644** Manchurians found Qing dynasty in China (until 1912).
AUSTRALIA AND THE PACIFIC ISLANDS			**1642** Dutch navigator, Abel Tasman, charts southern coast of Tasmania (named Van Diemen's Land) and South Island, New Zealand.	

MAIN LANGUAGE	MAIN RELIGION	CURRENCY	MAIN EXPORTS	GNP PER CAPITA
English	Christianity	East Caribbean dollar	Lobsters, salt	Est. US $3,000-8,000
Dutch	Christianity	Aruban florin	Petroleum products	Est US $3,000-8,000
Portuguese	Christianity	Escudo	Petroleum products	Not available
English	Christianity	Bermudan dollar	Fuel, pharmaceuticals	Est. over US $8,000
English	Christianity	Cayman Island dollar	Turtle products, consumer goods	Est. over US $8,000
French, English	Christianity	Bailiwick of Jersey pound, Bailiwick of Guernsey pound	Flowers, vegetables, dairy products	Est. over US $ 8,000
English	Christianity	Cook Island dollar	Fruit, vegetables, clothing	Not available
Spanish	Christianity	Chilean peso	Not available	Est. US £700-3,000
Faroese, Danish	Christianity	Faroese krona	Fish and fish products, cattle	Est. over US $8,000
English	Christianity	Falkland Island pound	Farm products, transport equipment	Not available
English	Christianity	Gibraltar pound	Re-exports of petroleum and petroleum products	Est. US $3,000-8,000
French	Christianity	French franc	Bananas, sugar, rum	Est. US $3,000-8,000
English	Christianity	US dollar	Textiles, electronic products	Est. US $3,000-8,000
English	Christianity	Pound sterling, Manx pound	Farm products	Est. US $3,000-8,000
Portuguese	Christianity	Escudo	Wine	Not available
French	Christianity	French franc	Petroleum products, bananas, rum	Est. US $3,000-8,000
English	Christianity	US dollar	Not available	Not available
English	Christianity	East Caribbean dollar	Clothing, electronic parts, plants	Est. US $3,000-8,000
French	Islam	French franc	Ylang-ylang, vanilla	Est. US $3,000-8,000
Dutch	Christianity	Netherlands Antilles guilder	Crude oil and petroleum products	Est. US $3,000-8,000
English	Christianity	New Zealand dollar	Copra, limes, passion fruit	Est. US $700-3,000
English	Christianity	Australian dollar	Postage stamps, seeds, avocados	Not available
English	Christianity	US dollar	Manufactured goods, food	Est. US $700-3,000
English	Christianity	Pitcairn dollar	Fruit, vegetables	Not available
French	Christianity	French franc	Sugar	Est. US $3,000-8,000
English	Christianity	Pound sterling	Fish, handicrafts	Not available
French	Christianity	French franc	Fish, shellfish, fishmeal	Est. over US $8,000
English	Christianity	New Zealand dollar, Tokelau souvenir coin	Copra, stamps, handicrafts	Not available
English	Christianity	US dollar	Lobster products, conch	Est. US $3,000-8,000
English	Christianity	US dollar	Rum, fish, gravel, sand, fruit	Est. US $700-3,000
English	Christianity	US dollar	Petroleum products	Est. over US $8,000
English	Christianity	US dollar	Copra, handicrafts	Est. under US $700
French	Christianity	Franc CFP	Not available	Not available

1660			AD1760
1660 Restoration of monarchy in England.	**1684** France at peak of power under Louis XIV (the Sun King).		**1760s** Industrial Revolution begins in Britain.
	1689 Ashanti state founded, West Africa.		**1779-93** War between Xhosa people and Dutch (Boer) settlers in southern Africa.
1670 Hudson Bay Company set up, Canada.	**1682** Louisiana claimed by France.		**1775-83** American Revolution and Declaration of Independence, creation of USA.
1658 Aurangzeb empire in India (until 1707).		**1757** After Battle of Plassey, Britain extends control of India.	
	1699 English navigator William Dampier explores northwestern Australia and names it New Britain.	**1768-71** English explorer Captain James Cook claims New South Wales, Australia, for Britain.	

591

POPULATION

There are well over 5,000 million people living in the world today and the number is expected to grow to 10,000 million by 2050. Some parts have far more people than others. These are mostly regions where there is fertile agricultural land, such as China, or where big industrial cities have grown up, as has happened in many European countries. From time to time populations change in size. War, drought, famine and disease may kill huge numbers of people or drive them from their homes. Poverty can force whole communities to move elsewhere in search of a better life.

Populations also grow at different rates. Most Europeans and North Americans are now living longer than ever before because they have good supplies of food and healthcare. However, most of these people are choosing to have fewer children, so the population is growing very slowly. By contrast, in Africa, South America and Asia, the population is growing rapidly. Many people there lack nutritional food, clean water, medical care and sanitation. These problems may become even worse if population growth is not controlled.

Most of the world's governments carry out population surveys called censuses, which not only count the number of people, but also record where they live and what they do. These help countries to measure changes in population and plan for the future.

THE WORLD HEALTH ORGANIZATION
The World Health Organization (WHO) is part of the United Nations. It aims to improve standards of health and health education around the world. The WHO works with governments to provide safe drinking water and adequate sewage disposal. Prevention of disease is another major goal.

▶ *A child in Mali, West Africa, is vaccinated against the dangerous disease of meningitis. Vaccination programmes are now carried out in most countries. Eighty percent of the world's children are immunized against the killer diseases of polio, tuberculosis, measles, diphtheria, tetanus and whooping cough.*

		AD1800			
EUROPE	**1789** French Revolution begins (until 1799), ends monarchy.	**1801** Act of Union unites Britain with Ireland to form United Kingdom.	**1804** Napoleon declares himself emperor of France.	**1806** End of Holy Roman Empire.	
AFRICA		**1795** British take the Cape of Good Hope from the Dutch in Africa.	**1804** Fulani people conquer Hausa people in West Africa.		
THE AMERICAS	**1789** George Washington becomes first president of USA.		**1803** Louisiana Purchase – USA buys land from France, doubling size of country.		**1809** South American wars of independence from Spain begin.
ASIA					
AUSTRALIA AND THE PACIFIC ISLANDS	**1788** British transport convicts to Sydney, Australia.	**1793** Free settlers arrive in Australia from Britain.	**1803** Settlement of Van Diemen's Land (Tasmania).		

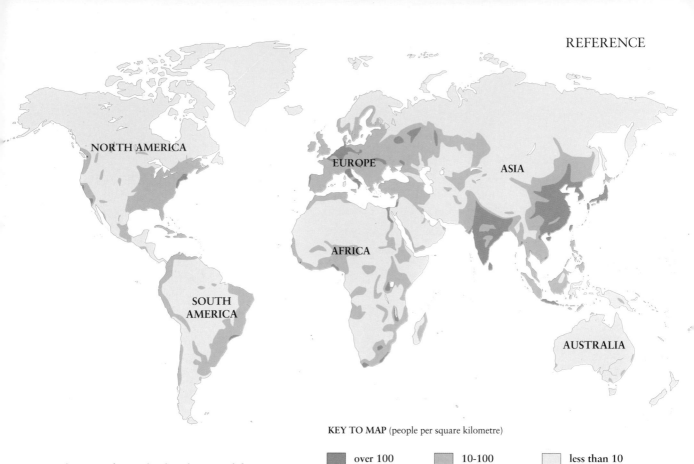

KEY TO MAP (people per square kilometre)

<table>
<tr><td>■ over 100</td><td>■ 10-100</td><td>□ less than 10</td></tr>
</table>

▲ This map shows the distribution of the world's population. The densest populations are in parts of Asia, Europe and North America. More than 3,000 million people live in Asia alone. Australia has the least dense population of all the populated continents.

► A Chinese poster encourages couples to have just one child. In China government campaigns have been very successful in persuading people to have fewer children. This has limited China's rapid population growth. Other countries that have carried out successful family planning programmes include Sri Lanka, Chile, Thailand and Colombia.

1810			AD1830	
	1815 Napoleon defeated at Waterloo by Britain and Prussia.	1825 World's first passenger railway opens in Britain.	1833 Slavery banned in British empire.	
	1818 Shaka becomes king of the Zulus.	1822 Liberia founded as haven for freed slaves from USA.	1830 Algeria invaded by French.	1835 Boers (farmers of Dutch descent) leave Cape to set up new colonies in north.
1812 War between USA and Britain (until 1814).	1819 USA buys Florida from Spain.		1834-8 Slavery abolished in Antigua, Barbuda and Jamaica.	1840 Upper and Lower Canada unite.
	1819 Singapore becomes British colony.			
1810 Lachlan Macquarie becomes governor of Australia (until 1821).	1813 Australian interior opened to settlement.	1828 Tasmanian Aborigines ordered onto reserves.	1830 Tasmanian settlers attempt mass murder of Aborigines.	1840 New Zealand becomes British colony.

RELIGION

Since prehistoric times, people everywhere have tried to make sense of the world around them. This search for a meaning to life grew into religious belief. The first religions were based on the worship of natural forces, such as air, fire and wind, or animals, mountains and rivers. These became linked to powerful supernatural beings – gods and goddesses, spirits and demons. Today some religions, such as Hinduism, have many gods. Others, such as Islam, Judaism and Christianity, have only one god. The Chinese religion of Confucianism has no god at all.

Many religions have developed from older faiths. Christianity sprang from Judaism. Religions are often divided into different groups whose members believe in the same principles, but may interpret them in different ways. Christianity, for example, includes Protestant, Roman Catholic and Eastern Orthodox groups.

Religion has played a major role in shaping world history and remains a powerful force. There are hundreds of religions in the world today and the main ones are described opposite. Although they differ in many ways, they all teach their followers to live by a moral code (knowing the difference between right and wrong).

▼ *A Hindu family lights candles to celebrate Divali, the festival of the goddess of wealth. Light plays an important part in the festivals and celebrations of many religions. Some believe that light has healing powers.*

▶ *This chart shows how the peoples of the world worshipped at the beginning of the 1990s. The largest religious group, the Christians, is followed by Muslims (believers in Islam) and Hindus. People who have no religious belief make up a large proportion. Other religions include Confucianism, Taoism, Shintoism and Jainism.*

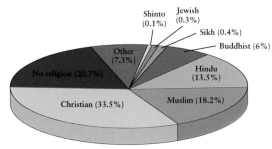

Shinto (0.1%)
Jewish (0.3%)
Sikh (0.4%)
Buddhist (6%)
Hindu (13.5%)
Muslim (18.2%)
Christian (33.5%)
No religion (20.7%)
Other (7.3%)

		AD1845		1855	
![] EUROPE		1845 Irish potato famine (ends 1847).	1848 Year of revolutions in France, Italy, Germany, Austria and Hungary. Communism founded by German, Karl Marx.		
![] AFRICA			1847 Liberia independent.	1855 Ethiopia united under Emperor Theodore II.	
![] THE AMERICAS	1841 US wagons carry settlers to Oregon.	1845 Texas joins USA.	1848 Gold Rush in California. USA gains New Mexico and California after Mexican War.		
![] ASIA	1842 Hong Kong becomes British colony (until 1997).				1858 India becomes part of British empire
![] AUSTRALIA AND THE PACIFIC ISLANDS		1845 Maoris fight British settlers to protect land.	1851 Gold rush starts in Australia and settlers pour in from Europe.	1854-5 Australian colonies (except Western Australia) gain self-government.	1856 New Zealand gains self-government.

Christianity

Christianity is based on the life and teachings of Jesus Christ, who was born in Palestine (now Israel). Christians believe that Jesus is the son of God and that he rose from the dead after being crucified on a cross. The Christian Bible includes the Jewish Old Testament and Christ's teachings, as recorded in the New Testament.

Islam

Islam was founded in Arabia by the prophet Muhammad in about AD622. The Muslims' (followers of Islam) most sacred book is the Koran, which is the direct word of the one God, Allah. Islamic life is based on a set of rules called the five pillars of Islam. By following these rules Muslims believe they will reach heaven.

Hinduism

Hinduism is the major religion of India. It began in about 1500BC, although nobody knows who founded the religion. Hindus worship many gods. The three most important are called Shiva, Vishnu and Brahma. They believe in reincarnation (rebirth) of the soul after death and are born into castes (ranks in society).

Buddhism

Buddhism is based on the teachings of an Indian prince, Gautama Siddhartha, who was born in 563BC. He became known as Buddha, which means Enlightened One. Buddhists share the Hindu belief in rebirth and aim to achieve nirvana (absolute peace). Meditation is used to achieve enlightenment (complete understanding).

Confucianism and Taoism

Confucianism has no gods or belief in life after death, but stresses good behaviour and duty to society. It follows the teachings of Confucius, who was born in China in about 551BC. Taoism began in about 300BC. Based on the teachings of Lao-Tzu, its many gods are taken from folk religions.

Judaism

Judaism was the first religion to teach that there is one God. Its main laws come from the Torah, the first five books of the Hebrew Bible (the Old Testament in Christianity). According to tradition, the ancient religion of the Jews was founded by Abraham. He was a Hebrew who lived in Canaan (now Israel) in about 2000BC.

Sikhism

Sikhism was founded in India in the late 1400s by Guru (teacher) Nanak, who had been a Hindu. The Sikhs believe in only one God who is the true guru. Sikh men have five 'k' symbols which they wear. They are kesh (uncut hair), kangha (comb), kara (bracelet), kaccha (breeches) and kirpan (dagger).

Shintoism

Shintoists worship the spirits of animals, rocks, trees, springs and other elements of nature. Shinto is Japan's oldest surviving religion and developed from early folk beliefs. Until the mid-1900s the Japanese worshipped their emperor, believing he was directly descended from the sun goddess, their most important god.

1860				AD1870		
	1861 Italy unites as a kingdom.		**1867** Austro-Hungarian empire founded.		**1871** Germany unites with Wilhelm I of Prussia as emperor.	
				1869 Suez Canal opens, linking Mediterranean Sea to Red Sea.		**1879** Zulu leader, Cetwayo, defeats British at Isandhlwana.
	1861-5 American Civil War.	**1865** Slavery abolished in USA.	**1867** Dominion of Canada established. USA buys Alaska from Russia.	**1869** East-West railway crosses USA.	**1872** Yellowstone, in USA, becomes first national park.	**1876** US troops defeated by Native Americans at Little Bighorn.
		1863 French gain control of Indo-China.	**1867** Mutsuhito becomes emperor of Japan and a new era of modernization begins.			
1860 Second Maori War.	**1861** Gold discovered on South Island, New Zealand.		**1868** British stop sending convicts to Western Australia.	**1870s** Pacific islands colonized by European powers.	**1874** Fiji becomes British colony.	

ENVIRONMENT

The environment is the surroundings in which we live. Some parts of it are living, such as plants, animals and people, while other parts are non-living, such as air and water. All these elements work together to keep life going.

People have always had an effect on the environment, but today human activities are causing serious damage. The air is being polluted with harmful gases from vehicles and factories. Water is polluted with pesticides, industrial waste and domestic sewage. Forests are cut down for timber and to make way for farmland, which is causing many plants and animals to die out.

Air pollution can damage the Earth's atmosphere and affect the climate. Chemicals called chlorofluorocarbons (CFCs) are destroying the ozone layer, a protective barrier around the Earth that keeps out harmful radiation from the Sun. Pollution from burning coal, oil and car exhausts increases the greenhouse effect, a process which traps heat from the Sun to warm the Earth. Many scientists believe that this pollution is already making the Earth warmer. Governments are being urged to find ways of reducing pollution to prevent irreparable damage.

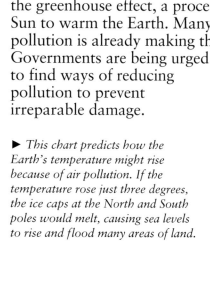

▼ *A worker checks for leaks of radioactivity at a disposal site for nuclear waste. Disposal of nuclear waste is a major problem for many countries. It can remain lethal (deadly) for thousands of years and no one yet knows how to dispose of it safely and permanently.*

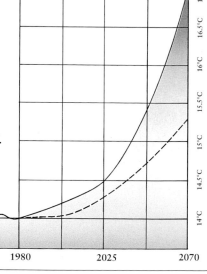

▶ *This chart predicts how the Earth's temperature might rise because of air pollution. If the temperature rose just three degrees, the ice caps at the North and South poles would melt, causing sea levels to rise and flood many areas of land.*

	AD1880				1910	
EUROPE					**1911** Norwegian Roald Amundsen reaches South Pole.	**1914** World War I starts.
AFRICA	**1880** Start of wars between the Boers and the British.		**1907** World's largest game reserve established at Etosha (now in Namibia).		**1912** African National Congress set up, South Africa.	**1914** World War I starts.
THE AMERICAS	**1885** Canadian-Pacific Railroad completed.	**1898** Spanish-American War.	**1900** Birth of jazz music, New Orleans, USA.	**1909** US Robert Peary reaches North Pole.	**1910** Mexican revolution.	**1914** Panama Canal opens.
ASIA	**1895** Japan gains Korea and Taiwan from China.		**1905** Japan defeats Russia.		**1912** China becomes a republic, emperor overthrown.	**1914** World War I starts.
AUSTRALIA AND THE PACIFIC ISLANDS	**1893** New Zealand is first country in the world to give women the vote.		**1907** New Zealand independent.			**1914** World War I starts.

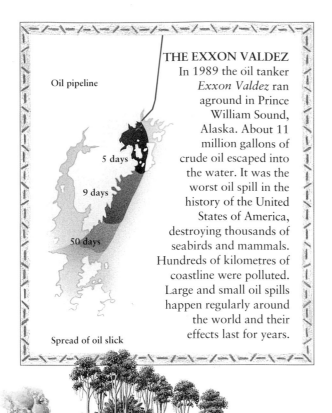

THE EXXON VALDEZ

In 1989 the oil tanker *Exxon Valdez* ran aground in Prince William Sound, Alaska. About 11 million gallons of crude oil escaped into the water. It was the worst oil spill in the history of the United States of America, destroying thousands of seabirds and mammals. Hundreds of kilometres of coastline were polluted. Large and small oil spills happen regularly around the world and their effects last for years.

Oil pipeline

5 days

9 days

50 days

Spread of oil slick

▼ Children collect newspapers and aluminium cans for recycling. Many materials that we use in everyday life, such as paper, glass, metal and some plastics, can be recycled. By reusing these materials people have found an important way of conserving the Earth's resources and preventing waste.

◄ Clearing forests can damage the environment. If many trees are cleared from high ground rainwater quickly runs downhill, taking some of the soil with it. This floods the ground below and may cause rivers to silt (block) up. In the dry season the exposed soil can become baked and cracked.

1920					AD1940
1918 End of World War I. Break-up of Austro-Hungarian empire.	**1921** Irish Free State founded. Fascists seize power in Italy.		**1936-9** Spanish Civil War.	**1939** World War II begins when Germany invades Poland.	
				1939 Outbreak of World War II. Heavy fighting in North Africa.	
1917 USA enters World War I (until 1918).	**1920-33** Prohibition (alcohol ban) in USA.		**1929** The Wall Street Crash in USA marks start of a world economic depression.		**1941** USA enters World War II.
1917 Socialist revolution in Russia, monarchy overthrown.	**1920** Ottoman empire collapses.	**1922** Soviet Union founded.	**1931** Japanese invade Manchuria.	**1937** War between Japan and China.	**1941** Japan enters World War II.
		1927 Canberra becomes capital of Australia.	**1930s** Economic depression in Australia and New Zealand.	**1939** Australia and New Zealand enter World War II.	**1941-2** Japan invades the Pacific islands.

CONFLICT

Conflicts and wars have been part of human life since ancient times. Wars of invasion and conquest usually break out when one country tries to dominate another. Civil wars (a war within one country) and revolutions happen when people attempt to overthrow the existing government or power in their country. Disputes over land borders, political beliefs, religion, trade and ownership of valuable resources also cause conflicts.

During this century two huge conflicts involved most of the world's powerful nations. Millions of people lost their lives and many countries' borders were redrawn as a result of both World War I (1914-1918) and World War II (1939-1945). After World War II ended the long Cold War started between the United States of America and the Soviet Union. These two superpowers threatened each other with nuclear war and supported opposing sides in other countries' conflicts. The early 1990s saw the break-up of the Soviet Union and the end of the Cold War, but, unfortunately, this led to further civil wars in places such as Bosnia-Herzegovina and Azerbaijan. As new conflicts begin, others finish. Talks to end conflicts in the Middle East and Northern Ireland have taken place in the 1990s.

▲ *Russian troops invade Grozny, capital of Chechnya, in 1994. Chechnya, a republic within Russia, declared its independence in 1991. This led to a full-scale conflict. All over the world, parts of countries try to become independent for many different reasons.*

▶ *Refugees, fleeing from civil war in Rwanda, cross into Tanzania in April 1994. After wars break out, large numbers of people are often forced to leave their homes to seek safety in neighbouring countries.*

		AD1945		1950	
	EUROPE	1945-8 Communist governments come to power in Eastern and Central Europe. Start of Cold War.	1949 North Atlantic Treaty Organization set up.		1955 Warsaw pact unites countries of Eastern bloc.
	AFRICA		1948 Apartheid adopted as offical policy in South Africa.	1952 Mau-Mau rising against British in Kenya (ends 1959).	1956 Suez Crisis.
	THE AMERICAS	1945 United Nations organization set up with headquarters in New York.	1948 Organization of American States founded.	1954 Revolution in Guatemala.	
	ASIA	1945 Atomic bomb dropped on Japan by USA. World War II ends. 1947 India and Pakistan independent.	1948 State of Israel founded in Palestine. 1949 China officially becomes Communist.	1950-3 Korean war.	
	AUSTRALIA AND THE PACIFIC ISLANDS	1945 Australia receives millions of European immigrants.	1948 South Pacific Commission set up.	1950-53 Australia and New Zealand enter Korean war. 1950s Testing of nuclear weapons in the Pacific.	

◀ *Red Cross trucks take food and medical supplies to Kabul, the war-torn capital of Afghanistan, in early 1994. International relief organizations, such as the Red Cross and the United Nations relief agency, provide shelter, food and healthcare for the victims of conflict throughout the world.*

▼ *This map shows areas where the United Nations (UN), the international peacekeeping organization, was involved in conflicts at the beginning of 1995. The UN's charter states that it must never use force when trying to settle disputes.*

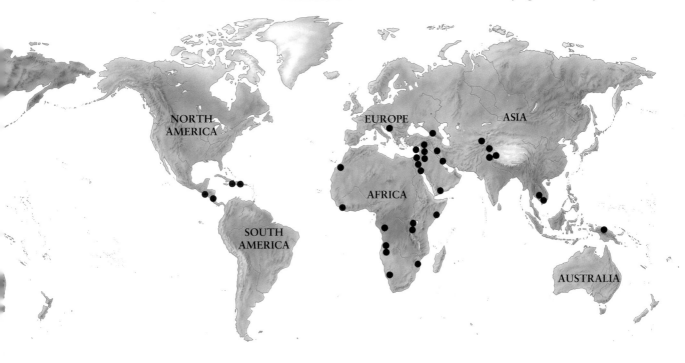

KEY TO MAP

● United Nations peace-keeping operations

	1960		AD1965	
1957 European Economic Community set up (becomes European Union in 1993).	**1961** Berlin Wall built, dividing the east and west of Germany's capital (pulled down 1989).			
1957 Ghana independent. In the following decades most African states become independent.		**1962** French leave Algeria after 8-year war of independence.	**1963** Foundation of Organization for African Unity set up.	
1959 Alaska joins USA.	**1961** Latin American Free Trade Association set up.	**1962** Jamaica and Trinidad independent.	**1965** USA enters Vietnam war (until 1973).	
1957 Vietnam war starts.	**1960** Sirimavo Bandaranaike of Ceylon (Sri Lanka) becomes world's first woman prime minister.			**1966** Cultural Revolution starts in China under Mao Zedong.
	1962 Western Samoa independent.		**1965** Australia enters Vietnam war (until 1970).	**1967** Aboriginal peoples gain full citizenship and vote in Australia.

599

GOVERNMENT

Many terms are used to describe the way a country is governed.
Monarchy: A country where the head of state is a monarch (a king or a queen). In a modern constitutional monarchy the monarch's power to govern is strictly limited.
Republic: The opposite of a monarchy, in which the head of state is often an elected president.
Democracy: Any form of government which is elected by popular vote. A multi-party democracy is one where the voters may choose between two or more political parties.

Federalism: The power in federal countries is divided between one central and several regional (state or provincial) governments.
Dependency: A state ruled by another country.
Communism: A political system in which the economy is directed by the state, which may own businesses, industries and farms.
Free market: An economic system in which the state does not direct the economy. States which have both public and private ownership are said to have a mixed economy.

All countries have governments that decide how the country is run. They make laws, set taxes and spend public money on projects and services of national importance, such as education and defence. Sometimes governments make agreements with other governments. A typical example of this is a trade agreement where countries benefit from selling goods to one another. They can also oppose other governments by either banning trade or taxing their imports.

Today most countries are democratic republics. This means the people have elected their government from a choice of political parties and have also elected their head of state. The opposite of democracy is dictatorship, a form of government in which one person or a small group of people has absolute power. In a dictatorship there are no elections and people are not free to choose a political party to support. Dictatorships are often run by the army or a monarch. Communist countries are usually run by one political party, the Communist Party, which believes that property is owned by everyone and that wealth should be shared equally between all the people.

◀ *The General Assembly of the United Nations (UN) meets in New York. Membership of the UN helps the world's governments keep in touch with each other. Most countries send representatives to the UN, which is an organization that works towards world peace.*

		AD1970					1985
EUROPE		1969 Violence breaks out in Northern Ireland between Protestants and Catholics.		1975 Death of Franco ends decades of dictatorship in Spain.			
AFRICA		1971 Idi Amin becomes dictator in Uganda (until 1979).				1980 Black majority rule in Zimbabwe.	
THE AMERICAS		1969 US astronauts walk on the Moon.				1979 Civil war in Nicaragua and El Salvador.	
ASIA		1971 Bangladesh breaks away from Pakistan.		1975 Vietnam war ends.	1976 North and South Vietnam unite.	1980 Iran-Iraq war starts (ends 1988).	1985 South Asian Association for Regional Co-operation set up
AUSTRALIA AND THE PACIFIC ISLANDS	1970 Fiji independent.	1973 South Pacific Bureau for Economic Co-operation set up.	1975 Papua New Guinea independent.	1976 Land rights granted to Aborigines in Australia.	1978 Solomon Islands and Tuvalu independent.		

► *People in the United States of America protest against their government's involvement in the Vietnam War (1957-1975). Although governments have the power to go to war and decide how the country is run, their decisions may be changed by public opinion.*

▼ *This map shows how the countries of the world were governed at the beginning of 1995. The main types of government are republic, monarchy and communist.*

KEY TO MAP

Republic	Communist	
Dependency	Islamic socialist state	
Monarchy		

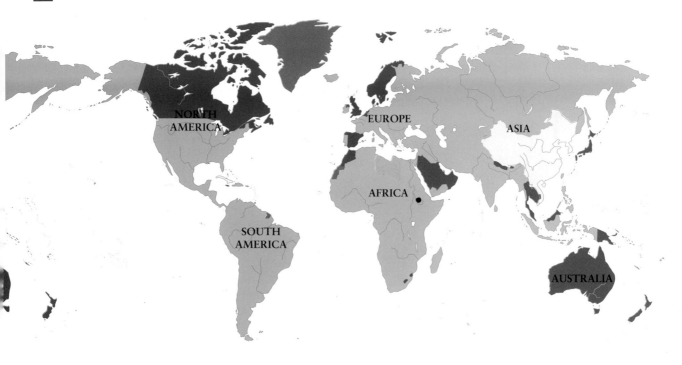

NORTH AMERICA

EUROPE

ASIA

AFRICA

SOUTH AMERICA

AUSTRALIA

	1990			AD1994
1986 Nuclear reactor accident at Chernobyl, Ukraine, devastates large areas.	1990 East and West Germany reunite.	1991 Yugoslavia breaks up.	1993 Czechoslovakia divides into Slovakia and Czech Republic.	1994 Cease-fire declared in Northern Ireland.
		1991 Apartheid ends in South Africa.		1994 First democratic elections in South Africa. Nelson Mandela elected president.
1987 USA and Soviet Union agree to ban certain kinds of nuclear weapons.		1992 Vote to create a self-governing homeland for Inuit. Earth Summit in Rio de Janeiro, Brazil.		1994 North America Free Trade Agreement set up.
1989 Pro-democracy movement crushed in Beijing, China.	1990 Iraq invades Kuwait, starting Gulf war (ends 1991).	1991 Soviet Union breaks up. Formation of Commonwealth of Independent States.		
1987 Rarotonga Treaty declares Pacific a nuclear-free zone.	1990 Micronesia independent.	1992 Mabo decision in Australian High Court confirms Aboriginal land rights.		1994 Palau independent.

UNITED NATIONS

The United Nations (UN) is an organization that works for world peace, security and co-operation between countries. Its members include most of the world's independent nations. The main aims of the UN are to prevent wars and settle international disputes. It also helps deal with issues such as refugees and provides disaster relief. The UN was founded in 1945 and its headquarters are in New York. By mid-1995, it had 185 member states. The dates on which they joined the UN are listed below.

Member – Date of admission	Member – Date of admission	Member – Date of admission	Member – Date of admission
Afghanistan – 1946	Denmark – 1945	Lebanon – 1945	St Christopher-Nevis – 1983
Albania – 1955	Djibouti – 1977	Lesotho – 1966	St Lucia – 1979
Algeria – 1962	Dominica – 1978	Liberia – 1945	St Vincent and the
Andorra – 1993	Dominican Republic – 1945	Libya – 1955	Grenadines – 1980
Angola – 1976	Ecuador – 1945	Liechtenstein – 1990	Samoa – 1976
Antigua and Barbuda – 1981	Egypt – 1945	Lithuania – 1991	San Marino – 1992
Argentina – 1945	El Salvador – 1945	Luxembourg – 1945	São Tomé and Príncipe – 1975
Armenia – 1992	Equatorial Guinea – 1968	Macedonia – 1993	Saudi Arabia – 1945
Australia – 1945	Eritrea – 1993	Madagascar – 1960	Senegal – 1960
Austria – 1955	Estonia – 1991	Malawi – 1964	Seychelles – 1976
Azerbaijan – 1992	Ethiopia – 1945	Malaysia – 1957	Sierra Leone – 1961
Bahamas – 1973	Federated States of	Maldives – 1965	Singapore – 1965
Bahrain – 1971	Micronesia – 1991	Mali – 1960	Slovakia – 1993
Bangladesh – 1974	Fiji – 1970	Malta – 1964	Slovenia – 1992
Barbados – 1966	Finland – 1955	Marshall Islands – 1991	Solomon Islands – 1978
Belarus – 1945	France – 1945	Mauritania – 1961	Somalia – 1960
Belgium – 1945	Gabon – 1960	Mauritius – 1968	South Africa – 1945
Belize – 1981	Gambia – 1965	Mexico – 1945	South Korea – 1991
Benin – 1960	Georgia – 1992	Moldova – 1992	Spain – 1955
Bhutan – 1971	Germany – 1973	Monaco – 1993	Sri Lanka – 1955
Bolivia – 1945	Ghana – 1957	Mongolia – 1961	Sudan – 1956
Bosnia-Herzegovina – 1992	Greece – 1945	Morocco – 1956	Surinam – 1975
Botswana – 1966	Grenada – 1974	Mozambique – 1975	Swaziland – 1968
Brazil – 1945	Guatemala – 1945	Myanmar (Burma) – 1948	Sweden – 1946
Brunei – 1984	Guinea – 1958	Namibia – 1990	Syria – 1945
Bulgaria – 1955	Guinea-Bissau – 1974	Nepal – 1955	Tajikistan – 1992
Burkina Faso – 1960	Guyana – 1966	Netherlands – 1945	Tanzania – 1961
Burundi – 1962	Haiti – 1945	New Zealand – 1945	Thailand – 1946
Cambodia – 1955	Honduras – 1945	Nicaragua – 1945	Togo – 1960
Cameroon – 1960	Hungary – 1955	Niger – 1960	Trinidad and Tobago – 1962
Canada – 1945	Iceland – 1946	Nigeria – 1960	Tunisia – 1956
Cape Verde – 1975	India – 1945	North Korea – 1991	Turkey – 1945
Central African	Indonesia – 1950	Norway – 1945	Turkmenistan – 1992
Republic – 1960	Iran – 1945	Oman – 1971	Uganda – 1962
Chad – 1960	Iraq – 1945	Pakistan – 1947	Ukraine – 1945
Chile – 1945	Ireland – 1955	Palau – 1994	United Arab Emirates – 1971
China – 1945	Israel – 1949	Panama – 1945	United Kingdom – 1945
Colombia – 1945	Italy – 1955	Papua New Guinea – 1975	United States of America – 1945
Comoros – 1975	Jamaica – 1962	Paraguay – 1945	Uruguay – 1945
Congo – 1960	Japan – 1956	Peru – 1945	Uzbekistan – 1992
Costa Rica – 1945	Jordan – 1955	Philippines – 1945	Vanuatu – 1981
Côte d'Ivoire – 1960	Kazakhstan – 1992	Poland – 1945	Venezuela – 1945
Croatia – 1992	Kenya – 1963	Portugal – 1955	Vietnam – 1977
Cuba – 1945	Kuwait – 1963	Qatar – 1971	Yemen – 1947
Cyprus – 1960	Kyrgyzstan – 1992	Romania – 1955	Yugoslavia – 1945
Czech Republic – 1993	Laos – 1955	Russia – 1945	Zambia – 1964
Dem Rep of Congo – 1960	Latvia – 1991	Rwanda – 1962	Zimbabwe – 1980

GLOSSARY

Words in *italics* have their own separate glossary entry.

Acid rain Rain that has been made very acidic by waste gases from factories and cars. These gases *pollute* the atmosphere and so also pollute rainfall. Acid rain can cause great damage to plants and animals. It can even damage the surface of buildings.

Agriculture Using land for growing crops and/or for keeping and grazing animals.

Ancestor Relative from whom a person is descended, such as a grandparent or great-great-grandparent.

Apartheid Policy of separating people of different races. This policy was once followed by the white government in South Africa. Black and white people were kept apart and black people's rights, such as the right to vote and the freedom to choose where to live, were severely restricted. Apartheid in South Africa ended in 1994, when *democratic elections* were held. The elections gave South Africa black majority rule and a black president.

Archipelago Group of islands.

Atoll Coral reef or island that forms a partial or complete ring around a *lagoon*.

Atomic bomb Highly destructive bomb. Its energy comes from splitting tiny chemical particles called atoms.

Bazaar Market made up of many different shops and stalls.

Cash crop Crop grown to sell rather than to feed the grower's own family.

Cassava Tropical plant with starchy roots. The roots are used to make flour for bread and tapioca for puddings.

Censorship System that prevents certain facts or opinions being made available to the public in newspapers, books, films or on television. Censorship rules vary from one country to another.

Chemical industry Industry that uses naturally occurring and chemically produced materials to make all kinds of products. These products include plastics, paints, medicines and fabrics.

Civil war War between opposing groups of people within the same country.

Civilization Society where people are highly developed in *agriculture*, government, art and science.

Colony Area *settled* or taken over by people from another country.

Communications network Huge system that links equipment so that people can send information to each other and swap ideas. Telecommunication is the electronic exchange of information via telephones, computers and fax machines.

Communism Political system where land, industry and all property and goods are controlled by the government or *state*.

Conservation Actions taken to protect the natural environment.

Consumer goods Necessary and/or desirable ready-to-use products, made for people to buy.

Copra Dried coconut kernels from which an oil is extracted.

Corruption Dishonest behaviour that often takes the form of offering people bribes or extra payments, especially people in business and government. The bribes are given to persuade people to support a particular individual or take a certain action.

Cultivation Preparing and using land for growing crops.

Currency Type of money used within a country, such as rupees in India.

Cyclone Very stormy weather with violent spiralling winds. A tropical cyclone is another name for a *hurricane*.

Deforestation Loss of areas of forest. Some forests are cut down for their timber. Others may be cleared to make way for buildings or *agriculture*. In many parts of the world *conservationists* are carrying out projects to replace trees.

Delta Area at the mouths of some rivers where the stream of water divides into several channels. The water then flows through deposits of sand and mud.

Democracy System of government where the people have a certain amount of power because they elect those who govern them.

Democratic election Election that allows the people of a country to choose who governs the country. Each person has one vote.

Democratic reform Change that gives the people in a country more rights and opportunities.

Dependency Area of land that is controlled or supported by another country.

Descendant Person who comes from particular ancestors. You are a *descendant* of your great-grandparents and the Aboriginal peoples in Australia are descendants of the very first people to settle in that land.

Dialect Special way of speaking within a language. People use some specific words and pronounce everything in a certain way. A dialect is spoken by a certain group of people or within a limited area.

Dike Bank or wall built to hold back the sea or a river to prevent flooding. It is also a channel or ditch dug to help the drainage of wet land.

Drought Long period of dry weather, causing a shortage of water.

Economy The way a country produces, uses and distributes its money, resources, goods and services. Examples of economic unions include the European Union, the North America Free Trade Agreement (between USA, Canada and Mexico), the South Pacific Bureau for Economic Co-operation and the Foundation of Organization for African Unity.

Elder Older person in a community who is greatly respected.

Emigrant Person who moves from his or her own country to live in another.

Empire Group of *colonies* or *territories* that is controlled by a country or power.

Environmental movement Groups of people working to put a stop to the many things that damage the natural environment, such as the *pollution* produced by industry.

Equator Imaginary line around the middle of the Earth, at an equal distance from the North and South poles. Countries on or near the Equator are very hot.

Equatorial The area around the *Equator* or the conditions there.

Erosion Wearing away of rock, land or buildings by the weather or the sea.

Escarpment Steep slope of a hill or rock.

Ethnic group Group of people within a larger community or country who have different characteristics, such as language, religion or customs. They may have different racial or geographical origins.

Exile A person who is forced by circumstances to leave his or her home country. Many people have become exiles because they hold different religious or political beliefs from the government of their home country.

Exploit a) To develop land or resources. b) To use land, resources or people for selfish reasons. *Colonists* in many parts of the world have often forced local people to work on their farms. Money earned from the farms has frequently gone to make the owners wealthy and not to help the local people.

Export Product made in one country and sold to another.

Extinct No longer in existence. Many groups of people, animals and plants have died out over the centuries, for all kinds of reasons. Volcanoes are also said to be extinct when they are no longer active.

Famine Extreme shortage of food. This may lead to people dying of starvation.

Federal A system where a nation is divided into several different *states*, *provinces* or *territories*. Usually each separate area is self-governing in local matters, but there is a central government for national matters such as foreign affairs and defence. The United States of America has a federal system.

Fertile land Land where conditions are suitable for plants, particularly crops, to grow. This often means that the land is well-watered and the soil has plenty of the nutrients that plants need to grow.

Fertilizer Substance added to soil to improve the size and quality of crops.

Fiesta Celebration or festival. A fiesta is often held to mark a religious occasion such as a saint's day.

Fiord Narrow, deep and steep-sided inlet of the sea in a mountainous area. Countries that are famous for their fiords include Norway, Greenland and New Zealand. Fiords formed long ago during the *Ice Ages*, when massive *glaciers* gouged out deep *valleys* as they moved towards the sea.

Fossil Remains or impression of an animal or plant that lived a long time ago. Fossils are usually found hardened in rock.

Free market *Economic* system where the government does not control the *economy*. A mixed *economy* is one where some things are state-controlled and others are privately owned.

Geothermal electricity Electricity produced from steam that occurs naturally, deep inside the Earth. This steam forms because of the intense heat beneath the Earth's crust.

Geyser Natural hot spring that throws up jets of steam or hot water.

Glacier Huge mass of ice that moves slowly downhill, along a river *valley*. Glaciers form high up in the mountains, where the snow never melts.

GNP (Gross National Product) This is often presented per capita, which means per head (or per person). GNP is a figure calculated by adding up the total value of all goods and services produced in a country in one year. It includes *investments* made abroad by that country. Money earned within the country by non-nationals is subtracted from the total. This figure is then divided by the number of people in the country. GNP is often expressed in US dollars and means that the *economic* progress of different countries can be compared.

Gorge Deep, narrow, steep-sided *valley*.

Guerrilla Member of a group of armed rebels fighting which is against the controlling force of a country.

Habitat The specific natural surroundings in which animals and plants live. The icy waters and shores of the far North form the polar bear's habitat.

Humid Moist or damp, as in air or climate.

Hurricane storm, with winds that travel at speeds of more than 120 kilometres per hour. Hurricanes occur in tropical areas.

Hydroelectric power Electricity made by using the power of water from rivers and lakes.

Ice Age Period of time on a planet when temperatures are extremely low for a very long time. Ice Ages took place on Earth long ago and lasted millions of years. The last one ended around 10,000 years ago.

Immigrant Person who has come to live in a country that is not his or her homeland.

Import Product that is brought into a country from abroad.

Independent Free from the control of others. An independent country is completely self-governing.

Inflation Overall rise in the price of goods and services. This in turn leads to a fall in the value of money. When money is devalued, it means that more is needed to buy the same goods.

Intensive farming Ways of getting the greatest amount of *agricultural* produce possible from a piece of land. Intensive farming methods might include increasing the workforce or using *fertilizers* and modern farming machinery.

Investment Money that people put into developing a project such as a business, an industry or a shopping centre.

Irrigation System for providing a supply of water to crops. This is often needed in areas where the rainfall is not enough to ensure good growth.

Lagoon Freshwater or saltwater lake that is separated from the sea by a sandbank or coral reef.

Land reclamation Bringing flooded or waste land back into use by either draining or clearing it. Large areas of the low-lying Netherlands have been reclaimed from the sea over the years.

Legislation The laws of a country and how these laws are drawn up and put into action.

Manufacturing industry Large-scale factory production of a wide variety of goods.

Military rule Government by the army of a country.

Mineral resource Naturally occurring substance found in the ground that needs extracting or collecting before it can be used by humans. Gold, salt and precious stones are all minerals.

Monarchy Land ruled by a king, queen, emperor or empress. Monarchs have varying degrees of power. In a constitutional monarchy most of the power is held by a *democratically elected* government. A monarch's title is hereditary, which means that it is passed down from one generation to the next.

Monsoon Extremely strong seasonal wind that can be accompanied by very wet, stormy weather. The best-known monsoons occur in southern Asia. They blow from the land to the sea in the winter and from the sea to the land during the summer.

Multinational company Business that operates in several countries.

Multiparty election Election where voters can choose between several different political groups or parties.

Native Person born and living in a particular area.

Natural resource Part of the natural environment, such as *fertile land* and minerals, that humans can use to satisfy their wants and needs. People are also a natural resource.

Navigation The skill of trying to find the easiest, quickest route from one place to another. This term is mostly used when people talk about travel by sea, river or air, but it is also used for journeys over land.

Nomad Person who regularly moves from place to place in search of food or grazing for animals. The land where nomads live is usually not hospitable or *fertile* enough to support settled communities.

Nuclear power Energy released by causing reactions to take place within the nuclei (central parts) of atoms. This energy can be produced and used in power stations to provide electricity.

Pagan Someone who does not believe in any of the world's main religions.

Peninsula Area of land jutting out from the mainland and surrounded by sea on three sides.

Pesticide Poison that is used to kill pests and weeds because they often interfere with crop-growing. Many people are looking for ways to avoid the use of pesticides, because they can cause a lot of damage to the environment.

Petrochemical industry *Manufacturing industry* using chemicals that are made from crude oil or natural gas. Products of this industry include plastics, *fertilizers* and medicines.

Plain Large, flat area of open land.

Plantation Large farm or estate where crops such as tea, coffee, sugar or cotton are grown. Just one crop is often grown on a plantation.

Plateau Large area of flat, or fairly flat, land that is raised above the surrounding country.

Poaching Stealing animals from private land. These animals may be prized as food, or for some other valuable product. Many poachers steal animals that are endangered and protected by law. For example, elephants are killed for their ivory tusks and certain birds and monkeys are stolen so that they can be sold as pets.

Pollution The result of damaging the air, land or water with harmful substances. These substances include waste products from industry, power stations, cars and modern farming methods.

Principality Area of land ruled by a prince. As with a *monarchy*, the ruler may have a small or large amount of real power.

Protectorate Area of land that is under the protection and partial control of another country.

Province Area of land that is part of a country or *empire*.

Public spending The spending of money collected from the people in taxes. The government decides how this will be spent.

Racism Unfair treatment of one race by another because of unreasonable fear or hatred. As a result people may be insulted and attacked or denied jobs, decent housing and an education.

Raw material Natural substance that can be made into other products. Iron ore is a raw material that is used to make steel.

Refinery Factory where *raw materials* are broken down and processed so that they can be used to make other products.

Refugee Person forced to flee his or her home country. This might be because of war, *famine* or religious and political beliefs.

Republic Country where the people vote for the head of *state* and/or the head of the government. The country is usually headed by a president, rather than a *monarch*. In a *democratic* republic the people elect their government from a choice of political parties.

Revolution Overthrow of an existing system of government, replacing it with another. Force or violence are frequently used to achieve this.

Riot Disturbance that involves a crowd of people. A riot may be very violent.

Robot Complex piece of machinery that can perform certain repetitive tasks. Robots are used in some factories to carry out jobs that used to be done by workers, such as making cars.

Sanction Action taken as a way of making a protest against an organization or country. A sanction is usually in the form of trading restrictions. Several countries might refuse to trade with another country where a certain group of people are being treated very badly. This is done in the hope that it will force the country to change its policies.

Savanna Large, grassy *plain*, found in tropical or sub-tropical areas, which has few or no trees.

Service industry Industry providing services for people rather than goods. Tourism, healthcare, entertainment, education, catering and banking are all service industries.

Settler Someone who goes to live permanently in an undeveloped area.

Shaman Priest or priest-doctor figure found mainly in Asia.

Shantytown Area of poor, makeshift dwellings, usually on the edge of a town. These areas grow up because there is not enough housing for everyone in the town.

Shrine Holy place with a special meaning for a certain religious group.

Slash and burn agriculture Growing crops on land that has been cleared for this purpose by cutting down trees and burning off plant life. Land that has been cleared like this does not stay *fertile* for very long.

Slavery Buying and selling of humans, who then become the property of the buyer.

Sorghum Kind of grass. Sorghum produces grain that is used to make a type of bread.

State Large community that is organized under one local or national government. The word is also used to mean the government of a country, especially a communist country.

Strike When workers stop working as a protest against low wages or poor conditions.

Subsidy Money given by governments to certain industries or organizations in order to keep prices down or to help improve production.

Subsistence farming When farmers can only grow enough food to support themselves and their families, with few or no extra crops to sell.

Territory When it is used as an official term, territory means an area of land that is controlled by a *state* or country.

Terrorist Someone who tries to achieve political ends by using violence and intimidation.

Textiles Woven or machine-knitted fabrics.

Time zone International system of measuring time. The Earth is constantly revolving, so sunrise occurs at different times in different parts of the world. Because of this 24 main time zones were established in the 1880s. Within one zone all the clocks are set to the same time, but one zone differs from the next by one hour and so on around the world. This means that people need to adjust their watches when they move from one zone to another.

Trawling Method of catching large numbers of fish by dragging a big, wide-mouthed net through the sea.

Tributary River that flows into another, larger river.

Tundra Treeless *plain* in the far North that supports mainly mosses, lichens and small, hardy shrubs. The subsoil of the tundra (soil beneath the top layer) is permanently frozen.

Typhoon Another name for a *hurricane*.

Valley Area of low land between hills or mountains.

Veld Large stretch of open grassland found in parts of southern Africa.

INDEX

H

I

J

INDEX

ACKNOWLEDGEMENTS

The publishers would like to thank the following for contributing to this book:

Page 6 RHPL; 7 RHPL; 8 Rex Features; 9 Rex Features; 14 Panos Pictures; 16 Travel Photo International; 17 RHPL; 19 Ancient Art & Architecture Collection *t*, RHPL *b*; 21 Hutchison Library *b*; 22 Rex Features; 24 RHPL; 25 Trip/Richard Powers *t*; 27 Trip/Richard Powers *t*, National Museum, Copenhagen *m*; 29 RHPL; 32 Panos Pictures; 33 RHPL *b*; 35 RHPL *t*, J Allan Cash *b*; 37 Mary Evans Picture Library *t*, Imperial War Museum *m*, Camera Press *b*; 40 Trinity College, Dublin; 41 Chris Fairclough Colour Library *b*; 42 J Allan Cash; 43 Popperfoto *l*, RHPL *r*; 45 Trip/J W Wallace *t*; 46 J Allan Cash *t*, RHPL *b*; 48 RHPL; 49 Popperfoto *t*; 50 Mary Evans Picture Library; 51 J Allan Cash *t*, Popperfoto *m*; 53 RHPL; 54 AeroCamera; 56 Mansell Collection; 59 RHPL; 60 RHPL; 63 RHPL; 66 RHPL; 67 RHPL; 68 RHPL *l*; 69 RHPL; 70 RHPL; 71 RHPL; 73 Allsport *t*, RHPL *b*; 74 RHPL; 75 Bridgeman Art Library/Giraudon *m*, Range Pictures/Bettmann Archive *b*; 76 Chris Fairclough Colour Library *b*; 77 Camera Press; 78 Life File/ Xavier Catalan; 79 Life File/ Tony Abbott *t*, Life File/Iain Haggarty *b*; 80 RHPL; 81 Panos Pictures *b*; 82 RHPL; 83 RHPL *t*, Panos Pictures *b*; 84 Range Pictures/Bettmann Archive; 85 J Allan Cash; 88 J Allan Cash *t*; 95 Chris Fairclough Colour Library; 96 J Allan Cash; 97 Bridgeman Art Library/Victoria & Albert Museum, London *l*, Mansell Collection *r*; 101 Hutchison Library; 104 Hutchison Library; 105 Trip/Marc Dubin *b*; 106 Comstock; 107 RHPL; 108 Rex Features; 109 Trip/V Shuba; 110 Hutchison Library; 111 Trip/M O'Brien; 112 Panos Pictures; 114 Panos Pictures; 115 Hutchison Library; 116 Panos Pictures; 117 Panos Pictures *t*, Comstock *b*; 118 RHPL; 120 Hutchison Library; 121 J Allan Cash *t*, Trip/M Bartholomew *b*; 122 Trip/Marc Dubin; 123 Trip/ H Sayer *t*, Hutchison Library *m*; 124 Panos Pictures; 126 Hutchison Library; 127 Hutchison Library; 128 Mary Evans Picture Library *t*, Rex Features *b*; 130 Sue Cunningham; 131 Panos Pictures; 132 Camera Press; 133 Rex Features *l*, Hutchison Library *r*; 134 RHPL; 135 Hutchison Library; 137 Hutchison Library; 138 Panos Pictures; 139 Panos Pictures *t*,

RHPL *b*; 141 Panos Pictures; 146 Hutchison Library; 147 Popperfoto *t*, Hutchison Library *b*; 149 RHPL; 150 RHPL *t*, Chris Fairclough Colour Library *b*; 151 RHPL; 152 J Allan Cash; 153 J Allan Cash *t*, Rex Features *b*; 154 Trip; 155 Camera Press; 156 J S Library International; 159 Christine Osborne Pictures *t*, NHPA *b*; 160 J S Library International; 161 Hulton-Deutsch Collection *r*; 162 Trip/Helene Rogers; 163 Christine Osborne Pictures *t*, J S Library International *b*; 165 RHPL *t*, J Allan Cash *b*; 166 Hutchison Library; 167 Panos Pictures; 168 Panos Pictures; 169 Hutchison Library *t*; 170 Panos Pictures; 171 Panos Pictures; 172 Edward Parker; 173 Trip/ M Jelliffe; 175 Panos Pictures; 177 Panos Pictures; 178 VSO; 180 Christine Osborne Pictures; 181 Panos Pictures; 184 British Museum; 185 Trip/M Jelliffe *t*, VSO *b*; 186 Panos Pictures; 187 Hutchison Library *m*; 188 Bridgeman Art Library/Museum für Völkerkunde, Berlin; 189 Panos Pictures *b*; 190 Panos Pictures *t*; 191 Panos Pictures; 192 Trip/Juliet Highet; 193 RHPL; 195 Christine Osborne Pictures *t*, Hutchison Library *b*; 197 Hutchison Library; 198 Hutchison Library; 199 Panos Pictures; 200 Trip/Dave Saunders; 203 RHPL *t*, Allsport *b*; 204 Panos Pictures; 205 Hutchison Library; 206 VSO; 207 Museum für Naturkinde der Humboldt, Berlin; 208 Hutchison Library; 209 Panos Pictures; 210 Panos Pictures; 211 Hutchison Library; 213 Hutchison Library *b*; 214 Bridgeman Art Library/ Horniman Museum, London *t*, J Allan Cash *b*; 215 Hutchison Library; 216 Trip/M Jelliffe; 217 Associated Press *t*, Greg Evans International *b*; 218 Allsport; 219 J Allan Cash; 220 Panos Pictures; 221 Panos Pictures; 222 Hutchison Library; 223 Hutchison Library *r*, Camera Press *l*; 224 British Museum *t*; 226 Panos Pictures; 227 Panos Pictures; 229 RHPL; 231 South African Embassy; 232 Satour; 233 Satour *t*; 234 Trip/Dave Saunders; 235 Hutchison Library *t*, Trip/Dave Saunders *b*; 236 Panos Pictures; 237 Mary Evans Picture Library *t*, South African Embassy *b*; 238 Hutchison Library; 240 Hutchison Library; 242 Panos Pictures; 243 Panos Pictures; 244 Environment Investigation Agency; 245 Panos Pictures; 247 Hutchison Library *t*; 249 Panos Pictures; 250 Hutchison Library; 252 Hutchison Library; 253 Mansell Collection *l*, Hutchison Library

r; 258 Hutchison Library *m*; 260 Panos Pictures *l*, RHPL *r*; 261 Trip/Eye Ubiquitous; 264 RHPL; 265 Trip/A Gasson; 266 J Allan Cash; 267 Trip/P Craven; 268 Dagnall Worldwide Photo Library; 271 RHPL; 272 Government of Quebec; 273 RHPL; 274 Mansell Collection *l*, National Archives of Canada, Ottawa *r*; 275 Canadian Pacific *t*, Associated Press *l*, Rex Features *r*; 277 RHPL; 278 Eye Ubiquitous; 282 Hutchison Library *l*; 283 J Allan Cash *b*; 284 Peter Newark Pictures *l*, Bettmann Archive *r*; 285 Peter Newark Pictures *t*, Bettmann Archive *b*; 287 Christine Osborne Pictures *l*; 288 British Museum *t*, RHPL *b*; 289 Panos Pictures; 290 Panos Pictures; 291 RHPL; 292 Trip/Chris Rennie *l*, Trip/Eye Ubiquitous *r*; 293 RHPL; 295 Hutchison Library *t*, Panos Pictures *b*; 296 RHPL; 299 RHPL *t*, Panos Pictures *b*; 301 Panos Pictures; 302 Life File/Richard Powers; 303 Panos Pictures; 304 RHPL; 305 RHPL; 306 RHPL; 307 RHPL; 310 Panos Pictures; 311 RHPL; 312 RHPL; 313 RHPL; 314 RHPL; 315 Travel Photo International; 316 J Allan Cash; 317 Austin Brown/Aviation Picture Library; 318 Dagnall Worldwide Photo Library; 319 RHPL; 320 Rod Panichelli; 322 Sue Cunningham *t*; 323 Trip/Life File *t*, Science Photo Library *b*; 324 Trip/Rob Cousins *t*, RHPL *b*; 325 Sue Cunningham; 326 Trip/Brian Gadsby; 327 Edward Parker; 328 Cinecontact; 329 Dave Saunders; 330 RHPL; 333 Panos Pictures; 334 Booker/Tate *l*, Hutchison Library *r*; 335 Hutchison Library; 337 Panos Pictures *t*; 339 Eye Ubiquitous *t*, Ariane Space *b*; 340 John Moss; 341 Hutchison Library; 343 Panos Pictures *t*, Sue Cunningham *m*; 344 VW Press Office; 345 Hutchison Library *t*, John Moss *b*; 346 Panos Pictures; 347 Sue Cunningham *t*, Popperfoto *b*; 348 Bridgeman Art Library/British Library, London *t*, Sue Cunningham *b*; 349 Bridgeman Art Library/ Victoria & Albert Museum, London *t*, Rex Features *b*; 351 Frank Spooner Pictures *t*; 352 Hutchison Library; 353 Trip/Richard Powers; 354 Hutchison Library; 355 Hutchison Library; 357 Hutchison Library; 358 Trip/Life File; 359 Hutchison Library; 361 Trip/Dave Saunders; 362 Sue Cunningham; 363 Trip/Chris Rennie; 364 Hutchison Library; 365 Daniel Gianoni *t*, Hutchison Library *b*; 366 Trip/A Gasson; 367 Hutchison Library *t*, John Moss *m*; 368 Royal Geographic

Society; 369 Chilean Embassy *t*, Frank Spooner Pictures *b*; 370 Hutchison Library; 371 Hutchison Library; 372 Panos Pictures; 373 Trip/N D Price; 374 Sue Cunningham; 376 RHPL; 377 A G E Fotostock; 378 Frank Spooner Pictures; 379 Trip/Dave Saunders *t*, Panos Pictures *b*; 380 Trip/Brian Gadsby *r*; 381 RHPL; 383 Andes Press Agency/Carlos Reyes; 384 Hulton-Deutsch Collection *t*, Mansell Collection *b*; 386 Paul Ratigan; 387 Paul Ratigan *t*, R Warburton/Middle East Pictures *b*; 388 Rex Features *l*, Panos Pictures *r*; 389 Camera Press; 390 Prodeepta Das; 391 RHPL; 393 Hutchison Library *b*; 394 Russia & Republics Photo Library; 396 Trip; 397 Trip/ V Kolpakov; 399 Liam Muir *b*; 400 Range Pictures/Bettmann Archive *t*; 401 Novosti Photo Library *t*, Fotomas Index *b*; 402 Hutchison Library; 403 Trip/ A Tjagny-Rjadno; 404 Trip/ V Kolpakov; 407 J Allan Cash; 411 RHPL; 413 Panos Pictures *b*; 414 Trip/Life File; 415 Hutchison Library; 417 Trip/Malcolm Jenkin; 420 RHPL; 423 Panos Pictures; 426 Panos Pictures; 429 RHPL; 430 Frank Spooner Pictures; 431 Camera Press; 432 British Museum; 433 Comstock *t*, Panos Pictures *b*; 434 RHPL; 436 Hutchison Library; 437 British Museum; 438 Panos Pictures; 439 Rex Features; 440 RHPL; 441 Trip; 443 RHPL; 445 Christine Osborne Pictures; 446 Trip/Helene Rogers; 450 Panos Pictures; 451 RHPL *b*; 452 Panos Pictures; 453 Panos Pictures *b*; 455 J Allan Cash; 456 Panos Pictures; 457 Images of India/Roderick Johnson *t*, Prodeepta Das *b*; 458 Liam Muir; 459 Panos Pictures *r*, Liam Muir *b*; 460 Trip/Helene Rogers; 461 Trip/Roger Lemoyne *t*, Panos Pictures *m*; 462 Trip/Helene Rogers; 463 Popperfoto *b*; 465 VSO; 466 Prodeepta Das; 467 Panos Pictures; 468 Panos Pictures; 469 Panos Pictures *b*; 471 Hutchison Library; 474 Panos Pictures; 475 Hutchison Library *t*, Panos Pictures *b*; 477 RHPL; 478 Panos Pictures; 479 Paul Ratigan *t*, Colin Edwards *b*; 480 Paul Ratigan; 482 RHPL; 485 Panos Pictures; 486 Trip/Dave Saunders; 487 RHPL *t*, Panos Pictures *b*; 488 Associated Press; 489 RHPL; 496 Trip/Linda Jackson; 497 Trip *t*, Panos Pictures *b*; 498 Panos Pictures; 499 Japan Information & Cultural Centre *m*; 501 Paul Ratigan *r*, 502 Mary Evans Picture Library; 503 Mary Evans Picture Library *m*, Panos Pictures

b; 505 RHPL; 514 Trip/Mark
Both b; 516 Topham/Associated
Press; 517 RHPL; 518 Camera
Press; 519 Trip/Robin Smith;
521 Hutchison Library; 522
RHPL; 526 Hutchison Library;
527 Trip/Robin Smith t,
Trip/Dave Saunders b; 529 Panos
Pictures t, RHPL b; 530
Australian Information Services
b; 531 E T Archive t, Panos
Pictures b; 533 J S Library
International t; 534 Trip/Warren
Jacobs; 535 RHPL m; 536
RHPL; 537 Trip/Warren Jacobs;
538 Fotomas Index t, Hutchison
Library b; 539 RHPL; 543
RHPL; 544 Hutchison Library;
546 RHPL; 547 RHPL; 548
Panos Pictures; 550 Trip/Warren
Jacobs; 551 Hutchison Library;
552 Planet Earth Pictures t,
Bruce Coleman Ltd b; 553 Planet
Earth Pictures; 554 Michael
Holford; 555 Popperfoto t,
Science Photo Library m, NHPA
b; 556 Bruce Coleman Ltd t,
Planet Earth Pictures b; 557
NHPA; 558 E T Archive t; 559
Mansell Collection m, Planet
Earth Pictures b; 560 Science
Photo Library; 561 Planet Earth
Pictures t; 562 Science Photo
Library b; 563 Greenpeace/
Morgan l, Mansell Collection r,
British Library b; 564 RHPL t,
Bryan and Cherry Alexander b;
566 British Antarctic Survey t;
567 Science Photo Library m;
568 NHPA t, Royal Geographic
Society b; 569 Bryan and Cherry
Alexander; 572 Science Photo
Library; 576 NASA; 584 Bruce
Coleman Ltd l, Novosti Photo
Library r; 585 Prodeepta Das t,
South American Pictures b; 588
Mary Evans Picture Library t,
Frank Spooner Pictures b; 589
RHPL b; 592 Panos Pictures;
593 Panos Pictures; 594 David
Rose; 596 Science Photo Library;
598 UN Photo; 599 The
Environmental Picture
Library/Tim Lambon; 600 Rex
Features t, UNHCR b; 601
Panos Pictures
All other photographs ZEFA

The publishers would like to thank
the following artists for
contributing to this book:

Jenny Abbot 318m
Hemesh Alles (Maggie Mundy
Illustration Agency) 70-1b; 73tr;
86-7bm, 198tr; 244tr; 273tl;
300t; 313br; 358tl; 366m; 370;
374br; 375t; 408b; 415t; 418tl;
420bl; 429r; 432b; 444ml; 452t;
485r; 506b;
Marion Appleton 231br; 595
Julian Baker 574b; 586; 602l;
Julie Banyard 19ml; 25ml; 38tr;
48t; 60mr; 72ml; 80; 82tl; 95ml;
105ml; 112tr; 140; 150tr; 172br;
185ml; 192ml; 196tr; 206tl;
243ml; 255mr; 293ml; 311br;
327t; 345b; 398l; 421bl; 425br;
431br; 437tl; 440bl; 460tl; 470bl;
486t; 495mr; 521tr; 528t; 538m
Sue Barclay 160tl
David Barnett 153b; 165m; 174-
5b; 191b

Tim Beer (Maggie Mundy
Illustration Agency) 500bl
Richard Bonson 178tr; 263t
Simon Calder 307b
Harry Clow 12tl; 16-17m; 28b;
30b; 36-37b; 38b; 45m; 47t;
57tl; 69b; 79m; 81m; 91b; 93b;
130; 131b; 138t; 159m; 164b;
185mr; 223b; 233m; 258-9b;
268t; 271ml; 278br; 279br;
316bl; 331t; 331b; 338br; 342tl;
343ml; 356; 363t; 365; 371;
381b; 386bl; 395m; 396-7;
423b; 441t; 457m; 465b; 470-
1b; 482-3m; 497b; 524b; 534-5t;
587
David Cook (Linden Artists) 156t;
191t; 192br; 235ml; 284tl; 289b;
300bl; 328tl; 333b; 361tl; 380tl;
388b;
Sandra Doyle 143tl; 153tr; 166bl;
188ml; 262bl; 263t; 302bl;
326tl; 339tr; 361ml; 371bl;
392bl;
James Field (Simon Girling Assoc.)
331m
Michael Fisher 50tl; 98ml; 481b
Chris Forsey 19tr; 33m; 34b;
41mr; 49mr; 56-7m; 60-1tm; 82-
3; 107m; 139; 151b; 166-7m;
170-1m; 188b; 200br; 212b;
227m; 264; 272br; 302br; 304m;
306tl; 308-9b; 317b; 322tl;
322br; 352-3; 362bl; 369m;
375mr; 383b; 396-7b; 413m;
415; 417b; 473b; 509br; 527;
529; 554-5m
Matthew Gore 595br
Karen Hiscock 519t
David Holmes 326bl
Mark Iley 10br; 11; 52t; 62tr;
76mr; 102br; 106tr; 126bl;
135tr; 204br; 263bl,t; 277;
294tr; 312tr; 323tr; 357br;
378bl; 391t; 416bl; 450bl; 454l;
466; 494bl; 518t; 519b; 532t;
556
Delyth Jones 286bl; 312bl; 333mr
Kevin Jones Assoc. 243br
Kuo Kang Chen 592t; 594b
Deborah Kindred (Simon Girling
Assoc.) 144tl; 176mr; 207br;
252r; 290-1b; 297tr; 298b;
309tr; 330tl; 353t; 363br; 498;
511
Peter Komarnyckj 158; 161b;
164tl; 339b; 362-3m; 436b;
439tl; 442t;
Mike Lacey (Simon Girling Assoc.)
15; 40; 42br; 100bl; 236-7tm;
256; 283tr; 333; 346; 376; 382b;
410br; 459ml; 484-5b; 496b;
537; 545br
Ruth Lindsay (Linden Artists)
278tl; 340br; 345m; 456b

Bernard Long 480br; 518b
Kevin Maddison 147m; 419r
Alan Male (Linden Artists) 228bl
Maltings Partnership 341ml; 596;
597
Peter Massey 118; 119m
John Marshall 8t; 31mr; 57tr;
71tr; 110-1bm; 270b; 394mr;
493mr; 510b; 516; 526; 536
Josephine Martin (Garden Studio)
10tl; 390r; 508t
Jamie Medlin 12-13b; 21mr; 47b;
103ml; 113b; 232b; 237b;
241br; 245br; 247mr
Janos Middletons 579t
Brian McIntyre 195mr
Doreen McGuiness 578-9b
Justin Moat 148bl; 190bl; 209bl;
211tl
Tony Morris 182br
Frank Nichols (Linda Rogers
Assoc.) 328-9b; 348br; 353bl
Steve Noon (Garden Studio) 35mr;
38mr; 54-5m; 94-5tm; 202b;
205br; 207ml; 264-5b; 273tr;
280bl; 293b; 358-9b; 378tl;
383r; 469mr; 479; 480bl; 483b;
495b; 500t; 503t; 525
Jenny Norton 169m; 179tr; 382t;
458b; 477mr
William Oliver 16t; 88br
Ralph Orm (Swanston) 290tl;
305b; 343b
Chris Orr (Simon Girling Assoc.)
287
Alex Pang (Simon Girling Assoc.)
145m; 335b; 344b
Darren Pattenden (Garden Studio)
137tr; 149b; 152tl; 156-7t;
165tr; 173t; 183b; 196; 199;
215m; 248; 266; 281m; 282tl;
291tr; 296mr; 297br; 298tl;
324ml; 334tl; 349tr; 359ml;
368tl; 399m; 406b
Justin Peek 350bl
Rob Perry 32tl; 93bl; 120tl; 141tl;
145tl; 201tm; 234tl; 487r
Eric Robson 134bl; 208bl
Eric Rowe (Linden Artists) 95br;
140br; 367br; 402-3b; 443r;
446b; 462-3m; 491b
Mike Roffe 463bl; 576r
Bernard Robinson 216l
Liz Sawyer (Simon Girling Assoc.)
272tl; 295mr; 315bl; 359br;
372tr
Roger Stewart 514; 535b; 558;
570; 572b
John Storey 260tl
Clive Spong (Linden Artists) 26t;
53bl; 58mr; 62bl; 116; 137tl;
142tr; 149t; 153tl; 168br; 180tr;
213tr; 218b; 229mr; 254bl;
314mr; 346tl; 361br; 373bl;
376tl; 398br; 407r; 412bl; 426-
7tl,m; 445t; 455t 461bl; 467b;
472bl; 499; 500r; 505tr; 520tl;
542m; 547m; 550
Treve Tamblin 560
George Thompson 488
Guy Troughton 54br; 66br
Peter Ware 163m; 182bl
Phil Weare 327b
Ann Winterbottom 297mr
David Wright 135ml; 62tl,tr
John York (Simon Girling Assoc.)
475tl

National Emblems Matthew Gore
Locator Globes Eugene Fleury
Opener Globes Mel Pickering
(Contour Publishing)
Map Artworks Mel Pickering

(Contour Publishing), Malcolm
Porter, Swanston Graphics with
additional help from Roy Flooks
and Mark Franklin
Language Scrolls Roy Flooks
Food & Feature borders
Roy Flooks
Flags Lovell Johns Ltd

The publishers would like to thank
the following for their assistance:

Áras na nGael (Brent Irish Cultural
and Community Association)
British Museum
Canadian High Commission
Education Office, Spanish Embassy
Egyptian Cultural and Education
Bureau
Embassy of Algeria
Embassy of the Grand Duchy of
Luxembourg
Embassy of Israel
Embassy of the People's Republic
of China in the United Kingdom
Embassy of the Republic of
Armenia
Embassy of Romania
Embassy of the Russian Federation
Embassy of Sierra Leone
Embassy of Western Samoa
Fiji Embassy
Flag Institute, Chester
Government of British Columbia
Government of the Province of
Alberta
Haringey Somali Community and
Cultural Association
High Commission of the Republic
of Trinidad and Tobago
Dr Rosaleen Howard-Malverde,
Lecturer in Latin American
Linguistics, Institute of Latin
American Studies, University of
Liverpool
Iranian Community Centre
Italian Cultural Institute
Japan Information and Cultural
Centre
Japan National Tourist
Organisation
Mrs Esther Jessop QSM
Kenya High Commission
Korea National Tourism
Organisation
Lebanese Embassy
Custodia Lima, Diplomat of
the Embassy of Cape Verde
in the USA
Madagascar Consulate
Malaysian High Commission
Ministry of Forests/Forestry
Canada
Namibian High Commission
Ms Thembi Ncube, Botswana
High Commission
Papua New Guinea High
Commission
Philippine Embassy
Polish Cultural Institute
Kirankumar D Purohit
Royal Botanic Gardens, Kew
Royal Danish Embassy
South African High Commission
Swedish Embassy
Tourist Office of North Cyprus
Turkish Embassy
United States Information Service
Université Française du Pacifique
Mr T F Vaipuna, Tonga High
Commission
Jehannes Ytsma, Fryske Akademy
Zairean Community Association

640